Test Bank

For Wayne Weiten's

PSYCHOLOGY
Themes and Variations
FIFTH EDITION

S. A. Hensch
University of Wisconsin – Marshfield/Wood County

William E. Addison
Eastern Illinois University

Australia • Canada • Mexico • Singapore • Spain • United Kingdom • United States

COPYRIGHT © 2001 Wadsworth, a division of Thomson Learning, Inc. Thomson Learning™ is a trademark used herein under license.

ALL RIGHTS RESERVED Instructors of classes adopting *Psychology: Themes and Variations, Fifth Edition* by Wayne Weiten as a required text may photocopy transparency masters for classroom use, but material may not be loaded on any type of network without the written permission of the publisher. In other words, no part of this work covered by the copyright hereon may be reproduced or used in any form or by any means—photographic, video, audio, digital, or any other form or method of copying, recording, or transmission, now known or hereafter devised including, without limitation, copying or recording by phonographic, photographic, magnetic, laser, electronic, or any other means and whether on photographic records, film, microfilm, microfiche, slides, filmstrips, transparencies, CD-ROM, Internet, World Wide Web, magnetic tape, cassettes, videodiscs, floppy disks, or any other human- or machine-readable medium, and the broadcast or transmission thereof—without the written permission of the publisher.

Printed in the United States of America

2 3 4 5 6 7 04 03 02

For permission to use material from this text, contact us by **Web**: http://www.thomsonrights.com
Fax: 1-800-730-2215 **Phone**: 1-800-730-2214

ISBN 0-534-36722-4

For more information, contact
Wadsworth/Thomson Learning
10 Davis Drive
Belmont, CA 94002-3098
USA

For more information about our products, contact us:
Thomson Learning Academic Resource Center
1-800-423-0563
http://www.wadsworth.com

International Headquarters
Thomson Learning
International Division
290 Harbor Drive, 2nd Floor
Stamford, CT 06902-7477
USA

UK/Europe/Middle East/South Africa
Thomson Learning
Berkshire House
168-173 High Holborn
London WC1V 7AA
United Kingdom

Asia
Thomson Learning
60 Albert Complex, #15-01
Singapore 189969

Canada
Nelson Thomson Learning
1120 Birchmount Road
Toronto, Ontario M1K 5G4
Canada

Contents

Introduction iv

Part I Psychology: Themes and Variations, Fourth Edition

Chapter 1	The Evolution of Psychology 1
Chapter 2	The Research Enterprise in Psychology 31
Chapter 3	The Biological Bases of Behavior 67
Chapter 4	Sensation and Perception 97
Chapter 5	Variations in Consciousness 131
Chapter 6	Learning Through Conditioning 161
Chapter 7	Human Memory 197
Chapter 8	Language and Thought 229
Chapter 9	Intelligence and Psychological Testing 265
Chapter 10	Motivation and Emotion 299
Chapter 11	Human Development Across the Life Span 331
Chapter 12	Personality: Theory, Research, and Assessment 369
Chapter 13	Stress, Coping, and Health 403
Chapter 14	Psychological Disorders 435
Chapter 15	Psychotherapy 473
Chapter 16	Social Behavior 507
Appendix B	Statistical Methods 541
Appendix C	Industrial/Organizational Psychology 551

Part II Psyk.trek

Unit 1	History & Methods 561
Unit 2	Biological Bases of Behavior 569
Unit 3	Sensation & Perception 580
Unit 4	Consciousness 592
Unit 5	Learning 599
Unit 6	Memory & Thought 609
Unit 7	Testing & Intelligence 616
Unit 8	Motivation & Emotion 623
Unit 9	Human Development 630
Unit 10	Personality Theory 637
Unit 11	Abnormal Behavior & Therapy 643
Unit 12	Social Psychology 652

Introduction

This test-item file was developed as an instructional aid for use with the textbook *Psychology: Themes and Variations, Fifth Edition*, by Wayne Weiten.

Part I of the test-item file contains approximately 230 multiple-choice questions for each chapter in the main text and approximately 60 multiple-choice questions for Appendices B and C. In addition, there are 4-5 essay questions provided for each of the text's 16 chapters. These items are arranged by chapter, and within each chapter the order of the items follows the order of presentation for the text material.

Part II of the test-item file typically contains 12 multiple-choice questions for each module on the Psyk.trek CD-ROM. These items are arranged by module number, and within each module the order of the items follows the order of the multimedia presentation.

New Features

The updated test bank for the 5th edition of Psychology: Themes and Variations incorporates several new features.

First, the majority of the test items that were retained from the previous version of the test bank now include test item analysis information in a separate line to the left of each question. This information indicates the average percentage of students who responded correctly to each item on term exams; it can be used to estimate the difficulty level for the various questions.

Second, new CRITICAL THINKING test items have been provided for each chapter. These questions tap key critical thinking skills such as analogical reasoning, counterfactual thinking, and inductive reasoning.

Third, the proportion of conceptual and applied questions has been increased in each chapter, and new conceptual and applied test items are included for most of the learning objectives in each of the chapters.

Finally, the on-line Psychology Study Center for Weiten's text gives students an opportunity to test their knowledge of key concepts. The self-quiz questions from that web site correspond to the last ten multiple-choice questions for each chapter.

Types of Questions

Multiple-Choice Questions

Several basic principles guided the construction of the multiple-choice questions. First, each item is worded to mirror the words and level of language used in the textbook and on the CD-ROM. Second, the number of items reflects the importance given to various topics. More items are provided on topics that are discussed extensively or stressed. Third, in Part I of the test file several alternative items are provided for major ideas and concepts whenever possible. This should allow for constructing alternative forms of tests or repeated testing without using the same items again.

For each question, the left-hand column provides up to 5 lines of information. The first line categorizes the type of knowledge that is assessed by the question; the second line identifies the learning objective to which the question is tied; the third line identifies the corresponding page number in the text; the fourth line provides test item analysis information which reflects the proportion of students who answered this question correctly (this information is not available for all the questions), and the last line provides the correct alternative.

For the questions in Part II of the test file no page numbers have been provided and the questions are keyed only to the separate modules of the Psyk.trek CD-ROM.

Six categories have been used in classifying questions:

(1) **Factual**: these questions evaluate student mastery of terminology, concepts, theories, principles, and research findings. The information required to answer these questions is spelled out explicitly in the text.

(2) **Concept/Applied**: these questions require that the student extend core concepts to new situations and settings, or evaluate new information using core concepts.

(3) **Critical Thinking**: these questions require more complex reasoning skills and test the ability of the student to think critically about core concepts from each chapter. These questions require analogical reasoning, counterfactual thinking, inductive reasoning, or other key critical thinking skills.

(4) **Integrative**: these questions require students to link, synthesize, and interrelate information from different sections of the chapter. Given the broader nature of these questions, they are not keyed to specific learning objectives or pages in the text.

(5) **Study Guide**: these questions are found at the end of the multiple-choice section for each chapter in Part I of the test file. Each of these questions is drawn directly from the student study guide for the text. These questions assess various aspects of student mastery of course material, but students who have completed the study guide self-quiz will have previously encountered each of these questions.

(6) **Online Quiz**: these questions are also found at the end of the multiple-choice section for each chapter in Part I of the test file. These questions assess various aspects of student mastery of course material, but students who have completed the online study guide for the course will have previously encountered each of these questions.

Essay Questions

Four to five essay questions can be found at the end of each chapter. The essay questions typically require students to synthesize information from more than one section of the chapter, so they are not keyed to specific learning objectives or to pages in the text. We have also provided brief outlines of suggested answers.

Interface With Other Materials

Ideally, students' learning should be evaluated through diverse methods, including essays, research papers, oral reports, and creative projects, in addition to multiple-choice tests. Many suggestions for creative approaches to student evaluation can be found in the *Instructor's Resource Package* developed for the text. However, practical considerations lead most instructors to depend heavily on multiple-choice exams in the introductory course. Hence, we have attempted to create a high-quality multiple-choice test bank made up of questions that accurately reflect the emphasis and interpretations in the text and that will mesh well with the pedagogical aids in the text and the study guide.

The multiple-choice questions in Part I of this test-item file are closely coordinated with the *Study Guide* and the pedagogical aids in the text. Each factual or conceptual question is based on one of the learning objectives listed at the beginning of each chapter in the test-item file.

In the *Study Guide*, the "Review of Key Terms" for each chapter is organized around the same learning objectives. Questions that assess students' knowledge of psychology's technical vocabulary are limited to those terms that are clearly identified and defined in the text's integrated running glossary. These terms are listed at the back of each chapter in the text. Students can check their mastery of this vocabulary by completing the "Review of Key Terms" in the *Study Guide*. Questions about the contributions and ideas of important theorists and researchers are limited to those individuals listed under "Key People" at the end of each text chapter. Students can assess their mastery of this information by completing the "Review of Key People" in the *Study Guide*.

This interface serves two purposes. First, it increases the utility of the review materials in the text and the *Study Guide* by ensuring they have direct relevance to the exams you'll be constructing. Second, it means that you can sample from the test-item file and feel confident that your students have been warned about what is important (if they used the review materials).

Using This Test Bank Effectively

Sound tests characterized by appropriate difficulty are a product of careful item selection. The questions in this test-item file were constructed to vary considerably in difficulty level, so that instructors can tailor their exams according to their personal needs and preferences. Whatever your unique preferences in testing are, it's a good idea to communicate them as clearly as possible to your students before the first exam. To make exams learning experiences, as well as evaluation devices, it's also wise to go over exams in class after the fact. These class debriefings can help students to better prepare for subsequent exams.

The Computerized Test Bank

The items from this test file are also available on computer disks that are compatible with a variety of computer configurations. The testing software is offered at no charge to instructors who adopt the text. The computerized testing program is user-friendly and it allows you to edit the questions provided, or create your own questions. It also permits you to select items in a variety of ways. Although the software will allow you to create tests using randomly selected questions, this is not recommended. Tests constructed from randomly selected questions may overemphasize some areas and ignore other areas. In addition, tests constructed in this way may inadvertently include alternative forms of the same question which have been supplied to allow instructors to test across course sections, or across semesters, without repeating identical test items.

To obtain a computerized version of the test-time file, contact Wadsworth directly at 800-354-0092, or talk to your Thomson Learning sales representative.

Chapter One
The Evolution of Psychology

LEARNING OBJECTIVES

1. Summarize Wundt's accomplishments and contributions to psychology.
2. Summarize Hall's accomplishments and contributions to psychology.
3. Describe structuralism and its impact on the subsequent development of psychology.
4. Describe functionalism and its impact on the subsequent development of psychology.
5. Summarize Watson's views on the appropriate subject matter of psychology, nature versus nurture, and animal research.
6. Summarize Freud's principal ideas and why they inspired controversy.
7. Summarize Skinner's work, views, and influence.
8. Summarize Rogers' and Maslow's ideas and the contributions of humanistic psychology.
9. Explain how historical events since World War I have contributed to the emergence of psychology as a profession.
10. Describe two recent trends in research in psychology that reflect a return to psychology's intellectual roots.
11. Explain why Western psychology traditionally had scant interest in other cultures and why this situation has begun to change.
12. Summarize the basic tenets of evolutionary psychology.
13. Discuss the growth of psychology and the most common work settings for contemporary psychologists.
14. List and describe seven major research areas in psychology.
15. List and describe the four professional specialties in psychology.
16. Summarize the text's three unifying themes relating to psychology as a field of study.
17. Summarize the text's four unifying themes relating to psychology's subject matter.
18. Discuss three important considerations in designing a program to promote adequate studying.
19. Describe the SQ3R method and explain what makes it effective.
20. Summarize advice provided on how to get more out of lectures.
21. Summarize advice provided on improving test-taking strategies.
22. Explain the nature of critical thinking skills and why they need to be taught.
23. Discuss some weaknesses in evolutionary explanations for gender differences in spatial abilities.

MULTIPLE-CHOICE QUESTIONS

Factual
LO 1
Page: 3
b

1. According to historians, the "birth" of psychology occurred in _____ in _____.
   a. 1859; England
   b. 1879; Germany
   c. 1883; the United States
   d. 1909; the United States

Factual
LO 1
Page: 3
d

2. The person responsible for establishing psychology as an independent discipline with its own subject matter is
   a. G. Stanley Hall
   b. René Descartes
   c. William James
   d. Wilhelm Wundt

Factual
LO 1
Page: 3
c

3. According to Thomas Leahey, Wilhelm Wundt brought the empirical methods of _____ to the questions of _____.
   a. philosophy; biology
   b. physiology; sociology
   c. physiology; philosophy
   d. philosophy; physiology

Factual
LO 1
Page: 3
b

4. According to Wilhelm Wundt, the focus of psychology was on the scientific study of
   a. observable behavior
   b. conscious experience
   c. unconscious motivation
   d. the functions of behavior

Concept/Applied
LO 1
Page: 3
d

5. Which of the following best reflects what Wilhelm Wundt thought the focus of psychology should be?
   a. questioning the nature of existence
   b. studying stimulus-response associations
   c. determining people's unconscious motivation for behavior
   d. examining people's awareness of their immediate experience

Factual
LO 2
Page: 3
c

6. Which of the following individuals is recognized for establishing America's first research laboratory in psychology and for launching America's first psychology journal?
   a. John Watson
   b. William James
   c. G. Stanley Hall
   d. Edward Titchener

Factual
LO 2
Page: 3
b

7. The first president of the American Psychological Association (APA) was
   a. Sigmund Freud
   b. G. Stanley Hall
   c. William James
   d. John Watson

Factual
LO 2
Page: 3
Correct = 92%
c

8. The world's largest organization devoted to the advancement of psychology is the
   a. World Psychology Organization
   b. American Psychological Society
   c. American Psychological Association
   d. Psychologists of North America

Factual LO 3 Page: 4 Correct = 95% c	9.	The first two major "schools" of psychology were a. behaviorism and psychoanalysis b. functionalism and behaviorism c. structuralism and functionalism d. behaviorism and Gestalt psychology
Factual LO 3 Page: 4 c	10.	Which of the following "schools" of psychology focused on identifying and examining the fundamental components of conscious experience, such as sensations, feelings, and images? a. humanism b. behaviorism c. structuralism d. functionalism
Critical Thinking LO 3 Page: 4 c	11.	Melissa is participating in a study in which she is asked to carefully observe and report her conscious reactions to several stimuli. Melissa is most likely participating in a study conducted by which of the following types of psychologists? a. humanist b. behaviorist c. structuralist d. psychoanalyst
Concept/Applied LO 3 Page: 4 a	12.	In an attempt to learn something about his conscious experience, William looked at an abstract painting and wrote down all of his impressions as they came to him. This technique is called a. introspection b. retrospection c. empiricism d. psychoanalysis
Factual LO 4 Page: 5 Correct = 98% b	13.	What was the term used by William James to describe a continuous flow of thoughts? a. existential awareness b. stream of consciousness c. transcendental meditation d. phenomenological flow
Factual LO 4 Page: 5 Correct = 44% a	14.	The school of psychology associated with understanding the purpose of behavior was a. functionalism b. behaviorism c. neodynamism d. psychoanalysis
Critical Thinking LO 4 Page: 5 a	15.	Professor Rice believes that it is not possible to completely understand emotions unless we understand the purpose that emotions play in survival and adaptation. Professor Rice's view is most consistent with which of the following "schools" of psychology? a. functionalism b. structuralism c. behaviorism d. psychoanalysis

Factual LO 4 Page: 5 Correct = 74% **a**	16.	William James, who was a pioneer in the development of functionalism, was most heavily influenced by which of the following individuals? a. Charles Darwin b. Sigmund Freud c. John Watson d. B. F. Skinner
Factual LO 4 Page: 5 Correct = 96% **b**	17.	Stressing that psychology should study the purpose of consciousness rather than its structure is associated with the "school" of psychology known as a. structuralism b. functionalism c. psychoanalysis d. Gestalt psychology
Concept/Applied LO 4 Page: 5 Correct = 45% **d**	18.	Which of the following concepts is least closely associated with functionalism as a "school" of psychology? a. mental testing b. stream of consciousness c. adapting to the environment d. elements of consciousness
Factual LO 4 Page: 5 Correct = 49% **c**	19.	Which early approach in psychology fostered the development of modern-day applied psychology? a. structuralism b. behaviorism c. functionalism d. pragmatism
Concept/Applied LO 4 Page: 5 Correct = 73% **c**	20.	Which of the following was least likely to be the focus of study for the functionalists? a. mental testing b. development in children c. sensation and perception d. the effectiveness of educational practices
Factual LO 4 Page: 6 **a**	21.	Which of the following was the first woman to serve as President of the American Psychological Association? a. Mary Calkins b. Margaret Washburn c. Leta Hollingworth d. Anna Freud
Factual LO 4 Page: 6 Correct = 40% **b**	22.	Which of the following was the first woman to receive a Ph.D. in psychology? a. Mary Calkins b. Margaret Washburn c. Leta Hollingworth d. Anna Freud
Factual LO 4 Page: 6 Correct = 26% **d**	23.	Leta Hollingworth is noted for which of the following? a. being the first woman to receive a Ph.D. in psychology b. being the first woman president of the American Psychological Association c. founding one of the early psychology laboratories in America d. collecting objective data on gender differences in behavior

Factual LO 5 Page: 5 Correct = 87% **a**	24.	Which psychologist proposed that the study of consciousness should be replaced by the study of behavior? a. John B. Watson b. Abraham Maslow c. G. Stanley Hall d. Sigmund Freud
Concept/Applied LO 5 Page: 6 **c**	25.	The theoretical orientation that insisted on verifiability of observation was a. structuralism b. functionalism c. behaviorism d. psychoanalysis
Concept/Applied LO 5 Page: 5 Correct = 77% **d**	26.	With which of the following would a behaviorist agree? a. Conscious experiences can be studied in an objective, precise way. b. In order to understand behavior, one must understand the motives behind the behavior. c. Behavior can only be explained in terms of phenomenology, that is, an individual's interpretation of experience. d. Psychology should be the science of behavior that can be observed by others.
Concept/Applied LO 5 Page: 6 Correct = 28% **d**	27.	John B. Watson argued that psychologists should a. use the method of introspection to establish the structural aspects of consciousness b. be concerned with the purposiveness (function) of behavior c. confine their work to people who are diagnosed as mentally ill d. abandon the study of consciousness
Factual LO 5 Page: 7 Correct = 70% **c**	28.	According to John Watson, behavior is governed primarily by a. heredity b. personal motives c. the environment d. unconscious desires
Concept/Applied LO 5 Page: 7 Correct = 66% **b**	29.	Strict behaviorists would be most sympathetic to which one of the following statements? a. Human behavior is primarily caused by inherited factors. b. Human behavior is primarily caused by environmental factors. c. Human behavior is primarily caused by equal contributions of inherited and environmental factors. d. No one really knows what the primary causes for human behavior are.
Critical Thinking LO 5 Page: 7 Correct = 81% **a**	30.	Response is to stimulus as a. pain is to cut b. light is to moth c. joke is to laugh d. pen is to paper
Factual LO 5 Page: 7 Correct = 79% **a**	31.	Another name for the behavioral approach in psychology is a. stimulus-response psychology b. structuralism c. applied psychology d. Gestalt psychology

Factual LO 5 Page: 7 Correct =90% **a**	32.	Which of the following "schools" of psychology was most responsible for the rise of animal research in psychology? a. behaviorism b. structuralism c. psychoanalysis d. Gestalt psychology
Concept/Applied LO 5 Page: 7 **a**	33.	Which of the following types of psychologists would be most likely to study rats in a laboratory setting? a. behaviorist b. structuralist c. psychoanalyst d. Gestalt psychologist
Critical Thinking LO 5 Page: 7 Correct = 81% **a**	34.	Christine is a psychologist who conducts research on the effects of reward on maze learning in rats. Christine would most likely be considered a a. behaviorist b. structuralist c. psychoanalyst d. Gestalt psychologist
Concept/Applied LO 5 Page: 7 **d**	35.	Which of the following statements best reflects the main advantage of conducting psychological research with animals? a. It is much cheaper to conduct research on animals than on humans. b. In their biological makeup, animals are fundamentally similar to humans. c. With research on animals, there are no ethical issues to be concerned with. d. A researcher can exert more control over an animal than over a human subject.
Factual LO 5 Page: 8 **b**	36.	Gestalt psychologists were primarily concerned with which of the following? a. emotions b. perception c. overt behavior d. unconscious desires
Factual LO 6 Page: 8 **a**	37.	Sigmund Freud received his educational training in which of the following fields? a. medicine b. sociology c. psychology d. philosophy
Factual LO 6 Page: 8 **c**	38.	Sigmund Freud developed an innovative procedure for treating people with psychological problems, which he called a. behavior modification b. primal therapy c. psychoanalysis d. rational-emotive therapy
Factual LO 6 Page: 8 Correct = 97% **d**	39.	According to Sigmund Freud, an individual's personality is largely determined by a. self-actualizing tendencies b. forces in the environment c. strivings for superiority d. forces in the unconscious

Concept/Applied LO 6 Page: 8 **d**	40.	The notion that unconscious motivations can influence our overt behavior is most consistent with the views of which of the following theorists? a. Carl Rogers b. Wilhelm Wundt c. B. F. Skinner d. Sigmund Freud
Factual LO 6 Page: 8 **b**	41.	Freud concluded that psychological disturbances are largely caused by a. unrealistic demands from family and friends b. personal conflicts existing at an unconscious level c. genetic predispositions to behave in a particular way d. conflicts between conscious desires and environmental constraints
Concept/Applied LO 6 Page: 8 Correct = 81% **b**	42.	The major departure of Freud's position from prevailing viewpoints around the early 1900s was that he a. saw abnormal behavior as resulting from biological causes b. saw people as not fully aware of the forces that control their behavior c. proposed the existence of free will d. emphasized environmental forces on behavior
Concept/Applied LO 6 Page: 9 **a**	43.	People resisted psychoanalysis main because of its emphasis on a. unconscious motivation b. introspection c. the role of heredity d. stimulus-response associations
Critical Thinking LO 6 Page: 9 **d**	44.	Which of the following statements about Freud's psychoanalytic theory is most accurate? a. Freud's views have been largely abandoned and they exert relatively little, if any, influence on current mainstream psychology. b. Freud's views exert a tremendous influence on other disciplines, but not on psychology. c. Freud's views exert a tremendous influence on developmental and abnormal psychology, but not on other areas of mainstream psychology. d. Many psychoanalytic concepts have filtered into the mainstream of psychology.
Critical Thinking LO 7 Page: 9 **a**	45.	With which of the following individuals is B. F. Skinner most in agreement on the issue of internal mental events? a. John Watson b. Sigmund Freud c. Wilhelm Wundt d. Abraham Maslow
Factual LO 7 Page: 9 Correct = 90% **b**	46.	Which of the following psychologists took the position that organisms tend to repeat responses that lead to positive outcomes and tend not to repeat responses that lead to neutral or negative outcomes? a. Sigmund Freud b. B. F. Skinner c. Carl Rogers d. Abraham Maslow

Critical Thinking LO 7 Page: 9 Correct = 85% **a**	47.	Janet trained her dog to sit on command by following this behavior with a reward of a dog biscuit and praise. Janet used the principles of which of the following "schools" of psychology? a. behaviorism b. humanism c. psychoanalysis d. functionalism
Concept/Applied LO 7 Page: 9 Correct = 94% **c**	48.	"Organisms tend to repeat responses that lead to positive outcomes, and they tend not to repeat responses that lead to neutral or negative outcomes." These words would most likely have been said by which of the following individuals? a. Wilhelm Wundt b. William James c. B. F. Skinner d. Abraham Maslow
Concept/Applied LO 7 Page: 10 **a**	49.	The notion that all behavior is fully governed by external stimuli is most consistent with which of the following schools of thought? a. behaviorism b. humanism c. structuralism d. functionalism
Concept/Applied LO 7 Page: 10 Correct = 60% **d**	50.	Skinner's behaviorism a. left room for free will b. included constructs about motives c. permitted limited statements about consciousness d. made the study of behavior and its outcome the basis of the whole approach
Concept/Applied LO 7 Page: 10 Correct = 93% **b**	51.	Which of the following psychologists would have been most likely to assert that "free will is an illusion"? a. Abraham Maslow b. B. F. Skinner c. Wilhelm Wundt d. Carl Rogers
Factual LO 7 Page: 10 Correct = 49% **b**	52.	Which of the following was the dominant school of thought in psychology during the 1950s and 1960s? a. Gestalt psychology b. behaviorism c. structuralism d. functionalism
Factual LO 7 Page: 10 **c**	53.	The principal criticism leveled at both behaviorism and psychoanalytic theory was that they were a. sexist b. nonscientific c. dehumanizing d. too empirical
Factual LO 8 Page: 10 Correct = 97% **c**	54.	Which of the following groups of psychologists would be most likely to focus on individual uniqueness, freedom, and potential for growth as a person? a. behaviorists b. psychoanalysts c. humanists d. Gestalt psychologists

Critical Thinking LO 8 Page: 10 **a**	55.	Which of the following "schools" of psychology takes the most optimistic view of human nature? a. behaviorism b. functionalism c. humanism d. psychoanalysis
Factual LO 8 Page: 11 Correct = 84% **b**	56.	Which theoretical viewpoint is most closely associated with Carl Rogers and Abraham Maslow? a. cognitive approach b. humanism c. structuralism d. biological approach
Factual LO 8 Page: 11 **c**	57.	Which of the following individuals is most closely associated with the humanistic approach to psychology? a. William James b. B. F. Skinner c. Abraham Maslow d. Sigmund Freud
Critical Thinking LO 8 Page: 11 **b**	58.	Which of the following statements is least to be made by a humanist? a. Humans are unique. b. The behavior of humans tends to be dictated by environmental circumstances. c. Humans have a basic need to fulfill their potentials. d. Research on animals has little relevance to understanding human behavior.
Critical Thinking LO 8 Page: 11 Correct = 84% **c**	59.	Which type of psychologist would be least likely to generalize from studies of animal subjects to human behavior? a. a psychoanalyst b. a behaviorist c. a humanist d. a cognitive psychologist
Factual LO 8 Page: 11 **a**	60.	Humanists believe that people's behavior is governed by which of the following? a. their self-concepts b. unconscious sexual urges c. the outcomes of their responses d. biochemical processes
Critical Thinking LO 8 Page: 11 Correct = 90% **b**	61.	Manny tends to be very passive and allows people to take advantage of him. What would a humanist be most likely to say about Manny? a. Manny will find it difficult to change because he probably has deep-seated feelings of inferiority. b. Manny can become more assertive once he begins to feel better about himself and recognizes that he has the ability to fulfill his potential. c. Manny simply needs to take an assertiveness training class in which he can learn and practice assertive behaviors. d. Manny should undergo analysis so that he can begin to resolve whatever unconscious conflict is at the root of his passivity.
Concept/Applied LO 8 Page: 11 **d**	62.	Which of the following psychologists would be most likely to stress that each person has a drive to grow and fulfill his or her potential? a. Sigmund Freud b. B. F. Skinner c. G. Stanley Hall d. Abraham Maslow

Factual LO 9 Page: 12 Correct = 83% **c**	63.	The branch of psychology concerned with everyday, practical problems is called _____ psychology. a. developmental b. abnormal c. applied d. cognitive
Concept/Applied LO 9 Page: 12 Correct = 92% **b**	64.	Margaret is an industrial psychologist who advises companies on how to improve worker morale. As a psychologist who attempts to solve practical problems, Margaret would most likely be considered a(n) _____ psychologist. a. academic b. applied c. behavioral d. humanistic
Critical Thinking LO 9 Page: 12 Correct = 62% **b**	65.	Which of the following sounds least like the work of an applied psychologist? a. finding ways to teach learning disabled children b. studying basic learning processes in rats c. treating someone with a phobia d. looking for ways to increase efficiency in an organization
Factual LO 9 Page: 12 Correct = 72% **b**	66.	Which of the following factors contributed most to the development of applied psychology? a. the advent of high-speed computers b. the high demand for mental testing of military recruits c. the increase in the number of people earning advanced degrees in psychology d. the increase in public awareness of the symptoms of psychological disorders
Factual LO 9 Page: 12 **b**	67.	One of the first areas of applied psychology to develop was a. counseling psychology b. mental testing c. personnel psychology d. sports psychology
Factual LO 9 Page: 12 Correct = 98% **d**	68.	The branch of psychology concerned with the diagnosis and treatment of psychological disorders is called a. counseling psychology b. social psychology c. developmental psychology d. clinical psychology
Concept/Applied LO 9 Page: 12 Correct = 82% **c**	69.	If you were having problems with depression, which of the following kinds of psychologists would be the greatest help to you? a. a developmental psychologist b. a social psychologist c. a clinical psychologist d. an experimental psychologist
Concept/Applied LO 9 Page: 12 Correct = 74% **a**	70.	Michael is having problems relating to other people because he is exhibiting delusions (false beliefs) and hallucinations. Michael would most likely seek help from a(n) _____ psychologist. a. clinical b. developmental c. experimental d. physiological

Critical Thinking LO 9 Page: 12 **b**	71.	Sarah was a member of the American Psychological Association in the 1920s. Sarah was most likely to be doing which of the following? a. conducting therapy b. giving psychological tests c. conducting cross-cultural research d. studying the role of the self-concept in personality
Factual LO 9 Page: 12 **b**	72.	The area of applied psychology most stimulated by World War II was _____ psychology. a. quantitative b. clinical c. child d. educational
Concept/Applied LO 9 Page: 12 Correct = 92% **c**	73.	A clinical psychologist would probably be most interested in which of the following? a. determining how small groups make decisions b. studying facial expressions of emotion c. figuring out the most effective ways of treating anxiety d. studying the nature of optical illusions
Factual LO 9 Page: 12 **a**	74.	During World War II, many academic psychologists were pressed into service, mainly as a. clinicians b. physicians c. teachers d. military leaders
Factual LO 9 Page: 13 **b**	75.	Which of the following organizations was established in 1988 to serve exclusively as an advocate for the science of psychology? a. American Psychological Association b. American Psychological Society c. Society for the Study of Scientific Psychology d. American Association for the Advancement of Science
Critical Thinking LO 9 Page: 13 **c**	76.	Which of the following is least likely to be included under the umbrella of applied psychology? a. school psychology b. counseling psychology c. experimental psychology d. industrial/organizational psychology
Factual LO 10 Page: 13 Correct = 94% **a**	77.	Which of the following terms refers to the mental processes involved in acquiring knowledge? a. cognition b. pedagogy c. empiricism d. introspection
Factual LO 10 Page: 13 **b**	78.	Which of the following approaches contends that psychology must study internal mental events in order to fully understand behavior? a. behaviorism b. cognitive psychology c. evolutionary psychology d. humanism

Factual LO 10 Page: 13 Correct = 69% d	79.	Which of the following is a recent movement in psychology that has revived the old interest in mental and conscious events? a. physiological psychology b. psychoanalysis c. behavioral psychology d. cognitive psychology
Concept/Applied LO 10 Page: 13 a	80.	Which of the following is most likely to be studied by a cognitive psychologist? a. strategies used by college students to solve a particular problem b. play behavior in preschool children c. whether or not a job incentive program is effective d. factors that determine group cohesiveness
Factual LO 10 Page: 13 d	81.	Which of the following individuals is most closely associated with the cognitive perspective in psychology? a. David Buss b. B. F. Skinner c. Abraham Maslow d. Noam Chomsky
Factual LO 10 Page: 14 c	82.	Research findings from the 1950s and 1960s clearly established that a. the mind has unequivocal control over the body b. the body has unequivocal control over the mind c. the mind and body reciprocally influence each other d. the cognitive viewpoint will reconcile many research findings
Factual LO 10 Page: 14 a	83.	Which of the following psychologists demonstrated that electrical stimulation of the brain could evoke emotional responses such as pleasure and rage in animals? a. James Olds b. Roger Sperry c. B. F. Skinner d. Abraham Maslow
Factual LO 10 Page: 14 c	84.	The results from a recent study suggest that the cognitive perspective surpassed the behavioral perspective in influence sometime around a. 1920 b. 1950 c. 1970 d. 1990
Concept/Applied LO 10 Page: 14 a	85.	Advocates of the _____ perspective maintain that much of human and animal behavior can be explained in terms of the bodily structures and biochemical processes that allow organisms to behave. a. biological b. cognitive c. behavioral d. psychoanalytic
Concept/Applied LO 10 Page: 14 c	86.	Professor Vasquez believes that nearly all psychological disorders can ultimately be traced to abnormalities in brain chemistry. Professor Vasquez's beliefs are most consistent with which of the following theoretical perspectives in psychology? a. behavioral b. cognitive c. biological d. humanistic

Factual LO 11 Page: 14 Correct = 99% **d**	87.	Historically, most of psychology's research has been conducted in a. China b. Japan c. Mexico d. the United States
Factual LO 11 Page: 14 Correct = 67% **d**	88.	Which of the following groups is most likely to have been used as subjects for psychological research? a. a variety of individuals b. lower-class males c. lower-class males and females d. middle- and upper-class white males
Factual LO 11 Page: 14 **c**	89.	The tendency to view one's own group as superior to others and as the standard for judging the worth of foreign ways is called a. racism b. egocentrism c. ethnocentrism d. functionalism
Factual LO 11 Page: 14 **a**	90.	Which of the following is cited in the textbook as a reason for the narrow focus of Western psychology? a. Cross-cultural research is time-consuming and costly. b. Psychology traditionally has emphasized the study of groups rather than individuals. c. Anthropologists are more research-oriented than psychologists. d. The influence of behaviorism narrowed the perspective of Western psychologists.
Critical Thinking LO 11 Page: 15 Correct = 83% **a**	91.	The recent increased interest in research dealing with "cultural" variables in psychology can be attributed to <u>all but</u> which of the following? a. depersonalization of human beings by modern psychology b. various groups (such as civil rights groups, women's groups) arguing that society has paid little attention to human diversity c. increased ethnic diversity in the United States d. increased contact with non-Western cultures due to advances in communication and travel
Factual LO 12 Page: 15 **b**	92.	Which of the following individuals is most closely associated with the recent development of evolutionary psychology? a. Alfred Binet b. David Buss c. Roger Sperry d. James Olds
Factual LO 12 Page: 15 **c**	93.	_____ psychology examines behavioral processes in terms of their adaptive value for a species over the course of many generations. a. Clinical b. Cognitive c. Evolutionary d. Physiological

THE EVOLUTION OF PSYCHOLOGY

Concept/Applied LO 12 Page: 15 **d**	94.	Professor Hensch believes that behaviors that are predominant in certain species probably serve some adaptive function. Professor Hensch's beliefs are most consistent with which of the following theoretical perspectives in psychology? a. behavioral b. cognitive c. humanistic d. evolutionary
Factual LO 12 Page: 15 Correct = 93% **c**	95.	The basic premise of evolutionary psychology is that natural selection favors behaviors that enhance organisms' success in a. establishing a territory b. locating a source of food c. passing on their genes to the next generation d. aggressive interactions with members of other species
Factual LO 12 Page: 15 **c**	96.	On the average, males tend to perform slightly better than females on all but which of the following visual-spatial tasks? a. map reading b. maze learning c. memory for locations d. mental rotation of images
Concept/Applied LO 12 Page: 16 Correct = 59% **b**	97.	Which of the following early psychologists would be most likely to endorse the tenets of evolutionary psychology? a. Sigmund Freud b. William James c. John Watson d. Wilhelm Wundt
Concept/Applied LO 12 Page: 16 Correct = 72% **a**	98.	Evolutionary psychologists would most likely explain females' greater emphasis on potential mates' economic resources by suggesting that it a. increases resources available for their children b. supports their innate need for a large territory c. allows them to acquire a greater variety of time-saving appliances d. increases females' confidence about the maternity of their children
Critical Thinking LO 12 Page: 16 **d**	99.	Which of the following statements best reflects the current thinking about evolutionary psychology? a. It is a widely-accepted approach to the study of human behavior. b. It is a simplistic rehash of ideas proposed by Charles Darwin over 140 years ago. c. It is a radical perspective supported by a small group of "revolutionary" scientists. d. It is a thought-provoking, innovative perspective that is rapidly gaining influence.
Factual LO 13 Page: 17 Correct = 96% **a**	100.	According to the definition of psychology that appears in your textbook, psychology is both a _____ and a(n) _____. a. science; profession b. theory; academic discipline c. school of thought; occupation d. cognitive process; undergraduate major

Factual LO 13 Page: 17 Correct = 92% c	101.	Over the last 50 years membership in the American Psychological Association has a. decreased b. remained the same c. increased dramatically d. first increased and then decreased
Factual LO 13 Page: 17 d	102.	One of the changes that has occurred in psychology over time is that a. psychology has become increasingly less applied in its focus b. the number of clinicians is decreasing c. psychologists have gone from being specialists to being generalists d. fewer psychologists now work in colleges and universities
Factual LO 13 Page: 17 Correct = 75% b	103.	Psychology accounts for about _____ of all doctoral degrees awarded in the sciences and humanities. a. 5% b. 10% c. 20% d. 50%
Factual LO 14 Page: 20 Correct = 72% c	104.	Which of the following is <u>not</u> listed in the textbook as a major area of research in psychology? a. physiological psychology b. cognitive psychology c. industrial/organizational psychology d. social psychology
Factual LO 14 Page: 20 Correct = 95% b	105.	Which of the following areas of research in psychology is concerned with assessing individual differences, developing tests, and developing new statistical techniques? a. social psychology b. psychometrics c. cognitive psychology d. physiological psychology
Factual LO 14 Page: 20 Correct = 83% b	106.	Which of the following areas of research in psychology is concerned with understanding the role of the endocrine system in the regulation of behavior? a. developmental psychology b. physiological psychology c. psychometrics d. cognitive psychology
Concept/Applied LO 14 Page: 20 Correct = 97% b	107.	A psychologist whose major interest focuses on how behavior changes as a function of age would probably be considered a _____ psychologist. a. physiological b. developmental c. social d. cognitive
Concept/Applied LO 14 Page: 20 c	108.	A psychologist who studies attitude formation and change would probably be considered a _____ psychologist. a. physiological b. developmental c. social d. cognitive

Concept/Applied LO 14 Page: 20 **d**	109.	A psychologist who studies information processing and decision making would probably be considered a _____ psychologist. a. physiological b. developmental c. social d. cognitive
Critical Thinking LO 14 Page: 20 **c**	110.	Which of the following would not be expected of an experimental psychologist? a. to study the effects of reward on learning b. to examine the relationship between sleep deprivation and task performance c. to conduct psychotherapy d. to study the factors that motivate behavior
Concept/Applied LO 14 Page: 20 Correct = 89% **b**	111.	A cognitive psychologist is most likely to be interested in which of the following topics? a. behavior in small groups b. information processing c. the adolescent identity crisis d. interpersonal attraction
Concept/Applied LO 14 Page: 20 Correct = 96% **d**	112.	Which of the following is likely to be of most interest to a developmental psychologist? a. the dynamics of small group decision making b. the effect of anxiety on problem-solving behavior c. the use of physical exercise as a means of combating depression d. the effects on children of being raised in a single-parent home
Factual LO 14 Page: 20 Correct = 96% **a**	113.	A psychologist who is interested in the psychological effect of aging would most likely specialize in which of the following? a. developmental psychology b. experimental psychology c. cognitive psychology d. psychometrics
Factual LO 14 Page: 20 Correct = 88% **a**	114.	A psychologist who specializes in psychometrics would most likely be concerned with which of the following? a. developing tests b. counseling c. animal experimentation d. the relationship between brain chemistry and behavior
Concept/Applied LO 14 Page: 20 Correct =83% **b**	115.	Which of the following questions would a social psychologist be most likely to ask? a. How stable is personality over the lifespan? b. Why do we like some people and not others? c. What effect does anxiety have on test performance? d. Do depressed people think differently than nondepressed people?
Concept/Applied LO 14 Page: 20 Correct = 87% **a**	116.	Which of the following questions would a physiological psychologist be most likely to ask? a. How do hormones affect behavior? b. Why do we like some people and not others? c. What effect does reward have on learning? d. What are the stages of problem solving?

Factual LO 15 Page: 21 **b**	117.	Which of the following areas is most likely to be classified as an applied area of specialization in psychology? a. psychometrics b. counseling psychology c. experimental psychology d. developmental psychology
Critical Thinking LO 15 Page: 21 Correct = 94% **d**	118.	Which of the following areas is most similar to clinical psychology? a. social psychology b. school psychology c. industrial psychology d. counseling psychology
Critical Thinking LO 15 Page: 21 Correct = 58% **d**	119.	Which of the following areas is <u>least</u> likely to be considered an applied area of psychology? a. industrial psychology b. clinical psychology c. educational psychology d. developmental psychology
Concept/Applied LO 15 Page: 21 **d**	120.	A psychologist who works on trying to increase job satisfaction and productivity in a large company would most likely have received training in which of the following specialties? a. clinical psychology b. counseling psychology c. educational and school psychology d. industrial and organizational psychology
Concept/Applied LO 15 Page: 21 **b**	121.	An industrial/organizational psychologist would be most likely to be involved in which of the following activities? a. providing assistance to people struggling with everyday problems b. working to improve employee morale and attitudes c. testing and counseling children who are having difficulty in school d. providing group or individual psychotherapy
Factual LO 15 Page: 21 **c**	122.	Which of the following is a medical doctor who specializes in diagnosing and treating mental disorders? a. a clinical psychologist b. a counseling psychologist c. a psychiatrist d. a physiological psychologist
Critical Thinking LO 15 Page: 21 **d**	123.	Which of the following statements regarding the difference between a clinical psychologist and a psychiatrist is accurate? a. Psychiatrists cannot prescribe drugs. b. A clinical psychologist has a medical degree. c. Both clinical psychologists and psychiatrists receive medical training. d. Clinical psychologists tend to take a nonmedical approach to the treatment of psychological disorders.
LO 15 Page: 21 Correct = 87% **b**	124.	A psychiatrist typically has which of the following degrees? a. Doctorate in Psychology b. Medical Degree c. Doctorate in Physiology d. Doctorate in Education

Factual LO 16 Page: 22 Correct = 88% **c**	125.	Psychology is based on systematic observation rather than pure reasoning or common sense. We can say, therefore, that psychology is a. behavioral b. speculative c. empirical d. rational
Factual LO 16 Page: 22 Correct = 85% **d**	126.	Empiricism means that knowledge should be acquired through which of the following? a. logical reasoning b. common sense c. historical tradition d. direct observation
Concept/Applied LO 16 Page: 22 **a**	127.	Researchers in psychology have "to see it to believe it." This orientation is most consistent with which of the following? a. empiricism b. structuralism c. functionalism d. humanism
Factual LO 16 Page: 22 Correct = 77% **b**	128.	The position that knowledge should be obtained or acquired through observation is referred to as a. structuralism b. empiricism c. functionalism d. nativism
Factual LO 16 Page: 22 Correct = 85% **c**	129.	Empiricism refers to a a. "school" of psychology b. sub-field of psychology c. position on how information should be acquired d. theoretical orientation about life
Concept/Applied LO 16 Page: 22 Correct = 54% **d**	130.	Which of the following qualifies as empirically based knowledge? a. intuition b. insight c. logical consistency d. observed actions
Critical Thinking LO 16 Page: 22 Correct = 42% **b**	131.	Which of the following is least characteristic of empiricism? a. documentation b. speculation c. skepticism d. observation
Concept/Applied LO 16 Page: 22 Correct = 52% **c**	132.	The idea that psychology is empirical suggests that a. reason and logic are primary to psychology b. conclusions should be guided by theories c. conclusions should be based on direct observation d. research should focus on underlying, internal events
Factual LO 16 Page: 22 Correct = 84% **a**	133.	A system of interrelated ideas used to explain a set of observations is called a. a theory b. an empirical set c. a hypothesis d. a sociohistorical context

Factual LO 16 Page: 22 **b**	134.	Which of the following best describes what a theory is? a. an explanation of unobservable phenomena b. a system of interrelated ideas used to explain some observation c. a string of unrelated observations d. related speculations that are based on common sense
Critical Thinking LO 16 Page: 22 Correct = 75% **d**	135.	Which of the following is <u>not</u> a reason for psychology's theoretical diversity? a. One theory does not adequately cover the variety of data we have today. b. Different theories focus on different aspects of behavior. c. "Facts" lend themselves to different interpretations. d. Psychology lacks adequate objective data to support theory.
Critical Thinking LO 16 Page: 23 **a**	136.	One psychologist explains a phobia in terms of learning principles whereas another looks to the unconscious for an explanation. Given this scenario, which of the following conclusions is most accurate? a. The two psychologists are using different theoretical perspectives. b. Only one of the two psychologists can be correct. c. Insufficient data have been collected to support either explanation. d. The two psychologists are probably using different sociohistorical contexts.
Factual LO 16 Page: 23 **d**	137.	The development of psychology as a science has been influenced by a. historical factors but not social factors b. social factors but not historical factors c. neither historical nor social factors d. both historical and social factors
Critical Thinking LO 16 Page: 23 **c**	138.	Which of the following statements is the most accurate? a. Social trends influence psychology's development. b. Psychology influences social trends and practices. c. Interconnections exist between what happens in psychology and what happens in society at large. d. There is little relationship between what happens in psychology and what happens in society at large.
Factual LO 16 Page: 23 **a**	139.	In the late 19th century, psychology's rapid growth as a laboratory science was due, in part, to its fascination with _____ as the model discipline. a. physics b. zoology c. sociology d. philosophy
Concept/Applied LO 16 Page: 23 **d**	140.	The idea that Freud's theory was based, in part, on prevailing values during his lifetime implies that psychology's development is influenced by the _____ context. a. social b. empirical c. historical d. sociohistorical
Concept/Applied LO 17 Page: 24 **c**	141.	A multifactorial approach to explaining your performance in a course would most likely focus on a. personal factors more than situational factors b. situational factors more than personal factors c. both personal and situational factors d. the relationship between you and your professor

Concept/Applied 142. The fact that your performance in this course will be affected by both personal and
LO 17 situational factors best supports which of the following?
Page: 24 a. a multifactorial causation of behavior approach
Correct = 87% b. the single-cause explanation of behavior
a c. the dual-cause explanation of behavior
 d. a psychoanalytic approach to explaining behavior

Factual 143. The concept of culture is most closely related to which of the following?
LO 17 a. an individual's collective unconscious
Page: 24 b. a genetic predisposition to behave in a particular way
d c. unconscious urges to satisfy one's basic instincts
 d. widely shared customs, beliefs, and values among members of a group

Factual 144. Widely shared customs, beliefs, values, and norms refer to which of the following?
LO 17 a. ideographic nature
Page: 24 b. culture
Correct = 98% c. ontogeny
b d. phylogeny

Critical Thinking 145. Which of the following statements about the concept of cultural heritage is not
LO 17 accurate?
Page: 24 a. It can be applied to small as well as to large groups.
d b. Much of one's cultural heritage is invisible.
 c. It can influence educational success and physical health.
 d. We generally feel a need to discuss our cultural heritage with others.

Factual 146. A host in which of the following countries is most likely to be insulted if dinner
LO 17 guests eat all the food they are served?
Page: 24 a. China
b b. India
 c. Korea
 d. the United States

Critical Thinking 147. Which of the following statements about the influence of culture is not accurate?
LO 17 a. The influence of culture is everywhere.
Page: 24 b. Our cultural heritage has a pervasive impact on our thoughts, feelings, and
c behavior.
 c. There is not much diversity in the behavior among members of the same culture.
 d. There are both differences and similarities across cultures in behavior.

Critical Thinking 148. Nature is to nurture as _____ is to environment.
LO 17 a. experience
Page: 25 b. learning
Correct = 82% c. heredity
c d. behavior

Factual 149. Which of the following best characterizes people's understanding of reality?
LO 17 a. highly objective
Page: 25 b. highly subjective
Correct = 92% c. genetically determined
b d. a passive process

Concept/Applied 150. The fact that Princeton students "saw" Dartmouth students engage in twice as many
LO 17 infractions as the Dartmouth students did in a Princeton-Dartmouth football game is
Page: 25 most consistent with which of the following?
c
  a. reliance on empirical evidence
  b. multifactorial causation of behavior
  c. subjectivity of perception
  d. unconscious motivation

Critical Thinking 151. Which of the following statements is least consistent with the position that reality is
LO 17 highly subjective?
Page: 25
b
  a. People tend to perceive what they expect to perceive.
  b. The nature of reality is the same for most people because of innate mechanisms.
  c. We tend to impose organization on the stimuli that we pay attention to.
  d. The perception of sights and sounds is an active process.

Concept/Applied 152. Based on Harold Kelley's research, if you are led to believe that you are going to
LO 17 hear a lecture given by a warm and friendly instructor, you
Page: 25
Correct = 86^
b
  a. will probably not be affected much by this expectation unless the instructor is, in fact, warm and friendly
  b. will probably perceive the instructor as being warm and friendly
  c. will probably not be affected unless you are allowed to compare the instructor to one who is cold
  d. may perceive the instructor as warm and friendly, but only if the lecture topic is interesting to you

Factual 153. The scientific method is designed to _____ subjectivity.
LO 17
Page: 26
Correct = 56%
b
  a. utilize
  b. counteract
  c. ignore
  d. enhance

Concept/Applied 154. Which of the following approaches do researchers in psychology take to address the
LO 17 fact that our experiences of the world are highly subjective?
Page: 26
c
  a. They also try to remain somewhat subjective.
  b. They try to simplify their research problems.
  c. They consistently apply the scientific method.
  d. They emphasize the study of internal mechanisms.

Concept/Applied 155. Which of the following is the best advice for developing sound study habits?
LO 18
Page: 27
a
  a. Plan your study schedule in advance.
  b. Make yourself comfortable in your study area by having your favorite music playing.
  c. Try to avoid interrupting your study time with breaks.
  d. Tackle simple, routine tasks before taking on larger tasks.

Critical Thinking 156. Which of the following is not good advice for developing sound study habits?
LO 18
Page: 28
c
  a. Spread out your studying over a period of time.
  b. Allow time for study breaks.
  c. Try to tackle simple, routine tasks first, saving larger tasks for later.
  d. Find a place to study where distractions are likely to be minimal.

Factual 157. Which of the following is not listed in the textbook as an effective study technique?
LO 18
Page: 28
c
  a. Set up a schedule for studying.
  b. Study in a place where distractions are minimal.
  c. Concentrate your study time immediately before an exam.
  d. Break major assignments down into smaller component tasks.

Concept/Applied LO 18 Page: 28 **d**	158.	The idea that you should reward yourself for achieving study goals is based on which of the following concepts? a. empiricism b. genetic predisposition c. unconscious motivation d. behavior modification
Concept/Applied LO 18 Page: 28 **b**	159.	The systematic use of rewards in developing effective study habits is most consistent with which of the following "schools" of psychology? a. humanism b. behaviorism c. functionalism d. structuralism
Factual LO 19 Page: 28 **c**	160.	SQ3R refers to which of the following? a. a mnemonic device used to recall key information b. a method of preparing a study schedule c. a study system designed to promote effective reading d. a technique designed to reduce test anxiety
Factual LO 19 Page: 28 Correct = 92% **a**	161.	The "Q" in the SQ3R method of studying refers to which of the following? a. question b. quiet c. quantify d. quiz
Factual LO 19 Page: 28 **b**	162.	Which of the following is <u>not</u> one of the "Rs" in the SQ3R method of studying? a. review b. remember c. recite d. read
Factual LO 19 Page: 29 **b**	163.	Saying out loud the answers to key questions in the textbook constitutes which of the following steps in the SQ3R method? a. read b. recite c. review d. survey
Factual LO 20 Page: 29 **c**	164.	Which of the following conclusions is supported by research comparing "successful" to "unsuccessful" students? a. Successful students and unsuccessful students attended class equally often. b. Paradoxically, successful students attended class less often than unsuccessful students. c. Successful students attended class more often than unsuccessful students. d. Successful students used an instructor's office hours more than students.
Factual LO 20 Page: 29 **a**	165.	According to research findings, which of the following is most likely to be associated with poor grades? a. being absent from class b. rewarding yourself for studying c. overlearning the material d. changing answers on a multiple-choice test

Factual LO 20 Page: 29 Correct = 92% **b**	166.	According to research findings, which of the following has been found to be associated with higher grades? a. not changing answers on tests b. attending class regularly c. writing down everything your instructor says d. putting off studying until just before an exam
Factual LO 20 Page: 30 **d**	167.	Which of the following is good advice for getting more out of lectures? a. Resist the temptation to anticipate what is coming next. b. When you take notes, try to be a "human tape recorder." c. Avoid reading ahead in the textbook, especially if the material is complex. d. Pay attention to clues from the instructor about what is important.
Factual LO 20 Page: 30 Correct = 71% **d**	168.	Which of the following is most likely to help you get more out of lectures? a. skipping lectures on topics you find confusing; instead, relying exclusively on the textbook b. trying to write down everything the lecturer says c. avoiding the temptation to anticipate what the lecturer will say next d. paying attention to clues about what is most important
Critical Thinking LO 20 Page: 30 Correct = 81% **b**	169.	Which of the following is <u>not</u> good advice for getting more out of lectures? a. Ask questions during the lecture. b. Try to record the lecturer's comments verbatim. c. When the material is especially complex, read ahead on the topic to be covered in class. d. During the lecture, try to anticipate what's coming next and search for deeper meanings.
Factual LO 21 Page: 30 Correct = 64% **c**	170.	Students are said to be "testwise" if they a. have a knack for identifying "trick" questions b. are particularly knowledgeable about the subject matter being tested c. are skilled at using clues contained within a test to improve their scores d. tend to score high on standardized tests
Factual LO 21 Page: 30 Correct = 65% **b**	171.	Research findings indicate that when changing answers on a multiple-choice test, most people: a. change a right answer to a wrong answer b. change a wrong answer to a right answer c. change a wrong answer to another wrong answer d. change a right answer to a wrong answer and back again to the right answer
Critical Thinking LO 21 Page: 30 **a**	172.	Which of the following is <u>not</u> good advice for improving your test-taking ability? a. Don't change answers on a multiple-choice test; your first answer is usually your best. b. Don't waste time thinking too much about difficult-to-answer questions. c. Do not "read things into" test items–that is, make an item more complicated than it is. d. If you have time left after you've answered all the questions, go back and review the test.
Critical Thinking LO 21 Page: 30 **d**	173.	Which of the following is <u>not</u> good advice for someone about to take a multiple-choice test? a. Anticipate the answer before looking at the options. b. Read all the options and eliminate those that are highly implausible. c. Be cautious of options that make broad, sweeping generalizations. d. Once you find your anticipated answer, don't waste time reading the other options.

Concept/Applied LO 21 Page: 30 **b**	174.	Which of the following is good advice for someone about to take a multiple-choice test? a. Do the most difficult and time-consuming questions first. b. Always read each question completely. c. It's a good idea to stick with your first answer. d. As you read the question, try to avoid the temptation to anticipate the answer.
Factual LO 22 Page: 32 **b**	175.	According to modern cognitive psychologists, critical thinking has two main components: the _____ component, and the _____ component. a. intellectual; social b. cognitive; emotional c. behavioral; cognitive d. emotional; attitudinal
Critical Thinking LO 22 Page: 32 **b**	176.	Which of the following is <u>not</u> likely to be considered a critical thinking skill? a. working systematically toward a desired goal b. accepting the views of an appropriate authority figure c. distinguishing among facts, opinions, and reasoned judgements d. understanding how reasons and evidence support or refute conclusions
Factual LO 22 Page: 32 **b**	177.	The word "critical" in the term "critical thinking" is generally meant to convey that a. thinking is essential to success in our culture b. critical thinkers are vigilant about their thinking c. the skills of effective thinking are learned early in life d. effective critical thinkers tend to be judgmental of others' views
Factual LO 23 Page: 33 **b**	178.	The spatial tasks on which males tend to do better than females generally involve which of the following? a. remembering locations b. mentally rotating objects c. identifying objects in a visual field d. processing verbal directions to a specific location
Concept/Applied LO 23 Page: 33 **d**	179.	Which of the following explanations is most likely to be used by an evolutionary psychologist to explain gender differences in spatial abilities? a. The principles of natural selection tend to operate differently in males and females. b. Through evolution, males were classically conditioned to develop certain kinds of spatial abilities. c. When they are young, males are more likely than females to be encouraged to engage in spatially-oriented activities. d. Division of labor between the sexes in hunting and gathering societies created different adaptive pressures for males and females.
Integrative **a**	180.	John Watson argued that psychology should study only observable behavior. This position is most consistent with which of the textbook's unifying themes? a. Psychology is empirical. b. Psychology evolves in a sociohistorical context. c. Heredity and environment jointly influence behavior. d. Our experience of the world is highly subjective.
Integrative Correct = 84% **c**	181.	In the 1920s, there were many fundamental disputes between competing schools of thought in psychology. These disputes illustrate which of the textbook's unifying themes? a. Psychology is empirical. b. Psychology evolves in a sociohistorical context. c. Psychology is theoretically diverse. d. Our experience of the world is highly subjective.

Integrative Correct = 67% **a**	182.	In the 19th century, Wilhelm Wundt attempted to shape the new discipline of psychology along the lines of physics, because in his era physics was admired as a "model" science. Wundt's attempt to imitate physics illustrates which of the textbook's unifying themes? a. Psychology evolves in a sociohistorical context. b. Psychology is theoretically diverse. c. Our experience of the world is highly subjective. d. Behavior is determined by multiple causes.
Integrative **a**	183.	The growth of psychology as a profession was stimulated by World War I and World War II. This influence illustrates which of the textbook's unifying themes? a. Psychology evolves in a sociohistorical context. b. Psychology is theoretically diverse. c. Psychology is empirical. d. Our experience of the world is highly subjective.
Integrative **d**	184.	In criticizing the structuralists' reliance on the method of introspection, William James argued that two people can view the same stimulus quite differently. James's argument illustrates which of the textbook's unifying themes? a. Psychology evolves in a sociohistorical context. b. Psychology is empirical. c. Heredity and environment jointly influence behavior. d. Our experience of the world is highly subjective.
Integrative Correct = 56% **d**	185.	Which of the following do behaviorism and psychoanalytic theory have in common? a. an emphasis on the role sexuality in behavior b. a resistance to the use of animal subjects in psychological research c. the notion that unconscious motives have a major influence on behavior d. the implication that people are not masters of their own destinies
Study Guide LO 1 Page: 3 **c**	186.	Of the two parents of psychology, physiology and philosophy, which provided the method? What is the method? a. philosophy; logic, reasoning b. philosophy; intuition, introspection c. physiology; observation, science d. physiology; anatomy, surgery
Study Guide LO 1 Page: 3 **a**	187.	Who is Wilhelm Wundt? a. He founded the first experimental laboratory. b. He founded the American Psychological Association. c. He discovered the classically conditioned salivary reflex. d. He founded behaviorism.
Study Guide LO 3 Page: 4 **b**	188.	Structuralism is the historical school of psychology that asserted that the purpose of psychology was to a. study behavior b. discover the smaller elements that comprise consciousness c. explore the unconscious d. examine the purposes of conscious processes
Study Guide LO 5 Page: 7 **a**	189.	For John B. Watson, the appropriate subject matter of psychology was a. animal behavior b. the unconscious c. consciousness d. human physiology

Study Guide LO 6 Page: 8 **d**	190.	Within the field of psychology, Freud's ideas encountered resistance because he emphasized a. human consciousness b. human behavior c. introspection d. the unconscious
Study Guide LO 7 Page: 9 **b**	191.	Which of the following would be considered the major principle of operant conditioning? a. Human behavior derives in part from free will; animal behavior is determined by the environment. b. Humans and other animals tend to repeat responses followed by positive outcomes. c. The majority of human behavior is based on thoughts, feelings, and wishes of which we are unaware. d. Human beings are fundamentally different from other animals.
Study Guide LO 8 Page: 11 **a**	192.	Which of the following theorists would tend to emphasize explanations in terms of freedom and potential for personal growth? a. Carl Rogers b. Sigmund Freud c. B. F. Skinner d. All of the above
Study Guide LO 9 Page: 12 **b**	193.	Which of the following represents a major breakthrough in the development of applied psychology? a. the use of the method of introspection b. Binet's development of the intelligence test c. establishment of the first animal laboratory d. Wundt's founding of experimental psychology
Study Guide LO 10 Page: 13 **b**	194.	Recent research trends in psychology involve two areas largely ignored by early behaviorists. These two areas are a. observable and measurable responses b. cognition (thinking) and physiological processes c. classical and operant conditioning d. the effect of environmental events and the behavior of lower animals
Study Guide LO 14 Page: 20 **c**	195.	Which core psychological research area is primarily devoted to the study of such topics as memory, problem solving, and thinking? a. physiological b. social c. cognitive d. personality
Study Guide LO 16 Page: 22 **c**	196.	The assertion that "psychology is empirical" means that psychology is based on a. introspection b. logic c. observation d. mathematics
Study Guide LO 17 Page: 24 **b**	197.	In looking for the causes of a particular behavior, psychologists assume a. one cause or factor b. multifactorial causation c. free will d. infinite causation

Study Guide LO 17 Page: 25 c	198.	Contemporary psychologists generally assume that human behavior is determined by a. heredity b. environment c. heredity and environment acting jointly d. heredity, environment, and free will
Study Guide LO 19 Page: 28 d	199.	What does SQ3R stand for? a. search, question, research, recommend, reconstitute b. silence, quietude, reading, writing, arithmetic c. summarize, quickly, read, research, reread d. survey, question, read, recite, review
Study Guide LO 22 Page: 32 d	200.	Critical thinking refers to a. analysis of problems in terms of scientific principles b. making decisions based on formal and informal logic c. thinking that includes consideration of probabilities d. all of the above
Online Quiz LO 1 Page: 3 b	201.	The scientific study of conscious experience was _____ notion of what the subject matter of psychology should be. a. James's b. Wundt's c. Weiten's d. Watson's
Online Quiz LO 3 Page: 4 c	202.	Introspection was most likely to be used by which of the following types of psychologists? a. humanist b. behaviorist c. structuralist d. functionalist
Online Quiz LO 5 Page: 5 b	203.	That psychology should study only what can be objectively observed is the focus of which of the following "schools" of psychology? a. humanism b. behaviorism c. structuralism d. functionalism
Online Quiz LO 6 Page: 8 d	204.	Which position seeks to explain behavior by focusing on unconscious determinants of behavior? a. structuralism b. functionalism c. Gestalt psychology d. psychoanalytic theory
Online Quiz LO 8 Page: 10 a	205.	Which of the following "schools" of psychology emphasizes the unique qualities of humans, and suggests that we have a drive for personal growth? a. humanism b. psychoanalysis c. behaviorism d. functionalism

Online Quiz LO 10 Page: 13 **c**	206.	Which of the following would be <u>least</u> likely to be studied by a cognitive psychologist? a.　how we remember things b.　the development of language c.　shaping behavior by reinforcement d.　how people reason to solve problems
Online Quiz LO 13 Page: 17 **d**	207.	Which of the following undergraduate majors is more popular than psychology in the United States? a.　accounting b.　engineering c.　general teacher education d.　business administration and management
Online Quiz LO 15 Page: 20 **a**	208.	Which of the following is the most widely practiced professional specialty in psychology? a.　clinical psychology b.　experimental psychology c.　educational and school psychology d.　industrial/organizational psychology
Online Quiz LO 17 Page: 25 **a**	209.	Nature is to nurture as heredity is to a.　environment b.　instincts c.　genetics d.　maturation
Online Quiz LO 20 Page: 29 **a**	210.	Research finding suggest that when students engage in attentive note taking, they are more likely to a.　be able to identify and remember the most important points from a lecture b.　recall the information they find particularly interesting c.　have problems distinguishing important from unimportant information d.　participate in class discussions

ESSAY QUESTIONS

1. Compare and contrast the philosophical approach with the scientific method.

   Both the philosophical approach and the scientific method can be used to answer psychological questions. The philosophical method does so by starting with an assumption and then using reasoning, intuition, and logic to reach a conclusion. In contrast, the scientific method begins with a hypothesis and then uses direct observation to test it. In other words, the philosophical method asks how the world must be (hypothetical), while the scientific method asks how the world is (empirical).

2. Discuss the contributions of structuralism and functionalism to the evolution of psychology as a discipline.

   Both perspectives reflect the early view that consciousness is the appropriate subject matter for the new science, but they differed in regard to how consciousness should be studied.

   With Wilhelm Wundt, the structuralists believed that consciousness should be broken down into its basic elements through introspection. This approach generated numerous laboratory studies of sensory and perceptual phenomena. Structuralism eventually died out due to the inconsistent results of introspective studies.

   Along with William James, the functionalists emphasized the adaptive purposes of consciousness, arguing that psychologists should look at the continuous flow of thought rather than its static elements. Its practical and applied focus generated advances in the study of mental testing, child development, and gender differences. Functionalism, too, gradually faded away, but left applied psychology and behaviorism as its enduring descendants.

3. Compare and contrast the psychoanalytic, behaviorist, and humanist perspectives with regard to their assumptions about human nature.

   Psychoanalysts view humans as essentially "bad"–primitive, animalistic, sexual, irrational, and unconsciously driven to behave in certain ways. This is a pessimistic view of humanity.

   Behaviorists view human nature as nonexistent. Rather, behavior develops under the control of the environment. Since behavior is regarded as conditioned reactions to observable stimuli, the implication is that there is no such thing as free will.

   Humanists view humans as essentially "good"–unique among species in that they have free will (conscious and rational), a natural potential for growth, and a basic need to fulfill this potential. This is an optimistic view of humanity.

4. Provide an overview, from the 1870s to the present, of psychology's interest in the study of mental processes.

   At its inception, psychology was defined as the study of consciousness, both its structure and functions. However, introspection yielded inconsistent results, and both schools of thought were gradually displaced by behaviorism, which redefined the field as the study of observable behavior. The behaviorists advocated abandonment of the study of consciousness altogether, on the grounds that mental events are not directly observable and are therefore unverifiable. This trend began to reverse itself in the 1950s with new research on cognitive development, problem solving, and language. It was recognized that the behaviorist picture of humanity is incomplete. Interest in the study of mental events was also revitalized by new, verifiable methods to study cognition scientifically.

This page intentionally left blank

Chapter Two
The Research Enterprise in Psychology

LEARNING OBJECTIVES

1. Explain science's main assumption and describe the goals of the scientific enterprise in psychology.
2. Explain the relations between theory, hypotheses, and research.
3. Outline the steps in a scientific investigation.
4. Discuss the advantages of the scientific approach.
5. Describe the experimental method of research, explaining independent and dependent variables, experimental and control groups, and extraneous variables.
6. Describe the Featured Study on the efficacy of subliminal self-help audio tapes.
7. Explain the major advantages and disadvantages of the experimental method.
8. Discuss three descriptive/correlational research methods: naturalistic observation, case studies, and surveys.
9. Explain the major advantages and disadvantages of descriptive/correlational research.
10. Describe three measures of central tendency and one measure of variability.
11. Distinguish between positive and negative correlations.
12. Discuss correlation in relation to prediction and causation.
13. Explain the logic of hypothesis testing and the meaning of statistical significance.
14. Explain what makes a sample representative and discuss the problem of sampling bias.
15. Explain when placebo effects are likely to be a problem.
16. Describe the typical kinds of distortions that occur in self-report data.
17. Describe Rosenthal's research on experimenter bias.
18. Discuss the pros and cons of deception in research with human subjects.
19. Discuss the controversy about the use of animals as research subjects.
20. Explain how this chapter highlighted two of the text's unifying themes.
21. Describe the nature of technical journals.
22. Explain how to use *Psychological Abstracts* and discuss the advantages of computerized literature searches.
23. Describe the standard organization of journal articles reporting on psychological research.
24. Explain why anecdotal evidence is flawed and unreliable.

MULTIPLE-CHOICE QUESTIONS

Factual
LO 1
Page: 38
Correct = 87%
a

1. The scientific approach assumes that
   a. events are governed by some lawful order
   b. each event is completely unique
   c. there are no general laws or principles that apply to human behavior
   d. the search for absolute truth is the ultimate goal

Factual
LO 1
Page: 38
Correct = 86%
d

2. Which is <u>not</u> among the goals of psychology?
   a. the development of measurement techniques for describing behavior precisely and accurately
   b. understanding why certain behaviors occur
   c. applications of research findings to solve everyday problems
   d. searching for absolute truths about behavior

Concept/Applied
LO 1
Page: 38
Correct = 56%
c

3. Answering the question of "how" something works is <u>most</u> closely associated with which goal of science?
   a. the search for truth
   b. application and control
   c. measurement and description
   d. understanding and prediction

Factual
LO 1
Page: 38
Correct = 98%
c

4. Any measurable conditions, events, characteristics, or behaviors that are controlled or observed in a study are called
   a. hypotheses
   b. correlations
   c. variables
   d. confounds

Concept/Applied
LO 1
Page: 38
Correct = 86%
d

5. The use of reinforcement principles to modify a child's unruly behavior reflects the goal of science that deals with
   a. understanding and prediction
   b. measurement and description
   c. deterministic and teleological
   d. application and control

Factual
LO 2
Page: 38
a

6. A system of interrelated ideas used to explain a set of observations is called
   a. a theory
   b. a hypothesis
   c. a conceptualization
   d. an application

Factual
LO 2
Page: 38
Correct = 63%
b

7. A theory is
   a. a tentative statement about the relationship between two or more variables
   b. a system of interrelated ideas used to explain a set of observations
   c. a statement of research results that have been proven to be correct
   d. a preliminary proposal that has yet to be tested

Factual
LO 2
Page: 38
Correct = 83%
c

8. A scientific theory has to be
   a. true
   b. accepted by others
   c. testable
   d. well established and not disputed

Concept/Applied LO 2 Page: 38 Correct = 66% **d**	9.	Theories permit researchers to move from a. understanding to application b. concept to description c. application to control d. description to understanding
Factual LO 2 Page: 38 Correct = 87% **a**	10.	Theory construction is a. a gradual iterative process that is always subject to revision b. a standard step-like process that quickly moves toward the truth c. a circular process that typically leads nowhere d. a process that results in concrete findings that are accepted by other scientists
Concept/Applied LO 2 Page: 38 Correct = 84% **b**	11.	Dr. Marqueta believes that "misery loves company." Based on this belief, Dr. Marqueta predicts that people who have received bad news will seek out other people. Dr. Marqueta's belief is an example of _____, and her prediction is an example of _____. a. a hypothesis; a theory b. a theory; a hypothesis c. a variable; an application d. a hypothesis; a variable
Factual LO 3 Page: 39 Correct = 81% **b**	12.	A hypothesis is a. a random guess as to what might happen in an experiment b. a tentative statement about the relationship between two or more variables c. a conclusion drawn from an experiment d. a system of interrelated ideas used to explain a set of observations
Factual LO 3 Page: 39 Correct = 85% **c**	13.	Hypotheses are typically expressed as a. theories b. variables c. predictions d. statistics
Concept/Applied LO 3 Page: 39 **a**	14.	Dr. Licciardi predicts that if people are observed while they perform a complex task they will make more errors. Dr. Licciardi's prediction is an example of a. a hypothesis b. an operational definition c. a theory d. inferential statistics
Concept/Applied LO 3 Page: 39 **d**	15.	Dr. Malm predicts that if teachers ignore students who act up in class, fewer students will act up in class. Dr. Malm's prediction is an example of a. an operational definition b. a theory c. inferential statistics d. a hypothesis
Concept/Applied LO 3 Page: 39 **d**	16.	A researcher is measuring the heart rate of subjects as an index of anxiety. In this study heart rate is a. A confounded variable b. negatively correlated with anxiety c. an independent variable d. an operational definition of anxiety

Factual LO 3 Page: 39 Correct = 82% a	17.	An operational definition a. describes the actions and procedures used to measure or control a variable b. separately defines each term used c. provides a logical basis for each term d. states relationships to other variables
Concept/Applied LO 3 Page: 39 c	18.	Dr. Critelli is studying aggression in children and plans to define aggression as the number of times one child pushes or strikes another child. Defining aggression in this way would a. be an example of a hypothesis b. violate ethical guidelines for psychological research c. represent an operational definition d. require a double-blind research design
Concept/Applied LO 3 Page: 39 c	19.	Dr. Dieringer wants to study attachment patterns in single-parent families. She plans to define the strength of attachment as the time it takes for the parent to respond when the infant starts to cry. Defining attachment in this way would a. be an example of a hypothesis b. violate ethical guidelines for psychological research c. represent an operational definition d. require a double-blind research design
Factual LO 3 Page: 40 Correct = 96% b	20.	When subjects are administered a series of written questions designed to assess their attitudes, opinions, or behavior, this is called a. direct observation b. a questionnaire c. an interview d. a psychological test
Concept/Applied LO 3 Page: 40 Correct = 60% c	21.	A psychologist monitors changes in the subject's heart rate as the subject watches a violent movie. The data collection technique being used is a. direct observation b. psychological testing c. physiological recording d. archival records
Factual LO 3 Page: 40 Correct = 49% a	22.	A standardized measure used to obtain a sample of a person's behavior is called a. a psychological test b. a case study c. an experiment d. a survey
Concept/Applied LO 3 Page: 40 b	23.	Jackson is working with a company to help them develop more effective training programs for their employees. He has spent a great deal of time reviewing all the documentation the company has about previous training opportunities they have provided for their employees. Up to this point in time, Jackson has been engaged in a. psychological testing b. archival research c. direct observation d. meta-analysis
Concept/Applied LO 3 Page: 40 a	24.	Two of the data collection techniques that are <u>most</u> likely to involve direct contact between the researcher and the research participant are a. direct observation and interviews b. archival research and psychological testing c. questionnaires and interviews d. archival research and questionnaires

Concept/Applied LO 3 Page: 40 **d**	25.	Laura answered a series of written questions that asked about her attitudes and opinions on a number of current issues. The method of data collection that was being used in this case was a. a standardized psychological test b. archival research c. direct observation d. a questionnaire
Factual LO 3 Page: 41 Correct = 95% **d**	26.	The <u>final</u> step in a scientific investigation is to a. conduct the study b. analyze the data c. decide whether or not the hypothesis was supported d. report the findings
Concept/Applied LO 3 Page: 41 Correct = 92% **a**	27.	Publication of research findings is extremely important to the scientific method because a. it allows for critique and self-correction b. it brings recognition to the research worker c. it forces the writer to be clear d. the royalties help the researcher pay for the research
Factual LO 3 Page: 41 Correct = 81% **b**	28.	A scientific journal refers to a. a personal diary kept by a scientist b. a periodical that publishes technical and scholarly articles c. a detailed record of the daily procedures followed in conducting a study d. a collection of biographies of famous scientists
Factual LO 4 Page: 42 Correct = 79% **d**	29.	Which of the following is <u>not</u> true regarding commonsense analyses of behavior? a. they tend to be vague and ambiguous b. they often tolerate contradictory generalizations c. they usually involve little effort to verify ideas or detect errors d. they are typically based on precise definitions and hypotheses
Factual LO 4 Page: 42 Correct = 77% **a**	30.	A general strategy for collecting empirical data is called a. a research method b. a case study c. a descriptive statistic d. a hypothesis
Factual LO 4 Page: 42 Correct = 85% **b**	31.	Differing approaches to the observation, measurement, manipulation, and control of variables in empirical studies are referred to as a. validity operationalizations b. research methods c. inductive techniques d. statistical analyses
Factual LO 5 Page: 42 Correct = 94% **d**	32.	The experiment is a research method in which the investigator a. systematically observes two variables to see whether there is an association between them b. observes behavior as it occurs in its natural environment c. conducts an in-depth investigation of an individual subject d. manipulates a variable under carefully controlled conditions and observes whether there are changes in a second variable as a result

Factual LO 5 Page: 42 Correct = 99% **c**	33.	Manipulating a variable under carefully controlled conditions and observing the changes in a second variable defines a. the testing approach b. the survey approach c. the experimental approach d. naturalistic observation
Factual LO 5 Page: 43 Correct = 82% **b**	34.	In an experiment, the variable that is controlled or manipulated by the researcher is called the a. dependent variable b. independent variable c. control variable d. stimulus variable
Factual LO 5 Page: 43 Correct = 86% **b**	35.	An independent variable in an experiment refers to a. the variable that is held constant across experimental conditions b. the variable deliberately manipulated by the experimenter c. the variable that the experimenter believes will change in value because of systematic correlations that exist in the experiment d. the variable that provides an alternative explanation for the results of the experiment
Concept/Applied LO 5 Page: 43 **b**	36.	A group of researchers is investigating the effects of gingko biloba on memory. During the first part of the study the animals learn to run a maze while they are not receiving the supplement; in the second part of the study the animals learn to run a different maze while they are receiving the supplement. In each case the researchers count how many trials it takes before the animals can run the maze pattern without making any errors. In this study the independent variable is a. the type of animal that the researchers select for the study b. the presence or absence of the food supplement in the animal's diet c. the number of trials it takes to run the maze without making any errors d. the age of the animals in the study
Concept/Applied LO 5 Page: 43 **c**	37.	A group of researchers wanted to determine if people will eat more food in a room with red paint and red decorations than in a room that is decorated blue. Half the participants in this study ate in a red room and half ate in a blue room. The researchers then measured how much food was consumed in each of the two rooms. In this study the independent variable was a. the type of food that was available during the study b. the amount of food that was consumed c. the color of the decorations in the room d. how hungry the participants were at the end of the study
Concept/Applied LO 5 Page: 43 **d**	38.	Researchers who were studying plant growth raised plants in two separate rooms. One room had taped conversations playing 24 hours a day; the other room was silent. The researchers found that the plants grew better in the room which had the conversations playing. In this study, the type of room (conversation or silence) would be a. the dependent variable b. an extraneous variable c. a placebo d. the independent variable

Concept/Applied LO 5 Page: 43 a	39.	Researchers who were studying memory had participants learn a list of words after consuming a soft drink with caffeine or a decaffeinated version of the same soft drink. The researchers then counted the number of words that were recalled from the list. In this study, the type of beverage (caffeinated or decaffeinated) would be a. the independent variable b. an extraneous variable c. the dependent variable d. a placebo
Factual LO 5 Page: 43 Correct = 55% c	40.	A dependent variable in an experiment refers to the variable a. held constant across the experimental conditions b. deliberately manipulated by the experimenter c. that changes value because of the systematic manipulation in the experiment d. that the experimenter is depending on to cause something to happen in the experiment
Concept/Applied LO 5 Page: 43 b	41.	Researchers studying the effects of sleep deprivation tested the physical coordination skills of 25-year-old males who had been sleep deprived for either 24, 36, or 48 hours. In this study the dependent variable would be a. the age of the research participants b. the physical coordination skills of the men in the study c. the length of time the participants had been sleep deprived d. the type of physical coordination task the researchers use
Concept/Applied LO 5 Page: 43 a	42.	A group of researchers wants to determine if people are more likely to follow directions if the person giving the directions is in a uniform. Half the participants are directed to a parking spot by a uniformed security guard, the other half are directed to a parking spot by an individual wearing blue jeans and a t-shirt. In this study the dependent variable would be a. the number of participants who park in the spot they are directed to b. the type of clothing worn by the person giving the directions c. the gender of the person driving into the parking lot d. the distance between the parking spot and the entrance
Concept/Applied LO 5 Page: 43 d	43.	A group of researchers conducts a study to determine if children's performance is affected by the presence of other children. First the children are taken to a room with no other children and timed while they complete a puzzle. Later the same children are taken to a room with four other children and timed while they complete a similar puzzle. In this study, the length of time it takes to complete the puzzle would be a. the independent variable b. an extraneous variable c. a control variable d. the dependent variable
Concept/Applied LO 5 Page: 43 b	44.	An industrial designer wants to determine if the new design for a piece of office equipment will result in fewer errors. The designer sets up a machine with the old design in one room, and a machine with the new design in a second room. He counts how many errors are made using each of the two machines. In this study, the number of errors that are made would be a. a control variable b. the dependent variable c. the independent variable d. an extraneous variable

Concept/Applied LO 5 Page: 43 Correct = 93% **b**	45.	If we view an experiment as an attempt to establish a cause-effect relationship, the _____ variable would be the cause, and the _____ variable would be the effect. a. dependent; independent b. independent; dependent c. control; experimental d. independent; confounded
Concept/Applied LO 5 Page: 43 Correct = 76% **a**	46.	A researcher found that clients who were randomly assigned to same-sex groups participated more in group therapy sessions than clients who were randomly assigned to coed groups. In this experiment, the dependent variable was a. the amount of participation in the group therapy sessions b. whether or not the group was coed c. the clients' attitudes toward group therapy d. how much the clients' mental health improved
Factual LO 5 Page: 43 Correct = 79% **a**	47.	The experimental group a. consists of the subjects who receive some special treatment with regard to the independent variable b. consists of the subjects who receive some special treatment with regard to the dependent variable c. consists of the subjects who do not receive the special treatment d. must be chosen so as to be as different from the control group as possible
Concept/Applied LO 5 Page: 43 **c**	48.	In an experiment designed to test memory processes one group was given special instructions and asked to group the items on a list into categories while they tried to memorize them. A second group of participants was given the same list, but they did not receive any special instructions. In this study, the experimental group is a. the group in which the participants remember the least items from the list b. the group who did not receive any special instructions c. the group who received the special instructions d. the group in which the participants remember the most items from the list
Concept/Applied LO 5 Page: 43 **b**	49.	In a study designed to test the effects of a new drug developed to treat Alzheimer's disease half the patients were given the actual drug while the other half of the patients were given a placebo (sugar pill). In this study, the experimental group is a. the patients who show evidence of an improvement in their memory b. the group who received the actual drug c. the group who received the placebo d. the patients who were not included in the study
Concept/Applied LO 5 Page: 43 **b**	50.	David and Alexandra both take part in a research study that is investigating the effects of sleep deprivation on reaction time. David is kept awake for 24 hours straight while Alexandra follows her normal sleep routine. In this study David is a. part of the hypothesis group b. part of the experimental group c. part of the control group d. part of the dependent variable group
Critical Thinking LO 5 Page: 43 Correct = 75% **b**	51.	The purpose of the control group is to a. make the experiment more complex b. isolate the effect of the independent variable on the dependent variable c. make statistical significance more likely d. isolate the effect of the dependent variable on the independent variable

Concept/Applied LO 5 Page: 43 Correct = 97% **d**	52.	A researcher wants to see if a protein-enriched diet will enhance the maze-running performance of rats. One group of rats is fed the high-protein diet for the duration of the study; the other group continues to receive ordinary rat chow. In this experiment, the group of rats that is fed the high-protein diet is _____ group; the group that receives ordinary rat chow is _____ group. a. a control; a control b. a control; an experimental c. an experimental; an experimental d. an experimental; a control
Concept/Applied LO 5 Page: 43 **c**	53.	A researcher has children watch 30 minutes of violent television, and then counts the number of times they hit each other afterward in a one-hour play period as a measure of aggression. The researcher concludes that television violence causes aggression. However, this conclusion is invalid because a. the study is strictly correlational b. aggression wasn't operationally defined c. there was no control group d. it is unethical to force children to watch violent television
Concept/Applied LO 5 Page: 43 **b**	54.	A group of researchers wanted to determine whether children would behave more aggressively after watching violent television programming. Half the children in the study watched a violent television show; the other children watched a non-violent television program. In this study, the control group is a. the children who behave the most aggressively at the end of the study b. the children who watch the non-violent program c. the children who watch the violent show d. the children who behave the least aggressively at the end of the study
Concept/Applied LO 5 Page: 43 **c**	55.	Jason believes that patrons in his bar will be more likely to leave a tip if the tip jar already has some money in it, than if the tip jar is completely empty. To test this belief he has the tip jar empty about half the time when a customer approaches the bar; the rest of the time he ensures there is at least $5.00 in the jar when a customer approaches. In Jason's experiment, the control group would be a. all the patrons who leave a tip when they leave the bar b. the patrons who see a tip jar that contains at least $5.00 c. the patrons who see an empty tip jar d. all the patrons who leave the bar without tipping Jason
Concept/Applied LO 5 Page: 43 **b**	56.	Dr. Prutherow believes that people who are under stress will develop more colds than people who are not under stress. When he randomly selects 10 participants and exposes them to high levels of stress, he finds that 9 of the participants develop colds. Based on these results he concludes that stress causes an increase in colds. Dr. Prutherow's reasoning may be flawed because in this study a. there was no dependent variable in his study b. there was no control group for comparison c. he didn't formulate a hypothesis before he collected his data d. he didn't measure the independent variable when the study ended
Factual LO 5 Page: 44 Correct = 83% **d**	57.	By definition, an extraneous variable is a. a variable that affects the control group but not the experimental group b. the same thing as a dependent variable c. a variable that is completely irrelevant to both the independent and dependent variables d. a variable, other than the independent variable, that may influence the dependent variable

Factual LO 5 Page: 44 Correct = 92% **b**	58.	A variable, other than the independent variable, that appears to have influenced the dependent variable in a study is referred to as a. a covariate b. an extraneous variable c. a redundant variable d. an inverse bias
Factual LO 5 Page: 44 Correct = 77% **c**	59.	When two variables are linked and their individual effects cannot be separated out, we speak of the variables as being a. independent variables b. dependent variables c. confounded variables d. codependent variables
Critical Thinking LO 5 Page: 44 **d**	60.	Diaz conducts a decision-making experiment to determine if people reason more logically when they have more time to decide. All the participants who are under 40 are allowed 15 minutes to reach a decision about a problem; all the participants who are over 40 are allowed 20 minutes to reach a decision about the same problem. Diaz has a problem with his experimental design because a. there are two control groups and no experimental group b. the length of time allowed for the decision is confounded with the independent variable c. there is no dependent variable in the experiment d. the age of the participants is confounded with the independent variable
Factual LO 5 Page: 44 Correct = 54% **d**	61.	In experiments, placing subjects in experimental groups such that each subject has an equal probability of ending up in any experimental group is referred to as. a. random selection b. random sampling c. random forecasting d. random assignment
Factual LO 5 Page: 44 Correct = 97% **c**	62.	Random assignment of subjects occurs when a. subjects are allowed to choose which group or condition they would like to be in b. a different method is used to assign each subject to a group or condition c. all subjects have an equal chance of being assigned to any of the groups or conditions d. all topics have an equal chance of being assigned to a particular experimenter
Concept/Applied LO 5 Page: 44 **a**	63.	Dr. Kalmagura plans on introducing a new exam review procedure in his chemistry classes. To check the effectiveness of the new procedure he is going to have half his students try the new technique for one semester, while the remaining students review in the way they have always done in the past. He asks each student to decide which of the techniques they would like to use, the new technique or the standard technique. In this example, Dr. Kalmagura's procedure illustrates a. the use of non-random assignment b. a correlational research design c. a double-blind research design d. what is meant by informed consent in research

Critical Thinking LO 5 Page: 44 **d**	64.	Bill received a poor performance evaluation in his job last year. Since then Bill has started working through his lunch hour, he has taken on four special projects, and enrolled in night classes to upgrade his computer skills. If Bill receives a better evaluation at his next performance it will be hard for him to figure out why because a. he failed to use a double-blind procedure to test his hypothesis b. he didn't formulate a research hypothesis before implementing the changes c. none of the actions he took are likely to be related to his overall job performance d. the three actions he took are confounded with each other
Factual LO 5 Page: 45 **a**	65.	An interaction between two variables means that a. the effect of one independent variable depends on the effect of another b. the effects of one independent variable get added to the effects of another c. the measurements of one dependent variable get added to the measurements of another d. the measurement of one dependent variable depends on the measurement of another
Concept/Applied LO 5 Page: 45 **b**	66.	Derrick designed an experiment in which participants listened to a persuasive speech delivered either by a person who was very tall or a person who was average in height. In addition, the speeches were delivered either by individuals wearing business clothes or by people wearing casual clothes. In this example, Derrick a. has two dependent variables, and will be able to determine if persuasion interacts with any other factors b. has two independent variables, and will be able to determine if height and style of clothing interact c. does not have a control group, which should reduce the impact of self-reporting bias in his study d. is using a double-blind procedure, which should reduce experimenter bias
Factual LO 6 Page: 46 **d**	67.	In the Featured Study on the use of subliminal self-help tapes, one of the dependent variables was a. the actual purpose of the tape (memory or self-esteem) b. the group that the subject was assigned to (experimental or control) c. the labeling of the tape (accurate or mislabeled) d. the subject's beliefs about their personal improvement
Factual LO 6 Page: 46 **b**	68.	In the Featured Study on the use of subliminal self-help tapes, one of the dependent variables was a. the actual purpose of the tape (memory or self-esteem) b. the actual improvement in memory or self-esteem c. the group that the subject was assigned to (experimental or control) d. the labeling of the tape (accurate or mislabeled)
Factual LO 6 Page: 46 **a**	69.	In the Featured Study on the use of subliminal self-help tapes, one of the independent variables was a. the actual purpose of the tape (memory or self-esteem) b. the group that the subject was assigned to (experimental or control) c. the actual improvement in memory or self-esteem d. the subject's beliefs about their personal improvement
Factual LO 6 Page: 46 **c**	70.	In the Featured Study on the use of subliminal self-help tapes, one of the independent variables was a. the group that the subject was assigned to (experimental or control) b. the actual improvement in memory or self-esteem c. the labeling of the tape (accurate or mislabeled) d. the subject's beliefs about their personal improvement

Factual LO 6 Page: 46 **b**	71.	In the Featured Study on the use of subliminal self-help tapes, the researchers found a. the observed changes matched the content of the tapes, not the labels on the tapes b. the observed changes matched the labels on the tapes, not the content of the tapes c. none of the participants increased either their memory or their self-esteem d. all the participants increased both their memory and their self-esteem
Concept/Applied LO 6 Page: 46 **c**	72.	The Tapes'R'Us factory had a production problem last month all the subliminal tapes were accidentally shipped with the wrong labels. The tapes to promote happiness were labeled "Becoming a more assertive person," and the assertiveness tapes were labeled "Becoming a happier person." Based on the results reported in the Featured Study on the use of subliminal self-help tapes, you should predict that people who buy the tapes labeled "Becoming a happier person" will report that they a. feel happier and more assertive after listening to the tapes b. have not noticed any change in either their overall level of happiness or their level of assertiveness c. feel happier, but have not noticed any change in their level of assertiveness d. feel more assertive, but have not noticed any change in their level of happiness
Concept/Applied LO 6 Page: 46 **d**	73.	The Tapes'R'Us factory had a production problem last month and all the subliminal tapes they produced were accidentally shipped with the wrong labels. The tapes to promote happiness were labeled "Becoming a more assertive person," and the assertiveness tapes were labeled "Becoming a happier person." Based on the results reported in the Featured Study on the use of subliminal self-help tapes, you should predict that people who buy the tapes labeled "Becoming a happier person" will a. score higher in both assertiveness and happiness on objective tests of these traits b. score higher on objective tests on happiness, but not on tests of assertiveness c. score higher on objective tests on assertiveness, but not on tests of happiness d. not show evidence of any significant change in either assertiveness or happiness on objective tests of these traits
Concept/Applied LO 6 Page: 46 **b**	74.	You are reading the ads in "The Global Insider" as you wait to pay for your gasoline. You notice one ad for subliminal tapes that claim they will increase your IQ score by over 90 points in just 2 weeks. Based on the results reported in the Featured Study on the use of subliminal self-help tapes, you should a. buy the magazine and send in the $200 they are requesting, because the evidence suggests that subliminal messages have a significant impact b. put the magazine down and pay for your gas, because the evidence suggests that subliminal messages have a minimal impact c. warn your friends because the evidence suggests that these tapes are often used by people who recruit individuals for cults d. buy the magazine and send in the $200 they are requesting, realizing that you IQ score is only likely to increase by 45 points, and it will probably take 4 weeks
Concept/Applied LO 7 Page: 47 Correct = 82% **a**	75.	The main advantage associated with the experimental method is a. its precise control b. its ability to duplicate real life in the laboratory c. that it can be used to explore just about everything d. participants usually enjoy taking part in the study
Factual LO 7 Page: 47 Correct = 64% **c**	76.	The ability to infer a cause-and-effect relationship is associated only with the a. correlational research method b. case history research method c. experimental research method d. empirical research method

Factual LO 7 Page: 47 Correct = 44% **d**	77.	One of the disadvantages of the experimental method is a. the inability to generate cause-and-effect conclusions b. the length of time necessary to complete the study c. the fact that only one variable can be studied at a time d. the fact that experiments often can't be done for practical or ethical reasons
Concept/Applied LO 7 Page: 48 Correct = 55% **d**	78.	Which of the following is <u>not</u> a disadvantage of the experimental method of conducting research? a. It cannot be used to study certain issues. b. It produces artificial situations that may not be applicable to real life. c. It is impossible to manipulate certain variables. d. It is virtually impossible to conduct a true experiment with human beings.
Factual LO 8 Page: 48 Correct = 69% **a**	79.	In descriptive/correlational research, the investigator a. systematically observes two variables to see whether there is an association between them b. manipulates a variable under carefully controlled conditions and observes whether there are changes in a second variable as a result c. exposes subjects to two closely related treatment conditions d. simultaneously manipulates two or more independent variables
Factual LO 8 Page: 48 Correct = 92% **a**	80.	Which of the following is <u>not</u> listed in the textbook as a descriptive research method? a. criterion-based induction b. case studies c. surveys d. naturalistic observation
Concept/Applied LO 8 Page: 48 Correct = 90% **b**	81.	Naturalistic observation, case studies, and surveys all have in common that a. they do not directly observe behavior b. they do not manipulate the variables under study c. they can show causal relationships d. the results obtained cannot be analyzed statistically
Concept/Applied LO 8 Page: 48 Correct = 97% **c**	82.	Going to a playground for an hour each day for two weeks and recording girl-boy exchanges would be an example of a. a case study b. a survey c. a naturalistic observation d. an experiment
Concept/Applied LO 8 Page: 48 Correct = 79% **d**	83.	Recording all instances of an event for a particular time period (such as how many times an older brother strikes his younger brother) without the subjects' awareness is an example of a. compiling a case study b. correlational research c. conducting an experiment d. naturalistic observation
Concept/Applied LO 8 Page: 48 Correct = 93% **b**	84.	You are sitting on a park bench in a major metropolitan area from 7 A.M. to 7 P.M. and you note the number of people who walk by, whether or not they litter, and their gender. You are engaging in a. casual observation b. naturalistic observation c. case study research d. experimental research

Concept/Applied LO 8 Page: 49 Correct = 99% c	85.	An advantage of naturalistic observation is that it a. approximates the experimental method b. allows for cause-and-effect conclusions to be drawn c. allows behavior to be studied in realistic settings d. involves random assignment
Concept/Applied LO 8 Page: 49 a	86.	A group of researchers wanted to investigate allegations of sexual harassment on a company's assembly line. To make their observations, the researchers took jobs working on the assembly line and pretended to be new employees. In this example, the researchers were using a. naturalistic observation b. correlational research c. survey research d. the case study method of research
Concept/Applied LO 8 Page: 49 b	87.	A local hospital wanted to assess the way its patients were being treated. The hospital hired several researchers to act as patients and record the way hospital personnel handled the admitting and preliminary evaluation procedures. In this example, the researchers hired by the hospital were engaged in a. case study research b. naturalistic observation c. correlational research d. survey research
Concept/Applied LO 8 Page: 49 c	88.	Jolyn believed that there were gender differences in driving habits. To test this assumption she stood near a quiet intersection. Jolyn recorded the gender of each driver who approached a stop sign, and also whether the individual came to a complete stop before proceeding into the intersection. Jolyn is conducting a. an experiment with two dependent variables b. case study research c. naturalistic observation d. psychological testing
Concept/Applied LO 8 Page: 50 Correct = 89% d	89.	Which of the following techniques is most likely to prove useful in determining why a <u>particular</u> child is afraid to go to school? a. experiment b. descriptive study c. naturalistic observation d. case study
Concept/Applied LO 8 Page: 50 a	90.	Dr. Kincaid was interested in the topic of autistic savants (individuals with limited abilities in many areas, but with an exceptional talent in one specific area). In the initial part of the investigation Dr. Kincaid carefully observed and compiled detailed files on three individuals who were autistic savants. Dr. Kincaid is conducting a. case study research b. survey research c. correlational research d. experimental research
Critical Thinking LO 8 Page: 50 Correct = 33% d	91.	Subjectivity and the danger of focusing attention selectively is probably greatest in a. experimental studies b. surveys c. naturalistic observation d. compiling a case study

Concept/Applied LO 8 Page: 50 d	92.	NASA wanted to know if extended periods of weightlessness would have an impact on long-term circulatory function. The agency located seven former astronauts who had spent more than one month in space under conditions of weightlessness, and tested all aspects of their cardiovascular function. NASA's research with these seven astronauts would be considered to be a. survey research b. experimental research c. correlational research d. case study research
Critical Thinking LO 8 Page: 50 d	93.	One of your friends is writing a research paper, and wants to obtain information about the depth of personal information people typically reveal during a first date. Directly observing a large number of people during a first date will be difficult, so your friend asks for your advice on the best way to collect this type of data. The best suggestion would be for your friend to use a. the case study approach b. archival research c. a double-blind observational study d. a survey
Concept/Applied LO 8 Page: 50 a	94.	Estavan received a questionnaire in the mail asking about his general buying habits. He was asked to identify the specific products that he typically buys, and the amount of each product that he typically uses. If Estavan completes the questionnaire and returns it, he will have taken part in research that incorporates a. the survey method b. naturalistic observation c. a case study approach d. archival research
Concept/Applied LO 9 Page: 51 Correct = 52% a	95.	Broadening the scope of phenomena that psychologists are able to study is associated with a. descriptive research methods b. introspective research methods c. hypothetical deductive research methods d. functional research methods
Concept/Applied LO 9 Page: 51 Correct =52% c	96.	Perhaps the greatest disadvantage or limitation associated with descriptive research methods is a. the inability to look at important variables like nutritional effects on behavior b. an insensitivity to ethical concerns c. the inability to control events and isolate cause and effect linkages d. the fact these methods usually focus attention too narrowly on a single variable
Concept/Applied LO 9 Page: 51 Correct = 57% d	97.	Perhaps the greatest advantage associated with descriptive research methods is a. a sensitivity to ethical concerns b. the isolation of cause and effect linkages in behavior c. the ability to focus on specific, isolated behaviors d. the ability to explore questions that cannot be examined using experimental procedures

Concept/Applied
LO 9
Page: 51
d

98. Trevor plans to study the relationship between people's responses to highly stressful situations and their overall health. He decides he must use correlational research, rather than experimental research, to investigate this problem because correlational studies
    a. tend to be more accurate than experiments
    b. have higher internal validity than experiments when there are two dependent variables
    c. can be used to study either positive or negative relationships, whereas experiments can only be used to study positive relationships
    d. can be used to investigate factors that would be unethical to manipulate in an experimental study

Critical Thinking
LO 9
Page: 52
c

99. Maria plans to study the relationship between self-esteem and being raised in a single-parent or a two-parent family. She decides she must use correlational research, rather than experimental research, to investigate this problem because correlational studies
    a. tend to be more accurate than experiments
    b. have higher internal validity than experiments when there are two dependent variables
    c. can be used to investigate factors that would be impossible to manipulate in an experimental study
    d. can be used to study either positive or negative relationships, whereas experiments can only be used to study positive relationships

Factual
LO 10
Page: 53
Correct = 79%
c

100. The use of mathematics to organize, summarize, and interpret numerical information is referred to as
    a. calculus
    b. functional analysis
    c. statistics
    d. algebra

Factual
LO 10
Page: 53
Correct = 73%
d

101. Statistics can be used to do all of the below except
    a. summarize observations
    b. organize observations
    c. interpret observations
    d. prove observations

Factual
LO 10
Page: 53
Correct = 90%
a

102. The two basic types of statistics are
    a. descriptive and inferential
    b. central tendency and variability
    c. sampling and correlative
    d. parametric and nonparametric

Factual
LO 10
Page: 53
Correct = 67%
a

103. Statistics that are used to summarize and organize data are called
    a. descriptive statistics
    b. numerical statistics
    c. inferential statistics
    d. computational statistics

Factual
LO 10
Page: 53
Correct = 94%
d

104. The score that falls exactly in the center of a distribution of scores such that half the scores fall below that score and half the scores fall above it is the
    a. mean
    b. standard deviation
    c. range
    d. median

Factual	105.	The median is
LO 10		a. the score that falls exactly in the center of a distribution
Page: 53		b. the arithmetic average of the scores in a distribution
Correct = 92%		c. the score that occurs most frequently in a distribution
a		d. the difference between the largest and the smallest scores in a distribution

Concept/Applied	106.	Your grade point average is an example of which measure of central tendency?
LO 10		a. median
Page: 53		b. mean
Correct = 95%		c. mode
b		d. midpoint

Factual	107.	The mode in a group of scores describes the _____ for that group of scores.
LO 10		a. central tendency
Page: 53		b. association with another group of scores
Correct = 77%		c. halfway point
a		d. variability

Concept/Applied	108.	When the scores for a recent Chemistry exam were calculated the mean was 60 and the median was 65. Later the professor discovered that one score had been recorded incorrectly; it had been entered into the computer as a 5, instead of as a 50. When this correction is made
LO 10		a. the median for the exam will change, but the mean will stay the same
Page: 53		b. both the mean and the median for the exam will change
c		c. the mean for the exam will change, but the median will stay the same
		d. neither the mean nor the median for the exam will be affected

Concept/Applied	109.	Charley tells you that 17 out of the 30 students enrolled in his English class scored exactly 62 points on the last exam. Conceptually, this is the same as saying
LO 10		a. the mean for that particular English exam was 62 points
Page: 53		b. the median for that particular English exam was 62 points
d		c. the standard deviation for that particular English exam was 62 points
		d. the mode for that particular English exam was 62 points

Concept/Applied	110.	Carla earned 78 points on her statistics exam. Ten of the students in her class earned higher scores than she did, and ten students earned lower scores than Carla. Based on this information, you can conclude that Carla's score of 78 points is
LO 10		a. the standardized score for her class
Page: 53		b. the median for her class
b		c. the mean for her class
		d. the mode for her class

Concept/Applied	111.	In Margaritte's sociology discussion group 4 of the 5 students are between the ages of 19 and 23; the fifth student is 54 years old. If Margaritte wants to report the statistic that best represents the "average" age for her discussion group, she should report either
LO 10		a. the mean or the median, because these numbers are typically the same
Page: 53		b. the mean or the mode, because these number are not affected by extreme scores
c		c. the median or the mode, because these numbers will be more representative
		d. the mean or the standard deviation, so additional statistics can be calculated

Concept/Applied	112.	When variability in a data set is large, the standard deviation will be _____; when variability is small, the standard deviation will be _____.
LO 10		a. large; small
Page: 53		b. large; large
Correct = 84%		c. small; large
a		d. small; small

Concept/Applied LO 10 Page: 53 **a**	113.	Georgeanne calculated descriptive statistics for the age of residents in a nursing home. She reported the mean age as 75 years, with a standard deviation of 10 years. Later she found that she had made an error in her calculations. One resident's age was entered as 27 when it should have been 72. When this correction is made a. the standard deviation for the data set will decrease b. the standard deviation for the data set will not change c. the standard deviation for the data set will increase d. the correlation coefficient for the data set will become negative
Critical Thinking LO 10 Page: 53 **b**	114.	Carmella is in a class where the scores on the second midterm exam ranged from 75 to 85 points. Conrad is taking the same course, but in his section the scores ranged from 50 to 98 points. In this example the standard deviation in Carmella's class should be a. negatively correlated with the standard deviation in Conrad's class b. lower than the standard deviation in Conrad's class c. higher than the standard deviation in Conrad's class d. the same as the standard deviation in Conrad's class
Factual LO 11 Page: 54 Correct = 72% **b**	115.	The statistic that indexes the degree to which we may predict the value of one variable from a second variable is the a. mean b. correlation coefficient c. standard deviation d. mode
Factual LO 11 Page: 54 Correct = 84% **c**	116.	The correlation coefficient is a measure of a. central tendency b. the amount of variability in a data set c. the degree of relationship between two variables d. the difference between the largest and smallest scores in a data set
Concept/Applied LO 11 Page: 54 Correct = 74% **d**	117.	If we were to measure the height and weight of 100 adult women, we would find that these two measures are a. uncorrelated b. increasingly correlated c. negatively correlated d. positively correlated
Concept/Applied LO 11 Page: 54 Correct = 79% **c**	118.	A correlation coefficient of zero describes a. a positive relationship between two variables b. a negative relationship between two variables c. the lack of a relationship between two variables d. a perfect relationship between two variables
Concept/Applied LO 11 Page: 54 **a**	119.	Suppose a researcher discovered a +.87 correlation between the length of a person's toes and the number of shoes the person owns. In general, people who own the fewest number of shoes would have a. small toes b. large toes c. medium-sized toes d. either very large or very small toes

Concept/Applied LO 11 Page: 54 **d**	120.	Dr. Macator predicts that people will act more aggressively during the heat waves of summer than they will during the cold spells of winter. This suggests that Dr. Macator believes that temperature and level of aggression are a. negatively correlated b. independent variables c. uncorrelated d. positively correlated
Concept/Applied LO 11 Page: 54 **c**	121.	The FDA found that people who used a particular diet drug combination had more heart valve defects than people who had not taken the diet drug combination. This suggests that the use of the diet drug combination and heart valve defects are a. negatively correlated b. independent variables c. positively correlated d. interactive variables
Concept/Applied LO 11 Page: 54 **a**	122.	Imagine that the personality traits of openness and extroversion are positively correlated. If Andrea's score in openness is extremely low a. she would most likely score at the low end of the extroversion scale b. it is impossible to predict how she is likely to score on the extroversion scale without more information c. she would most likely score at the high end of the extroversion scale d. she would probably score close to the median on the extroversion scale
Concept/Applied LO 11 Page: 54 **a**	123.	Dr. Barton has found that students who score higher than 85% on the first midterm tend to earn scores of 75% or better on the final exam, while students who score less than 60% on the first midterm often end up with a failing grade on the final exam. This suggests that a. the scores on the first midterm and the final exam are positively correlated b. the scores on the first midterm and the final exam are negatively correlated c. students who do poorly on the first midterm give up and study less for the final d. Dr. Barton should change the final so it is more fair to students who are not doing well in the course
Concept/Applied LO 11 Page: 54 Correct = 59% **a**	124.	Suppose a researcher discovered a strong negative correlation between the length of people's hair and the amount of money they paid for their automobile. In general, people who paid the least amount of money for their automobile also had a. the longest hair b. mid-length hair c. the shortest hair d. either extremely long or extremely short hair
Concept/Applied LO 11 Page: 54 Correct = 74% **d**	125.	Suppose that students who work more hours at their jobs tend to have lower grade point averages, and also tend to get less sleep. If we were to correlate the two variables of grade point average and number of hours of sleep, we would find that the correlation coefficient is a. greater than one b. equal to zero c. less than zero d. greater than zero, but less than one
Concept/Applied LO 11 Page: 54 **b**	126.	Mice who received gingko biloba in their diets made fewer errors in a maze running task than mice who had not received gingko biloba. This suggests that, in mice, the use of gingko biloba and errors in maze running are a. dependent variables b. negatively correlated c. positively correlated d. uncorrelated

Concept/Applied LO 11 Page: 54 **a**	127.	As the number of bystanders increases, people are less likely to help someone who is in distress. This suggests that the size of a crowd and helping behavior are a. negatively correlated b. uncorrelated c. positively correlated d. dependent variables
Concept/Applied LO 11 Page: 54 **b**	128.	Imagine that the personality traits of conscientiousness and extroversion are negatively correlated. If Wilfred's score in conscientiousness is extremely low a. he would probably score close to the median on the extroversion scale b. he would most likely score at the high end of the extroversion scale c. he would most likely score at the low end of the extroversion scale d. it is impossible to predict how he is likely to score on the extroversion scale without more information
Concept/Applied LO 11 Page: 54 **c**	129.	Dr. Hackle has found that no matter how students score on the first midterm, all the students in her class tend to score between 75% and 80% on her final exam. This suggests that a. the scores on the final exam and the first midterm are negatively correlated b. the scores on the final exam and the first midterm are positively correlated c. the scores on the final exam and the first midterm are not very highly correlated d. Dr. Hackle should change the final so it is more fair to the students who are doing well in her course
Concept/Applied LO 12 Page: 55 **c**	130.	Of the following correlation coefficients, the one that would allow the <u>most</u> accurate predictions of one variable based on the other variable would be a. 0.00 b. +1.24 c. +1.00 d. -0.49
Concept/Applied LO 12 Page: 55 **a**	131.	Of the following correlation coefficients, the one that would yield the <u>least</u> accurate predictions of one variable based on the other variable would be a. 0.00 b. +0.99 c. +0.17 d. -0.49
Concept/Applied LO 11 Page: 55 **b**	132.	Of the following, the correlation coefficient that indicates the strongest relationship between the two variables being measured is a. +0.65 b. -0.89 c. 0.00 d. +3.45
Concept/Applied LO 11 Page: 55 **c**	133.	Of the following, the correlation coefficient that indicates the weakest relationship between the two variables being measured is a. +0.95 b. -0.69 c. +0.01 d. -4.50

Concept/Applied LO 12 Page: 55 **d**	134.	Dr. Zelke surveys 50 university students to discover the relationship between textbook price and ratings of readability. Dr. Zelke finds that for these two variables the correlation coefficient is -0.70. This indicates that a. more expensive books tend to receive higher readability ratings than less expensive books b. there is no relationship between textbook price and ratings of readability c. increasing a textbooks price will cause a decrease in its readability rating d. more expensive books tend to receive lower readability ratings than less expensive books
Concept/Applied LO 12 Page: 55 **c**	135.	Dr. Redding has found a correlation of +0.65 between snoring and weight. This indicates that a. overweight individuals tend to snore less than underweight individuals b. there is no relationship between weight and snoring c. overweight individuals tend to snore more than underweight individuals d. individuals who go on a diet will most likely begin to snore
Concept/Applied LO 12 Page: 56 Correct = 81% **d**	136.	If the correlation coefficient between amount of exposure to television violence and aggressive behavior was found to be +0.43, we could conclude that a. watching television violence tends to cause aggressive behavior b. being an aggressive person tends to cause one to watch more violent television c. people who watch the most television tend to be the least aggressive d. there is a positive relationship between these two variables
Concept/Applied LO 12 Page: 56 Correct = 51% **a**	137.	Which of the following statements about correlations is <u>false</u>? a. A and B correlate +1.00; therefore, they are causally related. b. A and B correlate +1.00; if you know A you can predict B without error. c. A and B correlate -1.00; if you know A you can predict B without error. d. A correlation of +.90 gives better predictability than a correlation of +.60.
Factual LO 13 Page: 56 **b**	138.	Statistics that are used to interpret data and draw conclusions are called a. descriptive statistics b. inferential statistics c. numerical statistics d. significant statistics
Concept/Applied LO 13 Page: 56 Correct = 85% **a**	139.	Inferential statistics help us determine whether _____ played a role in an experiment. a. chance b. a dependent variable c. a normal distribution d. genetics
Concept/Applied LO 13 Page: 56 Correct = 48% **c**	140.	The logic of hypothesis testing requires us to determine whether a. the experimental group differs from the control group on the independent variable b. the scores of the experimental group are higher than the scores of the control group c. any observed difference between the two groups is too large to have easily occurred by chance d. the scores of the experimental group are lower than the scores of the control group

Concept/Applied LO 13 Page: 57 Correct = 72% **b**	141.	"Statistically significant" means that the results of an experiment most likely a. resulted from chance variations b. were not due to chance c. had practical significance d. were important
Concept/Applied LO 13 Page: 57 **b**	142.	Paulo tells you that he just completed an experiment in his botany class and the results he obtained were statistically significant. This means that the results he obtained a. are important and will likely have an impact in the field of botany b. were unlikely to be a result of chance variations in his sample c. will be of interest to people, even if they are not botanists d. were likely to be the result of chance variations in his sample
Concept/Applied LO 13 Page: 57 Correct = 28% **d**	143.	Helen conducted a study in which she measured the response time for males and females to complete a spatial task. She found that the mean response time was 1.48 minutes for males and 1.63 minutes for females. For Helen to be confident that an actual difference exists between the males and females in her study, she must a. calculate a correlation coefficient b. redo the experiment c. obtain a larger sample d. calculate an inferential statistic
Concept/Applied LO 13 Page: 57 **a**	144.	Rebecca reads a published research study about children's memory for sequences of actions. She uses the same procedures and the same materials to test children who are slightly older than the children in the original study. Rebecca is engaged in the scientific process known as a. replication b. plagiarism c. validation d. signification
Concept/Applied LO 13 Page: 58 **c**	145.	Gilda has located 7 studies that reported on the long-term impact of nutritional deficiencies during pregnancy. Each of the studies is from a different country, and Gilda would like to be able to combine the results of these studies in some way to discover if the overall results are consistent across the different countries. The best way for Gilda to do this would be through a. replication b. signification c. meta-analysis d. resampling
Factual LO 14 Page: 58 Correct = 93% **b**	146.	By definition, a sample a. is that group of people to whom the conclusion of the study will apply b. is a subset of the population who actually participate in a research study c. contains less than 50 people or animals d. must only include volunteers who express an interest in the study
Concept/Applied LO 14 Page: 58 **a**	147.	To determine whether students would like more courses scheduled in the late afternoon and evening hours the Student Services department sends questionnaires to 50 students selected at random from the 5,000 who are registered at the campus. In this instance, the 5,000 students who are registered at the campus would be a. a population b. a representative sample c. a biased sample d. the independent variable

Concept/Applied LO 14 Page: 58 **d**	148.	To discover whether residents of a city are in favor of building a new sports stadium the team's owner randomly selected and interviewed 500 of the city's 500,000 residents. In this instance, the 500 people that the owner interviewed would be a. a biased sample b. a population c. the dependent variable d. a representative sample
Factual LO 14 Page: 58 **a**	149.	By definition, a population a. is the group of people to whom the conclusion of the study will apply b. is a subset of the sample c. consists of those individuals who actually participate in the study d. is any group that contains more than 100 people or animals
Concept/Applied LO 14 Page: 58 **c**	150.	To generalize results to a population, we must first a. select a biased sample from the population of interest b. oversample selected subgroups in the population c. draw a representative sample from the population of interest d. ensure that all the variables have been operationally defined
Critical Thinking LO 14 Page: 58 **c**	151.	A researcher who is conducting an opinion survey asks viewers who are watching a political debate to dial a 1-800 number and record their opinion to the "question of the day." In this case the researcher is likely to have a. a representative sample b. a random sample c. a biased sample d. a random population
Concept/Applied LO 14 Page: 58 Correct = 92% **d**	152.	The subjects who participate in an experiment should a. all be chosen from the same geographical area and socioeconomic class b. be allowed to choose which group they would like to be in c. come from a wide range of different age groups d. be carefully chosen so they are a representative sample of the population
Factual LO 14 Page: 58 **d**	153.	A sample is representative if a. only volunteer subjects are used b. it is as different from the population as possible c. all subjects are chosen from a single, unusual segment of the population d. its composition is similar to the composition of the population
Concept/Applied LO 14 Page: 58 Correct = 63% **a**	154.	Sampling bias is a problem because it a. limits the generality of the findings b. makes it impossible to use inferential statistics c. makes it difficult to avoid a confounding of variables d. makes the effect of the independent variable appear to be bigger than it really is
Concept/Applied LO 14 Page: 58 Correct = 66% **c**	155.	Dr. Stillingsworth is interested in people's reactions to a controversial jury verdict. Dr. Stillingsworth calls people at their home between the hours of 1:00 p.m. and 3:30 p.m. on a Tuesday afternoon. In this example Dr. Stillingsworth has most likely selected a. a representative sample b. a biased population c. a biased sample d. a statistically significant population

Factual LO 15 Page: 59 **d**	156.	Sometimes a subject's expectations may lead to behavior change in the absence of any effective treatment. This is referred to as an example of a. sampling bias b. experimenter bias c. socially desirable responding d. the placebo effect
Factual LO 15 Page: 59 Correct = 90% **d**	157.	Placebo effects occur when a. the sample is not representative of the population b. two variables are confounded c. subjects are influenced by the social desirability bias d. due to their expectations, subjects experience some change from a nonexistent or ineffective treatment
Critical Thinking LO 15 Page: 59 **b**	158.	Dr. Limmex is trying to win FDA approval for a new drug to treat anxiety. Dr. Limmex claims that 14% of the people who took this new drug reported reduced anxiety, however other researchers claim that 14% of patients who receive no treatment also report reductions in their anxiety levels. It appears that the patients who improved after taking Dr. Limmex's drug a. had a self-report bias b. may have been experiencing placebo effects c. were a non-representative sample d. should have been placed in the control group, rather than the experimental group
Concept/Applied LO 15 Page: 59 **d**	159.	In an investigation of the effects of caffeine on concentration, half the participants were given regular colas which contained caffeine and half were given decaffeinated colas. In this study, the decaffeinated colas are being used as a. a confounding variable b. a random factor c. the dependent variable d. a placebo
Factual LO 16 Page: 60 Correct = 94% **c**	160.	The social desirability bias is a tendency to answer questions about oneself a. by agreeing with nearly every statement b. by disagreeing with nearly every statement c. in a socially approved manner d. in a socially disapproved manner
Factual LO 16 Page: 60 Correct = 90% **a**	161.	One is <u>most</u> apt to encounter problems with the social desirability bias when using a. self-reports b. case studies c. naturalistic observations d. the experimental method
Concept/Applied LO 16 Page: 60 Correct = 95% **c**	162.	Subjects' self-reports often indicate that they are healthier, happier, and less prejudiced than other types of evidence would suggest. The <u>most</u> likely explanation is a. experimenter bias b. faulty memory c. the social desirability bias d. a tendency to agree with almost every statement
Factual LO 16 Page: 60 Correct = 69% **b**	163.	The tendency to respond to questions in a manner unrelated to the content of a question is called a. cognitive confabulation b. response set c. counter confound d. counter placebo effect

Concept/Applied LO 16 Page: 60 Correct = 61% **d**	164.	John dislikes completing questionnaires, so each time he fills one out he always circles the same item (such as "strongly agree" or "strongly disagree"). John's behavior reflects a. the placebo effect b. a sampling bias c. social desirability d. a response set
Concept/Applied LO 16 Page: 60 **b**	165.	Darla has sent out a survey in which she is asking people to provide information about their attitudes on a number of sensitive subjects. When the surveys are returned Darla needs to be aware that the responses may be distorted due to a. placebo effects b. self-report biases c. statistical artifacts d. meta-analytic controls
Concept/Applied LO 16 Page: 60 **a**	166.	Reinhold is filling out the Minnesota Multiphasic Personality Inventory (MMPI) and as he reads each question he thinks about the way most other people would probably respond. When he answers, he selects the alternative that he thinks will present the most favorable impression. Reinhold's answers reflect a. a social desirability bias b. a negative response set c. the placebo effect d. non-representative sampling
Concept/Applied LO 16 Page: 60 **c**	167.	Malinda is filling out a survey for a marketing agency in order to be eligible for a grand prize drawing. She doesn't actually read many of the questions, and simply answers "yes" to everything. Malinda's answers to the survey reflect a. a social desirability bias b. the placebo effect c. a positive response set d. an interaction effect
Concept/Applied LO 17 Page: 60 **a**	168.	The fact that many times researchers unintentionally influence the outcome of their studies implies the existence of a. experimenter bias b. a placebo effect c. sampling bias d. social desirability
Factual LO 17 Page: 60 Correct = 87% **c**	169.	Experimenter bias occurs when a. experimenters explicitly instruct the subjects to behave in a way that will be consistent with the hypothesis b. experimenters desire to make a favorable impression on their subjects c. experimenters' beliefs in their own hypotheses affect either the subjects' behavior or their observations of the subjects d. experimenters conduct their studies in a completely objective manner
Factual LO 17 Page: 61 Correct = 91% **b**	170.	Experimenter bias typically results in a. the effects of the bias disconfirming the experimenter's expectations b. the effects of the bias confirming the experimenter's expectations c. results that are not statistically significant d. the placebo effect

Critical Thinking LO 17 Page: 61 **d**	171.	Melvin and Leigh are interviewing students at their campus to determine if the students agree or disagree with a proposed policy change. Melvin believes the proposed policy change is a good idea, but Leigh believes the change will be bad for students. Nearly all the students who Melvin interviewed supported the policy change, but nearly all the students who Leigh interviewed disapproved of the change. The differences in the results illustrate the potential impact of a. the placebo effect b. double-blind research studies c. confounded dependent variables d. experimenter bias
Concept/Applied LO 17 Page: 61 Correct = 93% **c**	172.	One method to control for experimenter bias effects in research is to use a. a socially desirable procedure b. reverse control groups c. a double-blind procedure d. a non-representative sample
Factual LO 17 Page: 61 Correct = 96% **d**	173.	The experimental procedure in which both the experimenter and subject are unaware of who is in the experimental and who is in the control group is referred to as the a. placebo control procedure b. stereotaxic procedure c. single-blind procedure d. double-blind procedure
Concept/Applied LO 17 Page: 61 **c**	174.	Dr. Hugo designs an experiment to test the effectiveness of a new antidepressant drug. Half the participants will receive the actual drug and half will receive a sugar pill, but neither the participants nor the researchers who administer the drug will know who is receiving the actual drug and who is receiving the placebo. In this case, Dr. Hugo has designed a. a study that will minimize self-report bias b. an unethical research procedure c. a double-blind research study d. a correlational study with two confounded factors
Concept/Applied LO 17 Page: 61 **a**	175.	Scarlett is a graduate student who is observing children playing together after watching a film. She knows that some children saw a film that contained graphic scenes of violence and some children saw a non-violent film, but she doesn't know which film each child she is observing watched. In this case, Scarlett is recording data for a. a double-blind research study b. a study with two independent variables c. an unethical research study d. a correlational study with confounded variables
Concept/Applied LO 17 Page: 61 **d**	176.	Dr. Webb designs a research study in which neither the subjects nor the individuals who interact directly with the subjects know which is the control group and which is the experimental group in the study. Dr. Webb probably chose this type of research design in order to a. avoid the need to obtain ethics approval for the study b. minimize the possibility of self-report bias c. ensure that her sample is not biased d. reduce the impact of experimenter bias

Factual LO 18 Page: 62 Correct = 70% **d**	177.	Which of the following statements is <u>true</u>? a. Deception has never been used in psychological research. b. Although deception has been used in the past, it has recently been banned by the American Psychological Association. c. In recent years, there has been a steady increase in the use of deception in psychological research. d. Deception has been fairly common in psychological research since the 1960s.
Factual LO 18 Page: 62 Correct = 63% **c**	178.	Which of the following is <u>not</u> one of the arguments that critics have used to argue against the use of deception in psychological research ? a. Lying is inherently immoral b. Subjects' ability to trust others may be undermined c. Subjects are likely to experience severe physical or psychological harm in this type of research d. Subjects may be made to feel foolish when the true purpose of the study is revealed
Concept/Applied LO 18 Page: 62 **a**	179.	Deception is used in some research in order to a. help control for placebo effects. b. help aid in double-blind procedures. c. prevent socially desirable responding. d. encourage socially desirable responding.
Factual LO 18 Page: 62 Correct = 67% **c**	180.	Research has revealed that subjects who participated in research involving deception a. were psychologically distressed at being deceived b. suffered extreme embarrassment at being "fooled" c. didn't mind being misled and generally enjoyed taking part in research d. lost the ability to trust others
Factual LO 19 Page: 63 Correct = 55% **c**	181.	Which of the following is <u>not</u> a criticism of using animals in psychological research? a. Many of the studies are trivial. b. It is unethical to subject an animal to pain. c. The studies cost too much for the limited amount of information they provide. d. The studies are a waste of time, as the results often do not apply to humans.
Factual LO 19 Page: 63 Correct = 71% **b**	182.	The single issue citizens write about most often to their congresspersons and the President is a. homelessness b. animal welfare c. the drug problem d. crime
Factual LO 19 Page: 63 Correct = 53% **a**	183.	What percentage of psychological studies involve animals? a. 7-8 percent b. 1-2 percent c. 50-60 percent d. 15-20 percent
Factual LO 19 Page: 64 Correct = 85% **b**	184.	Which of the following statements is <u>true</u>? a. More than one-third of all psychological studies involve animals. b. The American Psychological Association has developed strict ethical guidelines for research involving animals. c. There have been few if any major advances in the treatment of mental or physical disorders in humans that are attributable to animal research. d. The majority of psychological studies using animals involve painful or harmful manipulations.

Concept/Applied LO 18 Page: 64 **b**	185.	Zigfried Rosenblat, Jr. took part in a study on sexual deviance last year. He was somewhat dismayed when he read an article in a weekly journal discussing sexual deviance in which one patient was referred to as ZRJ. Although the article claimed all names had been disguised to protect personal identities, Zigfried is convinced he is the individual described in the article. In this case, it is possible that the researchers who conducted the study violated the ethical principle of a. informed consent b. right to privacy c. full disclosure d. adequate debriefing
Critical Thinking LO 18 Page: 64 **d**	186.	Dr. Jacobsen is investigating the link between social support networks and grades in school. Students in his classes are required to complete surveys forms related to this research. If a survey form is not completed by the end of the semester a student's grade is reduced by 10 points. In this case, some researchers might argue that Dr. Jacobsen's research violates the ethical principle of a. right to privacy b. protection for harm c. full disclosure d. informed consent
Concept/Applied LO 18 Page: 64 **a**	187.	Mackenzie took part in an experiment where she was told she would be required to sit alone in a darkened room for 30 minutes, after which she would be asked to complete a brief questionnaire about her future goals and plans. When she finished the questionnaire she was told the experiment was over. Mackenzie never really understood the purpose of the study, and she wasn't sure why she had to wait in the darkened room before filling out the short questionnaire. In this case, it would appear that the researchers who conducted the experiment a. did not use an adequate debriefing procedure b. failed to obtain informed consent c. violated Mackenzie's right to privacy d. did not provide adequate protection from harm
Concept/Applied LO 20 Page: 65 Correct = 51% **d**	188.	Publishing research results so others can subject the methods and conclusions to critical scrutiny illustrates which of your text's unifying themes? a. Behavior is determined by multiple causes. b. Psychology is theoretically diverse. c. Our experience of the world is highly subjective. d. Psychology is empirical.
Concept/Applied LO 20 Page: 65 Correct = 62% **b**	189.	The fact that researchers focus their attention on findings that are unlikely to have occurred by chance illustrates which of your text's unifying themes? a. Our experience of the world is highly subjective. b. Psychology is empirical. c. Behavior is determined by multiple causes. d. Psychology is theoretically diverse.
Concept/Applied LO 20 Page: 65 Correct = 89% **a**	190.	The fact that subjects sometimes report beneficial effects from a placebo treatment illustrates which of your text's unifying themes? a. Our experience of the world is highly subjective. b. Psychology is empirical. c. Heredity and environment jointly influence behavior. d. Our behavior is shaped by our cultural heritage.

Concept/Applied LO 20 Page: 65 Correct = 80% c	191.	The fact that research results can be affected by experimenter bias illustrates which of your text's unifying themes? a. Our behavior is shaped by our cultural heritage. b. Psychology is theoretically diverse. c. Our experience of the world is highly subjective. d. Behavior is determined by multiple causes.
Factual LO 21 Page: 66 Correct = 56% b	192.	Articles published in technical and scholarly journals are written for a. students majoring in that field b. other professionals in that field c. the general public d. anyone with an interest in the topic
Concept/Applied LO 21 Page: 66 Correct = 79% a	193.	<u>Most</u> journals in the field of psychology a. are highly selective about the articles they publish b. publish any studies or reports that are submitted c. rewrite highly technical articles to make them easier to understand d. do not publish articles that cross more than one discipline or field
Concept/Applied LO 21 Page: 66 Correct = 49% d	194.	Which of the following would <u>not</u> be a reason for a journal to reject an article for publication? a. The research was theoretically unimportant. b. The methodology used was unsound. c. The article was not well written. d. The article summarized and analyzed the findings from a number of earlier studies, but did not present any original research.
Factual LO 22 Page: 67 Correct = 65% b	195.	A summary of research literature in psychology can be obtained by looking in a. Psychological Review b. Psychological Abstracts c. Psychology Today d. the card catalog at your public library
Factual LO 23 Page: 69 Correct = 94% d	196.	The hypotheses for a research study are most likely to be found in the a. methodology section of a journal article b. reference section of a journal article c. results section of a journal article d. introduction section of a journal article
Factual LO 23 Page: 69 Correct = 90% b	197.	The data obtained in a research study, along with the statistical analyses, are reported in the a. introduction section of a journal article b. results section of a journal article c. method section of a journal article d. discussion section of a journal article
Factual LO 23 Page: 69 Correct = 81% a	198.	The correct sequencing of the sections of the main body of a journal article would be a. introduction, method, results, discussion b. introduction, discussion, method, results c. discussion, introduction, method, results d. method, introduction, results, discussion
Factual LO 23 Page: 69 Correct = 87% c	199.	The reference list at the end of a research article lists a. bibliographic information for all the previous research studies on the same topic b. bibliographic information for all the previous research studies by the same author c. bibliographic information for any studies referred to in the article d. the author's phone number, address, and web site

Factual LO 24 Page: 70 a	200.	Anecdotal evidence consists of a. personal stories about specific incidents and experiences b. general information that has little direct bearing on the issue under consideration c. statistical information that has been altered to support a specific point of view d. information that is gathered from a variety of sources
Factual LO 24 Page: 70 b	201.	Studies that have investigated the influence of anecdotal information have found that a. people are not influenced by anecdotal information, and tend to view it as non-representative and biased b. people tend to be influenced by anecdotal information, even when they are forewarned that the information is not representative c. people are only influenced by anecdotal evidence when they have not been forwarded that it may be misleading d. people are only influenced by anecdotal evidence when it is provided by someone they know and trust
Factual LO 24 Page: 71 c	202.	Individuals who think critically do not rely on anecdotal evidence because this type of evidence a. is too general and can be applied to too many unrelated situations b. is based on inferential statistical analysis, which is generally unreliable c. can be distorted by reporting biases d. involves only negative instances, and cannot be used to make an unbiased decision
Factual LO 24 Page: 71 d	203.	Of the following, which is not a concern related to anecdotal evidence? a. Anecdotal evidence often consists of self-reports that are subject to distortions in reporting. b. The evidence may be based on a single case and therefore the information may not representative. c. The information may be distorted and inaccurate because it has been passed from one person to another. d. The evidence is often too general and cannot be applied to specific situations.
Concept/Applied LO 24 Page: 71 a	204.	Annabel is planning to buy a cordless phone. She has narrowed her choice down to a Northtech X7 model and a Telecom G-Pro model. Alfred tells Annabel: "Consumer Reports did extensive testing and rated the Northtech X7 as the highest overall. The same article indicated that the Telecom phone was unreliable and needed frequent service." Francine tells Annabel: "The Consumer Reports article is probably flawed because my uncle had a Northtech X7 phone, and he had nothing but problems with it. He decided to switch to the Telecom phone, and he hasn't had any problems." Based on the research results reported in the critical thinking application, you should predict that Annabel will most likely a. buy the Telecom phone because she will be more persuaded by the anecdotal evidence b. buy the Northtech X7 phone because she will be more persuaded by objective evidence c. do further research on her own before buying either of the two phones d. decide not to buy a cordless phone because the two reports her friends provided conflict with each other
Integrative Correct = 71% b	205.	The scientific method's clarity and precision is to operational definitions as its intolerance of error is to a. placebo effects b. replication c. hypotheses d. subjects

Integrative Correct = 75% **a**	206.	Because our experience of the world is highly subjective, researchers use a. the double-blind procedure as a safeguard b. case studies as a safeguard c. extraneous variables as a safeguard d. psychoanalytic methods as a safeguard
Integrative **d**	207.	Which set of concepts is <u>not</u> a closely related set? a. mean, median, mode b. method, results, discussion c. experiment, independent variable, control group d. correlation, sample, journal
Integrative **b**	208.	Imagine that a group of researchers designed a study to test the effectiveness of subliminal-message weight-loss tapes. Half the participants receive real tapes, and half receive similar tapes with the subliminal messages removed. All the participants are told that their tapes contain subliminal messages. This study would be an example of a. the case study research b. the single-blind research method c. anecdotal research d. experimenter bias in selecting a random sample
Integrative **c**	209.	Imagine that a group of researchers conducted a single-blind study designed to test the effectiveness of subliminal-message weight-loss tapes. Suppose the researchers found that everyone lost weight during the study, even those who were given tapes without any subliminal messages. This type of result would a. indicate that the independent and dependent variables in the study are negatively correlated b. provide evidence that subliminal tapes are effective in promoting weight loss c. be evidence of a placebo effect d. be evidence that the study contained confounding variables
Study Guide LO 5 Page: 43 **c**	210.	An experimenter tests the hypothesis that physical exercise helps people's mood (makes them happier). Subjects in the experimental group participate on Monday and Tuesday and those in the control group on Wednesday and Thursday. What is the independent variable? a. the hypothesis b. day of the week c. the exercise d. the mood (degree of happiness)
Study Guide LO 5 Page: 43 **d**	211.	An experimenter tests the hypothesis that physical exercise helps people's mood (makes them happier). Subjects in the experimental group participate on Monday and Tuesday and those in the control group on Wednesday and Thursday. What is the dependent variable? a. the hypothesis b. day of the week c. the exercise d. the mood (degree of happiness)

Study Guide
LO 5
Page: 44
b

212. An experimenter tests the hypothesis that physical exercise helps people's mood (makes them happier). Subjects in the experimental group participate on Monday and Tuesday and those in the control group on Wednesday and Thursday. What is an extraneous (confounding) variable?
   a. the hypothesis
   b. day of the week
   c. the exercise
   d. the mood (degree of happiness)

Study Guide
LO 7
Page: 47
a

213. The major advantage of the experimental method over the correlational approach is that the experimental method
   a. permits one to make causal conclusions
   b. allows for prediction
   c. is generally less artificial than correlational procedures
   d. permits the study of people in groups

Study Guide
LO 10
Page: 53
a

214. What is the mode of the following data? 2, 3, 3, 3, 5, 5, 7, 12
   a. 3
   b. 4
   c. 5
   d. 6

Study Guide
LO 10
Page: 53
b

215. What is the median of the following data? 1, 3, 4, 4, 5, 6, 9,
   a. 3
   b. 4
   c. 4.57
   d. 6

Study Guide
LO 11
Page: 55
b

216. Researchers find an inverse relationship between alcohol consumption and speed of response. Which of the following fictitious statistics could possibly represent that correlation?
   a. -4.57
   b. -0.87
   c. +0.91
   d. +0.05

Study Guide
LO 13
Page: 56
c

217. The term statistical significance refers to
   a. how important the data are for future research on the topic
   b. the conclusion that there are no reasonable alternative explanations
   c. the inference that the observed effects are unlikely to be due to chance
   d. the representativeness of the sample

Study Guide
LO 17
Page: 61
c

218. An instructor wishes to find out whether a new teaching method is superior to his usual procedures, so he conducts an experiment. Everyone in his classes is quite excited about the prospect of learning under the new procedure, but of course he cannot administer the new teaching method to everyone. A random half of the students receive the new method and the remaining half receive the old. What is the most obvious flaw in this experiment?
   a. Subjects should have been systematically assigned to groups.
   b. The sample is not representative of the population.
   c. Placebo effects or experimenter bias are likely to affect results.
   d. Distortions in self-report will affect results.

Study Guide LO 17 Page: 61 **d**	219.	What procedure helps correct for experimenter bias? a. extraneous or confounding variables b. sleep learning or hypnosis c. a higher standard for statistical significance d. use of the double-blind procedure
Study Guide LO 18 Page: 62 **b**	220.	With regard to the topic of deception in research with human subjects, which of the following is true? a. Researchers are careful to avoid deceiving subjects. b. Some topics could not be investigated unless deception was used. c. It has been empirically demonstrated that deception causes severe distress. d. All psychological research must involve some deception.
Online Quiz LO 1 Page: 38 **b**	221.	IQ score, age, weight, grade point average, and income are all examples of a. constants b. variables c. correlations d. statistics
Online Quiz LO 3 Page: 39 **d**	222.	If you believe that increasing levels of anxiety are associated with drug abuse, you have just formulated a(n) a. epiphenomenon b. theory c. correlation d. hypothesis
Online Quiz LO 5 Page: 43 **c**	223.	A researcher wants to see if a protein-enriched diet will enhance the maze-running performance of rats. One group of rats is fed the high-protein diet for the duration of the study; the other group continues to receive ordinary rat chow. In this experiment, the rats' maze-running performance is the a. correlated variable b. control variable c. dependent variable d. independent variable
Online Quiz LO 7 Page: 47 **b**	224.	One of the disadvantages of the experimental method is a. the inability to generate cause-and-effect conclusions b. the artificial, contrived situations in which experiments are often conducted c. the length of time necessary to complete the study d. the fact that only one variable can be studied at a time
Online Quiz LO 8 Page: 50 **c**	225.	If you interviewed a person over a period of time to understand that person to the greatest degree possible, you would be using the a. experimental method of research b. correlational method of research c. case study method of research d. independent variable method of research
Online Quiz LO 10 Page: 53 **c**	226.	The standard deviation is a measure of a. central tendency b. the degree of relationship between two variables c. the amount of variability in a data set d. the difference between the largest and smallest scores in a data set

Online Quiz LO 11 Page: 54 **b**	227.	As interest rates increase, house sales decline, indicating a. a direct correlation between the two variables b. a negative correlation between the two variables c. a positive correlation between the two variables d. no correlation between the two variables
Online Quiz LO 15 Page: 59 **b**	228.	Placebos are used in research to control for a. nontreatment effects b. the subjects' expectations about treatment c. secondary drug effects d. random fluctuations in the independent variable
Online Quiz LO 16 Page: 60 **d**	229.	The tendency for survey subjects to provide answers that place them in a favorable light is referred to as a. sampling bias b. response stereotyping c. a placebo effect d. socially desirable responding
Online Quiz LO 23 Page: 69 **a**	230.	The abstract of a journal article provides a. a concise summary of the entire article b. an overview of the research problem, relevant theories, and previous research c. a description of the research methods used in the study d. a concise summary of the raw data and statistical analyses

ESSAY QUESTIONS

1. Design a simple experiment to investigate the effects of television violence on children's aggressive behavior, being sure to identify the independent and dependent variables, and the experimental and control groups.

    There are numerous possible experimental designs. Make sure there is an explicit, testable hypothesis; that "television violence" and "aggressive behavior" are operationally defined; that children are randomly assigned to groups; that the control group is exposed to nonviolent television rather than to no television at all.

2. Design a simple descriptive/correlational study to investigate the relationship between television violence and children's aggressive behavior.

    Again, there are numerous possibilities. Make certain that both variables are operationally defined; that a specific descriptive/correlational method (such as naturalistic observation or survey) is selected; that causation is neither stated nor implied.

3. What are the relative weaknesses and strengths of descriptive/correlational research as opposed to experimental research? Under what conditions would a psychologist choose one method as opposed to the other?

    Experimental research is the more powerful of the two methods, in that it allows precise control over the independent variable and therefore yields cause-and-effect conclusions. On the other hand, experiments may be somewhat artificial and often cannot be done for ethical reasons.

    Descriptive/correlational studies are conducted in the subjects' natural environment, are easier and faster to do than experiments, and can be done ethically in many circumstances in which experiments cannot. However, the researcher has little control over extraneous variables, and so cause-and-effect conclusions cannot be drawn.

    The choice between the two methods is a function of practical and ethical considerations.

4. What is the difference between a positive correlation and a negative correlation? List some specific variables that you predict would be positively correlated, and variables that would be negatively correlated, with alcohol consumption by college students.

    Positive correlation: As scores on variable X increase, scores on variable Y tend to increase, too.
    Examples: alcohol consumption and body weight; alcohol consumption and number of missed classes

    Negative correlation: As scores on variable X increase, scores on variable Y tend to decrease.
    Examples: alcohol consumption and coordination; alcohol consumption and grade point average

5. How do you feel about the use of animals as research subjects in psychological studies? Back up your position with evidence.

    Pro: Relatively few psychological studies involve animals, and of those that do, few expose animals to harm or pain; researchers can more precisely control the environment of animal subjects; animal research has generated important advances in the treatment of mental and physical disorders in humans; the knowledge gained justifies the risks.

    Con: Animals should have the same rights as human subjects; research animals are sometimes treated inhumanely; many psychological studies using animals are trivial; the results of animal studies may not generalize to humans.

This page intentionally left blank.

Chapter Three
The Biological Bases of Behavior

LEARNING OBJECTIVES

1. Describe the main functions of the two types of nervous tissue.
2. Describe the various parts of the neuron and their functions.
3. Describe the neural impulse.
4. Describe how neurons communicate at chemical synapses.
5. Describe the two types of postsynaptic potentials and how cells integrate these signals.
6. Discuss some of the functions of acetylcholine and the monoamine neurotransmitters.
7. Explain what endorphins are and how they are related to behavior.
8. Provide an overview of the peripheral nervous system, including its subdivisions.
9. Distinguish between the central nervous system and the peripheral nervous system.
10. Describe how the EEG, lesioning, and ESB are used to investigate brain function.
11. Describe the new brain imaging methods that are used to study brain structure and function.
12. Summarize the key functions of the medulla, pons, and cerebellum.
13. Summarize the key functions of the midbrain.
14. Summarize the key functions of the thalamus and hypothalamus.
15. Describe the nature and location of the limbic system and summarize some of its key functions.
16. Name the four lobes in the cerebral cortex and identify some of their key functions.
17. Summarize evidence that led scientists to view the left hemisphere as the dominant hemisphere and describe how split-brain research changed this view.
18. Describe how neuroscientists conduct research on cerebral specialization in normal subjects and what this research has revealed.
19. Describe some of the ways in which hormones regulate behavior.
20. Describe the structures and processes involved in genetic transmission.
21. Explain the difference between genotype and phenotype and the meaning of polygenic inheritance.
22. Explain the special methods used to investigate the influence of heredity on behavior.
23. Explain the four key insights that represent the essence of Darwin's theory of evolution.
24. Describe some subsequent refinements to evolutionary theory.
25. Provide some examples of animal behavior that represent adaptations.
26. Explain the relationship between parental investment and species' mating systems.
27. Discuss some common misconceptions about evolution.
28. Explain how this chapter highlighted three of the text's unifying themes.
29. Critically evaluate each of the five ideas on cerebral specialization and cognitive processes in light of available evidence.
30. Explain how neuroscience research has been overextrapolated by some education and child care advocates who have campaigned for infant schooling.

MULTIPLE-CHOICE QUESTIONS

Factual
LO 1
Page: 76
Correct = 80%
a

1. The cells that provide structural support and insulation for neurons are called
   a. glia
   b. somata
   c. neuromodulators
   d. dendrites

Factual
LO 1
Page: 76
Correct = 88%
b

2. Glia cells
   a. release neuromodulators
   b. provide structural support for neurons
   c. release neurotransmitters
   d. form the primary components of the spinal cord

Factual
LO 1
Page: 76
Correct = 94%
a

3. The cells of the nervous system that do the work of receiving, integrating, and transmitting information are the
   a. neurons
   b. glia
   c. neuroblasts
   d. neurilemma

Conceptual
LO 2
Page: 76
Correct = 82%
a

4. Which of the following is not one of the main functions of neurons?
   a. generating information
   b. transmitting information
   c. receiving information
   d. integrating information

Concept/Applied
LO 2
Page: 76
Correct = 66%
c

5. Which of the following statements regarding neurons is true?
   a. All neurons are similar in size and complexity.
   b. Only neurons in the brain are insulated with myelin sheaths.
   c. All neurons receive, integrate, and transmit signals within the nervous system.
   d. All of these statements are true.

Factual
LO 2
Page: 76
Correct = 90%
b

6. The basic parts of a neuron are
   a. vesicles, terminal buttons, synapse
   b. cell body, axon, dendrites
   c. myelin, nodes, axon terminals
   d. hindbrain, midbrain, forebrain

Critical Thinking
LO 2
Page: 76
Correct = 52%
c

7. Branches are to trees as _____ are to neurons.
   a. axons
   b. cell bodies
   c. dendrites
   d. nuclei

Factual
LO 2
Page: 76
Correct = 80%
b

8. _____ receive information from other neurons; _____ transmit information to other neurons.
   a. Axons; synapses
   b. Dendrites; axons
   c. Synapses; dendrites
   d. Axons; dendrites

Critical Thinking LO 2 Page: 76 c	9.	In computers, the keyboard receives input and passes that information along to the computer's central processing unit (CPU). In comparing a computer to a neuron, the keyboard would be equivalent to a. the soma b. the axon c. the dendrites d. the terminal buttons
Factual LO 2 Page: 77 c	10.	Exchange of information between neurons takes place at the a. axon b. cell body c. synapse d. myelin sheath
Factual LO 2 Page: 77 c	11.	The insulating material that encases some axons is referred to as the a. soma b. corpus callosum c. myelin sheath d. dendritic tree
Factual LO 2 Page: 77 d	12.	The disease multiple sclerosis seems to be due to a breakdown of a. neural impulses b. neural inhibition c. dendritic trees d. myelin sheath
Factual LO 2 Page: 77 Correct = 73% a	13.	Faster neural impulses occur in a. insulated or myelinated axons b. uninsulated or unmyelinated axons c. shorter axons d. neurons with extensive dendrites
Factual LO 2 Page: 77 Correct = 34% a	14.	Which of the following is the correct sequence of structures through which information flows in a neuron? a. dendrites to cell body to axon b. axon to cell body to dendrites c. glia to dendrites to axon d. dendrites to axon to glia
Factual LO 2 Page: 77 a	15.	The _____ is the junction between two neurons. a. synapse b. terminal button c. postsynaptic membrane d. myelin sheath
Factual LO 2 Page: 77 Correct = 60% b	16.	Neurotransmitters are secreted from the a. myelin sheath b. terminal buttons c. neuromodulators d. dendrites
Factual LO 3 Page: 77 b	17.	A neural impulse is initiated when a neuron's charge a. momentarily changes from positive to negative b. momentarily becomes less negative, or even positive c. suddenly becomes even more positive than it was during the resting state d. suddenly becomes even more negative than it was during the resting state

Factual LO 3 Page: 77 Correct = 81% **c**	18.	The minimum length of time between action potentials is determined by a. transduction capacity b. transduction incapacity c. the absolute refractory period d. the relative threshold period
Critical Thinking LO 3 Page: 79 Correct = 41% **d**	19.	Which of the following statements about the neural impulse is <u>false</u>? a. It travels faster in larger diameter fibers than in smaller fibers. b. It follows the all-or-none principle. c. It is a brief change in polarization of the cell membrane. d. It produces stronger neural impulses from stronger stimuli.
Factual LO 4 Page: 79 Correct = 81% **d**	20.	The distance between a terminal button and a dendrite is referred to as the a. midsynaptic potential range b. transmission gap c. neuromodulator d. synaptic cleft
Factual LO 4 Page: 79 **d**	21.	A chemical that transfers information from one neuron to another is referred to as a(n) a. synaptic vesicle b. enzyme c. neural impulse d. neurotransmitter
Factual LO 4 Page: 79 Correct = 58% **b**	22.	Neurotransmitters are stored in a. mitochondria b. synaptic vesicles c. dendrites d. nacelles
Factual LO 4 Page: 79 **c**	23.	Synaptic vesicles are structures that a. control the speed with which a neuron fires b. manufacture myelin c. store neurotransmitters d. provide energy for a neuron's activity
Factual LO 5 Page: 80 **c**	24.	An electric potential that increases the likelihood that the postsynaptic neuron will fire is called an a. all-or-none potential b. inhibitory postsynaptic potential c. excitatory postsynaptic potential d. excitatory presynaptic potential
Factual LO 5 Page: 80 **a**	25.	An inhibitory postsynaptic potential _____ the likelihood that the postsynaptic neuron will fire action potentials. a. increases b. decreases c. blocks d. does not affect
Factual LO 5 Page: 80 **d**	26.	Reabsorption of neurotransmitters into the presynaptic neuron is referred to as a. cyclomyosis b. regrading c. uploading d. reuptake

Factual LO 5 Page: 80 **a**	27.	Which of the following is the correct sequence of steps through which neurotransmitters progress during synaptic transmission? a. synthesis, release, binding, inactivation, reuptake b. release, synthesis, binding, reuptake, inactivation c. binding, synthesis, release, inactivation, reuptake d. synthesis, binding, release, reuptake, inactivation
Concept/Applied LO 4 Page: 81 **b**	28.	A good analogy for the way in which a neurotransmitter binds to receptor sites is a. the opening and closing of a window b. a key fitting in the lock of a door c. the lowering of a drawbridge d. the pulling of the trigger of a gun
Factual LO 6 Page: 81 Correct = 50% **d**	29.	Which of the following neurotransmitters is primarily involved in the activation of motor neurons controlling skeletal muscles? a. GABA b. dopamine c. serotonin d. acetylcholine
Factual LO 6 Page: 81 Correct = z78% **c**	30.	An agonist a. blocks the action of neurotransmitters b. prevents reuptake of neurotransmitters c. mimics the action of a neurotransmitter d. extends the absolute refractory period of neural transmission
Concept/Applied LO 6 Page: 82 Correct = 60% **a**	31.	Nicotine functions as an agonist when it a. stimulates some of the acetylcholine synapses b. inhibits some of the acetylcholine synapses c. occupies the acetylcholine receptor sites, thus blocking the action of the neurotransmitter d. prevents the release of acetylcholine into the synapse, thus blocking the action of the neurotransmitter
Factual LO 6 Page: 82 Correct = 63% **b**	32.	When curare blocks the action of acetylcholine by occupying its receptor sites, it is acting as a. an agonist b. an antagonist c. a neurotransmitter d. a placebo
Concept/Applied LO 6 Page: 82 **b**	33.	Parkinson's disease appears to be a function of a. damage to glia cells b. degeneration of neurons that use dopamine as a neurotransmitter c. agonistic chemical action on the receptor sites of the cerebrum d. enzymatic deficiency that does not allow for the proper cleanup of waste products in the nervous system
Factual LO 6 Page: 82 **c**	34.	The regulation of the sleep-wake cycle has been linked to a. amino acid release cycles b. gamma-aminobutyric acid c. serotonin d. phenylalanine hydroxylase

Factual LO 6 Page: 82 **b**	35.	Abnormalities at norepinephrine and serotonin synapses appear to play a role in which of the following? a. hyperactivity b. depression c. high anxiety d. increased appetite
Concept/Applied LO 6 Page: 82 Correct = 62% **c**	36.	The use of a drug that functions as a dopamine agonist would probably lead to which of the following? a. chronic insomnia b. excessive anxiety c. schizophrenic-like symptoms d. Parkinson-like symptoms
Factual LO 7 Page: 82 Correct = 74% **b**	37.	Which of the following has been implicated in pain alleviation? a. dopamine b. endorphins c. acetylcholine d. norepinephrine
Factual LO 7 Page: 82 Correct = 77% **a**	38.	A family of chemicals produced in the body that resemble the opiates are the a. endorphins b. dopamines c. biogenic amines d. acetylcholines
Concept/Applied LO 7 Page: 82 **b**	39.	A marathon runner may well experience a phenomenon known as "runner's high" because the pain of a long run may trigger the release of _____ in the brain. a. morphine b. endorphins c. placebos d. naloxone
Concept/Applied LO 7 Page: 82 **c**	40.	The release of endorphins is <u>most</u> closely associated with which of the following two reactions? a. obsessions and compulsions b. kindness and aggression c. pain and pleasure d. mania and depression
Factual LO 8 Page: 83 **b**	41.	The two most basic divisions of the nervous system are a. the sympathetic division and the parasympathetic division b. the central nervous system and the peripheral nervous system c. the somatic nervous system and the autonomic nervous system d. the brain and the spinal cord
Factual LO 8 Page: 83 Correct = 76% **a**	42.	Nerves outside the skull and spine comprise the a. peripheral nervous system b. vascular nervous system c. vagus nervous system d. skeletal nervous system
Factual LO 8 Page: 83 **b**	43.	The somatic nervous system and the autonomic nervous system comprise the a. central nervous system b. peripheral nervous system c. skeletal nervous system d. afferent nervous system

Factual LO 8 Page: 84 Correct = 50% **a**	44.	_____ nerves receive information, while _____ nerves carry out instructions. a. afferent; efferent b. motor; sensory c. somatic; autonomic d. autonomic; skeletal
Concept/Applied LO 8 Page: 84 Correct = 63% **a**	45.	The movement of voluntary skeletal muscles involved in doing calisthenics is under the control of the a. somatic nervous system b. parasympathetic nervous system c. sympathetic nervous system d. autonomic nervous system
Concept/Applied LO 8 Page: 84 Correct = 32% **a**	46.	When you are walking, the brain sends messages to the skeletal muscles in the legs by way of a. efferent fibers b. sensory fibers c. afferent fibers d. central fibers
Factual LO 8 Page: 84 **b**	47.	Internal functions such as heartbeat, breathing, and stomach contractions are controlled by the _____ nervous system. a. central b. autonomic c. somatic d. endocrine
Factual LO 8 Page: 84 **d**	48.	That part of the nervous system that controls digestion and flow of blood is the a. somatic nervous system b. motor nervous system c. sensory nervous system d. autonomic nervous system
Factual LO 8 Page: 84 **b**	49.	The conservation of body resources, including blood pressure reduction and the promotion of digestion, is handled by the a. somatic division b. parasympathetic division c. sympathetic division d. unsympathetic division
Factual LO 8 Page: 84 Correct = 67% **c**	50.	The _____ is most likely to be in control of bodily processes during periods of rest and recovery for the body. a. somatic nervous system b. sympathetic nervous system c. parasympathetic nervous system d. hypothalamus
Factual LO 8 Page: 84 **c**	51.	The _____ nervous system mobilizes the body when one needs to exert tremendous energy (such as flee from an attacker). a. somatic b. central c. sympathetic d. parasympathetic

Factual LO 8 Page: 84 Correct = 75% **d**	52.	The sympathetic nervous system operates (or is in primary control) during periods of a. calm b. circadian activity c. relaxation d. stress
Concept/Applied LO 8 Page: 85 Correct = 69% **b**	53.	Robyn has just eaten a full meal and is now relaxing. Robyn's _____ is in primary control at this time. a. sympathetic nervous system b. parasympathetic nervous system c. hormonal system d. thyroid gland
Factual LO 9 Page: 85 **a**	54.	The enclosing sheaths that protect the brain and spinal cord are referred to as a. meninges b. glia c. ventricles d. cerebrospinal sheaths
Factual LO 9 Page: 85 Correct = 64% **b**	55.	The _____ fluid nourishes the brain and provides a protective cushion for it. a. amniotic b. cerebrospinal c. parasympathetic d. somatic
Factual LO 9 Page: 86 **b**	56.	The blood-brain barrier is a semipermeable membrane-like mechanism that a. keeps neurotransmitters from entering the bloodstream b. stops some chemicals from passing from the bloodstream to the brain c. prevents ions in the blood from entering the brain d. regulates the flow of blood to the brain and spinal cord
Factual LO 9 Page: 86 **a**	57.	The structure that connects the peripheral nervous system to the brain is the a. spinal cord b. corpus callosum c. pineal gland d. medulla
Factual LO 10 Page: 86 Correct = 61% **c**	58.	Which of the following devices monitors the electrical activity of the brain? a. a stereotaxic recorder b. an electrocardiograph c. an electroencephalograph d. any of these can be used
Factual LO 10 Page: 87 Correct = 81% **c**	59.	If brain damage is suspected, a patient may be tested with which of the following methods? a. the electrocardiograph b. lesioning c. the electroencephalograph d. electrode implantation
Factual LO 10 Page: 87 Correct = 93% **b**	60.	Destroying a piece of brain tissue to observe its effect on behavior is referred to as which of the following? a. ESB b. lesioning c. tumor ligation d. stereotaxic inversion

Critical Thinking LO 10 Page: 87 Correct = 62% **a**	61.	Standing outside a football stadium and judging the excitement of the game by the crowd's screams is analogous to "eavesdropping" on the brain using which of the following? a. an electroencephalograph b. electrical stimulation c. MRI scanning d. CT scanning
Critical Thinking LO 10 Page: 87 **c**	62.	Which of the following research techniques is <u>least</u> likely to be used to study the human brain? a. electrical stimulation b. recording electrical signals with the EEG c. lesioning d. cortex mapping
Factual LO 10 Page: 87 **d**	63.	The implantation of electrodes in the brains of animals is accomplished through the use of which of the following? a. a stereotypical instrument b. a tachistoscope c. the electroencephalograph d. a stereotaxic instrument
Critical Thinking LO 10 Page: 87 Correct = 87% **b**	64.	Electrical stimulation of its lateral hypothalamus causes an animal to overeat and become obese. Therefore, we would expect that lesioning the lateral hypothalamus would produce a. overeating and obesity b. undereating and weight loss c. no effect on eating or body weight d. alternating periods of overeating and undereating
Factual LO 11 Page: 88 **a**	65.	Which of the following brain-imaging techniques is the <u>most</u> widely used? a. CT scanning b. PET scanning c. MRI scanning d. EEG recording
Factual LO 11 Page: 89 **b**	66.	Which of the following brain-imaging techniques is <u>most</u> likely to be used to study the activity of specific neurotransmitters? a. CT scanning b. PET scanning c. MRI scanning d. EEG recording
Concept/Applied LO 11 Page: 89 **d**	67.	MRI scanning uses <u>all but</u> which of the following to map out brain structure and brain function? a. radio waves b. magnetic fields c. computerized enhancement d. radioactively tagged sugars
Factual LO 11 Page: 89 **b**	68.	The technique in which radioactively tagged chemicals are introduced into the brain and then equipment monitors where the chemicals appear in the brain is a. computerized tomography b. positron emission tomography c. magnetic resonance imaging d. electrographic tomography

Factual LO 11 Page: 89 **b**	69.	MRI scans of schizophrenic patients have indicated that a. schizophrenic subjects have higher levels of dopamine than nonschizophrenic subjects b. schizophrenic subjects have larger ventricles than nonschizophrenic subjects c. schizophrenic subjects have lower levels of catecholamines than nonschizophrenic subjects d. the amygdala of schizophrenic subjects is structurally defective relative to nonschizophrenic subjects
Concept/Applied LO 11 Page: 89 Correct = 37% **b**	70.	Which of the following techniques is likely to be most useful for locating specific neurotransmitter substances in the brain? a. computerized tomography b. positron emission tomography c. magnetic resonance imaging d. electrographic tomography
Concept/Applied LO 11 Page: 89 **d**	71.	Which of the following techniques can be used with the functioning, working brain? a. EEG only b. PET only c. MRI only d. EEG, PET or MRI can all be used.
Factual LO 12 Page: 91 **a**	72.	The portion of the human brain that mediates simple reflexes, such as sneezing, coughing, and salivating is the a. hindbrain b. midbrain c. cerebellum d. thalamus
Factual LO 12 Page: 91 Correct = 77% **b**	73.	Which of the following structures is <u>not</u> part of the hindbrain? a. cerebellum b. thalamus c. medulla d. pons
Factual LO 12 Page: 91 Correct = 57% **b**	74.	The brain structure that controls unconscious but essential functions such as breathing and circulation is the a. pons b. medulla c. cerebellum d. corpus callosum
Concept/Applied LO 12 Page: 91 Correct = 30% **b**	75.	Shot in the head, the victim died instantly because the bullet entered the _____, that portion of the hindbrain that regulates breathing. a. cerebellum b. medulla c. thalamus d. pons
Factual LO 12 Page: 91 **c**	76.	The primary function of the cerebellum is to a. process visual information b. control blood pressure c. coordinate body movement d. store semantic memory

Factual LO 12 Page: 91 **a**	77.	Damage to the cerebellum is <u>most</u> likely to result in a. problems with coordination of movement b. impairment of short-term memory c. difficulties in judging distance d. eating irregularities
Concept/Applied LO 12 Page: 91 Correct = 61% **a**	78.	The drunken driving suspect was unable to hold his hand out to the side and bring his finger to a stop on his nose because one of the brain structures depressed first by alcohol is the a. cerebellum b. corpus callosum c. hypothalamus d. medulla
Factual LO 12 Page: 91 Correct = 40% **d**	79.	The hindbrain structure involved with sleep and arousal is the a. hypothalamus b. cerebrum c. thalamus d. pons
Factual LO 12 Page: 91 **c**	80.	The _____ serves as a bridge between the brainstem and the cerebellum. a. corpus callosum b. thalamus c. pons d. reticular formation
Concept/Applied LO 13 Page: 91 **c**	81.	When you hear a sudden noise behind you and you reflexively turn your head, an area in the _____ is at work. a. brainstem b. hindbrain c. midbrain d. forebrain
Factual LO 13 Page: 91 **c**	82.	The dopamine system involved in Parkinsonism is located in which of the following areas of the brain? a. brainstem b. hindbrain c. midbrain d. forebrain
Factual LO 13 Page: 93 **b**	83.	The structure that begins in the hindbrain and terminates in the midbrain is the a. hypothalamus b. reticular formation c. pons d. medulla
Concept/Applied LO 13 Page: 93 **a**	84.	A person might end up in a coma if the following area of the brain is damaged a. reticular formation b. medulla c. hypothalamus d. pons
Concept/Applied LO 13 Page: 93 Correct = 24% **d**	85.	Which area of the brain is <u>most</u> likely to be affected by surgical anesthesia? a. hypothalamus b. medulla c. pons d. reticular formation

Factual LO 14 Page: 93 Correct = 40% **c**	86.	Which brain structure appears to play an active role in integrating sensory information? a. hypothalamus b. limbic system c. thalamus d. cerebrum
Factual LO 14 Page: 93 **c**	87.	The brain structure responsible for relaying sensory information to various locations in the brain is the a. frontal lobe of the cerebral cortex b. cerebellum c. thalamus d. limbic system
Factual LO 14 Page: 93 Correct = 88% **d**	88.	The function of the hypothalamus is to regulate a. hunger b. thirst c. body temperature d. hunger, thirst, and body temperature
Critical Thinking LO 14 Page: 93 Correct = 52% **d**	89.	If a key part of the _____ is destroyed, an animal will lose all interest in food and may well starve to death. a. medulla b. cerebellum c. thalamus d. hypothalamus
Critical Thinking LO 14 Page: 93 **d**	90.	If a person has a brain tumor that results in a disruption of his/her eating behavior, which of the following areas is the most likely location of the tumor? a. brainstem b. cerebellum c. thalamus d. hypothalamus
Factual LO 15 Page: 94 **b**	91.	Pleasure centers in the brain appear to be concentrated most heavily in the a. endocrine system b. limbic system c. corpus callosum d. brainstem
Factual LO 15 Page: 94 **d**	92.	Which of the following brain structures is most closely associated with the regulation of emotion? a. cerebellum b. reticular formation c. brainstem d. limbic system
Factual LO 15 Page: 94 **c**	93.	Research by Olds and Milner (1954) identified a "pleasure center" in rat brains. Rats will press a lever thousands of times as long as a small electric current stimulates a. the brainstem b. the corpus callosum c. the hypothalamus d. the frontal lobe of the occipital cortex

Concept/Applied LO 15 Page: 94 Correct = 20% **c**	94.	Electrodes placed in which location are likely to produce the highest rates of self-stimulation by an animal? a. amygdala b. cerebral cortex c. medial forebrain bundle d. posterior
Factual LO 16 Page: 95 Correct = 61% **b**	95.	The _____ is the largest and most complex part of the human brain. a. medulla b. cerebrum c. cerebellum d. limbic system
Factual LO 16 Page: 95 **b**	96.	Which of the following is responsible for the human ability to engage in higher mental activity such as thinking and philosophizing? a. the corpus callosum b. the cerebrum c. the cerebellum d. the hypothalamus
Factual LO 16 Page: 95 Correct = 91% **a**	97.	The structure that connects the two cerebral hemispheres is the a. corpus callosum b. pineal gland c. thalamus d. parietal lobe
Factual LO 16 Page: 95 **a**	98.	Which of the following is not considered a lobe of the cerebral cortex? a. cranial b. temporal c. occipital d. parietal
Factual LO 16 Page: 95 Correct = 67% **a**	99.	The lobe of the brain with primary responsibility for processing bodily sensations is the a. parietal lobe b. occipital lobe c. frontal lobe d. thalamic lobe
Factual LO 16 Page: 95 **b**	100.	The primary processing for auditory sensations is in the _____ lobe of the cerebrum. a. parietal b. temporal c. frontal d. occipital
Concept/Applied LO 16 Page: 95 **d**	101.	If you have damaged your temporal lobe, you can expect to have problems with which of the following? a. tasting b. thinking c. seeing d. hearing

THE BIOLOGICAL BASES OF BEHAVIOR

Critical Thinking
LO 16
Page: 95
Correct = 73%
a

102. Damage to the temporal lobe of the brain would probably be most harmful to the career of
    a. a musician
    b. an actor
    c. an architect
    d. a painter

Concept/Applied
LO 16
Page: 95
Correct = 75%
b

103. When this lobe of the brain is electrically stimulated people report physical sensations, as if they had been touched, for example, on the arm.
    a. frontal
    b. parietal
    c. temporal
    d. occipital

Factual
LO 16
Page: 96
Correct = 51%
c

104. The amount of motor cortex devoted to each body area is determined by
    a. the size of the body area
    b. the location of the body area
    c. the diversity of movements of the body area
    d. none of these factors

Concept/Applied
LO 17
Page: 97
b

105. People who suffer damage to the _____ often show deficits in attention, planning, and getting organized.
    a. corpus callosum
    b. prefrontal cortex
    c. hindbrain
    d. medial forebrain bundle

Concept/Applied
LO 17
Page: 97
b

106. Some theorists believe that a sort of "executive control system," which is responsible for monitoring, directing, and organizing thought processes, is housed in the
    a. corpus callosum
    b. prefrontal cortex
    c. hindbrain
    d. medial forebrain bundle

Concept/Applied
LO 17
Page: 98
c

107. If you experience damage to Broca's area, you can expect to have difficulty
    a. being creative
    b. controlling your arms and legs
    c. speaking
    d. hearing

Factual
LO 17
Page: 98
Correct = 78%
b

108. The area of the frontal lobe that plays an important role in the production of speech is called
    a. Wernicke's area
    b. Broca's area
    c. Cannon's area
    d. Sperry's area

Factual
LO 17
Page: 98
a

109. The brain structure that controls your ability to understand speech is
    a. Wernicke's area
    b. the thalamus
    c. the occipital lobe of the cerebral cortex
    d. Broca's area

Concept/Applied LO 17 Page: 98 Correct = 39% **b**	110.	If you have difficulty understanding the meaning of someone's speech, you may suspect damage to a. the pituitary gland b. Wernicke's area c. the corpus callosum d. Korsakoff's area
Concept/Applied LO 17 Page: 98 **a**	111.	The main reason for the characterization of the left hemisphere as the "dominant" hemisphere was a. the evidence that the left hemisphere usually processes language b. the evidence that the left hemisphere usually processes complex information c. the fact that the majority of people are right-handed d. that split-brain patients use only their left hemisphere for processing information
Concept/Applied LO 17 Page: 98 Correct = 75% **d**	112.	The production of language for most persons resides in the a. posterior cerebral hemisphere b. central cerebral hemisphere c. right cerebral hemisphere d. left cerebral hemisphere
Factual LO 17 Page: 98 **d**	113.	Which of the following researchers won a Nobel prize for his landmark research on "split-brain" patients? a. Charles Darwin b. Robert Plomin c. Roger Sperry d. James Olds
Factual LO 17 Page: 98 **d**	114.	A split-brain person has a severed a. cerebral cortex b. cerebellum c. medulla d. corpus callosum
Factual LO 17 Page: 98 Correct = 82% **a**	115.	Surgically disconnecting the cerebral hemispheres has its origins in the treatment of a. epileptics b. people in comas c. schizophrenics d. psychopaths
Factual LO 17 Page: 98 Correct = 97% **b**	116.	If the left hemisphere of the brain is damaged, which part of the body would be most directly affected? a. the left half b. the right half c. the upper portion d. the entire body
Critical Thinking LO 17 Page: 98 Correct = 82% **b**	117.	If a right-handed subject whose corpus callosum has been cut is asked to reproduce a drawing, you would predict a. best performance by the right hand b. best performance by the left hand c. equal performance by the two hands d. an inability to draw with either hand

Concept/Applied LO 17 Page: 99 Correct = 54% **b**	118.	In order to best study the functional specialization of the two sides of the brain a. one side is temporarily paralyzed b. the two sides must be surgically disconnected c. the subject must be ambidextrous d. information must be sent to only one eye and one ear and both on the same side of the body
Critical Thinking LO 17 Page: 99 Correct = 38% **a**	119.	Because the speech center is generally located in the left hemisphere of the brain, a split-brain patient is unable to describe stimuli that are a. seen in the left visual field b. seen in the right visual field c. presented directly in front of him or her d. felt with the right hand
Critical Thinking LO 17 Page: 99 **c**	120.	If you sent the word "banana" to a split-brain patient's left hemisphere and the word "cucumber" to his right hemisphere, which of the following would he be able to name verbally? a. both of the items b. neither of the items c. only the banana d. only the cucumber
Concept/Applied LO 18 Page: 100 **a**	121.	Which of the following parts of the brain is most likely to play a major role in the work of artists, architects, and engineers, who must rely heavily on visual-spatial skills? a. the right hemisphere b. the left hemisphere c. cerebellum d. corpus callosum
Factual LO 18 Page: 100 Correct = 82% **c**	122.	Research has found that the left side of the brain typically exercises primary control over all of the following except a. language b. the right side of the body c. visual-spatial abilities d. linguistic processing
Concept/Applied LO 18 Page: 100 Correct = 91% **c**	123.	For most persons the _____ cerebral hemisphere controls _____. a. left; the right cerebral hemisphere b. right; the left cerebral hemisphere c. left; language production d. right; motivation for sexual behavior
Factual LO 18 Page: 100 Correct = 92% **d**	124.	In studies of neurologically intact people, researchers have concluded that a. there is no cerebral specialization in the intact brain b. the left hemisphere normally handles nonverbal processing c. the right hemisphere normally handles verbal processing d. none of these statements is accurate
Factual LO 18 Page: 100 Correct = 72% **a**	125.	In both split-brain people and neurologically intact people, the left hemisphere specializes in a. verbal processing b. visual recognition c. spatial perception d. all of these things

Critical Thinking LO 18 Page: 100 Correct = 90% **b**	126.	Which of the following is <u>least</u> closely associated with left hemisphere functioning? a. speaking b. musical recognition c. reading d. writing words
Factual LO 19 Page: 101 **c**	127.	The system of glands that secrete hormones directly into the bloodstream is known as the a. atopic system b. exocrine system c. endocrine system d. blood-brain system
Factual LO 19 Page: 101 Correct = 95% **b**	128.	The endocrine system a. connects the two cerebral hemispheres of the brain b. secretes hormones c. manufactures myelin d. forms the basis of reflexive behaviors
Factual LO 19 Page: 101 Correct = 94% **a**	129.	A hormone is a. a chemical secreted into the blood by a gland b. a brain structure below the hypothalamus c. a location in the brain where a specific memory is stored d. none of these
Factual LO 19 Page: 101 **a**	130.	People who have hormonal imbalances have problems with their a. endocrine system b. reticular formation c. limbic system d. left brain/right brain communication
Factual LO 19 Page: 101 Correct = 46% **c**	131.	Hormones are transported throughout the body via the a. nervous system b. limbic system c. bloodstream d. secretionary system
Factual LO 19 Page: 101 **b**	132.	Much of the endocrine system is controlled by the nervous system through the a. medulla b. hypothalamus c. thalamus d. cerebellum
Factual LO 19 Page: 101 **d**	133.	The master gland of the endocrine system is the a. thyroid gland b. adrenal gland c. pancreas d. pituitary gland
Critical Thinking LO 19 Page: 101 **c**	134.	Which of the following does not belong with the other three? a. gonads b. thyroid c. thalamus d. pituitary

THE BIOLOGICAL BASES OF BEHAVIOR

Factual LO 19 Page: 102 **b**	135.	_____ are released by the pituitary gland and affect the development of external sexual organs. a. Acetylcholines b. Gonadotropins c. Endorphins d. All of these
Factual LO 19 Page: 102 **c**	136.	The appearance of secondary sex characteristics is the responsibility of hormones secreted by the a. thyroid b. pancreas c. gonads d. thalamus
Concept/Applied LO 19 Page: 102 **a**	137.	The fact that Maria was a little later than her sisters in going through puberty can be attributed to the action of her a. gonads b. adrenal glands c. thyroid glands d. pancreas
Factual LO 20 Page: 102 Correct = 79% **d**	138.	The interdisciplinary field that studies the influence of genetic factors and behavioral traits is a. ethology b. cross-cultural anthropology c. physiological psychology d. behavioral genetics
Factual LO 20 Page: 102 Correct = 94% **b**	139.	The result of the fertilization of an egg by a sperm is a a. chromosome b. zygote c. gene d. fetus
Factual LO 20 Page: 102 **d**	140.	Which of the following are generally considered the key functional units in hereditary transmission? a. dichromats b. limens c. chromosomes d. genes
Factual LO 20 Page: 102 Correct = 95% **a**	141.	The carriers of genetic information in the form of DNA are the a. chromosomes b. ribosomes c. nucleotides d. rizomes
Factual LO 20 Page: 102 **b**	142.	With the exception of the sex cells, every cell in the human body contains a. 23 chromosomes b. 46 chromosomes c. 23 recessive genes and 23 dominant genes d. 46 heterozygous pairs

Factual LO 20 Page: 103 Correct = 86% **c**	143.	When a dominant gene is paired with a recessive gene, the gene pair is said to be a. homozygous b. phenotypic c. heterozygous d. polygenic
Factual LO 20 Page: 103 **d**	144.	When one member of a gene pair is more influential, such that its trait is expressed over the trait of the other gene, it is said to be a. expressive b. genotypic c. phenotypic d. dominant
Factual LO 20 Page: 103 **a**	145.	A gene that must be paired with another gene just like itself to determine the phenotype is known as a a. recessive gene b. heterozygous gene c. dominant gene d. co-dominant gene
Factual LO 21 Page: 104 Correct = 75% **d**	146.	The specific pattern of genes inherited at conception defines an individual's a. phenotype b. polygenic inheritance c. stereotype d. genotype
Factual LO 21 Page: 104 Correct = 93% **d**	147.	A person's genotype refers to his or her a. observable characteristics and traits b. being dominated by the paternal contribution to genetic makeup c. being dominated by the maternal contribution to genetic makeup d. genetic makeup
Factual LO 21 Page: 104 **a**	148.	The observable characteristics of an individual are referred to as one's a. phenotype b. zygotype c. genotype d. heritability
Concept/Applied LO 21 Page: 104 Correct = 87% **b**	149.	We would expect the greatest degree of phenotypic similarity among a. fraternal twins b. identical twins c. siblings d. parents and their children
Factual LO 21 Page: 104 Correct = 83% **d**	150.	It appears that most human characteristics are influenced by a. a single gene b. a single pair of genes c. the father's genetic endowment more than the mother's d. more than one pair of genes
Concept/Applied LO 21 Page: 104 Correct = 88% **c**	151.	Skin color is determined by three to five gene pairs. This makes skin color a. a monogenic trait b. a dominant trait c. a polygenic trait d. a polymorphous trait

Factual LO 21 Page: 104 Correct = 92% c	152.	Which of the following is determined at conception and is fixed forever? a. phenotype b. somatotype c. genotype d. prototype
Factual LO 22 Page: 104 Correct = 94% a	153.	Family studies, twin studies, and adoption studies are primarily designed to a. disentangle the effects of genetics and experience on behavioral traits b. establish the groundwork for genetic engineering programs c. demonstrate the empirical nature of psychological research d. assess the effects of modern child-rearing methods
Factual LO 22 Page: 104 d	154.	Which of the following techniques is used by scientists to determine the relative influence of the effects of genetics and experience on behavioral traits? a. twin studies b. family studies c. adoption studies d. all of these techniques
Critical Thinking LO 22 Page: 104 c	155.	Which of the following is not a method of study to determine genetic effects on human behavior? a. family studies b. adoption studies c. experimental longitudinal studies d. twin studies
Critical Thinking LO 22 Page: 105 d	156.	What is the major difficulty associated with the use of family studies to establish whether traits run in families? a. Researchers lack an agreed upon definition as to what constitutes a trait. b. Because of the rising divorce rates and adoption rates, fully intact families that cross several generations are becoming more difficult to locate. c. Genetic mutations and abnormalities are more prevalent than recently thought and make it difficult, if not impossible, to disentangle their effects from normal genetic patterns. d. The data are correlational, thus leading to a great deal of interpretational difficulty as to what traits occur because of shared genetics versus because of shared environments.
Concept/Applied LO 22 Page: 105 d	157.	Which of the following pairs of people would have the greatest proportion of shared genes? a. brothers of same parents b. sisters of same parents c. fraternal twins d. they are all the same
Factual LO 22 Page: 105 Correct = 85% b	158.	As far as we know, the only humans who have the same genotype are a. fraternal twins b. identical twins c. dizygotic twins d. no two people have the same genotype
Factual LO 22 Page: 105 d	159.	The genetic relatedness of identical twins is equal to a. 25% b. 50% c. 75% d. 100%

Factual LO 22 Page: 105 **b**	160.	The genetic relatedness of fraternal twins is equal to a. 25% b. 50% c. 75% d. 100%
Concept/Applied LO 22 Page: 106 Correct = 88% **c**	161.	Adoption studies of intelligence suggest that a. genetics is the only determinant of intelligence b. family environment more strongly determines intelligence than genetics c. both genetics and environment contribute to intelligence d. no clear method exists to assess the relative contributions of genetics and experience on intelligence
Factual LO 22 Page: 106 Correct = 62% **c**	162.	The research on adopted children and intelligence has found that there is a significant similarity between them and a. their biological parents b. their adoptive parents c. both sets of parents d. their adoptive siblings
Factual LO 22 Page: 106 Correct = 84% **a**	163.	Determining the location of specific genes on specific chromosomes is referred to as a. genetic mapping b. phenomapping c. chromosomal atlasing d. all of the above
Factual LO 22 Page: 107 **c**	164.	Which of the following involves the examination of blood relatives to determine the degree of resemblance for a specific trait? a. a twin study b. a family study c. genetic mapping d. genetic engineering
Concept/Applied LO 22 Page: 107 Correct = 92% **c**	165.	With regard to human behavior, it is fairly clear that a. heredity controls the vast majority of behavior b. the environment controls the vast majority of behavior c. heredity and environment interact to control the vast majority of behavior d. none of these statements is accurate
Factual LO 22 Page: 108 Correct = 80% **c**	166.	It appears that schizophrenia a. is an inherited trait that is uninfluenced by one's environment b. has no relationship to one's genetic endowment and is primarily social in origin c. has a strong inherited predisposition that interacts with one's environment d. has an early age of vulnerability; if someone has a sufficient amount of stress before that age, there is a high probability schizophrenia will develop
Critical Thinking LO 23 Page: 108 **a**	167.	Which of the following statements about Charles Darwin and the theory of evolution is <u>not</u> accurate? a. He was the first person to describe the process of evolution. b. He identified natural selection as the mechanism that orchestrates the process of evolution. c. He noted that some of the characteristics of organisms are passed down from one generation to the next. d. He suggested that variations in hereditary traits might affect organisms' ability to obtain resources.

Concept/Applied LO 23 Page: 109 c	168.	According to Darwin's theory of evolution, which of the following is the key factor in evolutionary change? a. the genetic transmission of learned behavior b. the relative success of aggressive predators c. variations in reproductive success d. the interaction of heredity and the environment
Factual LO 23 Page: 109 b	169.	In evolutionary theory, _____ refers to the reproductive success (number of descendants) of an individual organism relative to the average reproductive success in the population. a. selection b. fitness c. mutation d. adaptation
Factual LO 23 Page: 109 c	170.	The notion that heritable characteristics that provide a survival or reproductive advantage are more likely to be passed on to subsequent generations is known as a. natural selection b. polygenic transmission c. genetic mapping d. gene flow
Factual LO 24 Page: 110 d	171.	The gene pool of a population is directly affected by which of the following? a. gene flow b. mutations c. natural selection d. all of these
Concept/Applied LO 24 Page: 110 b	172.	Which of the following is best described as an "error" in DNA replication? a. gene flow b. a mutation c. genetic drift d. natural selection
Factual LO 24 Page: 110 a	173.	When gene frequencies in a population shift because some individuals leave the population (emigration) and others enter it (immigration), _____ is said to have occurred. a. gene flow b. a mutation c. genetic drift d. natural selection
Concept/Applied LO 24 Page: 110 c	174.	Which of the following is most likely to contribute to the emergence of new species? a. genetic drift within a single generation b. mutations within a given population c. minimal gene flow between populations d. natural selection among different species
Factual LO 24 Page: 110 b	175.	_____ is the sum of an individual's own reproductive success, plus the effects the organism has on the reproductive success of related others. a. Genetic drift b. Inclusive fitness c. Reproductive fitness d. Reproductive drift

Concept/Applied LO 25 Page: 111 **d**	176.	Studying the evolution of behavior is more difficult than studying the evolution of physical traits mainly because a. behaviors tend to evolve more slowly b. natural selection generally does not operate on behaviors c. behaviors are more susceptible to genetic drift d. behaviors may occur infrequently and may not last very long
Concept/Applied LO 25 Page: 112 **c**	177.	According to evolutionary theory, mating strategies are adaptive if they a. increase the probability of natural selection b. decrease the amount of genetic drift in the population c. aid the survival of an organism and its offspring d. increase the likelihood of favorable mutations
Concept/Applied LO 26 Page: 112 **a**	178.	Evolutionary theorists tend to be most interested in studying which of the following behaviors? a. mating b. aggression c. information processing d. maternal attachment
Concept/Applied LO 26 Page: 112 **c**	179.	According to evolutionary theorist Robert Trivers, a species' courtship and mating strategies depend primarily on sex differences in a. aggression b. body size c. parental investment d. spatial orientation
Factual LO 26 Page: 112 **b**	180.	In most mammalian species, the parental investment of males tends to focus on a. nourishing of the offspring b. the act of copulation c. defense of the home territory d. hunting for food
Factual LO 26 Page: 112 **c**	181.	When parental investment is high for females and low for males, the mating system that typically results is a. monogamy b. polyandry c. polygyny d. homogamy
Factual LO 26 Page: 112 **c**	182.	A mating system in which each male seeks to mate with multiple females, whereas each female mates with only one male is called a. monogamy b. polyandry c. polygyny d. homogamy
Factual LO 26 Page: 112 **d**	183.	Which of the following is the most common mating system in nature? a. monogamy b. homogamy c. polyandry d. polygyny

Factual LO 26 Page: 113 c	184.	A mating system in which each female seeks to mate with multiple males, whereas each male mates with only one female is called a. monogamy b. homogamy c. polyandry d. polygyny
Factual LO 26 Page: 113 a	185.	When parental investment is roughly equal for males and females, the mating system that typically results is a. monogamy b. polyandry c. polygyny d. homogamy
Factual LO 26 Page: 113 a	186.	A mating system in which one male and one female mate exclusively, or almost exclusively with one another is called a. monogamy b. homogamy c. polyandry d. polygyny
Concept/Applied LO 27 Page: 114 b	187.	Which of the following statements best reflects current thinking about the theory of evolution? a. Evolutionary theory is basically just speculation. b. The theory of evolution is well-supported by empirical evidence. c. There is active debate on the central hypotheses of evolutionary theory. d. The assertion that organisms are the product of evolutionary processes is not well-established.
Critical Thinking LO 27 Page: 114 c	188.	Which of the following statements about the theory of evolution is not accurate? a. In some respects, evolution is about how organisms respond to changing environments. b. The central hypotheses of evolutionary theory are well-supported by empirical evidence. c. Evolutionary theory assumes that most organisms have a motive to maximize reproductive fitness. d. The assertion that organisms are the product of evolutionary processes is well-established.
Concept/Applied LO 28 Page: 114 a	189.	The current interest in the right brain/left brain phenomenon highlights the importance of approaching topics such as this from a(n) _____ point of view. a. empirical b. subjective c. anecdotal d. conjectural
Factual LO 28 Page: 114 Correct = 83% c	190.	In this chapter, we saw that schizophrenia may be a function of abnormalities in neurotransmitter activity, structural defects in the brain, and genetic vulnerability. These findings support which of the following unifying themes of your textbook? a. Psychology is empirical. b. Psychology evolves in a sociohistorical context c. Behavior is determined by multiple causes d. Our behavior is shaped by our cultural heritage

Concept/Applied LO 28 Page: 114 Correct = 68% **c**	191.	Which of the following statements most accurately reflects the roles of heredity and environment in shaping our behavior? a. Genetic factors have little influence on behavior. b. Researchers have identified genes for specific behaviors such as sarcasm. c. Hereditary endowment plays an indirect role in molding our behavior. d. Genes exert their influence on behavior with little impact from environmental factors.
Factual LO 29 Page: 116 **b**	192.	Some researchers have suggested that the left hemisphere of the brain is likely to be involved in <u>all but</u> which of the following types of tasks? a. writing b. music c. speech d. language
Critical Thinking LO 29 Page: 116 **b**	193.	Kim is good at reading maps and enjoys listening to music. Some researchers would suggest that these characteristics indicate that Kim is probably a. left-brained b. right-brained c. mid-brained d. hemispheric
Factual LO 29 Page: 117 Correct = 56% **d**	194.	Your text asserts that school reform should focus on a. providing students with more right-brain activities b. encouraging students to become ambidextrous so as to exercise both sides of the brain equally c. providing students with more left-brain activities d. encouraging more holistic, intuitive thinking rather than worrying about exercising one or the other half of the brain
Concept/Applied LO 29 Page: 119 **c**	195.	Which of the following statements about hemispheric control is <u>true</u>? a. The right hemisphere controls analytical and logic skills, while the left hemisphere controls spatial and musical skills. b. Left-handed persons' behavior is controlled almost exclusively by the left hemisphere, while right-handed persons' behavior is controlled almost exclusively by the right hemisphere. c. Conclusions about hemispheric dominance and control often lead to overgeneralizations concerning which hemisphere controls what activities. d. One can increase one's IQ by engaging in activities designed to "build up" the nondominant hemisphere.
Factual LO 30 Page: 120 **a**	196.	In summarizing recent research in neuroscience, science writer Ronald Kotulak concluded that which of the following periods is critically important to an individual's brain development? a. the first 3 years of life b. 6 to 10 years of age c. adolescence d. the college years
Factual LO 30 Page: 120 **d**	197.	Research on environment and brain development indicates that, compared to rats raised in an impoverished environment, rats raised in an enriched environment a. had slightly heavier brains b. performed better on problem solving tasks c. had a thicker cerebral cortex in some areas of the brain d. All of these statements are true.

Factual LO 30 Page: 120 **a**	198.	All of the studies that highlighted the possible importance of early experience in animals had which of the following features in common? a. They used extreme conditions to make their comparisons. b. They used relatively crude measures of brain growth. c. The researchers used very small samples. d. They were supported by a grant from the United States Department of Education
Integrative Correct = 80% **c**	199.	Agonist is to _____ as afferent is to _____. a. efferent; antagonist b. axon; synapse c. antagonist; efferent d. phenotype; genotype
Integrative **b**	200.	_____ function in the endocrine system much like _____ in the nervous system. a. Hormones; dendrites b. Hormones; neurotransmitters c. Endorphins; sensory neurons d. Neurotransmitters; hormones
Integrative Correct = 59% **a**	201.	Which of the following does <u>not</u> belong with the others? a. a neuromodulator b. an EEG c. a CT scan d. a stereotaxic instrument
Study Guide LO 1 Page: 76 **a**	202.	Most neurons are involved in transmitting information a. from one neuron to another b. from the outside world to the brain c. from the brain to the muscles d. none of the above
Study Guide LO 2 Page: 76 **d**	203.	Which part of the neuron has the responsibility for receiving information from other neurons? a. the cell body b. the soma c. the axon d. the dendrites
Study Guide LO 2 Page: 77 **c**	204.	The myelin sheath serves to a. permit faster transmission of the neural impulse b. keep neural impulses on the right track c. both of the above d. none of the above
Study Guide LO 3 Page: 77 **d**	205.	The change in the polarity of a neuron that results from the inflow of positively charged ions and the outflow of negatively charged ions is called the a. presynaptic potential b. postsynaptic potential c. synaptic potential d. none of the above

Study Guide LO 3 Page: 79 **d**	206.	The task of passing a message from one neuron to another is actually carried out by a. the myelin sheath b. the glial cells c. the action potential d. neurotransmitters
Study Guide LO 10 Page: 87 **b**	207.	Which of the following techniques is often used by neurosurgeons to map the brain when performing brain surgery? a. EEG recordings b. ESB c. lesioning d. all of the above
Study Guide LO 21 Page: 104 **b**	208.	A person's current weight and height could be said to exemplify his or her a. genotype b. phenotype c. both of the above d. none of the above
Study Guide LO 22 Page: 105 **d**	209.	Which of the following kinds of studies can truly demonstrate that specific traits are indeed inherited? a. family studies b. twin studies c. adoption studies d. none of the above
Study Guide LO 22 Page: 108 **c**	210.	Current evidence indicates that schizophrenia results from a. genetic factors b. environmental factors c. multiple causes that involve both genetic and environmental factors d. completely unknown factors
Online Quiz LO 1 Page: 76 **d**	211.	The basic communication links of the nervous system are the a. glia b. bones c. muscles d. neurons
Online Quiz LO 3 Page: 77 **d**	212.	The electrical charge inside a neuron when it is in its resting state is approximately a. +600 volts b. +60 millivolts c. -700 volts d. -70 millivolts
Online Quiz LO 4 Page: 79 **a**	213.	An impulse moves from one neuron to another through the action of a. neurotransmitters b. hormones c. action potentials d. neuromodulators
Online Quiz LO 6 Page: 81 **a**	214.	A chemical substance that mimics the action of a neurotransmitter is known as an a. agonist b. impeder c. antagonist d. anticholinergic

Online Quiz LO 8 Page: 84 **a**	215.	Sensory information is carried from your eyes to your brain by way of a. afferent fibers b. autonomic fibers c. efferent fibers d. motor fibers
Online Quiz LO 11 Page: 88 **b**	216.	The brain imaging method that uses multiple X rays to generate a picture of a horizontal slice of the brain is a. an electroencephalograph b. computerized tomography c. stereotaxic instrumentation d. EKG
Online Quiz LO 15 Page: 94 **b**	217.	The rewarding effects of electrical stimulation of the brain seem to be mediated by a. excitation of the reticular formation b. activation of dopamine-releasing neurons c. activation of endorphins d. stimulation of the hypothalamus
Online Quiz LO 20 Page: 103 **a**	218.	In the _____ condition, the two genes in a specific pair are the same. a. homozygous b. phenotypic c. heterozygous d. polygenic
Online Quiz LO 26 Page: 112 **b**	219.	When parental investment is high for males and low for females, the mating system that typically results is a. monogamy b. polyandry c. polygyny d. homogamy
Online Quiz LO 30 Page: 120 **d**	220.	The seminal research on critical periods in neural development was conducted in the 1960s on which of the following subjects? a. rats b. adult monkeys c. preschool children d. newborn kittens

ESSAY QUESTIONS

1. Choose a specific neurotransmitter or class of neurotransmitters and discuss its impact on behavior.

   Acetylcholine: The only neurotransmitter between motor neurons and voluntary muscles, therefore mediates all voluntary movement. Also contributes to attention, arousal, and memory. Alzheimer's disease is associated with an insufficient supply of this neurotransmitter.

   Biogenic amines (dopamine, serotonin, norepinephrine): Dopamine--mediates voluntary movement. A deficiency is associated with Parkinsonism; overactivity is associated with schizophrenia. Serotonin--regulates sleeping and waking. Norepinephrine--also regulates arousal. A deficiency is associated with depression.

   GABA: Has inhibitory effects only. Too little GABA is associated with anxiety.

2. Compare and contrast the nervous system and the endocrine system.

   Both are internal communication systems; both use chemical messengers. The nervous system utilizes neurotransmitters, which travel short distances at high speeds; the endocrine system uses hormones, which are slow-acting and travel long distances.

3. Compare and contrast lesioning and electrical stimulation of the brain.

   Both are methods of studying brain function; both involve the introduction of electric current into a specific brain structure via an implanted electrode.

   Lesioning uses a fairly strong electric current to destroy brain tissue, thus eliminating the relevant behavior from the subject's repertoire. Since lesioning produces permanent brain damage, it is employed with animal subjects only.

   Electrical stimulation of the brain introduces a weak current to artificially stimulate a brain structure and produce a behavioral response. It does not permanently damage the brain and so, under certain medical circumstances, may be used with humans; however, the technique is more frequently applied to animals.

4. Assume that trait X is primarily an inherited characteristic. Imagine that trait X is investigated using family studies, twin studies, and adoption studies. Briefly describe each of these three methods and indicate what information each would be expected to yield regarding trait X.

   Family studies: There should be more phenotypic similarity on trait X among relatives who share a greater percentage of genes. For example, there should be more similarity on trait X between identical twins than among siblings, who in turn should exhibit more similarity than cousins.

   Twin studies: Identical twins should exhibit more similarity on trait X than fraternal twins.

   Adoption studies: Children adopted in early infancy should more closely resemble their biological parents on trait X than they do their adoptive parents.

5. Imagine the following scenario: Administrators at the local high school have been impressed by recent media reports of cerebral hemispheric specialization, and are considering curricular reform to achieve a better balance between "left-brained" and "right-brained" activities. You have been hired to advise them on this issue. What would your recommendation be, and why?

   Although there is some evidence that the cerebral hemispheres are specialized to a degree, there is no basis for saying that people have two independent streams of consciousness or that each hemisphere has its own cognitive style. There is little basis for labeling some people as "left-brained" and others as "right-brained," or for relating these differences to distinctive task preferences, personalities, or vocations. All information reaches both hemispheres, since they communicate via the corpus callosum. Thus, cerebral specialization is not a sound basis for educational reform.

This page intentionally left blank.

Chapter Four
Sensation and Perception

LEARNING OBJECTIVES

1. Explain how stimulus intensity is related to absolute thresholds.
2. Explain Weber's law, Fechner's law.
3. Explain the basic thrust of signal detection theory.
4. Describe some evidence on perception without awareness and discuss the practical implications of subliminal perception.
5. Discuss the meaning and significance of sensory adaptation.
6. List the three properties of light and the aspects of visual perception that they influence.
7. Describe the role of the lens and pupil in the functioning of the eye.
8. Describe the role of the retina in light sensitivity and in visual information processing.
9. Describe the routing of signals from the eye to the brain and the brain's role in visual information processing.
10. Discuss the trichromatic and opponent process theories of color vision, and the modern reconciliation of these theories.
11. Distinguish between top-down and bottom-up processing.
12. Explain the basic premise of Gestalt psychology and describe Gestalt principles of visual perception.
13. Explain how form perception can be a matter of formulating perceptual hypotheses.
14. Describe the monocular and binocular cues employed in depth perception and cultural variations in depth perception
15. Summarize the Featured Study and follow-up research on the perception of geographical slant.
16. Describe perceptual constancies and illusions in vision, and discuss cultural variations in susceptibility to certain illusions.
17. List the three properties of sound and the aspects of auditory perception that they influence.
18. Summarize information on human hearing capacities and describe how sensory processing occurs in the ear.
19. Compare and contrast the place and frequency theories of pitch perception and discuss the resolution of the debate.
20. Discuss the cues employed in auditory localization.
21. Describe the stimulus and receptors for taste and discuss individuals differences in taste sensitivity.
22. Describe the stimulus and receptors for smell, and human olfactory capabilities.
23. Describe the processes involved in the perception of pressure and temperature.
24. Describe the two pathways along which pain signals travel and discuss evidence that the perception of pain is subjective.
25. Explain the gate-control theory of pain perception and recent findings related to it.
26. Describe the perceptual experiences mediated by the kinesthetic and vestibular systems.
27. Explain how this chapter highlighted three of the text's unifying themes.
28. Discuss how the Impressionists, Cubists, and Surrealists used various principles of visual perception
29. Discuss how Escher, Vasarely, and Magritte used various principles of visual perception.
30. Explain how contrast effects can be manipulated to influence or distort judgments.

MULTIPLE-CHOICE QUESTIONS

Factual
LO 1
Page: 126
Correct = 93%
a

1. The term used to refer to the stimulation of the sense organs is
   a. sensation
   b. transduction
   c. perception
   d. sensory adaptation

Factual
LO 1
Page: 126
Correct = 66%
a

2. Technically, your absolute threshold is the point which you can detect
   a. a stimulus 50 percent of the time
   b. a stimulus 75 percent of the time
   c. any stimulus set point
   d. any stimulus that registers on sensory memory

Concept/Applied
LO 1
Page: 126
a

3. William was having his hearing tested, and a number of the tones that were presented were so faint he was not able to detect them. These faint sounds would
   a. fall below William's absolute threshold for sound
   b. cause more inhibitory than excitatory synapses
   c. fall below William's adaptation level for sound
   d. cause action potentials that were too weak to reach the terminal buttons

Concept/Applied
LO 1
Page: 126
d

4. Juanita was drinking some warm punch and she thought she could just detect a faint taste of nutmeg in the punch. However when she took another sip the taste wasn't there. On the third sip she could just make out the taste of nutmeg again. It is very likely that the amount of nutmeg in the punch was
   a. just below her taste constancy level
   b. producing inhibitory synapses rather than excitatory synapses
   c. producing action potentials that were too weak to reach the terminal buttons
   d. just at her absolute threshold for taste

Concept/Applied
LO 1
Page: 126
c

5. Giovanni was watching the night sky on a clear evening in November. He noticed that sometimes when he looked directly over head he could detect a very faint star. A few minutes later it seemed that the star had disappeared, and then it "appeared" again. In this case, it is very likely that the light from the star was
   a. just below Giovanni's level for perceptual invariance
   b. producing action potentials that were too weak to reach the terminal buttons
   c. just at Giovanni's absolute threshold for light
   d. producing inhibitory synapses rather than excitatory synapses

Concept/Applied
LO 2
Page: 127
Correct = 81%
b

6. If a subject is presented with a series of pairs of light bulbs of different wattages and is asked whether the members of each pair differ in brightness, which of the following is being measured?
   a. the physical intensity difference between the two lights
   b. the subject's just noticeable difference for brightness
   c. the subject's absolute threshold for brightness
   d. the subject's visual acuity

Concept/Applied
LO 2
Page: 127
Correct = 87%
c

7. If a 100-Hz tone had to be increased to 110 Hz for a subject to just notice the difference, you would predict that a 1000-Hz tone would have to be increased to
   a. 1010 to be noticed
   b. 1050 to be noticed
   c. 1100 to be noticed
   d. 1200 to be noticed

CHAPTER FOUR

Concept/Applied LO 2 Page: 127 c	8.	Evelyn turned the thermostat up from 68 degrees to 70 degrees; however, she doesn't think it feels any warmer and she wants to turn it up even higher. Her roommate thinks that it is now too hot, and she wants to turn the thermostat back down. Apparently Evelyn has a. a smaller just noticeable difference for temperature than her roommate does b. a lower absolute threshold for temperature than her roommate does c. a larger just noticeable difference for temperature than her roommate does d. a higher absolute threshold for temperature, compared to her roommate
Concept/Applied LO 2 Page: 127 b	9.	Ron is making potato soup. His roommate tastes it and tells Ron it is great, but Ron thinks it needs more salt. He adds just a little salt, and thinks the soup now tastes perfect. However, his roommate tastes it again and tells Ron that the soup is ruined because it is too salty. Apparently, for the taste of salt a. Ron can detect a smaller just noticeable difference than his roommate b. Ron's roommate can detect a smaller just noticeable difference than Ron can c. Ron has a higher absolute threshold than his roommate does d. Ron has a lower absolute threshold than his roommate does
Concept/Applied LO 2 Page: 127 d	10.	When Celeste was playing her stereo at 40 decibels and she turned it up to 44 decibels, she could notice that it was louder. Based on this information you could predict that if Celeste has her stereo playing at 80 decibels, her just noticeable difference for loudness would be a. 4 decibels, the same as it was at 40 decibels b. 2 decibels, half as much as it was at 40 decibels c. impossible to determine without more information d. 8 decibels, twice as much as it was at 40 decibels
Concept/Applied LO 2 Page: 127 Correct = 78% b	11.	You turn on a 3-way light bulb at 50 watts, then click it up to 100 watts, then up to 150 watts. The apparent increase in brightness from 50 to 100 is _____ the apparent increase in brightness from 100 to 150. a. less than b. more than c. the same as d. indeterminate relative to the other intensities
Concept/Applied LO 2 Page: 128 Correct = 41% c	12.	Which of the following is true regarding our inner "measurements" of sensory experiences? a. There is generally a one-to-one correspondence with the physical intensity of the stimulus. b. Although there is a one-to-one correspondence with the physical intensity of the stimulus at lower intensity levels, the correspondence virtually disappears at higher intensity levels. c. There is no one-to-one correspondence with the physical intensity of the stimulus, especially at the higher intensity levels. d. Although there is a one-to-one correspondence with the physical intensity of the stimulus for vision, there is no similar correspondence for hearing.
Factual LO 3 Page: 129 Correct = 79% c	13.	In the signal-detection method, if a subject detects a stimulus when no stimulus is actually present, this would be a a. hit b. miss c. false alarm d. correct rejection

Concept/Applied LO 3 Page: 129 Correct = 66% **a**	14.	Which type of signal-detection error becomes more likely when the expectation of a stimulus is weak? a. a miss b. a false alarm c. a correct rejection d. an accurate hit
Concept/Applied LO 3 Page: 129 Correct = 85% **b**	15.	The stronger your expectation that a signal is present, the greater the likelihood that you will a. miss a signal b. report a false alarm c. correctly reject a signal when it appears d. be aware of background noise
Concept/Applied LO 3 Page: 129 Correct = 82% **a**	16.	Jerry, a nuclear operator, must monitor 50 different gauges that keep track of various aspects of the nuclear reactor. According to _____, Jerry's detection of any problems will be influenced by the probability of any problem occurring in conjunction with the payoff associated with detecting the problem. a. signal-detection theory b. Frazier Kannard c. sensory conversion theory d. the Gestaltists
Concept/Applied LO 3 Page: 129 **a**	17.	Joan was sitting talking with some friends when she suddenly left the room to check on her baby. She was sure she heard little Emily cry out, but when she checked, Emily was sleeping peacefully. Based on signal detection theory, the fact that Joan thought she detected a baby's cry would be considered a. a false alarm b. a correct rejection c. a hit d. a miss
Concept/Applied LO 3 Page: 129 **b**	18.	Dalton was sitting in the hallway outside his chemistry class. Some students said they thought they could smell smoke, but Dalton didn't smell anything. When they all checked the lab to see if there were any problems, everything was fine and nothing was burning. Based on signal detection theory, the fact that Dalton didn't smell any smoke would be considered a. a false alarm b. a correct rejection c. a hit d. a miss
Concept/Applied LO 3 Page: 129 **d**	19.	The fact that your criterion for "hearing" mysterious noises at night may change after a rash of burglaries in your neighborhood can best be explained by a. Weber's law b. Fechner's law c. sensory adaptation d. signal-detection theory
Factual LO 4 Page: 129 Correct = 63% **a**	20.	Subliminal means a. below threshold b. barely perceptible c. deceptive d. superimposed

Factual LO 4 Page: 130 Correct = 58% **a**	21.	Which of the following statements is <u>true</u>? a. Although subliminal perception was once dismissed by scientists as preposterous, recent data have made the notion less implausible. b. Scientists have conclusively demonstrated that perception simply cannot take place without conscious awareness. c. Recent research suggests that subliminal messages can be quite persuasive, convincing us to buy products we don't want, promoting satanic rituals, and facilitating weight loss. d. Subliminal perception is only possible if sensory adaptation has taken place.
Factual LO 4 Page: 130 Correct = 80% **c**	22.	The 1992 study of attitudes and subliminal perception, conducted by Krosnick and his colleagues, found that a. paradoxically, people who were exposed to subliminal negative emotion-arousing photos rated a target person more positively than people exposed to subliminal positive emotion-arousing photos b. exposure to subliminal information had no effect on subjects' attitudes c. people exposed to subliminal negative emotion-arousing photos rated a target person more negatively than people exposed to subliminal positive emotion-arousing photos d. females were more influenced by subliminal messages than males
Factual LO 4 Page: 130 Correct = 62% **c**	23.	When researchers have attempted to demonstrate subliminal perception effects in the real world, they have typically found that a. such effects are substantial and a potential cause for public concern b. people are much more likely to be influenced by "positive" subliminal stimuli (e.g., self-help tapes) than "negative" ones (e.g., subliminal advertising) c. such effects are so weak as to be of little, if any, practical importance d. people are much more likely to be influenced by "negative" subliminal stimuli than "positive" ones
Factual LO 5 Page: 130 Correct = 75% **b**	24.	If one is subjected to prolonged stimulation, eventually a. sensory overload will occur b. sensory adaptation will occur c. perceptual agnosia will occur d. perceptual inversion will occur
Factual LO 5 Page: 130 Correct = 95% **c**	25.	Sensory adaptation refers to a. a weakening of a neurotransmitter substance b. a perceptual inversion principle c. a decline in sensitivity after prolonged stimulation d. an increase in sensitivity after prolonged stimulation
Concept/Applied LO 5 Page: 130 Correct = 98% **d**	26.	You enter a room and notice a distinctive new smell. After a bit of time you no longer smell the odor. This illustrates the phenomenon of a. progressive desensitization b. sensory contrast c. sensory novelty d. sensory adaptation
Concept/Applied LO 5 Page: 130 **d**	27.	Jacob has been working at his computer for the past 2 hours, and the hum that he found so annoying when he started no longer bothers him. The change in Jacob's sensitivity to the noise from the computer illustrates the process known as a. perceptual invariance b. perceptual assimilation c. adjusting just noticeable differences d. sensory adaptation

Concept/Applied LO 5 Page: 130 **a**	28.	Sonja put on a new watch this morning and found it uncomfortable because it was so much heavier than her old watch. However, at noon, when a friend asks her if she knows what time it is, Sonja finds she has forgotten she is even wearing the watch. The change in Sonja's sensitivity to the pressure of the watch illustrates the process known as a. sensory adaptation b. perceptual invariance c. perceptual assimilation d. adjusting just noticeable differences
Concept/Applied LO 5 Page: 130 Correct = 97% **b**	29.	Sensory adaptation can explain all of the following <u>except</u> a. getting used to the smell of the perfume you are wearing b. hearing your name spoken in a noisy room c. feeling comfortable in a cold swimming pool after being in for a few minutes d. getting used to the touch of your clothes on your skin
Concept/Applied LO 5 Page: 131 Correct = 81% **a**	30.	Overall, it appears that we perceive a. changing stimuli better than constant ones b. constant stimuli better than changing ones c. long-acting better than short-acting stimuli d. stimuli that are steady in the environment
Factual LO 6 Page: 131 Correct = 85% **a**	31.	The wavelength of light mainly affects our perception of a. color b. brightness c. saturation d. light purity
Factual LO 6 Page: 131 Correct = 70% **b**	32.	Our perception of the brightness of a color is affected mainly by a. the wavelength of light waves b. the amplitude of light waves c. the purity of light waves d. the saturation of light waves
Critical Thinking LO 6 Page: 131 Correct = 81% **c**	33.	If the human eye was not responsive to differences in the wavelength of light, we would not be able to perceive differences in a. brightness b. saturation c. color d. purity
Concept/Applied LO 6 Page: 131 **b**	34.	Jose is wearing a blue shirt and Evan is wearing a red shirt. In this case, Jose's shirt is reflecting a. higher amplitude light waves than Evan's shirt b. shorter light waves than Evan's shirt c. longer light waves than Evan's shirt d. lower amplitude light waves than Evan's shirt
Critical Thinking LO 6 Page: 131 **d**	35.	If the human eye was not responsive to differences in the amplitude of light waves we would not be able to perceive differences in a. saturation b. purity c. color d. brightness

Critical Thinking LO 6 Page: 131 **d**	36.	If the human eye was not responsive to differences in the purity of light waves we would not be able to perceive differences in a. hue b. brightness c. color constancies d. saturation
Factual LO 7 Page: 132 Correct = 88% **c**	37.	The lens in the eye a. converts light energy into neural energy b. controls the amount of light entering the eye c. bends entering light rays and focuses them onto the retina d. is the part of the eye that gives it its color
Concept/Applied LO 7 Page: 132 **d**	38.	As people age the lens of the eye loses its ability to accommodate, and it tends to remain flat, instead of becoming fat and round. This suggests that as people age they will a. lose their ability to focus on objects in the distance b. be less likely to detect differences in light purity c. be more likely to detect differences in brightness and hue d. lose their ability to focus on objects that are close
Concept/Applied LO 7 Page: 132 **c**	39.	Courtney wears glasses to correct the far-sightedness in her left eye. If she were not wearing her glasses a. the lens would focus images in front of the retina in her left eye b. the pupil in her left eye would dilate and let in too much light energy c. the lens would focus images behind the retina in her left eye d. the pupil in her left eye would constrict and not let in sufficient light energy
Factual LO 7 Page: 132 Correct = 62% **b**	40.	The structure that controls the size of the pupil is the a. lens b. iris c. ciliary muscle d. vitreous humor
Factual LO 7 Page: 133 Correct = 94% **a**	41.	The amount of light entering the eye is regulated by changes in the size of the a. pupil b. lens c. cornea d. retina
Factual LO 7 Page: 133 Correct = 86% **c**	42.	In bright sunlight, the pupil of the eye is a. the same size as it is in a dark room b. dilated c. constricted d. closed
Concept/Applied LO 7 Page: 133 **b**	43.	Isaiah is having his eyes checked. The doctor has put drops in Isaiah's eyes that will cause the pupils to open wide. As the drops begin to work, Isaiah will most likely notice that a. he will lose some of his color vision b. his vision will start to become quite blurry c. his vision will become extremely sharp and clear d. colors will appear to be "super" saturated

Concept/Applied LO 7 Page: 133 Correct = 64% **d**	44.	In dim light, the pupil of the eye is a. dilated, producing a sharper image b. constricted, producing a sharper image c. constricted, producing an image that is not as sharp d. dilated, producing an image that is not as sharp
Factual LO 8 Page: 134 Correct = 73% **a**	45.	The optic disk is a. where the optic nerve exits the retina b. the brain structure responsible for the merging of visual fields from both eyes c. where light enters the eye d. another term for the lens
Factual LO 8 Page: 134 Correct = 82% **c**	46.	The blind spot in the eye is a. where photoreceptor cells do not "bleach" b. the point at which ganglion cells synapse with bipolar cells c. where the optic nerve exits the back of the eye d. what leads to color blindness
Concept/Applied LO 8 Page: 135 **b**	47.	In order to maximize visual acuity at night, you should a. look directly at the object you wish to see b. turn your head at a slight angle to the object c. close one eye d. blink your eyes several times to hasten dark adaptation
Concept/Applied LO 8 Page: 135 **c**	48.	Petra looked directly into a very bright light and damaged her retina. The opthamologist has told her that she has sustained massive damage to her cones, but for the most part her rods have not been affected. One change that you could predict for Petra's vision is that she will now have a. poor vision in low illumination b. poor peripheral vision c. no color vision d. more accurate depth perception
Critical Thinking LO 8 Page: 135 **b**	49.	Imagine that biologists have discovered an animal that has eyes very similar to human eyes, but that the only receptor cells in the retina are rods; there are no cones. Based on what is known about human vision you might expect that this animal would a. have poor vision in low illumination b. have no color vision c. have poor peripheral vision d. be able to detect extremely fine details
Critical Thinking LO 8 Page: 135 **b**	50.	Imagine that biologists have discovered an animal that has eyes very similar to human eyes, but that the only receptor cells in the retina are cones; there are no rods. Based on what is known about human vision you might expect that this animal would have a. poor visual acuity b. poor peripheral vision c. poor vision in bright illumination d. no color vision

CHAPTER FOUR

Concept/Applied LO 8 Page: 135 **c**	51.	Devin looked directly into a very bright light and damaged his retina. The opthamologist has told him that he has sustained massive damage to his rods, but for the most part his cones have not been affected. One change that you could predict for Devin's vision is that he will now have a. no color vision b. poor vision in bright illumination c. poor peripheral vision d. more accurate depth perception
Concept/Applied LO 8 Page: 135 **d**	52.	Fifteen minutes after Zigfried left the brightly lit hallway and entered the dark passageway, dark adaptation was a. complete in his rods, but still taking place in his cones b. complete in both his rods and cones c. still taking place in both his rods and his cones d. complete in his cones, but still taking place in his rods
Factual LO 8 Page: 136 **d**	53.	The receptive field of a visual cell refers to the a. range of wavelengths of light the cell reacts to b. length of time necessary for the cell to integrate information at the ganglion level of the retina c. cell's degree of sensitivity or receptivity d. the collection of rod and cone receptors that funnel signals to a particular visual cell in the retina
Concept/Applied LO 8 Page: 136 **b**	54.	Our visual acuity will be best when a ganglion cell a. transmits its neural signal directly to the visual cortex b. has a small receptive field c. has a large receptive field d. transmits its neural signal to the cerebellum, instead of the visual cortex
Factual LO 8 Page: 136 Correct = 56% **c**	55.	The center-surround arrangement of visual fields contributes to the eye being a. an absolute-intensity detector b. insensitive at low illumination c. a contrast detector d. insensitive to low amplitude light waves
Concept/Applied LO 9 Page: 138 Correct = 60% **b**	56.	"Parallel processing" in the visual pathways suggests that separate neural channels a. do the same things at different locations b. extract different information from visual inputs c. send the same information to many different places d. provide safety backups for each other
Concept/Applied LO 9 Page: 138 **d**	57.	If the pathway through the superior colliculus were not functioning correctly, you might expect that a person would have difficulty a. distinguishing colors b. perceiving depth c. detecting differences in texture d. integrating visual and auditory information
Concept/Applied LO 9 Page: 138 **a**	58.	If the parvocellular system within the thalamus was not functioning correctly, you might expect that a person would have difficulty a. distinguishing colors b. detecting movement c. localizing sounds d. perceiving depth

Concept/Applied LO 9 Page: 138 **b**	59.	If the magnocellular system within the thalamus was not functioning correctly, you might expect that a person would have difficulty a. distinguishing colors b. perceiving depth c. perceiving fine details d. localizing sounds
Factual LO 9 Page: 138 Correct = 68% **a**	60.	The primary visual cortex is located in the a. occipital lobes b. temporal lobes c. parietal lobes d. frontal lobes
Factual LO 9 Page: 139 Correct = 34% **b**	61.	Cells in the visual cortex that respond selectively to specific features of complex stimuli are called a. ganglion cells b. feature detectors c. selective detectors d. hypocomplex cells
Factual LO 9 Page: 139 Correct = 67% **c**	62.	The cells in the visual cortex that respond to a line of the correct width, oriented at the correct angle, and located in the correct position in its receptive field are called a. hypercomplex cells b. triarchic cells c. simple cells d. binary cells
Factual LO 9 Page: 139 Correct = 74% **b**	63.	Complex cells in the visual cortex respond to a. circles of light anywhere in their receptive field b. specific widths and orientation of lines anywhere in their receptive field c. figure-ground disparity in their receptive field d. different colors in their receptive field
Concept/Applied LO 9 Page: 139 **a**	64.	A microelectrode is recording the activity from a single cell in the visual cortex of a cat. The cell begins to fire rapidly when a line is presented at a 45-degree angle directly in front of the cat, but stops firing when the line is shifted to a position that is off to the left. In this case, the microelectrode is most likely monitoring activity from a. a simple cell b. a cell in the superior colliculus c. a complex cell d. a hypercomplex cell
Concept/Applied LO 9 Page: 139 **b**	65.	A microelectrode is recording the activity from a single cell in the visual cortex of a cat. The cell begins to fire rapidly when a vertical line sweeps across the visual field to the left, but stops firing when the same line sweeps back across the visual field to the right. In this case, the microelectrode is most likely monitoring activity from a. a hypercomplex cell b. a complex cell c. a simple cell d. a cell in the parvocellular channel
Concept/Applied LO 10 Page: 140 Correct = 23% **c**	66.	While finger painting, Chris mixed yellow paint and blue paint and ended up with green, an example of a. trichromatic theory b. additive color mixing c. subtractive color mixing d. multiplicative color mixing

CHAPTER FOUR

| Concept/Applied
LO 10
Page: 140
Correct = 86%
b | 67. | Mixing many, varied paints together would tend to produce a _____, while projecting many varied colored spots on the same area of a screen would tend to produce a _____.
a. bright, light color; dark, dull color
b. dull, dark color; light, whitish color
c. reddish color; bluish color
d. dull, dark color; dull, dark color |

| Concept/Applied
LO 10
Page: 140
Correct = 87%
c | 68. | If you project a red, a green, and a blue light into space, the point at which the three lights cross will lead to the perception of
a. black light
b. ultraviolet light
c. white light
d. infrared light |

| Concept/Applied
LO 10
Page: 140
Correct = 87%
d | 69. | If you mix red, green, and blue paint, you will get
a. purple
b. white
c. orange
d. black |

| Concept/Applied
LO 10
Page: 140
a | 70. | At the musical he attended over the weekend, Andrew noticed that whenever the red and green spotlights overlapped, they seemed to change to a yellow spotlight. This can be explained using the principles of
a. additive color mixing
b. subtractive color mixing
c. hypercomplex feature detection
d. opponent-processing of colors |

| Concept/Applied
LO 10
Page: 141
d | 71. | Television sets are able to recreate the entire visible spectrum by additively mixing three primary colors. This process is similar to the view of human color vision called
a. opponent-process theory
b. saturation theory
c. complementary color theory
d. trichromatic theory |

| Factual
LO 10
Page: 142
Correct = 76%
b | 72. | Hering's opponent-process theory suggests that receptors are linked antagonistically in pairs. His opposed pairs were
a. red-yellow; blue-green; black-white
b. red-green; yellow-blue; black-white
c. red-black; yellow-white; green-blue
d. yellow-green; red-blue; black-white |

| Concept/Applied
LO 10
Page: 142
d | 73. | Eric has been wearing green welding goggles for the past 30 minutes. Based on the opponent-process theory of color vision, when Eric takes off the green goggles he should expect that objects will temporarily appear to be
a. blue
b. yellow
c. orange
d. red |

| Factual
LO 10
Page: 142
Correct = 60%
a | 74. | According to one theory of color vision, colors are signaled in pairs by neurons that fire faster to one color and slower to another color. This theory is known as the
a. opponent process theory
b. trichromatic theory
c. signal-detection theory
d. feature-detection theory |

Concept/Applied LO 10 Page: 142 **a**	75.	Denise was momentarily blinded when a paparazzi snapped her picture using a blue flash. Following the flash, she saw spots for several minutes. Based on the opponent-process theory of color vision, the spots that Denise saw a. would be yellow b. were most likely red c. were probably green d. would also appear to be blue
Concept/Applied LO 10 Page: 142 Correct = 80% **b**	76.	After having your picture taken with a yellow flash, you momentarily see blue spots floating before your eyes. This phenomenon is best explained by a. subtractive color mixing b. opponent process theory c. additive color mixing d. trichromatic theory
Concept/Applied LO 10 Page: 142 **d**	77.	The action of the visual receptors supports the a. Hering theory of color vision b. opponent process theory of color vision c. James-Lange theory of color vision d. trichromatic theory of color vision
Concept/Applied LO 10 Page: 142 Correct = 32% **b**	78.	The action of the lateral geniculate nucleus supports the a. Young-Helmholtz theory of color vision b. opponent process theory of color vision c. trichromatic theory of color vision d. Yerkes-Dodson theory of color vision
Factual LO 10 Page: 142 Correct = 77% **a**	79.	The best desciprion of the current view of the way in which color is coded in the visual system would be that color coding a. begins with a trichromatic process and then switches to an opponent process. b. begins with rods and then switches to cones. c. begins with cones and then switches to rods. d. begins with an opponent process and then switches to a trichromatic process.
Concept/Applied LO 11 Page: 143 **b**	80.	Three people look at the same sketch and report seeing three different things. This illustrates the contribution to perception of a. stimulus ambiguity b. perceptual set c. sensory readiness d. cognitive interpretation
Concept/Applied LO 11 Page: 143 **a**	81.	A perceptual set implies that a. people often see what they expect to see b. visual perception is based on a bottom-up processing strategy c. feature analysis is a "hard-wired" process d. the focused-attention stage of processing is often overridden by preattentive processes
Concept/Applied LO 11 Page: 144 **b**	82.	Ashlynn was listening to a tape recording of a famous speech that was being played backward. She just heard gibberish until a classmate said the phrase "meet me in St. Louis" was clearly spoken. The tape was rewound and as Ashlynn listened this time, she also clearly heard the same phrase. Ashlynn's ability to detect the phrase the second time through the tape illustrates a. the opponent-process model of perception b. the top-down processing model of perception c. the bottom-up processing model of perception d. the eclectic model of perception

Factual LO 11 Page: 144 Correct = 86% **a**	83.	Feature analysis assumes that we progress from individual elements to the whole in the formation of our perceptions. This is a case of a. bottom-up processing b. bottom-down processing c. top-down processing d. top-to-bottom processing
Critical Thinking LO 11 Page: 144 **c**	84.	Psychologists who took the structuralist approach to the study of consciousness believed that the best way to understand an individual's conscious experiences was to understand all the component parts that combined to produce the experience. This view is most consistent with a. the top-down processing model of perception b. the eclectic model of perception c. the bottom-up processing model of perception d. the opponent-process model of perception
Concept/Applied LO 11 Page: 144 Correct = 62% **a**	85.	The ability to rapidly process words in reading depends most on a. top-down processing b. bottom-up processing c. bottom-to-top processing d. lateral processing
Concept/Applied LO 11 Page: 144 **d**	86.	Vanessa describes a new melody that she heard at a concert by telling you each of the individual notes, in the order that they were played. In providing this type of description, it appears that Vanessa processed the melody using a. top-down processing b. figure-ground processing c. opponent-processes d. bottom-up processing
Concept/Applied LO 12 Page: 145 Correct = 88% **c**	87.	Rather than provide details about the party she just attended, Patty tried to give her overall impression, operating on the assumption of _____, that the whole may be greater than the mere sum of its parts. a. psychophysics b. holistic psychology c. Gestalt psychology d. psychodynamics
Concept/Applied LO 12 Page: 145 **a**	88.	The successive blinking on and off of the lights on the neon sign gave the impression of beer filling a glass. This illusion of motion is the a. phi phenomenon b. constancy principle c. common-fate principle d. motion parallax effect
Concept/Applied LO 12 Page: 145 **a**	89.	The lights around the movie marquee flashed on-and-off in succession. However, Jerome did not perceive them as separate lights flashing, but instead saw a continuous band of light moving around the edge of the marquee. Jerome's perception illustrates a. the phi phenomenon b. bottom-up processing c. feature detection d. preattentive processing

Concept/Applied LO 12 Page: 145 **b**	90.	Shelby created an animated scene using her computer. She drew a frog as he started to jump, and then drew the frog landing. The computer created 24 pictures between these two points, which adjusted the frog's position very slightly. When the entire sequence of 26 pictures is displayed in rapid succession, the frog appears to hop smoothly. This perception of smooth action is one example of a. preattentive processing b. the phi phenomenon c. bottom-up processing d. feature detection
Concept/Applied LO 12 Page: 145 **b**	91.	It is difficult to see a chameleon that has blended in with its background because a. of the principle of common fate b. we cannot easily distinguish between figure and ground c. of the perceptual principle of shape constancy d. of the illusion of relative size
Concept/Applied LO 12 Page: 145 **d**	92.	Zachary is looking at a reversible figure which first appears to be a vase and then appears to be two faces. His perception of the figure keeps switching between these two interpretations. This switching perception is caused by the fact that a. reversible figures cause people to experience the phi phenomenon b. the Gestalt principle of simplicity doesn't work for reversible figures c. The Gestalt principles of proximity and closure are both at work in reversible figures d. the figure-ground distinction in reversible figures is often ambiguous
Concept/Applied LO 12 Page: 145 Correct = 54% **a**	93.	Paintings or drawings that lead to ambiguous interpretations often invert the a. figure and ground b. sensation and perception c. top and bottom d. open processing and closed processing
Factual LO 12 Page: 145 Correct = 84% **d**	94.	The Gestalt principle of proximity refers to the idea that a. people tend to gravitate toward a common interaction distance b. center-surround cells are closer fire more often c. perception occurs in discrete time frames d. objects nearer to each other are seen as forming a unit
Concept/Applied LO 12 Page: 145 **c**	95.	Natalie sat on her porch looking out at the field of soybeans. The fact that Natalie perceived the soybean plants as being grouped into a series of separate rows is consistent with the Gestalt principle of a. closure b. simplicity c. proximity d. similarity
Concept/Applied LO 12 Page: 146 **b**	96.	Blake was at a football game, and even though people wearing green jackets were spread fairly evenly throughout the stands, he still perceived all the people in green jackets as a single group of visiting fans. Blake's perception is most consistent with the Gestalt principle of a. proximity b. similarity c. closure d. simplicity

Concept/Applied LO 12 Page: 146 a	97.	Christina was skiing down an intermediate run when the run broke into two separate trails. One trail turned off at a 90-degree angle; the second trail appeared to continue in the same general direction she had been headed. If Christina takes the second trail her actions would be consistent with the Gestalt principle of a. continuity b. closure c. proximity d. common region
Concept/Applied LO 12 Page: 146 c	98.	We often perceive a series of dots on a printed form as a "solid" line because of the Gestalt principle of a. constancy b. similarity c. closure d. symmetry
Concept/Applied LO 12 Page: 146 b	99.	When Justin looked up at the night sky he perceived the three stars that make up the belt in the constellation, Orion, as a single complete figure, rather than as individual stars. Justin's perception of the night sky illustrates the Gestalt principle of a. proximity b. closure c. similarity d. figure-ground
Factual LO 13 Page: 147 Correct = 57% a	100.	If you are looking at an object such as a book, the object itself can be referred to as a. a distal stimulus b. a proximal stimulus c. an approximate stimulus d. a distilled stimulus
Concept/Applied LO 13 Page: 147 Correct = 88% b	101.	You may interpret the trapezoid shape projected on your retina as a rectangular book, in which case you are formulating a a. Gestalt principle b. perceptual hypothesis c. psychophysical law d. phenomenological principle
Factual LO 14 Page: 149 Correct = 87% a	102.	Our ability to see three dimensions based on having only a two-dimensional retina is known as a. depth perception b. sensory accommodation c. visual acuity d. rod-cone refractance
Concept/Applied LO 14 Page: 149 c	103.	Amanda had an operation on her eyes, but the doctors were unable to save the vision in her left eye. One major change that will affect Amanda's perception is the fact that she will a. no longer have any perception of depth b. be more likely to misinterpret perceptual illusions c. no longer be able to utilize binocular depth cues d. lose her ability to perceive colors accurately

Concept/Applied LO 14 Page: 149 **a**	104.	As the large butterfly flew toward Richard, he could tell it was getting closer because he could feel his eyes turning inward toward his nose as he watched it. In this instance, Richard was able to judge how far away the butterfly was using the depth cue of a. convergence b. binocular disparity c. accommodation d. relative size
Factual LO 14 Page: 149 Correct = 93% **b**	105.	In order to keep focusing on an object as it moves closer to your face, you must a. rotate your eyes outward b. rotate your eyes inward c. look straight ahead d. focus at a point some distance beyond the approaching object
Concept/Applied LO 14 Page: 149 **d**	106.	As Briana drove down the highway the pickets of the fences moved past her in a blur, but the mountains in the distance didn't appear to move at all. Briana was experiencing a. the pictorial cue for depth called texture gradient b. the binocular cue for depth called convergence c. the binocular cue for depth called retinal disparity d. the monocular cue for depth called motion parallax
Factual LO 14 Page: 149 Correct = 78% **d**	107.	Images that occupy more space on your retina are seen as nearer relative to images that occupy less space. This is a cue to depth perception known as a. accommodation b. foveal disparity c. phrenetic search d. relative size
Factual LO 14 Page: 149 **c**	108.	Interposition refers to a. the relationship between bipolar and ganglion cells b. the processing of auditory information at the cochlear level c. an environmental depth cue in which closer objects overlap objects farther away d. the lens's ability to change shape and focus light directly on the retina
Concept/Applied LO 14 Page: 149 **c**	109.	Timothy was painting a picture of a jet on a runway; however in his painting the sides of the runway are parallel to each other. Timothy's picture will seem to lack depth because he has failed to make use of the monocular depth cue of a. convergence b. motion parallax c. linear perspective d. height in plane
Concept/Applied LO 14 Page: 149 **b**	110.	Gabriella was looking for shelter from the sudden cloud burst, and at first she had difficulty judging whether the old barn or the farmhouse was closer. However, when she noticed that the barn partially obscured the corner of the house she headed for the barn. She was able to judge which building was closer based on a. texture gradient b. interposition c. relative size d. linear perspective

Concept/Applied LO 14 Page: 149 **d**	111.	The sand at Jason feet appeared coarse, and he could see the individual grains of sand. However, the sand down the beach appeared to be much finer and less granular. This apparent difference in the sand may have partially resulted from the depth cue of a. interposition b. light and shadow c. relative size d. texture gradient
Concept/Applied LO 14 Page: 149 **a**	112.	Sydney had an operation on his right eye and has to wear an eye patch for three weeks. While he is wearing the eye patch, Sydney will lose his ability to a. utilize binocular depth cues b. perceive colors accurate c. utilize any depth cues d. perceive motion parallax
Concept/Applied LO 14 Page: 149 **b**	113.	Ashley is trying to create a small Christmas village on the mantle of her fireplace. She bought 3-inch high figures to put at the front of the mantle and smaller figures to put near the back. Ashley is trying to increase the impression of depth in her Christmas village through the use of a. light and shadow b. relative size c. convergence d. texture gradient
Concept/Applied LO 14 Page: 149 **d**	114.	Based on the evidence obtained in numerous cross-cultural investigations of depth perception, it seems reasonable to conclude that a. depth perception, whether in pictures or real space, is innate and invariant across cultures b. the basic processes in depth perception, whether in pictures or real space, are learned and are quite variable across cultures c. perception of depth using monocular cues is innate, but perception of depth using binocular cues must be learned d. the application of pictorial depth cues to pictures is partly an acquired skill, but the basic processes of depth perception in real space appear to be much the same across cultures
Factual LO 15 Page: 152 Correct = 28% **d**	115.	In the Featured Study on perceiving geographical slant, Proffitt and his colleagues (1995) found a. participants tended to overestimate the slant of 20-degree or steeper hills, while underestimating the slant of hills less than 20-degrees b. participants tended to underestimate the slant of 20-degree or steeper hills, while overestimating the slant of hills less than 20-degrees c. verbal and visual estimates of steepness were accurate but haptic estimates tended to overestimate steepness d. haptic estimates of steepness were accurate but verbal and visual estimates tended to overestimate steepness
Factual LO 15 Page: 152 Correct = 67% **c**	116.	In the Featured Study on perceiving geographical slant, Proffitt and his colleagues (1995) found that participants tended to overestimate a. steepness when standing at the bottom of hills but not when standing at the top of hills b. steepness when standing at the top of hills but not when standing at the bottom of hills c. steepness whether standing at the bottom or at the top of hills d. the steepness of inclines in the lab but not the steepness of actual hills

Factual LO 15 Page: 152 **b**	117.	In the Featured Study on perceiving geographical slant, Proffitt and his colleagues (1995) found that participants tended to overestimate a. steepness when standing at the bottom of hills and underestimate steepness when standing at the top of hills b. the steepness of hills to a greater degree when standing at the top than when standing at the bottom c. steepness when standing at the top of hills and underestimate steepness when standing at the bottom of hills d. the steepness of hills to a greater degree when standing at the bottom than when standing at the top
Factual LO 15 Page: 152 Correct = 87% **a**	118.	In the Featured Study on perceiving geographical slant, Proffitt and his colleagues (1995) found that participants tended to a. overestimate the steepness of hills to a greater degree when they were physically tired b. underestimate the steepness of hills to a greater degree when they were physically tired c. make accurate estimates of steepness when they were physically tired and overestimate steepness when they were rested d. make accurate estimates of steepness when they were physically tired and underestimate steepness when they were rested
Concept/Applied LO 15 Page: 153 **c**	119.	Ernest has just finished a 5-mile run. He is asked to estimate the geographical slant of a hill near his home while he is still exhausted from his workout. Based on research by Proffitt and his colleagues, Ernest is likely to a. underestimate the slant to a greater degree than he would have before his run b. give the same estimate of slant as he would have before his run c. overestimate the slant to a greater degree than he would have before his run d. underestimate the slant, instead of overestimating it as he would have before his run
Concept/Applied LO 15 Page: 153 **d**	120.	Carmella is at a water park. She watches several sliders ride the "Max" and decides to try it for herself. Based on the work by Proffitt and his colleagues you might predict that when she gets to the top, Carmella will a. ride the slide because it will appear less steep from the top than it did from the bottom b. ride the slide because it will appear shorter from the top than it did from the bottom c. have second thoughts because the slide will appear longer from the top than it did from the bottom d. have second thoughts because the slide will appear steeper from the top than it did from the bottom
Concept/Applied LO 16 Page: 153 Correct = 35% **d**	121.	The phenomenon of size constancy implies that a. the perception of size is not related to the perception of distance b. the farther away an object is, the more we underestimate its true size c. two objects will be perceived as the same size whenever they produce the same size retinal image d. two objects may be perceived as being the same size even though they produce different size retinal images
Factual LO 16 Page: 153 Correct = 83% **b**	122.	Perceptual constancy refers to a. the same thing as functional fixedness b. our perception of objects remaining stable despite the fact that sensory information changes c. the existence of schemas that guide our perceptions d. visual fields in the retina that allow our perception of the world to remain stable

Concept/Applied LO 16 Page: 153 **c**	123.	Three-year-old Kevin was flying in a plane for the first time. As the plane descended for its landing Kevin became very excited at all the toy houses and cars he saw, and he couldn't wait for the plane to land so he could play with the toys. Kevin's misinterpretation of the true size of the houses and cars the plane passed over shows that he is still not fully utilizing a. binocular depth cues b. linear perspective c. size constancy d. visual accommodation
Concept/Applied LO 16 Page: 153 Correct = 54% **c**	124.	The fact that the corner of a building thrust toward the viewer looks shorter than an inside corner thrust away from the viewer can be accounted for by the a. horizontal-vertical illusion b. Ponzo illusion c. Müller-Lyer illusion d. illusion of relative size
Concept/Applied LO 16 Page: 154 Correct = 38% **a**	125.	The Ames room, in which people are seen to get small or enlarge as they move about, demonstrates that our perception of the world depends strongly on a. the assumptions we make about it b. the actual, distal stimuli c. the proximal stimulus elements d. bottom-up processing
Factual LO 16 Page: 155 Correct = 81% **b**	126.	The moon illusion occurs when a. you perceive the moon to be smaller on the horizon than overhead b. you perceive the moon to be larger on the horizon than overhead c. you perceive the moon to be the same size when viewed on the horizon and overhead d. you think you see the moon when in fact it is not there
Concept/Applied LO 16 Page: 156 Correct = 92% **a**	127.	Optical illusions tend to be a. influenced by our experiences b. more pronounced in children c. less pronounced in adults d. genetically determined
Factual LO 17 Page: 157 Correct = 72% **b**	128.	The perception associated with the amplitude of a sound wave is a. timbre b. loudness c. tonal quality d. richness
Factual LO 17 Page: 157 Correct = 75% **d**	129.	The perception of timbre corresponds to a sound wave's a. pitch b. panache c. amplitude d. purity
Concept/Applied LO 17 Page: 157 **a**	130.	Compared to the low notes on a piano, the high notes always produce sound waves that have a. a higher frequency b. a lower amplitude c. a higher amplitude d. a lower frequency

Concept/Applied LO 17 Page: 157 **d**	131.	When a clarinet plays a high C followed by a low C, these two notes are perceived differently because they differ in a. amplitude b. purity c. complexity d. frequency
Critical Thinking LO 17 Page: 157 **c**	132.	If the human ear could not detect differences in the amplitude of sound waves, people would not be able to detect differences in the a. pitch of sounds b. timbre of sounds c. loudness of sounds d. saturation of sounds
Factual LO 17 Page: 157 Correct = 88% **b**	133.	The amplitude of sound waves is measured in _____; the frequency of sound waves is measured in _____. a. hertz; wavelengths b. decibels; hertz c. centimeters; nanometers d. wavelengths; hertz
Factual LO 17 Page: 158 Correct = 88% **c**	134.	Humans can hear sounds that range from a. 5 to 50 Hz b. 10 to 100 Hz c. 20 to 20,000 Hz d. 10,000 to 100,000 Hz
Factual LO 18 Page: 159 Correct = 94% **a**	135.	The structure of the ear that conducts sound waves to the middle ear is the a. auditory canal b. auditory conduction tube c. auditory tract d. auditory lineal
Factual LO 18 Page: 159 Correct = 83% **a**	136.	The structure of the ear that transduces sound vibrations into nerve impulses is the a. cochlea b. oval window c. temporal lobe d. stirrup
Concept/Applied LO 18 Page: 160 **b**	137.	Jefferson has had years of exposure to high amplitude sound through his work as a helicopter mechanic. Lately he has noticed that he is losing his ability to detect high frequency sounds. Jefferson has most likely damaged: a. his eardrum b. his cochlea c. his auditory canal d. the tiny bones of his middle ear
Concept/Applied LO 18 Page: 160 Correct = 69% **d**	138.	The retina is to the eye as the a. eardrum is to the ear b. ossicles are to the ear c. pinna is to the ear d. cochlea is to the ear

CHAPTER FOUR

| Factual
LO 18
Page: 160
Correct = 57%
c | 139. | The actual, direct receptors for hearing are the
a. ossicles
b. cochleas
c. hair cells
d. basilar cells |

| Concept/Applied
LO 19
Page: 160
Correct = 65%
b | 140. | According to place theory, the ability to hear pitch corresponds to
a. specific hair cells being stimulated along the length of the semicircular canals
b. vibrations occurring at specific locations down the length of the basilar membrane
c. the entire cochlea vibrating at a speed equivalent to the wavelengths the ear is being stimulated with
d. differential movement of specific ossicles |

| Critical Thinking
LO 19
Page: 160
a | 141. | Imagine the basilar membrane in the human ear were longer. Based on place theory, you might expect that humans would be able to
a. hear a wider range of sounds, especially high frequency sounds
b. hear a wider range of sounds, especially low frequency sounds
c. detect sound waves that had a lower amplitude
d. localize sounds more accurately |

| Concept/Applied
LO 19
Page: 160
Correct = 59%
c | 142. | The theory of hearing that views the basilar membrane as being like a drumhead is
a. place theory
b. timpani theory
c. frequency theory
d. opponent process theory |

| Concept/Applied
LO 19
Page: 161
d | 143. | The maximum firing rate for individual neurons is 1000 neural impulses per second. This biological limitation would make it difficult for
a. place theory to fully explain pitch perception
b. opponent-process theory to fully explain color perception
c. trichromatic theory to fully explain color perception
d. frequency theory to fully explain pitch perception |

| Critical Thinking
LO 19
Page: 161
c | 144. | Imagine that human neurons reach a maximum firing rate of 5000 impulses per second, rather than only 1000 impulses per second. Using the volley principle, this would mean that
a. place theory could explain the full range of human pitch perception
b. neither frequency theory nor place theory could fully explain human pitch perception
c. frequency theory could explain the full range of human pitch perception
d. both place theory and frequency theory would be necessary to fully explain human pitch perception |

| Concept/Applied
LO 19
Page: 161
Correct = 71%
b | 145. | The frequency theory of pitch perception is flawed because
a. structurally, it is impossible for the basilar membrane to vibrate
b. neurons cannot fire fast enough to account for hearing tones higher than 1,000 cycles/second
c. it places the transduction process in the semicircular canals and not the cochlea
d. the action of the ossicles interacting with the auditory nerve was misidentified |

Concept/Applied LO 19 Page: 161 Correct = 53% **d**	146.	The volley principle suggests that a. spreading effects from one semicircular canal to another interact to produce pitch perception for frequencies higher than 5,000 Hz b. ossicles of the middle ear "echo" or "volley" auditory transmission back and forth to stimulate hair cells c. sound localization is an interpretation of time discrepancies between the time when the same sound reaches each ear d. groups of auditory neurons are able fire neural impulses in rapid succession, sending signals that exceed the firing rate of any single neuron
Factual LO 19 Page: 161 Correct = 74% **d**	147.	Pitch perception can best be explained by _____ for very low-pitched sounds, _____ for very high-pitched sounds, and _____ for pitches in the middle range. a. place theory; frequency theory; place theory b. frequency theory; both theories; place theory c. place theory; both theories; frequency theory d. frequency theory; place theory; both theories
Concept/Applied LO 20 Page: 161 **a**	148.	Clifford was in an accident and he has lost all the hearing in his right ear. The deafness in this ear will mostly affect Clifford's ability to a. localize sounds accurately b. separate speech sounds from background noise c. detect high frequency sounds d. detect high amplitude sounds
Concept/Applied LO 20 Page: 161 **a**	149.	Juan and Karletta were walking one night when they heard a car backfire. Juan was convinced the sound came from directly in front of them, and Karletta was convinced the sound came from directly behind them. One reason they might have difficulty localizing the sound is a. the sound waves would have arrived at both ears at the same instant b. we are able to judge distance better than direction for sounds c. sound localization is more difficult in the dark d. only speech sounds can be accurately localized
Concept/Applied LO 20 Page: 161 Correct = 99% **a**	150.	Dan was able to tell that the voice he heard calling his name was coming from the building on his left because of a. auditory localization b. depth perception c. perceptual constancy d. perceptual set
Concept/Applied LO 20 Page: 161 Correct = 89% **d**	151.	Auditory localization is to hearing as a. size constancy is to vision b. optical illusion is to vision c. retinal disparity is to vision d. depth perception is to vision
Factual LO 20 Page: 161 Correct = 67% **b**	152.	The two major cues we use to localize sound sources in space are a. distance and loudness b. intensity and timing differences at the ears c. pitch and loudness differences at the ears d. loudness and timbre differences at the ears

Concept/Applied LO 20 Page: 161 Correct = 78% **d**	153.	You would predict from a knowledge of distance cues that accuracy of localizing sounds would be poorest for a source a. 90 degrees to the right b. 90 degrees to the left c. 45 degrees to the front left d. directly in front of the person
Factual LO 20 Page: 161 Correct = 29% **c**	154.	People can detect timing differences between each ear as small as a. 1/10 of a second b. 1/1,000 of a second c. 1/100,000 of a second d. 1/1,000,000 of a second
Concept/Applied LO 20 Page: 161 Correct = 36% **a**	155.	If you are sitting in a room facing exactly north and a sound emanates exactly from the south, you will perceive the sound as coming from a. either the north or the south b. either the east or the west c. directly over your head d. all directions at the same time
Factual LO 20 Page: 161 Correct = 85% **d**	156.	The loudness difference between the two ears is greatest when the sound source is a. directly behind the listener's head b. directly in front of the listener c. a long distance away d. well off to one side
Factual LO 21 Page: 162 Correct = 89% **a**	157.	The sense associated with the perception of taste is referred to as the a. gustatory system b. olfactory system c. vagus system d. vestibular system
Concept/Applied LO 21 Page: 162 Correct = 73% **b**	158.	Which statement about the gustatory system is <u>false</u>? a. Taste cells are concentrated in taste buds on the tongue. b. The physical stimulus for taste is any molecular substance. c. Taste cells live only about ten days. d. Taste cells are not distributed evenly across the surface of the tongue.
Factual LO 21 Page: 162 Correct = 99% **a**	159.	Generally, the four basic tastes are considered to be a. salty, sweet, sour, and bitter b. salty, spicy, bland, and sour c. sour, bitter, bland, and hot d. sweet, sour, spicy, and smooth
Concept/Applied LO 21 Page: 162 Correct = 87% **c**	160.	The rods and cones are to vision as the taste buds are to a. olfaction b. kinesthesis c. gustation d. flavation
Factual LO 21 Page: 162 Correct = 86% **d**	161.	Newborn infants react _____ to sweet tastes and _____ to strong sour tastes. a. neutrally; negatively b. positively; neutrally c. positively; positively d. positively; negatively

Factual LO 21 Page: 163 c	162.	Compared to nontasters, people characterized as supertasters have a. about 10 times as many taste buds per square centimeter b. three or four additional types of taste buds c. about 4 times as many taste buds per square centimeter d. taste buds in more locations within their mouth and throat
Factual LO 21 Page: 163 d	163.	One key gender difference that has been found with respect to tasting is that a. men are more likely than women to be supertasters b. women tend to react more to sweet tastes while men react more to bitter tastes c. men tend to react more to sweet tastes while women react more to bitter tastes d. women are more likely than men to be supertasters
Concept/Applied LO 21 Page: 163 b	164.	Eloise is an individual who is classified as a supertaster. She is likely to be especially sensitive to a. sweet and salty tastes b. sweet and bitter tastes c. salty and sour tastes d. sour and bitter tastes
Concept/Applied LO 21 Page: 164 Correct = 92% d	165.	Food generally tastes bland when you have a severe head cold because a. you cold will cause the sweet receptors in your mouth to become inactivated b. your high temperature will cause your brain to block signals from the taste buds in the mouth c. because your naturally produced antibodies interfere with chemical molecules stimulated by your taste buds d. flavor is influenced by smell as well as taste, and with a reduced sense of smell your sense of taste will be diminished
Concept/Applied LO 21 Page: 164 c	166.	Mike broke his nose in a recent boxing match. The doctors packed his nose and told him he will need to breathe through his mouth for the next 10 to 14 days. Mike is likely to find that while his nose is packed, a. food will taste better because his sense of taste will be temporarily enhanced to compensate for his missing sense of smell b. he will have problems with his equilibrium and balance c. food will have little taste because much of a food's flavor depends on our sense of smell d. he will have trouble detecting motion because the main pathway to his superior colliculus will be blocked
Factual LO 22 Page: 164 Correct = 96% b	167.	The sense associated with the perception of smell is a. gustation b. olfaction c. kinesthesis d. audition
Factual LO 22 Page: 164 Correct = 73% d	168.	Of the following, the only sensory system that does not project upward to the cerebral cortex through the thalamus, is a. vision b. hearing c. gustation d. olfaction
Factual LO 22 Page: 164 Correct = 90% c	169.	The sensory receptors for smell are referred to as a. smell buds b. gustatory bulbs c. olfactory cilia d. psiatic receptors

Factual LO 22 Page: 164 Correct = 84% **a**	170.	Our sense of smell shows evidence of sensory adaptation. The perceived strength of an odor usually a. fades to less than half its original strength within about four minutes b. increases to more than twice its original strength within about four minutes c. fades to less than half its original strength within a few seconds d. slowly increases over time, reaching a maximum in about 15 minutes
Concept/Applied LO 22 Page: 164 Correct = 74% **b**	171.	Which of the following is a <u>true</u> statement regarding the olfactory capacity of humans? a. With specialized training, we could track a timber wolf through a mountain range. b. Although there are some species whose sense of smell is superior, human olfaction compares favorably with that of many animals. c. Since our capacity is so limited, we can only detect fairly powerful odors. d. Although we are especially sensitive to food odors, we are not particularly sensitive to other odors.
Factual LO 23 Page: 165 **c**	172.	Stimulation of sensory receptors of the skin is processed by the a. septal cortex, which is located in the cerebellum b. limbic system, which is located in the hypothalamus c. somatosensory cortex, which is located in the parietal lobes d. medial forebrain bundle, which is located in the temporal lobes
Factual LO 23 Page: 165 Correct = 87% **b**	173.	Cells in the nervous system that report touch show all of the following except a. localization for areas of the skin b. unlimited life span c. center-surround receptive fields d. sensory adaptation
Factual LO 23 Page: 165 Correct = 65% **c**	174.	Temperature receptors in the skin are a. pacinian corpuscles b. hair follicles c. free nerve endings d. Krause end-bulbs
Factual LO 23 Page: 165 Correct = 53% **d**	175.	If heat is applied to the skin, the skin's "warm" receptors _____, and the skin's "cold" receptors _____. a. begin to fire; fire more slowly b. fire more rapidly; begin to fire c. begin to fire; continue not to fire d. fire more rapidly; cease their spontaneous firing
Concept/Applied LO 23 Page: 165 Correct = 84% **b**	176.	You place your left hand in a pan of cool water and your right hand in a pan of warm water, for a minute. If you then place both your hands in a pan of lukewarm water, the lukewarm water will feel a. lukewarm to both hands b. warm to your left hand but cool to your right hand c. cool to your left hand but warm to your right hand d. cool to both hands
Concept/Applied LO 24 Page: 165 Correct = 96% **a**	177.	Information that an injury has just occurred is carried to the brain via the _____ pain pathway; information that the injury has not yet healed is carried to the brain via the _____ pain pathway. a. fast; slow b. fast; fast c. slow; fast d. slow; slow

Factual LO 24 Page: 165 Correct = 64% **c**	178.	The pathway for pain that results in the experience of pain being less localized and longer lasting is the a. thalamic pathway b. endorphin pathway c. slow pathway d. generic pathway
Factual LO 24 Page: 166 Correct = 51% **d**	179.	Which of the following has <u>not</u> been shown to influence the perception of pain in humans? a. mood b. personality c. expectations d. age
Factual LO 24 Page: 166 **b**	180.	Neural transmission in the slow pain pathway depends on a. thicker, myelinated neurons called A-fibers b. thin, unmyelinated neurons called C-fibers c. pulsating neural impulses called pain spindles d. opponent process receptors in the area surrounding the injury
Concept/Applied LO 24 Page: 166 **b**	181.	Catelin has had a slow throbbing pain in her ankle since she twisted it roller blading last week. These pain signals are traveling along a. ungated endorphin pathways in the hypothalamus b. thin, unmyelinated C fibers c. thick, myelinated A-delta fibers d. periaqueductal gray neurons in the midbrain
Concept/Applied LO 24 Page: 166 **d**	182.	Derek dropped a hammer on his foot and shrieked a split second later at the intense pain from a newly broken toe. The almost instantaneous pain signals traveled along a. thin, unmyelinated C fibers b. gated endorphin pathways in the hypothalamus c. periaqueductal gray neurons in the midbrain d. thick, myelinated A-delta fibers
Concept/Applied LO 25 Page: 166 **a**	183.	A theory that can account for the fact that people suffering from pain sometimes report pain relief from a sugar pill placebo is a. gate-control theory b. sensory adaptation theory c. perceptual constancy theory d. cognitive control theory
Concept/Applied LO 25 Page: 166 Correct = 84% **d**	184.	One's ability to overcome tremendous amounts of pain in certain situations (such as an athlete who plays with a broken foot and does not feel the pain until later) can be explained by a. sympathetic nervous system control mechanisms b. the hypnotic induction control theory of pain c. an overactive thyroid response (hormone release) d. the gate-control theory of pain
Factual LO 25 Page: 167 Correct = 42% **b**	185.	The pathway that researchers believe mediates the perception of pain originates in a. the septal nucleus b. the periacqueductal gray c. the medulla d. the medial forebrain bundle

Concept/Applied LO 25 Page: 167 Correct = 21% **c**	186.	Cutting fibers in the neural pathway leading away from the periacqueductal gray in the midbrain a. reduces the perception of pain b. enhances the effects of morphine and other opiate drugs c. increases the perception of pain d. causes the release of endorphins
Factual LO 26 Page: 167 Correct = 86% **b**	187.	The brain receives information about the positions of the various parts of the body through the a. vestibular sense b. kinesthetic sense c. kinetic sense d. homeostatic sense
Factual LO 26 Page: 167 Correct = 68% **a**	188.	The kinesthetic system relates to a. maintaining the relative position of body parts b. the location of the body in space c. the sense of forward acceleration d. sensing body movement, as in a car
Factual LO 26 Page: 167 Correct = 61% **d**	189.	Receptors for the kinesthetic sense are found in the a. cochlea b. semicircular canals c. basilar membrane d. joints and muscles
Concept/Applied LO 26 Page: 167 **d**	190.	A police officer asked Stanley to close his eyes and touch the tip of his nose using first his right index finger and then his left index finger. To complete this test of coordination Stanley would need to rely on a. his vestibular sense b. his reticular sense c. sensory accommodation d. his kinesthetic sense
Factual LO 26 Page: 167 Correct = 73% **c**	191.	The vestibular sense reports information from a set of receptors in a. the joints b. the muscles c. the inner ear d. the skin
Factual LO 26 Page: 167 Correct = 51% **c**	192.	Which of the following parts of the ear has a role in maintaining balance? a. the cochlea b. the basilar membrane c. the semicircular canals d. the ossicles
Concept/Applied LO 26 Page: 167 **a**	193.	Loreen has a bad case of vertigo. She feels like the room is spinning, and she has trouble keeping her balance. It is possible that this sense of disequilibrium is a result of excess activity in neurons originating in the a. semicircular canals b. periaqueductal gray c. olfactory bulb d. parvocellular system

Concept/Applied LO 26 Page: 167 **b**	194.	You have a severe ear infection. One potential side effect would be a. blurred vision b. loss of balance c. loss of ability to taste the "flavor" of food d. an enhanced sense of smell
Concept/Applied LO 27 Page: 168 Correct = 77% **d**	195.	Our construction of perceptual hypotheses illustrates which of your text's unifying themes? a. Psychology is empirical. b. Psychology evolves in a sociohistorical context. c. Behavior is determined by multiple causes. d. Our experience of the world is highly subjective.
Concept/Applied LO 27 Page: 168 **c**	196.	The fact that many Americans might be reluctant to try the Japanese delicacy of raw fish illustrates which of your text's unifying themes? a. Psychology is empirical. b. Psychology evolves in a sociohistorical context. c. Behavior is shaped by our cultural heritage. d. Our experience of the world is highly subjective.
Factual LO 28 Page: 169 Correct = 56% **d**	197.	In order to create the illusion of three-dimensional reality, a painter must use a. bivariate depth cues b. binocular depth cues c. myopic depth cues d. pictorial depth cues
Factual LO 28 Page: 169 Correct = 48% **c**	198.	The _____ were more concerned with interpreting a viewer's fleeting perception of reality than with recreating the photographic "reality" of a scene. a. Medievalists b. Realists c. French Impressionists d. Cubists
Factual LO 28 Page: 169 Correct = 46% **c**	199.	The Impressionist technique of pointillism relies on the use of a. subtractive color mixing b. feature analysis c. additive color mixing d. binocular disparity as a cue for depth
Factual LO 28 Page: 170 Correct = 78% **a**	200.	The school of painting that reduces reality to combinations of geometric forms laid out in a flat space is a. cubism b. surrealism c. impressionism d. pointillism
Concept/Applied LO 28 Page: 171 Correct = 70% **a**	201.	The organizational principles that are evident in the paintings of Cubists are a. Gestalt principles b. functional principles c. zeitgeist principles d. psychoanalytic principles
Factual LO 28 Page: 171 Correct = 93% **b**	202.	By exploring the world of dreams and fantasy, Surrealists reflected the influence of a. Abraham Maslow b. Sigmund Freud c. Gustav Fechner d. B. F. Skinner

CHAPTER FOUR

Concept/Applied LO 29 Page: 172 Correct = 46% **d**	203.	M. C. Escher's paintings are viewed as examples of a. pointillism b. Cubism c. structuralistic functionalism d. perceptual ambiguity
Factual LO 30 Page: 174 **a**	204.	The door-in-the-face technique involves a. making a very large request that is likely to be turned down to increase the chances that people will agree to a smaller request later b. making a very small request that is likely to be accepted to increase the chances that people will agree to a larger request later c. concealing some of the costs associated with a request until after the request has been accepted d. adding incentives to a request that has been turned down until people finally agree to go along with the initial request
Factual LO 30 Page: 175 **b**	205.	It is fairly easy to manipulate many types of judgments by selecting a. average comparitors that are typical b. extreme comparitors that may be unrepresentative c. comparitors that both better and worse than the event that is being judged d. as many comparitors as possible that are similar to event being judged
Concept/Applied LO 30 Page: 175 **c**	206.	Last year Fiona had a yard sale. She marked the prices of items very reasonably, and she refused to reduce them when people tried to "deal." This year she had another yard sale, but this time she marked the prices of items quite high, and then reduced them by 50% or more when people asked to "deal." Fiona was surprised to find that she made much more money this year. When she asks you why this might have happened you explain how judgments can be affected by a. absolute thresholds b. sensory adaptation c. contrast effects d. subliminal comparitors
Concept/Applied LO 30 Page: 175 **d**	207.	Roberta and Phil have been arrested for vandalism. Their defense attorney may be able to get a lighter sentence for her clients if she emphasizes that a. this is the first offense for both her clients b. both her clients are good students who always score at the top of their class c. her clients are both active in a number of extra-curricular activities at their school d. the other students involved in the incident did much more damage than her clients did
Integrative **c**	208.	The visual cortex is to the auditory cortex as the occipital lobe is to the a. occipital lobe b. frontal lobe c. temporal lobe d. parietal lobe
Integrative Correct = 83% **b**	209.	The retina is to the basilar membrane as depth perception is to a. auditory adaptation b. auditory localization c. auditory afterimages d. auditory feature detection

Integrative **c**	210.	Hue is to pitch as brightness is to a. timbre b. purity c. loudness d. retinal disparity
Study Guide LO 3 Page: 129 **d**	211.	Which of the following places a major emphasis on subjective factors in the perception of thresholds? a. Weber's law b. Fechner's law c. Steven's power factor d. signal detection theory
Study Guide LO 5 Page: 130 **b**	212.	The fact that we are generally much more aware of the changes in our sensory environments than we are of the constants is the general idea behind a. signal detection theory b. sensory adaptation c. the method of constant stimuli d. sensory equalization
Study Guide LO 6 Page: 131 **c**	213.	The major difference between a green light and a blue light is the a. wave frequency b. wave purity c. wavelength d. wave saturation
Study Guide LO 9 Page: 136 **d**	214.	The receiving area of a retinal cell is called the a. cone b. foveal field c. rod d. receptive field
Study Guide LO 10 Page: 142 **b**	215.	Which theory of color vision best explains why the color of an afterimage is the complement of the original color? a. the trichromatic theory b. the opponent process theory c. both theories explain this phenomenon equally well d. neither theory adequately explains this phenomenon
Study Guide LO 12 Page: 145 **d**	216.	When watching a wild car chase scene in a movie, we can be thankful for a. chunking b. lateral processing c. bottom-up processing d. the phi phenomenon
Study Guide LO 14 Page: 149 **a**	217.	Which of the following is not one of the pictorial depth cues? a. convergence b. linear perspective c. relative height d. texture gradients
Study Guide LO 21 Page: 162 **c**	218.	Which of the following is not considered to be one of the four fundamental tastes? a. sour b. sweet c. burnt d. bitter

CHAPTER FOUR

Study Guide LO 25 Page: 166 **a**	219.	Gate-control theory is an attempt to explain a. why the perception of pain is so subjective b. how subliminal perception works c. how receptive fields influence one another d. how the optic chiasm directs visual information
Study Guide LO 27 Page: 168 **c**	220.	Which of the following terms perhaps best describes human perception? a. accurate b. objective c. subjective d. unknowable
Online Quiz LO 1 Page: 126 **d**	221.	_____ refers to physical stimulation, while _____ refers to the interpretation of that physical stimulation. a. Internal; external b. Afferent; efferent c. Efferent; perception d. Sensation; perception
Online Quiz LO 6 Page: 131 **b**	222.	The purity of a wavelength of light corresponds to the perception of a. hue b. saturation c. brightness d. color constancies
Online Quiz LO 8 Page: 134 **c**	223.	Light is converted into neural energy that travels to the brain to produce visual experience by the a. pupil b. lens c. retina d. optic disk
Online Quiz LO 8 Page: 135 **a**	224.	Night and peripheral vision depend mainly on _____, while daylight and acute vision depend mainly on _____. a. rod cells; cone cells b. cone cells; rod cells c. rod cells; bipolar cells d. bipolar cells; cone cells
Online Quiz LO 12 Page: 146 **d**	225.	The Gestalt principle of _____ implies that people organize visual perception in the _____. a. continuity; most complex manner possible b. proximity; top-down processing manner c. closure; bottom-up processing manner d. *Pragnanz*; simplest manner possible
Online Quiz LO 13 Page: 147 **a**	226.	If you look at a sheet of notebook paper set on a table, the distal stimulus is the _____, and the proximal stimulus is the _____. a. sheet of paper; projection on the retina b. projection on the retina; sheet of paper c. square shape; square shape d. trapezoidal shape; square shape

Online Quiz LO 19 Page: 160 **a**	227.	Which of the following describes how we hear according to place theory? a. Different sound frequencies vibrate different portions of the basilar membrane, producing different pitches. b. Our perception of pitch corresponds to the rate or frequency at which the entire basilar membrane vibrates. c. We perceive differences in pitch according to the number of hair cells that vibrate at any one time. d. Different sound frequencies affect the intensity with which the membrane separating the middle ear from the inner ear vibrates, producing different pitches.
Online Quiz LO 21 Page: 162 **b**	228.	Which of the following is <u>not</u> one of the four basic tastes? a. salty b. citrus c. sweet d. bitter
Online Quiz LO 26 Page: 167 **a**	229.	Which of the following can cause disruption of your vestibular system? a. riding on an amusement park thrill ride that spins you around b. having an upset stomach c. having a cold that temporarily robs you of your sense of taste d. temporarily losing sensation in your arm because you slept on it
Online Quiz LO 29 Page: 172 **b**	230.	Victor Vasarely pioneered an approach called a. pointillism b. kinetic art c. cubism d. proximal-closure

CHAPTER FOUR

ESSAY QUESTIONS

1. From a distal light source to the brain, sequentially trace a visual stimulus through the eye and nervous system.

   Light passes through the cornea, enters the pupil, is focused by the lens, and projected onto the retina. The retina converts the light rays into nerve impulses, which then travel via the optic nerve to the optic chiasm. At the optic chiasm, the axons from the inside half of each eye cross over and project along two divergent pathways to the opposite cerebral hemisphere.

2. Provide an overview of the trichromatic and opponent process theories of color vision, and resolve the "debate" between the two.

   The trichromatic theory proposes that the eye has three types of receptors, each responsive to one of the three primary colors of light: red, blue, and green. The eye then additively mixes different proportions of these three colors to produce the colors we see.

   The opponent process theory proposes that color is signaled in pairs by receptors that fire faster to one color and slower to a second, complementary color. The three pairs of opponent colors are red-green, blue-yellow, and black-white.

   Both theories are needed to adequately explain color vision. In the earliest stage of information processing, there are three types of cones, each responsive to a different band of wavelengths, consistent with trichromatic theory. In later stages, cells in the retina, the lateral geniculate nucleus, and the visual cortex respond in opposite ways to complementary colors. Thus, color coding begins with a trichromatic process and then switches to an opponent process.

3. Compare vision and hearing with regard to the proximal stimulus and information processing for each sense.

   The proximal stimulus for vision is light waves oscillating over distance. Light waves have three properties: (1) amplitude, affecting the perception of brightness; (2) wavelength, affecting the perception of color; and (3) purity, affecting the perception of saturation.

   Similarly, the proximal stimulus for hearing is sound waves oscillating over time. Sound waves have the same three properties as light waves: (1) amplitude, affecting the perception of loudness; (2) wavelength, affecting the perception of pitch; and (3) purity, affecting the perception of timbre.

   Both the eye and the ear convert physical energy (light and sound waves, respectively) into the neural energy that travels to the brain, producing sensory experience. In the eye, this conversion is done by the rods and cones at the retina; in the ear, this conversion is done by the hair cells, located on the basilar membrane in the inner ear. Visual information is routed to the visual cortex in the occipital lobes; auditory information is routed to the auditory cortex in the temporal lobes.

4. Provide an overview of the place and frequency theories of pitch perception, and resolve the "debate" between the two.

   Place theory proposes that specific sound frequencies vibrate specific portions of the basilar membrane, producing different pitches. Frequency theory, on the other hand, proposes that pitch perception corresponds to the frequency at which the entire basilar membrane vibrates.

   Currently, it is believed that both theories are needed to fully account for pitch perception. It appears that, for low-frequency sounds (under 1000 Hz), pitch perception depends on frequency coding only; for moderate-frequency sounds (1000 Hz to 5000 Hz), pitch perception depends on a combination of place and frequency coding; for high-frequency sounds (over 5000 Hz), pitch perception depends on place coding only.

This page intentionally left blank.

Chapter Five
Variations in Consciousness

LEARNING OBJECTIVES

1. Discuss the nature and evolution of consciousness.
2. Discuss the relationship between consciousness and EEG activity.
3. Summarize what is known about our biological clocks and their relationship to sleep.
4. Summarize the evidence on the value of melatonin for resetting biological clocks.
5. Describe how sleep research is conducted.
6. Describe how the sleep cycle evolves through the night.
7. Compare and contrast REM and NREM sleep.
8. Summarize age trends in patterns of sleep.
9. Summarize how culture influences sleep patterns.
10. Discuss the neural and evolutionary bases of sleep.
11. Summarize evidence on the effects of complete and partial sleep deprivation, including the chapter's Featured Study.
12. Discuss the effects of selective deprivation of REM sleep and slow-wave sleep.
13. Discuss the prevalence, causes, and treatment of insomnia.
14. Describe the symptoms of narcolepsy, sleep apnea, night terrors, nightmares, and somnambulism.
15. Discuss the nature of dreams.
16. Summarize findings on dream content.
17. Describe some cultural variations in beliefs about the nature and importance of dreams.
18. Describe the three theories of dreaming covered in the chapter.
19. Discuss hypnotic susceptibility and list some prominent effects of hypnosis.
20. Explain the role-playing and altered-state theories of hypnosis.
21. Summarize evidence on the short-term and long-term effects of meditation.
22. List and describe the major types of abused drugs and their effects.
23. Explain why drug effects vary and how psychoactive drugs exert their effects in the brain.
24. Summarize which drugs carry the greatest risk of tolerance, physical dependence, and psychological dependence.
25. Summarize evidence on the major physical health risks associated with drug abuse.
26. Discuss how drug abuse is related to psychological health.
27. Explain how the chapter highlighted four of the text's unifying themes.
28. Summarize evidence on common questions about sleep discussed in the Application.
29. Summarize evidence on common questions about dreams discussed in the Application.
30. Discuss the influence of definitions and how they are sometimes misused as explanations for the phenomena they describe.

MULTIPLE-CHOICE QUESTIONS

Concept/Applied
LO 1
Page: 179
b

1. One can learn to control alpha brain-wave patterns through the use of _____ techniques.
   a. reciprocal inhibition
   b. biofeedback
   c. mnemonic
   d. invasive therapy

Factual
LO 1
Page: 180
d

2. Consciousness includes awareness of
   a. external events only
   b. internal sensations only
   c. self only
   d. external events, internal sensations, and self

Concept/Applied
LO 1
Page: 180
c

3. The idea that one's consciousness continually changes, fluctuates, and wanders characterizes William James's concept that consciousness is
   a. an incomplete picture puzzle
   b. a partially submerged iceberg
   c. a stream
   d. a flower garden

Concept/Applied
LO 1
Page: 180
c

4. If you could tape-record your thoughts, you would find
   a. a system of hierarchically organized cognitions
   b. one central thought and multiple, related subsidiary thoughts
   c. an endless flow of ideas that constantly shifts and changes
   d. an organized system of parallel thoughts

Factual
LO 1
Page: 180
d

5. During sleep, there is
   a. no awareness of external stimuli
   b. no awareness of either external or internal stimuli
   c. awareness of all external stimuli
   d. selective awareness of external stimuli

Concept/Applied
LO 1
Page: 181
b

6. Which of the following statements best reflects current thinking regarding the evolutionary roots of consciousness?
   a. Researchers generally agree that there is no plausible evolutionary explanation of consciousness.
   b. The evolutionary bases of consciousness remain elusive.
   c. Unobservable behaviors such as consciousness are not subject to the laws of evolution.
   d. Plenty of empirical evidence exists to support the adaptive quality of consciousness.

Factual
LO 2
Page: 181
b

7. The electroencephalograph is used in sleep research to measure brain-wave activity in the
   a. corpus callosum
   b. cerebral cortex
   c. hypothalamus
   d. medulla

Factual
LO 2
Page: 181
d

8. An electroencephalograph is a device that measures
   a. glucose metabolism in the brain
   b. muscle tension in the body
   c. respiration rates as an index of arousal
   d. electrical activity of the brain

Concept/Applied LO 2 Page: 181 **a**	9.	An EEG would indicate primarily _____ activity in a person who is meditating with eyes closed. a. alpha b. beta c. delta d. theta
Factual LO 2 Page: 181 Correct = 58% **b**	10.	The EEG pattern associated with normal, waking, alert states is a. gamma b. beta c. alpha d. delta
Factual LO 2 Page: 181 Correct = 79% **b**	11.	The delta wave EEG pattern is associated with a. dreaming b. deep sleep c. a waking state d. none of these states
Critical Thinking LO 2 Page: 181 Correct = 88% **a**	12.	Which of the following does not belong with the other three? a. omega b. theta c. alpha d. delta
Critical Thinking LO 2 Page: 181 Correct = 78% **c**	13.	Which of the following instruments is not usually used to monitor sleep in the laboratory? a. EEG b. EMG c. PET d. EOG
Factual LO 3 Page: 182 **b**	14.	A circadian rhythm involves a biological cycle that fluctuates a. every 8 hours b. daily c. monthly d. yearly
Factual LO 3 Page: 182 **a**	15.	According to recent research, we are most likely to fall asleep a. as our body temperature begins to drop b. when it gets dark c. when our body temperature stabilizes at normal d. as our body temperature begins to climb
Critical Thinking LO 3 Page: 182 **d**	16.	Which of the following statements about circadian rhythms in humans is accurate? a. Humans generally show no indication of having circadian rhythms. b. Circadian rhythms are apparently a uniquely human development. c. Circadian rhythms in humans tend to function on a 30-day cycle. d. Circadian rhythms in humans actually appear to be regulated by several internal clocks.
Factual LO 3 Page: 182 Correct = 73% **a**	17.	The hormone _____ appears to play a key role in adjusting our biological clocks. a. melatonin b. cholecystokinin c. serotonin d. phenylalanine

Factual LO 3 Page: 182 Correct = 46% **d**	18.	Signals sent from the suprachiasmatic nucleus to the pineal gland have been implicated in a. inducing sleep b. causing one to dream c. alpha rhythm generation d. resetting circadian rhythms
Concept/Applied LO 3 Page: 182 Correct = 71% **c**	19.	Which of the following appears to be the sequence of events associated with resetting one's biological clock? a. The hypothalamus signals the thalamus, which in turn sends signals to the medial forebrain bundle. b. The thalamus signals the optic chiasm, which in turn causes a release of the hormone philoxin, which activates the renal gland. c. The suprachiasmatic nucleus signals the pineal gland, which in turn secretes the hormone melatonin. d. The superior colliculus signals the thalamus, which stimulates Broca's area.
Concept/Applied LO 3 Page: 182 **d**	20.	Which of the following would require some adjustment of your biological clock? a. springing ahead to daylight savings time b. flying west from Los Angeles to Hawaii c. shifting back to an earlier work shift d. all of these would require some adjustment
Factual LO 3 Page: 183 Correct = 89% **d**	21.	Research has shown that people who work on a rotating shift schedule are _____ to have accidents and be _____ productive than people who do not work on a rotating shift schedule. a. more apt; just as b. less apt; less c. less apt; more d. more apt; less
Factual LO 4 Page: 183 **a**	22.	The evidence from a number of studies indicates that _____ can reduce the effects of jet lag. a. melatonin b. caffeine c. nicotine d. endorphins
Factual LO 4 Page: 184 **d**	23.	In the United States, melatonin is classified as a. a steroid b. a narcotic c. a form of caffeine d. a dietary supplement
Factual LO 4 Page: 184 **d**	24.	The results of scientific research have consistently supported the effectiveness of melatonin in a. enhancing sex b. fighting cancer c. slowing the aging process d. none of these
Factual LO 5 Page: 184 Correct = 37% **a**	25.	The electromyograph records a. muscular activity and tension b. contractions of the heart c. brain wave activity d. eye movements

Concept/Applied LO 5 Page: 184 **a**	26.	Felicia is a participant in a study on stress reactions. Which of the following instruments would <u>most</u> likely be used to measure her muscle tension? a. electromyograph b. circadiometer c. electroencephalograph d. polygraph
Factual LO 6 Page: 185 **a**	27.	Stage 1 sleep is represented by EEG brain-wave patterns referred to as a. alpha waves b. REM waves c. synchronisitic waves d. zeta waves
Factual LO 6 Page: 185 **d**	28.	Slow-wave sleep refers to stages _____ and an EEG rhythm of _____. a. 1 and 2; theta b. 2 and 3; alpha c. 1 and 4; theta d. 3 and 4; delta
Concept/Applied LO 6 Page: 185 **c**	29.	Alexander is hooked up to an electroencephalograph (EEG) in a sleep lab. As the researcher watches the printout from the EEG, theta waves appear. Based on this information, the researcher can conclude that Alexander a. has just entered Stage 3 sleep b. is still awake, but is relaxed and drowsy c. has just entered Stage 1 sleep d. is currently in REM sleep
Factual LO 6 Page: 185 Correct = 29% **b**	30.	Sleep spindles, which appear against a background of mixed, mostly lower frequency EEG activity, are characteristic of a. stage 1 sleep b. stage 2 sleep c. stage 4 sleep d. REM sleep
Factual LO 6 Page: 185 Correct = 67% **d**	31.	The stage of sleep in which the slowest brain waves occur is a. stage 1 b. stage 2 c. REM d. stage 4
Factual LO 7 Page: 185 Correct = 92% **d**	32.	Which of the following is (are) characteristic of REM sleep? a. dreams b. rapid eye movements c. relaxed muscle tone d. all of these
Concept/Applied LO 7 Page: 185 **b**	33.	Olivia has trouble staying asleep for more than 4 hours at a time. Olivia is likely to experience a. more vivid dreams than people who sleep for a full 8 hours b. less REM sleep than people who sleep for a full 8 hours c. less deep sleep than people who sleep for a full 8 hours d. more sleep spindles than people who sleep for a full 8 hours

Factual LO 7 Page: 185 Correct = 90% c	34.	A rapid EEG (beta), dreaming, rapid eye movements, and profound muscle relaxation go with a. stage 1 sleep b. stage 2 sleep c. REM sleep d. relaxed wakefulness
Factual LO 7 Page: 185 Correct = 90% a	35.	Dreaming typically goes with which sleep stage? a. REM b. stage 1 c. stage 2 d. stage 4
Concept/Applied LO 7 Page: 185 b	36.	REM sleep is also known as paradoxical sleep because a. subjects in REM sleep are deeply asleep, but are extremely easy to awaken b. brain activity during REM sleep is similar to that observed in wide-awake subjects c. muscular tension during REM sleep is similar to that observed in wide-awake subjects d. the eyes are open even though the person is sleeping
Factual LO 7 Page: 185 a	37.	Voluntary muscle activity a. is at its lowest during REM sleep b. is at its highest during REM sleep c. does not occur in NREM sleep d. does not occur during either REM or NREM sleep
Critical Thinking LO 7 Page: 185 c	38.	"Manny got out of bed and began doing calisthenics during REM sleep, probably because he was dreaming about boot camp." What is wrong with this statement? a. Sleep is a relaxed condition of the body and, as such, precludes physical activity. b. Research shows that no dreaming takes place in REM sleep. c. Research shows that we are virtually paralyzed in REM sleep. d. Manny was never in boot camp so he is not likely to be dreaming about it.
Factual LO 7 Page: 185 b	39.	Among the physiological changes that occur when you are dreaming is (are) a. transition to alpha waves b. rapid eye movements c. increased voluntary muscle activity d. all of these
Concept/Applied LO 7 Page: 185 c	40.	David is asleep and his eyelids are evidencing little ripples back and forth. We can conclude that David is a. in alpha state b. having a seizure c. dreaming d. doing none of these
Critical Thinking LO 7 Page: 185 a	41.	Which of the following is not associated with REM sleep? a. heightened muscle tension b. dreaming c. irregular breathing d. irregular pulse rate

Factual LO 7 Page: 186 Correct = 68% **d**	42.	In general, as the cycle of sleep recurs through the night, it tends to contain a. more stage 4 and less REM b. more stage 4 and more REM c. less stage 4 and less REM d. less stage 4 and more REM
Concept/Applied LO 7 Page: 186 Correct = 62% **d**	43.	Given the cyclical nature of sleep, we can expect to do the <u>most</u> dreaming a. toward the beginning of the night's sleep b. in the middle of the night's sleep c. in NREM sleep d. toward the end of the night's sleep
Factual LO 8 Page: 187 Correct = 80% **d**	44.	The general course of development of sleep patterns from infancy to adulthood includes a. greater REM percentage in infancy than adulthood b. total sleep time decreasing from infancy to adulthood c. fewer but longer sleep periods in adulthood d. all of these
Factual LO 8 Page: 187 Correct = 37% **c**	45.	During adulthood, the proportion of _____ gradually decline(s). a. stage 1 sleep b. stage 2 sleep c. slow-wave sleep d. stage 1, stage 2, and slow wave sleep all
Critical Thinking LO 9 Page: 187 **b**	46.	Which of the following statements about co-sleeping (i.e., parents and children sleeping together) is <u>not</u> accurate? a. Co-sleeping is widely accepted in Japanese culture. b. Co-sleeping is actively encouraged in most Western societies. c. American parents generally teach their children to sleep alone. d. Around the world as a whole, co-sleeping is the norm rather than the exception.
Critical Thinking LO 9 Page: 188 Correct = 52% **d**	47.	Which of the following statements about napping practices is <u>not</u> accurate? a. Napping practices vary along cultural lines. b. Industrialization tends to undermine the siesta tradition. c. The siesta tradition is found mostly in tropical regions. d. The siesta tradition is generally found in most nomadic groups.
Concept/Applied LO 9 Page: 188 **a**	48.	Cody is visiting his pen pal in a tropical, non-industrialized village. Cody is likely to find that the inhabitants of the village a. take a 1-to-2 hour midday nap each day b. are less likely than Americans are to encourage co-sleeping c. experience less REM sleep than is typical for Americans d. experience less slow-wave sleep than is typical for Americans
Factual LO 10 Page: 188 **a**	49.	The brain structure that appears to be the <u>most</u> important to sleep and wakefulness is the a. reticular formation b. hippocampus c. cerebellum d. corpus callosum
Critical Thinking LO 10 Page: 188 **c**	50.	Imagine that a mammal was discovered that had no pons in the hindbrain. You should predict that this mammal would a. never experience NREM sleep b. sleep for most of the day c. never experience REM sleep d. seldom sleep

VARIATIONS IN CONSCIOUSNESS

Concept/Applied LO 10 Page: 189 **d**	51.	Research on brain regulation of sleep has, in general, suggested that a. there is a single sleep-wakefulness center that uses serotonin b. there is a single sleep-wakefulness center that uses serotonin, norepinephrine, dopamine, and acetylcholine c. there are several brain areas involved in sleep but they all use serotonin d. several areas of the brain affect sleep, and they use serotonin, acetylcholine, norepinephrine, and dopamine
Concept/Applied LO 10 Page: 189 **a**	52.	Overall, the evidence seems strongest for which of the following hypotheses regarding the adaptive value of sleep? a. Sleep reduces exposure to predators and other dangers. b. Sleep helps animals restore energy depleted by waking activities. c. Sleep helps organisms conserve energy. d. None of these hypotheses has been supported.
Factual LO 11 Page: 190 Correct = 22% **a**	53.	Total sleep deprivation for several days has been shown to a. have surprisingly little effect on subjects who are highly motivated b. greatly affect performance on a number of tasks c. result in the onset of psychological disorders d. have profound effects on performance but not on emotional state
Factual LO 11 Page: 190 **b**	54.	The effects of partial sleep deprivation generally depend on the amount of sleep lost and a. one's gender b. the nature of the task at hand c. how much sleep one is accustomed to getting d. one's typical level of anxiety when awake
Factual LO 11 Page: 191 **b**	55.	The results of the Featured Study on the effects of sleep deprivation show that when compared to members of the control group, participants who were deprived of sleep a. performed at about the same level on cognitive tasks b. rated their effort, concentration, and performance higher c. scored significant lower on a measure of mood d. maintained a significant level of irritability weeks after the study
Critical Thinking LO 11 Page: 191 **c**	56.	The Featured Study is representative of a great deal of recent research which suggests that the effects of sleep deprivation a. are substantially different in males and females b. vary as a function of one's normal sleeping habits c. are more serious than widely believed d. are practically nonexistent in healthy adults
Factual LO 11 Page: 191 **d**	57.	Studies indicate that partial sleep deprivation can impair which of the following? a. attention b. reaction time c. decision making d. attention, reaction time, or decision making
Factual LO 12 Page: 192 Correct = 80% **d**	58.	If selectively deprived of REM sleep, a person will experience _____ later. a. hypochondriasis b. emotionality c. NREM d. REM rebound

Concept/Applied LO 12 Page: 192 Correct = 78% **a**	59.	Kara has just fallen asleep and immediately slips into REM. Kara has probably experienced or undergone a. sleep deprivation b. alcohol overdose c. NREM rebound d. biofeedback training
Concept/Applied LO 12 Page: 192 **a**	60.	Mateen has been selectively deprived of slow-wave sleep for five nights. You would expect that on the sixth, undisturbed night, he will a. show increased stage 4 sleep b. show increased REM sleep c. show decreased stage 4 sleep d. show decreased REM sleep
Concept/Applied LO 12 Page: 192 Correct = 54% **a**	61.	While serving as a subject at a sleep clinic, Erica was deprived of dreaming for several nights with the result that she a. experienced REM rebound and spent more time in REM sleep on subsequent nights b. became accustomed to going without dreaming and spent less time in REM sleep on subsequent nights c. immediately returned to a normal sleep cycle when she was allowed to sleep through the night d. had difficulty achieving REM on subsequent nights
Factual LO 12 Page: 192 **c**	62.	People who are selectively deprived of slow-wave sleep for several nights in a row a. will suffer no ill effects whatsoever b. need to be awakened less and less frequently as the deprivation goes on c. will make up for the lost slow-wave sleep when allowed to sleep normally again d. will spend more time in REM sleep to compensate
Factual LO 13 Page: 192 Correct = 89% **b**	63.	When a person has chronic problems not getting adequate sleep, he or she is said to suffer from which of the following? a. hypersomnia b. insomnia c. somnambulism d. any of these could be the problem
Factual LO 13 Page: 192 Correct = 92% **c**	64.	The <u>most</u> common sleep disorder we know of is a. sleep apnea b. night terrors c. insomnia d. somnambulism
Critical Thinking LO 13 Page: 192 **b**	65.	Insomnia is associated with <u>all</u> <u>but</u> which of the following? a. daytime fatigue b. night terrors c. impaired functioning d. increased health problems
Concept/Applied LO 13 Page: 192 **a**	66.	Sheri has no trouble falling asleep, but she has difficulty remaining asleep. Sheri is suffering from a. insomnia b. narcolepsy c. sleep apnea d. pseudoinsomnia

Factual LO 13 Page: 193 **d**	67.	People who think they are not getting enough sleep even when they tend to sleep very well are most likely to have a. sleep apnea b. insomnia c. hypersomnia d. pseudoinsomnia
Factual LO 13 Page: 193 Correct = 98% **d**	68.	Insomnia can be caused by a. excessive anxiety b. depression c. health problems d. any of these
Factual LO 17 Page: 193 **a**	69.	Which of the following is the most common treatment for insomnia? a. prescription of sleeping pills b. relaxation training c. stress-reduction exercises d. group therapy
Critical Thinking LO 13 Page: 193 Correct = 88% **a**	70.	Which of the following statements regarding the use of sleeping pills is not accurate? a. They are a good long-range solution for insomnia. b. There is some danger of overdose. c. They reduce the proportion of time spent in REM sleep. d. They gradually become less effective with continued use.
Concept/Applied LO 13 Page: 193 **c**	71.	Lauren has been having trouble sleeping, and she decides to take a sedative to help her get a good night's sleep. The use of a sedative is likely to a. increase the amount of time she spends in both slow-wave and REM sleep b. increase the amount of time she spends in slow-wave sleep, but decrease her overall REM sleep c. decrease the amount of time she spends in both slow-wave and REM sleep d. increase the amount of time she spends in REM sleep, but decrease her overall slow-wave sleep
Concept/Applied LO 13 Page: 193 **d**	72.	Abruptly stopping the use of a sedative for the treatment of insomnia can lead to a. REM rebound b. narcolepsy c. microsleep d. rebound insomnia
Factual LO 13 Page: 194 **c**	73.	One recent study suggested that _____ treatments produce more long-lasting benefits in the treatment of insomnia than do drug therapies. a. hypnosis b. psychoanalytic c. cognitive-behavioral d. electroconvulsive shock
Factual LO 14 Page: 194 Correct = 89% **b**	74.	A disease characterized by sudden and irresistible onsets of sleep during normal waking periods is a. epilepsy b. narcolepsy c. hypersomnia d. sleep agnosia

Concept/Applied LO 14 Page: 194 Correct = 86% **a**	75.	Valerie has episodes in which she experiences a sudden and irresistible urge to sleep during normal waking periods. Valerie <u>most</u> likely suffers from a. narcolepsy b. hypersomnia c. cretinism d. a lack of REM rebound
Concept/Applied LO 14 Page: 194 Correct = 81% **b**	76.	The rare sleep disorder in which a person will, without warning, go directly from being awake into REM sleep is a. sleep apnea b. narcolepsy c. hypersomnia d. somnambulism
Factual LO 14 Page: 194 **d**	77.	Which of the following has been used with modest success in the treatment of narcolepsy? a. group therapy b. cognitive-behavioral therapy c. sedative drugs d. stimulant drugs
Concept/Applied LO 14 Page: 194 Correct = 82% **b**	78.	One hypothesis regarding the cause of crib death in babies is that they stop breathing during sleep, a sleep disorder known as a. narcolepsy b. sleep apnea c. night terror d. hypersomnia
Factual LO 14 Page: 194 Correct = 83% **b**	79.	Sleep apnea is characterized by a. a sudden, irresistible urge to sleep during normal waking hours b. a reflexive gasping for air during sleep c. an extremely low rate of REM d. "night terrors"
Concept/Applied LO 14 Page: 194 **c**	80.	Joshua experiences reflexive gasping for air during sleep several times a night and frequently wakes up because of it. Joshua <u>most</u> likely has a. night terrors b. narcolepsy c. sleep apnea d. lack of NREM rebound
Factual LO 14 Page: 194 Correct = 67% **b**	81.	Which of the following usually occurs in REM sleep? a. night terrors b. nightmares c. sleepwalking d. enuresis
Factual LO 14 Page: 194 **c**	82.	In adults, there is a correlation between nightmares and a. depression b. schizophrenia c. neurotic symptoms d. sleepwalking
Critical Thinking LO 14 Page: 194 **d**	83.	Night terrors are most closely associated with which of the following? a. a somnambulistic episode b. emotional disturbance c. severe depression d. NREM sleep

Concept/Applied LO 14 Page: 194 **a**	84.	Kelli wakes up abruptly from NREM sleep with intense autonomic arousal and feelings of panic. Kelli has just experienced a a. night terror b. nightmare c. psychotic dream d. somnambulistic break
Concept/Applied LO 14 Page: 194 **b**	85.	Sara had been asleep for just over 2 hours when she suddenly let out a piercing cry and sat straight up in her bed. When her parents asked what had scared her, she really couldn't remember, and she soon fell back to sleep. From this description, it appears that Sara experienced a. an episode of sleep apnea b. a night terror c. a nightmare d. REM deprivation
Concept/Applied LO 14 Page: 194 Correct = 74% **c**	86.	Stephen wanders about while remaining asleep. Stephen's condition is called a. narcology b. sleep tremors c. somnambulism d. agnosia
Concept/Applied LO 14 Page: 194 Correct = 32% **d**	87.	Of the following statements regarding sleepwalking, which is <u>most</u> accurate? a. Sleepwalking occurs in REM sleep. b. It is not safe to awaken a sleepwalker. c. Sleepwalkers rarely hurt themselves. d. Sleepwalkers are not acting out a dream.
Critical Thinking LO 14 Page: 194 **c**	88.	Which of the following statements regarding sleepwalking is <u>not</u> accurate? a. Sleepwalking occurs mostly in children. b. It is safe to awaken a sleepwalker. c. Sleepwalking typically occurs while the person is dreaming. d. There appears to be a genetic predisposition to sleepwalking.
Critical Thinking LO 15 Page: 194 Correct = 61% **a**	89.	Which of the following statements about dreams is <u>not</u> true? a. Dreams only occur during REM sleep. b. Dreams have sometimes changed the world. c. Dreams are not as bizarre as widely assumed. d. Dreamers occasionally realize that they are dreaming.
Factual LO 16 Page: 195 Correct = 62% **a**	90.	Research has revealed that <u>most</u> dreams are a. about fairly normal activities b. about fairly bizarre activities c. random bursts of activity with little coherence d. focused on others rather than oneself
Concept/Applied LO 16 Page: 196 Correct = 70% **c**	91.	According to research evidence on dream content, which of the following would a person be <u>least</u> likely to dream about? a. falling off a cliff b. being chased by black-robed creatures, all bearing the face of your most feared instructor c. a political candidate trying to muster enthusiasm in his audience d. missing an important exam

Factual LO 16 Page: 196 Correct = 57% c	92.	According to research on the content of dreams, which of the following is the <u>least</u> likely dream theme? a. personal misfortune b. conflict c. current affairs d. aggression
Concept/Applied LO 16 Page: 196 Correct = 91% b	93.	Men are more likely than women to dream about a. children b. automobiles c. clothing d. all of these things
Factual LO 16 Page: 196 a	94.	What did Freud call the contents of our waking life that spill into our dreams? a. the day residue b. manifest content c. nocturnal spillover d. wish fulfillment
Concept/Applied LO 16 Page: 196 d	95.	Which of the following statements regarding the content of dreams is accurate? a. Men and women generally dream about the same things. b. The content of dreams has little to do with what goes on in one's waking life. c. People's dreams rarely involve themselves. d. The content of dreams can be affected by external stimuli.
Critical Thinking LO 17 Page: 197 b	96.	Which of the following dream themes is <u>least</u> likely to be consistently reported by individuals from a variety of cultures? a. having sex b. eating food c. falling d. being pursued
Factual LO 17 Page: 197 Correct = 41% b	97.	In the _____ culture, dreams are viewed as the focal point of existence that determines an individual's way of life. a. Marakesh of Morocco b. aborigines of Australia c. Arapesh of New Guinea d. Parintinin of Brazil
Critical Thinking LO 17 Page: 197 b	98.	Which of the following statements about culture and dreams is <u>not</u> accurate? a. Some basic dream themes appear to be nearly universal across cultures. b. People in Western societies tend to recall their dreams vividly. c. In many cultures, dreams are seen as a window into the spiritual world. d. In Western cultures, dreams are largely written off as insignificant.
Factual LO 18 Page: 197 c	99.	The use of dreams to satisfy ungratified needs is referred to as a. id idealization b. self-centeredness c. wish fulfillment d. sublimation
Factual LO 18 Page: 197 Correct = 76% d	100.	The theorist who advanced the wish-fulfillment idea about dreaming was a. Cartwright b. Hobson c. McCarley d. Freud

Concept/Applied LO 18 Page: 197 Correct = 56% **c**	101.	According to Freud, a sexually frustrated person would probably have highly erotic dreams because, according to him, the principal purpose of a dream is a. sexual gratification b. conflict resolution c. wish fulfillment d. the repression of unconscious desires
Concept/Applied LO 18 Page: 198 Correct = 70% **a**	102.	If you interpreted Peter's dream of arguing with a larger-than-life faceless authority figure as an attempt on his part to decide which approach to take in convincing his father of the merits of his future plans, you would be subscribing to the a. problem-solving theory of dreams b. activation-synthesis theory of dreams c. wish-fulfillment theory of dreams d. neural overflow hypothesis of dreams
Critical Thinking LO 18 Page: 198 Correct = 65% **b**	103.	The idea that dreams are times when people can think creatively about what is going on in their lives and then use that information later when awake is consistent with the _____ view of dreams. a. wish fulfillment b. problem-solving c. synergistic d. James-Verduin
Critical Thinking LO 18 Page: 198 **b**	104.	The idea that dreams are the cortex's attempt to make sense out of bursts of general firing from lower brain centers is the core of _____ theory of dreaming. a. the wish fulfillment b. the activation-synthesis c. the problem-solving d. no current
Concept/Applied LO 19 Page: 200 **b**	105.	Which of the following statements regarding hypnotic susceptibility is <u>most</u> accurate? a. Everyone can be hypnotized. b. Not everyone can be hypnotized. c. Only those with weak egos can be hypnotized. d. Only those who believe in the power of hypnosis can be hypnotized.
Factual LO 19 Page: 200 **a**	106.	About _____ percent of the population appear to be exceptionally good subjects for hypnosis. a. 10 b. 25 c. 50 d. 75
Factual LO 19 Page: 200 **a**	107.	About _____ percent of the population don't respond at all to hypnosis. a. 10 b. 25 c. 50 d. 75
Concept/Applied LO 19 Page: 200 **d**	108.	Which of the following personality factors is most closely related to hypnotic susceptibility? a. neuroticism b. compulsiveness c. extraversion d. imaginativeness

Concept/Applied LO 19 Page: 200 **a**	109.	Robert experienced much severe punishment in childhood and, as a way to cope, he developed an active fantasy life. Robert would be a good candidate for a. hypnosis b. meditation c. insomnia research d. drug research
Critical Thinking LO 19 Page: 200 Correct = 89% **d**	110.	Which of the following is <u>not</u> a common effect of hypnosis? a. auditory and visual hallucinations b. the reduction of inhibitions c. some resistance to pain d. total loss of personal control
Critical Thinking LO 19 Page: 201 Correct = 88% **c**	111.	A stage hypnotist is sometimes successful in getting people to disrobe in public. What is the best explanation for this phenomenon? a. When hypnotized, a subject comes under the total control of the hypnotist and will follow any instructions to the letter. b. The subject is a confederate of the hypnotist and disrobes while pretending to be hypnotized. c. When hypnotized, subjects are able to convince themselves that they cannot be held responsible for their actions and so end up doing things they might not otherwise do. d. The hypnotist is careful to select only those subjects who look as if they would enjoy disrobing in public.
Factual LO 19 Page: 201 Correct = 82% **b**	112.	Which of the following is the <u>most</u> common posthypnotic suggestion given to people? a. to act infantile b. to forget something—that is, to exhibit amnesia c. to perform a behavior unusual for the person d. to act like an animal
Concept/Applied LO 20 Page: 201 Correct = 68% **c**	113.	Which of the following statements regarding the EEG patterns of a hypnotized person is <u>most</u> accurate? a. The patterns are similar to those of someone in REM sleep. b. The patterns are similar to those of someone who has been diagnosed with a multiple personality. c. The patterns are similar to those of an awake person. d. The patterns are similar to those of a young child.
Concept/Applied LO 20 Page: 201 Correct = 70% **d**	114.	The role-playing theory of hypnosis offered by Barber and Spanos suggests that the hypnotized subject a. actually fakes the hypnotic state b. enters into a trance and acts out suggestions c. knows that he or she is only pretending d. is in a normal state but acts out the role of a hypnotized person
Concept/Applied LO 20 Page: 201 Correct = 94% **d**	115.	The idea that hypnotized persons are acting in the manner they believe a hypnotized person would is the basic tenet behind the _____ theory of hypnosis. a. Freudian b. dissociative c. divided consciousness d. role-playing

Concept/Applied
LO 20
Page: 201
a

116. The fact that nonhypnotized subjects can be suspended rigidly between two chairs with only their heads and feet supporting them
a. supports the role-playing view of hypnosis
b. provides support for the notion of posthypnotic suggestion
c. supports the idea that hypnosis is a unique altered state
d. suggests that hypnosis can tap into the subjects unconscious

Factual
LO 20
Page: 202
Correct = 85%
c

117. Dissociation refers to
a. a loss of inhibition by hypnotized subjects
b. a hypnotized subject's willingness to act out the hypnotist's suggestions
c. a splitting of mental processes into two separate, simultaneous streams of awareness
d. role playing by hypnotized subjects in response to situational cues

Critical Thinking
LO 20
Page: 202
Correct = 50%
d

118. The idea that hypnosis is associated with divided consciousness and is an altered state is most consistent with which of the following theories of hypnosis?
a. Barber's role theory
b. Schachter's cognitive theory
c. Freud's psychoanalytic theory
d. Hilgard's dissociation theory

Factual
LO 21
Page: 202
Correct = 96%
a

119. A conscious attempt to focus one's attention in a nonanalytical manner is called
a. meditation
b. dissociation
c. Zen Buddhism
d. hypnosis

Factual
LO 21
Page: 202
Correct = 84%
b

120. Meditation has its roots in
a. early Christianity
b. Eastern religions
c. transcendental psychology
d. the scientific study of the relaxation response

Factual
LO 21
Page: 202
Correct = 63%
c

121. Research has shown that meditation can produce a physiological state similar to
a. the REM stage of sleep
b. that produced by hypnosis
c. relaxation
d. a drug-induced trance

Critical Thinking
LO 21
Page: 202
c

122. Which of the following does not happen when a person is in a meditative state?
a. Alpha waves become more prominent in EEG recordings.
b. Heart rate decreases.
c. Oxygen consumption increases.
d. Respiration rate decreases.

Concept/Applied
LO 21
Page: 202
c

123. Scott is in a state of alpha rhythm, with decreased heart rate, oxygen consumption, and carbon dioxide elimination. Scott is probably
a. hypnotized
b. in a drug-induced trance
c. meditating
d. in REM sleep

Critical Thinking
LO 21
Page: 203
b

124. Which of the following has not been claimed as a long-term effect associated with meditation?
a. increased sex drive
b. increased longevity among the elderly
c. reduction in stress
d. improvement in mood

Factual LO 22 Page: 204 Correct = 94% **d**	125.	Psychoactive drugs are chemicals that alter one's a. emotional state b. behavioral functioning c. mental condition d. emotional state, behavioral functioning, and mental condition
Factual LO 22 Page: 204 Correct = 94% **a**	126.	Opiates such as morphine and heroin have a capacity to a. alleviate pain b. improve memory c. enhance sensory awareness d. do all of these things
Factual LO 22 Page: 204 Correct = 93% **b**	127.	A drug that depresses central nervous system activity is referred to as a(n) a. hallucinogen b. sedative c. narcotic d. amphetamine
Factual LO 22 Page: 204 Correct = 98% **b**	128.	Sleep-inducing drugs are classified as a. narcotics b. sedatives c. hallucinogens d. soporifics
Critical Thinking LO 22 Page: 204 **a**	129.	Which of the following does not belong with the others? a. alcohol b. cocaine c. nicotine d. amphetamines
Concept/Applied LO 22 Page: 204 Correct = 83% **b**	130.	Adam has just consumed a substance that provides him with increased alertness and energy, along with reduced fatigue. However, it also makes him more talkative, increases his blood pressure, reduces his appetite, and makes him restless. Adam has likely ingested a. THC b. an amphetamine c. LSD d. a sedative
Concept/Applied LO 22 Page: 204 Correct = 56% **d**	131.	Robert has just taken a drug that has made him feel euphoric. He has probably taken a. a narcotic b. a hallucinogen c. a sedative d. any of these drugs
Factual LO 22 Page: 205 Correct = 55% **b**	132.	_____ is a type of amphetamine that may be snorted or injected intravenously. a. Crack b. Crank c. Ice d. Ecstasy
Critical Thinking LO 22 Page: 205 **a**	133.	Which of the following does not belong with the others? a. cocaine b. LSD c. mescaline d. psilocybin

Concept/Applied LO 22 Page: 205 Correct = 78% **a**	134.	Renee is experiencing distortions in her sensory and perceptual processes. Additionally, she is exhibiting paranoia, nausea, and "jumbled" thought processes. Renee is most likely under the influence of a a. hallucinogen b. sedative c. narcotic d. stimulant
Concept/Applied LO 22 Page: 205 **d**	135.	Heather is taking a prescription drug to control her back pain. She finds that when she takes the drug she experiences some short-term drowsiness and nausea. It is likely that Heather's physician has prescribed a. a stimulant b. a sedative c. a hallucinogen d. a narcotic
Critical Thinking LO 22 Page: 205 **b**	136.	Caffeine is to alcohol as a. opiate is to stimulant b. stimulant is to depressant c. stimulant is to opiate d. opiate is to sedative
Factual LO 22 Page: 206 Correct = 95% **b**	137.	The most widely used recreational drug in the United States is a. cocaine b. alcohol c. marijuana d. the barbiturates
Factual LO 22 Page: 206 **d**	138.	Alcohol appears to contribute to about _____ percent of student rapes on college campuses. a. 25 b. 50 c. 75 d. 90
Factual LO 23 Page: 206 Correct = 97% **d**	139.	The overall effect of a drug on an individual is influenced by which of the following? a. the individual's motivation and expectations b. the personality of the individual taking the drug c. the dose and potency of the drug d. all of these factors
Critical Thinking LO 23 Page: 206 Correct = 87% **c**	140.	The idea of multifactorial causation in drug effects suggests a. that taking several different drugs at the same time reduces their effects b. that taking several different drugs at once increases their effectiveness c. that the effect of a drug depends on dosage, user's age, mood, motivation, experience, and personal makeup d. none of these things
Factual LO 23 Page: 206 Correct = 98% **d**	141.	A progressive decrease in one's response to a drug with repeated and prolonged use is called a. withdrawal b. habituation c. dependency d. tolerance

Concept/Applied LO 23 Page: 206 Correct = 95% **b**	142.	Bryan finds that, where he used to need only one, he now needs two or more sleeping pills to fall asleep. This development indicates that Bryan a. is using sleeping pills as a recreational drug b. has developed a tolerance to sleeping pills c. has become physically addicted to sleeping pills d. has become psychologically addicted to sleeping pills
Factual LO 23 Page: 206 Correct = 52% **d**	143.	Among the following, which drug tends to produce tolerance most <u>slowly</u>? a. narcotics b. stimulants c. sedatives d. alcohol
Factual LO 23 Page: 206 Correct = 75% **b**	144.	For which of the following drugs does the tolerance level develop the most <u>rapidly</u>? a. cannabis b. sedatives c. alcohol d. hallucinogens
Factual LO 23 Page: 207 **d**	145.	The effects of sedatives and alcohol appear to be associated with which of the following neurotransmitter systems? a. serotonin b. norepinephrine c. dopamine d. GABA
Factual LO 23 Page: 208 Correct = 56% **d**	146.	The combined effect of certain drugs can be much greater than the sum of the effects of each one alone. Such an effect is said to be a. additive b. polymorphous c. multiplicative d. synergistic
Factual LO 23 Page: 208 Correct = 59% **b**	147.	A synergistic effect is one in which a. a drug suppresses the action of a neuromodulator b. the combined effects of two drugs are more than what would be predicted by the simple addition of the effects in isolation c. a person addicted to one drug is more susceptible to be addicted to a similar drug d. a drug affects the myelin sheath of a neuron and "short-circuits" its insulation properties
Factual LO 24 Page: 208 **a**	148.	Which of the following drugs carries the <u>least</u> amount of risk for physical and/or psychological dependence? a. LSD b. cocaine c. amphetamines d. heroin
Factual LO 24 Page: 208 **d**	149.	Which of the following drugs carries the <u>greatest</u> risk for physical and/or psychological dependence? a. LSD b. cocaine c. alcohol d. heroin

Factual LO 24 Page: 208 **b**	150.	Which of the following drugs has the <u>highest</u> degree of risk for psychological dependence? a. LSD b. cocaine c. cannabis d. mescaline
Factual LO 24 Page: 208 Correct = 96% **c**	151.	A strong mental and emotional craving for a drug is termed a. physical dependence b. tolerance c. psychological dependence d. withdrawal
Concept/Applied LO 24 Page: 208 **c**	152.	Aaron has been taking a mild amphetamine for the past four months to help him cope with being a full-time student while holding down a full-time job. Now that his classes have ended he wants to stop taking the amphetamine, but each time he tries to skip the medication he starts sweating and he develops tremors. It appears that Aaron has a. developed a drug tolerance for amphetamines b. become amphetamine intolerant c. developed a physical dependence for amphetamines d. habituated to the effects of amphetamines
Factual LO 24 Page: 208 **a**	153.	Physical dependence would be <u>least</u> likely with which of the following drugs? a. marijuana b. alcohol c. morphine d. seconal
Factual LO 24 Page: 208 **c**	154.	Many theorists believe that virtually all abused drugs eventually increase activity in a particular neural pathway, called the _____ pathway. a. monoamine reticular b. GABA cortical c. mesolimbic dopamine d. prefrontal pleasure
Critical Thinking LO 25 Page: 209 Correct = 82% **d**	155.	Which of the following drugs would be <u>most</u> likely to result in a fatal overdose? a. LSD b. mescaline c. marijuana d. barbiturates
Factual LO 25 Page: 209 Correct = 100% **d**	156.	A lethal overdose can occur with which of the following drugs? a. only with stimulants b. only with sedatives c. only with narcotics d. with stimulants, sedatives, or narcotics
Critical Thinking LO 25 Page: 209 **a**	157.	Which of the following drugs is <u>least</u> likely to result in a fatal overdose? a. LSD b. heroin c. cocaine d. barbiturates

Factual LO 25 Page: 210 **c**	158.	Which of the following drugs has the greatest number (and most diverse) negative effects on physical health? a. LSD b. heroin c. alcohol d. cocaine
Factual LO 25 Page: 210 Correct = 90% **a**	159.	There is the greatest amount of debate on the risks associated with which of the following drugs? a. marijuana b. alcohol c. cocaine d. heroin
Factual LO 25 Page: 210 Correct = 72% **d**	160.	There is strong evidence that marijuana causes _____ in humans. a. permanent brain damage b. male sterility c. birth defects d. none of these effects
Critical Thinking LO 26 Page: 210 Correct = 76% **c**	161.	Which of the following statements regarding drug abuse and psychological health is <u>most</u> accurate? a. Drug abuse causes maladjustment. b. Maladjustment causes drug abuse. c. Drug abuse and maladjustment are positively correlated. d. Drug abuse and maladjustment are negatively correlated.
Critical Thinking LO 26 Page: 210 **d**	162.	Which of the following statements regarding drug abuse and psychological health is accurate? a. Drug abuse may contribute to the development of psychological disorders. b. Psychological maladjustment may cause drug abuse. c. Drug abuse and psychological maladjustment may be caused by ineffective parenting. d. All of these statements are accurate.
Factual LO 27 Page: 211 Correct = 71% **c**	163.	Research on consciousness dwindled in the early part of the 20th century after _____ redefined psychology as the science of behavior. a. Sigmund Freud b. Roger Sperry c. John Watson d. Wilhelm Wundt
Critical Thinking LO 27 Page: 211 Correct = 62% **c**	164.	Which of the following statements regarding the study of consciousness is accurate? a. Psychology began as the study of behavior rather than the study of consciousness. b. John Watson and others viewed psychology as the science of consciousness. c. The 1960s saw an increase in the study of variations of consciousness. d. Today, psychologists are generally not interested in studying issues related to consciousness.
Critical Thinking LO 27 Page: 211 Correct = 74% **d**	165.	The fact that the alterations of consciousness produced by drugs depend significantly on personal experience illustrates which of the following unifying themes? a. Psychology is empirical. b. Psychology evolves in a sociohistorical context. c. Behavior is determined by multiple causes. d. Our experience of the world is highly subjective.

Critical Thinking
LO 27
Page: 211
c	166.	The fact that the importance people place on dreams varies across societies best illustrates which the textbook's unifying themes?
a. Psychology is empirical.
b. Psychology evolves in a sociohistorical context.
c. Our behavior is shaped by our cultural heritage.
d. Our experience of the world is highly subjective.
Factual
LO 28
Page: 212
Correct = 91%
d	167.	The amount a person sleeps at night tends to
a. be the same for everyone of the same age
b. be different across cultures, indicating a strong learned component to how much sleep one needs
c. be greatly reduced if one takes a 15-minute nap at midday
d. vary from person to person
Concept/Applied
LO 28
Page: 212
Correct = 77%
d	168.	Mark's mother is worried because he only sleeps about 4 to 5 hours per night. What would you tell her?
a. She has reason to be concerned because, in the long run, Mark's lack of sleep will take its toll physically.
b. There is nothing to worry about because young people need less sleep than older people.
c. There is no problem as long as Mark spends most of his sleep time in REM sleep.
d. There is probably nothing to be worried about since different people need differing amounts of sleep.
Critical Thinking
LO 28
Page: 212
c	169.	Which of the following statements regarding naps is <u>not</u> accurate?
a. Many highly productive people have made effective use of naps.
b. Most naps enhance subsequent alertness and task performance.
c. Naps are generally considered very efficient ways to sleep.
d. Overly long naps can disrupt nighttime sleep.
Factual
LO 28
Page: 212
Correct = 79%
d	170.	Depressant drugs have been found to
a. facilitate falling asleep
b. disrupt the normal sleep cycle
c. reduce REM sleep
d. do all of these things
Concept/Applied
LO 28
Page: 212
Correct = 89%
a	171.	As a result of taking sleeping pills, Elian has been getting 8 hours of sleep per night but he does not feel rested. Why is this the case?
a. Sleeping pills suppress REM sleep.
b. Sleeping pills suppress stage 2 sleep.
c. Sleeping pills increase the amount of time spent in REM sleep.
d. Sleeping pills increase the amount of time spent in NREM sleep.
Factual
LO 28
Page: 212
Correct = 75%
b	172.	Alcoholics may spend a good deal of time sleeping, but their sleep is not refreshing because they
a. wake up many times during a single sleep cycle
b. spend less time in REM sleep
c. spend less time in NREM sleep
d. spend too much time in stage 4 sleep
Concept/Applied
LO 28
Page: 212
Correct = 97%
d	173.	Research indicates that
a. people who get less sleep clearly live longer
b. males who get less sleep clearly live longer than males who sleep more, but no differences are observed in females
c. females who get less sleep clearly live longer than females who sleep more, but no differences are observed in males
d. none of these statements is accurate

Critical Thinking
LO 28
Page: 212
b	174.	Which of the following statements regarding yawning is <u>not</u> accurate?
a. Yawning is seen in all cultures.
b. Yawning is a response to a buildup of carbon dioxide.
c. Yawning is correlated with sleepiness and boredom.
d. Yawning is seen in other mammals, as well as in birds, fish, and reptiles.
Critical Thinking
LO 28
Page: 213
a	175.	Which of the following statements regarding snoring is <u>not</u> accurate?
a. Snoring tends to decrease as people get older.
b. Snoring is more common among men than women.
c. Snoring is associated with sleep apnea and cardiovascular disease.
d. Snoring is more frequent among people who are overweight.
Critical Thinking
LO 28
Page: 213
b	176.	Which of the following is <u>not</u> good advice for avoiding sleep problems?
a. Minimize consumption of stimulants such as caffeine and nicotine.
b. Vary the time when you go to bed at night.
c. Establish a daytime exercise program.
d. Avoid daytime naps if you're having trouble sleeping at night.
Critical Thinking
LO 28
Page: 213
d	177.	Which of the following is <u>not</u> good advice for combating insomnia?
a. Develop a bedtime sleep ritual.
b. Read a dull textbook before going to bed.
c. Avoid taking naps during the day.
d. Have a cup of warm coffee just before going to bed.
Critical Thinking
LO 29
Page: 214
Correct = 74%
c	178.	Which of the following statements about dreams is <u>most</u> accurate?
a. Only about 75 percent of all people dream.
b. The reason we do not remember our dreams is that the content of the dream is repressed.
c. People cannot remember their dreams because of too much time passing between when they dreamed and when they try to recall the dream.
d. Most dreams people can remember deal with sexually oriented topics.
Critical Thinking
LO 29
Page: 214
b	179.	Which of the following statements regarding dreams is <u>not</u> accurate?
a. Dream recall is best when people are awakened during or very soon after a dream.
b. Dreams flash through consciousness instantaneously.
c. We dream whether we remember our dreams or not.
d. Trying to remember dreams can aid dream recall.
Factual
LO 29
Page: 215
d	180.	According to Freud, the manifest content of a dream is the
a. hidden meaning of the dream
b. sexual content of the dream
c. content of the dream indicative of the person's hostility
d. actual content of the dream at the surface level
Concept/Applied
LO 29
Page: 215
Correct = 44%
a	181.	The psychoanalyst interpreted his patient's dream of riding a horse as indicative of her repressed sexual urges. This interpretation constitutes the _____ content of the dream.
a. latent
b. manifest
c. overt
d. subliminal

Concept/Applied LO 29 Page: 215 Correct = 54% **b**	182.	Michael dreamed that he was being chased through the galaxy by ferocious interplanetary creatures. This is the _____ content of Michael's dream. a. latent b. manifest c. subliminal d. true
Concept/Applied LO 29 Page: 215 Correct = 44% **a**	183.	Alice decided that her dream of flying reflects her desire to escape from an unfulfilling marriage. What would a contemporary dream theorist say to Alice? a. Her interpretation may be accurate because she is the person best equipped to decipher her dream. b. Her interpretation is too superficial and does not get at the latent meaning of the dream. c. Alice needs an analyst to interpret her dream for her because the dream is a reflection of unconscious wishes. d. Before any credibility is given to her interpretation, she needs to have a series of similar dreams.
Factual LO 29 Page: 215 Correct = 74% **b**	184.	Thinking clearly about the circumstances of your waking life while recognizing that you are dreaming is referred to as a a. latent dream b. lucid dream c. manifest dream d. confabulated dream
Critical Thinking LO 29 Page: 215 **b**	185.	Michelle insists she never dreams; she is convinced of this because she has never recalled a single dream. If Michelle were tested in a sleep lab it is likely that a. she would experience REM sleep, but she would only report a dream if she were awakened from slow-wave sleep b. she would experience REM sleep, and she would report a dream if she were awakened from REM sleep c. she would not experience REM sleep d. she would experience REM sleep, but she would not report any dreams if she were awakened from REM sleep
Concept/Applied LO 29 Page: 215 **c**	186.	Hunter was dreaming, but he knew that he was dreaming. During his dream he was able to control some of the events that occurred in the dream. In this case, Hunter is a. dreaming during Stage 4 of the sleep cycle b. having a theta-wave dream c. having a lucid dream d. experiencing pseudo-REM sleep
Concept/Applied LO 29 Page: 215 Correct = 84% **c**	187.	Bill has had many dreams in which he has fallen off a cliff, but he has always awakened before hitting the bottom. He has become an insomniac because of his fear that if he ever hits the bottom, he will die. What would you tell Bill? a. He has reason to be afraid. b. He should take sleeping pills to repress REM sleep so that he will not dream. c. His belief has no substance and is merely a myth. d. He simply needs to train himself to wake up whenever he has a falling dream.
Critical Thinking LO 30 Page: 216 **d**	188.	Which of the following statements regarding the debate over whether alcoholism is a disease is <u>not</u> accurate? a. One can inherit a genetic vulnerability to alcoholism. b. Alcoholism disrupts a variety of vital functions. c. More research is needed to determine whether or not alcoholism is a disease. d. The question of whether alcoholism is a disease is a matter of definition.

Concept/Applied LO 30 Page: 216 c	189.	Which of the following statements regarding the use of definitions in psychology is the <u>most</u> accurate? a. Definitions generally emerge out of research. b. Definitions can be useful as explanations for phenomena. c. Definitions are typically crafted by experts in a specific field. d. The source of a definition is unimportant in evaluating its validity.
Concept/Applied LO 30 Page: 217 b	190.	Concluding that a person drinks too much because he/she is an alcoholic, is an example of _____ reasoning. a. logical b. circular c. inductive d. deductive
Integrative Correct = 80% d	191.	Which of the following are generally associated with non-REM sleep? a. rapid eye movements b. dreams c. nightmares d. night terrors
Integrative b	192.	Alpha waves are likely to be prominent if you are a. programming a computer b. meditating c. under hypnosis d. doing any of these things
Integrative Correct = 82% c	193.	The effects of many psychoactive drugs depend to a large extent on users' expectations. This finding illustrates which of your text's unifying themes? a. Psychology is empirical. b. Psychology evolves in a sociohistorical context. c. Our experience of the world is highly subjective. d. All of these.
Study Guide LO 1 Page: 180 c	194.	What did William James mean by his term "the stream of consciousness"? a. Consciousness always remains at the same level. b. Consciousness never stops. c. Consciousness is always changing. d. Consciousness is beyond personal control.
Study Guide LO 2 Page: 181 b	195.	Which brain wave is probably operating while you are taking this quiz? a. alpha b. beta c. theta d. delta
Study Guide LO 3 Page: 182 c	196.	The circadian rhythm operates around a a. 1-year cycle b. 28-day cycle c. 24-hour cycle d. 90-minute cycle
Study Guide LO 3 Page: 182 d	197.	What appears to be responsible for regulating the circadian rhythm? a. amount of time spent sleeping b. amount of time spent awake c. cultural practices d. exposure to light

Study Guide LO 6 Page: 186 **a**	198.	The most vivid dreams generally occur a. during REM sleep b. during NREM sleep c. during the early hours of sleep d. when alpha brain waves are present
Study Guide LO 10 Page: 188 **d**	199.	Severing the ascending reticular activating system in cats caused them to a. become very aggressive b. become very fearful c. remain in continuous wakefulness d. remain in continuous sleep
Study Guide LO 14 Page: 194 **b**	200.	Which of the following sleep disorders is <u>most</u> life threatening? a. nightmares b. narcolepsy c. sleep apnea d. somnambulism
Study Guide LO 16 Page: 196 **a**	201.	The content of <u>most</u> dreams is a. mundane b. exotic c. exciting d. erotic
Study Guide LO 21 Page: 202 **d**	202.	Which of the following physiological changes is unique to meditation? a. increased alpha rhythms b. decreased heart rate c. decreased oxygen consumption d. All of these things are common to many forms of relaxation.
Study Guide LO 23 Page: 207 **b**	203.	Psychoactive drugs exert their effect on the brain by a. decreasing blood supply to the brain b. altering neurotransmitter activity c. breaking down essential brain amino acids d. penetrating the nucleus of the neurons
Study Guide LO 27 Page: 211 **d**	204.	Which of the following is likely to produce highly subjective events? a. hypnosis b. meditation c. psychoactive drugs d. all of these
Study Guide LO 29 Page: 214 **d**	205.	Which of the following statements is correct? a. Most people do not dream in color. b. Practice will not improve the ability to recall dreams. c. Dreams generally last only 1 or 2 minutes at most. d. From birth until death everyone dreams.
Online Quiz LO 2 Page: 181 **d**	206.	The four basic EEG patterns are a. alpha, beta, gamma, delta b. beta, theta, omega, gamma c. theta, delta, beta, omega d. alpha, beta, theta, delta

Online Quiz LO 3 Page: 182 **a**	207.	Which of the following glands is responsible for secreting the hormone involved in adjustments to our biological clocks? a. the pineal gland b. the pituitary gland c. the thyroid d. the gonads
Online Quiz LO 5 Page: 184 **b**	208.	The electrooculograph measures and records a. heart rate b. eye movement c. brain wave activity d. galvanic skin response
Online Quiz LO 6 Page: 185 **b**	209.	Stages 3 and 4 of sleep are associated with _____ waves in EEG recordings. a. alpha b. delta c. REM d. asynchronistic
Online Quiz LO 10 Page: 188 **b**	210.	Which of the following functions would most likely be impaired by damaging the reticular activating system? a. menstruation b. sleep-wake cycle c. visual sensory processing d. coordination of motor movement
Online Quiz LO 13 Page: 192 **b**	211.	Matthew has persistent early-morning awakening from sleep. He is <u>most</u> likely a. a hypersomniac b. an insomniac c. a somnambulist d. a phototrapist
Online Quiz LO 16 Page: 196 **c**	212.	Women are more likely than men to dream about a. sex with strangers b. acting aggressively c. jewelry d. all of these things
Online Quiz LO 19 Page: 199 **b**	213.	Hypnosis owes its beginnings to the work of which of the following? a. Sigmund Freud b. Franz Anton Mesmer c. Ernest Hilgard d. Harry Houdini
Online Quiz LO 22 Page: 206 **c**	214.	According to a study of drinking on college campuses, drinkers are prone to which of the following behaviors? a. increased anxiety b. hallucinations c. aggression d. increased alertness
Online Quiz LO 28 Page: 213 **a**	215.	Snoring is a common phenomenon that is seen in about _____ percent of adults. a. 25 b. 40 c. 60 d. 80

ESSAY QUESTIONS

1. Compare REM and NREM sleep with regard to EEG activity, muscular activity, and cognitive activity.

   NREM sleep refers to stages 1 through 4, collectively, and thus is characterized by varied EEG activity. As sleep progresses through these stages, sleep becomes progressively deeper; brain waves correspondingly decrease in frequency and increase in amplitude. Muscle tension also decreases as sleep deepens, but even in stage 4, there is sufficient muscle tone to allow the possibility of sleepwalking. Dreams occasionally occur during NREM sleep, but these tend to be brief and fragile.

   REM sleep is also a deep sleep, in the sense that it is relatively difficult to awaken a person from this stage. Muscle tone is so relaxed as to leave the body virtually paralyzed, precluding the possibility of sleepwalking. The eyes, however, move beneath closed lids. The EEG shows beta activity, as if the person was wide awake. This paradoxical finding can be accounted for by the fact that REM is the stage during which most dreaming occurs.

2. Describe the effects of complete, partial, and selective sleep deprivation. What, if anything, do these effects tell us about why we sleep?

   Complete sleep deprivation for one or more nights is associated with feelings of sleepiness, irritability, and difficulty concentrating. Nevertheless, sleep-deprived people function surprisingly well, thus telling us little about why we sleep.

   Partial sleep deprivation likewise has inconsistent effects. People who get substantially less sleep than they are accustomed to do feel sleepy, and may suffer impaired performance on tasks that are long, difficult, or tedious. These results also tell us little about the functions of sleep.

   The existence of distinct sleep stages implies that each stage may have its own function. To investigate this possibility, researchers have selectively deprived subjects of either REM sleep or slow-wave sleep. In both kinds of selective deprivation, subjects experience an increased need for that stage of sleep specifically. In addition, both REM deprivation and slow-wave deprivation produce a "rebound effect" in which subjects make up for lost time when allowed to sleep normally again. None of these studies tell us the precise functions of sleep, but they do demonstrate definite and independent needs for both REM and slow-wave sleep.

3. What do people tend to dream about, and what theories have been proposed to explain why people dream at all?

   Above all, dreams tend to be personal. They generally involve people we now, in settings that are familiar to us. We are particularly likely to dream about current worries, conflicts, and stressors.

   There is no universally agreed upon explanation for why we dream. Freud proposed that dreams are a form of "wishful thinking" in which we have the opportunity to gratify impulses that have gone unfulfilled in our waking lives. Other theorists take a more cognitive view, proposing that dreams provide an opportunity to engage in creative problem solving. Both of these views mesh nicely with available data regarding the typical content of dreams.

   A very different view is the activation-synthesis model of dreaming, which proposes that dreams are simply by-products of neural activation during REM sleep. In this view, the content of dreams is almost incidental. Whereas the wish-fulfillment and problem-solving theories both regard the "wide awake" brain as the effect of dreaming, the activation-synthesis model views the "wide awake" brain as the cause of dreaming.

4. Compare and contrast the "role-playing" and "altered state" views of hypnosis.

Both views are attempts to account for known hypnotic phenomena, which include heightened suggestibility, relaxation, focused attention, and enhanced fantasy.

Proponents of the "role-playing" view regard hypnosis as a normal state of consciousness in which suggestible people act "as if" they are hypnotized by enacting their role expectations about how hypnotized people should behave. In support of this view, there is evidence that many supposed hypnotic phenomena can be duplicated by nonhypnotized subjects.

Other theorists continue to insist that hypnosis is a unique, altered state of consciousness. For example, Ernest Hilgard maintains that hypnosis creates a dissociation in consciousness—a splitting off of mental processes into two separate, simultaneous streams of awareness. This view is made plausible by the fact that divided consciousness is a common, normal experience (as in "highway hypnosis," for example).

At present, there is no resolution to the debate between these two opposing views.

This page intentionally left blank.

Chapter Six
Learning Through Conditioning

LEARNING OBJECTIVES

1. Describe Pavlov's demonstration of classical conditioning and the key elements in this form of learning.
2. Discuss how classical conditioning may shape phobias and physiological processes, including sexual arousal.
3. Describe the classical-conditioning phenomena of acquisition, extinction, and spontaneous recovery.
4. Describe the processes of generalization and discrimination and summarize the classic study of Little Albert.
5. Explain what happens in higher-order conditioning.
6. Discuss the nature of operant responding in comparison to the types of responding typically governed by classical conditioning.
7. Describe Thorndike's work and explain his law of effect.
8. Describe Skinner's principle of reinforcement and the prototype experimental procedures used in studies of operant conditioning.
9. Describe the operant conditioning phenomena of acquisition, shaping, and extinction.
10. Explain how stimuli govern operant behavior and how generalization and discrimination occur in operant conditioning.
11. Discuss the role of delayed reinforcement and conditioned reinforcement in operant conditioning.
12. Identify various types of schedules of reinforcement and discuss their typical effects on responding.
13. Explain how operant psychologists study choice and summarize what they have learned.
14. Explain the distinction between positive and negative reinforcement.
15. Describe and distinguish between escape learning and avoidance learning.
16. Explain two-process theory and the role of negative reinforcement in avoidance behavior.
17. Describe punishment and its effects.
18. Discuss the phenomena of instinctive drift, conditioned taste aversion, and preparedness.
19. Explain the evolutionary perspective on learning.
20. Describe research on signal relations and response-outcome relations, and explain their theoretical importance.
21. Discuss the nature and importance of observational learning.
22. List the basic processes in observational learning and discuss Bandura's view on whether reinforcement affects learning or performance.
23. Explain how the chapter highlighted two of the text's unifying themes.
24. Describe how to specify your target behavior and gather baseline data for a self-modification program.
25. Discuss your options for increasing or decreasing a response in designing a self-modification program.
26. Discuss how to execute, evaluate, and end a self-modification program.
27. Describe how classical conditioning is used to manipulate emotions.

MULTIPLE-CHOICE QUESTIONS

Factual
LO 1
Page: 222
Correct = 91%
b

1. Another name for classical conditioning is
   a. operant conditioning
   b. respondent conditioning
   c. observational learning
   d. trial-and-error learning

Factual
LO 1
Page: 222
Correct = 95%
a

2. Pavlov became interested in conditioning when he observed laboratory dogs
   a. salivating right before food was placed in their mouths
   b. failing to salivate when food was placed in their mouths
   c. salivating only when food was placed in their mouths
   d. salivating right after they had swallowed food

Factual
LO 1
Page: 223
Correct = 66%
d

3. When a neutral stimulus acquires the capacity to evoke a response that was originally evoked by another stimulus the process is
   a. operant conditioning
   b. instrumental conditioning
   c. Skinnerian conditioning
   d. classical conditioning

Factual
LO 1
Page: 223
Correct = 77%
a

4. Pavlov found that meat powder placed on a dog's tongue will make the dog salivate. In Pavlov's terms, the meat powder is
   a. an unconditioned stimulus
   b. an unconditioned response
   c. a conditioned stimulus
   d. a conditioned response

Factual
LO 1
Page: 223
Correct = 79%
d

5. In Pavlov's original experiment on classical conditioning, the unconditioned response (UCR) was
   a. the sound of a tone
   b. salivation elicited by a tone
   c. the presentation of meat powder following a tone
   d. salivation elicited by meat powder

Factual
LO 1
Page: 223
Correct = 85%
b

6. In classical conditioning, the stimulus that naturally evokes an unlearned response is the
   a. conditioned stimulus
   b. unconditioned stimulus
   c. unconditioned reinforcer
   d. conditioned reinforcer

Factual
LO 1
Page: 223
Correct = 58%
c

7. In classical conditioning, the stimulus that is originally neutral in regard to the response to be learned is the
   a. unconditioned stimulus
   b. unconditioned response
   c. conditioned stimulus
   d. conditioned response

Factual
LO 1
Page: 223
c

8. A conditioned stimulus is
   a. a stimulus that elicits an unconditioned response without previous conditioning
   b. an unlearned reaction that occurs without previous conditioning
   c. a previously neutral stimulus that has, through conditioning, acquired the capacity to elicit a conditioned response
   d. a learned reaction that occurs because of previous conditioning

Factual LO 1 Page: 223 **b**	9.	The major difference between a CS and a UCS is a. the order in which they are presented b. that one reliably elicits the response of interest prior to conditioning while the other does not c. that during conditioning the response to one increases while the response to the other decreases d. the strength of the response that each stimulus elicits
Concept/Applied LO 1 Page: 223 **d**	10.	Carson used to really enjoy lime sherbet and when he was in Mexico he tried frozen lime margaritas. After his fourth margarita Carson became extremely ill. Now he finds that even the sight of lime sherbet in a bowl can make him feel queasy. In this example, the unconditioned stimulus is a. the lime margaritas that Carson consumed b. the illness that followed the fourth margarita c. the sight of lime sherbet d. the queasiness that Carson feels when he sees lime sherbet
Concept/Applied LO 1 Page: 223 **d**	11.	Darrel was dancing with his new girlfriend at an Elvis tribute. When the band started playing "Can't Help Falling in Love with You" his girlfriend gave him a long passionate kiss, which Darrel found very enjoyable. Now Darrel finds that every time he hears "Can't Help Falling in Love with You" on the radio, he becomes mildly excited. In this example, the long, passionate kiss is a. a conditioned stimulus b. an unconditioned response c. a conditioned response d. an unconditioned stimulus
Concept/Applied LO 1 Page: 223 **c**	12.	Veronica had been working at Zenex Industries for 8 months when her boss asked to see her in his office. She thought he wanted to talk about a promotion so she was quite excited, but instead of giving her a promotion, the boss told Veronica she was being laid off as a result of company downsizing. Veronica could feel her heart pounding as she listened to the news. Veronica was able to get a new job, but every time her new boss asks to talk to her in private, Veronica feels a little faint. In this example, the unconditioned response is a. the bad news from her boss at Zenex Industries b. her new boss asking for a private meeting c. her pounding heart when she heard she was being laid off d. the faintness she feels when her new boss wants to talk to her in private
Concept/Applied LO 1 Page: 223 **c**	13.	One Saturday Lacey was sitting at home when the telephone rang. A local company was making promotional calls and told Lacey she had just won a $1000 gift certificate. She felt a rush of excitement at the thought of what she could do with $1000. Now Lacey finds that whenever she hears a telephone ring, she feels a surge of excitement. In this example, the rush of excitement that Lacey felt when she heard she had won the gift certificate is a. the conditioned stimulus b. the unconditioned stimulus c. the unconditioned response d. the conditioned response

Concept/Applied LO 1 Page: 223 **b**	14.	Holly was dancing with her new boyfriend at an Elvis tribute. When the band started playing "Can't Help Falling in Love with You" her boyfriend gave her a long, passionate kiss, which Holly found very enjoyable. Now Holly finds that every time she hears "Can't Help Falling in Love with You" on the radio, she becomes a little flushed. In this example, the conditioned stimulus is a. the long, passionate kiss b. the song "Can't Help Falling in Love with You" c. the enjoyment she experienced after the kiss from her boyfriend d. the flushing she experiences when she hears the song on the radio
Concept/Applied LO 1 Page: 223 **d**	15.	Floyd had been working at Qualton Enterprises for 2 years when his boss asked to see him in her office. He thought she wanted to talk about a promotion so he was quite excited, but instead of giving him a promotion, the boss told Floyd he was being laid off as a result of company downsizing. Floyd could feel his heart pounding as he listened to the news. Floyd has a new job now, but every time his new boss asks to talk to him in private, Floyd feels a little faint. In this example, Floyd's new boss asking for a private talk is a. an unconditioned response b. a conditioned response c. an unconditioned stimulus d. a conditioned stimulus
Concept/Applied LO 1 Page: 223 **a**	16.	One Saturday Clayton was sitting at home when the telephone rang. A local company was making promotional calls and told Clayton he had just won a $500 gift certificate. He felt a rush of excitement at the thought of what he could do with $500. Now Clayton finds that whenever he hears a telephone ring, he feels a little surge of excitement. In this example, the conditioned response is a. the surge of excitement that Clayton feels whenever he hears a telephone ring b. the ringing of a telephone c. the news that he had just won a $500 gift certificate d. the rush of excitement he felt when he won the certificate
Concept/Applied LO 1 Page: 223 **b**	17.	Charity used to really enjoy potato salad and at a family reunion she ate a large helping. Unfortunately the potato salad had not been kept cold, and Charity became quite ill after eating it. Now she finds that even the sight of potatoes in the grocery store can make her feel sick to her stomach. In this example, the sick feeling Charity experiences when she sees potatoes in the grocery store is a. an unconditioned response b. a conditioned response c. an unconditioned stimulus d. a conditioned stimulus
Critical Thinking LO 1 Page: 224 **c**	18.	The dependent variable in a classical conditioning experiment is a. the conditioned stimulus b. whether or not the UCS is presented c. the strength of the conditioned response d. the number of conditioning trials
Concept/Applied LO 2 Page: 224 Correct = 89% **d**	19.	Classical conditioning could account for how a child learns to a. sing a song b. tie shoe laces c. print letters d. fear the dark

Concept/Applied LO 2 Page: 224 Correct = 85% **d**	20.	Classical conditioning could account for how a child learns to a. talk b. play baseball c. walk d. love the smell of her father's after shave
Concept/Applied LO 2 Page: 225 Correct = 61% **a**	21.	When advertisers pair their products with attractive people or enjoyable surroundings, in the hope that the pairings will cause their products to evoke good feelings, they are using principles derived from a. classical conditioning b. instrumental conditioning c. observational learning d. operant conditioning
Concept/Applied LO 2 Page: 225 Correct = 58% **b**	22.	Mary woke up one night with a spider dangling in front of her face. She screamed, and from that point on she could not stand to be near spiders. Mary's fear of spiders is based on a. a response-outcome association b. classical conditioning c. observational learning d. operant conditioning
Concept/Applied LO 2 Page: 225 **c**	23.	Eduardo's mother always wore Chantille perfume and when she would hug him or hold him close he could smell that scent. Today, whenever he catches a whiff of Chantille perfume, it makes him feel calm and relaxed. The learning process that could best account for Eduardo's response to the scent of Chantille perfume is a. operant conditioning b. observational learning c. classical conditioning d. delayed reinforcement
Concept/Applied LO 2 Page: 225 **d**	24.	Caitlyn is afraid of all spiders because her brother once dropped a spider down her shirt when she was younger. Today, even the sight of a rubber spider is enough to send shivers down her spine. The learning process that could best account for Caitlyn's fear of spiders is a. operant conditioning b. observational learning c. delayed reinforcement d. classical conditioning
Concept/Applied LO 2 Page: 225 **a**	25.	A major auto maker has developed a series of television commercials which show its cars in the great outdoors, in peaceful settings, away from the hustle and bustle of big cities. They hope that seeing the cars in these settings will condition good feelings about their cars. This particular auto maker is attempting to use a. classical conditioning in its advertising campaign b. operant conditioning in its advertising campaign c. observational learning in its advertising campaign d. noncontingent reinforcement in its advertising campaign
Concept/Applied LO 2 Page: 225 Correct = 72% **a**	26.	When an individual has a phobia, the irrational fear and anxiety that the person experiences is a. a conditioned response b. an unconditioned response c. a conditioned stimulus d. an unconditioned stimulus

Concept/Applied LO 2 Page: 225 Correct = 23% **b**	27.	Frederick cringes every time he hears a dentist's drill, even when he is sitting in the waiting room of his dentist's office. In this example, the pain of dental drilling is a. a conditioned response b. an unconditioned stimulus c. an unconditioned response d. a conditioned stimulus
Concept/Applied LO 2 Page: 225 **c**	28.	Simon cringes every time he hears a dentist's drill, even when he is sitting in the waiting room of his dentist's office. In this example, cringing in the waiting room is a. an unconditioned response b. a conditioned stimulus c. a conditioned response d. an unconditioned stimulus
Concept/Applied LO 2 Page: 225 **d**	29.	A woman reported feeling "weak in the knees" whenever she smelled cigarette smoke and Beemans gum, because of the association of these smells with her first love. In this example, her "weak knees" would be a. an unconditioned response b. a conditioned stimulus c. an unconditioned stimulus d. a conditioned response
Concept/Applied LO 2 Page: 225 Correct = 79% **c**	30.	A woman reported feeling "weak in the knees" whenever she smelled cigarette smoke and Beemans gum, because of the association of these smells with her first love. In this example, the combined smell of cigarettes and Beemans gum would be a. a conditioned response b. an unconditioned response c. a conditioned stimulus d. an unconditioned stimulus
Concept/Applied LO 2 Page: 225 Correct = 81% **b**	31.	A woman reported feeling "weak in the knees" whenever she smelled cigarette smoke and Beemans gum, because of the association of these smells with her first love. The positive emotional response that this woman experienced developed through a. instrumental conditioning b. classical conditioning c. observational learning d. operant conditioning
Factual LO 2 Page: 226 **a**	32.	In the study by Domjan et al. (1988), which investigated the adaptive significance of sexual conditioning, the conditioned stimulus was a. a distinctive chamber with white walls and a mesh floor b. a sexually receptive female quail c. a taxidermically-prepared female quail made of terrycloth and polyester fiber d. the act of copulation
Factual LO 2 Page: 227 **b**	33.	In the study by Domjan et al. (1988), which investigated the adaptive significance of sexual conditioning, the researchers found that the quail in the experimental group a. had a higher percentage of viable sperm in their semen b. ejaculated a greater volume of semen c. ejaculated more frequently when a receptive female was present d. ejaculated more quickly after mounting a receptive female

Factual LO 2 Page: 227 c	34.	The study by Domjan et al. (1988), which investigated the adaptive significance of sexual conditioning, may shed some light on a. how erectile dysfunction may develop in humans b. why some species fail to reproduce and become extinct c. how sexual fetishes develop in humans d. the evolutionary causes in infertility in humans
Factual LO 3 Page: 227 Correct = 86% c	35.	The initial stage of learning a response is called a. extinction b. contiguity c. acquisition d. conditioning
Concept/Applied LO 3 Page: 227 Correct = 77% d	36.	According to Pavlov, the key to classical conditioning is the a. strength of the UCS b. strength of the CS c. resistance to extinction brought about by sign-releasing stimuli d. pairing of stimuli in time--that is, temporal contiguity
Critical Thinking LO 3 Page: 228 a	37.	On Tuesday morning Chloe prepared her typical breakfast of corn flakes with milk, and a cup of coffee. However, instead of having grapefruit with her breakfast, she tried eating guava for the first time. Later she became extremely ill. If her illness causes her to develop a conditioned response to one of her breakfast items, the conditioned response will most likely be to a. guava because it was a novel stimulus b. milk because the milk may have been sour c. grapefruit because that was the one thing missing from her typical breakfast d. coffee because coffee is a stimulant
Factual LO 3 Page: 228 a	38.	The best temporal arrangement for establishing a new conditioned response is a. short-delayed conditioning b. simultaneous conditioning c. trace conditioning d. backward conditioning
Factual LO 3 Page: 228 Correct = 51% b	39.	When the CS is presented and stopped before the UCS is presented, the arrangement is called a. simultaneous conditioning b. trace conditioning c. instrumental conditioning d. short-delayed conditioning
Concept/Applied LO 3 Page: 228 d	40.	Dominic is playing with some balloons. He counts "one, two, three," and just as he says "three" he pops the balloon with a pin. His sister is listening in the next room and begins to cringe when she hears Dominic start counting, and before she actually hears the balloon pop. In this example, the conditioned stimulus of Dominic's counting and the unconditioned stimulus of the balloon pop were arranged in a a. simultaneous conditioning pattern b. trace conditioning pattern c. negative reinforcement conditioning pattern d. short-delayed conditioning pattern

Critical Thinking LO 3 Page: 228 **b**	41.	Gavin wants to condition his dog to wag its tail whenever the phone rings. He waits while the phone is ringing, and a few seconds after the ringing stops, he scratches his dog behind the ears to elicit some vigorous tail wagging. In the example, the conditioned stimulus of the ringing telephone, and the unconditioned stimulus of the ear scratches are arranged using a a. short-delayed conditioning pattern b. trace conditioning pattern c. simultaneous conditioning pattern d. variable interval pattern
Concept/Applied LO 3 Page: 228 **c**	42.	Mikayla wants to condition her dog to drool at the sound of the telephone, so she plans to pair the sound of the ringing telephone with a tasty dog treat. To use classical conditioning most effectively, Mikayla should present the tasty dog treat a. a few seconds before the telephone starts to ring b. at the same instant that the telephone rings c. a half second after the telephone has started ringing d. a few seconds after the telephone has stopped ringing
Concept/Applied LO 3 Page: 228 **b**	43.	Edward's assignment for his experimental psychology class is to condition a classmate to blink each time a clicking noise is played. Edward plans to pair the clicking noise with a puff of air directed at the eyelid. To use classical conditioning most effectively, Edward should play the clicking noise a. several seconds before he directs the puff of air at his classmate's eyelid b. a half second before he directs the puff of air at his classmate's eyelid c. a half second after he directs the puff of air at his classmate's eyelid d. at the same instant that he directs the puff of air at his classmate's eyelid
Factual LO 3 Page: 229 Correct = 80% **a**	44.	The continued presentation of the CS without the UCS will result in the gradual disappearance of the CR. This phenomenon is known as a. extinction b. inhibition c. suppression d. conditioned forgetting
Concept/Applied LO 3 Page: 229 Correct = 82% **d**	45.	After training one of his dogs to salivate in response to a tone, Pavlov continued to present the tone periodically without the food, with the result that the dog a. kept responding with undiminished intensity despite extended exposure to the tone alone b. stopped responding immediately c. initially responded to the tone at an even greater intensity than before d. gradually stopped responding to the tone
Concept/Applied LO 3 Page: 229 **b**	46.	In order to weaken or eliminate a conditioned response you would a. present the UCS before the CS several times b. present the CS alone several times c. present the UCS alone several times d. present extra pairings of the CS and UCS
Concept/Applied LO 3 Page: 229 **b**	47.	Carly used to be afraid of visits to her family doctor because she associated the sight of his waiting room with the pain of having a blood sample drawn. However, Carly's new doctor's lab worker is "painless" and the sight of the waiting room is no longer associated with pain. Consequently, Carly finds her fear of visits to her family doctor has disappeared. This illustrates the classical conditioning process known as a. spontaneous recovery b. extinction c. second-order conditioning d. avoidance

Concept/Applied LO 3 Page: 229 **c**	48.	Ken used to drool at the smell of peanut butter cookies as they baked, and he couldn't wait to sink his teeth into that first cookie. However, Ken's new roommate makes terrible peanut butter cookies and the smell of them baking is no longer associated with a wonderful taste experience. Consequently, Ken finds that the smell of the cookies no longer makes him drool in anticipation. This illustrates the classical conditioning process known as a. spontaneous recovery b. second-order conditioning c. extinction d. avoidance
Factual LO 3 Page: 229 Correct = 83% **d**	49.	The reappearance of a conditioned response after extinction and a period of rest is called a. disinhibition b. reconditioning c. stimulus generalization d. spontaneous recovery
Concept/Applied LO 3 Page: 229 **d**	50.	Mariah developed a fear of the water when she fell off a river raft last summer. This year she took swimming lessons and thought she had finally overcome her fear of water. She was eagerly looking forward to an upcoming rafting trip, however, as soon as she stepped onto the raft she was instantly terrified again. This illustrates the classical conditioning process known as a. extinction b. second-order conditioning c. stimulus generalization d. spontaneous recovery
Critical Thinking LO 3 Page: 229 **b**	51.	The phenomenon of spontaneous recovery suggests that a. classical conditioning can only be used to condition biologically meaningful responses b. even if a person is able to extinguish a conditioned response, there is an excellent chance that it will reappear later c. once a conditioned response has been extinguished a person will also stop responding to other stimuli that are similar d. when a conditioned response is extinguished, higher-order responses replace the original response
Concept/Applied LO 3 Page: 229 **d**	52.	Kaleb developed a fear of snowstorms two winters ago when his car spun off the road and hit a tree during a blizzard. As the winter progressed, and he had no further accidents, Kaleb thought his fear of snowstorms had pretty well disappeared. To his surprise, this winter when the first heavy snow started to fall, he found his heart was pounding and he was trembling. This illustrates the classical conditioning process known as a. extinction b. second-order conditioning c. stimulus generalization d. spontaneous recovery
Factual LO 3 Page: 229 Correct = 70% **a**	53.	When a conditioned response shows spontaneous recovery, the rejuvenated response typically a. is weaker than the previously conditioned response b. is stronger than the previously conditioned response c. occurs before the conditioned stimulus d. changes to an unconditioned stimulus

Concept/Applied
LO 3
Page: 229
a

54. Cody developed a severe fear of flying when he was piloting a small plane through some severe turbulence. He has been seeing a therapist, and it appears that his fear response has been successfully extinguished. The therapist used a flight simulator to help Cody practice his piloting skills in a safe setting. However, the first time Cody stepped back into a real plane, his fear returned. This example illustrates the phenomenon known as
   a. the renewal effect
   b. second-order conditioning
   c. negative reinforcement
   d. stimulus generalization

Critical Thinking
LO 3
Page: 229
a

55. Anthony classically conditioned his cat to purr whenever the phone rang. One day the phone rang for nearly two hours straight when Anthony wasn't home and the cat's conditioned purring response underwent extinction. Today the response has spontaneously recovered, but if the conditioned purring response were to undergo extinction again Anthony should expect that it will
   a. take less time to extinguish than it took for the original extinction
   b. take more time to extinguish than it took for the original extinction
   c. take the same amount of time to extinguish as it took for the original extinction
   d. not be possible to extinguish the response now that spontaneous recovery has occurred

Concept/Applied
LO 3
Page: 229
Correct = 77%
b

56. Imagine a conditioned response is extinguished in a different setting than the one in which it was originally acquired. When the animal is returned to the environment where the acquisition originally took place, you should expect to see evidence of
   a. stimulus generalization
   b. response renewal
   c. avoidance
   d. superstitious responding

Concept/Applied
LO 3
Page: 229
Correct = 87%
c

57. The renewal effect and spontaneous recovery both suggest that extinction
   a. permanently erases conditioned responses
   b. alters the meaning of the unconditioned stimulus
   c. suppresses, but does not erase a learned association
   d. only has a permanent effect in animals, not in people

Factual
LO 4
Page: 230
d

58. Stimulus generalization occurs when
   a. there is a temporal association between two stimuli
   b. an organism fails to respond to stimuli that are similar to the original stimulus used in conditioning
   c. an unconditioned stimulus fails to elicit the unconditioned response
   d. an organism responds to new stimuli that are similar to the original conditioned stimulus

Concept/Applied
LO 4
Page: 230
b

59. When Diana was three years old she became terrified when the neighbor's budgie bird kept flying near her head. Today she is afraid of all birds, including robins, pigeons, and blue jays. Diana's fear illustrates the classical conditioning process of
   a. instinctive drift
   b. stimulus generalization
   c. stimulus discrimination
   d. negative avoidance

Concept/Applied LO 4 Page: 230 **a**	60.	When Luis was a child he really liked the smell of the rose-scented perfume his mother always used to wear. He came to associate that scent with snuggles and hugs from his mom. As an adult Luis likes any floral scent, including the smell of lilacs and wildflowers. This example illustrates the classical conditioning process of a. stimulus generalization b. stimulus discrimination c. instinctive drift d. spontaneous recovery
Concept/Applied LO 4 Page: 230 Correct = 94% **a**	61.	The general principle governing stimulus generalization in classical conditioning is that generalization is greater a. when stimuli are very similar to the original conditioned stimulus b. when stimuli are very different from the original conditioned stimulus c. when tactile stimulation is used rather than auditory stimulation d. when auditory stimulation is used rather than visual stimulation
Factual LO 4 Page: 230 Correct = 35% **c**	62.	In the Little Albert experiment on conditioned emotional responses, the unconditioned stimulus was a. the rabbit b. the rat c. the loud noise d. the fear reaction
Concept/Applied LO 4 Page: 230 Correct = 99% **b**	63.	In the Watson and Rayner experiment on conditioned emotional responses, Little Albert could be expected to evidence a fear response to all of the following <u>except</u> a. a roll of cotton b. a baseball bat c. a Santa Claus beard d. a white rat
Concept/Applied LO 4 Page: 230 **a**	64.	Continuing to pair a specific CS and UCS, but periodically presenting stimuli similar to the CS and not pairing them with the UCS, should result in a. stimulus discrimination b. stimulus generalization c. extinction d. response attenuation
Concept/Applied LO 4 Page: 230 Correct = 92% **d**	65.	If a dog salivates to a blue light and not to a yellow light, the dog is showing evidence of a. spontaneous recovery b. conditioned emotional reactions c. stimulus generalization d. stimulus discrimination
Factual LO 4 Page: 230 Correct = 93% **d**	66.	In classical conditioning, a subject can learn to respond to one CS but not to another similar CS. This is the phenomenon of a. extinction b. stimulus generalization c. conditioned forgetting d. stimulus discrimination
Concept/Applied LO 4 Page: 230 **b**	67.	When Lindsay was nine years old the neighbor's chihuahua bit her on the ankle. Today Lindsay is still terrified of chihuahuas, but she likes almost all other types of dogs. Lindsay's fear illustrates the classical conditioning process of: a. instinctive drift b. stimulus discrimination c. stimulus generalization d. negative avoidance

Concept/Applied LO 4 Page: 230 **c**	68.	When Antonio was sick as a child his mother would always make him vanilla pudding; to Antonio it seemed like the vanilla pudding made him feel better. Even now, he still gets a good feeling when he starts to prepare some vanilla pudding, but not when he starts to make any other type of pudding. This example illustrates the classical conditioning process of a. stimulus generalization b. instinctive drift c. stimulus discrimination d. negative avoidance
Critical Thinking LO 4 Page: 230 Correct = 99% **b**	69.	_____ means treating two stimuli alike; _____ means treating two stimuli differently. a. Acquisition; extinction b. Generalization; discrimination c. Extinction; acquisition d. Discrimination; generalization
Factual LO 5 Page: 231 Correct = 77% **b**	70.	A dog is first conditioned to salivate to a tone. Then, a light is paired with the tone for a number of trials; finally, the light is presented alone, and the dog responds. This procedure is known as a. chaining b. higher-order conditioning c. compound conditioning d. sensory preconditioning
Concept/Applied LO 5 Page: 231 Correct = 56% **a**	71.	In higher-order conditioning _____ now functions as if it were _____. a. a conditioned stimulus; an unconditioned stimulus b. an unconditioned stimulus; a conditioned stimulus c. a conditioned response; an unconditioned response d. an unconditioned response; a conditioned response
Factual LO 5 Page: 231 Correct = 79% **c**	72.	In higher-order conditioning, new conditioned responses are a. conditioned to discriminative stimuli b. built on the foundation of innate unconditioned responses c. built on the foundation of previously established conditioned responses d. blocked by sensory adaptation
Concept/Applied LO 5 Page: 231 Correct = 24% **d**	73.	You have conditioned a fear response to a 1000-Hz tone. Now the tone is paired with a green light. Later, the green light alone elicits fear. This is an example of a. stimulus generalization b. response generalization c. discriminated conditioned response d. higher-order conditioning
Concept/Applied LO 5 Page: 231 **a**	74.	Six-year-old Kristen is afraid of balloons because a balloon once popped in her face while she was holding it. Last week she went to the circus and there was a clown holding a huge assortment of helium balloons. Now she is also afraid of clowns, even though none of the balloons the clown was holding popped. Kristen's fear of clowns illustrates the classical conditioning process of a. higher-order conditioning b. instinctive drift c. spontaneous recovery d. the renewal effect

Factual LO 6 Page: 232 **a**	75.	Operant conditioning is a type of learning in which a. responses come to be controlled by their consequences b. an organism's responding is influenced by the observation of others' behavior c. involuntary responses are slowly replaced by voluntary responses d. a neutral stimulus acquires the ability to elicit a response that was originally elicited by another stimulus
Concept/Applied LO 6 Page: 232 Correct = 68% **a**	76.	Learning to tie one's shoes is most likely acquired via the process of a. operant conditioning b. reflexive conditioning c. spontaneous recovery d. classical conditioning
Concept/Applied LO 6 Page: 232 **d**	77.	Dillon is four years old, and his parents want to teach him to say "please" and "thank you." They will be most successful in altering Dillon's behavior if they use a. classical conditioning b. higher-order conditioning c. non-contingent reinforcement d. operant conditioning
Concept/Applied LO 6 Page: 232 **d**	78.	April wants to teach her cat not to claw at the arms of her couch. She will be most successful in reducing the cat's scratching behavior if she uses a. classical conditioning b. higher-order conditioning c. observational learning d. operant conditioning
Factual LO 7 Page: 232 Correct = 68% **c**	79.	Operant conditioning is another name for a. classical conditioning b. respondent conditioning c. instrumental learning d. observational learning
Factual LO 7 Page: 232 Correct = 57% **d**	80.	The law of effect states that _____ lead to _____ of the association between the stimulus and a response. a. reinforcers; weakening b. punishers; strengthening c. strong unconditioned stimuli; quickening d. satisfying events; strengthening
Factual LO 8 Page: 233 Correct = 92% **c**	81.	According to Skinner, a stimulus is a reinforcer if it a. reduces a biological need b. induces a biological need c. increases the probability of the response that produced it d. decreases the probability of the response that produced it
Concept/Applied LO 8 Page: 233 Correct = 53% **b**	82.	Cassie asked her father for a candy bar at the grocery store, and her father bought her the candy bar. If Cassie asks for more candy bars in the future, the candy bar has acted as a. a discriminative stimulus b. a reinforcer c. a conditioned response d. a conditioned stimulus

Factual LO 8 Page: 233 Correct = 77% **a**	83.	The rules that determine whether responses lead to the presentation of a reinforcer are called a. reinforcement contingencies b. stimulus contiguities c. schedules of reinforcement d. antecedents
Factual LO 8 Page: 234 Correct = 75% **d**	84.	In a Skinner box, the cumulative recorder a. permits the experimenter to control the reinforcement contingencies b. provides a complete record of everything the animal does c. delivers the reinforcers d. creates a graphic record of operant responding as a function of time
Concept/Applied LO 8 Page: 234 Correct = 82% **b**	85.	In the cumulative record, a rapid response rate is indicated by _____; a slow response rate is indicated by _____. a. a shallow slope; a steep slope b. a steep slope; a shallow slope c. an upward slope; a downward slope d. a downward slope; an upward slope
Concept/Applied LO 8 Page: 234 Correct = 88% **c**	86.	In a cumulative record of responses from a Skinner box, a steep slope in the line indicates a. poorly planned reinforcement contingencies b. slow responding taking place c. fast responding taking place d. extinction has occurred
Critical Thinking LO 8 Page: 234 **b**	87.	You are watching a pigeon pecking a disk in a small chamber. There is a cumulative recorder connected to the disk. While you are watching, the pigeon is pecking at a slow, steady rate. Based on this information, you can predict that the line on the cumulative recorder will a. have a steep, upward slope b. have a shallow, upward slope c. have a shallow, downward slope d. have a steep, downward slope
Concept/Applied LO 8 Page: 234 **c**	88.	Nathan is watching the cumulative recorder that is connected to a box where a rat is pressing a lever to receive food reinforcement. The slope of the line is becoming flatter and flatter over time. Based on this output, Nathan can conclude that the rat's response rate a. is increasing over time b. will soon show spontaneous recovery c. is decreasing over time d. is caused by inadequate stimulus generalization
Critical Thinking LO 8 Page: 234 **c**	89.	You are watching a cumulative recorder that is connected to a small disk in a chamber. The pigeon has been trained to peck the disk when a red light is turned on, and not to peck the disk when a green light is turned on. Based on this information you should observe that when the green light is turned on, a. the slope of the line on the cumulative recorder will be steeper than when the red light is turned on b. the pen on the cumulative recorder will start to move downward c. the slope of the line on the cumulative recorder will be shallower than when the red light is turned on d. the roll of paper in the cumulative recorder will stop moving

| Factual
LO 9
Page: 235
Correct = 71%
c | 90. | The process of selectively reinforcing responses that are closer and closer approximations of some desired response is called
a. stimulus discrimination
b. selection
c. shaping
d. step-wise conditioning |

| Concept/Applied
LO 9
Page: 235
Correct = 77%
b | 91. | Learning to ride a bicycle is most likely acquired via the process of
a. classical conditioning
b. shaping
c. spontaneous recovery
d. innate stimulus release |

| Concept/Applied
LO 9
Page: 235
Correct = 94%
a | 92. | Danny's skill at hitting a baseball gradually improves as his attempts produce more frequent and longer-distance hits. This is an example of
a. shaping
b. stimulus generalization
c. extinction
d. stimulus discrimination |

| Factual
LO 9
Page: 235
Correct = 43%
d | 93. | The technique used to teach animals complex tricks, such as teaching pigeons to play ping-pong, is
a. respondent conditioning
b. continuous reinforcement
c. programming
d. shaping |

| Concept/Applied
LO 9
Page: 235
Correct = 55%
c | 94. | Arranging information and questions in a sequence of small steps to permit active learning by individuals relies on principles derived from
a. classical conditioning
b. observational or vicarious learning
c. operant conditioning
d. stimulus generalization |

| Concept/Applied
LO 9
Page: 235
c | 95. | Nicolas has autistic disorder and he was mute. A therapist working with Nicolas initially gave him a piece of chocolate any time he made a sound with his lips. This slowly changed until Nicolas only received a piece of chocolate for saying complete words, and eventually only for saying complete sentences. In this example, Nicolas developed speech skills through the use of
a. classical conditioning
b. modeling
c. shaping
d. negative reinforcement |

| Concept/Applied
LO 9
Page: 235
d | 96. | Jerome is training to be a vacuum cleaner sales person. Initially, he got paid for each customer he called on, even if the customer did not ask for a demonstration. Currently, he only gets paid for actually demonstrating the product. Eventually, he will only get paid for actually closing a sale. In this example, Jerome's sales skills are being developed through the use of
a. classical conditioning
b. modeling
c. negative reinforcement
d. shaping |

Concept/Applied   97. Summer is teaching herself to type using a computer software package. The first
LO 9   time she used the program, the sentences she was supposed to type scrolled very
Page: 235   slowly across the computer screen and when she finished the computer played a
c   clapping sound. However, now she has to type the material faster than her previous
                        "best time" before the computer plays the clapping sound. This computer software
                        package incorporates
                        a. classical conditioning
                        b. modeling
                        c. shaping
                        d. negative reinforcement

Concept/Applied   98. When reinforcement for a behavior is removed, the consequence will be
LO 9   a. an immediate weakening and eventual disappearance of the behavior
Page: 236   b. a short increase in the frequency with which the behavior is performed,
b   followed by the weakening and eventual disappearance of the behavior
                        c. the emergence of superstitious behavior designed to reinstitute the
                            reinforcement
                        d. unpredictable unless more information about the nature of the behavior is
                            provided

Concept/Applied   99. Kylee used to bring drawings home from her kindergarten class every day, and her
LO 9   parents would put the pictures on the refrigerator and tell Kylee how nice the
Page: 236   pictures were. Lately her parents haven't been putting her artwork on the
d   refrigerator, and now Kylee has stopped bringing drawings home with her. This
                        example illustrates the operant conditioning process of
                        a. punishment
                        b. avoidance
                        c. resistance
                        d. extinction

Concept/Applied   100. Bart used to go to his health club every day after work because he almost always
LO 9   saw Abigail there. For two full weeks Abigail wasn't at the club when Bart went
Page: 236   there for his workout, and now Bart has stopped going to his health club. This
a   example illustrates the operant conditioning process of
                        a. extinction
                        b. punishment
                        c. avoidance
                        d. resistance

Concept/Applied   101. Jeremy stops gambling five minutes after his slot machine last paid off; Jessica is
LO 9   still gambling, even though her slot machine hasn't paid off in over an hour. In this
Page: 236   example, Jeremy's behavior _____ while Jessica's behavior _____
Correct = 66%   a. shows low resistance to extinction; shows high resistance to extinction
a   b. has been classically conditioned; has been operantly conditioned
                        c. shows high resistance to extinction; shows low resistance to extinction
                        d. is controlled by conditioned stimuli; is controlled by unconditioned stimuli

Concept/Applied   102. When resistance to extinction is high it means that
LO 9   a. responding will continue for a long time after reinforcement is discontinued
Page: 236   b. responding will taper off quickly when reinforcement is discontinued
a   c. responding will fail to show spontaneous recovery following a period of
                            extinction
                        d. shaping was done incorrectly when the initial response was acquired

Concept/Applied LO 9 Page: 236 **b**	103.	Raul's parents make certain they thank Raul every time he clears the dishes from the table without being asked. Sadie's parents try to remember to thank Sadie every time she clears the table without being asked, but about half the time they forget. Based on principles of operant conditioning, you should predict that a. both children's table clearing will be equally resistant to extinction b. Sadie's table clearing will be more resistant to extinction than Raul's c. Raul's table clearing will be more resistant to extinction than Sadie's d. Raul will develop stimulus generalization and Sadie will develop stimulus discrimination
Factual LO 10 Page: 236 Correct = 53% **c**	104.	A discriminative stimulus is a. the same thing as a reinforcer b. the same thing as a conditioned stimulus c. a cue that indicates the probable consequences of an operant response d. a cue that indicates whether the unconditioned stimulus will be pleasant or aversive
Concept/Applied LO 10 Page: 236 Correct = 80% **d**	105.	A pigeon learns to peck at a disk lighted green to receive reinforcement, but not at a disk lighted red. The color of the disk is _____ for the pigeon. a. a reinforcer or nonreinforcer b. a punisher or nonpunisher c. a generalization stimulus d. a discriminative stimulus
Concept/Applied LO 10 Page: 236 **d**	106.	You are watching a rat in a Skinner box, and every time a red light comes on the rat presses the lever in the box. However, when a green light comes on the rat never presses the lever. In this case it appears that the color of the light is acting as a. a positive reinforcer for bar pressing b. a negative reinforcer for bar pressing c. an unconditioned stimulus for bar pressing d. a discriminative stimulus for bar pressing
Concept/Applied LO 10 Page: 236 **c**	107.	Julie has a desk right next to her manager's office. Whenever her manager is in his office Julie makes sure that she works hard at her computer. However, if the manager is away from his office she often works much more slowly and takes more breaks. In this case the manager being in his office is acting as a. a positive reinforcer for working hard b. a negative reinforcer for working hard c. a discriminative stimulus for working hard d. an unconditioned stimulus for working hard
Concept/Applied LO 10 Page: 237 Correct = 39% **d**	108.	A child asks to be allowed to stay up an extra half hour only when his mother is in a good mood. This is an example of a. acquisition b. shaping c. stimulus generalization d. stimulus discrimination
Concept/Applied LO 10 Page: 237 **b**	109.	After owning a car with a manual transmission, Don buys a car with an automatic transmission. When first driving his new car, he keeps reaching for the nonexistent clutch and gear shift. This is an example of a. acquisition b. stimulus generalization c. stimulus discrimination d. shaping

Concept/Applied LO 10 Page: 237 **b**	110.	When Kristen asks her grandmother for a cookie, her grandmother usually gives her one. Last week at the park Kristen's mother was embarrassed when Kristen walked up to five different elderly ladies and asked them for cookies. Kristen's behavior illustrates the concept of a. unconditioned reinforcement b. stimulus generalization c. stimulus discrimination d. observational learning
Concept/Applied LO 10 Page: 237 **a**	111.	Micah really liked his mom's homemade apple pie, and he would eat a huge slice whenever she made some. When he went to visit with a friend, he tried some apple pie that the friend's brother had made, and it tasted terrible. Now Micah will only eat his mom's apple pie; if anyone else offers him apple pie he politely turns them down. Micah's behavior toward apple pie illustrates the concept of a. stimulus discrimination b. stimulus generalization c. noncontingent reinforcement d. observational learning
Concept/Applied LO 10 Page: 237 **a**	112.	The basic principles of gradual acquisition, extinction, stimulus generalization, and discrimination apply a. to both classical and instrumental conditioning b. only to classical conditioning c. only to instrumental conditioning d. learning by animals, but not to learning by people
Concept/Applied LO 11 Page: 237 Correct = 92% **c**	113.	In order for a reinforcer to be most effective, it should be a. delayed for a short period of time to allow the person to coalesce the information in long-term memory b. delayed for varying periods of time depending on the behavior being reinforced c. delivered as soon as possible after the behavior has been performed d. a secondary reinforcer
Factual LO 11 Page: 237 Correct = 93% **c**	114.	In general, the longer the delay between a response and reinforcement, a. the faster conditioning proceeds b. the more effective the reinforcer becomes c. the more slowly conditioning proceeds d. the more likely it is that stimulus generalization will occur
Critical Thinking LO 11 Page: 237 **b**	115.	With computer-based study guides students typically receive immediate reinforcement for correct responses. With noncomputer-based study guides the reinforcement for correct responses may be delayed for some time. Based on what is known about operant conditioning, you should predict that learning a. with both types of study guides should proceed at the same rate b. will proceed more quickly with computer-based study guides c. will be more resistant to extinction when a noncomputer-based study guide is used d. will proceed more slowly with computer-based study guides
Concept/Applied LO 11 Page: 237 Correct = 86% **b**	116.	Food is an example of _____; praise is an example of _____. a. a primary reinforcer; a primary reinforcer b. a primary reinforcer; a secondary reinforcer c. a secondary reinforcer; a secondary reinforcer d. a secondary reinforcer; a primary reinforcer

Concept/Applied LO 11 Page: 237 **b**	117.	Primary reinforcers _____, while secondary reinforcers _____. a. depend on learning; satisfy biological needs b. satisfy biological needs; depend on learning c. are associated with classical conditioning; are associated with operant conditioning d. are associated with operant conditioning; are associated with classical conditioning
Factual LO 12 Page: 238 Correct = 68% **d**	118.	Continuous reinforcement occurs when a. reinforcement is delivered continually, regardless of whether or not a response is made b. it is not known in advance what responses will be reinforced c. every behavior engaged in by the subject is reinforced d. every occurrence of the designated response is reinforced
Concept/Applied LO 12 Page: 238 Correct = 51% **a**	119.	Assuming the reinforcer is the sound of the rattle, a baby's response of shaking a rattle is reinforced according to which type of schedule? a. continuous reinforcement b. fixed-interval c. variable-interval d. variable-ratio
Concept/Applied LO 12 Page: 238 **c**	120.	Katrina is trying to put a dollar bill into a vending machine in her office. Sometimes the machine will take a dollar bill on the first try, other times it can take up to five or six tries before the dollar bill is finally accepted. In this example, inserting a dollar bill into the vending machine is reinforced on a. a continuous reinforcement schedule b. a noncontingent reinforcement schedule c. an intermittent reinforcement schedule d. a short-delay reinforcement schedule
Factual LO 12 Page: 238 Correct = 65% **a**	121.	Relative to extinction following continuous reinforcement, extinction following intermittent reinforcement a. proceeds more slowly b. proceeds more rapidly c. occurs at the same rate d. is longer lasting
Factual LO 12 Page: 238 Correct = 49% **c**	122.	The behavior that would be most difficult to extinguish would be one that was a. reinforced every time it occurred b. shaped c. reinforced intermittently d. reinforced by your parents
Concept/Applied LO 12 Page: 238 Correct = 89% **a**	123.	Marie works in a dress factory where she earns $10 for each three dresses she hems. Marie is paid on a a. fixed-ratio schedule b. variable-ratio schedule c. fixed-interval schedule d. variable-interval schedule
Concept/Applied LO 12 Page: 238 **a**	124.	Maxwell runs a lawn care service and he charges his clients based on the square footage of their yard, rather than charging an hourly rate for his services. In this example, Maxwell is working on a. a fixed-ratio schedule of reinforcement b. a fixed-interval schedule of reinforcement c. a variable-ratio schedule of reinforcement d. a variable-interval schedule of reinforcement

Critical Thinking LO 12 Page: 238 **d**	125.	You are watching a rat pressing a lever in a Skinner box to obtain food pellets. The rat is pressing the lever at a very high rate, but it takes a break from lever pressing each time a food pellet is delivered. In this example, the reinforcement schedule that is in place is most likely a. a fixed-interval schedule b. a variable-ratio schedule c. a variable-interval schedule d. a fixed-ratio schedule
Factual LO 12 Page: 238 Correct = 74% **b**	126.	In a variable-ratio schedule, the reinforcer is given a. after a fixed number of nonreinforced responses b. after a variable number of nonreinforced responses c. for the first response that occurs after a fixed amount of time has elapsed d. for the first response that occurs after a variable amount of time has elapsed
Concept/Applied LO 12 Page: 238 **c**	127.	Shaquille is a professional basketball player. He never knows for sure which of his shots will result in a basket, but the more shots he takes the more baskets he makes. In this example, Shaquille's shooting is being reinforced on a. a fixed-ratio schedule b. a fixed-interval schedule c. a variable-ratio schedule d. a variable-interval schedule
Critical Thinking LO 12 Page: 238 **b**	128.	You are watching a rat pressing a lever in a Skinner box to obtain food pellets. The rat is pressing the lever at a very high rate, and does not stop, even when a food pellet is delivered. In this example, the reinforcement schedule that is in place is most likely a. a fixed-interval schedule b. a variable-ratio schedule c. a fixed-ratio schedule d. a variable-interval schedule
Concept/Applied LO 12 Page: 238 **d**	129.	The newest winning numbers in the state lottery are announced on the local television station every Saturday night, at the end of the news hour. People who are watching for the lottery numbers, will have their "watching" reinforced on a. a fixed-ratio schedule b. a variable-ratio schedule c. a variable-interval schedule d. a fixed-interval schedule
Critical Thinking LO 12 Page: 238 **b**	130.	You are watching a rat pressing a lever in a Skinner box to obtain food pellets. The rat pauses for a long time after each food pellet is delivered, but slowly increases its rate of lever pressing as more time elapses. In this example, the reinforcement schedule that is in place is most likely a. a variable-ratio schedule b. a fixed-interval schedule c. a variable-interval schedule d. a fixed-ratio schedule
Concept/Applied LO 12 Page: 239 **a**	131.	Josiah checks his electronic mail several times throughout the day. Some days there is mail each time he checks; sometimes several days go by with no new messages arriving. In this example, Josiah's behavior of checking his electronic mail is being reinforced on a. a variable-interval schedule b. a fixed-ratio schedule c. a fixed-interval schedule d. a variable-ratio schedule

Critical Thinking
LO 12
Page: 239
c

132. You are watching a rat pressing a lever in a Skinner box to obtain food pellets. The rat is pressing the lever at a slow, steady rate, but it does not stop, even when a food pellet is delivered. In this example, the reinforcement schedule that is in place is most likely
a. a variable-ratio schedule
b. a fixed-interval schedule
c. a variable-interval schedule
d. a fixed-ratio schedule

Concept/Applied
LO 12
Page: 239
Correct = 78%
c

133. Mary takes a course in which she is tested every two weeks. Her studying falls off right after a test, followed by a gradual increase to a rapid rate of studying as the next test approaches. Her studying conforms to the typical pattern of responding maintained on _____ schedules.
a. fixed-ratio
b. variable-ratio
c. fixed-interval
d. variable-interval

Concept/Applied
LO 12
Page: 239
Correct = 25%
c

134. Given the same frequency of reinforcement, _____ schedules generate higher rates of responding than do _____ schedules.
a. interval; ratio
b. fixed; variable
c. ratio; interval
d. variable; fixed

Factual
LO 13
Page: 240
a

135. Two or more reinforcement schedules that operate simultaneously and independently, each for a different response, are termed
a. concurrent schedules of reinforcement
b. classical-operant schedules of reinforcement
c. variable-fixed schedules of reinforcement
d. interval-ratio schedules of reinforcement

Critical Thinking
LO 13
Page: 240
b

136. Donavon is trying to decide whether he should spend the evening studying for his Economics midterm or researching the term paper for his History class. In making his choice, Donavon must choose between
a. positive and negative reinforcement
b. concurrent schedules of reinforcement
c. punishment and reinforcement
d. classical and operant conditioning

Factual
LO 13
Page: 240
c

137. The matching law states that under concurrent schedules of reinforcement, organisms' relative rate of responding to each alternative
a. tends to increase steadily over time
b. tends to decrease steadily over time
c. tends to match each alternative's relative rate of reinforcement
d. tends to fluctuate randomly across the alternatives

Factual
LO 13
Page: 241
d

138. According to optimal foraging theory, predatory animals will usually
a. pursue small prey that requires little effort to catch
b. pursue large prey that requires greater effort to catch
c. pursue small prey only if foraging in large groups
d. maximize nutritional value relative to the energy they expend in hunting

LEARNING THROUGH CONDITIONING

Factual LO 14 Page: 241 Correct = 93% a	139.	Positive reinforcement involves a. the presentation of a pleasant stimulus b. the presentation of an unpleasant stimulus c. the removal of a pleasant stimulus d. the removal of an unpleasant stimulus
Concept/Applied LO 14 Page: 241 c	140.	Tessa really likes to mow the lawn during the summer months, but her parents will only let her mow the lawn if all the dishes are washed. Consequently, every Saturday Tessa has the table cleared and all the dishes washed as soon as everyone has finished breakfast. In this case a. mowing the lawn is a negative reinforcer for doing the dishes b. doing the dishes is a positive reinforcer for mowing the lawn c. mowing the lawn is a positive reinforcer for doing the dishes d. doing the dishes is a negative reinforcer for mowing the lawn
Concept/Applied LO 14 Page: 241 d	141.	When Skyler was first training Smooches, his dog, to heel he would give Smooches a treat when she stayed close during walks. Now Smooches stays right by Skyler's side, even when she is not on her leash. In this case a. the dog treats were negative reinforcers for staying close b. the staying close was a positive reinforcer for receiving dog treats c. the staying close was a negative reinforcer for receiving dog treats d. the dog treats were positive reinforcers for staying close
Factual LO 14 Page: 241 Correct = 61% d	142.	Negative reinforcement involves a. the presentation of a pleasant stimulus b. the presentation of an unpleasant stimulus c. the removal of a pleasant stimulus d. the removal of an unpleasant stimulus
Concept/Applied LO 14 Page: 241 Correct = 68% d	143.	Your teenaged daughter has not cleaned her room in a month. You go in and begin yelling at her to clean her room. She begins to clean up, and you stop yelling. Your daughter's cleaning behavior can be viewed as responding to a. classical conditioning b. positive reinforcement c. punishers d. negative reinforcement
Concept/Applied LO 14 Page: 241 Correct = 63% c	144.	Which of the following is an example of negative reinforcement? a. giving a child a sweet dessert as a reward for finishing his dinner b. paying a child $1 for each "A" received on her report card c. stopping nagging a child when he finally cleans his room d. cutting a child's TV time by 30 minutes each time she "talks back"
Concept/Applied LO 14 Page: 241 b	145.	A student who studies in order to earn high grades is working for _____; a student who studies in order to avoid low grades is working for _____. a. negative reinforcement; positive reinforcement b. positive reinforcement; negative reinforcement c. negative reinforcement; negative reinforcement d. positive reinforcement; positive reinforcement
Concept/Applied LO 14 Page: 241 a	146.	Henry got a bad sunburn on his face when he was skiing last winter. Now, before he starts a day of skiing he uses a sunscreen on his face to prevent another sunburn. In this case, avoiding a sunburn functions as a. a negative reinforcer for using a sunscreen b. a positive reinforcer for using a sunscreen c. a conditioned stimulus for using a sunscreen d. an unconditioned stimulus for using a sunscreen

Concept/Applied LO 14 Page: 241 **d**	147.	McKenna had an unplanned pregnancy when she was 19 years old. Following her pregnancy McKenna started taking a birth control pill each day to prevent another pregnancy. In this case a. preventing a pregnancy acts as a positive reinforcer for taking birth control pills b. taking birth control pills acts as a negative reinforcer for preventing a pregnancy c. taking birth control pills acts as a positive reinforcer for preventing a pregnancy d. preventing a pregnancy acts as a negative reinforcer for taking birth control pills
Factual LO 15 Page: 242 **b**	148.	Escape learning is a type of learning in which a. an organism's responding is influenced by the observation of others' behavior b. an organism engages in a response that brings aversive stimulation to an end c. a neutral stimulus acquires the ability to elicit a response that was originally elicited by another stimulus d. an organism engages in a response that prevents aversive stimulation from occurring
Concept/Applied LO 15 Page: 242 Correct = 92% **b**	149.	A rat is placed on one side of a two-compartment shuttle box. On each trial, a light is turned on and is followed 10 seconds later by a painful electric shock for one minute. The rat can terminate the trial by jumping a barrier into the other compartment. If the rat jumps during the light, it has learned to _____ the shock; if the rat jumps during the shock, it has learned to _____ the shock. a. escape; avoid b. avoid; escape c. escape; escape d. avoid; avoid
Concept/Applied LO 15 Page: 242 **b**	150.	Nolan has learned to drink a cup of coffee whenever he gets a tension headache because drinking coffee makes the pain of the headache go away. This is an example of a. avoidance learning b. escape learning c. positive reinforcement d. classical conditioning
Concept/Applied LO 15 Page: 242 **a**	151.	Hanna finds that when her kids become too rowdy and noisy, she can successfully block out their noise if she closes the door to her study. In this example, closing the door is an example of a. an escape response b. an avoidance response c. an unconditioned response d. positive reinforcement
Factual LO 15 Page: 242 Correct = 74% **c**	152.	Escape conditioning is maintained by a. modeling b. punishment c. negative reinforcement d. positive reinforcement
Factual LO 15 Page: 242 Correct = 65% **a**	153.	Avoidance conditioning is maintained by a. negative reinforcement b. positive reinforcement c. punishment d. modeling

Factual
LO 15
Page: 242
d

154. Acquiring a behavior that prevents the occurrence of an aversive event is
    a. escape learning
    b. negative reinforcement
    c. punishment learning
    d. avoidance learning

Concept/Applied
LO 15
Page: 242
d

155. Brenda has learned to take an over-the-counter medication 30 minutes before she eats a spicy meal. When she does this she is able to prevent the heartburn and indigestion that she would experience otherwise. This is an example of
    a. escape conditioning
    b. positive reinforcement
    c. classical conditioning
    d. avoidance conditioning

Concept/Applied
LO 15
Page: 242
Correct = 86%
a

156. When Jackie watches slasher movies she covers her eyes when the blood starts to splatter; when Clarice watches slasher movies she covers her eyes as soon as she hears ominous music start to play. Jackie's response is consistent with _____ while Clarice's response is consistent with _____.
    a. escape responding; avoidance responding
    b. avoidance responding; escape responding
    c. negative reinforcement; positive reinforcement
    d. classical conditioning; operant conditioning

Concept/Applied
LO 16
Page: 243
Correct = 41%
d

157. In Mowrer's two-process theory of avoidance learning, the source of reinforcement for continued avoidance behavior is
    a. periodically receiving shock
    b. escaping shock
    c. fear not occurring
    d. reduction of conditioned fear

Factual
LO 16
Page: 243
Correct = 46%
c

158. According to Mowrer, the response of successfully avoiding a feared stimulus
    a. is classically conditioned
    b. is positively reinforced by a reduction in fear
    c. is negatively reinforced by a reduction in fear
    d. should quickly extinguish, since the feared stimulus never occurs

Factual
LO 17
Page: 243
Correct = 81%
c

159. Any event that follows a behavior and results in the behavior having a lower probability of happening in the future is known as
    a. negative reinforcer
    b. positive reinforcer
    c. punisher
    d. vicarious conditioner

Concept/Applied
LO 17
Page: 243
Correct = 38%
c

160. Jane, your teenage daughter, was ridiculed at school for wearing a particular style of shirt. Now she no longer wears that style of shirt at school. Being ridiculed is an example of
    a. negative reinforcement
    b. positive reinforcement
    c. punishment
    d. modeling

Concept/Applied
LO 17
Page: 243
a

161. Your spouse withdraws attention from you each time you begin criticizing her cooking. Eventually you stop criticizing your spouse's cooking. The withdrawal of attention can be categorized as
    a. punishment
    b. observational learning
    c. negative reinforcement
    d. modeling

Concept/Applied LO 17 Page: 243 **c**	162.	Miguel used to enjoy occasionally drinking a glass of red wine, but when he drank too much red wine at a friend's party a few months ago he woke up with a terrible hangover. Since then Miguel refuses to drink any red wine. In this case, Miguel's hangover acted as a. negative reinforcement for drinking red wine b. a conditioned response to wine drinking c. punishment for drinking red wine d. a secondary reinforcer for attending parties
Concept/Applied LO 17 Page: 243 **a**	163.	Angela used to really enjoy diving for her school team, but at their most recent diving practice she hit her head on the diving board during her last dive. Since then she hasn't attended any of the team practices, and she refuses to dive. In this case, hitting her head on the board acted as a. punishment for diving b. negative reinforcement for diving c. an unconditioned response to diving d. a discriminative stimulus for attending team practices
Factual LO 17 Page: 244 Correct = 75% **a**	164.	Negative reinforcement _____ the rate of a response; punishment _____ the rate of a response. a. increases; decreases b. decreases; increases c. increases; increases d. decreases; decreases
Concept/Applied LO 17 Page: 244 Correct = 68% **c**	165.	The difference between punishment and negative reinforcement is that a. punishment strengthens negative behavior while negative reinforcement weakens negative behavior b. punishment weakens negative behavior while negative reinforcement strengthens negative behavior c. punishment weakens behavior while negative reinforcement strengthens behavior d. there is no difference between punishment and negative reinforcement in their effects on behavior
Critical Thinking LO 17 Page: 244 **c**	166.	Typically, most people would a. enjoy being negatively reinforced or punished b. dislike being negatively reinforced or punished c. enjoy being negatively reinforced and dislike being punished d. enjoy being punished and dislike being negatively reinforced
Factual LO 18 Page: 246 Correct = 80% **b**	167.	When an animal's innate response tendencies interfere with the conditioning process, it is referred to as a. learned helplessness b. instinctive drift c. counterconditioning d. misbehavior
Concept/Applied LO 18 Page: 246 Correct = 80% **c**	168.	Breland and Breland's work with "miserly raccoons" demonstrated a. how principles of reinforcement (derived from studies of rats and pigeons) easily generalize to raccoons b. differences in appropriate rewards for different species c. that there are biologically imposed limits to the generality of conditioning principles d. that raccoons are less conditionable, and therefore less intelligent, than rats and pigeons

Concept/Applied LO 18 Page: 246 Correct = 74% a	169.	Breland's trained raccoons would deposit single tokens into a slot but would not deposit two tokens, which they rubbed together. This is due to a. instinctive drift to food-washing behavior b. poor conditioning of token placing c. insufficient reinforcement of token placing d. lack of interest in the single tokens
Concept/Applied LO 18 Page: 246 Correct = 29% d	170.	Which of the following most clearly shows that an animal's biological makeup greatly affects ease of learning an association? a. Pavlov's dogs, bells, and salivation b. Thorndike's cats in a puzzle box c. Skinner's rats in an operant chamber d. Seligman's sauce béarnaise phenomenon
Factual LO 18 Page: 246 Correct = 79% b	171.	The experience Seligman had with the sauce béarnaise was unique in that a. it suggested that generalization is more pervasive than originally thought b. a conditioned response was established even though there was a long delay between the conditioned stimulus and the unconditioned stimulus c. it appears that discriminative cues can lose their predictive influence in a fairly short period of time d. operant conditioning dynamics take precedence over classical conditioning principles
Factual LO 18 Page: 247 Correct = 76% d	172.	The studies of Garcia and his colleagues demonstrate that rats very easily learn to associate a taste CS with a. a shock UCS b. a visual UCS c. an auditory UCS d. a nausea-inducing UCS
Concept/Applied LO 18 Page: 247 Correct = 35% a	173.	You eat a new food and that night become ill with nausea and vomiting. Later you experience nausea whenever you taste or smell the new food. Why did you not associate your nausea with the cues of the room, the people present, the bathroom, the toilet, and so on? a. You were biologically predisposed to associate taste and nausea. b. The nontaste cues were too weak. c. The taste cues were more immediate. d. There was less contiguity for the other cues.
Concept/Applied LO 18 Page: 247 d	174.	Clara and Ashley ate dinner at a new restaurant last night. The entire restaurant was decorated in green, and the sound of waterfalls played in the background. Both Clara and Ashley ordered "trapper casserole," which tasted like nothing they had ever eaten before. Four hours after they had eaten they both became extremely ill and were taken to the hospital by ambulance, with the sirens wailing. Based on research conducted by Garcia and his colleagues, you might predict that in the future Clara and Ashley will both show conditioned responses to a. anything that is colored green b. the sound of falling water c. the sound of sirens d. foods that smell or taste like trapper casserole

Concept/Applied LO 18 Page: 247 Correct = 54% **b**	175.	The evolutionary history of rats has rendered them _____ to associate a taste CS with an illness UCS, and _____ to associate that same CS with an electric shock UCS. a. prepared; prepared b. prepared; unprepared c. unprepared; unprepared d. unprepared; prepared
Factual LO 18 Page: 248 Correct = 74% **a**	176.	A species-specific predisposition to be conditioned in certain ways and not others is referred to as a. preparedness b. sign-releasing predisposition c. reification d. phobia
Concept/Applied LO 18 Page: 248 **d**	177.	Zane has been shocked on six separate occasions while making toast. However, he doesn't seem to have developed a phobia toward toasters. Zane's only phobia is toward spiders, because he once had a big spider fall in his shirt when he was child. Zane's pattern of phobias illustrates the concept of a. signal relations b. negative avoidance c. superstitious responding d. preparedness
Concept/Applied LO 19 Page: 249 Correct = 32% **d**	178.	The evolutionary perspective on learning suggests that a. most species respond to classical conditioning, but only mammals show operant conditioning b. most species respond to operant conditioning, but only mammals show classical conditioning c. basic mechanisms of learning are unique for each species d. basic mechanisms of learning are similar across species
Concept/Applied LO 19 Page: 249 Correct = 87% **c**	179.	The evolutionary perspective on learning suggests that a. most species respond to classical conditioning, but only mammals show operant conditioning b. most species respond to operant conditioning, but only mammals show classical conditioning c. differences in the adaptive challenges faced by various species have led to some species-specific learning tendencies d. because all species face the same adaptive challenges, species-specific learning tendencies will disappear as a species evolves
Concept/Applied LO 20 Page: 249 Correct = 79% **d**	180.	Group A rats receive 30 paired buzzer-shock trials. Group B rats get the same, but also 20 more trials with shock alone (no buzzer). You would predict that a. Group A and B later show equal fear response to the buzzer b. Group B shows a stronger fear response to the buzzer c. Group A extinguishes fear to the buzzer more rapidly d. Group A shows a stronger fear response to the buzzer
Concept/Applied LO 20 Page: 249 Correct = 22% **d**	181.	According to Rescorla, the single best way to ensure a strong CR is to arrange that the CS a. remains constantly present throughout training b. be one that is well above the absolute threshold of the animal being trained c. always occurs simultaneously with presentations of the UCS d. be the most predictive signal of the UCS

Concept/Applied LO 20 Page: 249 **b**	182.	Rafael's brother always says, "I'm going to get you" just before he hits Rafael. Alan's brother sometimes says, "I'm going to get you" just before he hits Alan; other times he just hits Alan with no warning. Based on the work by Rescorla you should predict that when these boys hear the words, "I'm going to get you," Rafael will show a. an unconditioned response, while Alan will show a conditioned response b. a stronger conditioned response than Alan will show c. a weaker conditioned response than Alan will show d. a conditioned response, while Alan will show an unconditioned response
Critical Thinking LO 20 Page: 249 **c**	183.	A school in Kansas had always used a loud siren as a tornado warning to indicate students should seek shelter. Last summer, to accommodate the needs of hearing-impaired students, they enhanced the system and included a bright flashing light along with the siren. During one warning the sirens didn't function the way they were supposed to, and only the flashing light came on. The teachers were surprised that the students didn't seek shelter during the warning. This lack of response was likely the result of a. negative avoidance b. instinctive drift c. poor signal relations d. noncontingent reinforcement
Concept/Applied LO 21 Page: 250 Correct = 89% **d**	184.	Your younger daughter watches your older daughter wash the breakfast dishes. Later your younger daughter attempts to wash some dishes. The older daughter has acted as a. a noncontingent reinforcer b. a negative reinforcer c. a positive reinforcer d. a model
Concept/Applied LO 21 Page: 250 Correct = 97% **c**	185.	Learning that takes place by observing another person is referred to as a. operant conditioning b. noncontingent learning c. observational learning d. classical conditioning
Concept/Applied LO 21 Page: 251 **a**	186.	A three-year-old boy observes his father yelling at his mother every time she says something the father doesn't like. Based on principles of observational learning, in the future whenever the mother says something to the boy that the he does not like, the boy is most likely to do which of the following? a. yell at his mother b. yell at his sister c. go and tell his father what the mother said d. yell at his father
Factual LO 21 Page: 251 Correct = 55% **d**	187.	Which of the following statements is <u>true</u>? a. Observational learning is entirely separate from both classical and operant conditioning. b. Observational learning is a form of classical conditioning. c. Observational learning is a form of operant conditioning. d. Both classical and operant conditioning can take place vicariously through observational learning.

Concept/Applied LO 21 Page: 251 Correct = 97% c	188.	After watching his father wash the car, five-year-old Bob washes his bike. This is an example of a. superstitious behavior b. classical conditioning c. observational learning d. positive reinforcement
Factual LO 22 Page: 251 Correct = 40% c	189.	Which of the following focuses on or highlights the importance of cognitions in observational learning? a. reproduction of behavior b. motivation to perform the behavior c. retention of information d. ability to execute the behavior effectively
Concept/Applied LO 23 Page: 253 b	190.	The principles of learning and conditioning have a. turned out to have little relevance to real-world concerns b. been widely applied in education, business, and industry c. attracted little interest outside of psychology d. proven worthless when applied to humans as opposed to animals
Concept/Applied LO 23 Page: 253 Correct = 62% b	191.	Research on conditioning generally has demonstrated the importance of _____, but findings regarding the biological constraints on conditioning have shown that _____ is also very important. a. nature; nurture b. nurture, nature c. heredity; biology d. instincts; training
Concept/Applied LO 23 Page: 253 a	192.	The biological preparedness explanation for conditioned taste aversions illustrates which of your text's unifying themes? a. Heredity and environment jointly influence behavior. b. Our experience of the world is highly subjective. c. Psychology evolves in a sociohistorical context. d. Our behavior is shaped by our cultural heritage.
Concept/Applied LO 23 Page: 253 Correct = 67% b	193.	In today's business world, management often emphasizes positive reinforcement more than in the past. This illustrates which of your text's unifying themes? a. Our experience of the world is highly subjective. b. Psychology evolves in a sociohistorical context. c. Behavior is determined by multiple causes. d. Psychology is empirical.
Factual LO 24 Page: 256 Correct = 75% a	194.	Application of operant principles to solve behavior problems is generally known as a. behavior modification b. cognitive engineering c. modeling d. insight training
Concept/Applied LO 24 Page: 256 Correct = 45% d	195.	Which of the following goals is specified in an appropriate format for designing a self-modification program? a. increasing your motivation b. decreasing your irritability c. increasing your happiness d. stopping smoking

Factual LO 24 Page: 256 Correct = 75% **c**	196.	The first step in a behavior modification program is to a. gather baseline data b. specify the antecedents c. specify the target behavior d. design a program
Factual LO 24 Page: 257 **b**	197.	An antecedent in a behavior modification program is a. a source of a reinforcement b. an event that precedes a behavior c. a consequent of performing a behavior d. an emotional component associated with the receipt of reinforcement or punishment
Concept/Applied LO 24 Page: 257 Correct = 44% **a**	198.	Harold begins to chew his fingernails every time his teacher enters the classroom. In this case the antecedent is a. the teacher entering the classroom b. the fear associated with the teacher c. anticipated punishment d. chewing the fingernails
Concept/Applied LO 25 Page: 257 Correct = 42% **a**	199.	In setting up reinforcement contingencies in a self-modification program, you should a. choose a reinforcer that is readily available and relatively potent b. use delayed reinforcement c. arrange to reinforce yourself only after there has been a drastic change in the frequency of the target response d. use continuous rather than intermittent reinforcement
Factual LO 25 Page: 258 **b**	200.	A system for administering symbolic reinforcers that can later be exchanged for "genuine" reinforcers is referred to as a. vicarious conditioning b. a token economy c. a behavioral contract d. antecedent control
Factual LO 25 Page: 258 Correct = 42% **c**	201.	Which of the following is not a strategy for decreasing the frequency of an undesirable behavior? a. positive reinforcement for withholding the response b. punishment for making the response c. increasing exposure to antecedents of the response d. decreasing exposure to antecedents of the response
Factual LO 25 Page: 258 Correct = 76% **d**	202.	When using punishment in a self-modification program, you should a. make the punishment fairly severe b. increase the intensity of the punishment over time c. get a friend or family member to administer the punishment d. make sure you have the opportunity to earn some reinforcers, too
Concept/Applied LO 26 Page: 259 Correct = 83% **b**	203.	With most behavior modification programs, once a terminal goal has been reached, it is a good idea to a. stop the program abruptly b. phase the program out gradually by reducing the frequency or potency of the reinforcers c. switch from positive to negative reinforcement d. switch from a ratio to an interval schedule of reinforcement

Critical Thinking LO 27 Page: 261 **b**	204.	Tia wants to be the governor for her state. In all her television ads she plays patriotic music and has the American flag displayed in the background. If voters develop positive feelings toward Tia as a result of these ads, those positive feelings would represent a. an unconditioned response b. a conditioned response c. positive reinforcement d. negative reinforcement
Concept/Applied LO 27 Page: 261 **c**	205.	Bette creates a television ad that alternates between images of garbage dumps and people drinking in a bar. She is hoping that people who watch the ad will develop negative feelings toward drinking. Bette is relying on a. observational learning b. positive reinforcement c. classical conditioning d. negative reinforcement
Concept/Applied LO 27 Page: 261 **c**	206.	Marvin creates a television ad that alternates between images of garbage dumps and people drinking in a bar. He is hoping that people who watch the ad will develop negative feelings toward drinking after seeing these ads. In Marvin's ad the conditioned stimulus would be a. the images of garbage dumps b. people's feelings of disgust when viewing garbage c. the images of people drinking in a bar d. the feelings people have toward drinking before they see the ad
Critical Thinking LO 27 Page: 261 **d**	207.	Skyler creates a television ad that alternates between images of garbage dumps and people drinking in a bar. If people develop negative feelings about drinking as a result of watching Skyler's ad, those negative feelings would represent a. an unconditioned response b. positive reinforcement c. negative reinforcement d. a conditioned response
Integrative Correct = 64% **c**	208.	Stimulus discrimination is to stimulus generalization as reinforcement is to a. acquisition b. shaping c. punishment d. resistance
Integrative **b**	209.	If you devise a self-modification program in which you systematically reward yourself for studying, you are applying the principles of a. classical conditioning b. operant conditioning c. observational learning d. Pavlovian conditioning
Integrative Correct = 88% **a**	210.	Classical conditioning is to the autonomic nervous system as _____ is to the somatic nervous system. a. operant conditioning b. observational learning c. negative reinforcement d. partial reinforcement

Study Guide LO 1 Page: 223 **b**	211.	Sally developed a fear of balconies after almost falling from a balcony on a couple of occasions. What was the conditioned response? a. the balcony b. fear of the balcony c. almost falling d. fear resulting from almost falling
Study Guide LO 3 Page: 229 **d**	212.	When the UCS is removed and the CS is presented alone for a period of time, what will occur? a. classical conditioning b. generalization c. acquisition d. extinction
Study Guide LO 4 Page: 230 **c**	213.	Sally developed a fear of balconies from almost falling. Although she has had no dangerous experiences on bridges, cliffs, and the view from tall buildings, she now fears these stimuli as well. Which of the following is likely to have produced a fear of these other stimuli? a. instinctive drift b. spontaneous recovery c. generalization d. discrimination
Study Guide LO 9 Page: 235 **a**	214.	A researcher reinforces closer and closer approximations to a target behavior. What is the name of the procedure she is using? a. shaping b. classical conditioning c. discrimination training d. extinction
Study Guide LO 10 Page: 236 **a**	215.	John says, "Please pass the salt." Ralph passes the salt. "Thank you," says John. John's request precedes a behavior (salt passing) that is reinforced ("Thank you"). Thus, the request "Please pass the salt" is a _____ for passing the salt. a. discriminative stimulus b. response c. positive reinforcer d. conditioned stimulus (CS)
Study Guide LO 12 Page: 239 **d**	216.	A rat is reinforced for the first lever-pressing response that occurs, on the average, after 60 seconds. Which schedule is the rat on? a. FR b. VR c. FI d. VI
Study Guide LO 15 Page: 242 **b**	217.	When the rat presses a lever, the mild electric shock on the cage floor is turned off. What procedure is being used? a. punishment b. escape c. discrimination training d. avoidance
Study Guide LO 16 Page: 243 **b**	218.	In the two-process explanation of avoidance, the cue stimulus acquires the capacity to elicit fear through the process of a. operant conditioning b. classical conditioning c. generalization d. discrimination

Study Guide
LO 17
Page: 243
c

219. The contingencies are as follows: if the response occurs, a stimulus is presented; if the response does not occur, the stimulus is not presented. Under this procedure the strength of the response decreases. What procedure is being used?
a. positive reinforcement
b. negative reinforcement
c. punishment
d. avoidance training

Study Guide
LO 18
Page: 246
a

220. In terms of the traditional view of conditioning, research on conditioned taste aversion was surprising because
a. there was a very long delay between CS and UCS
b. the dislike of a particular taste was operantly conditioned
c. conditioning occurred to all stimuli present when the food was consumed
d. the sense of taste seems to be relatively weak

Online Quiz
LO 1
Page: 223
d

221. Classical conditioning is a type of learning in which
a. responses come to be controlled by their consequences
b. an organism's responding is influenced by the observation of others' behavior
c. an organism engages in a response that brings aversive stimulation to an end
d. a neutral stimulus acquires the ability to elicit a response that was originally elicited by another stimulus

Online Quiz
LO 3
Page: 228
c

222. When the CS occurs just before the UCS and stops at the same time as the UCS, the arrangement is called
a. simultaneous conditioning
b. trace conditioning
c. short-delayed conditioning
d. backward conditioning

Online Quiz
LO 4
Page: 230
c

223. When shown a Santa Claus beard, Little Albert showed evidence of
a. stimulus discrimination
b. superstitious behavior
c. stimulus generalization
d. extinction

Online Quiz
LO 7
Page: 232
c

224. Responses that are followed by satisfying consequences increase in probability. This is a statement of Thorndike's law of
a. exercise
b. contiguity
c. effect
d. operants

Online Quiz
LO 11
Page: 237
d

225. When Diana finished washing the supper dishes, her mother gave her a dollar. In this case, the dollar can be viewed as a _____ if it leads to Diana _____ in the future.
a. discriminative reinforcer; washing other things (such as clothes)
b. primary reinforcer; having an increased probability of washing the dishes
c. negative reinforcer; having a decreased probability of washing the dishes
d. secondary reinforcer; having an increased probability of washing the dishes

Online Quiz
LO 12
Page: 238
a

226. A salesperson earns a commission for each item of clothing she sells. Commission on the clothing sales is an example of which type of reinforcement schedule?
a. fixed-ratio
b. variable-interval
c. fixed-interval
d. variable-ratio

Online Quiz
LO 14
Page: 241
a

227. Negative reinforcement
a. is the removal of an aversive condition following a response
b. weakens the preceding behavior
c. is the onset of an aversive condition following a response
d. works just the opposite to positive reinforcement

Online Quiz
LO 17
Page: 244
b

228. Which of the following statements about punishment is not correct?
a. Punishment may take the form of removal of a rewarding stimulus.
b. Punishment occurs whenever a response terminates an aversive condition.
c. Punishment may take the form of giving aversive stimulation after a response.
d. Punishment, by definition, weakens preceding behavior.

Online Quiz
LO 22
Page: 251
b

229. According to Bandura, your motivation to perform an observed response depends on
a. the amount of attention you paid to the model's behavior originally
b. your expectation of being reinforced for the response
c. the degree to which you can remember the model's behavior
d. your ability to perform the observed response

Online Quiz
LO 26
Page: 259
a

230. A successful self-modification program may end spontaneously when
a. the new, improved patterns of behavior become self-reinforcing
b. a new behavior problem suddenly takes the place of the old one
c. the reinforcer loses its effectiveness
d. the frequency of the target behavior drops to zero

ESSAY QUESTIONS

1. Explain how a specific phobia could be acquired through classical conditioning, being sure to identify the unconditioned stimulus, unconditioned response, conditioned stimulus, and conditioned response in your example. Also, using classical conditioning, indicate how the phobia could be eliminated.

   Example of an appropriate response

   NS - - - - - - - - - - - - - - - UCS ----> UCR
   dog approaches   dog bites   fear

   CS ----------------> CR (fear may generalize to other dogs, particularly dogs that resemble the one that bit you)
   dog approaches   fear

   Fear can be eliminated by extinction-exposure to the CS without the expected UCS (in this example, exposure to dogs that do not bite).

2. Provide specific, everyday examples (for instance, from child-rearing) of the following operant-conditioning phenomena: positive reinforcement, negative reinforcement, and punishment.

   In evaluating students' examples, make certain they know the difference between negative reinforcement (removal of an aversive-stimulus contingent on a desirable response) and punishment (presentation of an aversive-stimulus contingent on an undesirable response or removal of a pleasant stimulus contingent on an undesirable response).

3. Compare the acquisition procedures in classical and operant conditioning. What is the essential difference between the two types of conditioning?

   In classical conditioning, a neutral stimulus is repeatedly paired with an unconditioned stimulus until the once-neutral stimulus becomes conditioned--that is, capable of eliciting the same response as the UCS. Thus the procedure sets up a contingency between two stimuli. The reinforcer (UCS) is contingent on the neutral stimulus (later, the CS) having been presented, not on any specific behavior of the organism. In operant conditioning, a specific response is targeted and is paired with a consequent stimulus. In positive reinforcement, for example, the subject must make the target response in order to earn the reinforcer. Similarly, in punishment, delivery of an aversive stimulus is contingent on performance of a designated response. Thus, in operant conditioning, consequent stimuli are contingent on the operant response; in classical conditioning, UCSs are contingent on the conditioned stimulus.

4. Briefly describe observational learning, and explain how it relates to classical and operant conditioning.

   Observational learning occurs when an organism's behavior is influenced by having watched the behavior of another organism (a "model"). In order for observational learning to take place, the organism must (1) pay attention to the behavior of the model, (2) remember the behavior of the model, (3) be capable of imitating the model's behavior, and (4) be motivated to imitate the model's behavior.

   Observational learning is not independent of classical and operant conditioning, but rather allows for the possibility that both types of conditioning can take place vicariously through watching another organism be conditioned. Thus, you may acquire a phobia by observing someone else's classically conditioned fear response; or you may acquire a new operant after observing someone else be rewarded for this response.

5. Design a self-modification program to improve your study habits.

   Make sure that observable target responses are specified (for example, study at least two hours each night), as opposed to personality traits; that time is set aside to monitor baseline frequencies of these responses; that realistic, obtainable reinforcers (or punishers) are selected and are related appropriately to the target responses; that the student knows the conditions under which the program can be terminated (for example, studying has become self-sustaining due to improved grades).

This page intentionally left blank.

Chapter Seven
Human Memory

LEARNING OBJECTIVES

1. List and describe the three basic human memory processes.
2. Discuss the role of attention in memory, and contrast the early- and late-selection theories of attention.
3. Describe the three levels of information processing proposed by Craik and Lockhart.
4. Discuss three techniques for enriching encoding and research on each.
5. Describe the role of the sensory store in memory.
6. Discuss the characteristics of short-term memory.
7. Describe Baddely's model of working memory.
8. Evaluate the hypothesis that all memories are stored permanently in long-term memory.
9. Explain the issues in the debate about whether short-term and long-term memory are really separate.
10. Describe conceptual hierarchies, schemas, and semantic networks, and their role in long-term memory.
11. Describe schemas and scripts and their role in long-term memory.
12. Explain how retrieval cues and context cues influence retrieval.
13. Discuss Bartlett's work and research on the misinformation effect.
14. Discuss the implications of evidence on source monitoring and reality monitoring.
15. Describe Ebbinghaus' forgetting curve and three measures of retention.
16. Explain how forgetting may be due to ineffective encoding.
17. Compare and contrast decay and interference as potential causes of forgetting.
18. Explain how forgetting may be due to factors in the retrieval process.
19. Summarize evidence for the view that most recovered memories of childhood sexual abuse are genuine.
20. Summarize evidence for the view that most recovered memories of childhood sexual abuse are inaccurate.
21. Describe the Featured Study on the creation of hypnotic pseudomemories.
22. Summarize evidence on the biochemistry and neural circuitry underlying memory.
23. Distinguish between two types of amnesia and identify the anatomical structures implicated in memory.
24. Distinguish between implicit versus explicit memory and their relationship to declarative versus procedural memory.
25. Explain the distinctions between episodic versus semantic memory and prospective versus retrospective memory.
26. Explain how the chapter highlighted two of the text's unifying themes.
27. Discuss the importance of rehearsal, distributed practice, and interference in efforts to improve everyday memory.
28. Discuss the value of deep processing, transfer-appropriate processing, and good organization in efforts to improve everyday memory.
29. Describe some verbal and visual mnemonic devices that can be used to improve everyday memory.
30. Explain how hindsight bias and overconfidence contribute to the frequent inaccuracy of eyewitness testimony.

MULTIPLE-CHOICE QUESTIONS

Factual
LO 1
Page: 265
a

1. The three basic processes in memory are
   a. encoding, storage, and retrieval
   b. acoustic, semantic, and eidetic
   c. recall, recognition, and relearning
   d. sensation, perception, and cognition

Factual
LO 1
Page: 265
a

2. Which of the following terms does <u>not</u> refer to a basic process of memory?
   a. inclusion
   b. retrieval
   c. storage
   d. encoding

Concept/Applied
LO 1
Page: 265
Correct = 93%
d

3. In order for a memory to be stored it must first be
   a. ablated
   b. modeled
   c. retrieved
   d. encoded

Concept/Applied
LO 1
Page: 266
c

4. If you were attempting to recall a memory, the memory process you would be using is
   a. encoding
   b. storage
   c. retrieval
   d. acquisition

Factual
LO 1
Page: 266
Correct = 98%
a

5. The process of recalling information from memory is referred to as
   a. retrieval
   b. encoding
   c. storage
   d. information registry

Concept/Applied
LO 1
Page: 266
Correct = 91%
b

6. The order of the basic memory processes in which information enters our memory system and is used later is
   a. encoding->retrieval->storage
   b. encoding->storage->retrieval
   c. storage->retrieval->acquisition
   d. acquisition->encoding->retrieval

Concept/Applied
LO 1
Page: 266
d

7. Shayla is able to retain the vocabulary she learned in her first semester Spanish class after the class has ended. The main memory process that accounts for the fact that Shayla can hold information in her memory for extended periods of time is
   a. encoding
   b. retrieval
   c. chunking
   d. storage

Factual
LO 2
Page: 267
Correct = 81%
b

8. _____ involves focusing awareness on a narrow range of stimuli or events.
   a. Encoding
   b. Attention
   c. Elaboration
   d. Clustering

198   CHAPTER SEVEN

Factual LO 2 Page: 267 Correct = 78% **c**	9.	Most theories of attention a. emphasize the nonselective nature of the process b. propose that our attention is distributed equally among all stimulus inputs c. liken it to a filter that screens out most potential stimuli while allowing a select few to pass through d. assume that the vast majority of potential stimuli reach conscious awareness
Factual LO 2 Page: 267 Correct = 68% **a**	10.	"Early-selection" theories of attention propose that a. stimuli are screened out before the brain processes the meaning of sensory input b. stimuli are screened out after the brain processes the meaning of sensory input c. attention is distributed equally among all stimulus inputs that are above threshold d. stimuli are screened out before they reach the sense organs
Factual LO 2 Page: 268 **d**	11.	Which statement best represents current thinking about early- versus late-selection theories of attention? a. The preponderance of evidence supports early selection. b. The preponderance of evidence supports late selection. c. The preponderance of evidence supports intermediate selection. d. The location of the attention filter may be flexible.
Factual LO 3 Page: 268 **a**	12.	A memory code that emphasizes the physical structure of the stimulus is called a(n) _____ code. a. structural b. phonemic c. semantic d. episodic
Factual LO 3 Page: 268 Correct = 55% **c**	13.	_____ code is a memory code that emphasizes the meaning of verbal input. a. A structural b. A phonemic c. A semantic d. An episodic
Factual LO 3 Page: 268 Correct = 70% **d**	14.	Which of the following sequences represents progressively deeper levels of processing? a. phonemic, semantic, structural b. structural, semantic, phonemic c. semantic, phonemic, structural d. structural, phonemic, semantic
Critical Thinking LO 3 Page: 268 **a**	15.	Kiana was given a list of words as part of a memory test that included: "dog, pail, and hate." Later, she recalled these words as: "dig, paint, and hard." Kiana's errors in recall suggest that she had encoded the original word list a. phonemically b. semantically c. implicitly d. structurally
Factual LO 3 Page: 268 Correct = 72% **d**	16.	Which of the following was not a level of processing associated with verbal information as suggested by Craik and Lockhart (1972)? a. semantic b. structural c. phonemic d. functional

Factual LO 3 Page: 268 Correct = 82% **b**	17.	The deepest level of processing of information in memory, emphasizing the meaning of the information being processed, is a. the triarchic level of encoding b. the semantic level of encoding c. attentional encoding d. dyadic encoding
Concept/Applied LO 3 Page: 268 Correct = 68% **c**	18.	Which level of processing results in longer-lasting memory codes? a. structural encoding b. mnemonic encoding c. semantic encoding d. phonemic encoding
Concept/Applied LO 3 Page: 268 Correct = 89% **b**	19.	In which level of processing is an emphasis placed on the sounds of words? a. morphemic b. phonemic c. mnemonic d. platonic
Factual LO 4 Page: 269 **d**	20.	Elaboration involves a. the creation of visual images to represent the words to be remembered b. decreasing the complexity of the material to be remembered c. forming two kinds of memory code for each word d. linking a stimulus to other information at the time of encoding
Concept/Applied LO 4 Page: 269 **a**	21.	Visual imagery may facilitate memory because it a. provides a second kind of memory code and two codes are better than one b. increases the personal meaningfulness of the material to be remembered c. increases the complexity of the material to be remembered d. is easier to recall visual images than words
Concept/Applied LO 4 Page: 269 Correct = 45% **a**	22.	The use of imagery, according to Paivio, facilitates the encoding of a. concrete objects b. abstract ideas c. semantic bases d. all of these equally
Concept/Applied LO 4 Page: 269 **b**	23.	Karina is given a list of words to memorize, and she forms a mental image of each word on the list. Calvin is given the same list of words, and he thinks of words that rhyme with each of the words on the list. Based on the research that has focused on the process of encoding, you should expect that on a memory test a. both Karina and Calvin will recall the same number of words b. Karina will recall more words than Calvin c. Calvin will recall more words than Karina d. Karina is more likely to make "look-alike" errors in recall
Concept/Applied LO 4 Page: 270 Correct = 59% **a**	24.	The dual-coding theory argues that memory is a. enhanced by forming either semantic or visual codes b. composed of declarative and procedural elements c. composed of episodic and semantic codes d. composed of schematic and nonschematic elements
Factual LO 4 Page: 270 Correct = 91% **b**	25.	Self-referent encoding involves a. the creation of visual images to represent the words to be remembered b. making the material to be remembered personally meaningful c. forming two kinds of memory codes for each word d. linking a stimulus to other information at the time of encoding

Concept/Applied LO 4 Page: 270 Correct = 82% **b**	26.	With _____, personally relevant information is recalled better in the future relative to other forms of encoding. a. structural encoding b. self-referent encoding c. mnemonics d. semantics
Concept/Applied LO 5 Page: 270 **c**	27.	In their efforts to understand memory storage, theorists have historically related it to a. the change of seasons b. the water in a stream c. the technologies of their age d. a library of documents
Factual LO 5 Page: 270 Correct = 86% **d**	28.	The Atkinson-Shiffrin memory model proposes that memory has a. sensory, short-term, medium-term, and long-term stores b. short-, medium-, and long-term stores c. four different memory stores d. sensory, short-term, and long-term stores
Concept/Applied LO 5 Page: 271 Correct = 56% **a**	29.	The type of memory where information is stored for the shortest period of time is a. sensory memory b. short-term memory c. long-term memory d. working memory
Critical Thinking LO 5 Page: 271 **c**	30.	Which of the following statements regarding sensory memory is <u>not</u> accurate? a. Information can be stored in sensory memory for only a fraction of a second. b. Sensory memory is the first component of the memory system. c. Sensory memory preserves information according to the acoustic properties of the stimulus. d. Sensory memory can preserve information from a variety of sensory modalities (e.g., visual, auditory).
Factual LO 5 Page: 271 **d**	31.	Which of the following researchers conducted a classic experiment that demonstrated the brief duration of information in sensory memory? a. Richard Atkinson b. Hermann Ebbinghaus c. George Miller d. George Sperling
Factual LO 5 Page: 271 **d**	32.	A sensory memory a. usually lasts for about 30 seconds b. can be maintained by rehearsal c. is usually stored acoustically d. gives you additional time to try to recognize a stimulus
Critical Thinking LO 6 Page: 271 **a**	33.	Which of the following statements regarding short-term memory (STM) is <u>not</u> accurate? a. The capacity of STM is limited to about 30 items of information. b. STM can maintain unrehearsed information for about 20 seconds. c. STM is the second component of the memory system. d. Through rehearsal, information in STM can be stored indefinitely.

Concept/Applied LO 6 Page: 271 Correct = 75% c	34.	When you listen to a lecture, the information is held in _____ memory until you write it in your notes. a. trace b. sensory c. short-term d. long-term
Factual LO 6 Page: 271 b	35.	Information can be maintained indefinitely in short-term memory through the process of a. retrieval b. rehearsal c. encoding d. chunking
Factual LO 6 Page: 272 c	36.	With rehearsal, information in short-term memory can be maintained for some time. Without rehearsal, the duration of short-term memory is a. no longer than 1 second b. about 5 seconds c. about 20 seconds d. 1-2 minutes
Concept/Applied LO 6 Page: 272 Correct = 83% b	37.	You are absorbed in reading your psychology text when the phone rings. After talking on the phone, you can't remember the last thing you read. This information was lost from _____ memory, because the phone conversation distracted you from _____ the information. a. sensory; perceiving b. short-term; rehearsing c. long-term; rehearsing d. long-term; retrieving
Factual LO 6 Page: 272 c	38.	Which of the following researchers is known for identifying the capacity of short-term memory as "seven plus or minus two" items? a. Richard Atkinson b. Hermann Ebbinghaus c. George Miller d. George Sperling
Concept/Applied LO 6 Page: 272 b	39.	As Kayla was introduced to the seven members of the committee who would be interviewing her for a scholarship, she silently repeated all the names to herself, in order. Kayla was using a. chunking to increase the capacity of her short-term memory b. rehearsal to temporarily store the names in short-term memory c. filtering to temporarily bloc other information out of short-term memory d. acoustic encoding to process the names semantically
Concept/Applied LO 6 Page: 272 d	40.	Mark is listening as his roommate lists 14 things that they need to buy for their apartment before the end of the week. Based on George Miller's research into the capacity of short-term memory, if Mark doesn't write the items down as he hears them, he is <u>most</u> likely to remember a. less than 5 of the items from the list b. approximately 10 to 12 items from the list c. the entire list d. between 5 and 9 items from the list

Factual LO 6 Page: 272 **d**	41.	The "magic number seven" describes the a. duration of STM b. number of units that may be encoded in LTM at one time c. most frequently occurring number on a set of dice d. capacity of STM
Concept/Applied LO 6 Page: 273 Correct = 89% **b**	42.	Which of the following lists of letters would be easier for a person to maintain in short-term memory? a. CVX JLA DQS KRO GWN b. ABC CIA IRS XYZ FCC c. FL IJN A MKQR DW XGUH d. All of these could be kept in short-term memory with equal ease.
Factual LO 7 Page: 273 Correct = 62% **b**	43.	Which memory system is referred to in your text as "working memory"? a. sensory memory b. short-term memory c. long-term memory d. all of these collectively
Concept/Applied LO 7 Page: 273 Correct = 91% **a**	44.	When you mentally picture the road between your house and school, you are relying on which component of working memory? a. the visuospatial sketchpad b. the conceptual hierarchy c. the rehearsal loop d. the executive control system
Factual LO 7 Page: 273 Correct = 36% **b**	45.	Baddely's concept of working memory a. integrates sensory memory, short-term memory, and long-term memory into a single, complex system b. expands the functions and processes of short-term memory c. takes the place of the old concept of sensory memory d. expands the functions and processes of long-term memory
Factual LO 7 Page: 273 Correct = 30% **b**	46.	According to Baddely, short-term or working memory consists of all but which of the following components? a. a rehearsal loop b. a feature-detection element c. a visuospatial sketchpad d. an executive control system
Concept/Applied LO 7 Page: 274 **a**	47.	Mia was trying to figure out how to fit the box that contained her new computer into the trunk of her car. She mentally manipulated the position of the box, trying to figure out a way to make it fit. Based on Baddely's model of working memory, Mia was utilizing a. the visuospatial sketchpad to mentally manipulate the box's position b. the rehearsal loop while she worked repeatedly on the problem c. the executive control system to juggle all the information she needed to consider d. her prospective memory to remember the actions she would need to perform
Concept/Applied LO 7 Page: 274 Correct = 44% **a**	48.	The ability of people to "juggle" information in working memory in order to reason and make decisions is the _____ component of working memory. a. executive control system b. rehearsal loop c. visual imagery d. schematic

Concept/Applied LO 8 Page: 274 **b**	49.	The memory system that has an almost unlimited storage capacity is a. time-based memory b. long-term memory c. working memory d. auditory sensory memory
Factual LO 8 Page: 274 **d**	50.	Flashbulb memories are a. memories for information b. memories for actions, skills, and operations c. chronological recollections of personal experiences d. unusually vivid and detailed recollections of momentous events
Factual LO 8 Page: 274 **b**	51.	Unusually vivid and detailed recollections of momentous events are called a. episodic memories b. flashbulb memories c. sensory memories d. nondeclarative memories
Concept/Applied LO 8 Page: 274 **a**	52.	In Serena's law class they are discussing high-profile cases and when they get to the O. J. Simpson case, Serena suddenly has a vivid memory of watching the white Bronco driving slowly down the freeway. She feels like she can recall every detail of that night, right down to the snacks she and her roommate were eating. This would be an example of a. a flashbulb memory b. sensory memory c. procedural memory d. an implicit memory
Concept/Applied LO 8 Page: 274 **d**	53.	Evidence for the notion that LTM storage may be permanent includes a. the fact that everyone has memories that have lasted over a great many years b. the existence of flashbulb memories c. reports of exceptional recall through hypnosis d. all of these findings
Critical Thinking LO 8 Page: 274 **c**	54.	Which of the following statements regarding the storage of information in long-term memory is <u>not</u> accurate? a. Flashbulb memories tend to become less detailed and complete with time. b. Electrical stimulation of the brain (ESB) can elicit descriptions of past events. c. Hypnosis-aided recollections of age-regressed subjects are remarkably accurate. d. Psychologists cannot absolutely rule out the possibility that all memories are stored permanently in long-term memory.
Factual LO 9 Page: 275 **a**	55.	A handful of theorists have questioned the concept of sensory memory on the grounds that a. it may be nothing more than perceptual processes at work b. information doesn't last long enough to be tested c. it really isn't all that different from short-term memory d. it seems to work only for auditory stimuli
Factual LO 9 Page: 275 **d**	56.	A large number of theorists have questioned the concept of short-term memory on the grounds that a. its capacity is simply too limited b. information in short-term memory doesn't last long enough to be tested c. it really isn't all that different from sensory memory d. it really isn't all that different from long-term memory

Critical Thinking LO 9 Page: 275 a	57.	Which of the following statements regarding the current view of short-term memory and long-term memory is accurate? a. The view that short-term memory and long-term memory are separate is widely accepted. b. The effect of interference applies only to information in long-term memory. c. Information actually lasts longer in short-term memory than in long-term memory. d. Information in short-term memory can be encoded semantically as well as phonemically.
Factual LO 10 Page: 275 Correct = 76% d	58.	Which of the following statements is true? a. Long-term memories are generally stored in a completely random fashion. b. Long-term memory stores are organized as systematically and efficiently as a well-run library. c. Organization of information in long-term memory is unnecessary. d. People tend to use a hodgepodge of overlapping organizational frameworks in long-term memory.
Factual LO 10 Page: 276 Correct = 81% a	59.	Clustering occurs when one a. remembers similar or related items in groups b. uses a semantic network to encode new information c. recalls information based on the use of related schemata or scripts d. associates various stimuli in order to maintain a greater quantity of information in short-term memory
Concept/Applied LO 10 Page: 276 Correct = 88% b	60.	One of the notable features of LTM is that it is organized according to a clustering principle, which means a. grouping items in LTM that occurred close together in time b. the tendency to remember related items in groups or categories c. grouping words that look alike in LTM d. making a network of items in LTM
Concept/Applied LO 10 Page: 276 d	61.	Maria is trying to recall the names of all 48 of the contiguous United States. She begins by naming the New England states, followed by the mid-Atlantic states, the states in the Southeast, the Midwest, the Southwest, and finally the states in the Pacific Northwest. Maria's pattern of recall illustrates the concept of a. the primacy effect b. levels-of-processing c. the serial-position effect d. clustering
Factual LO 10 Page: 276 c	62.	A multilevel classification system based on common properties among items is called a. a script b. a schema c. a conceptual hierarchy d. a mnemonic device
Factual LO 10 Page: 276 Correct = 71% a	63.	A schema is a. an organized general knowledge structure b. a specific type of representative heuristic c. a specific type of availability heuristic d. a peculiar form of amnesia

Concept/Applied LO 10 Page: 276 Correct = 78% **a**	64.	A student's organized set of expectations about how a college professor is supposed to act is an example of a a. schema b. chunk c. semantic network d. script
Concept/Applied LO 10 Page: 276 **d**	65.	Brock was describing the inside of his doctor's office to one of his friends. In his description he mentions that there were two diplomas on the wall, even though this doctor does not have any diplomas displayed on the wall. Brock's error in recall illustrates a. the role of semantic networks in long-term memory b. the need for conceptual hierarchies in long-term memory c. the need for a good executive control system in short-term memory d. the role of schemas in long-term memory
Factual LO 10 Page: 277 Correct = 76% **b**	66.	Scripts are a. storage locations for memories b. schemata about procedures we use in daily life c. the associations we have with the denotative meaning of a word d. long-term sequences of actions that result from effective decision making
Concept/Applied LO 10 Page: 277 **a**	67.	A student's organized set of expectations about how to study for and take an exam is an example of a a. script b. cluster c. conceptual hierarchy d. semantic network
Concept/Applied LO 10 Page: 277 Correct = 88% **c**	68.	The fact that some people have an organized sequence of memories for driving their car to work implies the existence of a. prototypes b. analogies c. scripts d. chained connotations
Factual LO 10 Page: 277 Correct = 56% **d**	69.	Nodes representing concepts joined together by pathways that link related concepts is referred to as a(n) a. clustering hierarchy b. organizational schema c. lexical ordering d. semantic network
Critical Thinking LO 10 Page: 277 Correct = 81% **d**	70.	According to the notion of semantic networks, which pair of words would be linked <u>most</u> closely? a. car-nose b. boat-goat c. fill-feed d. tree-bird
Factual LO 10 Page: 277 **d**	71.	The idea that when you think about a word it triggers related words is referred to as a. a conceptual hierarchy response b. clustering c. elaborative rehearsal d. spreading activation within a semantic network

Critical Thinking LO 10 Page: 277 Correct = 87% **d**	72.	According to Collins and Loftus (1975), which of the following statements is true? a. When we think about a word, our thoughts naturally go to related words. b. The process of thinking about related words is called spreading activation within a semantic network. c. The strength of the activation decreases as it spreads outward. d. All of these statements.
Factual LO 11 Page: 277 **b**	73.	Connectionist models of memory tend to be based on a. how computers process information b. how neural networks handle information c. the principles of operant conditioning d. the principles of Gestalt psychology
Concept/Applied LO 11 Page: 277 **a**	74.	A parallel distributed processing system consists of a large network of interconnected computing units, nodes that operate much like a. neurons b. computer chips c. chromosomes d. wheels on a car
Critical Thinking LO 11 Page: 278 **d**	75.	Which of the following is <u>not</u> considered a strength of parallel distributed processing (PDP) models? a. They provide a plausible account of how mental structures may be derived from neural structures. b. They help explain the great speed of humans' cognitive functioning. c. They fit well with the observation that human memory is adept at filling in the gaps when information is missing. d. All of these are considered to be strengths of PDP models.
Factual LO 12 Page: 279 Correct = 99% **d**	76.	The "tip of the tongue" phenomenon refers to a. saying something before you've had a chance to think about it b. dreamlike material that you recall during alpha-wave presleep c. a mnemonic device to help you store information in long-term memory d. feeling like you know something but are unable to recall it
Concept/Applied LO 12 Page: 279 Correct = 85% **a**	77.	If you try to remember something but cannot, yet know the information is in memory, you are experiencing the a. tip-of-the-tongue phenomenon b. psuedoamnesia phenomenon c. Krensky syndrome d. retrieval-delay phenomenon
Factual LO 12 Page: 279 Correct = 89% **c**	78.	A retrieval cue is a. a brain structure stimulus used to locate a particular memory b. the same thing as an elaboration encoding variable c. a stimulus associated with a memory that is used to locate that memory d. always based on the mood you were in when a memory was first encoded
Critical Thinking LO 12 Page: 279 **a**	79.	Which of the following statements regarding the role of context in memory is accurate? a. Context cues often facilitate the retrieval of information. b. Context cues generally facilitate the retrieval of visual information, but interfere with the ability to recall auditory information. c. Context cues generally facilitate the retrieval of auditory information, but interfere with the ability to recall visual information. d. Context exerts no systematic influence on the encoding and retrieval of information.

Concept/Applied
LO 12
Page: 279
Correct = 60%
d

80. You attended your high school graduation over 20 years ago. You are now trying to recall as much as possible about the graduation ceremonies. Which of the following would be the best retrieval cue?
    a. the number of students who graduated
    b. the year the ceremony took place
    c. the time of day the ceremony took place
    d. the featured speaker at the ceremony

Concept/Applied
LO 12
Page: 279
Correct = 79%
b

81. We can probably attribute the failing memory of senior citizens who move from a home they've lived in for an extended time into another residence to
    a. a protein deficiency
    b. the lack of retrieval cues
    c. a lack of elaboration
    d. the confusion associated with a decaying memory

Critical Thinking
LO 12
Page: 280
b

82. Which of the following statements regarding hypnosis and memory is <u>not</u> accurate?
    a. Reinstatement of context can facilitate recall of information even without hypnosis.
    b. Research suggests that hypnosis generally increases subjects' ability to recall correct information.
    c. Courts tend to be very cautious about allowing hypnosis-aided recollections as admissible testimony.
    d. All of these statements are accurate.

Concept/Applied
LO 13
Page: 280
Correct = 70%
d

83. The work of researchers like Bartlett and Loftus on errors in memory suggests that memory is best viewed as
    a. a tape recording
    b. storage on a computer disc
    c. a literal record of events
    d. a reconstruction of events or materials

Concept/Applied
LO 13
Page: 280
Correct = 70%
c

84. Loftus' work on eyewitness testimony has clearly demonstrated that
    a. memory errors come mostly from erroneous original encoding
    b. most memory errors are constructive
    c. information given after an event can alter a person's memory of the event
    d. most memory errors are simply omissions of details of the event

Concept/Applied
LO 13
Page: 280
c

85. Tyler witnessed an automobile accident and heard one of the bystanders casually mention that the driver was probably intoxicated. Even though the driver had not been drinking, and had never crossed the center line, Tyler tells the police officer who is investigating the accident that the car had been "weaving all over the road." Tyler's faulty recall illustrates
    a. proactive interference
    b. implicit memory readjustment
    c. the misinformation effect
    d. mood-dependent memory

Factual
LO 13
Page: 280
Correct = 76%
d

86. Which of the following has been offered as an explanation for the misinformation effect?
    a. The new misinformation destroys and replaces the original memory of the event.
    b. The new misinformation interferes with the retrieval of the original memory.
    c. Individuals can access both the original memory and the altered memory, but they have difficulty distinguishing the original.
    d. All of these have been offered as explanations.

Factual LO 14 Page: 281 **b**	87.	The process of making attributions about the origins of memories is referred to as a. reality monitoring b. source monitoring c. buffering d. a contraindication
Factual LO 14 Page: 281 **c**	88.	The study of source monitoring – the process of making attributions about the origins of memories – is <u>most</u> closely associated with which of the following researchers? a. Brenda Milner b. Endel Tulving c. Marcia Johnson d. Elizabeth Loftus
Concept/Applied LO 14 Page: 281 **c**	89.	During a party, Michael was talking to a friend about the symbolism involved in a recent movie. Michael attributed the explanation of the symbolism to a prominent movie critic, when actually he heard it from his roommate. This example illustrates which of the following phenomena? a. amnesia b. cryptomnesia c. source-monitoring error d. serial-position effect
Factual LO 14 Page: 281 Correct = 21% **a**	90.	The process of deciding on whether a memory is based on an external source or an internal source is referred to as a. reality monitoring b. transmogrification c. either an internal or external attribution d. the locus of causality
Factual LO 14 Page: 281 **a**	91.	Inadvertent "plagiarism" that occurs when people come up with an idea that they think is original, when they were actually exposed to it earlier is known as a. cryptomnesia b. state-dependent memory c. the misinformation effect d. retroactive interference
Concept/Applied LO 14 Page: 281 **a**	92.	Jeannie believes her research idea was original with her, but it was really one she had heard from a colleague in an earlier discussion. Jeannie's belief is referred to as an example of a. cryptomnesia b. anterograde amnesia c. retrograde amnesia d. plagiarasmia
Factual LO 14 Page: 281 **c**	93.	The process of deciding whether a memory is based on external sources (one's perceptions of actual events) or internal sources (one' thoughts and imaginations) is called a. source monitoring b. reality monitoring c. memory reconstruction d. parallel distributed processing

Concept/Applied LO 14 Page: 282 **a**	94.	According to your textbook, it is likely that reports of alien abductions are actually the result of a. reality monitoring errors b. source monitoring errors c. cryptomnesia d. retrograde amnesia
Factual LO 14 Page: 283 **b**	95.	The first person to conduct scientific studies of forgetting was a. Sigmund Freud b. Hermann Ebbinghaus c. John Watson d. George Miller
Factual LO 14 Page: 283 **b**	96.	Ebbinghaus used which of the following as stimuli in his classic studies of forgetting? a. geometric shapes b. nonsense syllables c. common English words d. uncommon English words
Concept/Applied LO 14 Page: 283 **d**	97.	Ebbinghaus' original forgetting curves, which graphed his retention over time, suggested that most forgetting occurs a. very gradually over long periods of time b. only after several days have passed c. as a result of interference with other information d. very rapidly after learning something
Concept/Applied LO 15 Page: 283 **c**	98.	The probable reason that Ebbinghaus' forgetting curves were so steep was that Ebbinghaus a. had a poor memory b. learned too many lists c. used very meaningless materials d. used autobiographical materials
Factual LO 15 Page: 283 **b**	99.	In studies of forgetting, the retention interval is the length of time a. between the presentation of stimuli and the complete forgetting of the information b. between the presentation of stimuli and the measurement of forgetting c. during which the stimulus material is available to be studied by the subjects d. over which the subject has 100 percent recall of the material
Concept/Applied LO 15 Page: 284 **b**	100.	This multiple-choice question is an example of a _____ measure of retention. a. recall b. recognition c. relearning d. reiteration
Concept/Applied LO 15 Page: 284 **a**	101.	LeAnn had her purse snatched as she walked out to her car. The police who are investigating the crime ask LeAnn to try to pick the purse snatcher out of a line-up of eight suspects. The police are basically using a. a recognition task to recover information from LeAnn's memory b. a recall task to recover information from LeAnn's memory c. transfer-appropriate encoding to recover information from LeAnn's memory d. a misinformation task to recover information from LeAnn's memory

Concept/Applied LO 15 Page: 284 a	102.	If you are asked what your grandmother's maiden name was, this is a _____ question. a. recall b. recognition c. relearning d. reiteration
Critical Thinking LO 15 Page: 284 d	103.	Which of the following statements regarding recall and recognition is <u>not</u> accurate? a. Research conducted in the 1920s indicated that subjects' performance on recognition measures was far superior to their performance on recall measures. b. The difficulty of a recognition task can vary greatly, depending on the number, similarity, and plausibility of the options provided. c. Some researchers have suggested that recognition tasks are especially sensitive measures of retention. d. The findings from recent research suggest that college students actually perform better on recall tasks than they do on recognition tasks.
Factual LO 15 Page: 284 Correct = 76% a	104.	A relearning measure requires subjects to a. memorize information a second time to determine how much time or effort is saved b. select previously learned information from an array of options c. reproduce information on their own without any cues d. indicate whether a given piece of information is familiar
Concept/Applied LO 15 Page: 284 Correct = 98% c	105.	Generally, which type of test should be easiest? a. a short-answer test b. an essay test c. a multiple-choice test d. an oral test
Concept/Applied LO 15 Page: 284 Correct = 84% b	106.	An essay exam is most similar to the _____ method of measuring retention. a. recognition b. recall c. relearning d. production
Concept/Applied LO 15 Page: 284 c	107.	If it takes you 10 minutes to memorize a list the first time and only 2 minutes to memorize it a week later, then your "savings score" is _____ percent. a. 20 b. 50 c. 80 d. 90
Concept/Applied LO 16 Page: 285 Correct = 45% b	108.	Pseudoforgetting is viewed as a function of a. interference effects b. lack of attention c. hippocampal damage d. insufficient retrieval cues
Factual LO 16 Page: 285 Correct = 69% a	109.	Pseudoforgetting is information loss due to ineffective a. encoding only b. storage only c. retrieval only d. encoding, storage, and retrieval

Concept/Applied 110. If you're thinking about your plans for the weekend while you are reading your
LO 16   psychology textbook, the reason you will probably forget most of what you read is
Page: 285   that you've used _____ encoding, which is inferior to _____ encoding
Correct = 74% for retention of verbal material.
a
              a. phonemic; semantic
              b. semantic; reconstructive
              c. phonemic; proactive
              d. proactive; semantic

Factual   111. Decay theory suggests that forgetting is due to
LO 17   a. ineffective encoding
Page: 285   b. impermanent storage
Correct = 42%   c. retrieval failure
b   d. interference effects

Factual   112. The basic tenet of the _____ theory of forgetting is that if you fail to use a memory,
LO 17   over time its brain trace will fade.
Page: 285   a. interference
c   b. retrograde
                c. decay
                d. anterograde

Critical Thinking 113. Imagine that researchers find some memories are lost very quickly from memory
LO 17   while other memories are much longer lasting. This evidence would create the most
Page: 285   problems for
a   a. the decay theory of forgetting
                    b. the interference theory of forgetting
                    c. the repression theory of forgetting
                    d. the neurochemical theory of forgetting

Factual   114. In studies of long-term memory, researchers have found that
LO 17   a. the mere passage of time is the sole cause of forgetting
Page: 285   b. the passage of time is more influential than what happens during the time
Correct = 59%   interval
c   c. the passage of time is not as influential as what happens during the time interval
                d. subjects who sleep during the retention interval forget more than those who
                   remain awake

Concept/Applied 115. You have an exam at 8 A.M. and it is now 8 P.M. the night before. You have studied
LO 17   well. The best thing to do now is
Page: 285   a. study some other similar topic
Correct = 77%   b. study some other very different topic
d   c. play cards with others in the dorm
                   d. sleep all night

Factual   116. _____ occurs when new information impairs the retention of previously
LO 17   learned information.
Page: 285   a. Retroactive interference
Correct = 65%   b. Proactive interference
a   c. Retrograde amnesia
                d. Anterograde amnesia

Concept/Applied 117. You move to a new house and memorize your new phone number. Now, you can't
LO 17   remember your old phone number. This is an example of
Page: 285   a. retroactive interference
Correct = 51%   b. proactive interference
a   c. retrograde amnesia
                   d. motivated forgetting

212   CHAPTER SEVEN

Factual LO 17 Page: 286 Correct = 53% **b**	118.	Proactive interference occurs when a. new information impairs the retention of previously learned information b. previously learned information interferes with the retention of new information c. a person loses memories of events that occurred prior to a head injury d. a person loses memories of events that occur after a head injury
Concept/Applied LO 17 Page: 286 **a**	119.	Your female friend recently got married and changed her last name to that of her husband's. You have difficulty remembering her new last name because of a. proactive interference b. retroactive interference c. memory decay d. response inhibition
Concept/Applied LO 17 Page: 286 **c**	120.	Allen was recently traded to a new basketball team, and he is having a hard time remembering all the new plays because he keeps using the plays from his former team. Allen's problems illustrate the effects of a. retroactive interference b. state-dependent forgetting c. proactive interference d. memory reconstruction
Concept/Applied LO 17 Page: 286 **b**	121.	You recently moved to a different town and have a new telephone number. Now you have difficulty remembering your old telephone number because of a. proactive interference b. retroactive interference c. trace-decay d. memory organization deficiencies
Concept/Applied LO 17 Page: 286 **a**	122.	Interference effects on retention are greatest when the interfering learning is a. similar to the material to be remembered b. dissimilar to the material to be remembered c. unrelated to the material to be remembered d. similarity of the materials does not seem to affect retention
Factual LO 18 Page: 286 Correct = 98% **c**	123.	The encoding specificity principle states that a. forgetting is due only to the passage of time b. forgetting is usually due to interference from competing memories c. retrieval failure is often due to a mismatch between the available retrieval cues and the memory code d. forgetting involves purposeful suppression of memories
Concept/Applied LO 18 Page: 286 Correct = 79% **a**	124.	To be <u>most</u> effective, a retrieval cue should be a. congruent with the original encoding of material b. similar in meaning to the material c. similar in sensory appearance to the material d. very distinctive in character
Concept/Applied LO 18 Page: 286 Correct = 88% **a**	125.	You meet a man at a party and carefully store his name along with an image of his face. The next day, he calls you on the phone, but you can't remember his name. According to the encoding specificity principle, this is because a. the sound of his voice is an inappropriate retrieval cue b. you never paid attention to his name in the first place c. the name is no longer in your long-term memory d. the name is in your sensory store only

Factual LO 18 Page: 286 Correct = 85% **c**	126.	_____ has occurred when the initial processing of information is similar to the type of processing required for retention. a. Lexical matching b. Episodic processing c. Transfer-appropriate processing d. Phonemic processing
Factual LO 18 Page: 286 Correct = 60% **b**	127.	The concept of motivated forgetting is based largely on the work of which of the following early psychologists? a. Hermann Ebbinghaus b. Sigmund Freud c. John Watson d. Wilhelm Wundt
Factual LO 18 Page: 287 Correct = 91% **b**	128.	Which of the following terms is synonymous with "motivated forgetting"? a. regression b. repression c. sublimation d. rationalization
Critical Thinking LO 19 Page: 288 **b**	129.	Which of the following statements regarding the prevalence of childhood abuse is accurate? a. Data tend to support the view that very few people have actually been victimized by childhood sexual abuse. b. Males are more likely to have experienced physical abuse and females are more likely to have suffered from sexual abuse. c. Females are more likely to have experienced physical abuse and males are more likely to have suffered from sexual abuse. d. Males and females are equally likely to have experienced childhood sexual abuse.
Critical Thinking LO 19 Page: 288 **d**	130.	Which of the following statements regarding the repressed memories of childhood abuse is <u>not</u> accurate? a. Some accused parents have argued that their children's recollections are false memories created by therapists. b. Many clinical psychologists accept recovered memories of abuse at face value. c. Many psychologists involved in research on memory have expressed skepticism about the recent upsurge of recovered memories of abuse. d. All of these statements are accurate.
Critical Thinking LO 20 Page: 288 **b**	131.	Which of the following arguments is <u>least</u> likely to be made by psychologists who doubt the authenticity of repressed memories of childhood abuse? a. Self-assessments of memory are often distorted. b. People are probably lying about their previously repressed memories. c. Therapists sometimes operate under the assumption that virtually all psychological problems are attributable to childhood sexual abuse. d. There have been a number of cases in which recovered memories of childhood abuse have been discredited.
Concept/Applied LO 20 Page: 289 **a**	132.	Those who question the accuracy of repressed memories are <u>most</u> likely to cite research on which of the following? a. the misinformation effect b. flashbulb memories c. retroactive interference d. connectionist models of memory

Factual LO 21 Page: 289 **b**	133.	In studies of _____, subjects are given false information about an event while hypnotized and are subsequently tested for their recall of this event in a nonhypnotized state to see whether any false memories are reported. a. retrieval deficits b. hypnotic pseudomemory c. mood-congruence effects d. hypnotic age regression
Factual LO 21 Page: 290 **c**	134.	Based on the results of the Featured Study, which of the following factors is most likely to influence the likelihood of creating hypnotic pseudomemories? a. age of the subjects b. gender of the subjects c. hypnotist-subject rapport d. closeness of relationship between subjects and their parents
Factual LO 21 Page: 290 Correct = 90% **c**	135.	The results of the Featured Study on hypnotic pseudomemory indicate that a. hypnotic pseudomemories can be created in virtually anyone b. it is virtually impossible to create hypnotic pseudomemories c. hypnotic pseudomemories are most likely to occur among people who are highly susceptible to hypnosis d. hypnotic pseudomemories are most likely to occur in people who have strong negative feeling toward the hypnotist
Critical Thinking LO 21 Page: 291 **d**	136.	Which of the following statements best reflects the current view of the repressed memories controversy? a. It seems likely that most cases of recovered memories are authentic. b. It appears that many therapists are deliberately creating false memories in their patients. c. Recovered memories of childhood abuse can be summarily dismissed. d. We should be extremely careful about accepting recovered memories of abuse in the absence of convincing corroboration.
Factual LO 22 Page: 292 Correct = 74% **d**	137.	Research has related which of the following physiological processes to memory functioning? a. alterations in synaptic transmission b. the creation of localized neural circuits in the brain c. hormonal fluctuations d. All of these physiological processes have been related to memory functioning.
Critical Thinking LO 22 Page: 292 **b**	138.	Based on studies of the biochemistry of memory in animals, which of the following conclusions is not accurate? a. Hormonal changes can either facilitate or impair memory. b. Memories can be chemically transferred from one animal to another. c. The administration of drugs that interfere with protein synthesis impairs long-term memory in some animals. d. Memory formation may result in alterations in synaptic transmission at specific sites.
Concept/Applied LO 22 Page: 292 **a**	139.	Thompson's work with the conditioned eye blink in rabbits suggest that a. learning may depend on very specific and localized brain circuits b. there is little hope of finding localized brain changes in learning c. brain action in learning is too diffuse to map out d. none of these statements is accurate

Factual LO 22 Page: 292 Correct = 70% **b**	140.	The long-lasting increase in neural excitability at synapses of a specific neural pathway is referred to as a. spreading cortical activation b. long-term potentiation c. transfer-appropriate excitation d. an engram process
Critical Thinking LO 22 Page: 292 **a**	141.	Evidence from studies of which of the following <u>most</u> clearly supports the idea that memory traces consist of specific neural circuits? a. long-term potentiation b. retrograde amnesia c. electrical stimulation of the brain d. the transfer of RNA from one animal to another
Factual LO 23 Page: 292 **b**	142.	Retrograde amnesia refers to an inability to a. form or recall new memories b. recall old memories c. recall events about oneself d. do all of these things
Concept/Applied LO 23 Page: 292 Correct = 83% **a**	143.	Dave is thrown from his motorcycle and suffers a severe blow to the head, resulting in loss of memory for events that occurred before the accident. This is an example of a. retrograde amnesia b. anterograde amnesia c. motivated forgetting d. retroactive interference
Concept/Applied LO 23 Page: 293 **c**	144.	Faith had brain surgery to remove a small tumor from her temporal lobe. While recovering from the surgery Faith appeared to be fine, and she was able to talk about events from her childhood, and events from just prior to the surgery. However, she really cannot remember anything that has happened since the surgery. Faith's memory difficulties are consistent with those seen in a. retrograde amnesia b. cryptomnesia c. anterograde amnesia d. pseudoforgetting
Concept/Applied LO 23 Page: 293 Correct = 82% **b**	145.	If you suffer from an inability to recall old memories as a result of brain trauma, you have a case of a. anterograde amnesia b. retrograde amnesia c. Korsakov's syndrome d. limbic system inversion
Factual LO 23 Page: 293 **b**	146.	Damage to which of the following is most likely to cause deficits in long-term memory? a. limbic system b. hippocampal region c. sympathetic nervous system d. Broca's area
Concept/Applied LO 23 Page: 293 **a**	147.	Which of the following areas of the brain is associated with the severe memory impairment that occurs in Alzheimer's disease? a. limbic system b. hippocampal region c. sympathetic nervous system d. Broca's area

Factual LO 23 Page: 293 Correct = 51% **d**	148.	The gradual conversion of information into durable long-term memory codes is called a. long-term potentiation b. postsynaptic conversion c. elaboration d. consolidation
Factual LO 23 Page: 293 **b**	149.	The current thinking is that memories are consolidated in the _____ and stored in the _____. a. limbic system; cerebellum b. hippocampal region; cortex c. cortex; limbic system d. cerebellum; hippocampus
Concept/Applied LO 23 Page: 293 **b**	150.	According to the notion of consolidation, memories of visual information are most likely to be stored in a. the limbic system b. areas of the visual cortex c. the hippocampal region d. the cerebellum
Factual LO 23 Page: 294 **a**	151.	Evidence from recent studies indicates that the _____ may be critical to the formation of memories for learned fears and other emotional memories. a. amygdala b. hippocampus c. limbic system d. prefrontal cortex
Factual LO 23 Page: 294 **d**	152.	Evidence from recent studies indicates that the _____ may contribute to memory for temporal sequences and to short-term, working memory. a. amygdala b. hippocampus c. limbic system d. prefrontal cortex
Concept/Applied LO 24 Page: 294 **a**	153.	Implicit memory is _____, is accessed _____, and can be best assessed with _____ measures of retention. a. unconscious; indirectly; relearning b. unconscious; indirectly; recognition c. conscious; indirectly; relearning d. conscious; directly; recall
Factual LO 24 Page: 294 Correct = 71% **b**	154.	Which type of memory is reasonably unaffected by amnesia? a. explicit memory b. implicit memory c. episodic memory d. generative memory
Factual LO 24 Page: 295 **d**	155.	Explicit memory is likely to be affected by which of the following? a. age b. amnesia c. the length of the retention interval d. any of these factors

Factual LO 24 Page: 295 Correct = 75% **b**	156.	The memory system that contains words, definitions, events, and ideas is the a. episodic memory system b. declarative memory system c. procedural memory system d. assimilative memory system
Concept/Applied LO 24 Page: 295 **b**	157.	Your birth date and your mother's maiden name are most likely to be contained in your _____ memory system. a. procedural b. declarative c. episodic d. independent
Factual LO 24 Page: 295 Correct = 93% **b**	158.	Procedural memory a. is memory for factual information b. is memory for actions, skills, and operations c. is made up of chronological recollections of personal experiences d. contains general knowledge that is not temporally dated
Factual LO 24 Page: 295 Correct = 56% **d**	159.	Some theorists believe that implicit memory is handled by the _____ memory system. a. episodic b. state-dependent c. semantic d. procedural
Factual LO 24 Page: 295 **a**	160.	Some theorists believe that the _____ memory system may handle implicit remembering, while the _____ memory system handles explicit remembering. a. procedural; declarative b. declarative; procedural c. independent; procedural d. declarative; independent
Concept/Applied LO 24 Page: 295 **c**	161.	The memory system that contains the memory for how to type on a typewriter or drive an automobile is the _____ memory system. a. cerebellum b. schematic c. procedural d. episodic
Factual LO 24 Page: 296 **a**	162.	Declarative memory appears to be handled by the _____ and the areas of the cortex with which it communicates. a. cerebellum b. medulla c. limbic system d. hippocampal complex
Factual LO 25 Page: 296 **a**	163.	Which of the following researchers suggested that declarative memory be subdivided into episodic and semantic memory? a. Endel Tulving b. Brenda Milner c. George Miller d. Elizabeth Loftus

Factual LO 25 Page: 296 c	164.	The subdivision of the declarative memory system made up of chronological recollections of personal experiences is referred to as a. network memory b. nodal memory c. episodic memory d. event-evoked memory
Factual LO 25 Page: 296 Correct = 87% a	165.	_____ memory is made up of temporally dated recollections of personal experiences. a. Episodic b. Declarative c. Semantic d. Explicit
Factual LO 25 Page: 296 Correct = 71% d	166.	Memory of "chronological" and "dated" personal experiences is referred to as a. semantic memory b. declarative memory c. implicit memory d. episodic memory
Factual LO 25 Page: 296 Correct = 69% b	167.	General knowledge that is not tied to the time when the information was learned is contained in _____ memory. a. episodic b. semantic c. implicit d. procedural
Concept/Applied LO 25 Page: 296 Correct = 83% c	168.	Dave is reminiscing about the first car he owned in high school and how he felt the first time he drove it through town. This is an example of _____ memory. a. procedural b. declarative c. episodic d. semantic
Factual LO 25 Page: 296 Correct = 82% c	169.	_____ memory involves remembering to perform actions in the future. a. Proactive b. Retrograde c. Prospective d. Retrospective
Factual LO 25 Page: 296 d	170.	_____ memory involves remembering events from the past or previously learned information. a. Reactive b. Proactive c. Prospective d. Retrospective
Concept/Applied LO 25 Page: 296 d	171.	When, during a psychology test, you try to remember something your instructor said in class last week, you are using what researchers call _____ memory. a. proactive b. retrograde c. prospective d. retrospective

Critical Thinking
LO 25
Page: 297
b

172. Which of the following statements regarding prospective memory is not accurate?
    a. People seem to vary tremendously in their ability to carry out prospective memory tasks.
    b. Infrequent tasks tend to be easier to remember than habitual tasks.
    c. Older adults seem to be more vulnerable to problems with prospective memory than younger people.
    d. Event-based prospective tasks appear to be easier to remember than time-based tasks.

Critical Thinking
LO 26
Page: 297
d

173. The fact that what you see in the world around you depends on where you focus your attention best illustrates which of the following unifying themes of your textbook?
    a. Psychology is empirical.
    b. Psychology evolves in a sociocultural context.
    c. Behavior is determined by multiple causes.
    d. People's experience of the world is highly subjective.

Critical Thinking
LO 26
Page: 297
d

174. The reconstructive nature of memory best reflects which of the following unifying themes of your textbook?
    a. Psychology is empirical.
    b. Psychology evolves in a sociocultural context.
    c. Behavior is determined by multiple causes.
    d. People's experience of the world is highly subjective.

Critical Thinking
LO 26
Page: 297
b

175. The fact that your memory for a specific event may be influenced by the amount of attention you pay to the event, the level at which you process information about the event, how you organize the information, and the amount of interference you experience reflects which of the following unifying themes of your textbook?
    a. Psychology is empirical.
    b. Behavior is determined by multiple causes.
    c. Our behavior is shaped by our cultural heritage.
    d. Our experience of the world is highly subjective.

Factual
LO 27
Page: 298
Correct = 59%
b

176. Mnemonic devices
    a. can only be used to remember concrete words
    b. have existed since ancient times
    c. are generally ineffective and are unnecessary in modern times
    d. All of these statements accurately describe mnemonic devices.

Factual
LO 27
Page: 298
Correct = 71%
d

177. Practicing material already learned in order to improve retention is referred to as
    a. chunking
    b. memorization
    c. elaboration
    d. overlearning

Concept/Applied
LO 27
Page: 298
Correct = 73%
b

178. Overlearning material will
    a. not improve retention
    b. improve retention
    c. improve retention for nonsense syllables but not much else
    d. results in "burnout"

Factual
LO 27
Page: 298
c

179. The _____ effect occurs when subjects show better recall for items at the beginning and end of a list than for items in the middle.
    a. clustering
    b. elaboration
    c. serial-position
    d. consolidation

Factual LO 27 Page: 298 **a**	180.	According to the serial-position effect, subjects tend to show better recall for items _____ of a list than for items _____. a. at the beginning and end; in the middle b. in the middle; at the beginning and end c. at the end; at the beginning d. in the middle; at the beginning
Factual LO 27 Page: 298 Correct = 84% **b**	181.	Distributed practice refers to learning a. through several different senses b. over several sessions c. all at once d. from several different sources
Factual LO 27 Page: 298 Correct = 77% **b**	182.	Massed practice refers to learning material a. across several large sessions b. all at once c. in a quiet place with no distractions d. with large numbers of people (masses)
Concept/Applied LO 27 Page: 298 **c**	183.	Relative to massed practice, distributed practice is _____ when learning the information in a textbook. a. no different b. inferior c. superior d. there is no reliable information on the relative effects
Concept/Applied LO 27 Page: 298 **a**	184.	A good strategy for minimizing interference with retention of course material is to a. conduct a last, thorough review of material as close to exam time as possible b. engage in massed practice c. overlearn the material d. spend less time on rote repetition of the material
Concept/Applied LO 28 Page: 299 Correct = 90% **d**	185.	As a student, it's a good idea to tailor your study methods to the type of test you'll be given. This notion is based on the concept of a. deep processing b. distributed practice c. minimal interference d. transfer-appropriate processing
Factual LO 28 Page: 299 Correct = 67% **a**	186.	If you group information according to similarities as an aid for later remembering, you are _____ that information. a. organizing b. transferring c. processing d. encoding
Concept/Applied LO 28 Page: 299 **c**	187.	The empirical finding that outlining material from textbooks can enhance retention of the material is most consistent with which of the following approaches for improving memory? a. massed practice b. distributed practice c. organization d. deep processing

Concept/Applied 188. ROY G BIV is a fictitious name people use to help them remember the order of
LO 29   colors in the color spectrum. ROY G BIV is an example of
Page: 299   a. the method of loci
Correct = 87%   b. a mnemonic
b   c. Aristotle's method of memory
                     d. memoranda

Concept/Applied 189. Using the phrase "Every good boy does fine" to remember the order of musical
LO 29   notes is an example of a(n)
Page: 299   a. narrative
Correct = 44%   b. acrostic
b   c. rhyme
                     d. acronym

Concept/Applied 190. If you went to the grocery store to purchase a variety of items and did not take a list,
LO 29   which mnemonic would be the best to use?
Page: 300   a. an acrostic
d   b. a rhyme
                     c. the keyword method
                     d. the link method

Factual 191. If you associate a concrete word with a to-be-remembered abstract word and then
LO 29   generate an image to represent the concrete word, you are using
Page: 300   a. an acrostic
Correct = 35%   b. the link method
c   c. the keyword method
                     d. a semantic network

Concept/Applied 192. Which of the following mnemonics would be the most useful for helping you
LO 30   remember the name of a person you just met at a party?
Page: 300   a. rhyme
b   b. keyword method
                     c. an acrostic
                     d. link method

Critical Thinking 193. The fact that the recall of eyewitnesses can be distorted by information introduced
LO 30   after the event by police officers, attorneys, etc., is best explained by which of the
Page: 302   following?
a   a. the misinformation effect
                     b. the serial-position effect
                     c. errors in source-monitoring
                     d. memory reconstruction

Concept/Applied 194. Knowing that a particular person has been arrested and accused of the crime in
LO 30   question can influence the recollections of eyewitnesses. This finding can best be
Page: 302   explained by which of the following?
a   a. hindsight bias
                     b. the overconfidence effect
                     c. the misinformation effect
                     d. the serial-position effect

Factual 195. When tested for their memory of general information, people tend to
LO 30   a. overestimate their accuracy
Page: 303   b. underestimate their accuracy
a   c. correctly estimate their accuracy
                     d. be influenced by the person doing the testing

Factual LO 30 Page: 303 **c**	196.	The correlation between eyewitness confidence and eyewitness accuracy can best be characterized as a. strongly positive b. strongly negative c. moderate d. nonexistent
Factual LO 30 Page: 303 **d**	197.	Overconfidence in recalling information is most likely to be fueled by which of the following errors in thinking? a. source-monitoring errors b. reality-monitoring errors c. the fundamental attribution error d. the failure to seek disconfirming evidence
Integrative **c**	198.	If the three memory stores were ordered in terms of levels of processing, which of the following sequences would be the correct order for progressively deeper processing? a. long-term memory, short-term memory, sensory memory b. short-term memory, sensory memory, long-term memory c. sensory memory, short-term memory, long-term memory d. sensory memory, long-term memory, short-term memory
Integrative Correct = 95% **d**	199.	Mort hated his history professor last year and can never remember the professor's name. This instance of forgetting probably reflects a. ineffective encoding b. inadequate depth of processing c. poor organization in Mort's semantic memory d. motivated forgetting
Integrative Correct = 66% **a**	200.	Martin can't remember who invented flush toilets because he was flirting with a classmate when his history professor described this momentous event. His forgetting appears to be due to a. ineffective encoding b. motivated forgetting c. time decay d. proactive interference
Integrative Correct = 69% **a**	201.	The memory improvement strategies of elaboration, using visual imagery, and engaging in deeper processing all involve which memory process? a. encoding b. storage c. retrieval d. interference
Integrative **c**	202.	Which of the following terms includes all the others? a. semantic memory b. episodic memory c. long-term memory d. procedural memory
Study Guide LO 3 Page: 268 **a**	203.	Which one of the three levels of processing would probably be employed when attempting to memorize the following three-letter sequences WAB WAC WAD? a. structural b. semantic c. phonemic d. chunking

Study Guide LO 4 Page: 269 **d**	204.	According to Paivio's dual-coding theory a. words are easier to encode than images b. abstract words are easier to encode than concrete words c. visual imagery may hinder the retrieval of words d. it should be easier to remember the word "banana" than the word "justice"
Study Guide LO 5 Page: 275 **b**	205.	Retrieval from long-term memory is usually best when the information has been stored at which level of processing? a. structural b. semantic c. phonemic d. chunking
Study Guide LO 10 Page: 276 **c**	206.	Which of the following sequences of words would be most subject to a clustering effect? a. FAN HEAVEN JUSTICE CHAIR b. HOUSE VACATION MOUSE STATISTIC c. BLUE DOG CAMEL YELLOW d. CONVERSE ICICLE CONCEPT THINKING
Study Guide LO 11 Page: 278 **d**	207.	Which word best describes the speed of human cognitive functioning? a. slow b. moderate c. rapid d. blazing
Study Guide LO 12 Page: 279 **b**	208.	When you attempt to recall the name of a high school classmate by imagining yourself back in the English class with her, you are making use of a. retrieval cues b. context cues c. schemas d. recognition cues
Study Guide LO 14 Page: 281 **b**	209.	You recall being lost in a shopping mall at the age of five but your parents assure you that it never happened. Errors like this are most likely due to a. ineffective encoding b. a reality monitoring error c. a source monitoring error d. the misinformation effect
Study Guide LO 16 Page: 285 **c**	210.	Ineffective encoding of information may result in a. the primacy effect b. the recency effect c. pseudoforgetting d. chunking
Study Guide LO 17 Page: 285 **d**	211.	Decay theory is best able to explain the loss of memory in a. sensory store b. long-term memory c. short-term memory d. repressed memory
Study Guide LO 18 Page: 286 **c**	212.	When you violate the encoding specificity principle, you are likely to experience an inability to a. encode information b. store information c. retrieve information d. form a visual image of the material you want to retrieve

Study Guide LO 27 Page: 298 **d**	213.	It is very easy to recall the name of your high school because it has been subjected to extensive a. deep processing b. clustering c. chunking d. rehearsal
Study Guide LO 30 Page: 303 **a**	214.	The failure to seek out disconfirming evidence can often lead to a. the overconfidence effect b. the reconstructive bias c. the hindsight bias d. a source monitoring error
Online Quiz LO 2 Page: 267 **c**	215.	Curtis is working on a presentation and doesn't hear the phone ringing in the background. Later he is surprised to find three phone messages have come in for him, because he was totally unaware that the phone had even rung. Incidents of this type would lend support to which of the following? a. a late-selection model of attention b. a proactive model of attention c. an early-selection model of attention d. an acoustic-blocking model of attention
Online Quiz LO 4 Page: 270 **c**	216.	Which of the following is not listed in the textbook as a method to enrich encoding of to-be-stored information? a. self-referent encoding b. visual imagery c. rote memorization d. elaboration
Online Quiz LO 6 Page: 272 **d**	217.	Chunking is the a. elaboration of information in short-term memory for storage into long- term memory b. process of passing information from sensory memory to short-term memory c. actual storage process of information in long-term memory d. method used to increase the amount of information one can hold in short-term memory
Online Quiz LO 8 Page: 274 Correct = 77% **a**	218.	Penfield's studies suggest that long-lost memories can be elicited through electrical stimulation of the brain. This suggests the possibility that forgetting may be a matter of a. retrieval failure b. displacement c. gradual decay d. unconscious wishes to forget
Online Quiz LO 11 Page: 277 **d**	219.	Models of memory that are based on the assumption that cognitive processes depend on patterns of activation in interconnected computational networks that resemble neural networks are called _____ models. a. functional b. dual coding c. information processing d. parallel distributed processing

Online Quiz
LO 15
Page: 284
a

220. A _____ measure requires subjects to reproduce information on their own without any cues.
a. recall
b. recognition
c. relearning
d. reiteration

Online Quiz
LO 17
Page: 285
Correct = 89%
a

221. According to interference theory
a. people forget information because of competition from other material
b. forgetting is due to ineffective encoding
c. the principal cause of forgetting should be the passage of time
d. the events that occur during the retention interval do not affect forgetting

Online Quiz
LO 23
Page: 293
Correct = 78%
d

222. In anterograde amnesia
a. new information impairs the retention of previously learned information
b. previously learned information interferes with the retention of new information
c. a person loses memories of events that occurred prior to a head injury
d. a person loses memories of events that occur after a head injury

Online Quiz
LO 28
Page: 299
a

223. According to the notion of deep processing, you can learn material more effectively by relating the information to
a. your own life and experience
b. hypnotic pseudomemories
c. famous world events
d. similar material you have read

Online Quiz
LO 30
Page: 303
c

224. The tendency to mold our interpretation of the past to fit how events actually turned out is called
a. the misinformation effect
b. the serial-position effect
c. hindsight bias
d. the overconfidence effect

ESSAY QUESTIONS

1. Name the three human memory stores in the order in which information would encounter them. Using the Atkinson and Shiffrin (1971) model, describe the capacity of each system, the durability of storage in each system, and the format of information storage in each system. Also identify the processes that transfer information from one system to another.

    Sensory memory--preserves information in its original sensory form for a brief time, usually just a fraction of a second. Can hold about 25 stimuli at a time. If a stimulus is perceived, it is transferred to

    Short-term memory--holds 5 to 9 "chunks" of unrehearsed information for about 20 to 30 seconds. Since a stimulus is typically given a verbal label at the time it is perceived, information will generally be stored acoustically (or phonemically) in short-term memory. Information can be maintained indefinitely in short-term memory by rehearsal; rehearsal also increases the likelihood of transfer to

    Long-term memory--has a virtually unlimited capacity to hold information over an indefinite period of time. Format of information storage depends on the type of rehearsal used: simple recitation promotes acoustic storage in long-term memory; elaboration promotes semantic storage in long-term memory.

2. Compare the Atkinson and Shiffrin (1971) model of short-term memory with Baddely's (1976, 1989) more complex model of short-term memory.

    In the older model, short-term memory was a unitary memory store. Information in short-term memory was stored acoustically; displacement and decay were the only mechanisms by which information could be lost from short-term memory.

    Baddely characterizes short-term memory as "working memory," consisting of three components: (1) the rehearsal loop, analogous to the whole of short-term memory in the Atkinson and Shiffrin model; (2) a visuospatial sketchpad that allows one to hold and manipulate visual images; and (3) an executive control system, which holds the limited amount of information one can use in reasoning or decision making at any given time. Although the capacity and duration of information storage are unchanged in this newer model, the functions of short-term memory are greatly expanded.

3. Outline some strategies that can be used to improve retrieval of information from long-term memory.

    Use all available retrieval cues, such as partial recollection of the information to be retrieved; put yourself back in the context in which encoding originally took place; recreate the mood you were in when encoding originally took place.

4. Compare and evaluate decay theory and interference theory as explanations of forgetting.

    Decay theory maintains that memory traces gradually fade away over time. If decay theory is correct, then the mere passage of time should be the principal cause of forgetting; furthermore, memories may be permanently lost from long-term memory.

    Interference theory proposes that people forget due to competition from other information. If this is the case, then forgetting should depend on what happens during the retention interval rather than simply the length of the retention interval. Since interference is presumed to interrupt retrieval rather than storage, this view implies that information loss from long-term memory is only temporary.

    Despite many attempts, researchers have not been able to demonstrate decay from long-term memory. On the other hand, many studies have shown that forgetting does depend on the amount, type, and complexity of material subjects are exposed to during the retention interval, consistent with interference theory.

5. Distinguish between implicit and explicit memory, declarative and procedural memory, and semantic and episodic memory, and explain how these are interrelated.

    Declarative and procedural memory are hypothesized divisions of long-term memory. Declarative memory contains factual information; procedural memory contains memory of actions, skills, and operations.

    Semantic and episodic memory are hypothesized divisions of declarative memory. Semantic memory contains general facts that are not temporally tagged; episodic memory contains personal facts that are tagged with information about when these personal experiences occurred.

    Implicit and explicit memory are not distinct memory systems, but rather behavioral phenomena. Implicit memory is unconscious, must be accessed indirectly, and can best be assessed with relearning measures of retention. Explicit memory is conscious, can be accessed directly, and can best be assessed with recall or recognition measures of retention. Some theorists believe that implicit memory is handled by the procedural memory system and that explicit memory is handled by the declarative memory system.

Chapter Eight
Language and Thought

LEARNING OBJECTIVES

1. Describe the "cognitive revolution" in psychology.
2. Outline the key properties of language.
3. Outline the development of human language during the first year.
4. Describe children's early use of single words and word combinations.
5. Summarize the effects of bilingualism on language and cognitive development and the factors that influence the learning of a second language.
6. Summarize evidence on language acquisition in animals.
7. Discuss the possible evolutionary bases of language.
8. Compare and contrast the behaviorist, nativist, and interactionist perspectives on language acquisition.
9. Discuss culture and language and the status of the linguistic relativity hypothesis.
10. List and describe the three types of problems proposed by Greeno.
11. Explain the difference between well-defined and ill-defined problems.
12. Explain how irrelevant information and functional fixedness can hinder problem solving.
13. Explain how mental set and unnecessary constraints can hinder problem solving.
14. Describe a variety of general problem-solving strategies.
15. Discuss the distinction between field independence and dependence.
16. Discuss cultural variations in cognitive style as they relate to problem solving.
17. Compare the additive and elimination by aspects approaches to selecting an alternative.
18. Discuss conflict in decision making and the idea that one can think too much about a decision.
19. Explain the factors that individuals typically consider in risky decision making.
20. Describe the availability and representativeness heuristics.
21. Describe the base rate neglect and the conjunction fallacy and their causes.
22. Summarize the research on the alternative outcomes effect.
23. Explain evolutionary theorists' evaluation of cognitive research on flaws in human decision strategies.
24. Explain how the chapter highlighted four of the text's unifying themes.
25. Explain what is meant by the gambler's fallacy the law of small numbers.
26. Describe the propensity to overestimate the improbable and seek confirming information.
27. Discuss the overconfidence effect and the effects of framing on decisions.
28. Describe some language manipulation strategies that people use to shape others' thoughts.

MULTIPLE-CHOICE QUESTIONS

Factual
LO 1
Page: 308
Correct = 93%
d

1. Cognition refers to
   a. focusing awareness of a narrow range of stimuli or events
   b. the use of language in a social context
   c. widely shared beliefs that are transmitted socially across generations
   d. the mental processes involved in acquiring and using knowledge

Factual
LO 1
Page: 308
Correct = 40%
a

2. During the first half of the 20th century, the study of cognition was discouraged because
   a. earlier studies using the method of introspection had yielded unreliable results
   b. of the theoretical dominance of psychodynamic theories
   c. cognition was not considered to be a psychological function
   d. language acquisition was viewed as an innate process that could not be studied empirically

Factual
LO 1
Page: 308
Correct = 62%
a

3. The 1950s brought a "cognitive revolution" in psychology because
   a. some theorists recognized that an exclusive focus on observable behavior would yield an incomplete picture of human functioning
   b. it was finally recognized that cognition is a uniquely human capability
   c. introspection became more objective and reliable as a research tool
   d. behaviorists recognized that language could not be studied objectively

Concept/Applied
LO 1
Page: 308
Correct = 96%
d

4. Which of the following is <u>not</u> a cognitive activity?
   a. remembering something
   b. making a decision
   c. solving a problem
   d. blinking at something

Concept/Applied
LO 1
Page: 308
Correct = 77%
b

5. Our ability to reason constitutes primarily
   a. a behavioral activity
   b. a cognitive activity
   c. a learned activity
   d. an objective activity

Factual
LO 2
Page: 308
Correct = 63%
c

6. The four essential characteristics of language are that it must be
   a. symbolic, generative, phonemic, and structured
   b. syntactic, symbolic, generative, and semantic
   c. semantic, symbolic, structured, and generative
   d. generative, rule governed, phonemic, and syntactic

Concept/Applied
LO 2
Page: 308
Correct = 59%
d

7. The symbols used in a language are arbitrary. In other words
   a. there is a built-in relationship between the look of the symbols and the concepts they stand for
   b. there is a built-in relationship between the sound of the symbols and the concepts they stand for
   c. the symbols have the same meaning to everyone
   d. there is no built-in relationship between the symbols and the concepts they stand for

Concept/Applied
LO 2
Page: 308
Correct = 29%
c

8. The fact that there are different sounds across languages that all represent the same thing reflects the
   a. structural quality of language
   b. cross-cultural quality of language
   c. semantic quality of language
   d. generative quality of language

Factual LO 2 Page: 308 **b**	9.	When we say that language is generative, we mean that a. the symbols used in the language are arbitrary b. a limited number of symbols can be combined to produce an infinite variety of messages c. language is both written and oral d. sentences must be structured in a limited number of ways
Concept/Applied LO 2 Page: 308 Correct = 60% **a**	10.	The ability of language to allow a person to express new ideas refers to a. the generative quality of language b. the invention dimension of language c. the constructive function of language d. the symbolic dimension of language
Concept/Applied LO 2 Page: 309 Correct = 87% **d**	11.	The fact that language has rules that govern the arrangement of words into phrases and sentences refers to the a. generative aspect of language b. phonemic aspect of language c. continuity aspect of language d. structured aspect of language
Factual LO 2 Page: 309 Correct = 90% **c**	12.	The English language uses a. 26 phonemes, one for each letter of the alphabet b. approximately 450,000 phonemes, one for each word c. about 40 to 45 phonemes, corresponding to the letters of the alphabet plus several variations d. all of the 100 or so phonemes that humans are capable of producing
Critical Thinking LO 2 Page: 309 **c**	13.	Which of the following statements is <u>false</u>? a. Humans are capable of producing about 100 phonemes. b. A letter of the alphabet is represented by more than one phoneme if it has more than one pronunciation. c. All languages use all of the phonemes of which humans are capable. d. Phonemes are combined into morphemes.
Concept/Applied LO 2 Page: 309 **a**	14.	Three-year-old Johnny used to say "mikk" when he wanted a drink of milk. Now he is able to say "milk" quite clearly. In this instance Johnny has made a gain in his use of a. phonemes b. syntax c. morphemes d. linguistic heuristics
Concept/Applied LO 2 Page: 309 **d**	15.	Last Halloween 4-year-old Jillian called the decorations at her house "punkins." This year she is able to say "pumpkins" when she describes them. In this instance Jillian has made a gain in her use of a. syntax b. morphemes c. linguistic heuristics d. phonemes
Factual LO 2 Page: 309 Correct = 84% **a**	16.	Phonemes are the smallest units of _____ in a spoken language; morphemes are the smallest units of _____ in a language. a. sound; meaning b. sound; syntax c. meaning; sound d. meaning; syntax

Factual LO 2 Page: 309 Correct = 71% **d**	17.	The smallest unit of meaning in a language is a. the phoneme b. the word c. the phrase d. the morpheme
Concept/Applied LO 2 Page: 310 **c**	18.	When the word "oat" is changed to the word "boat," the number of a. phonemes and morphemes are both increased b. phonemes stays the same, but the number of morphemes is increased c. phonemes increases, but the number of morphemes stays the same d. phonemes decreases, but the number of morphemes increases
Concept/Applied LO 2 Page: 310 **c**	19.	When the word "jar" is changed to the word "jars," the number of a. phonemes increases, but the number of morphemes stays the same b. phonemes stays the same, but the number of morphemes is increased c. phonemes and morphemes are both increased d. phonemes decreases, but the number of morphemes increases
Concept/Applied LO 2 Page: 310 Correct = 52% **d**	20.	The word "unchangeable" consists of a. nine morphemes, one for each letter of the alphabet used b. one morpheme, for the entire word c. four morphemes, one for each syllable d. three morphemes: "un," "change," and "able"
Factual LO 2 Page: 310 **a**	21.	Semantics is the component of language concerned with a. understanding the meaning of words and word combinations b. specifying rules for how words can be arranged into sentences c. creating novel messages from a finite number of symbols d. correctly pronouncing the prefixes, suffices, and root words of a language
Factual LO 2 Page: 310 **b**	22.	The denotation of a word consists of a. its emotional overtones and secondary implications b. its dictionary definition c. the separate sounds that make up the word d. a complex interaction between the word's phonology and syntax
Factual LO 2 Page: 310 **c**	23.	The connotation of a word consists of a. its dictionary definition b. the separate sounds that make up the word c. its emotional overtones and secondary implications d. a complex interaction between the word's phonology and syntax
Factual LO 2 Page: 310 **d**	24.	The component of language that would be evident if an individual recognizes that "give" and "take" have opposite meanings is a. syntax b. phonology c. generativity d. semantics
Concept/Applied LO 2 Page: 310 Correct = 96% **a**	25.	The requirement that a declarative sentence have both a noun phrase and a verb phrase is an example of a a. rule of syntax b. transformational rule c. morpheme d. heuristic

Factual LO 2 Page: 310 Correct = 93% **a**	26.	Syntax refers to rules for a. arranging words into phrases and sentences b. combining phonemes to form morphemes c. using words symbolically d. combining morphemes into words
Factual LO 2 Page: 310 **a**	27.	Which of the following statements is <u>true</u>? a. Rules of syntax underlie all language use. b. If speakers can use a rule of syntax, they will also be able to verbalize it. c. The process by which we learn the rules of syntax is well understood by psycholinguists. d. Syntax is the first component of language to be mastered by children
Concept/Applied LO 2 Page: 310 **b**	28.	The sentence, "The nervous the stared thick at exam student" would be virtually impossible for an English speaker to understand because the sentence violates the rules of English a. psycholinguistics b. syntax c. morphemes d. phonemes
Concept/Applied LO 2 Page: 310 **d**	29.	Last year 5-year-old Alonda would say "No he coming" when explaining to her younger sister that their older brother would be staying home. Now Alonda will tell her sister "He's not coming." This example illustrates that Alonda has made gains in her use of a. linguistic relativity b. phonemes c. morphemes d. syntax
Critical Thinking LO 2 Page: 310 **a**	30.	Imagine that a race of extraterrestrials came to earth. These extraterrestrials quickly learned to use Earth words to convey meaningful messages, but they never created new combinations of words or learned how to use rules to create meaningful sentences. Their communications would a. not be generative or structured, but would be symbolic and semantic b. lack all the elements of language c. not be symbolic or semantic, but would be generative and structured d. have all the requirements for language
Critical Thinking LO 2 Page: 310 **b**	31.	Imagine that a race of extraterrestrials came to earth. These extraterrestrials quickly learned to use Earth words to convey meaningful messages, and they were able to communicate effectively about unique aspects of their planet in meaningful sentences. Their communications would a. not be symbolic or semantic, but would be generative and structured b. have all the requirements for language c. not be generative or structured, but would be symbolic and semantic d. not be semantic or generative, but would be structured and symbolic
Factual LO 3 Page: 310 Correct = 95% **b**	32.	In language development, babbling refers to producing a. different cries to signify different kinds of discomfort b. a wide variety of phonemes and consonant-vowel combinations c. sound by placing the tongue near the back of the mouth d. random combinations of words

Factual LO 3 Page: 310 Correct = 52% **d**	33.	Babies start babbling at about what age? a. birth b. 1 month c. 3 months d. 6 months
Factual LO 3 Page: 310 Correct = 71% **c**	34.	Which of the following statements is <u>true</u>? a. Babbling simply involves imitation of the parents' speech sounds. b. Babies only babble sounds that are part of the parents' language. c. Babies initially babble sounds used in many different languages. d. Babbling only emerges in infants who are not exposed to correct speech.
Critical Thinking LO 3 Page: 310 Correct = 70% **c**	35.	Which of the following statements is <u>false</u>? a. Infants' first words are similar, even in different languages. b. Infants' first words resemble the syllables they babble spontaneously. c. The sounds babbled by babies from different cultures are different right from the start. d. Infants' first words are likely to consist of sounds that are easy to produce.
Critical Thinking LO 3 Page: 310 **c**	36.	If you were to compare adult speech with the speech of infants under 6 months of age you should expect to find that a. infants produce more morphemes than adults do b. adults are capable of producing more phonemes than infants are c. infants produce more phonemes than adults do d. adults and infants both use the same number of phonemes
Concept/Applied LO 3 Page: 310 **d**	37.	You are at a daycare center and you hear three 12-month-old babies babbling; each baby from a different racial/ethnic background (Asian, Hispanic, and Caucasian). The babbling of each of these infants a. will sound very similar, because maturation is the major determinant of language acquisition during the first year b. will consist mainly of vowel sounds, because consonant sounds don't usually emerge until 14 months of age c. will consist mainly of two-word phrases (telegraphic speech) d. will sound very different, with each child's babbles sounding quite similar to the parents' native language
Factual LO 3 Page: 311 Correct = 65% **c**	38.	The child's first words are generally spoken at about what age? a. 3 to 5 months b. 6 to 8 months c. 10 to 13 months d. 18 to 21 months
Concept/Applied LO 4 Page: 311 Correct = 64% **b**	39.	Valerie is 18 months old. Her productive vocabulary probably consists of a. fewer than 3 words b. 3 to 50 words c. 100 to 200 words d. about 500 words
Critical Thinking LO 4 Page: 311 Correct = 86% **b**	40.	Which of the following situations would lead you to suspect that the child has a language development problem? a. A one-year-old child understands a few words and can say a few words. b. A two-year-old child babbles and uses a few words. c. A three-year-old child uses grammar correctly around 75% to 80% of the time. d. A five-year-old child can use language much better than a chimpanzee.

Concept/Applied LO 4 Page: 311 Correct = 88% **b**	41.	In general, toddlers can a. say more words than they understand b. understand more words than they can say c. understand and say about the same number of words d. use more "action" words than "object" words
Concept/Applied LO 4 Page: 311 **a**	42.	Jenna is 14 months old and uses only "bottle, no, up, bye-bye, mama, and dada" when she talks. However, when the family is on their way to visit Jenna's grandmother, and her father tells Jenna to get her blue bunny from the bedroom and bring it with her, Jenna quickly runs to get the bunny. This episode demonstrates that a. toddlers' receptive vocabularies are larger than their productive vocabularies b. toddlers' productive vocabularies are larger than their receptive vocabularies c. infants have difficulty pronouncing phonemes they have never heard d. Jenna is able to overextend her current vocabulary
Factual LO 4 Page: 311 **d**	43.	Fast mapping is a. the development of a mental representation of one's environment b. the pacing activity associated with genetics, allowing for anticipation of motivational events c. the type of play a child engages in at an early age d. mapping words to underlying concepts after only one exposure
Concept/Applied LO 4 Page: 311 **b**	44.	Dean ate ice cream for the first time yesterday. All day today he has been asking for ice cream. This would be an example of a. metalinguistic awareness b. fast mapping c. overextension d. semantic slanting
Factual LO 4 Page: 312 **a**	45.	Overextension occurs when a. a word is incorrectly used to describe a wider set of objects or actions than it applies to b. a word is incorrectly used to describe a narrower set of objects or actions than it applies to c. the child's vocabulary has become overly large d. a child uses a single word to signify an entire phrase or sentence
Concept/Applied LO 4 Page: 312 **a**	46.	Kailee has learned the word "kitty," but she uses this word when she is referring to cats, bunnies, squirrels, and other small furry animals. Kailee's use of this word illustrates a. overextension b. fast mapping c. telegraphic speech d. babbling
Concept/Applied LO 4 Page: 312 **d**	47.	Robert knows how to say "red," but when his cousin asks him to name the colors of the cars that drive past their house he says red for the red cars, the blue cars, the green cars, and the black cars. Robert's use of this word illustrates a. fast mapping b. telegraphic speech c. babbling d. overextension

LANGUAGE AND THOUGHT

Critical Thinking LO 4 Page: 312 Correct = 60% a	48.	The fact that overextensions are more common in children's production of words than in their comprehension of words implies that overextensions occur because a. toddlers must rely on a very limited vocabulary to express themselves b. toddlers can't consistently identify objects to which different words apply c. children's vocabulary growth occurs at such a rapid pace d. toddlers cannot yet combine words into sentences
Factual LO 4 Page: 312 b	49.	When a child incorrectly uses a word to describe a narrower set of objects or actions than it is meant to, that child is showing evidence of a. overextension b. underextension c. fast mapping d. telegraphic speech
Concept/Applied LO 4 Page: 312 c	50.	Underextension would be evident if a three-year-old child a. used a word too broadly b. used telegraphic speech to communicate complex ideas c. used a word too narrowly d. failed to utilize fast mapping
Factual LO 4 Page: 312 a	51.	A child's early two-word utterances a. are often described as telegraphic speech b. usually begin to appear at about age 12 months c. are always direct imitations of parents' speech d. have little or no communicative value, since the child does not yet use rules of syntax
Factual LO 4 Page: 312 Correct = 38% a	52.	Which of the following statements is true? a. Although telegraphic speech is not unique to the English language, it is not a cross-culturally, universal aspect of language development. b. The emergence of telegraphic speech is unique to the English language. c. The emergence of telegraphic speech is a cross-culturally, universal aspect of language development. d. Telegraphic speech is more prevalent in Western cultures than in non-Western cultures.
Concept/Applied LO 4 Page: 312 b	53.	You are listening to 2-year-old Annie as she says "No eat. No like." She is trying to let you know that she is not going to eat her broccoli because she doesn't like it. Annie's communication illustrates the use of a. underextension b. telegraphic speech c. semantic slanting d. overregularization
Concept/Applied LO 4 Page: 312 b	54.	Two-year-old Owen rushes into the kitchen and tells his sister: "Baby throw. Baby bad." He wants her to know that his baby brother is bad because he just threw his toys on the floor. Owen's communication illustrates the use of a. overregularization b. telegraphic speech c. semantic slanting d. underextension
Factual LO 4 Page: 312 Correct = 55% c	55.	The average length of youngsters' spoken statements ("mean length of utterance") is measured in a. letters b. phonemes c. morphemes d. words

Critical Thinking LO 4 Page: 312 **d**	56.	Dale is six and his sister Alina is four. One major difference that you would expect in comparing their language development would be a. Alina's expressions would have a longer mean length of utterance b. Dale would be more likely to incorporate overextensions into his expressions c. Alina would be less likely to use telegraphic speech in communicating ideas d. Dale's expressions would have a longer mean length of utterance
Concept/Applied LO 4 Page: 312 **c**	57.	A child who uses "wented" as the past tense of the verb "to go" a. is using a metalinguistic transformation b. is probably still at the stage of using semantic slanting c. is using a general rule in an irregular case where it does not apply d. is using motherese to express the past tense
Concept/Applied LO 4 Page: 312 **c**	58.	A child who says, "I sawed a cat in the yard," is making which of the following errors? a. overextension b. underextension c. overregularization d. underregularization
Concept/Applied LO 4 Page: 312 **d**	59.	Four-year-old Nina says: "I runned all the way home." This most likely indicates that a. Nina has forgotten the correct way to form the past tense b. Nina hears improper verb forms spoken in her home c. Nina is still relying on telegraphic speech to convey meaning d. Nina is overregularizing a grammatical rule
Critical Thinking LO 4 Page: 312 **a**	60.	Which of the following statements is _false_? a. Overregularizations occur only in English, which has numerous irregular verbs. b. Overregularizations reflect the fact that children do not acquire the rules of grammar in a single leap. c. Overregularizations decline when school-age children are formally taught subtle exceptions to grammatical rules. d. Overregularizations are more common in children's comprehension of words than in their production of words.
Factual LO 4 Page: 312 Correct = 72% **b**	61.	Metalinguistic awareness refers to a. the ability to recognize one's own grammatical errors b. the ability to reflect on the use of language c. knowledge of which verbs are irregular d. awareness of the role of positive reinforcement in language acquisition
Concept/Applied LO 4 Page: 312 **a**	62.	Seven-year-old Tracy heard a joke in school and asks you: "How could you find a lost dog in the woods." When you are stumped, she tells you: "You stand near a tree and listen for the bark." Tracy's play on words indicates that she is developing a. metalinguistic awareness b. psycholinguistic skills c. linguistic relativity d. the ability to use linguistic heuristics
Factual LO 5 Page: 313 **a**	63.	Evidence from research studies investigating bilingualism suggest that a. bilinguals score higher than monolinguals in analytical reasoning and metalinguistic awareness b. bilingualism has a significant negative effect on overall language development c. bilinguals are faster than monolinguals in language-processing speed d. bilinguals score lower than monolinguals in selective attention and cognitive flexibility

Concept/Applied LO 5 Page: 313 **c**	64.	Dr. Phrasnal is studying cognitive flexibility and selective attention in middle-class bilingual and monolingual subjects. Based on the evidence from previous research studies, Dr. Phrasnal will most likely find that the bilingual subjects score a. lower in both cognitive flexibility and selective attention b. higher in cognitive flexibility, but lower in selective attention c. higher in both cognitive flexibility and selective attention d. lower in cognitive flexibility, but higher in selective attention
Factual LO 5 Page: 313 Correct = 42% **d**	65.	Studies comparing acquisition of a second language by young children and adults suggest that a. young children are far superior to adults in acquiring a second language b. adults are far superior to young children in acquiring a second language c. which age group is superior depends on the specific language involved d. adults may learn a second language as readily as do young children
Concept/Applied LO 5 Page: 314 **b**	66.	A 40-year-old couple emigrate from Poland to the Untied States. They have an 18-year-old son and a 9-year-old daughter. Based on research that has investigated mastery of English as a second language, you should expect that a. the entire family will master English at about the same rate b. the 9-year-old daughter will master English more quickly than her parents and her brother c. both the son and the daughter will master English much more quickly than their parents d. the parents will master English much more quickly than either of their two children
Factual LO 6 Page: 314 **b**	67.	In some early studies researchers attempted to teach chimpanzees to speak. These studies were discontinued when the researchers concluded that a. chimpanzees lack the cognitive capacity to understand and produce language b. chimpanzees lack the necessary vocal equipment to produce human speech sounds c. humans are the only species that is capable of conscious communication d. chimpanzees mastered basic language skills more quickly than human children
Critical Thinking LO 6 Page: 315 **c**	68.	Kanzi's ability to distinguish between "Pour the Coke in the lemonade" and "Pour the lemonade in the Coke" illustrates an understanding of a. neither syntax nor semantics b. semantics, but not syntax c. both syntax and semantics d. syntax, but not semantics
Factual LO 6 Page: 315 **b**	69.	Results from studies in which researchers have attempted to teach chimpanzees to use non-verbal language (i.e., sign language or communication boards) indicate that a. chimpanzees are incapable of acquiring non-verbal communication b. some chimpanzees have appeared to learn many words, and have combined words in appropriate ways c. chimpanzees are capable of learning language to a level equivalent to that seen in 10-year-old children d. chimpanzees can use non-verbal methods to communicate with other chimps, but not with humans
Concept/Applied LO 7 Page: 315 Correct = 55% **a**	70.	Pinker and Bloom (1992) suggest that human language may be a result of evolutionary processes because language allows humans to a. acquire information about the world secondhand b. use trial-and-error learning more effectively c. avoid heuristic fallacies d. engage in more efficient introspection

Factual LO 7 Page: 315 Correct = 54% **d**	71.	Which of the following is <u>not</u> one of the evolutionary advantages that language may have provided? a. more efficient hunting and gathering b. avoidance of predators and other dangers c. reproductive and mating advantages d. more rapid classical conditioning
Factual LO 7 Page: 316 **b**	72.	According to Pinker and Bloom (1992), if the acquisition of language produced a 1% difference in mortality rates among overlapping Neanderthal and human populations, Neanderthals would have become extinct in a. 10 generations b. 30 generations c. 4000 generations d. 30,000 generations
Factual LO 7 Page: 316 Correct = 51% **c**	73.	According to Pinker and Bloom (1992), if the acquisition of language was a trait variation that produced just 1% more offspring, it would increase in prevalence from 0.1% to 99.9% in a. 3 generations b. 30 generations c. 4000 generations d. 40,000 generations
Factual LO 8 Page: 316 Correct = 79% **b**	74.	According to Skinner, children learn a language a. because they possess an innate language acquisition device b. through imitation, reinforcement, and shaping c. as the quality of their thought improves with age d. only when they have reached a certain level of brain maturation
Factual LO 8 Page: 316 Correct = 49% **a**	75.	According to learning theory, children's vocabularies increase and their pronunciation improves as a. parents insist on closer and closer approximations of the correct word before they provide reinforcement b. the quality of their problem-solving ability improves c. the brain matures with age d. transformational rules are mastered
Factual LO 8 Page: 316 **c**	76.	Which of the following is a criticism of Skinner's model of language acquisition? a. Its concepts are extremely vague. b. Children don't seem to learn transformational rules as Skinner said they should. c. It is unreasonable to expect children to learn an infinite number of sentences by imitation. d. Children don't respond to positive reinforcement until they are in preschool, after language is already established.
Critical Thinking LO 8 Page: 316 **b**	77.	The fact that overregularizations occur in many different languages as children master language skills provides evidence against a. the interactionist theory of language development b. the behavioral theory of language development c. the nativist theory of language development d. the linguistic relativity theory of language development

Critical Thinking LO 8 Page: 316 a	78.	Mrs. Bondle seldom corrects her 4-year-old's grammatical errors, such as "Her drinked my milk." However, she is careful to correct factual errors, such as "Tiger ate his milk." Assuming Mrs. Bondle's child develops normal language skills, her pattern of feedback would be inconsistent with a. the behavioral view of language development b. the nativist view of language development c. all major theories of language development d. the transformational theory of language development
Factual LO 8 Page: 316 c	79.	Noam Chomsky contended that a. language is almost wholly a matter of social learning b. biological factors play a relatively minor role in language development c. there is an inborn biological propensity that guides language learning d. reinforcement is the main factor in language learning
Concept/Applied LO 8 Page: 316 Correct = 63% b	80.	Which type of theory best accounts for the apparent rapidity and ease of language acquisition in early childhood? a. behaviorist theory b. nativist theory c. cognitive theory d. social communication theory
Factual LO 8 Page: 316 Correct = 67% a	81.	The hypothesized "language acquisition device" is associated with the a. nativist theory of language b. learning theory of language c. generativity theory of language d. stage theory of language
Critical Thinking LO 8 Page: 317 Correct = 74% b	82.	Which of the following is <u>not</u> an item of evidence Chomsky would use to support the idea of an inborn language learning mechanism? a. Children learn language very quickly and effortlessly. b. Language learning in young children is different across cultures. c. The errors in child speech are common and indicate lawfulness. d. The general rate of language learning is similar for kids from diverse backgrounds.
Critical Thinking LO 8 Page: 317 b	83.	Some researchers have reported that in the first few months babies who are born deaf still coo and babble, just like babies who can hear. This research result is <u>most</u> supportive of a. the cognitive theory of language development b. the nativist theory of language development c. the behavioral theory of language development d. the linguistic relativity theory of language development
Factual LO 8 Page: 317 b	84.	According to cognitive theories of language acquisition a. children learn language through imitation, reinforcement, and shaping b. language acquisition is tied to children's progress in thinking c. children possess a built-in language acquisition device d. thought can occur only after the child acquires language
Concept/Applied LO 8 Page: 317 d	85.	According to cognitive theorists, when children begin to add "s" to nouns to express plurals, it is because they a. have been reinforced for doing so b. have learned a transformational rule c. have learned a phrase-structure rule d. understand the concept of plurality

Critical Thinking LO 8 Page: 317 **d**	86.	Helen has just started to understand the idea that events can happen in the future. Now when she talks about things she is going to do tomorrow or next week she uses the future tense, rather than the present tense. This development in Helen's language skills is most consistent with a. the behavioral theory of language development b. the nativist theory of language development c. the linguistic relativity theory of language development d. cognitive theories of language development
Factual LO 8 Page: 317 Correct = 79% **b**	87.	_____ emphasize the functional value of interpersonal communication. a. Cognitive theorists b. Social communication theorists c. Nativistic theorists d. Behaviorists
Factual LO 8 Page: 317 Correct = 51% **c**	88.	Social communication theorists emphasize the _____ of interpersonal communication. a. linguistic relativity b. interaction between surface and deep structure c. functional value d. problem-solving aspects
Critical Thinking LO 8 Page: 317 **d**	89.	Dr. Grath believes that both an innate predisposition and a supportive environment contribute to language development. Dr. Grath's views are most consistent with those of a. behavioral theories b. nativist theories c. Whorfian theories d. interactionist theories
Concept/Applied LO 8 Page: 317 **d**	90.	Dr. Pratchard believes that experience determines which specific aspects of language an individual will eventually master. Dr. Partchard's views of language development most closely mirror those of a. Noam Chomsky b. Benjamin Whorf c. Herbert Simon d. B. F. Skinner
Concept/Applied LO 8 Page: 317 **a**	91.	Dr. Sciorro believes that because the majority of children acquire language without any effort, there must be a biological mechanism that facilitates language learning. Dr. Sciorro's views of language development most closely mirror those of a. Noam Chomsky b. Herbert Simon c. B. F. Skinner d. Benjamin Whorf
Concept/Applied LO 9 Page: 317 **a**	92.	The linguistic relativity hypothesis predicts that a. people should have difficulty thinking about things they cannot describe in words b. language and thought should develop independently c. people in all cultures should think alike, despite their language differences d. language development should consistently lag behind cognitive development

Factual LO 9 Page: 317 **c**	93.	The linguistic relativity hypothesis a. has yet to be tested experimentally b. has been tested experimentally and soundly rejected c. has received some tentative support in recent experimental studies d. has been tested experimentally and wholeheartedly endorsed
Critical Thinking LO 9 Page: 318 **b**	94.	When 3-year-old Garret is coloring a picture he carefully selects a brown crayon to color a tree trunk, a green crayon for the leaves in the tree and a red crayon for the bird in the tree. When Garret is asked to name the colors he has been using, he confidently answers "blue" each time. The fact that Garret can distinguish between the colors, even though he can't accurately name them yet, suggests that a. the linguistic relativity hypothesis provides an accurate description of the link between thought and language b. the linguistic relativity hypothesis does not accurately reflect the link between thought and language c. social communication theory does not accurately reflect the link between language and behavior d. social communication theory provides an accurate description of the link between language and behavior
Critical Thinking LO 9 Page: 318 **c**	95.	Imagine that anthropologists found a culture that had over 80 different words for rice. If researchers also found that the people in this culture thought about rice in different and more elaborate ways than people who have only one word for rice a. it would provide evidence that the linguistic relativity hypothesis is incorrect b. it would support social communication theory c. it would support the linguistic relativity hypothesis d. it would provide evidence that social communication theory is incorrect
Factual LO 10 Page: 319 Correct = 39% **a**	96.	Which of Greeno's basic kinds of problems requires the problem solver to discover the relations among the parts of the problem? a. inducing structure b. arrangement c. transformation d. recategorization
Factual LO 10 Page: 319 **a**	97.	Series-completion problems are examples of which of Greeno's (1978) categories? a. inducing structure b. arrangement c. transformation d. recategorization
Concept/Applied LO 10 Page: 319 **c**	98.	The entrance exam that Jaclyn is taking for graduate school has a number of questions such as: glove is to hand as sock is to _____. Questions of this type are considered to be a. problems of arrangement b. problems of transformation c. problems of inducing structure d. ill-defined problems
Concept/Applied LO 10 Page: 319 Correct = 77% **d**	99.	Reorganizing the letters "OSHUE" to form an English word is an example of an anagram, which constitutes a problem of a. inducing structure b. lexical analysis c. transformation d. arrangement

Factual LO 10 Page: 319 Correct = 69% **b**	100.	The sudden discovery of the correct solution following incorrect attempts based primarily on trial and error is called a. functional fixedness b. insight c. rearrangement d. transformation
Concept/Applied LO 10 Page: 319 **d**	101.	Marc loves to solve anagrams, and spends a great deal of time working through books of anagrams. It appears that Marc enjoys problems that require a. transformation b. inducing structure c. analogical reasoning d. arrangement
Concept/Applied LO 10 Page: 320 **a**	102.	Marie received a puzzle as a present for her birthday. The puzzle has three pegs, and to solve the puzzle a person is required to move nine disks from the center peg to one of the outside pegs. However, only one disk can be moved at a time, and a larger disk can never be placed on top of a smaller disk. Marie's puzzle is an example of: a. a problem of transformation b. a problem of arrangement c. a problem of inducing structure d. an ill-defined problem
Concept/Applied LO 10 Page: 320 Correct = 90% **d**	103.	"Apple is to fruit as hamburger is to _____" is an example of a. an arrangement problem b. a series-completion problem c. the representativeness heuristic d. an analogy problem
Factual LO 11 Page: 320 Correct = 88% **a**	104.	Laboratory studies of problem solving tend to focus on relatively _____ problems; in the real world most problems are _____ to some degree. a. well-defined; ill-defined b. well-defined; well-defined c. ill-defined; well-defined d. ill-defined; ill-defined
Concept/Applied LO 11 Page: 320 **d**	105.	John is a nationally known composer who has been asked to compose the musical score for a new science-fiction adventure movie. Since no one has ever done a movie of this type before, John will be working without any guidelines. John is faced with a. a problem of arrangement b. a problem of transformation c. a problem of inducing structure d. an ill-defined problem
Factual LO 12 Page: 320 Correct = 90% **c**	106.	When solving problems containing numerical information a. it is safe to assume that all of the information will be needed to solve the problem b. it is a good idea to start by trying to figure out how to use the numerical information c. you should start by figuring out which information is relevant to the problem d. insight will typically produce the fastest, most accurate solution to the problem

Factual LO 12 Page: 321 Correct = 92% c	107.	Functional fixedness is the a. inability to discover the relations among the parts of a problem b. inability to carry out a sequence of transformations in order to reach a specific goal c. tendency to perceive an item only in terms of its most common use d. sudden discovery of the correct solution following incorrect attempts based primarily on trial and error
Factual LO 12 Page: 321 Correct = 73% d	108.	Functional fixedness refers to a. continued use of problem solving strategies that have worked in the past b. arriving at a particularly insightful solution to a problem c. focusing on information that is irrelevant to the solution of the problem d. not seeing a new function for a familiar object
Concept/Applied LO 12 Page: 321 Correct = 80% a	109.	You have a pair of pliers and a bag of nuts in the shell. You are lamenting the fact that you can't shell the nuts because you do not have a nutcracker. Your inability to perceive the pliers as a makeshift nutcracker demonstrates _____ on your part. a. functional fixedness b. mental set c. insight insufficiency d. heuristic reasoning
Concept/Applied LO 12 Page: 321 c	110.	Claudia wants to send a fragile vase to her parents for their anniversary, but she can't find any appropriate packing material in her house. She decides to pop some popcorn and use that to pack around the vase. In this case, Claudia has a. demonstrated functional fixedness in solving her problem b. effectively utilized the availability heuristic in solving her problem c. overcome functional fixedness in solving her problem d. utilized an elimination-by-aspects strategy to solve her problem
Concept/Applied LO 12 Page: 321 b	111.	When Quentin sprained his ankle in a backyard softball game, his girlfriend grabbed a bag of frozen corn from the freezer to wrap around his ankle until they got him to the local clinic. In this case, Quentin's girlfriend a. effectively utilized the availability heuristic b. was able to overcome functional fixedness c. demonstrated functional fixedness in treating Quentin's sprained ankle d. successfully utilized an elimination-by-aspects strategy
Factual LO 13 Page: 321 c	112.	If you tend to persist in using the same problem-solving strategy time after time you are evidencing a. a delusion b. an illusion c. a mental set d. a generic insight
Concept/Applied LO 13 Page: 321 a	113.	Luchins' famous water jar problems illustrate the operation of _____ in problem solving. a. a mental set b. assuming constraints c. functional fixedness d. irrelevant focusing

Concept/Applied LO 13 Page: 321 **a**	114.	Eva just upgraded her software package. However, even though the updated version contains a number of more efficient methods for working with files, Eva continues to work with files the way she did before the upgrade. In this case, Eva is showing evidence of a. mental set b. belief perseverance c. priming d. the availability heuristic
Concept/Applied LO 13 Page: 321 **b**	115.	Rylee's algebra teacher is amazed at the creativity Rylee shows in solving homework problems. He seldom uses the same method on two consecutive problems, even when the problems are very similar in content and structure. Although Rylee makes lots of mistakes in algebra, he is unlikely to experience a. overregularization in his problem solving b. mental set in his problem solving c. functional fixedness in his problem solving d. noncompensatory problem solving
Concept/Applied LO 14 Page: 322 **c**	116.	When Alaina is working on her bicycle she brings her entire tool kit out on the driveway and starts pulling wrenches from the tool kit at random and trying them until she finds one that fits. Alaina's approach when she is working on her bicycle could be best described as a. alternate outcomes analysis b. working backward c. trial and error d. forming subgoals
Factual LO 14 Page: 322 Correct = 93% **d**	117.	Attempting possible solutions to a problem sequentially, then discarding the ones that don't work until you find one that does, is called the _____ method of problem solving. a. working backward b. heuristic c. algorithmic d. trial-and-error
Factual LO 14 Page: 322 Correct = 49% **c**	118.	An algorithm is a. the set of possible pathways to a solution considered by a problem solver b. a guiding principle or "rule of thumb" used in problem solving c. a methodical procedure for trying all possible solutions to a problem d. equivalent to a heuristic
Factual LO 14 Page: 322 Correct = 43% **c**	119.	Which of the following statements is <u>false</u>? a. Algorithms can be used to apply the trial-and-error approach systematically. b. If an algorithm is available for a problem, it guarantees that a solution can eventually be found. c. Algorithms exist for all well-defined problems. d. Algorithms may be impractical when the problem space is large.
Concept/Applied LO 14 Page: 322 **b**	120.	Lance is trying to solve a complex anagram puzzle. He systematically tries every potential solution by testing each possible combination of the letters provided. In this case, Lance is a. working backward to solve the anagram b. using an algorithm to solve the anagram c. using a heuristic to solve the anagram d. using means-ends analysis to solve the anagram

Concept/Applied 121. Vivian is making quiche for the very first time. She carefully follows the step-by-
LO 14   step directions provided in her cookbook. In this case, Vivian is using
Page: 322   a. an algorithm to help her prepare the quiche
a   b. a heuristic to help her prepare the quiche
                 c. functional fixedness to help her prepare the quiche
                 d. framing to help her prepare the quiche

Concept/Applied 122. Salvador hates to work through the problems on his calculus assignments step-by-
LO 14   step and he often tries shortcuts that might save him some time. It appears that
Page: 322   Salvador prefers to use
c   a. algorithms rather than heuristics in solving calculus problems
                 b. functional fixedness in solving calculus problems
                 c. heuristics rather than algorithms in solving calculus problems
                 d. analogies in solving calculus problems

Concept/Applied 123. Esmeralda wants to use her roommate's computer to work on her term paper.
LO 14   However the roommate has password protection on the computer's boot sequence.
Page: 322   Rather than starting at "a" and systematically testing every possible word in the
a   English language, Esmeralda makes some educated guesses about the passwords,
             based on what she knows about her roommate. In this case, Esmeralda is using
                 a. a heuristic to get past the password protection
                 b. an algorithm to get past the password protection
                 c. reframing to get past the password protection
                 d. representativeness to get past the password protection

Factual   124. Working backward is a good strategy to follow when
LO 14   a. a problem has obvious subgoals
Page: 323   b. you can recognize the similarity between two problems
Correct = 66%   c. the problem does not have a well-specified goal
d   d. you have many options available at the beginning of a problem, but few options
                    at the end

Concept/Applied 125. In which case will working backward to solve a problem be an effective strategy?
LO 14   a. when a problem has a well-defined endpoint
Page: 323   b. when a problem is unsolvable by heuristics
a   c. when it is necessary to change the representation of a problem
                 d. when a problem has multiphasic branch points

Concept/Applied 126. Mayra wants to generate a set of anagrams for a contest in the campus paper. To
LO 14   generate the anagrams she starts with the words that the contestants need to come up
Page: 323   with to win the contest, and then scrambles the letters. In this case, Mayra's method
c   of solving the problem is consistent with the problem-solving heuristic known as
                 a. means-end analysis
                 b. searching for analogies
                 c. working backward
                 d. trial-and-error

Factual   127. If you solve a current problem using the solution to a previous, similar problem,
LO 14   which heuristic are you applying?
Page: 323   a. working backward from the goal
Correct = 65%   b. the availability heuristic
c   c. searching for analogies
                 d. formulating subgoals

Concept/Applied LO 14 Page: 323 Correct = 67% **b**	128.	Observing the similarities between a new problem to be solved and one you've successfully solved in the past is called a. an algorithm b. searching for analogies c. shaping d. the alternative outcomes effect
Concept/Applied LO 14 Page: 323 **d**	129.	When Graham is printing copies from the computer in the computer classroom, the paper keeps jamming in the machine. He takes the paper out of the paper tray, fans it, and then flips it over, so the other side of the paper feeds first. This is the way he solves similar problems on the photocopy machine at the office where he works. In this case, Graham's method of solving the problem is consistent with the problem-solving heuristic known as a. means-end analysis b. working backward c. trial-and-error d. searching for analogies
Concept/Applied LO 14 Page: 324 Correct = 73% **c**	130.	Diagrams sometimes facilitate problem-solving because they a. aid in the search for analogies b. make it easier to execute algorithms c. change the representation of the problem d. relax constraints on problem solutions
Concept/Applied LO 15 Page: 326 Correct = 59% **d**	131.	Clarice has a tendency to accept the physical environment as given and makes little if any attempt at analyzing or restricting it. Clarice would be considered a. extrinsically motivated b. a novice at problem solving c. field independent d. field dependent
Concept/Applied LO 15 Page: 326 **a**	132.	Tiffany has gotten the same error message five times in a row as she has tried to print out her computer file. Each time she followed the same six steps, and she can't understand why she keeps getting the error message, because she is sure she is executing the steps in the correct order. Her friend, Daisy, suggests that Tiffany try moving to a different computer terminal, and when Tiffany uses a different computer she is able to print the file without any problems. Based on this incident, Witkin and his colleagues might suggest that Tiffany was a. field dependent b. field independent c. unable to use noncompensatory strategies d. high in metacognition
Concept/Applied LO 15 Page: 326 **c**	133.	Levi enjoys solving logical reasoning problems. He seems to have a knack for looking at problems in new ways, and reorganizing the components of problems in creative ways. It is likely that Levi a. relies more heavily on external than internal frames of reference b. uses algorithms more frequently than heuristics in solving problems c. relies more heavily on internal than external frames of reference d. will introduce unnecessary constraints into problems that he is working on
Concept/Applied LO 15 Page: 326 **d**	134.	Field _____ subjects are generally better at solving problems of arrangement; field _____ subjects are generally better at solving problems that depend on overcoming functional fixedness. a. dependent; independent b. dependent; dependent c. independent; dependent d. independent; independent

Concept/Applied LO 15 Page: 326 **d**	135.	During the Apollo 14 mission the ground engineers had to devise a new way of cleaning the capsule air supply, using only the materials the astronauts had on board the space capsule. Based on the work of Witkin and his colleagues, the engineers would have the greatest chance of success in solving this problem if they a. were field dependent b. were high in metacognition c. used a compensatory strategy d. were field independent
Concept/Applied LO 16 Page: 327 Correct = 45% **d**	136.	The concept of field dependence-independence highlights the importance of _____ in determining problem-solving skills. a. expertise b. behavioral factors c. nativistic factors d. cultural factors
Factual LO 16 Page: 327 Correct = 64% **a**	137.	The educational practices in modern Western societies seem to nourish a. field independence b. risk-averse behaviors c. field dependence d. algorithmic problem-solving
Concept/Applied LO 16 Page: 327 **c**	138.	In cultures that depend on hunting and gathering for subsistence, a(n) _____ style is more adaptive. a. field dependent b. risk-averse c. field independent d. algorithmic
Concept/Applied LO 16 Page: 327 **a**	139.	Eskimo hunters of the Arctic wastelands and the Aboriginal hunters of the desert wastelands in Australia are a. among the most field independent peoples of the world b. among the most risk-averse peoples of the world c. among the most field dependent peoples of the world d. two groups who are least likely to utilize heuristic reasoning skills
Concept/Applied LO 16 Page: 327 Correct = 63% **a**	140.	Sean was stranded in the desert when his plane crashed. He has the best chances for survival under these circumstances if his cognitive style is a. field independent b. risk-averse c. field dependent d. based on algorithms
Concept/Applied LO 16 Page: 327 **a**	141.	Tylo belongs to a nomadic hunter-gatherer tribe in the South American jungle. Based on what is known about cultural differences in cognitive style, it is quite likely that Tylo will score high in a. field independence b. field dependence c. belief perseverance d. fast mapping

Concept/Applied LO 16 Page: 327 **d**	142.	Darius belongs to a religious sect whose livelihood is based on agriculture. There are strict rules regarding dress and behavior, and children are expected to help in the fields as soon as they are old enough. Based on what is known about cultural differences in cognitive style, it is quite likely that Darius will score high in a. field independence b. belief perseverance c. fast mapping d. field dependence
Concept/Applied LO 17 Page: 328 Correct = 37% **c**	143.	Car A has good mileage, a low price, and low maintenance, or three pluses. Car B has only a low price and low maintenance, or two pluses. So, I'll choose Car A. This is an example of a. a weighted additive strategy b. a noncompensatory decision model c. a purely additive strategy d. elimination-by-aspects
Concept/Applied LO 17 Page: 328 **b**	144.	Marisa is trying to decide between two computers that are advertised at the same price. Both computers are the same in most respects; however, computer A has a 600 MHz processor and 64 MB of RAM while computer B has a slower 500 MHz processor but 128 MB of RAM. Because Marisa thinks that the speed of the processor matters more than the amount of RAM, she decides to buy computer A. In this case, Marisa has made her decision using a. elimination by aspects b. a compensatory decision model c. a noncompensatory decision model d. the representativeness heuristic
Concept/Applied LO 17 Page: 328 **a**	145.	Brett is trying to decide which graduate schools he will apply to. He is making up a list of all the positive and negative aspects he feels are associated with 100 different schools, and he plans to send applications to the 10 schools that score the highest when he adds up all the positive points and subtracts all the negative points. The decision strategy that Brett is using is referred to as a. a compensatory decision model b. elimination by aspects c. a noncompensatory decision model d. an expected value strategy
Factual LO 17 Page: 328 Correct = 79% **c**	146.	If an alternative is eliminated whenever it fails to satisfy some minimum criterion on an attribute, which decision-making strategy is being used? a. a purely additive strategy b. a weighted additive strategy c. elimination by aspects d. a compensatory strategy
Concept/Applied LO 17 Page: 328 Correct = 36% **a**	147.	When using elimination by aspects, it is best to evaluate the _____ aspect first. a. most important b. least important c. most favorable d. least favorable
Concept/Applied LO 17 Page: 328 Correct = 79% **c**	148.	Christine wants to buy a new television. She will not purchase a television with a screen smaller than 25 inches. She will also not purchase a television that costs more than $500. Her decision-making strategy is referred to as a. a purely additive strategy b. a weighted additive strategy c. elimination by aspects d. a compensatory strategy

Concept/Applied LO 17 Page: 328 **d**	149.	Dallas is planning to buy a new computer. He will not buy a computer that has a processor speed that is less than 500 MHz, and he will not buy a computer that does not have at least a 20GB hard drive. The decision strategy that Dallas is using is referred to as a. a purely additive decision strategy b. a compensatory decision strategy c. the availability heuristic d. elimination by aspects
Concept/Applied LO 17 Page: 328 **c**	150.	Kimba is trying to decide which graduate schools she will apply to. She has decided not to send applications to any university located in a city with a population greater than 500,000 people, and she does not plan to apply to any university more than 500 miles from the city where her parents live. The decision strategy that Kimba is using is referred to as a. a purely additive decision strategy b. a compensatory decision strategy c. elimination by aspects d. the availability heuristic
Concept/Applied LO 17 Page: 328 Correct = 61% **b**	151.	You apply to a graduate school that decides on who is accepted by demanding that three successive criteria be met: major GPA over 3.50; overall GPA over 3.00; GRE over 1000. Failure to meet any one eliminates an applicant. This is an example of a. a compensatory decision model b. a noncompensatory decision model c. a weighted decision strategy d. a purely additive decision strategy
Factual LO 17 Page: 329 **a**	152.	Research suggests that when a decision task involves many options and factors, people are more likely to use a. a noncompensatory strategy b. base rate strategies c. a compensatory strategy d. trial-and-error strategies
Concept/Applied LO 17 Page: 329 **a**	153.	Melva is trying to decide which of two different cars to purchase; Parker is trying to decide which one of eight different cars to buy. Based on the research conducted by John Payne, you might expect that under these circumstances a. Melva will be more likely to use a compensatory strategy and Parker will be more likely to use a noncompensatory strategy b. Melva will be more likely to use a noncompensatory strategy and Parker will be more likely to use a compensatory strategy c. both Melva and Parker will be likely to use a noncompensatory strategy d. both Melva and Parker will be likely to use a compensatory strategy
Concept/Applied LO 17 Page: 329 **c**	154.	Desiree and Jaimie are planning their schedules for next semester. Desiree is looking at the three available history classes and trying to decide which one she should take; Jamie is reading the descriptions of the ten literature classes that are scheduled and trying to decide which one to take. Based on the research conducted by John Payne, you might expect that under these circumstances a. Desiree will be more likely to use a noncompensatory strategy and Jaime will be more likely to use a compensatory strategy b. both Desiree and Jaime will be likely to use a noncompensatory strategy c. Desiree will be more likely to use a compensatory strategy and Jaime will be more likely to use a noncompensatory strategy d. both Desiree and Jaime will be likely to use a compensatory strategy

Factual LO 18 Page: 329 **a**	155.	Which of the following statements is <u>most</u> accurate? a. Delayed decisions are common when alternatives are not dramatically different in their overall attractiveness. b. In reaching a decision delays almost always lead to better decisions because there is additional time for reflection. c. Delay in reaching a decision reduces people's reliance on heuristics, and can help to eliminate the effects of framing. d. Additional deliberation in decision making often leads people to reconsider the attributes that have the most relevance to the final decision.
Factual LO 18 Page: 329 **d**	156.	Which of the following statements is <u>most</u> accurate? a. Delayed decisions are common when alternatives differ dramatically in their overall attractiveness. b. In reaching a decision delays almost always lead to better decisions because there is additional time for reflection. c. Delay in reaching a decision reduces people's reliance on heuristics, and can help to eliminate the effects of framing. d. Additional deliberation in decision making often leads people to consider attributes that have no relevance to the final decision.
Concept/Applied LO 19 Page: 330 Correct = 87% **b**	157.	You flip a fair coin ten times. Each time it comes up heads you get 10 cents. Each time it comes up tails you lose 5 cents. What is your expected value for each flip of the coin? a. +10 cents b. +5 cents c. -5 cents d. -10 cents
Concept/Applied LO 19 Page: 330 **b**	158.	Jacob is thinking of buying a $1 lottery ticket. In Lottery A his odds of winning are 1 out of a 1000, and he may win $500. In Lottery B his odds of winning are 1 out of 5000, but he may win $5000. Based on expected value theory, Jacob should a. buy either ticket because both lotteries have the same expected value b. buy a ticket from Lottery B because it has a higher expected value c. buy a ticket from Lottery A because it has a higher expected value d. not buy either ticket because both lotteries have very low odds of winning
Concept/Applied LO 19 Page: 330 **d**	159.	Wilson is watching two different roulette-type games at a local charity bazaar. Each game costs $1.00 to play. In one game there are ten different numbers, and if the number he selects comes up he will win $12.00. In the other game there are 100 different numbers, but if the number he selects comes up he will win $50.00. Based on expected value theory, Wilson should a. play the second game because it has a higher expected value b. play either one of the games because they both have the same expected value c. not play either game because they both have such low odds of winning d. play the first game because it has a higher expected value
Factual LO 19 Page: 330 Correct = 57% **b**	160.	Subjective utility refers to a. the expected value of an outcome b. what an outcome is personally worth to an individual c. a personal estimate of what the probability of an outcome is d. an individual's willingness to take risks
Factual LO 19 Page: 330 Correct = 78% **c**	161.	Subjective probability refers to a. the expected value of an outcome b. what an outcome is personally worth to an individual c. a personal estimate of what the probability of an outcome is d. an individual's willingness to take risks

Concept/Applied LO 19 Page: 330 Correct = 40% **b**	162.	Assume that odds of a new computer requiring any type of service in the first two years are less than 1 in 10,000, and the average cost any computer service calls is only $120. However, Karen pays $300 for a 2-year service contract on her new computer. She explains that her peace of mind is well worth the cost of the contract. In this case, Karen's decision to purchase the service agreement appears to be based primarily on a. expected value b. subjective utility c. subjective probability d. noncompensatory factors
Factual LO 19 Page: 330 **c**	163.	Research into the emotional impact of unexpected outcomes suggests that surprising wins provide _____ pleasure than expected victories, and surprising losses are _____ disappointing. a. more; less b. less; more c. more; more d. less; less
Concept/Applied LO 19 Page: 330 **c**	164.	Fernando and Isabelle are both seniors at Central High and their school's basketball tem just won the divisional championship. Fernando was certain the Central High team would be eliminated early, while Isabelle was certain their team would win the divisional title. Based on the research into the emotional impact of unexpected outcomes, you should predict that, compared to Fernando, Isabelle will a. be more excited by Central High's win, because it was what she expected b. tend to overestimate Central High's chances for future victories c. be less excited by Central High's win, because it was what she expected d. tend to underestimate Central High's chances for future victories
Concept/Applied LO 19 Page: 330 **a**	165.	Marina and Deven both received a "C" on their last English paper. When she handed her paper in, Marina didn't think she had done very well. However, Deven was convinced that she had written an "A" paper. Based on the research into the emotional impact of unexpected outcomes, you should expect that a. Deven will be more disappointed by the grade that she received b. Marina will be more disappointed by the grade that she received c. both students will be equally disappointed by the grades they received d. neither student will be disappointed by the grades they received, because a "C" is still a passing grade
Factual LO 20 Page: 330 Correct = 58% **d**	166.	Basing the estimated probability of an event on the ease with which instances come to mind is called the a. law of small numbers b. representativeness heuristic c. conjunction fallacy d. availability heuristic
Concept/Applied LO 20 Page: 330 **c**	167.	You can't think of a single instance when Cathy helped you out, and so you decide that Cathy must be an ungenerous person. Your judgment is based on a. subjective utility b. the representativeness heuristic c. the availability heuristic d. expected value

Concept/Applied LO 20 Page: 330 Correct = 76% a	168.	The availability heuristic implies that people will _____ the frequency of events that are easy to remember and _____ the frequency of events that are hard to remember. a. overestimate; underestimate b. underestimate; overestimate c. overestimate; overestimate d. underestimate; underestimate
Concept/Applied LO 20 Page: 330 Correct = 54% a	169.	When people overestimate the frequency of violent crimes because these events generate a great deal of media coverage, they are using a. the availability heuristic b. the representativeness heuristic c. a compensatory model d. the elimination by aspects strategy
Concept/Applied LO 20 Page: 330 d	170.	Juliana used to enjoy eating chicken, but since she has seen all the headlines about people becoming ill from eating chicken she has decided she will never eat chicken again. In this case, Juliana's decision to stop eating chicken may have been influenced by a. the representativeness heuristic b. the conjunction fallacy c. the overconfidence effect d. the availability heuristic
Concept/Applied LO 20 Page: 330 a	171.	Zackary's friend asks how well Zackary gets along with his younger brother. Zackary thinks about how irritating his younger brother was yesterday, and the big fight they had as a result, and tells his friend that he doesn't get along with his brother at all. In this instance, Zackary's response is consistent with a. the availability heuristic b. the representativeness heuristic c. the conjunction fallacy d. the hindsight bias
Factual LO 20 Page: 330 c	172.	The representativeness heuristic refers to our tendency to a. ignore subjective probabilities when making decisions b. estimate the probability of an event by judging the ease with which relevant instances come to mind c. estimate the probability of an event based on how similar it is to the typical prototype of that event d. ignore common stereotypes when estimating probabilities
Concept/Applied LO 20 Page: 331 d	173.	After seeing your new neighbor walking very stiffly and primly by your house wearing horn-rimmed glasses on a chain, a cardigan sweater, and her hair in a bun, you decide she must be a librarian. Your judgment is based on a. subjective probability b. subjective utility c. the availability heuristic d. the representativeness heuristic
Concept/Applied LO 20 Page: 331 b	174.	Elisa is entering survey data from adult males in a research study. One respondent has listed his height as 6 feet 5 inches, but the occupation is hard to decipher. Elisa thinks it might be basketball player or bank president. She decides to enter basketball player as the occupation. In this case, Elisa a. demonstrated the conjunction fallacy in making her decision b. probably relied on the representativeness heuristic to make her decision c. demonstrated overextension in making her decision d. probably relied on the availability heuristic to make her decision

| Concept/Applied
LO 20
Page: 331
c | 175. | Byron has been watching his new neighbor for a week. She drives a sporty car, carries a cell phone, and wears nothing but blue business suits. Byron decides his new neighbor must be a lawyer. In this case, Byron seems to have formed an opinion about his new neighbor's occupation based on
a. the hindsight bias
b. the availability heuristic
c. the representativeness heuristic
d. the base-rate fallacy |

| Concept/Applied
LO 21
Page: 331
d | 176. | Christine has been following the state lottery for over a year, and she has a record of the number of times every number has been selected. She is ready to invest $1000 in lottery tickets with the same six-number combination on each ticket. She is going to choose the six numbers that have occurred the least frequently in the last year because she is sure they will be picked eventually. In this case, Christine is showing evidence of
a. the availability heuristic
b. the gambler's fallacy
c. the conjunction fallacy
d. the base rate fallacy |

| Concept/Applied
LO 21
Page: 331
b | 177. | Malcolm has been watching a roulette-type game at a local charity bazaar. The game has only ten numbers on the wheel, and every number except 8 has come up as a winner during the last 15 minutes. Malcolm decides to bet $10 on number 8, because it has to come up eventually. In this case, Malcolm is showing evidence of
a. the availability heuristic
b. the gambler's fallacy
c. the conjunction fallacy
d. the base rate fallacy |

| Factual
LO 21
Page: 331
d | 178. | The conjunction fallacy is a tendency to
a. ignore information about base rates when estimating the probabilities of certain combinations of outcomes
b. overestimate the odds of a chance event if that event hasn't occurred recently
c. draw general conclusions based on a few isolated cases
d. believe that the odds of two uncertain events happening together are greater than the odds of either event happening alone |

| Concept/Applied
LO 21
Page: 331
d | 179. | Claude and Marie are excited because they have just bought a restaurant from the previous owners. The two partners know that the last seven restaurants that have been operated at that location have gone bankrupt within a year of their openings, but Claude and Marie are certain their restaurant will be successful because they plan on working hard to be a success. In this case, the two new business partners are
a. showing belief perseverance
b. showing evidence of the gambler's fallacy
c. showing the confirmation bias
d. apparently ignoring base rates |

| Concept/Applied
LO 21
Page: 331
c | 180. | Autumn has been figure skating since she was five years old. She has never placed higher than third in any of the competitions she has been in, but she is still convinced that she will be able to become a professional figure skater in a few years. Her coach and her parents have tried to tell her that not many people make it as professional skaters, but Autumn is convinced that she can beat the odds. In this case, Autumn is
a. displaying evidence of mental set
b. showing belief perseverance
c. apparently ignoring base rates
d. showing the confirmation bias |

Factual LO 22 Page: 333 a	181.	In the Featured Study on the alternative outcomes effect, Windschitl and Wells found that even when the probability of a focal outcome is held constant, the perceived likelihood of that outcome occurring depends on a. how the probabilities for the alternative outcomes are distributed b. the ease with which alternative outcomes can be brought to mind c. the base rate of occurrence for the alternative outcomes d. the representativeness of the alternative outcomes
Concept/Applied LO 22 Page: 333 b	182.	Serena has a raffle ticket for a drawing in which there are a total of 1000 tickets, and each person can only have one ticket. Garth has a raffle ticket for a drawing in which there are a total of 1000 tickets, but the remaining tickets are held by only 40 other people. Based on the alternative outcomes effect a. Serena should rate her chances of winning as being lower than Garth's b. Serena should rate her chances of winning as being higher than Garth's c. Garth should rate his chances of winning as being higher than Serena's d. Serena should rate her chances of winning as being the same than Garth's
Critical Thinking LO 22 Page: 333 c	183.	Arthur Andrews was running for county supervisor, and throughout his campaign the polls consistently indicated he held 30% of the popular vote. Initially there were seven other candidates, but as election day came closer five of the other candidates dropped out of the race. Based on the alternative outcomes effect, Arthur Andrews probably a. felt more confident of victory when there were fewer opposing candidates b. believed the polls were more accurate when there were fewer opposing candidates c. felt less confident of victory when there were fewer opposing candidates d. believed the polls were less accurate when there were fewer opposing candidates
Factual LO 23 Page: 334 d	184.	According to Gigerenzer (1997), the human mind is wired to think in terms of a. base rates and probabilities, rather than raw frequencies b. both raw frequencies and base rates c. neither raw frequencies nor base rates d. raw frequencies, rather than base rates and probabilities
Factual LO 23 Page: 334 a	185.	Evolutionary theorists argue that if decision problems were stated in terms of raw frequencies, then a. base rate neglect and the conjunction fallacy would both disappear b. base rate neglect and the conjunction fallacy would both become more pronounced c. base rate neglect would disappear, but the conjunction fallacy would become more pronounced d. base rate neglect would become more pronounced, but the conjunction fallacy would disappear
Concept/Applied LO 24 Page: 335 a	186.	Interactionist theories of language development help to illustrate which of your text's unifying themes? a. Heredity and environment jointly influence behavior. b. Psychology evolves in a sociohistorical context. c. Our experience of the world is highly subjective. d. Psychology is empirical.

Concept/Applied LO 24 Page: 335 **c**	187.	During the 1950s and 1960s creative new ways of measuring mental processes paved the way for the cognitive revolution. The development of new research methods helps to illustrate which of your text's unifying themes? a. Our experience of the world is highly subjective. b. Psychology is theoretically diverse. c. Psychology is empirical. d. Behavior is determined by multiple causes.
Concept/Applied LO 24 Page: 335 **c**	188.	The fact that variations in cognitive style sometimes reflect the ecological demands of one's environment helps to illustrate which of your text's unifying themes? a. Our experience of the world is highly subjective. b. Psychology is theoretically diverse. c. Our behavior is shaped by our cultural heritage. d. Psychology evolves in a sociohistorical context.
Concept/Applied LO 24 Page: 335 **d**	189.	The fact that choices which are objectively identical can seem very different when reframed in different terms helps to illustrate which of your text's unifying themes? a. Heredity and environment jointly influence behavior. b. Psychology is theoretically diverse. c. Our behavior is shaped by our cultural heritage. d. Our experience of the world is highly subjective.
Concept/Applied LO 25 Page: 336 **d**	190.	Mr. and Mrs. Jones have five daughters. Hoping for a son, they decide to have a sixth child, reasoning that a boy is long overdue. Is their reasoning correct, and why? a. Yes – the greater the number of girls a couple has had, the greater the likelihood that the next will be a boy b. Yes – after having so many daughters, a boy is almost a sure thing c. No – it is more likely that Mr. and Mrs. Jones will continue to produce girls d. No – the probability of a son is unaffected by the sex of the previous children
Factual LO 25 Page: 336 Correct = 73% **a**	191.	The likelihood of misleading results in a small sample is _____ the likelihood of misleading results in a large sample. a. greater than b. less than c. the same as d. sometimes greater and sometimes less than
Concept/Applied LO 25 Page: 336 **b**	192.	Reed is an avid basketball fan who is excited by the fact that the local professional team has won the first five games of the season. Based on this early performance, Reed is looking forward to a record-breaking season. This faulty logic illustrates an error in statistical reasoning because a. later performance is seldom related to early performance b. small samples cannot be expected to provide reliable indications of long-run performance c. winning streaks usually only last for a short period of time d. small samples are the most accurate representation of final outcomes
Concept/Applied LO 26 Page: 337 Correct = 53% **c**	193.	Many people mistakenly believe their chances of dying in an airplane crash are greater than their chances of dying in an automobile crash. This belief reflects the operation of a. confirmation bias b. the belief in the law of small numbers c. the availability heuristic d. the conjunction fallacy

Concept/Applied LO 26 Page: 337 a	194.	Maribel is on a jury and she is already convinced that the defendant in the case is not guilty. She listens very attentively to everything the defense attorneys have to say, but she tends to pay less attention when the prosecution is presenting evidence. In this instance, Maribel is showing evidence of a. a confirmation bias b. the conjunction fallacy c. the base-rate fallacy d. the overconfidence effect
Concept/Applied LO 26 Page: 337 c	195.	One of the implications of having a confirmation bias is that a. it allows people to make accurate decisions more quickly b. it interferes with our ability to accurately code and store information c. once a conclusion is drawn about something, subsequent information is interpreted as consistent with the conclusion d. it tends to produce mental set and functional fixedness
Concept/Applied LO 26 Page: 337 c	196.	Corey was serving on a jury in a criminal case, and the jury reached a unanimous "not guilty" verdict. Several months later some additional evidence came to light that strongly suggested that the defendant was, in fact, guilty of the crime in question. Corey is still not convinced by the new evidence, and claims he wouldn't have voted guilty, even if the new information had been presented during the trial. In this example, Corey is showing evidence of a. the conjunction fallacy b. the availability heuristic c. belief perseverance d. mental set
Factual LO 27 Page: 338 Correct = 71% c	197.	Overestimating the accuracy of your answer illustrates a. the conjunction fallacy b. the negative effects of framing c. the overconfidence effect d. the gambler's fallacy
Factual LO 27 Page: 338 c	198.	Which of the following statements is most accurate? a. The overconfidence effect is seen only when making predictions about events that have personal significance. b. In their predictions about personal matters, people tend to be more accurate than confident. c. Even professionals and experts tend to be overconfident about their own predictions. d. The overconfidence effect is seen only when making predictions about events that have no personal significance.
Factual LO 27 Page: 339 Correct = 33% b	199.	Kahneman and Tversky (1984) concluded that people are much more likely to take risks when a. they are not asked to provide rationales for their choices b. seeking to cut their losses c. the issue is framed in terms of probability of success d. the probability of success is equal to the probability of failure
Factual LO 27 Page: 339 Correct = 44% a	200.	When people are seeking gains they are _____ to make risky decisions than when they are attempting to cut their losses. a. less likely b. more likely c. equally likely d. less likely if female but more likely if male

Concept/Applied 201. Fred needs major heart surgery and he has consulted with two doctors about the
LO 27 operation. Dr. Marx tells Fred he has a 90% chance of surviving the surgery; Dr.
Page: 339 Scalli tells Fred there is a 10% chance that he won't survive the surgery. Based on
Correct = 86% Kahneman and Tversky's research
c
   a. Fred is most likely to let Dr. Scalli perform the operation.
   b. Fred will probably avoid making a decision until it is too late.
   c. Fred is most likely to let Dr. Marx perform the operation.
   d. Fred won't care who does the surgery because both doctors have presented the same information.

Concept/Applied 202. Researchers presented two groups of physicians with information regarding a
LO 27 surgical procedure. Half the physicians were told that on average 15 out of 100
Page: 339 people die as a result of the surgery; the remaining physicians were told that on
a average 85 out of 100 people survive the surgery. Based on the framing effect you should expect
   a. the second group of physicians would be more likely to recommend the surgical procedure to their patients
   b. the first group of physicians would be more likely to recommend the surgical procedure to their patients
   c. both groups of physicians would recommend the surgical procedure to their patients
   d. neither group of physicians would recommend the surgical procedure to their patients

Critical Thinking 203. A sales representative from an investment company is trying to convince a young
LO 27 couple to invest in one of the company's mutual funds. He will probably be most
Page: 339 successful if he
b
   a. mentions the names of other people who have invested in the fund
   b. stresses that the fund has had solid returns in 12 of the past 15 years
   c. stresses that the fund has only lost money in 3 of the past 15 years
   d. leaves a detailed prospectus containing a lot of statistical analyses

Factual 204. The deliberate choice of words to create specific emotional responses is referred to
LO 28 as
Page: 340
a
   a. semantic slanting
   b. linguistic relativity
   c. belief perseverance
   d. phonemic overextension

Concept/Applied 205. A local grocer wanted to cut down on the use of credit cards in his store. He found
LO 28 his business declined significantly when he imposed a "surcharge" for credit card
Page: 340 sales. However, his business boomed when he offered "rebates" for cash sales, even
b though customers paid the same amount for products in both cases. This situation illustrates the impact of
   a. phonemic overextension
   b. semantic slanting
   c. the alternative outcomes effect
   d. the conjunction fallacy

Factual 206. Implying that a negative label will be applied to a person who makes an unpopular
LO 28 decision is known as
Page: 340
c
   a. the alternative outcomes effect
   b. the belief perseverance effect
   c. anticipatory name calling
   d. the linguistic relativity effect

Concept/Applied LO 28 Page: 340 **d**	207.	According to the text, people who are critical thinkers recognize semantic slanting and understand that a. only negative language can have a significant influence in shaping thoughts b. neither negative and positive language have a significant influence in shaping thoughts c. only positive language can have a significant influence in shaping thoughts d. both negative and positive language can have a significant influence in shaping thoughts
Integrative Correct = 37% **a**	208.	In light of their views on language acquisition, which theorist would expect apes to progress the furthest in language development? a. B. F. Skinner b. Noam Chomsky c. Jean Piaget d. Herb Terrace
Integrative Correct = 29% **c**	209.	Alice is trying to decide whether to invest $5000 in the stock market or government bonds. She thinks, "My father lost his shirt in the stock market," and decides to put her money in government bonds. Alice is engaged in _____, and her decision was guided by _____. a. compensatory decision making; the availability heuristic b. compensatory decision making; the representativeness heuristic c. risky decision making; the availability heuristic d. risky decision making; anticipatory semantic slanting
Integrative Correct = 78% **c**	210.	To solve the "string problem" described in the text, you have to catch the screwdriver while holding the second string. This _____ problem is often solved in a burst of _____ when a person overcomes _____. a. transformation; insight; heuristic constraints b. arrangement; intuition; confirmation bias c. arrangement; insight; functional fixedness d. transformation; intuition; mental set
Study Guide LO 1 Page: 308 **b**	211.	Which of the following explanations best explains the success of the cognitive revolution? a. the refining of introspection as a research method b. the development of empirical methods c. the use of psychotherapy to explore the unconscious d. the success in teaching chimps to use language
Study Guide LO 2 Page: 308 **d**	212.	Which of the following is not one of the basic properties of language? a. generative b. symbolic c. structured d. alphabetical
Study Guide LO 4 Page: 312 **c**	213.	When a child says that "tub" and "but" are constructed of the same three letters, she is showing an awareness of a. morphemes b. phonemes c. metalinguistics d. syntax

Study Guide LO 8 Page: 316 **b**	214.	The fact that children appear to learn rules, rather than specific word combinations, when acquiring language skills argues most strongly against which theory of language development? a. cognitive b. behaviorist c. nativist d. social communication
Study Guide LO 10 Page: 319 **a**	215.	Which one of Greeno's problems is exemplified by the anagram? a. arrangement b. inducing structure c. transformation d. chunking
Study Guide LO 12 Page: 321 **b**	216.	Which barrier to problem solving are you overcoming when you use a piece of paperclip as a temporary replacement for the screw that fell out of your glasses? a. irrelevant information b. functional fixedness c. mental set d. unnecessary constraints
Study Guide LO 14 Page: 322 **d**	217.	Which of the following heuristics would you probably employ if assigned the task of carrying out a school election? a. work backwards b. representativeness c. search for analogies d. form subgoals
Study Guide LO 20 Page: 330 **c**	218.	Most persons mistakenly believe that more people die from tornadoes than from asthma. This is because they mistakenly apply a. a means/end analysis b. a compensatory decision model c. an availability heuristic d. a representativeness heuristic
Study Guide LO 26 Page: 337 **d**	219.	Failure to actively seek out contrary evidence may lead to a. overestimating the improbable b. the conjunction fallacy c. the gambler's fallacy d. confirmation bias
Study Guide LO 27 Page: 339 **c**	220.	People generally prefer a choice that provides an 80 percent chance of success over one that provides a 20 percent chance of failure. This illustrates the effect of a. the availability heuristic b. the representativeness heuristic c. framing d. mental set
Online Quiz LO 1 Page: 308 **b**	221.	During the first half of the 20th century, the study of cognition was discouraged because a. earlier studies using the method of introspection had reliably mapped the structure of consciousness b. of the theoretical dominance of behaviorism c. cognition was not considered to be a psychological function d. language acquisition was viewed as an innate process that could not be studied empirically

Online Quiz LO 2 Page: 309 **b**	222.	Phonemes are a. the same across all languages b. the smallest units of sound in a spoken language c. the smallest units of meaning in a spoken language d. rules for combining sounds to form meaning
Online Quiz LO 4 Page: 311 **c**	223.	After the first word is spoken a. vocabulary immediately grows at an extremely rapid pace b. further increases in vocabulary occur very slowly and steadily c. vocabulary growth is slow for several months, and then speeds up dramatically d. no further vocabulary growth takes place until around 18 months
Online Quiz LO 8 Page: 316 **b**	224.	The behavioral theorists emphasize the role of _____ in language acquisition. a. built-in brain mechanisms b. imitation and selective reinforcement c. the social context d. cognitive maturity
Online Quiz LO 10 Page: 319 **c**	225.	The need to discover the relationships between the elements of a problem is generally referred to as a problem of a. arrangement b. transformation c. inducing structure d. ideation
Online Quiz LO 14 Page: 322 **b**	226.	A "mental rule of thumb" for problem solving is referred to as a. an algorithm b. a heuristic c. a mental set d. a syllogism
Online Quiz LO 16 Page: 327 **d**	227.	The field dependent style is predominant in a. Western societies b. nomadic societies that depend on hunting and gathering for subsistence c. societies that stress lenient child-rearing practices d. sedentary agricultural societies
Online Quiz LO 17 Page: 328 **a**	228.	When a task involves few alternatives and attributes, people tend to use a _____ model; when a task is more complex, people tend to use a _____ model. a. compensatory; noncompensatory b. compensatory; compensatory c. noncompensatory; noncompensatory d. noncompensatory; compensatory
Online Quiz LO 19 Page: 329 **b**	229.	Risky decision making involves making decisions under conditions of a. positive expected value b. uncertainty c. high subjective utility d. low subjective utility
Online Quiz LO 20 Page: 330 **c**	230.	Basing the estimate of an event on how similar it is to the prototype of that event is called the a. law of small numbers b. conjunction fallacy c. representativeness heuristic d. availability heuristic

ESSAY QUESTIONS

1. Outline the key properties of language and use these to evaluate the ape-language controversy.

    Language is symbolic, and thus allows us to communicate about objects and events that are distant in time and place.

    Although the symbols in language are arbitrary, they have shared meanings for those who speak the same language, and so language is semantic.

    Language is generative--its limited symbols can be combined to form an infinite variety of messages.

    Language is structured. Although an infinite number of sentences is possible, these must be constructed in a limited number of ways. The communications of the trained chimps are clearly symbolic and semantic. Evidence regarding generativity is more questionable. Although chimps have generated many new combinations of symbols, doubts have been raised as to whether these sentences are truly spontaneous and creative. For the most part, evidence for chimps' grasp of language structure has been negative. A notable exception, however, is Sue Savage-Rumbaugh's training of the chimp Kanzi, who appeared to master rules of syntax. Her study raises the possibility that language may not be a uniquely human capacity.

2. Compare and contrast the behaviorist and nativist theories of language acquisition. What is the interactionist view, and how has it arisen out of dissatisfaction with the other two approaches?

    Behaviorists represent the extreme "nurture" position on this issue. First proposed by Skinner, the behaviorist view is that language is conditioned through imitation and reinforcement. Being understood, getting what you asked for, and being responded to in a conversation are powerful reinforcers that shape children's increasingly complex vocalizations.

    Nativists, as exemplified by Noam Chomsky, represent the extreme "nature" position on this issue. Impressed with the apparent ease and rapidity with which young children acquire language, and critical of the inefficiency of imitation and reinforcement as the underlying processes, Chomsky proposed that humans have an innate "language acquisition device." In this view, the brain is preprogrammed to acquire language effortlessly with minimal input. According to Chomsky, children learn the rules of language, rather than specific word combinations.

    Mirroring the history of the nature-nurture debate in general, the interactionist view regards both of these approaches as too extreme, asserting instead that heredity and environment both contribute significantly to language development. While acknowledging our biological preparedness for learning language, interactionists also regard children's social exchanges with parents and others as crucial. Thus, language depends on both an innate predisposition and a supportive environment.

3. Name and describe the three types of problems identified by Greeno (1978). Then, indicate which of the six approaches to problem solving discussed in your text would be helpful and unhelpful in solving each type of problem.

    Problems of inducing structure: The subject must discover the relations among the parts of the problem. Examples include series-completion problems and analogy problems. Working backward can't be applied since the goal state is unknown. It would be helpful to form subgoals. For instance, to solve analogy problems, the first subgoal is to figure out all the possible relations between the first two parts of the analogy.

    Problems of arrangement: The subject must arrange the parts of a problem in a way that satisfies some criterion (although the specific goal state is not known). These are generally solved in a flash of insight after a period of trial and error. Anagrams are an example of this type of problem. Trial and error might be effective if the number of possible solutions is small. Working backward, particularly if there are relatively few goal states, might be helpful. Changing the representation of the problem may help overcome mental set or functional fixedness.

    Problems of transformation: The subject must carry out a sequence of transformations in order to reach a specific goal. These problems are generally solved by carrying out a sequence of planned steps.

4. How does risky decision making differ from making decisions about preferences? How do people generally make each type of decision?

Making decisions about preferences involves selecting from an array of known options (for example, choosing an apartment). In this type of decision task, when the number of options is small, people generally use some form of compensatory decision model, such as a weighted additive strategy. When the number of options is large, people favor a noncompensatory model, such as elimination by aspects. In all decisions of this type, people demonstrate a limited ability to process and evaluate a large number of attributes and options.

Risky decision making involves making decisions under conditions of uncertainty. In such cases, people frequently make irrational decisions that deviate from an objective assessment of the probabilities of different outcomes. Sometimes people base risky decisions on what the different outcomes are personally worth to them (subjective utility). Sometimes they estimate subjective probabilities of various outcomes, using mental (often inaccurate) shortcuts such as the representativeness heuristic and the availability heuristic.

Overall, people are not as rational and systematic in their decision making as they believe themselves to be.

This page intentionally left blank.

Chapter Nine
Intelligence and Psychological Testing

LEARNING OBJECTIVES

1. List and describe the principal categories of psychological tests.
2. Explain the concepts of standardization and test norms.
3. Explain the meaning of test reliability and how it is estimated.
4. Explain the three types of validity and how they are assessed.
5. Summarize the contributions of Galton and Binet to the evolution of intelligence testing.
6. Summarize the contributions of Terman and Wechsler to the evolution of intelligence testing.
7. Explain the meaning of an individual's score on a modern intelligence test.
8. Discuss the reliability and validity of modern IQ test scores.
9. Discuss how well intelligence tests predict vocational success.
10. Discuss the use of IQ tests in non-Western cultures.
11. Describe how mental retardation is defined and divided into various levels.
12. Discuss what is known about the causes of mental retardation.
13. Discuss the role of IQ tests in the identification of gifted children.
14. Describe the personal characteristics of the gifted and adult achievements of the gifted.
15. Summarize empirical evidence that heredity affects intelligence.
16. Discuss the Burt affair and estimates of the heritability of intelligence.
17. Describe various lines of research that indicate that environment affects intelligence.
18. Using the concept of reaction range, explain how heredity and the environment interact to affect intelligence.
19. Discuss heritability and socioeconomic disadvantage as alternative explanations for cultural differences in average IQ.
20. Discuss the possible contributions of stereotype vulnerability and cultural bias to ethnic differences in average IQ.
21. Describe some new trends in the assessment of intelligence.
22. Describe Sternberg's and Gardner's theories of intelligence.
23. Discuss how the chapter highlighted three of the text's unifying themes.
24. Discuss popular ideas about the nature of creativity.
25. Describe creativity tests and summarize how well they predict creative achievement.
26. Discuss associations between creativity and personality, intelligence, and mental illness.
27. Explain how appeals to ignorance and reification have cropped up in various debates about intelligence.

MULTIPLE-CHOICE QUESTIONS

Factual
LO 1
Page: 346
Correct = 58%
c

1. Any psychological test should be seen as
   a. measuring the person's typical behavior
   b. tapping the constancies of a person's behavior
   c. a sample of a person's behavior
   d. tapping a person's absolute level of performance

Critical Thinking
LO 1
Page: 346
Correct = 62%
a

2. Which of the following does not characterize a psychological test?
   a. Psychological tests allow one to predict behavior with great accuracy.
   b. Psychological tests are samples of behavior.
   c. Psychological tests are standardized measures of behavior.
   d. Psychological tests measure individual differences.

Factual
LO 1
Page: 346
a

3. The two very broad categories of psychological tests are
   a. mental ability and personality tests
   b. intelligence and achievement tests
   c. interest tests and aptitude tests
   d. aptitude and attitude tests

Concept/Applied
LO 1
Page: 347
Correct = 88%
a

4. An elementary school child is given a test designed to determine whether or not she should be placed in a class of "gifted" children. The test is probably
   a. an intelligence test
   b. an achievement test
   c. a personality test
   d. a vocabulary test

Factual
LO 1
Page: 347
Correct = 88%
a

5. An achievement test measures
   a. a person's mastery and knowledge of a subject
   b. general mental ability
   c. talent for specific kinds of learning
   d. basic characteristics of one's personality

Concept/Applied
LO 1
Page: 347
Correct = 74%
a

6. At the end of her calculus course, Mary takes a test to determine how well she has mastered the material. Her calculus test is primarily
   a. an achievement test
   b. an intelligence test
   c. an aptitude test
   d. a test of her math potential

Concept/Applied
LO 1
Page: 347
a

7. If you wanted to gauge a person's mastery and knowledge in a specific area, such as mathematics, you would need to administer
   a. an achievement test
   b. an aptitude test, such as the Differential Aptitude Test (DAT)
   c. a self-report inventory
   d. an intelligence test, such as the Wechsler Adult Intelligence Scale (WAIS)

Concept/Applied
LO 2
Page: 347
d

8. Francis has applied for admission to a computer science program, and one of the requirements for admission is the completion of a test that measures sequencing skills and abstract reasoning skills. Her score on this test will be a major factor in the decision about whether to admit her to the program. In this case, the test that Francis is scheduled to take would be classified as
   a. an achievement test
   b. a projective test
   c. a normative test
   d. an aptitude test

Concept/Applied
LO 1
Page: 347
Correct = 76%
d

9. A spelling test is an example of an
   a. intelligence test
   b. analytical test
   c. aptitude test
   d. achievement test

Concept/Applied
LO 1
Page: 347
Correct = 81%
b

10. Interested in learning how to fly airplanes, Roger has just taken a test designed to predict how well he is likely to do in a pilot training program. Roger has taken a(n)
    a. achievement test
    b. aptitude test
    c. intelligence test
    d. test of general mental ability

Concept/Applied
LO 1
Page: 347
b

11. In trying to make a decision about a career that would fit your abilities and interest, you would probably want to take a test that would measure your potential or talent for specific kinds of activities. A test that would measure this sort of potential would most likely be
    a. an achievement test
    b. an aptitude test
    c. an intelligence test
    d. a test of general mental ability

Concept/Applied
LO 1
Page: 347
a

12. Standardized tests designed to predict how well you will do in college are most appropriately called
    a. aptitude tests
    b. intelligence tests
    c. personality tests
    d. predictive tests

Concept/Applied
LO 1
Page: 347
Correct = 76%
d

13. Exams given at the end of a course to determine how much you have learned in the course are most appropriately called
    a. intelligence tests
    b. abilities tests
    c. tests of general mental ability
    d. achievement tests

Factual
LO 1
Page: 347
a

14. _____ tests measure interests, values, and attitudes.
    a. Personality
    b. Achievement
    c. Aptitude
    d. All of these

Concept/Applied
LO 1
Page: 347
Correct = 93%
d

15. Walter has taken a test that attempts to assess his interests and attitudes. Walter has most likely taken
    a. an achievement test
    b. an aptitude test
    c. a correlational test
    d. a personality test

Critical Thinking
LO 2
Page: 348
Correct = 93%
b

16. The fact that two people taking the same test in two different places will receive the same instructions, the same questions, and the same time limits means that the test has been
    a. synchronized
    b. standardized
    c. validated
    d. regulated

INTELLIGENCE AND PSYCHOLOGICAL TESTING

Factual LO 2 Page: 348 Correct = 80% **a**	17.	If a psychological test is to tell you how you score relative to other people, the following must be developed a. test norms b. test scores c. test scales d. test levels
Factual LO 2 Page: 348 Correct = 66% **c**	18.	A norm refers to a. a test's reliability b. a test's validity c. a test's distribution of scores d. all of these things
Factual LO 2 Page: 348 Correct = 55% **d**	19.	Information about where a particular score on a test falls in relationship to some group is given by a. standardization information b. test outcome data c. test reliability d. test norms
Factual LO 2 Page: 348 Correct = 93% **c**	20.	Test norms allow you to convert your raw score on a test into a(n) _____ score, which indicates the proportion of people who scored below your obtained score. a. variation b. average c. percentile d. prototypical
Concept/Applied LO 2 Page: 348 Correct = 85% **b**	21.	If 30 percent of a reference group scored higher than you on a test, your score would be at the a. 30th percentile b. 70th percentile c. 29th percentile d. indeterminate from the available information
Factual LO 2 Page: 348 **b**	22.	An individual's percentile score is the percentage of people who a. score above his or her score b. score at or below his or her score c. score between the mean and his or her score d. score below the mean on a standardized test
Critical Thinking LO 2 Page: 348 **c**	23.	If your score falls at the 75th percentile on a standardized test, then which of the following is an accurate interpretation? a. You correctly answered 75% of the items on the test. b. Seventy-five percent of the people who took the test scored higher than you. c. Seventy-five percent of the people who took the test scored at or below your score. d. Your answers to pairs of similar items on the test were the same 75% of the time.
Concept/Applied LO 2 Page: 348 **b**	24.	Tamara scored at the 95th percentile on the logical reasoning component of the Graduate Record Exam (GRE). This means that for the logical reasoning section of the GRE a. she obtained a raw score of 95 b. she scored higher than 95% of the sample used to establish the test norms c. she correctly answered 95% of the questions on the exam d. she scored lower than 95% of the sample used to establish the test norms

Concept/Applied LO 3 Page: 348 **b**	25.	If a test yields nearly identical scores when it is retaken after a 2-month interval, the test is said to be a. valid b. reliable c. significant d. standardized
Factual LO 3 Page: 348 Correct = 77% **a**	26.	Reliability refers to the _____ of a measuring device such as a test. a. consistency b. predictability c. accuracy of inference d. representativeness
Concept/Applied LO 3 Page: 348 Correct = 67% **b**	27.	If you assess test-retest reliability, you hope that it leads to a a. strong negative correlation b. strong positive correlation c. either a or b as long as it is statistically significant d. a higher statistical probability of occurrence
Factual LO 3 Page: 348 Correct = 81% **b**	28.	Test-retest procedures are used to determine a test's a. content validity b. reliability c. criterion validity d. accuracy
Concept/Applied LO 3 Page: 348 **b**	29.	In correlating the scores from the even-numbered items on a test with those from the odd-numbered items, a researcher would be measuring which of the following? a. test-retest reliability b. split-half reliability c. face reliability d. inter-scorer reliability
Concept/Applied LO 3 Page: 349 Correct = 78% **d**	30.	Which of the following represents the strongest test-retest reliability for a test? a. 0 b. -75 c. .70 d. .90
Critical Thinking LO 3 Page: 349 **d**	31.	Which of the following statements regarding acceptable levels of test reliability is accurate? a. Reliability estimates must be equal to or higher than .50. b. Reliability estimates must be equal to or higher than .70. c. Reliability estimates must be .50 or higher for a personality test, and .70 or higher for a test of mental ability. d. There are no absolute guidelines about acceptable levels of reliability.
Concept/Applied LO 3 Page: 349 **c**	32.	Dr. Iverson has had 25 students who have repeated her advanced Economics class over the past five years. Each time, the student's grade for the second attempt in her course was nearly identical to the grade received on the first attempt. This leads Dr. Iverson to conclude that her testing procedures a. provide valid measures of student ability b. are well standardized c. provide reliable measures of student ability d. successfully measures abstract reasoning skills

Concept/Applied LO 3 Page: 349 **b**	33.	Dr. Carmody has designed a new critical thinking assessment test. He administers the test to a group of students in October. In April he tests the same students and finds that the overall correlation between the two sets of scores is +0.91. Based on this information, Dr. Carmody could conclude that his new test a. likely has low construct validity b. appears to have high test-retest reliability c. has been well standardized d. will have high criterion-related validity
Factual LO 4 Page: 349 Correct = 89% **a**	34.	If a test accurately measures what it was designed to measure, we would say that the test is a. valid b. empirical c. normative d. consistent
Factual LO 4 Page: 349 Correct = 78% **c**	35.	The degree to which the items on a test are representative of the "domain" it is supposed to cover is referred to as a. test reliability b. test convergence c. content validity d. criterion validity
Concept/Applied LO 4 Page: 349 **d**	36.	Lanette is arguing with her professor that questions on her last test were not covered during lectures or in the textbook. Lanette is basically arguing that the test was <u>not</u> a. criterion reliable b. test-retest reliable c. criterion valid d. content valid
Concept/Applied LO 4 Page: 349 Correct = 61% **b**	37.	Professor Ridley is known for giving fair exams that include only test items for which the student should have been prepared. Professor Ridley's exams can be said to be high in a. criterion-related validity b. content validity c. predictive validity d. standardized validity
Concept/Applied LO 4 Page: 349 **a**	38.	If you wanted to be able to predict how successful you would be at being an engineer, you would take a test that measured your potential for this profession. It is hoped that the test would be high in a. criterion-related validity b. internal validity c. construction validity d. hypothetical validity
Concept/Applied LO 4 Page: 350 **d**	39.	If the scores on a mechanical aptitude test are strongly correlated with performance in an auto mechanics training class, the test would be said to be high in a. reliability b. face validity c. construction validity d. criterion-related validity
Concept/Applied LO 4 Page: 350 **d**	40.	Criterion-related validity is established by a. logic and theory testing b. having experts in the field assess the items on the test c. examining correlation coefficients for repeated administrations of the test d. correlating scores on the test with another trait associated with the test

Concept/Applied LO 4 Page: 350 Correct = 55% c	41.	The correlation between a group's scores on an industrial aptitude test and actual performance on the industrial job would describe the test's a. content validity b. construct validity c. criterion-related validity d. reliability
Concept/Applied LO 4 Page: 350 a	42.	Dr. Clarke designs a test she believes will predict an individual's ability to perform in managerial positions. When Dr. Clark administers her test to 100 managers at Aldor Corporation, she finds that some of the best managers do well on the test, but others do quite poorly. Dr. Clarke should probably conclude that her test a. lacks criterion-related validity b. lacks content validity c. is not well standardized d. is unreliable
Critical Thinking LO 4 Page: 350 c	43.	If a test designed to measure extroversion correlates negatively with measures of social discomfort, correlates positively with measures of sociability, and has low correlations with measures of intelligence, you could conclude that the test has a. low construct validity b. low test norms c. high construct validity d. high reliability
Factual LO 4 Page: 350 Correct = 43% c	44.	The extent to which a test measures some abstract personal quality such as creativity or intelligence is a matter of a. criterion-related validity b. content validity c. construct validity d. face validity
Concept/Applied LO 4 Page: 350 Correct = 96% d	45.	For which of the following would it be the <u>most</u> difficult to demonstrate validity? a. a mechanical aptitude test b. a history test c. a secretarial aptitude test d. a test of creativity
Factual LO 5 Page: 352 d	46.	Sir Francis Galton is generally recognized for which of the following contributions? a. coined the phrase "nature versus nurture" b. invented the concept of correlation c. assessed mental ability by measuring reaction time d. all of these contributions
Factual LO 5 Page: 352 d	47.	The British scholar Sir Francis Galton assessed mental ability by measuring which of the following? a. reaction time b. color perception c. sensitivity to high-pitched sounds d. all of these characteristics
Factual LO 5 Page: 352 c	48.	Which of the following individuals is generally recognized as the "inventor" of the concept of correlation? a. Alfred Binet b. Lewis Terman c. Francis Galton d. Robert Sternberg

Factual LO 5 Page: 352 **a**	49.	The man responsible for developing the first intelligence tests designed to predict the school performance of children was a. Alfred Binet b. David Wechsler c. Lewis Terman d. Jean Piaget
Factual LO 5 Page: 352 **a**	50.	Alfred Binet and Theodore Simon devised the first intelligence test in 1905 in order to a. predict the school performance of children b. predict future life success c. provide support for the belief that intelligence is genetically determined d. provide support for the belief that intelligence is environmentally determined
Factual LO 5 Page: 352 **a**	51.	The Binet-Simon scale of intelligence expressed a child's score in terms of a. mental age b. a potential score c. a percentile score d. an intelligence quotient
Concept/Applied LO 6 Page: 352 Correct = 95% **b**	52.	When tested on the Stanford-Binet, Ada is found to have a mental age of 8. This means that a. she is intellectually impaired b. her performance was as good as that of an average 8-year-old child c. her score is 8 standard deviation units above the average score d. her IQ is 80
Factual LO 6 Page: 352 Correct = 77% **d**	53.	(Mental age/chronological age) x 100 yields a(n) a. Binet quotient b. achievement quotient c. maturity quotient d. intelligence quotient
Concept/Applied LO 6 Page: 352 Correct = 85% **a**	54.	If a child of age 10 made a mental age score of 8 on the Binet test, his IQ would be a. 80 b. 100 c. 125 d. 75
Factual LO 6 Page: 352 Correct = 88% **b**	55.	The letters IQ stand for a. intelligence quota b. intelligence quotient c. intuitive quality d. intellectual quota
Factual LO 6 Page: 352 Correct = 83% **c**	56.	If a child's chronological age matches his or her mental age, then the child's IQ would be approximately a. 50 b. 75 c. 100 d. 125

Concept/Applied LO 6 Page: 352 Correct = 53% **d**	57.	Jerome is 8 years old and has been determined to have a mental age of 10. What is Jerome's IQ? a. 80 b. 100 c. 110 d. 125
Critical Thinking LO 5 Page: 352 **b**	58.	Walter is 10 years old and has a mental age of 8, based on the Stanford-Binet Intelligence Scale. Alfred is 12 and has a mental age of 10, based on the Stanford-Binet Intelligence Scale. Using the intelligence quotient scoring system suggested by William Stern a. Walter would be considered "more" intelligent than Alfred b. Alfred would be considered "more" intelligent than Walter c. both boys would be considered equally intelligent d. the scores could not be meaningfully compared because the boys are not the same age
Concept/Applied LO 6 Page: 352 **b**	59.	The difficulties associated with the concept of mental age include a. the fact it's difficult to think of a person as having a mental age b. applying it to adults c. the calculation of the intelligence quotient from it d. all of these things
Factual LO 6 Page: 353 **c**	60.	Who was originally responsible for developing IQ tests for all ages with both verbal and performance items and with subtest scores? a. Alfred Binet b. Lewis Terman c. David Wechsler d. Jean Piaget
Factual LO 6 Page: 353 **a**	61.	The Wechsler IQ tests differ from the original Stanford-Binet in that a. they are divided into verbal and performance subtests b. they measure general intelligence c. they yield an overall score d. all of these ways
Factual LO 6 Page: 353 **c**	62.	Which of the following is not an individually administered IQ test? a. the Stanford-Binet Intelligence Scale b. the Wechsler Intelligence Scale for Children c. the Otis-Lennon School Ability Test d. the Wechsler Adult Intelligence Scale
Factual LO 6 Page: 353 **d**	63.	The test currently used to assess adult intelligence is the a. Galton IQ test b. Terman-Stanford-Binet Intelligence Scale c. California PF d. Wechsler Adult Intelligence Scale
Concept/Applied LO 6 Page: 353 **d**	64.	Tamara is completing The Wechsler Adult Intelligence Scale, and one section of the test evaluates her arithmetic reasoning skills using story problems. Tamara's score on this section of the test will be used in the computation of her score on the _____ scale. a. performance b. practical c. logical-mathematical d. verbal

Concept/Applied LO 6 Page: 353 **a**	65.	Austin is completing The Wechsler Adult Intelligence Scale, and one section of the test evaluates his ability to analyze patterns and copy designs using blocks. Austin's score on this section of the test will be used in the computation of his score on the _____ scale. a. performance b. verbal c. practical d. spatial
Concept/Applied LO 7 Page: 354 **b**	66.	Maranda tells you that her 12-year-old cousin recently completed an intelligence test that translated raw scores into deviation IQ scores. Maranda knows that her cousin's score was 75, but she is not sure what this means. You should tell her that her cousin a. answered 75% of the questions correctly on the test b. scored below the mean for 12-year-olds c. scored above the mean for 12-year-olds d. scored at the mean for the average 9-year-old
Factual LO 7 Page: 354 **b**	67.	The shape of a normal distribution approximates a. a rectangle b. a bell c. a "U" d. an "M"
Factual LO 7 Page: 354 **b**	68.	Wechsler developed the deviation IQ based on the normal distribution. On his test an overall IQ of 130 would mean a. the person has 130 units of intelligence b. the person scored two standard deviations above the mean c. the person's MA is 13 and CA is 10 d. none of these things
Factual LO 7 Page: 354 Correct = 81% **c**	69.	Most tests using the deviation IQ set the mean at _____ and the standard deviation at _____. a. 10; 5 b. 50; 10 c. 100; 15 d. 120; 20
Concept/Applied LO 7 Page: 354 Correct = 66% **b**	70.	Since IQ scores are assumed to be normally distributed, an IQ score of 100 would put you a. to the left of the center of the normal curve b. at the center of the normal curve c. to the right of the center of the normal curve d. somewhere on the curve, your exact location depending on the performance of others taking the test with you
Factual LO 7 Page: 354 Correct = 48% **a**	71.	Why is it that IQ scores do <u>not</u> routinely increase as we get older? a. because an IQ score is indicative of our relative standing in our particular age group b. because we do not accumulate that much more information as we get older c. because the tests are not designed to measure increases in knowledge as we get older d. because the tests for adults are not comparable to the tests for children

Factual LO 7 Page: 354 Correct = 62% **a**	72.	When a deviation IQ score is converted into a percentile score, it indicates a. percentage of cases scoring at a lower level b. percentage of cases scoring at a higher level c. percentage of the time one can be expected to score at a similar level if the test is taken again d. that the original score deviated too much from the average to be reliable
Factual LO 8 Page: 354 Correct = 76% **c**	73.	What do intelligence tests actually measure? a. only knowledge b. only potential c. a blend of knowledge and potential d. test-taking expertise
Concept/Applied LO 8 Page: 354 Correct = 76% **c**	74.	What would the ideal intelligence test measure? a. a person's understanding of language b. the extent of a person's accumulated knowledge c. a person's potential for acquiring knowledge d. a person's interests and preferences
Factual LO 8 Page: 355 **d**	75.	Although there may be some question as to exactly what IQ tests measure, there is little question that they tend to be consistent measures, that is, they are high in a. predictability b. validity c. generalizability d. reliability
Factual LO 8 Page: 355 **c**	76.	In comparison to most other types of psychological tests, IQ tests tend to be a. low in reliability b. similar in terms of reliability c. exceptionally reliable d. reliable for children, but unreliable for adults
Factual LO 8 Page: 356 **c**	77.	Correlations between IQ scores and school grades can best be characterized as a. nonsignificant b. moderately negative c. moderately positive d. positive, and nearly perfect
Concept/Applied LO 8 Page: 357 **b**	78.	The person who has the ability to see all aspects of a problem and make good decisions is demonstrating the _____ type of intelligence. a. verbal b. practical c. social d. academic
Factual LO 8 Page: 357 **d**	79.	According to Robert Sternberg, IQ tests tend to focus narrowly on which of the following types of intelligence? a. social b. mechanical c. quantitative d. academic/verbal
Factual LO 8 Page: 357 **a**	80.	Which of the following is a true statement regarding the validity of IQ tests? a. IQ tests do not appear to be valid indicators of intelligence in a general sense. b. IQ test scores are good predictors of success in life. c. IQ tests are valid measures of practical intelligence. d. IQ tests are valid measures of social intelligence.

Critical Thinking LO 8 Page: 357 Correct = 93% **d**	81.	The person who is sensitive to others' needs and accepts others for who they are is evidencing the _____ type of intelligence. a. fluid b. practical c. verbal d. social
Concept/Applied LO 8 Page: 357 Correct = 71% **a**	82.	Most intelligence tests over the years have tended to stress a. verbal and reasoning skills related to academics b. practical intelligence in everyday life c. social intelligence and human relationships d. all of these things
Factual LO 9 Page: 357 **c**	83.	The correlation between IQ scores and vocational success is best described as a. nonsignificant b. moderately negative c. moderately positive d. virtually nonexistent
Factual LO 9 Page: 358 **d**	84.	Court rulings and laws now require that tests used in employment selection measure which of the following? a. general intelligence b. academic/verbal intelligence c. the ability to get along with co-workers d. specific abilities that are clearly related to job performance
Critical Thinking LO 9 Page: 358 **d**	85.	Which of the following statements best characterizes the current view regarding the use of tests to predict vocational success? a. It is illegal to use mental ability tests to evaluate prospective employees. b. Employers can use any test of mental ability with prospective employees as long as the test has been shown to be reliable. c. Only tests designed to measure social or practical intelligence are permissible. d. Tests that measure mental abilities relevant to specific jobs continue to be valuable tools in selecting employees.
Factual LO 10 Page: 358 Correct = 61% **a**	86.	In which of the following countries are IQ tests <u>least</u> likely to be used? a. China b. Britain c. France d. Australia
Factual LO 10 Page: 358 Correct = 72% **c**	87.	In which of the following non-Western countries are IQ tests <u>most</u> likely to be used? a. China b. India c. Japan d. Malaysia
Critical Thinking LO 10 Page: 358 **b**	88.	Which of the following statements about the influence of culture on the use of IQ tests is true? a. IQ tests are widely used in virtually all cultures. b. Different cultures have different conceptions of what intelligence is. c. It is generally accepted across all cultures that it is possible to measure and quantify intellectual ability. d. Western IQ tests generally translate well into the language and cognitive framework of non-Western cultures.

Factual LO 11 Page: 359 **d**	89.	Mental retardation is defined in terms of which of the following? a. general mental ability b. deficient adaptive skills associated with self-care c. deficient adaptive skills associated with social interaction d. All of these items.
Factual LO 11 Page: 359 **a**	90.	Currently, the proportion of the population classified as retarded is about _____ percent. a. 1-3 b. 5-10 c. 15-20 d. 25-30
Factual LO 11 Page: 359 **a**	91.	The vast majority of retarded people are classified as _____ retarded. a. mildly b. moderately c. significantly d. severely
Concept/Applied LO 11 Page: 359 **a**	92.	Frank has an IQ of 60, completed the fifth grade, and is basically self-supporting; Frank would most likely be classified as _____ retarded. a. mildly b. moderately c. significantly d. severely
Factual LO 11 Page: 359 **a**	93.	If all the individuals classified as moderately, severely, or profoundly retarded were placed in one group, they would comprise approximately _____ percent of the retarded population. a. 15 b. 30 c. 50 d. 85
Concept/Applied LO 11 Page: 360 **c**	94.	Megan has an IQ score of 30 and she is able to perform simple tasks in highly structured environments. According to the system traditionally used to categorize various levels of mental retardation, Megan would most likely be classified as having a. mild mental retardation b. moderate mental retardation c. severe mental retardation d. profound mental retardation
Factual LO 11 Page: 360 Correct = 79% **d**	95.	The IQ of someone classified as severely mentally retarded is approximately a. 85 to 95 b. 70 to 85 c. 50 to 70 d. 20 to 35
Concept/Applied LO 11 Page: 360 Correct = 69% **c**	96.	Jamie is a 23-year-old female who can only pass the third grade. She is employed in a sheltered workshop and has a difficult time with mild stress. Jamie is most likely a. schizophrenic-hebephrenic subtype b. suffering from emotional lability brought on by a deficiency of serotonin c. moderately mentally retarded d. profoundly mentally retarded

Factual LO 12 Page: 359 **d**	97.	The form of mental retardation that is usually caused by the presence of an extra chromosome is a. phenylketonuria b. hydrocephaly c. organic d. Down syndrome
Factual LO 12 Page: 359 **b**	98.	_____ is a metabolic disorder (due to an inherited enzyme deficiency) that can lead to retardation if it is not caught and treated in infancy. a. Hydrocephaly b. Phenylketonuria c. Down syndrome d. Parkinson's disease
Factual LO 12 Page: 359 **a**	99.	Diagnosticians are able to pin down an organic cause for retardation in about _____ percent of all cases. a. 25 b. 40 c. 60 d. 85
Factual LO 12 Page: 359 **a**	100.	Hydrocephaly may lead to mental retardation because of a. a buildup of cerebrospinal fluid that destroys brain tissue b. the presence of an extra chromosome c. an inherited enzyme deficiency d. nutritional deficiencies
Factual LO 12 Page: 360 **c**	101.	The vast majority of mildly retarded children come from a. blended families b. predominantly rural areas c. the lower socioeconomic classes d. middle class, suburban families
Critical Thinking LO 12 Page: 360 Correct = 49% **d**	102.	The environmental hypothesis suggests that mental retardation is a. best defined as the inability to adjust satisfactorily to one's environment b. a label used to direct slow learners into special education programs c. caused by environmental deficiencies in about 50 percent of cases d. caused by various unfavorable environmental factors
Factual LO 12 Page: 360 **d**	103.	Which of the following would be considered an environmental factor in the development of retardation? a. parental neglect b. lower-quality schooling c. inadequate nutrition and medical care d. any of these factors
Factual LO 13 Page: 360 **a**	104.	Which of the following statements best reflects current government policy regarding the identification of gifted children? a. Schools should not rely too heavily on IQ tests to select gifted children. b. The use IQ scores in selecting gifted children is a violation of constitutional law. c. Schools should restrict their selection of gifted children to those with special talents. d. A child cannot be classified as gifted unless he or she has an IQ score of at least 130.

Factual LO 13 Page: 360 Correct = 94% **a**	105.	Designations of intellectual "giftedness" tend to be determined primarily by a. IQ test performance b. degree of social competence c. creativity d. physical appearance
Factual LO 13 Page: 360 **a**	106.	Most school districts consider children who fall in the upper _____ percent of the IQ distribution to be gifted. a. 2-3 b. 5 c. 10 d. 25
Factual LO 13 Page: 360 **c**	107.	In practice, the minimum IQ score for gifted programs usually falls somewhere around a. 100 b. 115 c. 130 d. 150
Concept/Applied LO 13 Page: 360 **a**	108.	Jamal recently completed an intelligence test and was told that his IQ score was 135. Based on the standard practices in most school districts, Jamal would a. be considered gifted and would be eligible for gifted programs b. not meet the criterion for giftedness unless he was also highly creative c. be mainstreamed and would attend regular classes for most of the day d. need to show superior potential in at least three other areas to be eligible for gifted programs
Factual LO 14 Page: 361 Correct = 55% **b**	109.	Research on gifted individuals, including Terman's longitudinal study, have shown that gifted children a. tend to be below average in physical and emotional health b. tend to be above average in physical and emotional health c. become adults who are no more successful than average d. tend to conform to society's traditional view of the gifted
Factual LO 14 Page: 361 **b**	110.	According to recent research conducted by Ellen Winner, profoundly gifted children (those with an IQ above 180) are often a. much taller than normal children b. introverted and socially isolated c. diagnosed as schizophrenic d. hostile toward their peers
Factual LO 14 Page: 361 **c**	111.	The results of recent research suggest that the incidence of _____ among profoundly gifted children (those with an IQ above 180) is about twice as high as in other children. a. drug abuse b. schizophrenia c. interpersonal and emotional problems d. childhood sexual abuse

Critical Thinking LO 14 Page: 362 **d**	112.	Which of the following statements regarding giftedness and achievement in life is <u>most</u> accurate? a. Children identified as gifted typically go on to make genius-level contributions to society as adults. b. There is a negative correlation between IQ as a child and significance of achievement as an adult. c. Most children identified as gifted tend to "burn out" by the time they reach their mid-20s. d. The vast majority of children selected for gifted school programs do not achieve eminence as adults.
Concept/Applied LO 15 Page: 362 **d**	113.	An implication of the belief that intelligence is largely a function of genetics is that a. an intellectually stimulating environment can increase a person's intellectual potential b. everyone has the potential to do well intellectually if given the chance c. educational opportunities should be made available to everyone d. you either are intelligent or you are not and no environmental circumstance can change that fact
Factual LO 15 Page: 363 Correct = 87% **b**	114.	In which of the following cases is the correlation between IQ scores the lowest? a. siblings reared together b. siblings reared apart c. fraternal twins reared together d. fraternal twins reared apart
Critical Thinking LO 15 Page: 363 **c**	115.	Which of the following statements regarding heredity and intelligence is <u>not</u> accurate? a. Siblings reared together have higher correlations on IQ than do siblings reared apart. b. Identical twins show higher correlations on IQ than do fraternal twins. c. Fraternal twins reared together have higher correlations on IQ than do identical twins reared apart. d. Fraternal twins reared together have higher correlations on IQ than do siblings reared together.
Critical Thinking LO 15 Page: 363 **a**	116.	The results of studies that compare IQ scores in identical and fraternal twins suggest that a. IQ is inherited to a considerable degree b. heredity plays virtually no role in IQ c. when it comes to IQ, environmental factors play a more important role than does heredity d. about 50% of IQ is due to heredity, and 50% is due to environmental factors
Factual LO 15 Page: 363 **d**	117.	"Rearing together" gives higher correlations in IQ than "rearing apart" for which groups? a. fraternal twins only b. identical twins only c. siblings only d. fraternal twins, identical twins, and non-twin siblings
Concept/Applied LO 15 Page: 363 **a**	118.	The fact that the correlation in IQ scores between identical twins reared apart is lower than that between identical twins reared together suggests that a. environmental factors can have an influence on intellectual development b. environmental factors have no impact on intellectual development c. genetic factors have no impact on intellectual development d. identical twins often do not have the same genotype

Factual LO 16 Page: 363 Correct = 95% **a**	119.	Cyril Burt's studies of the influence of heredity on intelligence were conducted on a. identical twins reared apart b. fraternal twins reared apart c. unrelated siblings raised together d. a group of genetically identical monkeys
Factual LO 16 Page: 364 Correct = 69% **b**	120.	The main reason that Cyril Burt's conclusions about the role of heredity in intelligence are controversial is that a. he provided no data to support the conclusions b. there is evidence that his data cannot be trusted c. his research was not well known during his lifetime d. subsequent research has contradicted his conclusions
Factual LO 16 Page: 364 **c**	121.	Why is it that the problems with Cyril Burt's data, which were either fabricated or ineptly collected, could go undetected for nearly 20 years? a. His data had no real application to everyday life. b. His research was never actually published in his lifetime. c. His data were fairly similar to the results of other studies. d. Other researchers simply weren't interested in this particular area of study.
Concept/Applied LO 16 Page: 364 Correct = 52% **b**	122.	Saying that the heritability of intelligence is 70 percent would mean that a. 70 percent of a person's intelligence is due to heredity b. 70 percent of the variability of intelligence scores in a group is accounted for by genetic variation c. 30 percent of a person's intelligence is due to environmental factors d. None of these statements is accurate.
Factual LO 16 Page: 364 Correct = 80% **d**	123.	The problem with heritability estimates for intelligence is that a. the estimates have been based largely on research with white, middle-class subjects b. they may vary from one group to another depending on a number of factors c. they are group statistics and therefore cannot be meaningfully applied to individuals d. all of these factors are concerns
Factual LO 16 Page: 364 Correct = 74% **b**	124.	Researchers such as Jensen who believe that IQ is largely genetic argue that _____ of one's IQ is inherited. a. 100 percent b. 80 percent c. 60 percent d. 50 percent
Factual LO 16 Page: 364 Correct = 87% **c**	125.	The consensus among researchers is that ____ percent of one's intelligence is inherited. a. 100 percent b. exactly 80 percent c. around 60 percent d. less than 40 percent
Concept/Applied LO 17 Page: 365 Correct = 91% **c**	126.	Which of the following would constitute the strongest evidence for environmental influence in intelligence? a. similarity in IQ between parents and their biological children b. similarity in IQ between identical twins reared together c. similarity in IQ between adopted children and their foster parents d. similarity in IQ between adopted children and their biological parents

Critical Thinking LO 17 Page: 365 c	127.	Which of the following statements regarding the findings from adoption studies and IQ is <u>not</u> accurate? a. Research with adopted children provides useful evidence about the impact of experience as well as heredity. b. Adopted children show some resemblance to their foster parents in IQ. c. Entirely unrelated children who are raised in the same home have no similarities in IQ. d. Siblings reared together are more similar in IQ than siblings reared apart.
Critical Thinking LO 17 Page: 365 a	128.	You would predict that the IQs of children who stay in understaffed orphanages a. will gradually decline as they grow older b. will show the normal increases with development c. will start out low, but gradually increase as they reach puberty d. will be fairly normal until they reach puberty, when there will be a sharp decline
Concept/Applied LO 17 Page: 365 Correct = 87% d	129.	Which of the following is an expression of the nurture side of the nature versus nurture argument? a. Environmental deprivation has little effect on intellectual performance. b. An intellectually stimulating environment would be wasted on those who did not have some innate intellectual potential. c. Intellectual potential is something with which you are born; it is not acquired. d. An intellectually stimulating environment can lead to noticeable increases in the IQs of disadvantaged children.
Factual LO 18 Page: 365 b	130.	The "Flynn effect" is best characterized by the fact that a. IQ scores are becoming less accurate predictors of academic performance b. IQ performance has been rising steadily all over the industrialized world since the 1930s c. verbal intelligence scores are decreasing, but students are getting better grades in school d. despite dramatic advancements in technology, IQ performance has remained stable over the last 50 years
Factual LO 18 Page: 366 d	131.	Which of the following has been offered as an explanation for the steady rise in IQ performance all over the industrialized world since the 1930s? a. improved schools b. advances in technology c. better-educated parents d. all of these factors
Factual LO 18 Page: 366 Correct = 93% d	132.	A tentative answer to the heredity versus environment question with respect to intelligence is that a. heredity is the major factor b. environment is the major factor c. the environment puts limits on the effects of heredity d. heredity may set certain limits on intelligence and environmental factors determine where we fall within those limits
Factual LO 18 Page: 366 c	133.	Which of the following researchers is <u>most</u> closely associated with the concept of reaction range in IQ? a. Alfred Binet b. Claude Steele c. Sandra Scarr d. David Wechsler

Factual LO 18 Page: 366 Correct = 61% **a**	134.	The term used to refer to genetically determined limits on IQ is a. reaction range b. the normal curve c. reaction time d. percentile range
Factual LO 18 Page: 366 Correct = 61% **b**	135.	According to theories that employ the concept of reaction range, the upper limits of an individual's intellectual potential are a. determined during the first year of life b. set by heredity c. determined by environmental experiences d. subject to modification until puberty
Factual LO 18 Page: 366 Correct = 78% **c**	136.	The reaction range of IQ has been estimated to be around _____ IQ points. a. 1-2 b. 5 c. 20 d. 50
Concept/Applied LO 18 Page: 366 **c**	137.	According to the reaction range model a. children with average IQ scores will not have very wide reaction ranges b. children with average IQ scores are being raised in average-quality environments c. children raised in high-quality environments should score near the top of their reaction range d. children raised in high-quality environments will have higher IQ scores than children raised in poor-quality environments
Critical Thinking LO 19 Page: 367 **b**	138.	Which of the following statements is the <u>most</u> debatable? a. Intelligence is at least somewhat genetic in origin. b. Genetic factors are strongly implicated in the cause of ethnic differences in intelligence. c. The average IQ in the lowest social classes is about 30 to 30 points lower than the average IQ in the highest social classes. d. The average IQ for some minority groups in the United States is about 3 to 15 points lower than the average for whites.
Factual LO 19 Page: 367 **b**	139.	Which of the following researchers sparked a heated debate by arguing that cultural differences in IQ are largely due to heredity? a. Alfred Binet b. Arthur Jensen c. Robert Sternberg d. David Wechsler
Factual LO 19 Page: 367 Correct = 49% **c**	140.	Which of the following statements corresponds <u>most</u> closely to Arthur Jensen's position on ethnic differences in average IQ scores? a. IQ differences are a function of relative nutritional levels for different ethnic groups, particularly the amount of protein in one's diet. b. IQ differences reflect the inherent bias in IQ tests toward different ethnic groups. c. IQ differences are a function of the relative nature of the gene pool for different ethnic groups. d. Jensen is an interactionist and would partially endorse all of these statements.

Factual LO 19 Page: 367 Correct = 65% **a**	141.	Whose research and conclusions triggered an emotional debate over ethnic differences in intelligence? a. Arthur Jensen b. David Wechsler c. Francis Galton d. Alfred Binet
Critical Thinking LO 19 Page: 367 **b**	142.	Which of the following statements regarding differences in IQ is <u>not</u> supported by research findings? a. Group differences in average IQ can be influenced by environmental factors even if the heritability of intelligence is high. b. The average difference in IQ between minority groups and whites is largely a function of genetic factors. c. Children from the lowest social classes score about 20-30 points lower on IQ tests than do children from the highest social classes. d. The average IQ for many of the larger minority groups in the United States is about 3-15 points lower than it is for whites.
Factual LO 19 Page: 367 Correct = 69% **d**	143.	In *The Bell Curve*, Richard Herrnstein and Charles Murray imply a. that intelligence is largely inherited b. that ethnic differences in average IQ are at least partly genetic c. that intellectual ability has become the prime determinant of individuals' success d. all of these things
Factual LO 19 Page: 369 Correct = 85% **a**	144.	The correlation between social class and intelligence is a. positive b. negative c. inverse d. zero
Factual LO 19 Page: 369 Correct = 69% **d**	145.	Which of the following appears to be the most responsible for ethnic differences in IQ? a. genetic differences between ethnic groups b. culturally biased tests c. poor rapport between a nonminority test giver and a minority test taker d. the cultural disadvantages associated with a lower-class upbringing
Critical Thinking LO 19 Page: 369 **d**	146.	When compared to children from middle- and upper-class backgrounds, lower-class children tend to a. be more likely to come from single-parent homes b. be exposed to fewer books c. have less privacy for concentrated study d. all of these factors
Factual LO 20 Page: 369 **c**	147.	Which of the following researchers proposed the notion of stereotype vulnerability to explain ethnic differences in IQ scores? a. Sandra Scarr b. Arthur Jensen c. Claude Steele d. Robert Sternberg

Critical Thinking LO 20 Page: 369 **b**	148.	Which of the following explanations of ethnic differences in IQ scores suggests that a person's beliefs that others will attribute his or her possible failure to racial inferiority will lead to performance anxiety and lower IQ scores? a. reaction range b. stereotype vulnerability c. self-monitoring hypothesis d. ethnic standardization
Factual LO 20 Page: 370 Correct = 75% **a**	149.	The results of the Featured Study on racial stereotypes and test performance suggest that a. stereotype vulnerability appears to impair minority group members' test performance b. members of minority groups tend to perform lower on tests regardless of the circumstances c. both black and white subjects are susceptible to the effects of stereotype vulnerability d. the effects of stereotype vulnerability are greatest for white students in all situations
Critical Thinking LO 20 Page: 371 **d**	150.	Which of the following statements best reflects your textbook's conclusion regarding research on the effects of stereotype vulnerability on test performance? a. Stereotype vulnerability has no discernible effect on test performance. b. Stereotype vulnerability has a greater effect on test performance that does socioeconomic disadvantage. c. Stereotype vulnerability clearly results in lower test performance for white students. d. More evidence is clearly needed on the effects of stereotype vulnerability.
Factual LO 20 Page: 371 Correct = 82% **a**	151.	In general, the balance of evidence suggests that the amount of cultural bias on IQ tests is a. modest b. substantial c. nonexistent d. No relevant studies have been conducted.
Critical Thinking LO 20 Page: 371 Correct = 74% **c**	152.	Which of the following statements concerning cultural factors in intelligence is <u>not</u> true? a. IQ tests are generally constructed by white, middle-class psychologists. b. The charges of cultural bias on IQ tests have received some empirical support. c. There is strong evidence in support of genetic explanations for ethnic differences in IQ. d. Most Asian American groups tend to perform better in school than other ethnic groups.
Critical Thinking LO 20 Page: 371 **a**	153.	Which of the following is the <u>most</u> widely accepted explanation for the outstanding intellectual and educational attainments of Asian Americans? a. Asian cultural values tend to encourage and nurture educational achievement. b. Asians are genetically predisposed to high intellectual achievement. c. Asian Americans are likely responding to a reverse-stereotype vulnerability. d. Asian Americans are, by nature, highly competitive in academic settings.
Factual LO 20 Page: 372 **b**	154.	According to the data presented in the text, which of the following groups has the highest high school graduation rate? a. White b. Korean c. Hispanic d. African-American

Factual LO 21 Page: 372 **a**	155.	In _____, correlations among many variables are analyzed to identify closely related clusters of variables. a. factor analysis b. analysis of variance c. inferential statistics d. descriptive statistics
Factual LO 21 Page: 372 **d**	156.	Because he believed that all cognitive abilities, including specific ones like numerical reasoning and memory, depend heavily on general intelligence, _____ contributed to the view that intelligence is a single general ability. a. L. L. Thurstone b. Howard Gardner c. Robert Sternberg d. Charles Spearman
Factual LO 21 Page: 372 Correct = 74% **b**	157.	Spearman argued that intelligence a. is a series of unrelated factors b. is made up of a "core factor" common to all intellectual abilities c. can change from time to time d. is only seen in certain "school-type" problems
Factual LO 21 Page: 372 Correct = 84% **c**	158.	In analyzing factors in intelligence, Charles Spearman emphasized a general intelligence factor known as a. crystallized intelligence b. *s* c. *g* d. the primary mental ability
Critical Thinking LO 21 Page: 372 **b**	159.	Based on Charles Spearman's view of intelligence, individuals who excel in a. academics are also likely to be gifted athletes and musicians b. one academic area are likely to excel in most academic areas c. one academic area are likely to show deficiencies in other academic areas d. academics early are likely to "burn out" when they are older
Factual LO 21 Page: 373 Correct = 59% **b**	160.	Thurstone argued that intelligence is really cluster of _____ distinct or primary mental abilities. a. three b. seven c. fifty d. one hundred and fifty
Factual LO 21 Page: 373 Correct = 39% **d**	161.	Which of the following is <u>not</u> one of the primary mental abilities suggested by Thurstone? a. word fluency b. spatial ability c. inductive reasoning d. sensory discrimination
Factual LO 21 Page: 373 Correct = 70% **c**	162.	Reasoning capacity, memory capacity, and speed of information processing are referred to by Horn as a. generative intelligence b. abstract intelligence c. fluid intelligence d. level-two intelligence

Factual LO 21 Page: 373 Correct = 51% **a**	163.	Crystallized intelligence, according to Horn, is associated with a. applying acquired knowledge and skills in problem solving b. memory capacity c. reasoning ability d. all of these things
Factual LO 21 Page: 373 Correct = 80% **a**	164.	The 1986 revision of the Stanford-Binet IQ test introduced which of the following major changes? a. divided the test into a set of subtests b. multiplied the intelligence quotient by two c. used different versions for different ethnic groups d. combined the Stanford-Binet test with a version of the Wechsler test
Concept/Applied LO 21 Page: 373 Correct = 73% **c**	165.	The most recent (1986) revision of the Stanford Binet test suggests that the "modern" trend in mental ability testing is a. to place greater emphasis on generalized intelligence b. to reaffirm the concept of mental age c. to put more stress on the assessment of specific abilities d. to make tests more global in character
Factual LO 21 Page: 374 Correct = 42% **b**	166.	In an attempt to develop a "culture-free" measure of intelligence, researchers are focusing on a. brain-wave pattern analysis b. reaction times c. sensory discrimination d. none of these measures
Factual LO 21 Page: 374 Correct = 65% **c**	167.	The correlation between reaction times and IQ scores is a. very high b. moderate c. weak d. nonexistent
Factual LO 21 Page: 374 **d**	168.	The correlations between inspection time and IQ scores are a. virtually nonexistent b. very weak, and negative c. fairly strong, but probably not of practical significance d. high enough to have practical value
Factual LO 22 Page: 374 **a**	169.	Historically, the investigation of intelligence has been approached primarily from a _____ perspective. a. testing b. cognitive c. biological d. evolutionary
Factual LO 22 Page: 374 **a**	170.	The _____ perspective on the investigation of intelligence emphasizes measuring the amount of intelligence people have and figuring out why some people have more than others. a. testing b. cognitive c. behavioral d. psychoanalytic

Factual LO 22 Page: 374 **b**	171.	The _____ perspective on the investigation of intelligence focuses on how people use their intelligence; that is, the interest is in the process of intelligence rather than the amount. a. testing b. cognitive c. behavioral d. psychoanalytic
Factual LO 22 Page: 375 Correct = 77% **b**	172.	Which of the following is <u>not</u> one of the parts of Sternberg's triarchic theory of intelligence? a. contextual subtheory b. general mental ability subtheory c. experiential subtheory d. componential subtheory
Factual LO 22 Page: 375 Correct = 58% **d**	173.	Analytical thinking (planning and monitoring progress and evaluating), according to Sternberg, is associated with testing for _____ intelligence. a. experiential b. schematic c. reductionistic d. componential
Factual LO 22 Page: 375 Correct = 59% **a**	174.	The name that Sternberg has given to the high-level processes used in planning how to attack a problem is a. metacomponents b. knowledge-acquisition components c. performance components d. information-processing components
Factual LO 22 Page: 375 Correct = 65% **b**	175.	Which of the following is <u>not</u> one of the subtheories of the triarchic theory of intelligence proposed by Sternberg? a. contextual b. generative c. componential d. experiential
Factual LO 22 Page: 375 Correct = 59% **a**	176.	Which subtheory of intelligence, as proposed by Sternberg, is associated with intelligence being a culturally defined concept? a. the contextual subtheory b. the geographic subtheory c. the apocalyptic subtheory d. the anachronistic subtheory
Factual LO 22 Page: 375 Correct = 48% **c**	177.	Which subtheory of intelligence, as proposed by Sternberg, is associated with dealing effectively with novelty and how one performs familiar tasks automatically and effortlessly? a. the contextual subtheory b. the operational subtheory c. the experiential subtheory d. the generative subtheory
Concept/Applied LO 22 Page: 375 Correct = 73% **b**	178.	According to Sternberg's triarchic theory of intelligence, a mnemonic device such as learning "Every good boy does fine" in order to remember which notes are on the lines of the treble clef in musical notation represents a. a metacomponent b. a knowledge-acquisition component c. a performance component d. an intelligence component

Concept/Applied LO 22 Page: 375 Correct = 63% **c**	179.	Sternberg suggests that traditional IQ tests have placed too much emphasis on a. reasoning ability b. abstract concepts c. speed d. metacomponents
Factual LO 22 Page: 376 **b**	180.	According to Howard Gardner, IQ tests have generally emphasized which of the following skills? a. spatial and linguistic b. verbal and mathematical c. analytical and practical d. academic and interpersonal
Concept/Applied LO 22 Page: 376 **d**	181.	Leticia is a prima ballerina with a New York ballet company. According to Howard Gardner's theory of multiple intelligences, Leticia is likely to score high in which of the following? a. interpersonal intelligence b. spatial intelligence c. experiential intelligence d. bodily-kinesthetic intelligence
Concept/Applied LO 22 Page: 376 **c**	182.	Roland is an architect who can design dream homes based on vague ideas and images that his clients bring to him. According to Howard Gardner's theory of multiple intelligences, Roland is likely to score high in which of the following? a. intrapersonal intelligence b. interpersonal intelligence c. spatial intelligence d. logical-mathematical intelligence
Factual LO 22 Page: 376 Correct = 88% **d**	183.	Howard Gardner has tried to expand our thinking on intelligence, contending that traditional IQ tests are too narrowly focused on verbal and mathematical skills. In addition to these, his list of human intelligence includes a. spatial skills b. musical skills c. interpersonal skills d. spatial, musical, and interpersonal skills
Factual LO 22 Page: 376 Correct = 72% **d**	184.	Which of the following is <u>not</u> one of the seven types of intelligence proposed by Gardner? a. linguistic b. interpersonal c. spatial d. emotional
Concept/Applied LO 22 Page: 376 Correct = 74% **a**	185.	Jeremy is very sensitive to sounds, rhythms, the meaning of words, and the different functions of language. According to Gardner, Jeremy has a high level of _____ intelligence. a. linguistic b. fluid c. musical d. crystallized

Concept/Applied LO 22 Page: 376 Correct = 82% **b**	186.	Reba has an uncanny ability to discern and respond appropriately to the moods, temperaments, motivations, and desires of other people. According to Gardner, Reba has a high level of _____ intelligence. a. socioemotional b. interpersonal c. linguistic d. parapsychotic
Critical Thinking LO 23 Page: 376 **b**	187.	The observed ethnic differences in average intelligence within Western societies best illustrate the importance of which of the following factors? a. genetic b. cultural c. cognitive d. evolutionary
Critical Thinking LO 23 Page: 377 **c**	188.	In the first half of the 20th century, a strong current of racial and class prejudice supported the idea that IQ tests measured innate ability and that "undesirable" groups scored poorly because of their genetic inferiority. This development best reflects which of the following themes of your textbook? a. Psychology is empirical. b. Psychology is theoretically diverse. c. Psychology evolves in a sociocultural context. d. Behavior is determined by multiple causes.
Factual LO 24 Page: 378 **d**	189.	Creativity involves the generation of ideas that are a. original b. novel c. useful d. original, novel, and useful
Critical Thinking LO 24 Page: 379 **a**	190.	Which of the following statements regarding the creative process is accurate? a. Creativity generally emerges out of normal problem-solving efforts. b. Most creative breakthroughs depend on unconscious thought processes. c. Creativity cannot be learned; you either have it or you don't. d. Creativity usually involves sudden flashes of insight and great leaps of imagination.
Concept/Applied LO 24 Page: 379 Correct = 69% **c**	191.	In convergent thinking one attempts to a. utilize a hypothetico-deductive reasoning strategy to solve a problem b. work from the very specific to the very general in solving a problem c. narrow down a list of alternatives to solve a problem d. involve a relevant schema in order to solve a problem
Concept/Applied LO 24 Page: 379 **a**	192.	This multiple-choice question requires a. convergent thinking b. divergent thinking c. creativity d. insight
Factual LO 24 Page: 379 **a**	193.	In _____ thinking, one tries to expand the range of alternatives by generating many possible solutions. a. divergent b. convergent c. contingent d. symbolic

Concept/Applied LO 24 Page: 379 c	194.	Everyone likes to have Sheri working on their committees because she seems to have the unique ability to consider a variety of options and quickly narrow the list of options down to the one or two best alternatives. In other words, Sheri is skilled in a. divergent thinking b. transformational logic c. convergent thinking d. field dependence
Concept/Applied LO 24 Page: 379 b	195.	Your group has been considering various ideas for a group project for the past three weeks. You currently have 16 different ideas, but you're required to hand in your final topic selection in class tomorrow morning. This task will be easiest to complete if most of your group members are skilled in which of the following? a. divergent thinking b. convergent thinking c. transformational logic d. field dependence
Concept/Applied LO 25 Page: 379 b	196.	The question "How many uses can you think of for a shoe?" would <u>most</u> likely appear on a. an intelligence test b. a test of creativity c. an aptitude test d. a personality test
Factual LO 25 Page: 379 Correct = 80% d	197.	Creativity test items that give respondents a starting point and then require them to generate as many possibilities as they can in a short period of time are scored on the basis of a. the quantity of alternatives generated b. the originality of the alternatives c. the usefulness of the alternatives d. all of these things
Factual LO 25 Page: 379 a	198.	Which of the following is a widely used test of creativity? a. Remote Associates Test b. Thematic Apperception Test c. Iowa Test of Basic Skills d. Graduate Record Exam
Factual LO 25 Page: 380 d	199.	According to your textbook, creativity tests may have limited value. Why is this the case? a. The tests are not very reliable. b. It is basically impossible to define creativity. c. Creativity is a subjective judgement. d. The tests measure creativity out of context.
Factual LO 25 Page: 380 d	200.	Creativity generally depends on which of the following? a. motivation b. intelligence c. situational factors d. all of these things
Factual LO 26 Page: 380 c	201.	Which of the following traits has <u>not</u> been linked to creativity? a. nonconformity b. independence c. submissive d. impulsive

Concept/Applied 202. Dr. Fuller needs a really creative student to assist with the design of a new research
LO 26   project. She's asked to see the IQ scores of a number of students so she can use the
Page: 380   scores to choose her new research assistant. What does Dr. Fuller need to know
b   before making her decision?
  a. Scores on some IQ tests are more related to creativity than others.
  b. Creativity is related to intelligence, but only weakly.
  c. Grade point averages would be just as good a predictor of creativity, and probably easier to obtain.
  d. There is no relationship at all between intelligence and creativity.

Critical Thinking 203. Which of the following statements best reflects current thinking regarding the
LO 26   relationship between creativity and mental illness?
Page: 380
d
  a. Creativity and psychological maladjustment are probably causally related.
  b. Creativity and psychological well-being appear to be completely unrelated.
  c. There is a weak but significant relationship between creativity and susceptibility to multiple personality disorder.
  d. There may be a correlation between major creative achievement and vulnerability to mood disorders.

Critical Thinking 204. Which of the following statements regarding the effect of enriched environments on
LO 27   IQ is <u>not</u> accurate?
Page: 383
b
  a. Educational enrichment programs (e.g., Head Start) generally have not produced substantial, long-term gains in IQ.
  b. The inability of enrichment programs to produce enduring increases in IQ indicates that intelligence is largely a product of heredity.
  c. The failure of enrichment programs to increase IQ scores may be due to the fact that the programs were poorly executed, or underfunded.
  d. Some adoption studies have demonstrated that an improved environment can lead to meaningful increases in IQ.

Factual   205. _____ occurs when a hypothetical, abstract concept is given a name and then
LO 27   treated as though it were a concrete, tangible object.
Page: 383
b
  a. Correlation
  b. Reification
  c. Standardization
  d. Crystallization

Factual   206. According to your textbook, "intelligence" is best thought of as a
LO 27
Page: 383
a
  a. useful abstraction
  b. tangible commodity
  c. score on an IQ test
  d. product of heredity

Integrative   207. Predictability is to criterion-related validity as _____ is to test-retest
d   reliability.
  a. correlation
  b. standardization
  c. predictability
  d. consistency

Integrative   208. Galton and Terman's belief that intelligence is largely inherited meshed well with
Correct = 83%   the social values of their era. This compatibility illustrates which of your text's
c   unifying themes?
  a. Psychology is empirical.
  b. Psychology is theoretically diverse.
  c. Psychology evolves in a sociohistorical context.
  d. All of these statements are true.

Integrative Correct = 84% **c**	209.	Intelligence tests measure _____ thinking; tests of creativity measure _____ thinking. a. divergent; convergent b. divergent; divergent c. convergent; divergent d. convergent; convergent
Study Guide LO 1 Page: 347 **b**	210.	The test you are now taking is an example of a. an aptitude test b. an achievement test c. an intelligence test d. a criterion-related test
Study Guide LO 3 Page: 348 **a**	211.	Which of the following statistics is generally used to estimate reliability and validity? a. the correlation coefficient b. the standard deviation c. the percentile score d. the median
Study Guide LO 4 Page: 349 **d**	212.	What kind of validity do tests such as the SAT and ACT particularly strive for? a. content validity b. construct validty c. absolute validity d. criterion-related validity
Study Guide LO 11 Page: 359 **a**	213.	Which of the following retarded groups can often pass for normal as adults? a. mild b. moderate c. profound d. both mild and moderate
Study Guide LO 14 Page: 361 **d**	214.	Terman's long-term study of gifted children found that they tended to a. excel in physical development b. excel in social development c. excel in emotional development d. excel in all three of these areas
Study Guide LO 15 Page: 363 **d**	215.	Which of the following groups shows the <u>lowest</u> correlation with respect to intelligence? a. fraternal twins reared together b. fraternal twins reared apart c. identical twins reared apart d. siblings reared together
Study Guide LO 18 Page: 366 **b**	216.	If the reaction range concept of human intelligence is correct, then a child with exactly normal intelligence will probably <u>not</u> get much higher than an IQ of a. 107 b. 112 c. 122 d. 130
Study Guide LO 20 Page: 369 **b**	217.	Steele's theory of stereotype vulnerability is an attempt to explain why a. Asian-Americans score higher than average on IQ tests b. African-Americans score lower than average on IQ tests c. cultural bias must necessarily be inherent in all intelligence tests d. general intelligence in a population declines over time

Study Guide LO 21 Page: 372 a	218.	Spearman's "g" infers that a. most kinds of intelligence are highly related b. most kinds of intelligence are not highly related c. intelligence is highly correlated with personality characteristics d. intelligence is primarily genetic in origin
Study Guide LO 28 Page: 383 c	219.	Which of the following statements is an example of reification? a. Birds of a feather flock together. b. Creative people are born not raised. c. She gets good grades in school because she is intelligent. d. Intelligence tests are only moderate predictors of vocational success.
Online Quiz LO 1 Page: 347 b	220.	An intelligence test is designed to measure a. a person's accumulated knowledge b. a person's intellectual potential c. a person's previous learning d. all of these things
Online Quiz LO 2 Page: 348 b	221.	If 80 percent of those who provided the basis for the test norms for a test earned scores below your score, you would be at the a. 20th percentile b. 80th percentile c. 25th percentile d. 75th percentile
Online Quiz LO 4 Page: 349 c	222.	Professor Meeny has been known to administer exams that have exam questions on topics not covered in the course. Professor Meeny's students are upset at the fact that his exams are so low in a. reliability b. predictive validity c. content validity d. concept validity
Online Quiz LO 7 Page: 354 a	223.	In a normal distribution of information, most persons will be found a. in the center of the distribution b. to the far right in the distribution c. to the far left in the distribution d. on both extremes of the distribution
Online Quiz LO 9 Page: 358 a	224.	The use of intelligence tests in making employment decisions a. has declined b. is becoming standard practice c. has been ruled unconstitutional by the Supreme Court d. is a relatively recent development in the United States
Online Quiz LO 14 Page: 361 d	225.	According to Joseph Renzulli, eminent adults who make enduring contributions to their fields tend to show high levels of all but which of the following? a. creativity b. motivation c. intelligence d. social skills
Online Quiz LO 16 Page: 364 a	226.	An estimate of the proportion of trait variability in a population that is determined by variations in genetic inheritance is known as a. a heritability ratio b. a percentile score c. an intelligence quotient d. a reaction range

Online Quiz LO 19 Page: 367 c	227.	The disparity in average IQ between large minority groups and whites in the United States is a. virtually zero b. nonsignificant c. from 3 to 15 points d. impossible to determine
Online Quiz LO 22 Page: 376 c	228.	According to Gardner's theory of seven types of intelligence, one would expect a navigator on a ship to possess a high level of _____ intelligence. a. bodily-kinesthetic b. linguistic c. spatial d. bodily-kinesthetic, linguistic, and spatial
Online Quiz LO 26 Page: 380 b	229.	Research shows that creative people a. are always of superior intelligence b. are more confident, independent, and nonconforming than average c. are less tolerant of complexity, contradiction, and ambiguity than others d. have all of these characteristics

ESSAY QUESTIONS

1. In what ways have changing views about the influence of heredity and environment on intelligence affected the development of intelligence tests?

   Several individuals discussed in the chapter theorized explicitly about the nature-nurture issue with regard to intelligence, whereas the views of others are implicit in their work. The best answers to this question should reveal students' understanding of (1) the general views of the following figures regarding intelligence, (2) what their views explicitly or implicitly entail about nature-nurture, and (3) how their views have influenced the development of intelligence tests.

   Galton: One's level of intellectual ability is genetically determined. Contents of the mind are built of elementary sensations, and brighter people have greater sensory acuity that, presumably, is biologically based and therefore influenced mainly by heredity. This view led him to try to measure simple sensory processes, for example, sensitivities to stimuli, reaction time. He had little success so his mental tests were a failure, but his work stimulated interest in the measurement of intelligence.

   Galton's view that intelligence is inherited was not seriously challenged by others working to develop intelligence tests (e.g., Binet, Terman, Wechsler, Guilford, Thurstone) until very much later.

   Cattell and Horn: Intelligence consists of fluid intelligence (determined mostly by biological factors) and crystallized intelligence (determined mostly by experience). This implies that fluid intelligence may be more influenced by heredity and crystallized intelligence may be more influenced by experience. The movement away from the notion of intelligence as a single factor and toward the idea that it is a collection of different abilities represents a current trend in theorizing about intelligence and in the development of intelligence tests. For instance, the most prominent modern theories (e.g., Gardner's, Sternberg's) view intelligence as multiple. These theories have few, if any, clear implications about the effects of heredity and environment on intelligence.

2. Most cases of mental retardation have no identifiable organic cause. From what you know of their views concerning intelligence, discuss what each of the following might say about these cases of mental retardation: Jensen, Wechsler, Gardner, Scarr.

   Answers to this question should acknowledge that an important criterion of mental retardation is IQ score. Jensen believes that intelligence is largely inherited, and that this accounts for differences between ethnic and racial groups in average IQ scores. So it's logical to assume that he would expect levels of mental retardation to differ between these groups and to correspond to a group's average IQ score standing.

   One of Wechsler's contributions that has implications for this issue is that he based IQ scores on the normal distribution rather than on the ratio between mental age and chronological age. His approach, then, is central to the way mental retardation is currently assessed, i.e., in terms of number of standard deviations below the mean.

   Gardner posits multiple intelligences that are independent of each other. An implication is that an individual may have widely varying levels of the different types of intelligence, so that scoring in the retarded range for one type of intelligence may have nothing to do with one's levels in the other forms.

   Scarr is a good example of a modern heredity-environment interactionist. She has emphasized the notion of "reaction range," which states that heredity may set certain limits on intelligence, and environmental factors determine where within that range one's intelligence actually ends up. From this point of view, mental retardation can result primarily from deficiencies in heredity, environment, or various combinations of the two.

3. Discuss the similarities and differences between current views on the nature and assessment of intelligence and creativity.

   Both are influenced to a considerable extent by experience. Both apparently are based largely on normal, conscious problem-solving processes.

   Intelligence is most often defined in such a way that it seems to depend on convergent thinking; creativity on divergent thinking.

   Regarding measurement, intelligence test items are more likely to require particular correct answers; creativity tests are more open-ended.

   Both are currently thought to consist of multiple factors rather than being a single factor. The trend is toward viewing both intelligence and creativity as collections of abilities, specific to particular areas.

   Creativity tests are mediocre predictors of creative achievement in the real world. Intelligence tests are mediocre predictors of vocational achievement, but pretty good predictors of school achievement. Manifestations of intelligence and creativity in the real world are both subject to considerable influence by many factors other than intelligence and creativity, respectively, including situational factors, training, motivation, and personality. In addition, intelligence and creativity are somewhat related to each other.

   Studies like Terman's show that very intelligent people tend to be physically and emotionally healthy. There seems to be a similar connection between these traits and creativity. On the other hand, there is some evidence of a connection between high levels of creativity and some forms of mental illness, especially mood disorders.

4. In what ways do you think sociohistorical context may have influenced the investigation of creativity?

   There's a lot of room for speculation in answering this question, and not much guidance from the text. Answers should demonstrate students' understanding of what sociohistorical influence means, i.e., that the zeitgeist, including widespread social, political, and economic assumptions, influences the questions that are asked and interpretations of findings. Some examples of ideas that students might try to develop include:

   Exceptional creativity is thought to be rare, but it's highly valued. This combination has led to its being viewed as mysterious. It's not surprising, then, that a common assumption has been that creativity is under the control of mysterious unconscious processes, and that it's usually manifested in sudden bursts of insight. An implication of these assumptions is that creativity is largely beyond the control of individuals and that one cannot therefore be held responsible for not being creative. These beliefs have inspired studies demonstrating that, in fact, creativity is a product of mostly normal, conscious problem-solving processes and that it can be fostered by hard work and accumulating experience in particular domains. This view does not sit well with today's impatient generation.

   This same set of assumptions about creativity--that it is rare, emerges out of the mysterious unconscious, and that we shouldn't be ashamed for not being creative--has contributed to the belief that high levels of creativity are usually accompanied by psychological disorders. This belief has stimulated research yielding findings that have been interpreted as agreeing with the stereotype. Prentky (1989) suggests there's no causal connection, but that certain cognitive styles may both foster creativity and predispose people to psychological disorders. Could it be that, because of long-held stereotypes about creative people, individuals who show creativity are treated by others in our society in ways that contribute to those disorders?

5. Can you think of areas of our society, other than education, the workplace, and clinical settings, that have been affected by the use of psychological tests? Have psychological tests led to improvement in these areas?

Possible areas that students might mention include:

Criminal justice: Criminal defendants, especially those who use the insanity defense, may be given psychological tests to determine whether they can be held responsible for their acts, whether they're competent to stand trial, or what type of sentencing might be most appropriate. The public seems to be highly skeptical about the value of tests used in this way.

Research: Especially in some types of psychological research, tests are widely used both to classify subjects into independent variable groups and as dependent measures. Undoubtedly many benefits have been derived from research that has made use of psychological tests. Self-understanding and personal development: Psychological tests have become widely available to the general public through popular magazines, self-help books, TV, and self-help groups. These tests are most often used to reveal something about the individual to oneself. Reasons for testing oneself in this way range from mild curiosity to serious efforts at modifying one's behavior. Though many tests of this type are probably trivial, it's quite likely that many people have experienced beneficial results from this kind of psychological testing.

Chapter Ten
Motivation and Emotion

LEARNING OBJECTIVES

1. Distinguish between the two major categories of motives found in humans.
2. Summarize evidence on the areas of the brain implicated in the regulation of hunger.
3. Summarize evidence on how fluctuations in blood glucose and hormones affect hunger.
4. Summarize evidence on how culture, learning, food cues, and stress influence hunger.
5. Discuss the contribution of genetic predisposition, dietary restraint, and set point to obesity.
6. Describe the impact of hormones and pheromones in regulating animal and human sexual behavior.
7. Summarize evidence on the impact of erotic materials, including aggressive pornography, on human sexual behavior.
8. Discuss parental investment theory and findings on human gender differences in sexual activity.
9. Describe the Featured Study on culture and mating preferences and evolutionary analysis of jealousy.
10. Summarize evidence on the nature of sexual orientation and on how common homosexuality is.
11. Summarize evidence on the determinants of sexual orientation.
12. Outline the four phases of the human sexual response.
13. Describe the affiliation motive and how it is measured.
14. Describe the achievement motive and discuss how individual differences in the need for achievement influence behavior.
15. Explain how situational factors and fear of failure affect achievement strivings.
16. Describe the cognitive component of emotion.
17. Describe the physiological underpinning of emotions.
18. Discuss the body language of emotions and the facial feedback hypothesis.
19. Discuss cross-cultural similarities and variations in emotional experience.
20. Compare and contrast the James-Lange and Cannon-Bard theories of emotion and explain how Schachter reconciled these conflicting views in his two-factor theory.
21. Summarize the evolutionary perspective on emotion.
22. Explain how the chapter highlighted five of the text's organizing themes.
23. Summarize information on factors that do not predict happiness.
24. Summarize information on factors that are moderately or strongly correlated with happiness.
25. Explain four conclusions that can be drawn about the dynamics of happiness.
26. Describe the key elements in arguments.
27. Explain some common fallacies that often show up in arguments.

MULTIPLE-CHOICE QUESTIONS

Critical Thinking
LO 1
Page: 388
a

1. Which of the following statements regarding human motives is <u>not</u> accurate?
   a. Everyone shares the same set of social needs.
   b. Most biological motives reflect survival needs.
   c. The strength of social needs varies from person to person.
   d. Humans have a larger number of social needs than biological needs.

Factual
LO 1
Page: 388
b

2. According to K. B. Madsen, most motivation theories identify _____ biological needs.
   a. less than 5
   b. 10-15
   c. 25-30
   d. more than 40

Critical Thinking
LO 1
Page: 388
c

3. What do the following have in common: achievement, autonomy, play, and dominance?
   a. They are all drives.
   b. They are all biological needs.
   c. They are all social needs.
   d. They are all social-based biological motives.

Concept/Applied
LO 1
Page: 388
a

4. According to motivation theorists, we would expect people generally to be
   a. more similar in biological than in social needs
   b. more similar in social than in biological needs
   c. highly varied in both social and biological needs
   d. quite similar in both biological and social needs

Concept/Applied
LO 1
Page: 388
b

5. Imogene grew up in a small town in northern England, Dexter grew up in a large city in West Germany. You should expect that Imogene and Dexter have
   a. the same social needs, but different biological needs
   b. the same biological needs, but different social needs
   c. different biological and social needs
   d. the same biological and social needs

Factual
LO 2
Page: 388
b

6. Cannon and Washburn (1912) proposed that hunger is caused by
   a. lack of food
   b. stomach contractions
   c. low blood sugar
   d. all of these things

Critical Thinking
LO 2
Page: 389
Correct = 67%
d

7. Which of the following statements related to Cannon's findings on hunger is true?
   a. There is a correlation between stomach contractions and feelings of hunger.
   b. People whose stomach has been surgically removed still experience hunger.
   c. Stomach contractions do not cause hunger.
   d. All of these statements are true.

Factual
LO 2
Page: 389
c

8. Animals that have lesions in the ventromedial nucleus of the hypothalamus
   a. go for days without sleep
   b. lose all interest in sex
   c. overeat and become obese
   d. ignore food and often starve

Concept/Applied LO 2 Page: 389 **a**	9.	A laboratory rat has had part of its hypothalamus destroyed by lesioning. The rat doesn't seem to know when to stop eating, and has ballooned to several times its normal size. In this case, it would appear that portions of the a. ventromedial hypothalamus have been destroyed b. lateral hypothalamus have been destroyed c. parvocellular hypothalamus have been destroyed d. magnocellular hypothalamus have been destroyed
Concept/Applied LO 2 Page: 389 **b**	10.	Dr. McCardle has implanted an electrode in the hypothalamus of a rat. When the rat's brain is electrically stimulated the rat stops eating. The electrode is <u>most</u> likely activating the a. magnocellular hypothalamus b. ventromedial hypothalamus c. lateral hypothalamus d. parvocellular hypothalamus
Factual LO 2 Page: 390 **b**	11.	Injection of which of the following neurotransmitters is likely to inhibit the consumption of carbohydrates? a. GABA b. serotonin c. norepinephrine d. neuropeptide Y
Factual LO 2 Page: 390 **a**	12.	In general, contemporary theories regarding brain regulation of hunger tend to focus on which of the following? a. neural circuits b. anatomical centers c. overall size of brain d. amount of electrical activity in the hindbrain
Factual LO 3 Page: 390 Correct = 70% **d**	13.	Manipulations that decrease blood glucose level cause _____; manipulations that increase blood glucose level cause _____. a. an increase in general arousal; a decrease in general arousal b. a decrease in general arousal; an increase in general arousal c. a decrease in hunger; an increase in hunger d. an increase in hunger; a decrease in hunger
Factual LO 3 Page: 390 Correct = 1% **a**	14.	Neurons that are sensitive to sugar levels in the blood are referred to as a. glucostats b. hypothalamic nuclei c. rheostats d. thalami
Factual LO 3 Page: 390 Correct = 95% **b**	15.	According to glucostatic theory, the level of _____ in the _____ is a primary control mechanism for the regulation of hunger. a. cholecystokinin; bloodstream b. glucose; blood c. lipids; liver d. metabolites; pancreas
Critical Thinking LO 3 Page: 390 Correct = 50% **d**	16.	How does the glucostatic idea account for the fact that diabetics feel hungry much of the time? a. Diabetics have high blood sugar, which stimulates hunger. b. Diabetics have low blood sugar, which stimulates hunger. c. Diabetics have high insulin levels, which stimulates hunger. d. Diabetics' cells do not take glucose from the blood effectively.

Critical Thinking LO 3 Page: 390 **d**	17.	Which of the following statements regarding the role of insulin in hunger is <u>not</u> accurate? a. Insulin is a hormone secreted by the pancreas. b. Insulin must be present for cells to utilize glucose. c. Increased insulin secretion causes increased hunger. d. Diabetics have too much insulin.
Critical Thinking LO 3 Page: 390 **c**	18.	Which of the following statements best reflects the current view regarding the role of leptin in hunger regulation? a. The presence of leptin in the bloodstream tends to increase feelings of hunger. b. Leptin levels apparently regulate the hunger centers located in the stomach. c. When leptin levels are high, the propensity to feel hungry diminishes. d. An excessive amount of leptin in the brain has been associated with obesity in rats.
Factual LO 3 Page: 390 **d**	19.	Leptin apparently activates receptors in the brain that inhibit the release of _____, thus resulting in an inhibitory effect on eating. a. insulin b. glucostats c. serotonin d. neuropeptide Y
Factual LO 4 Page: 391 **b**	20.	Which of the following would <u>not</u> be considered an environmental factor in the regulation of hunger? a. stress b. hormonal fluctuations c. food-related cues d. learned preferences and habits
Factual LO 4 Page: 392 **d**	21.	According to research conducted by Stanley Schachter, which of the following food-related cues is likely to influence eating behavior? a. how appealing food appears b. how obvious the availability of food is c. how much effort is required to eat the food d. All of these cues were found to influence eating behavior to some extent.
Critical Thinking LO 4 Page: 392 **b**	22.	Which of the following statements regarding the influence of stress on eating behavior is <u>not</u> accurate? a. Stress leads to increased eating in a substantial portion of people. b. Some studies suggest that stress-induced eating may be more common in men than women. c. Studies suggest that stress-induced eating may be more common among chronic eaters. d. It appears to be stress-induced arousal rather than stress itself that stimulated eating.
Factual LO 5 Page: 392 **b**	23.	Assuming that people whose body weight exceeds their ideal body weight by 20% are considered obese, then about _____ percent of men and women in the United States should be regarded as obese. a. 10 b. 25 c. 40 d. 60

Factual LO 5 Page: 392 **a**	24.	Recent surveys indicate that the incidence of obesity in the United States has a. increased b. decreased c. remained constant d. virtually disappeared
Factual LO 5 Page: 393 **c**	25.	Which of the following is a measure of weight that controls for variations in height, and is increasingly used in research on obesity? a. set point b. reaction range c. body mass index d. obesity quotient
Factual LO 5 Page: 393 **a**	26.	In adoption studies designed to examine the role of genetic disposition in obesity, researchers have found that adoptees a. were more like their biological parents in weight b. were more like their foster parents in weight c. did not resemble either set of parents in weight d. were more like their half-siblings than either set of parents
Factual LO 5 Page: 394 Correct = 98% **d**	27.	The set point for body weight refers to the a. lowest possible weight at which the person can survive b. highest weight the person can attain by unrestricted eating c. person's current weight d. person's natural point of stability in body weight
Factual LO 5 Page: 394 Correct = 57% **a**	28.	According to set-point theory, the body monitors the a. level of fat stores in the body to keep it fairly constant b. level of glucose in the bloodstream c. basal metabolic rate to keep it constant d. activity of the hypothalamus
Critical Thinking LO 5 Page: 394 **a**	29.	Which of the following statements regarding fat cells and weight loss is accurate? a. Weight loss reduces the average size of fat cells. b. Weight loss reduces the number of fat cells. c. Weight loss will reduce the number of fat cells, but only with regular exercise. d. Recent studies indicate that there is virtually no relationship between weight loss and fat cells.
Factual LO 5 Page: 394 **c**	30.	Set-point theorists propose that people's set point depends on a. their bone structure b. their activity level c. the number of fat cells they possess d. their current body weight
Concept/Applied LO 6 Page: 394 Correct = 76% **b**	31.	Typically a shift in body weight in an adult who gains weight involves a. an increase in the number of fat cells in the body b. an increase in the size of fat cells in the body c. an increase in the number of muscle cells in the body d. a general increase in the number of cells throughout the body
Concept/Applied LO 5 Page: 394 **c**	32.	Which of the following concepts best explains the behavior of a person who believes he/she has cheated on a diet, and then proceeds to go on an eating binge because "I've already blown my diet anyway"? a. set point b. reaction range c. dietary restraint d. genetic predisposition

Factual LO 6 Page: 395 Correct = 96% **c**	33.	The principal gonadal hormones in females are a. androgens b. teratogens c. estrogens d. pheromones
Factual LO 6 Page: 395 Correct = 58% **d**	34.	The principal gonadal hormones in males are a. teratogens b. estrogens c. bioamines d. androgens
Factual LO 6 Page: 395 Correct = 95% **d**	35.	Low levels of _____ have been associated with a lowered male sex drive. a. catecholamines b. pheromones c. estrogen d. testosterone
Critical Thinking LO 6 Page: 396 **c**	36.	Which of the following statements regarding the influence of hormones on human sexual behavior is not accurate? a. Hormones exert less influence over sexual behavior in humans than they do in rats. b. Androgen levels seem related to sexual motivation in both males and females. c. Hormonal fluctuations clearly have a major impact on sexual desire in humans. d. Rising testosterone levels predict the onset of sexual activity in adolescent females.
Factual LO 6 Page: 396 Correct = 97% **a**	37.	A chemical secreted by one animal that affects the behavior of another is called a(n) a. pheromone b. hormone c. aphrodisiac d. drive inducer
Factual LO 6 Page: 396 **c**	38.	In humans, pheromones a. often function as aphrodisiacs b. are the single most important determinant of sexual behavior c. may be responsible for ovulatory synchronization among women who live together d. do all of these things
Factual LO 6 Page: 396 Correct = 87% **c**	39.	Research suggests that the synchronization of menstruation in women living in group settings may be related to a. social factors b. group routines c. pheromones d. dietary factors
Critical Thinking LO 6 Page: 396 Correct = 58% **d**	40.	Which of the following statements about pheromones and humans is most accurate? a. Females secrete pheromones that attract males in the same manner with as other animals. b. It appears that pheromones disproportionately influence females relative to males. c. Perfume manufacturers have discovered that the scents associated with pheromones sell much more than scents that are not similar to pheromones. d. The effect of pheromones on human behavior is not really clear.

Factual LO 6 Page: 396 Correct = 94% **a**	41.	Aphrodisiacs are a. substances thought to increase one's sexual drive b. the same things as pheromones c. hormones used to stimulate sexual receptivity in females d. the cause of the "Coolidge Effect"
Factual LO 6 Page: 396 Correct = 66% **d**	42.	Which of the following substances is a genuine aphrodisiac? a. vitamin E b. oysters c. alcohol d. none of the above
Factual LO 7 Page: 396 **c**	43.	When physiological responses to erotic stimuli are measured in laboratory studies a. men are more aroused than women b. women are more aroused than men c. men and women show similar levels of arousal d. neither men nor women are aroused
Factual LO 7 Page: 397 **a**	44.	Which of the following effects has <u>not</u> been supported by research? a. Viewing erotic materials tend to cause sex crimes. b. Viewing erotic materials changes ones attitudes to be more liberal about sexual practices. c. Viewing erotic materials may make some people dissatisfied with their own sexual interactions. d. Viewing erotic materials elevates the likelihood of overt sexual activity for a few hours immediately after the exposure.
Critical Thinking LO 7 Page: 397 **c**	45.	Which of the following statements regarding exposure to erotic material is accurate? a. Most evidence demonstrates a strong association between use of pornography and committing sex crimes. b. Sexual desire reaches a peak during the exposure, and then quickly abates. c. It increases the likelihood of sexual activity for a few hours after the exposure. d. Women actually become more physiologically aroused by erotic material than men, but they are more likely to suppress their feelings.
Factual LO 7 Page: 397 **c**	46.	About what proportion of women surveyed on 32 college campuses (Koss, Gidycz, and Wisniewski, 1987) reported having been victimized by date rape? a. 2 in 3 b. 1 in 2 c. 1 in 7 d. 1 in 15
Factual LO 7 Page: 397 **d**	47.	Research on rape has found that about _____ percent of rapes are committed by someone who is known by the victim. a. 20 b. 40 c. 60 d. 90
Factual LO 8 Page: 398 **c**	48.	The "Coolidge effect" refers to which of the following? a. the fact that men have a stronger sex drive than women b. the tendency for women to be selective in their attraction to sexual partners c. the preference for variety in sexual partners that is seen in males of many species d. the notion that powerful men are likely to have a large number of sexual partners

Concept/Applied LO 8 Page: 398 Correct = 84% c	49.	Concern that one's intimate partner might be tempted to spice up his or her sex life by looking for greener pastures reflects most people's intuitive belief in the validity a. of monogamy b. of marriage counseling c. of the Coolidge effect d. of Freud's pessimistic view of human nature
Factual LO 8 Page: 398 c	50.	Psychologists who take an evolutionary view argue that natural selection favors behaviors that maximize an individual's a. self-actualization b. acquisition of territory c. reproductive success d. material wealth
Factual LO 8 Page: 398 c	51.	Which of the following researchers proposed parental investment theory? a. David Buss b. Walter Cannon c. Robert Trivers d. Stanley Schachter
Factual LO 8 Page: 398 c	52.	_____ theory asserts that a species' mating patterns depend on what each sex has to invest, in the way of time, energy, and survival risk, to maximize the transmission of its genes to the next generation. a. Drive b. Inclusive fitness c. Parental investment d. Physiological equilibrium
Concept/Applied LO 8 Page: 398 d	53.	Parental investment theory predicts that in comparison to women, men show _____ interest in sexual activity, and _____ willingness to engage in uncommitted sex. a. less; more b. more; less c. less; less d. more; more
Concept/Applied LO 8 Page: 398 c	54.	Parental investment theory predicts that in comparison to men, women show _____ desire for variety in sexual partners, and _____ interest in sexual activity. a. less; more b. more; less c. less; less d. more; more
Critical Thinking LO 8 Page: 400 d	55.	Evolutionary theory predicts that women should place more emphasis than men on all but which of the following partner characteristics? a. ambition b. intelligence c. social status d. physical attractiveness
Factual LO 9 Page: 400 Correct = 37% b	56.	In the Featured Study on mating preference, the hypothesis tested was that a. preferences in the characteristics of mating partners will differ from culture to culture b. preferences in the characteristics of mating partners will be the same from culture to culture c. preferences in the characteristics of mating partners will be basically the same for males but differ for females from culture to culture d. preferences in the characteristics of mating partners will the same for females but differ for males from culture to culture.

Factual	57.	According to the results of the Featured Study on culture and mating preferences, which of the following characteristics in a potential mate is likely to be rated highly by both males and females?
LO 9		
Page: 400		a. status
b		b. kindness
		c. youthfulness
		d. financial prospects

Factual	58.	According to the results of the Featured Study on culture and mating preferences, which of the following characteristics in a potential mate is likely to be rated more highly by women than by men?
LO 9		
Page: 400		a. status
a		b. kindness
		c. youthfulness
		d. physical attractiveness

Factual	59.	According to the results of the Featured Study on culture and mating preferences, which of the following characteristics in a potential mate is likely to be rated more highly by men than by women?
LO 9		
Page: 401		a. status
c		b. kindness
		c. youthfulness
		d. financial prospects

Factual	60.	The results from the Featured Study on culture and mating preferences indicate that the most prominent cross-cultural variation in mate preferences is the emphasis placed on which of the following?
LO 9		
Page: 401		a. status
b		b. chastity
		c. ambition
		d. financial prospects

Factual	61.	The results from the Featured Study on culture and mating preferences tend to support which of the following theories of sexual motivation?
LO 9		
Page: 401		a. observational learning
d		b. operant conditioning
		c. psychoanalytic theory
		d. evolutionary theory

Concept/Applied	62.	According to the notion of paternity uncertainty, which of the following should be the most threatening to the reproductive success of men?
LO 9		
Page: 402		a. bisexuality in one's partner
c		b. homophobia in one's partner
		c. sexual infidelity by one's partner
		d. emotional infidelity by one's partner

Concept/Applied	63.	According to evolutionary theory, which of the following should be the most threatening to the reproductive success of women?
LO 9		
Page: 402		a. bisexuality in one's partner
d		b. homophobia in one's partner
		c. sexual infidelity by one's partner
		d. emotional infidelity by one's partner

Factual LO 10 Page: 403 **a**	64.	A person who seeks emotional-sexual relationships with members of the other sex is referred to as a. heterosexual b. homosexual c. bisexual d. monogamous
Factual LO 10 Page: 403 **c**	65.	A person who seeks emotional-sexual relationships with members of either sex is referred to as a. heterosexual b. homosexual c. bisexual d. monogamous
Factual LO 10 Page: 403 **b**	66.	A person who seeks emotional-sexual relationships with members of the same sex is referred to as a. heterosexual b. homosexual c. bisexual d. monogamous
Factual LO 10 Page: 403 Correct = 96% **b**	67.	Which of the following terms is most likely to be used by a homosexual woman to describe her sexual orientation? a. gay b. lesbian c. bisexual d. straight
Concept/Applied LO 10 Page: 403 **a**	68.	Alfred Kinsey argued that homosexuality and heterosexuality are a. end points on a "sexual orientation" continuum b. orientations based on early learning c. orientations that are a function of genetics d. value judgments and should be of little concern to scientists
Factual LO 10 Page: 404 **b**	69.	Recent studies suggest that about _____ percent of the population could reasonably be characterized as homosexual. a. 1 b. 5-8 c. 15-20 d. 30-35
Factual LO 11 Page: 404 **a**	70.	Which of the following approaches to explaining the origins of homosexuality has received the <u>most</u> empirical support? a. biological b. psychoanalytic c. operant conditioning d. classical conditioning
Factual LO 11 Page: 405 **c**	71.	Which of the following statements regarding homosexuality has <u>not</u> been supported by empirical evidence? a. Male homosexuality is linked to genetic material on the X chromosome. b. There are anatomical differences in the brain between homosexual and heterosexual men. c. Homosexuality is a learned preference acquired when same-sex stimuli have been paired with sexual arousal. d. Identical twins of homosexual men are more likely to be homosexual than are fraternal twins of homosexual men.

Factual LO 11 Page: 405 **b**	72.	Several lines of research suggest that _____ during critical periods of prenatal development may influence sexual orientation as an adult. a. severe physical trauma b. hormonal secretions c. neural abnormalities d. loss of oxygen
Factual LO 11 Page: 405 **a**	73.	Which of the following researchers is known for his interactionist theory of sexual orientation? a. Daryl Bem b. David Buss c. Walter Cannon d. Stanley Schachter
Factual LO 11 Page: 405 **c**	74.	According to the interactionist theory of sexual orientation, genes and prenatal hormones shape a child's _____, which initiates a chain of events that ultimately shapes sexual orientation. a. body size b. facial features c. temperament d. need for affiliation
Factual LO 11 Page: 405 **c**	75.	Criticism of the interactionist theory of sexual orientation has focused on which of the following aspects? a. how prenatal hormones can affect organization of the brain b. the role that parents play in shaping the sexual orientation of their children c. how social discomfort around same-sex peers gets translated into sexual attraction to same-sex peers d. the notion that the pathway to homosexuality appears to be biological in males and environmental in females
Factual LO 12 Page: 406 Correct = 90% **b**	76.	Which of the following represents the correct sequence of the phases of the human sexual response? a. plateau, excitement, orgasm, resolution b. excitement, plateau, orgasm, resolution c. plateau, excitement, resolution, orgasm d. excitement, plateau, resolution, orgasm
Factual LO 12 Page: 406 Correct = 73% **a**	77.	Heart rate, respiration rate, and blood pressure increase sharply during which two phases of the human sexual response? a. excitement and orgasm b. orgasm and resolution c. plateau and orgasm d. excitement and plateau
Factual LO 12 Page: 406 **b**	78.	Penile erection in males and the swelling of the clitoris in females is due to a. muscular contractions b. engorgement of blood vessels c. increased blood pressure d. decrease in respiration

Concept/Applied LO 12 Page: 406 **a**	79.	Sean and his wife have been kissing and caressing for about 15 minutes. His level of arousal is still increasing and he has begun to secrete some seminal fluid from the tip of his penis. Based on the phases described by Masters and Johnson, Sean is in the a. plateau phase b. excitement phase c. orgasmic phase d. resolution phase
Concept/Applied LO 12 Page: 406 **b**	80.	Alayna and her husband have been kissing and caressing for about 15 minutes. Her level of arousal is still increasing and she can feel some tightening in her vagina. Based on the phases described by Masters and Johnson, Alayna is in the a. resolution phase b. plateau phase c. excitement phase d. orgasmic phase
Concept/Applied LO 12 Page: 407 **d**	81.	Scott just experienced an orgasm. For about an hour he cannot achieve another orgasm. Scott is in the _____ phase of the sexual response cycle. a. excitement b. plateau c. orgasmic d. resolution
Factual LO 12 Page: 407 Correct = 90% **c**	82.	During which phase of the human sexual response cycle does a series of muscular contractions pulsate through the pelvic area? a. excitatory phase b. resolution phase c. orgasm phase d. phallic phase
Concept/Applied LO 12 Page: 407 **c**	83.	Talia and her husband are having sex when Talia suddenly experiences a series of muscular contractions throughout her pelvis. Based on research conducted by Masters and Johnson a. Talia's muscular contractions are likely to produce an orgasm in her husband b. it will be at least 20 minutes before Talia can become sexually aroused again c. Talia may experience another orgasm without going through a refractory period d. Talia will now pass into the plateau stage of the sexual response cycle
Critical Thinking LO 12 Page: 407 **d**	84.	Which of the following statements regarding the human sexual response is <u>not</u> accurate? a. It is normal for sexual arousal to vary during lengthy foreplay. b. The subjective experience of orgasm is very similar for males and females. c. Women are far more likely than men to be multiorgasmic. d. Men are more likely than women to engage in intercourse without experiencing an orgasm.
Critical Thinking LO 12 Page: 407 Correct = 83% **c**	85.	Which of the following generalizations was <u>not</u> supported by Masters and Johnson's human sexuality research? a. Women are more apt than men to have intercourse without orgasm. b. The subjective experience of orgasm is very similar for men and women. c. Men are more apt to be multiorgasmic than women are. d. Sexual difficulties are most typically caused by psychological factors.

Concept/Applied LO 12 Page: 408 c	86.	Peter and his wife are having sex when Peter's blood pressure increases sharply and he experiences a series of muscular contractions throughout his pelvis. Based on research conducted by Masters and Johnson a. Peter is likely to experience several more orgasms before he enters a refractory period b. Peter's muscular contractions are likely to produce an orgasm in his wife c. Peter will be relatively unresponsive to sexual stimulation for a period of time following his orgasm d. Peter will now pass into the plateau stage of the sexual response cycle
Concept/Applied LO 12 Page: 408 c	87.	Which of the following best describes the refractory period? a. the time between orgasms in multiorgasmic women b. a time following female orgasm during which females are largely unresponsive to further stimulation c. a time following male orgasm during which males are largely unresponsive to further stimulation d. the time between initiation of intercourse and orgasm
Concept/Applied LO 12 Page: 408 Correct = 83% c	88.	Sexual motivation appears to be a. mostly biological b. mostly psychological c. a mixture of biological and psychological factors d. almost totally unexplainable
Factual LO 13 Page: 408 d	89.	The need to associate with others and maintain social bonds is referred to as the _____ motive. a. competence b. sociological c. psychosocial d. affiliation
Factual LO 13 Page: 408 b	90.	Which of the following needs is <u>not</u> generally considered a component of the affiliation motive? a. friendship b. esteem c. love d. companionship
Concept/Applied LO 13 Page: 408 Correct = 89% a	91.	Evelyn likes to be around people a lot. Additionally, she develops deep friendships and joins many social groups. Evelyn's behavior reflects a. an affiliation motive b. an achievement motive c. a level-four Maslowian motive d. all of these motives
Factual LO 13 Page: 408 a	92.	According to Baumeister and Leary, which of the following is a major determinant of people's happiness? a. the quality of their personal relationships b. the number of people the work with c. the number of people they consider "friends" d. the size of their immediate family
Factual LO 13 Page: 408 Correct = 07% d	93.	The Thematic Apperception Test has been used to assess an individual's a. arousal level b. competence motive c. psychocynbernetic motive d. affiliation motive

Factual LO 13 Page: 408 **b**	94.	The Thematic Apperception Test is considered _____ test. a. an aptitude b. a projective c. an achievement d. a criterion-based
Factual LO 13 Page: 408 Correct = 59% **a**	95.	The projective test that has been used a great deal to measure affiliation need is the a. Thematic Apperception Test b. Minnesota Multiphasic Personality Test c. Sarason Sociability Scale d. Rorschach Ink Blot Test
Factual LO 13 Page: 409 Correct = 82% **a**	96.	Compared to low scorers, people who score high in the need for affiliation a. devote more time to interpersonal activities b. worry less about acceptance from others c. are more argumentative in groups d. show all of these characteristics
Concept/Applied LO 13 Page: 409 Correct = 81% **d**	97.	People who score high on affiliation need tend to do or be all of the following except a. join more social groups b. spend more time with friends c. be less argumentative in groups d. worry less about being accepted by others
Critical Thinking LO 13 Page: 409 **d**	98.	Breana is telling a story about a character on a TAT card. In this story Breana focuses on the fact the character is daydreaming about being away from all the pressures of work and family, and spending quiet time in an isolated location. Breana's answer suggests that she <u>most</u> likely has a. a low need for achievement b. a high need for affiliation c. a high need for achievement d. a low need for affiliation
Factual LO 14 Page: 409 **c**	99.	Which of the following needs is <u>not</u> generally considered a component of the achievement motive? a. outperforming others b. meeting high standards of excellence c. being accepted by others d. desiring to excel
Factual LO 14 Page: 409 **d**	100.	Which of the following psychologists is <u>most</u> closely identified with research on the achievement motive? a. David Buss b. Henry Murray c. Walter Cannon d. David McClelland
Factual LO 14 Page: 409 Correct = 91% **d**	101.	The need to master difficult challenges, outperform others, and meet high standards of excellence is referred to as a(n) a. intellect motive b. power motive c. competence motive d. achievement motive

Factual LO 14 Page: 409 Correct = 84% c	102.	Estimates of the average need for _____ in entire societies at specific times correlate with progress and productivity in those societies. a. affiliation b. intimacy c. achievement d. esteem
Concept/Applied LO 14 Page: 409 Correct = 92% a	103.	McClelland's research with achievement themes in popular literature and the later economic success of a society suggested a. a positive relationship between story achievement themes and later economic success b. no relationship between story themes and economic activity c. a negative relationship between story themes and economic activity d. none of these things
Concept/Applied LO 14 Page: 409 a	104.	Imagine that a sociologist had been tracking the patent index in a developing country for the past 30 years. Over that time the number of patents applied for has been steadily increasing. Based on David McClelland's work, it is likely that this country's need for achievement a. will also have steadily increased over the past 30 years b. will have shown a steady decline over the past 30 years c. will not have changed over the past 30 years d. will have fluctuated randomly over the past 30 years
Concept/Applied LO 14 Page: 410 b	105.	Alisha is telling a story about a character on a TAT card. In this story Alisha focuses on the individual's lack of persistence when undertaking projects, and she also describes how the individual prefers situations that have little competition. Alisha's answer suggests that she most likely has a. a low need for affiliation b. a low need for achievement c. a high need for affiliation d. a high need for achievement
Critical Thinking LO 14 Page: 410 a	106.	Which of the following characteristics is least likely to be found in persons high in achievement motivation? a. tendency to select the hardest tasks b. tendency to delay gratification c. future-oriented d. persistent
Critical Thinking LO 14 Page: 410 c	107.	Which of the following statement regarding the need for achievement is the most accurate? a. The need for achievement is highly variable in a given person throughout his/her lifetime. b. Achievement motive is generally determined by situational factors. c. The need for achievement is a fairly stable aspect of one's personality. d. There is a strong genetic component in the need for achievement.
Concept/Applied LO 14 Page: 410 b	108.	Maria is pursuing a highly competitive career, and she works very hard and persistently at her tasks. Maria's behavior most likely reflects a. an external locus of control b. a high achievement motivation c. a high power need d. an obsessive-compulsive personality structure

Critical Thinking LO 14 Page: 410 **b**	109.	A person high in achievement motivation would be expected to show all but which of the following characteristics? a. greater persistence on tasks b. tendency to seek immediate gratification c. tendency to choose competitive occupations d. tendency to choose tasks of intermediate difficulty
Critical Thinking LO 14 Page: 410 Correct = 42% **b**	110.	Given a high level of achievement motivation, which type task should maximize one's sense of accomplishment? a. a very difficult task b. an intermediate difficulty task c. a very easy task d. task difficulty doesn't matter
Factual LO 15 Page: 410 **b**	111.	According to Atkinson's expectancy-value model, the pursuit of achievement increases as the probability of success _____ and the incentive value of success _____. a. increases; decreases b. increases; increases c. decreases; increases d. decreases; decreases
Factual LO 15 Page: 410 Correct = 98% **d**	112.	Which of the following has not been found to influence achievement-oriented behavior? a. one's level of achievement motivation b. one's subjective probability of success of accomplishing a task c. one's level of motivation to avoid failure d. all of these have been found to influence achievement-oriented behavior
Critical Thinking LO 14 Page: 410 **c**	113.	Austin is telling a story about a character on a TAT card. In this story Austin focuses on the character's desire to succeed, and he describes how unhappy the person will be if she does not succeed in reaching her goal. Austin's answer suggests that he most likely has a. a low need for achievement b. a high need for affiliation c. a high need for achievement d. a low need for affiliation
Concept/Applied LO 14 Page: 410 **b**	114.	Max has the need to master difficult challenges, to outperform others, and to meet high standards for excellence. According to researchers such as McClelland and Atkinson, Max most likely a. has high affiliation needs b. is high in achievement motivation c. is low in achievement motivation d. has a high fear of failure
Concept/Applied LO 14 Page: 410 **c**	115.	Stefan is an individual who has a high need for achievement. His boss has three jobs that need to be completed; one job is easy, one job is moderately difficult, and one job is extremely difficult. If Stefan is allowed to choose which of the three jobs he will undertake for his boss, you would expect that Stefan will a. maximize the task difficulty by selecting the hardest job b. choose the easy job, to maximize his chance for success c. choose the moderately difficult job d. ask his boss to make the choice, to avoid a potentially negative evaluation

Concept/Applied LO 14 Page: 410 **b**	116.	Cyndi is an individual who has a high need for achievement. She is trying to decide which one of four possible courses she should take as her final elective course for her degree. One of the courses is supposed to be an easy course with an "A" practically guaranteed for very little effort; one course is supposed to be moderately difficult, but with effort an "A" is possible; one course is supposed to be a "killer" course with little chance of earning a grade higher than a "B"; the fourth course is a seminar-style course with no grades assigned. You should expect that Cyndi will choose a. the course that has no assigned grades b. the moderately difficult course that requires effort for a high grade c. the easy course which practically guarantees a high grade d. the "killer" course to maximize her level of task difficulty
Critical Thinking LO 15 Page: 411 **d**	117.	Which of the following statements regarding the motive to avoid failure is <u>not</u> accurate? a. The fear of failure may stimulate achievement. b. People vary in their motivation to avoid failure. c. The fear of failure is a stable aspect of personality. d. Women score significantly higher than men on the motive to avoid failure.
Factual LO 16 Page: 412 Correct = 67% **a**	118.	The three components that any complete treatment of emotion should include are a. cognitive, behavioral, physiological b. cognitive, situational, physiological c. social, situational, cognitive d. behavioral, physiological, social
Factual LO 16 Page: 412 Correct = 64% **a**	119.	The _____ component of an emotion refers to the subjective conscious experience of that emotion. a. cognitive b. physiological c. affective d. behavioral
Factual LO 16 Page: 413 **c**	120.	In studying the cognitive components of emotions, psychologists generally rely on which of the following? a. heart rate b. galvanic skin response c. subjects' verbal reports d. scores on the Thematic Apperception Test
Factual LO 17 Page: 413 **d**	121.	Most of the discernible physiological arousal associated with emotion occurs through the actions of the a. medulla b. forebrain c. central nervous system d. autonomic nervous system
Factual LO 17 Page: 413 **d**	122.	The GSR is usually considered to be a(n) a. measure of conscious emotion b. index of honesty c. measure of the cognitive component of emotion d. general measure of autonomic arousal

Critical Thinking LO 17 Page: 413 Correct = 88% **b**	123.	Which of the following statements about polygraphs is most accurate? a. Polygraphs can detect lying with almost 100 percent accuracy. b. Polygraphs can detect emotionality that accompanies lying some of the time, but with a high error rate. c. Polygraphs cannot detect emotionality at all. d. Polygraphs can detect positive emotional states with a high degree of accuracy and negative emotional states with a low degree of accuracy.
Factual LO 17 Page: 413 Correct = 76% **a**	124.	A device that measures heart rate, respiration rate, and blood pressure (i.e., autonomic arousal) is a(n) a. polygraph b. galvanic response meter c. electromyocardiograph d. electroencephalograph
Factual LO 17 Page: 414 **a**	125.	Recent evidence suggests that the _____ plays a particularly central role in the modulation of emotion. a. amygdala b. thalamus c. temporal lobe d. pineal gland
Factual LO 17 Page: 414 **a**	126.	Research on the role of the amygdala in the modulation of emotion has focused mainly on which of the following emotions? a. fear b. sadness c. surprise d. happiness
Concept/Applied LO 17 Page: 414 **b**	127.	Malcolm is reading a mystery novel, and as the action builds he finds he is breathing more quickly than usual, and he feels like his stomach is tied in knots. These reactions are part of the a. objective component in Malcolm's emotional experience b. physiological component in Malcolm's emotional experience c. cognitive component in Malcolm's emotional experience d. behavioral component in Malcolm's emotional experience
Concept/Applied LO 17 Page: 414 **d**	128.	As Danica saw the headlights coming directly at her through the fog on the highway her blood pressure rose quickly, and she felt her heart start to race. These reactions are part of the a. behavioral component in Danica's emotional experience b. objective component in Danica's emotional experience c. cognitive component in Danica's emotional experience d. physiological component in Danica's emotional experience
Concept/Applied LO 17 Page: 414 **b**	129.	Victoria is extremely upset because she has been falsely accused of stealing money from her employer. Her lawyer has suggested that Victoria take a polygraph test to prove her innocence. She asks you whether she should agree to the test. Based on the research into the accuracy of polygraphs, you should tell Victoria that polygraphs a. are extremely accurate, and if Victoria is truly innocent she will pass with no problem b. are inaccurate 25% to 33% of the time c. sometimes wrongly indicate that innocent people are guilty, but are 100% accurate in detecting guilt d. sometimes wrongly indicate that guilty people are innocent, but are 100% accurate in detecting innocence

Factual LO 18 Page: 415 **d**	130.	The _____ component of an emotion consists of the "body language" used to express the emotion. a. affective b. cognitive c. physiological d. behavioral
Critical Thinking LO 18 Page: 415 **c**	131.	Which of the following statements regarding the behavioral expression of emotion is <u>not</u> accurate? a. Facial expressions reveal a variety of basic emotions. b. The facial expressions that go with the basic emotions seem to be innate. c. People who have been blind since birth do not smile and frown as sighted people do. d. People are reasonably skilled at deciphering emotions from others' facial expressions.
Factual LO 18 Page: 415 **d**	132.	Research by Paul Ekman and Wallace Friesen indicate that subjects are generally successful in identifying (from facial cues in photographs) all but which of the following emotions? a. fear b. anger c. happiness d. contentment
Concept/Applied LO 18 Page: 415 **a**	133.	Royce is describing a whitewater rafting trip. As he talks about the raft crashing through rapids, Janie's mouth drops and she finds she is clutching at the arms of her chair. These reactions are part of the a. behavioral component in Janie's emotional experience b. cognitive component in Janie's emotional experience c. physiological component in Janie's emotional experience d. objective component in Janie's emotional experience
Concept/Applied LO 18 Page: 415 **c**	134.	Ezra is watching a movie and as the star of the movie tries to deal with various difficulties, Ezra finds himself laughing uncontrollably, with tears streaming down his face. These reactions are part of the a. physiological component in Ezra's emotional experience b. cognitive component in Ezra's emotional experience c. behavioral component in Ezra's emotional experience d. objective component in Ezra's emotional experience
Concept/Applied LO 18 Page: 416 **c**	135.	The facial feedback hypothesis suggests that a. other people can identify your emotional state by observing your facial expressions b. a facial expression is simply an external sign of the internal feelings c. you can affect how you feel by making a certain facial expression d. the internal state causes the facial expression
Concept/Applied LO 18 Page: 416 **c**	136.	Warrick was posing for his girlfriend while she painted a picture for her art class. She had asked him to hold his mouth in a frown because she was trying to depict someone who was sad and dejected. Now that he has finished posing, Warrick finds that he is feeling somewhat unhappy, but he is not really sure why. This type of reaction is consistent with which of the following? a. the two-factor theory of emotion b. the James-Lange theory of emotion c. the facial feedback hypothesis d. the common-sense view of emotion

Concept/Applied LO 18 Page: 416 **d**	137.	Diane has been feeling somewhat down for the past few days. Her sister suggests that if Diane smiled a little more, she might feel better. This suggestion is consistent with a. the two-factor theory of emotion b. the James-Lange theory of emotion c. the common-sense view of emotion d. the facial feedback hypothesis
Factual LO 18 Page: 416 **d**	138.	The idea that muscles of the face send information to the brain and that this affects the emotion we feel is known as a. Schachter's cognitive theory b. the James-Lange theory c. Darwin's facial expression theory d. the facial feedback hypothesis
Factual LO 19 Page: 416 Correct = 78% **c**	139.	Research results have indicated considerable cross-cultural agreement in the identification of all but which of the following emotional expressions? a. fear b. sadness c. suspicion d. happiness
Factual LO 19 Page: 416 Correct = 72% **b**	140.	Ekman, who has conducted a number of studies of facial expressions associated with emotions, found a. expression of the same emotion varies from culture to culture b. six fundamental emotions that most everyone agrees on c. that there are too many different emotions to identify d. common expressions for happiness and sadness only
Critical Thinking LO 19 Page: 417 **a**	141.	Cross-cultural similarities exist in all but which of the following? a. the categorization of different emotions b. identification of basic emotions from facial expressions c. the types of events that trigger specific emotions d. the physiological arousal that accompanies emotion
Factual LO 19 Page: 418 Correct = 76% **c**	142.	Cultural norms that regulate the appropriate expression of emotions are called a. cognitions b. polygraphs c. display rules d. emotional cues
Factual LO 19 Page: 418 **a**	143.	Display rules are cultural norms that regulate the expression of a. emotions b. how interpersonal exchange will take place c. sexual mores d. all of these things
Factual LO 20 Page: 418 **b**	144.	According to the James-Lange theory of emotions, one's conscious experience of emotion results from one's perception of a. others' emotions b. autonomic arousal c. skin conductancy d. tension in the facial muscles

Factual LO 20 Page: 418 Correct = 48% **d**	145.	The James-Lange theory of emotions focuses on the _____ determinants of emotions. a. psychological b. behavioral c. cognitive d. physiological
Concept/Applied LO 20 Page: 418 Correct = 47% **b**	146.	Imagine that your house is on fire and you are afraid. Which of the following explanations best represents the James-Lange theory? a. "I'm shaking because I'm afraid." b. "I'm afraid because I'm shaking." c. "My shaking must be due to fear, since my house is on fire." d. "My fear is a built-in, primary reaction to a dangerous situation."
Concept/Applied LO 20 Page: 418 **d**	147.	Imagine that an individual has taken medication that has lowered his or her overall level of autonomic arousal. If this person reports less intense emotional experiences it would provide some support for a. the Cannon-Bard theory of emotion b. the common-sense view of emotion c. the facial feedback hypothesis d. the James-Lange theory of emotion
Concept/Applied LO 20 Page: 418 **b**	148.	Dylan is on a roller coaster that has just reached the top of the first climb and is starting to drop. Based on the James-Lange theory of emotions, Dylan should report a. "My racing heart must mean I'm terrified because everyone else is screaming." b. "I feel terrified because my heart is racing." c. "My heart is racing because I am terrified." d. "The sight of the drop makes my heart race and it makes me feel terrified."
Concept/Applied LO 20 Page: 418 **c**	149.	Recent studies have detected some subtle differences in the patterns of autonomic arousal that accompany basic emotions such as happiness, anger and fear. The results from these studies lend some support to a. the Cannon-Bard theory of emotion b. Izard's evolutionary theory of emotion c. the James-Lange theory of emotion d. Schachter's two-factor theory of emotion
Factual LO 20 Page: 418 Correct = 61% **d**	150.	Walter Cannon criticized the James-Lange theory by pointing out a. that physiological arousal may occur in the absence of emotion b. that physiological changes are too slow to be the source of conscious emotion c. that very different emotions are accompanied by highly similar patterns of physiological arousal d. all of these things
Concept/Applied LO 20 Page: 418 **a**	151.	As Erica watched the televised drawing of lottery numbers, she realized she had the winning combination. If her heart starts to race at the same instant that she feels euphoria over winning the lottery, Erica's response pattern would lend support to a. the Cannon-Bard theory of emotion b. the James-Lange theory of emotion c. Izard's evolutionary theory of emotion d. Schachter's two-factor theory of emotion

Factual LO 20 Page: 418 Correct = 31% **c**	152.	According to the James-Lange theory, the conscious experience of emotion _____ physiological arousal; according to the Cannon-Bard theory, the conscious experience of emotion _____ physiological arousal. a. precedes; follows b. coincides with; precedes c. follows; coincides with d. follows; precedes
Factual LO 20 Page: 419 Correct = 39% **c**	153.	Current evidence suggests that a. different emotions are associated with easily distinguishable patterns of autonomic arousal b. all emotions are accompanied by the identical pattern of autonomic arousal c. there are some subtle differences in patterns of visceral arousal that accompany different emotions, but these are very difficult to distinguish from one another d. different emotions produce different intensities of the same basic pattern of autonomic arousal
Factual LO 20 Page: 419 Correct = 83% **a**	154.	According to Schachter's two-factor theory of emotion a. the experience of emotion depends on autonomic arousal and your cognitive interpretation of that arousal b. different patterns of autonomic activation lead to the experience of different emotions c. emotion occurs when the thalamus sends signals simultaneously to the cortex and to the autonomic nervous system d. emotions develop because of their adaptive value
Concept/Applied LO 20 Page: 419 **c**	155.	Schachter's two-factor theory of emotion suggests that we distinguish between the experience of different emotions on the basis of a. the type of behavior involved b. the type of bodily pattern involved c. our interpretation of the situation d. the emotional expression of others
Concept/Applied LO 20 Page: 419 **d**	156.	"General bodily arousal contributes to emotion, but one's interpretation of what is happening gives the specific emotion" is a proposition that would be made by a. Pavlov b. James c. Cannon d. Schachter
Concept/Applied LO 20 Page: 419 Correct = 63% **c**	157.	Imagine that your house is on fire and you are afraid. Which of the following explanations best represents Schachter's two-factor theory? a. "I'm shaking because I'm afraid." b. "I'm afraid because I'm shaking." c. "My shaking must be due to fear, since my house is on fire." d. "My fear is a built-in, primary reaction to a dangerous situation."
Concept/Applied LO 20 Page: 419 Correct = 69% **b**	158.	Schachter's concept of emotion stresses that a. thoughts precede felt emotion b. both bodily arousal and our interpretation of the arousal play a role in emotion c. we can have emotions without bodily arousal d. different emotions must be based on different patterns of arousal

Concept/Applied LO 20 Page: 419 a	159.	Scott takes an antihistamine, but he doesn't realize that the medication will also increase his overall level of autonomic arousal. Thirty minutes after he has taken the medication he is introduced to Danielle. If Scott incorrectly attributes his increased arousal as attraction for Danielle it would lend support to a. Schachter's two-factor theory of emotion b. the James-Lange theory of emotion c. the Cannon-Bard theory of emotion d. Izard's evolutionary theory of emotion
Factual LO 20 Page: 419 a	160.	According to the Cannon-Bard theory, people look to _____ cues to differentiate and label their emotions; according to Schachter, people look to _____ cues to differentiate and label their emotions. a. physiological; situational b. physiological; physiological c. situational; physiological d. situational; situational
Factual LO 20 Page: 420 Correct = 61% b	161.	Research on Schachter's two-factor theory of emotion has been a. strongly supportive b. mixed – some research supportive and other research not c. strongly nonsupportive d. none of the above, as an insufficient amount of research has been conducted to evaluate Schachter's theory
Concept/Applied LO 21 Page: 420 Correct = 53% d	162.	According to evolutionary theories of emotion a. the experience of emotion depends on autonomic arousal and your cognitive interpretation of that arousal b. different patterns of autonomic activation lead to the experience of different emotions c. emotion occurs when the thalamus sends signals simultaneously to the cortex and to the autonomic nervous system d. emotions develop because of their adaptive value
Concept/Applied LO 21 Page: 420 Correct = 66% d	163.	Imagine that your house is on fire and you are afraid. Which of the following explanations best represents evolutionary theories of emotion? a. "I'm shaking because I'm afraid." b. "I'm afraid because I'm shaking." c. "My shaking must be due to fear, since my house is on fire." d. "My fear is a built-in, primary reaction to a dangerous situation."
Factual LO 21 Page: 420 a	164.	Evolutionary theorists believe that emotions evolved _____ thought. a. before b. after c. simultaneously with d. as a control on
Factual LO 21 Page: 420 Correct = 63% b	165.	Evolutionary theorists account for the many different emotions that humans are capable of experiencing by assuming that a. each emotion is associated with its own distinctive pattern of autonomic arousal b. a small number of primary emotions can occur in various combinations and at various intensities c. humans use their advanced cognitive skills to make fine distinctions between emotions d. each and every specific emotion evolved separately

Critical Thinking LO 21 Page: 420 Correct = 29% **b**	166.	Evolutionary theories of emotion assume all but which of the following? a. Emotions are largely innate. b. Emotions followed thought in the evolutionary sequence. c. Emotions originate in subcortical brain structures. d. Humans have a relatively small number of innate emotions with adaptive value.
Concept/Applied LO 21 Page: 421 Correct = 77% **d**	167.	Because the evolutionary theorists propose that there are only a few innate primary emotions, the great variety of emotions are held to arise from a. learning new reactions later in life b. suppressing natural reactions to stimuli c. forming new associations to original cues d. blends of primary emotions and variations in intensity
Concept/Applied LO 22 Page: 421 **c**	168.	The controversies surrounding evolutionary theory, aggressive pornography, and the determinants of sexual orientation are evidence for which of the following unifying themes of your textbook? a. Psychology is empirical. b. Psychology evolves in a sociohistorical context. c. Behavior is determined by multiple causes. d. Our behavior is shaped by our cultural heritage.
Concept/Applied LO 22 Page: 421 **b**	169.	Your textbook describes a number of approaches for explaining the experience of emotion. From this discussion, we can see that a. psychology is empirical b. psychology is theoretically diverse c. psychology evolves in a sociohistorical context d. behavior is determined by multiple causes
Factual LO 23 Page: 422 **c**	170.	When people are asked to rate their happiness a. the vast majority indicate that they are unhappy b. about half the respondents indicate that they are happy c. a small minority place themselves below the neutral point on the scale d. only those who are relatively healthy consider themselves happy
Factual LO 23 Page: 422 **b**	171.	Research has shown that which of the following is <u>not</u> very important in determining one's happiness? a. work b. money c. personality d. love and marriage
Factual LO 23 Page: 422 **c**	172.	Which of the following best characterizes the correlation between income and subjective feelings of happiness? a. negligible b. negative, but weak c. positive, but weak d. positive, and strong
Critical Thinking LO 23 Page: 423 **c**	173.	Which of the following statements regarding the relationship between parenthood and happiness is <u>most</u> accurate? a. People who have children are more happy than people without children. b. People who have children are less happy than people without children. c. People who have children are neither more, nor less, happy than people without children. d. The more children people have, the happier they tend to be.

Factual LO 23 Page: 423 **d**	174.	The correlation between physical attractiveness and happiness is a. negative b. moderately positive c. strongly positive d. negligible
Factual LO 24 Page: 423 **b**	175.	The correlation between health status and subjective well-being is a. negative b. moderately positive c. strongly positive d. negligible
Factual LO 24 Page: 423 **a**	176.	Which of the following variables would be considered the best predictor of happiness? a. health b. money c. parenthood d. intelligence
Concept/Applied LO 24 Page: 424 **a**	177.	Relationship harmony is likely to be an important determinant of happiness in which of the following types of cultures? a. collectivist b. empirical c. actualized d. individualistic
Factual LO 24 Page: 424 **c**	178.	Which of the following variables would be considered the best predictor of happiness? a. money b. health c. personality d. intelligence
Factual LO 24 Page: 424 **b**	179.	_____ involves putting personal goals ahead of group goals and defining one's identity in terms of personal attributes rather than group memberships. a. Attribution b. Individualism c. Collectivism d. Socialism
Factual LO 24 Page: 424 **b**	180.	Overall, the best predictor of individuals' future happiness is their a. financial status b. past happiness c. commitment to their religion d. degree of physical attractiveness
Critical Thinking LO 24 Page: 424 **b**	181.	Research evidence suggests that happiness depends more on _____ factors than on _____ factors. a. external; internal b. internal; external c. financial; personality d. age; cultural
Critical Thinking LO 25 Page: 425 **c**	182.	Which of the following statements regarding happiness is <u>not</u> accurate? a. The quest for happiness is never hopeless. b. When it comes to happiness, everything is relative. c. Increases in income generally bring increases in happiness. d. Objective realities are not as important as subjective feelings.

Critical Thinking LO 25 Page: 425 **d**	183.	Which of the following statements regarding the correlation between social activity and happiness <u>might</u> be accurate? a. Social activity causes happiness. b. Happiness causes people to be more socially active. c. Extraversion causes both greater social activity and greater happiness. d. All of these statements might be accurate.
Factual LO 26 Page: 426 **a**	184.	_____ are the reasons that are presented to persuade someone that a conclusion is true or probably true. a. Premises b. Arguments c. Assumptions d. Attributions
Factual LO 26 Page: 426 **c**	185.	_____ are premises for which no proof of evidence is offered. a. Statements b. Arguments c. Assumptions d. Attributions
Critical Thinking LO 26 Page: 426 **a**	186.	Premises are to conclusions as _____ is/are to _____. a. legs; a table b. a pencil; a pen c. a bird; feathers d. a floppy disk; a computer
Factual LO 26 Page: 426 **d**	187.	Reasons that take support away from a conclusion are called a. fallacies b. premises c. assumptions d. counterarguments
Factual LO 27 Page: 426 **c**	188.	A *non sequitur* is basically a. a weak analogy b. a false dichotomy c. an irrelevant reason d. a circular argument
Concept/Applied LO 27 Page: 426 **d**	189.	The statement, "We need to control cyberporn because it currently is unregulated," is an example of which of the following? a. weak analogy b. false dichotomy c. irrelevant reason d. circular argument
Concept/Applied LO 27 Page: 427 **b**	190.	The statement, "If marijuana is legalized, then the next thing you know heroin will be legal," is an example of which of the following? a. weak analogy b. slippery slope c. irrelevant reason d. circular argument
Factual LO 27 Page: 427 **a**	191.	_____ asserts that two concepts or events are similar in some way. a. An analogy b. A dichotomy c. An argument d. A slippery slope

Factual LO 27 Page: 427 **b**	192.	A _____ creates an either-or choice between two outcomes. a. weak analogy b. false dichotomy c. circular argument d. slippery slope
Factual LO 27 Page: 427 **b**	193.	The statement, "We can ban cyberporn, or we can hasten the moral decay of modern society," is an example of which of the following? a. weak analogy b. false dichotomy c. circular argument d. slippery slope
Integrative Correct = 67% **a**	194.	Which theorists agree that autonomic arousal precedes the conscious experience of emotion? a. James, Lange, and Schachter b. Cannon, Bard, and Atkinson c. Tomkins, Izard, and Plutchik d. Maslow, McClelland, and Murray
Study Guide LO 2 Page: 389 **c**	195.	What happens when a rat's lateral hypothalamus is lesioned? a. It starts eating. b. It looks for a sexual partner. c. It stops eating. d. It loses bladder and bowel control.
Study Guide LO 3 Page: 390 **a**	196.	The presence of the hormone Leptin in the bloodstream tends to a. decrease hunger b. accompany stress c. contribute to general arousal level d. signal sexual activity
Study Guide LO 5 Page: 393 **d**	197.	Which data from twin studies provide the most convincing evidence of the influence of heredity on body weight? a. Identical twins reared together are more similar than fraternal twins reared together. b. Identical twins reared together are more similar than fraternal twins reared apart. c. Identical twins reared apart are more similar than fraternal twins reared apart. d. Identical twins reared apart are more similar than fraternal twins reared together.
Study Guide LO 6 Page: 395 **c**	198.	The presence of testosterone is related to higher levels of sexual activity in a. males b. females c. both males and females d. androids
Study Guide LO 8 Page: 398 **b**	199.	According to this theory, the sex that makes the larger investment in offspring (bearing, nursing, etc.) will be more selective of partners than the sex that makes the smaller investment. a. adaptation level theory b. parental investment theory c. investment differentiation theory d. social learning theory

Study Guide LO 9 Page: 399 **c**	200.	According to the evolutionary theories, men seek as partners women who a. are similar to them in important attitudes b. have a good sense of humor c. are beautiful, youthful, and in good health d. have good financial prospects
Study Guide LO 19 Page: 417 **b**	201.	Evidence regarding facial expression in different cultures and observation of the blind suggests that a. Schachter's two-factor theory is correct b. facial expression of emotion is to a large extent innate c. emotions originate in the cortex d. learning is the major factor in explaining basic facial expressions
Study Guide LO 20 Page: 419 **a**	202.	Which of the following proposed that emotion arises from one's perception of autonomic arousal? a. Schachter b. Cannon-Bard c. LeDoux d. McClelland
Study Guide LO 21 Page: 420 **d**	203.	Which of the following theories assert that thinking or cognition plays a relatively small role in emotion? a. two factory theory b. James-Lange theory c. achievement theory d. evolutionary theory
Study Guide LO 24 Page: 424 **c**	204.	Of the following, which has been found to be most strongly associated with happiness? a. physical attractiveness b. health c. job satisfaction d. general intelligence
Study Guide LO 27 Page: 427 **c**	205.	Someone exhorts people to take action against company policy, as follows: "We can oppose these changes, or we can live out our lives in poverty." While the intent of the argument may be appropriate and persuasive, logically it would be which of the following fallacies? a. slippery slope b. weak analogy c. false dichotomy d. circular reasoning
Online Quiz LO 1 Page: 388 **b**	206.	Which of the following is <u>not</u> considered a social need in humans? a. affiliation b. aggression c. nurturance d. achievement
Online Quiz LO 3 Page: 390 **a**	207.	The recent discover of a previously undetected hormone, called _____, has shed new light on the hormonal regulation of hunger. a. leptin b. glucotin c. norepinephrine d. neuropeptide Y

Online Quiz LO 5 Page: 394 a	208.	The basic idea behind the set-point theory of body weight is that a. the body monitors fat stores and tries to keep them stable b. the body monitors carbohydrate stores and tries to keep them stable c. the body monitors protein levels and tries to keep them stable d. glucostats are critical in weight control
Online Quiz LO 8 Page: 398 d	209.	Studies by evolutionary theorists of which of the following topics have drawn the most attention? a. hunger b. aggression c. territoriality d. sexual behavior
Online Quiz LO 9 Page: 399 b	210.	At present, which of the following approaches appears to provide the most complete account for gender disparities in sexual behavior? a. operant conditioning b. evolutionary theory c. social learning theory d. sociopolitical theory
Online Quiz LO 12 Page: 408 b	211.	Which of the following statements about the sexual cycle studied by Masters and Johnson is true? a. Orgasm is quite different in males and females. b. During the refractory period, men cannot experience another orgasm. c. The excitement phase occurs much more rapidly in women than in men. d. The plateau phase involves a decrease in bodily functions.
Online Quiz LO 14 Page: 408 c	212.	One's need for achievement is usually assessed using which of the following instruments? a. Wechsler Adult Intelligence Scale b. Minnesota Multiphasic Personality Inventory c. Thematic Apperception Test d. Edwards Manifest Needs Scale
Online Quiz LO 17 Page: 413 c	213.	The galvanic skin response is a measure of a. blood flow through the skin b. muscle tension of the skin c. electrical conductivity of the skin d. two-point difference threshold of the skin
Online Quiz LO 20 Page: 418 c	214.	According to the Cannon-Bard theory of emotion a. the experience of emotion depends on autonomic arousal and your cognitive interpretation of that arousal b. different patterns of autonomic activation lead to the experience of different emotions c. emotion occurs when the thalamus sends signals simultaneously to the cortex and to the autonomic nervous system d. emotions develop because of their adaptive value
Online Quiz LO 24 Page: 424 c	215.	_____ culture is one whose members place a high priority on cooperation and shared values. a. An actualized b. An empirical c. A collectivist d. An individualistic

ESSAY QUESTIONS

1. In what ways are motivation and emotion similar to each other and different from each other?

   Some points students might mention and elaborate upon:

   Both can activate and influence behavior. But it's more difficult to predict the behavior that an emotion will lead to.

   The same motive or emotion can lead to different behaviors in different individuals, or in the same individual at different times. Also, the same behavior might result from different motives or emotions.

   Both can operate on us without our awareness.

   Both are most often activated by some internal or external stimulus. According to some prominent theories, there are both primary motives and primary emotions. Primary motives are biological in nature; there are also social motives. The text offers no comparable division of emotions into biological and social.

   According to prominent theories, the experiences of both motivation and emotion are influenced by cognitive factors.

   Similar areas of the brain (especially the hypothalamus and the ANS) appear to be involved in both.

2. Some psychologists have suggested that the function of emotions is to motivate the organism. What do you think this means? Illustrate your points with examples.

   It's hard to think of any explanation for why we have emotions unless it's to motivate behavior. Darwin believed emotions have adaptive value, that is, they promote individual and species survival by directing behavior that is beneficial to the individual or species. This included the notion that the apparently innate and universal facial expressions that accompany emotions serve as signals to others and thereby influence their behavior.

   When emotions are experienced, autonomic arousal occurs, probably for the purpose of preparing the body to respond to whatever stimuli led to the emotion's being activated. This also suggests that the purpose of emotion is to motivate.

   Schachter's two-factor theory suggests that environmental cues influence one's interpretation of the autonomic arousal being experienced so that particular labels are applied to emotional experiences. We then behave in accordance with the label. This also implies that the mechanism of emotion operates for the purpose of guiding behavior in particular directions.

3. Compare and contrast sexual motivation with the basic motives of hunger and thirst. How well do the concepts of drive and homeostasis contribute to understanding sexual motivation?

   Good answers will include and elaborate upon the following points: All are biologically based, though hunger and thirst are necessary for individual survival and sex is not (though some individuals might argue this point). All three seem to conform to the definition of "drive." But sexual motivation is not driven by deprivation as much as the other two, so that its satisfaction is not as easily explained in terms of homeostasis or maintaining equilibrium. Sexual motivation in humans appears to be more under the influence of incentives than are hunger and thirst. All are influenced by a complex network of biological and social factors.

4. Suppose you are a university counselor who wants to develop a program to improve students' academic performance. You believe that many students perform poorly because of motivational problems, including simple lack of motivation as well as being motivated by the wrong things. What are some of the considerations that should guide the design of your program?

   Much of what theory and research have to say about motivation is relevant in designing such a program. Good answers to this question should include and flesh out several of the following points:

   The problem of lack of incentive can be dealt with in part by remembering that motivation can be influenced by incentives. Expectancy-value models can be useful here.

   It's important to know that some motives are biological, some social. One's level of motivation to perform well in school depends on social experiences and can thus be manipulated through social experience.

   Maslow's theory implies that motivation to perform well academically must wait upon the satisfaction of lower-level motives.

   It may be possible to link motivation to perform well in school with other motives that are already stronger, such as the need for affiliation. Success along these lines will require understanding the nature of individual differences in levels of these other motives.

   People with different levels of achievement motivation respond differently to different levels of challenge.

   Fear of failure also influences efforts toward achievement.

5. As you'll learn in Chapter 11, research on temperament shows that from the earliest days of life infants differ from each other in things like emotional tone, tempo of activity, and sensitivity to environmental stimuli. Discuss these findings from the viewpoint of evolutionary theories of emotion.

   Answers should reveal students' understanding that when newborns exhibit characteristics such as these, this strongly suggests that those characteristics are innate, based on heredity rather than experience. The evolutionary perspective would state that such innate characteristics probably have adaptive value. Good answers should explore the possible adaptive benefits that temperamental differences might confer.

This page intentionally left blank.

Chapter Eleven
Human Development Across the Life Span

LEARNING OBJECTIVES

1. Outline the major events of the three phases of prenatal development.
2. Summarize the impact of environmental factors on prenatal development.
3. Describe general trends and principles and cultural variations in motor development.
4. Summarize the findings of Thomas and Chess's longitudinal study of infant temperament.
5. Summarize theories of attachment and research on patterns of attachment and their effects.
6. Discuss bonding at birth, day care, and culture in relation to attachment.
7. Explain Belsky's evolutionary perspective on attachment.
8. Outline the basic tenets of Erikson's theory and describe his stages of childhood personality development.
9. Outline Piaget's stages of cognitive development and discuss the strengths and weaknesses of Piaget's theory.
10. Summarize evidence which suggests that some cognitive abilities could be innate and describe how children's understanding of mental states progresses.
11. Describe children's progress in attention and memory.
12. Outline Kohlberg's stages of moral development and discuss the strengths and weaknesses of Kohlberg's theory.
13. Describe the major events of puberty and the Featured Study on the timing of sexual maturation.
14. Evaluate the assertion that adolescence is a time of turmoil.
15. Discuss some common patterns of identity formation.
16. Summarize evidence on the stability of personality and the prevalence of the midlife crisis.
17. Outline Erikson's stages of development in adulthood.
18. Describe typical transitions in family relations during the adult years.
19. Discuss patterns of career development in both men and women.
20. Describe the physical changes associated with aging.
21. Describe the cognitive changes associated with aging.
22. Explain how this chapter highlighted the interaction of heredity and environment.
23. Summarize evidence on gender differences in behavior, and discuss the significance of these differences.
24. Explain how biological factors are thought to contribute to gender differences.
25. Explain how environmental factors are thought to contribute to gender differences.
26. Explain the argument that fathers are essential for healthy development and some criticism of this line of reasoning.

MULTIPLE-CHOICE QUESTIONS

Factual
LO 1
Page: 432
Correct = 85%
d

1. Developmental psychology is primarily concerned with
   a. an analysis of individual differences in behavior
   b. an analysis of species differences in behavior
   c. the role of learning in behavior
   d. those aspects of behavior that change over the life span

Factual
LO 1
Page: 432
Correct = 89%
b

2. The prenatal period refers to
   a. the period from conception to implantation
   b. the nine months before birth
   c. the period of time immediately after birth
   d. the time period before conception takes place

Factual
LO 1
Page: 432
Correct = 60%
b

3. The first phase of prenatal development is the
   a. embryonic stage
   b. germinal stage
   c. fetal stage
   d. postnatal stage

Concept/Applied
LO 1
Page: 432
a

4. Omar's wife conceived a baby seven days ago, and does not yet know she is pregnant. His wife's pregnancy is currently in the
   a. germinal stage
   b. embryonic stage
   c. fetal stage
   d. placental stage

Factual
LO 1
Page: 433
Correct = 95%
d

5. The _____ is the structure that allows oxygen and nutrients to pass from the mother to the fetus.
   a. zygote
   b. amnion
   c. uterus
   d. placenta

Factual
LO 1
Page: 433
Correct = 78%
c

6. A _____ implants itself into the uterine wall and becomes a(n) _____.
   a. fetus; zygote
   b. sperm; egg
   c. zygote; embryo
   d. embryo; fetus

Factual
LO 1
Page: 433
Correct = 69%
c

7. The embryonic stage of prenatal development refers to
   a. the formation of a zygote
   b. the implantation of the fertilized egg into the uterine wall
   c. the second through eighth weeks of prenatal development
   d. the last seven months of the pregnancy

Factual
LO 1
Page: 433
Correct = 57%
d

8. During which stage of development do the heart, spine, and brain emerge?
   a. post-natal
   b. placental
   c. fetal
   d. embryonic

Factual LO 1 Page: 433 Correct = 60% **d**	9.	The stage of prenatal development during which most miscarriages are likely to occur is the a. zygotic stage b. germinal stage c. fetal stage d. embryonic stage
Concept/Applied LO 1 Page: 433 **d**	10.	Chelsey is pregnant and she is concerned about taking an over-the-counter medication for her allergies. She should be <u>most</u> concerned if her pregnancy is currently at the a. placental stage b. germinal stage c. fetal stage d. embryonic stage
Factual LO 1 Page: 433 Correct = 91% **c**	11.	The third stage of prenatal development, which lasts from two months through birth, is referred to as the a. postgerminal stage b. embryonic stage c. fetal stage d. postnatal stage
Factual LO 1 Page: 433 Correct = 68% **b**	12.	The developing organism becomes capable of physical movement during the a. germinal stage b. fetal stage c. embryonic stage d. postnatal stage
Concept/Applied LO 1 Page: 433 **c**	13.	Avery is excited by the fact she has begun to feel her baby kicking and moving in her uterus. If Avery can feel her baby moving, her pregnancy must be in the a. embryonic stage b. germinal stage c. fetal stage d. neonatal stage
Concept/Applied LO 1 Page: 433 Correct = 86% **a**	14.	The longest stage of prenatal development is the a. fetal stage b. embryonic stage c. germinal stage d. zygotic stage
Concept/Applied LO 1 Page: 434 Correct = 89% **c**	15.	Premature babies who survive were typically born during the a. germinal stage b. embryonic stage c. fetal stage d. postnatal stage
Factual LO 1 Page: 434 Correct = 85% **b**	16.	The age of viability, referring to the age at which the fetus _____, is reached _____. a. can first respond to stimulation; at about 9 weeks b. can survive if born prematurely; between 22 and 26 weeks c. first has a heartbeat; at about 16 weeks d. experiences no further cell division in the brain; between 36 and 38 weeks

Concept/Applied LO 1 Page: 434 **c**	17.	Felicia is pregnant and her blood pressure has become dangerously high. Her doctor wants to deliver her baby by Cesarean section, even though Felicia is only 27 weeks pregnant. If Felicia's baby is delivered at this point in her pregnancy, the baby will have a. less than a 10% chance of survival b. approximately a 25% chance of survival c. almost an 85% chance of survival d. virtually a 100% chance of survival
Concept/Applied LO 2 Page: 434 Correct = 78% **a**	18.	Any mechanical or chemical interference with prenatal development will have the <u>most</u> serious impact when the system to be affected is a. growing rapidly b. growing slowly c. growing at a constant pace d. not growing at all
Concept/Applied LO 2 Page: 435 Correct = 83% **b**	19.	If a baby is born with a small head, heart defects, and retarded mental and motor development, the mother is <u>most</u> likely to have a. had smallpox early in her pregnancy b. been an alcoholic c. continued to work during pregnancy d. smoked during pregnancy
Concept/Applied LO 2 Page: 435 Correct = 79% **d**	20.	The full-blown fetal alcohol syndrome is produced by a. heavy drinking during the first three months of pregnancy b. heavy drinking during the final three months of pregnancy c. one drunken binge at any time during pregnancy d. heavy drinking throughout pregnancy
Concept/Applied LO 2 Page: 435 Correct = 97% **c**	21.	Which of the following statements is <u>true</u>? a. As long as the pregnant woman isn't physiologically addicted to alcohol, it doesn't matter how much she drinks. b. Three drinks per day can be considered a safe level of alcohol consumption for most pregnant women. c. Even normal social drinking by the expectant mother may be harmful to the fetus. d. Alcohol consumption by the mother poses almost no risk to the developing fetus in the last three months of the pregnancy.
Concept/Applied LO 2 Page: 435 **b**	22.	Camille drank heavily during the first eight weeks of her pregnancy, but since that time she has abstained from all alcohol. It is most likely that Camille's baby will a. be unaffected by her drinking, because it occurred so early in the pregnancy b. have noticeable physical deformities, and an increased risk of mental retardation c. have noticeable physical deformities, but no risk of mental retardation d. have no physical deformities, but will have an increased risk of mental retardation
Factual LO 2 Page: 435 Correct = 40% **c**	23.	Which of the following has <u>not</u> been associated with women who smoke during pregnancy? a. increased risk for miscarriage, stillbirth, or prematurity b. increased risk of attention deficit disorder in the infant c. increased risk for microcephaly in the newborn d. increased risk for Sudden Infant Death Syndrome (SIDS)

Factual LO 2 Page: 435 Correct = 66% **d**	24.	Genital herpes and AIDS are typically passed from mother to offspring during the a. germinal stage b. embryonic stage c. fetal stage d. birth process
Factual LO 2 Page: 435 Correct = 65% **a**	25.	The potential damage due to prenatal exposure to maternal illness is primarily a function of a. when the mother contracts the disease b. the severity of the mother's symptoms c. the condition of the mother's overall health d. whether the unborn child is male or female
Concept/Applied LO 2 Page: 435 **d**	26.	Angelina and Dominque are best friends. Angelina contracts rubella and Dominque catches it from her. At the time they are sick with the disease, Angelina is 4 weeks pregnant and Dominque is 8 months pregnant. The <u>most</u> likely outcome in this situation is a. Angelina's baby will be unaffected by the disease, but Dominque's baby will have physical defects as a result of Dominque's rubella infection b. both babies will have physical defects as a result of their mothers' rubella c. neither baby will have physical defects as a result of their mothers' rubella d. Dominque's baby will be unaffected by the disease, but Angelina's baby will have physical defects as a result of Angelina's rubella infection
Factual LO 2 Page: 436 Correct = 59% **a**	27.	Of the countries listed below, which country has the <u>lowest</u> infant mortality rate? a. Sweden b. Great Britain c. United States d. Canada
Factual LO 2 Page: 436 Correct = 62% **c**	28.	Of the countries listed below, which country has the <u>highest</u> infant mortality rate? a. Singapore b. Hong Kong c. United States d. Ireland
Factual LO 2 Page: 436 Correct = 91% **c**	29.	Of the factors that may shape development prior to birth, which is the <u>least</u> understood? a. excessive alcohol use b. rubella (German measles) c. fluctuations in maternal emotions d. tobacco use
Concept/Applied LO 3 Page: 437 **d**	30.	The cephalocaudal trend in physical development suggests that infants will be able to control their a. hips and legs before they can control their shoulders and arms b. shoulders and arms before they can control their hands and fingers c. hands and fingers before they can control their shoulders and arms d. shoulders and arms before they can control their hips and legs
Concept/Applied LO 3 Page: 437 Correct = 51% **a**	31.	In learning to crawl, children initially depend on their arms to propel them and later shift to using their legs. This motor development sequence is an example of a. the cephalocaudal trend b. the proximodistal trend c. the cephalopedal trend d. encephalitis

Concept/Applied LO 3 Page: 437 Correct = 70% **b**	32.	The fact that babies can hold their head up _____ they can first sit up, is an example of the _____ trend in motor development. a. before; proximodistal b. before; cephalocaudal c. after; proximodistal d. after; cephalocaudal
Factual LO 3 Page: 438 Correct = 90% **a**	33.	The proximodistal trend in the motor development of children can be described simply as a a. center-outward direction b. head-to-foot direction c. outward-inward direction d. side-to-side direction
Concept/Applied LO 3 Page: 438 Correct = 88% **d**	34.	According to the basic sequences of progression of motor maturation, which of the following body structures should take the longest to come under effective control? a. torso b. shoulders c. arms d. fingers
Concept/Applied LO 3 Page: 438 **a**	35.	The proximodistal trend in physical development suggests that infants will be able to control their a. shoulders and arms before they can control their hands and fingers b. shoulders and arms before they can control their hips and legs c. hips and legs before they can control their shoulders and arms d. hands and fingers before they can control their shoulders and arms
Factual LO 3 Page: 438 Correct = 61% **a**	36.	With respect to maturation, it has been discovered that a. all children go through roughly the same sequence of physical development b. the sequence of physical development varies from culture to culture c. the sequence of physical development varies from individual to individual d. while sequence varies a lot, rates are fairly universal across children
Critical Thinking LO 3 Page: 438 Correct = 79% **b**	37.	The fact that children in different cultures _____ in the age at which basic motor skills appear demonstrates that _____. a. vary somewhat; genetic factors can slow or accelerate early motor development b. vary somewhat; environmental factors can slow or accelerate early motor development c. do not vary; genetic factors alone determine early motor development d. do not vary; environmental factors alone determine early motor development
Concept/Applied LO 3 Page: 439 Correct = 46% **a**	38.	Experience and training exert their effects on motor behavior a. more as the child becomes older b. less as the child becomes older c. most at the very first, and less as the child grows older d. about equally at all phases of development
Factual LO 3 Page: 439 Correct = 42% **b**	39.	As children grow older and acquire specialized motor skills, which of the following becomes increasingly critical? a. maturation b. experience c. genetic predispositions d. nutrition

Factual LO 4 Page: 440 Correct = 80% **a**	40.	When groups of subjects of differing age are compared at a single point in time, the study is called a a. cross-sectional study b. longitudinal study c. cross-cultural study d. sequential study
Concept/Applied LO 4 Page: 440 Correct = 79% **c**	41.	A researcher collects information about a group of people for 25 years in order to determine the nature of psychological changes these persons exhibit. This type of study is classified as _____ research. a. cross-sectional b. sequential c. longitudinal d. cross-cultural
Concept/Applied LO 4 Page: 440 **b**	42.	Tucker is a graduate student who is studying identity formation. He selects a group of 5-year-olds, a group of 10-year-olds, and a group of 15-year-olds, and interviews each group, asking them what they plan to be when they finish school. In this example, Tucker is using a. a longitudinal research design b. a cross-sectional research design c. a multi-factorial research design d. a nested condition research design
Concept/Applied LO 4 Page: 440 **a**	43.	Jade is a graduate student who is studying the way in which selective attention develops during the preadolescent years. She selects a group of 10-year-olds and she assesses their selective attention every six months over a two-year period. In this example, Jade is using a. a longitudinal research design b. a cross-sectional research design c. a multi-factorial research design d. a nested condition research design
Factual LO 4 Page: 440 Correct = 35% **a**	44.	Research suggests that a child's "temperamental individuality" is well established around a. two to three months of age b. six to seven months of age c. one year of age d. two years of age
Concept/Applied LO 4 Page: 440 **d**	45.	Gary is an active infant who always seems to be happy. He has a regular schedule and his parents know that he will sleep through the night without waking, even when he stays over night with his grandparents. Using the temperament categories outlined by Thomas and Chess, Gary would most likely be considered to have a. a difficult temperament b. a slow-to-warm-up temperament c. an uninhibited temperament d. an easy temperament
Factual LO 4 Page: 440 Correct = 95% **b**	46.	An infant who actively resists change, who fails to develop a regular sleeping and eating schedule, and who is generally irritable and unhappy is best described as temperamentally a. easy b. difficult c. slow to warm up d. mixed

Factual LO 4 Page: 440 Correct = 78% **d**	47.	Thomas and Chess refer to a child who tends to be glum, erratic in sleep and eating, and resistant to change as a. an easy child b. a slow-to-warm-up child c. a mixed temperament child d. a difficult child
Concept/Applied LO 4 Page: 440 **b**	48.	Mikaela is a quiet infant who doesn't seem to smile a lot, but who also seldom cries. She seems cautious and wary of changes in her surroundings, but eventually she adapts to the change. Using the temperament categories outlined by Thomas and Chess, Mikaela would most likely be considered to have a. a difficult temperament b. a slow-to-warm-up temperament c. an easy temperament d. an uninhibited temperament
Concept/Applied LO 4 Page: 440 **c**	49.	Ruby is an active infant who appears to be somewhat high-strung, and who protests loudly every time her parents try to change her routine in any way. Using the temperament categories outlined by Thomas and Chess, Ruby would most likely be considered to have a. an easy temperament b. a slow-to-warm-up temperament c. a difficult temperament d. an uninhibited temperament
Concept/Applied LO 4 Page: 440 Correct = 85% **d**	50.	According to Kagan and colleagues, infants who are shy, timid, and wary of unfamiliar persons are said to exhibit a. an uninhibited temperament b. a slow-to-warm-up temperament c. mixed temperaments d. inhibited temperament
Concept/Applied LO 4 Page: 440 **b**	51.	Ross is a shy, timid child who is uncomfortable around unfamiliar people. Using the temperament categories outlined by Kagan, Ross would most likely be considered to have a. an easy temperament b. an inhibited temperament c. a slow-to-warm-up temperament d. an uninhibited temperament
Concept/Applied LO 4 Page: 440 Correct = 68% **a**	52.	If an infant is temperamentally easy, what would be the best prediction to make about the child's temperament at age 10? a. The child is fairly likely to retain the easy temperament. b. The child is likely to overcompensate by becoming "difficult" later on. c. No reasonable prediction can be made. d. By the age of 10 the child is likely to develop whatever temperament the primary caregiver has.
Factual LO 5 Page: 441 Correct = 85% **a**	53.	The close, emotional bond of affection between an infant and its caregiver is called a. attachment b. dependency c. imprinting d. identification

Factual LO 5 Page: 442 Correct = 56% **c**	54.	At what age does an infant typically first exhibit separation anxiety? a. one to two weeks b. one to two months c. six to eight months d. around one year
Concept/Applied LO 5 Page: 442 **b**	55.	Four-month-old Wade and 14-month-old Macy are left with a babysitter while their mother runs a few errands. According to the research on separation anxiety, it is <u>most</u> likely that a. Wade will show more distress than Macy when he realizes that his mother has gone b. Macy will show more distress than Wade when she realizes that her mother has gone c. both Wade and Macy will show about the same degree of separation anxiety d. neither child is likely to show separation anxiety as long as the babysitter is responsive and caring
Concept/Applied LO 5 Page: 442 **c**	56.	One-year-old Tommy is extremely distressed whenever his mother leaves him, yet resists her attempts to comfort him when she returns. Tommy probably has _____ to his mother. a. no attachment b. a secure attachment c. an anxious-ambivalent attachment d. an avoidant attachment
Concept/Applied LO 5 Page: 442 **c**	57.	Mercedes takes her 1-year-old son, Justice, to visit a day-care center where she plans to enroll him. Justice eagerly explores the play room as long as Mercedes is present. When his mom leaves the room to fill out some forms, Justice becomes somewhat upset, but when Mercedes returns he quickly calms down. This is the type of interaction you might observe between a child and a parent who a. share an avoidant attachment relationship b. share an anxious-ambivalent attachment relationship c. share a secure attachment relationship d. have not yet developed an attachment relationship
Concept/Applied LO 5 Page: 442 **d**	58.	Kara takes her 1-year-old son, Delaney, to visit a day-care center where she plans to enroll him. Delaney appears very anxious and is unwilling to explore the play room, even though Kara is close by. When his mom leaves the room to fill out some forms, Delaney becomes extremely upset. When Kara returns he clings to her leg, but does not calm down and continues to sob. This is the type of interaction you might observe between a child and a parent who a. share a secure attachment relationship b. share an avoidant attachment relationship c. have not yet developed an attachment relationship d. share an anxious-ambivalent attachment relationship
Concept/Applied LO 5 Page: 442 **d**	59.	Jasmin takes her 1-year-old son, Randy, to visit a day-care center where she plans to enroll him. Randy eagerly explores the play room, and when his mom leaves the room to fill out some forms he shows no signs of concern. When Jasmin returns he shows little interest and continues to play with the toys he has collected. This is the type of interaction you might observe between a child and a parent who a. share an anxious-ambivalent attachment relationship b. share a secure attachment relationship c. have not yet developed an attachment relationship d. share an avoidant attachment relationship

Factual LO 6 Page: 443 **c**	60.	Which of the following statements is <u>true</u>? a. If mother and newborn are deprived of skin-to-skin contact immediately after birth, their relationship is irrevocably damaged. b. From the first moment they lay eyes on their babies, all mothers experience an instantaneous and overwhelming bond to them. c. There is no convincing evidence that skin-to-skin contact between mother and newborn immediately after birth leads to healthier attachment later on. d. Skin-to-skin contact immediately after birth leads to a much stronger, more secure attachment later in infancy.
Concept/Applied LO 6 Page: 443 **d**	61.	Which of the following statements most accurately summarizes the findings of studies of infant day care? a. The vast majority of infants in day care will develop insecure attachments to their mothers. b. Girls seem to be more vulnerable to the negative effects of infant day care than boys. c. Day-care infants are likely to be more aggressive than their peers later on. d. Negative effects of day care seem minimal and may even be outweighed by positive effects when day care is of high quality.
Concept/Applied LO 6 Page: 444 Correct = 56% **a**	62.	Cross-cultural studies of infant attachment suggest that attachment _____ universal, and that attachment patterns _____ influenced by a culture's child-rearing practices. a. is; are b. is not; are c. is; are not d. is not; are not
Factual LO 5 Page: 444 **c**	63.	According to Bowlby, parents and their infants become attached to one another because a. their social interactions are mutually reinforcing b. social roles dictate that parents should love their children and vice versa c. infants and adults are biologically programmed for mutual attachment d. parents become conditioned stimuli for reinforcing events
Factual LO 7 Page: 445 **a**	64.	According to Belsky, if the local environment is relatively safe and rich in resources, then individuals are more likely to form _____ attachments as children, and as adults they will be more likely to pursue a reproductive strategy that fosters _____ in mating relationships. a. secure; quality b. secure; quantity c. insecure; quality d. insecure; quantity
Factual LO 7 Page: 445 **b**	65.	According to Belsky, if the local environment is unsafe and resources are depleted, then individuals are more likely to form _____ attachments as children, and as adults they will be more likely to pursue a reproductive strategy that fosters _____ in mating relationships. a. secure; quality b. insecure; quantity c. insecure; quality d. secure; quantity

Concept/Applied LO 7 Page: 445 **c**	66.	Gilbert did not date much prior to his marriage, and he recently celebrated his 35th wedding anniversary. He spent a lot of time with his three children when they were growing up, and he has been very involved with the raising of his grandchildren. Based on Belsky's research, if you looked at Gilbert's early childhood, you might expect to find that he grew up in _____ environment, and that he formed _____ attachment with his parents. a. an unsafe, impoverished; an insecure b. an unsafe, impoverished; a secure c. a safe, enriched; a secure d. a safe, enriched; an insecure
Critical Thinking LO 7 Page: 445 **d**	67.	Pierre is telling you about a case study that he read for his Cultural Geography class. It focused on a country which, for the past 30 years, has experienced high levels of civil unrest, severe drought, and famine. Based on Belsky's research into the evolutionary aspects of attachment, you might expect that in this country you would find a. a high number of insecure attachments in the children and relatively unstable romantic relations in the adults b. a high number of insecure attachments in the children but relatively stable romantic relations in the adults c. a high number of secure attachments in the children but relatively unstable romantic relations in the adults d. a high number of secure attachments in the children and relatively stable romantic relations in the adults
Concept/Applied LO 8 Page: 445 Correct = 91% **a**	68.	Stage theories of development assume that a. individuals progress through specified stages in a particular order because each stage builds on the previous stage b. environmental circumstances can sometimes cause individuals to skip stages early on and return to them later c. progress through the sequence of stages is not related to age d. there are few, if any, discontinuities in development
Factual LO 8 Page: 445 **b**	69.	Erik Erikson's developmental stages are organized around potential turning points called a. fixation points b. psychosocial crises c. developmental tasks d. psychosexual crises
Concept/Applied LO 8 Page: 446 **d**	70.	A child who successfully completes stage 1 of Erikson's stages of psychosocial development will acquire a. an ability to initiate one's own activities b. self-sufficiency c. a sense of competence d. optimism and trust toward the world
Concept/Applied LO 8 Page: 446 **d**	71.	According to Erikson, the first stage of development (birth to one year) is a period when the infant develops the basic characteristic of a. initiative versus guilt b. autonomy versus shame and doubt c. industry versus inferiority d. trust versus mistrust

Concept/Applied LO 8 Page: 446 a	72.	Jerry is 8 months old. Based on Erikson's theory of personality development, the fundamental question that Jerry is dealing with at this point in his life is a. "Is my world predictable and supportive?" b. "Can I do things myself or must I always rely on others?" c. "Am I good or am I bad?" d. "Am I competent or am I worthless?"
Factual LO 8 Page: 446 Correct = 73% c	73.	For Erikson, the stage during which toilet training occurs is a. trust versus mistrust b. industry versus inferiority c. autonomy versus shame and doubt d. initiative versus guilt
Concept/Applied LO 8 Page: 446 b	74.	Craig is 2 years old and he likes to put on his own coat and shoes. However, his mother often becomes impatient waiting for him to get ready, and she usually finishes zipping his coat and tying his shoes for him. Based on Erikson's theory, it is likely that Craig will develop a. a general sense of mistrust b. feelings of shame and doubt c. a sense of inferiority d. feelings of autonomy
Concept/Applied LO 8 Page: 446 Correct = 58% c	75.	During the third stage of psychosocial development, the crisis that must be resolved is initiative versus guilt. By this Erikson meant that the child must learn a. who to trust or not trust b. how to deal with peers and adults c. how to pursue his or her own interests and also get along with others d. how to become self-sufficient
Concept/Applied LO 8 Page: 446 a	76.	Anne is 5 years old and she likes to help with jobs around the house. Tonight, when she was clearing the dishes from the table, she dropped a stack of plates and broke them all. Her father scolded her and told her that she could help more by staying out of the way and letting her older brothers clear the table. If her father's reaction is typical of the interactions she has with him, Erikson would suggest that Anne is likely to develop a. feelings of guilt b. feelings of inferiority c. a general sense of mistrust d. a sense of initiative
Factual LO 8 Page: 446 Correct = 67% d	77.	The challenge of learning to function in society and beyond the family marks Erikson's childhood stage of a. initiative versus guilt b. trust versus mistrust c. autonomy versus shame and doubt d. industry versus inferiority
Concept/Applied LO 8 Page: 446 Correct = 41% a	78.	Erikson's period of _____ corresponds to the early school years. a. industry versus inferiority b. initiative versus guilt c. trust versus mistrust d. autonomy versus shame and doubt

Concept/Applied 79. The elementary school-age child who does well in school and who receives praise
LO 8   and support at home will develop what Erikson calls a sense of
Page: 447   a. industry
Correct = 50%   b. superiority
a   c. generativity
                  d. trust

Concept/Applied 80. Kyler is 9 years old, and he likes to draw and paint. However, he doesn't receive
LO 8   very good grades on his art projects, and several times his friends have laughed at the
Page: 447   pictures Kyler has created. Based on Erikson's theory, it is likely that Kyler will
b   develop
                  a. feelings of guilt
                  b. feelings of inferiority
                  c. a sense of despair
                  d. a sense of industry

Concept/Applied 81. Shawn is concerned with how he compares to his peer group. For example, he is
LO 8   always trying to kick the football farther than his friends, and he constantly wonders
Page: 447   if he is doing as well in school as the other boys in his second grade class. According
d   to Erikson, Shawn is most likely in the stage of
                  a. initiative versus guilt
                  b. autonomy versus shame and doubt
                  c. identity versus role confusion
                  d. industry versus inferiority

Critical Thinking 82. The major shortcoming of Erikson's psychosocial stages theory of development is
LO 8   that
Page: 447   a. he failed to look at adult development
Correct = 85%   b. he placed too little emphasis on social forces in the development of personality
c   c. like many stage theories, it pays little attention to explaining individual
                      differences
                  d. it fails to account for continuity in personality development

Factual   83. To Piaget, cognitive development involves
LO 9   a. stages that are characterized by fundamentally different thought processes
Page: 447   b. increases in the quantity, but not the quality, of knowledge with age
a   c. passive reception of environmental stimuli
                  d. age-related changes in attention and memory

Factual   84. Piaget proposed four stages of cognitive development. Which of the following is not
LO 9   one of his stages?
Page: 447   a. sensorimotor
Correct = 66%   b. postoperational
b   c. preoperational
                  d. formal operational

Concept/Applied 85. During the sensorimotor stage of cognitive development, a child's relations with the
LO 9   world are through
Page: 448   a. logical reasoning
Correct = 92%   b. physical interaction
b   c. abstract operations
                  d. systematic hypothesis testing

Factual
LO 9
Page: 448
Correct = 81%
a

86. According to Piaget, during which stage of cognitive development do children come to realize that an object continues to exist even when they cannot see it or touch it?
    a. sensorimotor
    b. preoperational
    c. concrete operational
    d. formal operational

Concept/Applied
LO 9
Page: 448
Correct = 72%
c

87. For children in which Piagetian stage might we be correct with the old expression "Out of sight is out of mind"?
    a. concrete operational
    b. preoperational
    c. sensorimotor
    d. formal operations

Concept/Applied
LO 9
Page: 448
a

88. When Teresa's mother hides her favorite doll under a blanket, Teresa acts as if it no longer exists, and she makes no attempt to look for it. Based on this information, you can infer that Teresa is in Piaget's
    a. sensorimotor period of cognitive development
    b. formal period of cognitive development
    c. concrete period of cognitive development
    d. preoperational period of cognitive development

Concept/Applied
LO 9
Page: 448
b

89. Trey's older sister is playing a game with him. She hides the ball they are playing with behind her back, and Trey quickly loses interest in the game. He makes no attempt to look for the ball, and instead picks up another toy that is close by. This suggests that Trey has not yet developed
    a. the ability to assimilate new experiences
    b. an understanding of object permanence
    c. a strong attachment to his sister
    d. sensorimotor patterns of responding

Critical Thinking
LO 9
Page: 448
Correct = 81%
c

90. Timmy believes he can avoid getting any older by not having any more birthday parties. Timmy is probably in which stage of cognitive development?
    a. sensorimotor
    b. concrete operational
    c. preoperational
    d. formal operational

Concept/Applied
LO 9
Page: 448
c

91. Lane is currently attending preschool. According to the stages outlined by Piaget, Lane would most likely be in the
    a. sensorimotor period of cognitive development
    b. formal period of cognitive development
    c. preoperational period of cognitive development
    d. concrete period of cognitive development

Factual
LO 9
Page: 448
Correct = 82%
b

92. The idea that even if an object changes shape or appearance the underlying quantity of the object remains the same is Piaget's principle of
    a. object permanence
    b. conservation
    c. irreversibility
    d. assimilation

Factual LO 9 Page: 448 Correct = 87% **a**	93.	The term "conservation" refers to a child's a. awareness that changing the shape of something doesn't alter the amount of that something b. ability to understand that simply because something isn't visible doesn't mean it no longer exists c. ability to solve moral dilemmas in the most economical manner possible d. assimilating new experiences into an existing memory structure in order to conserve memory space
Concept/Applied LO 9 Page: 448 **c**	94.	Patricia is upset because she is convinced that her brother has a bigger piece of cake than she does. Her dad quickly slices Patricia's piece of cake in two and tells her that she now has "more" cake. If Patricia calms down and is convinced that she does have more cake than her brother, it would suggest that she a. has not yet mastered object permanence b. does not understand the process of assimilation c. does not yet understand conservation d. is displaying egocentric reasoning
Concept/Applied LO 9 Page: 448 **d**	95.	Mrs. Potter asks Malik if he wants his sandwich in one piece, or cut into two pieces. Malik asks her to keep it in one piece, because he isn't hungry enough to eat two pieces. Malik's answer suggests that he a. has not yet mastered object permanence b. cannot assimilate changes in the shape of the sandwich c. cannot accommodate changes in the shape of the sandwich d. does not yet understand conservation
Factual LO 9 Page: 448 Correct = 83% **b**	96.	The tendency to focus on just one feature of a problem while neglecting other important aspects is referred to as a. assimilation b. centration c. object impermanence d. reification
Concept/Applied LO 9 Page: 448 **a**	97.	Gretchen watches as her preschool teacher forms two identical balls of modeling clay. The teacher gives one of the balls of modeling clay to Gretchen, and then squashes the remaining ball into a flat pancake. She asks Gretchen if they both have the same amount of clay, and Gretchen confidently states that the teacher has more because the pancake is bigger than the ball. Gretchen's answer illustrates the flaw in thinking that Piaget labeled a. centration b. conservation c. egocentrism d. assimilation
Factual LO 9 Page: 448 Correct = 89% **d**	98.	The inability of a child to mentally "undo" something is referred to as a. assimilation b. object permanence c. egocentrism d. irreversibility
Concept/Applied LO 9 Page: 448 Correct = 91% **a**	99.	Preschoolers generally do not recognize that if 8 - 5 = 3, then 3 + 5 = 8. This is because their thought is characterized by a. irreversibility b. animism c. egocentrism d. centration

Concept/Applied 100. When Matthew saw his older brother's bicycle fall off its kick stand, Matthew told
LO 9 his brother that the bicycle must be tired from being ridden too much. Matthew's
Page: 448 statement illustrates the type of thinking that Piaget referred to as
b
a. centration
b. animism
c. preformal operations
d. conservation

Concept/Applied 101. The assumption of a preoperational child that a car is moving because she is in it is
LO 9 an example of
Page: 448
Correct = 65% a. egocentrism
a b. centration
c. conservation
d. reversibility

Concept/Applied 102. You ask a three-year-old why the sky is blue; she says it is because blue is her
LO 9 favorite color. This answer reflects the _____ thinking that is typical of
Page: 448 preschoolers.
Correct = 88%
c a. irreversible
b. animistic
c. egocentric
d. operational

Concept/Applied 103. A child sees his mother crying and brings her his own favorite teddy bear to comfort
LO 9 her. This child is demonstrating
Page: 448
Correct = 62% a. egocentrism
a b. animism
c. irreversibility
d. centration

Concept/Applied 104. Children's thought processes are particularly egocentric during which Piagetian
LO 9 stage?
Page: 448
Correct = 56% a. sensorimotor
b b. preoperational
c. concrete operations
d. formal operations

Concept/Applied 105. Bob is asked, "Do you have a brother?" He replies, "Yes." "What's his name?"
LO 9 "Joe." "Does Joe have a brother?" Bob answers, "No." Bob is most likely in which
Page: 448 stage of cognitive development?
Correct = 84%
b a. formal
b. preoperational
c. concrete operational
d. sensorimotor

Concept/Applied 106. Water is poured from a short, broad beaker into a tall, skinny beaker. Is there more or
LO 9 less water now? A child answers that it's the same amount, only it's taller. The child
Page: 449 is in which stage of cognitive development?
Correct = 80%
b a. sensorimotor
b. concrete operational
c. preoperational
d. preconventional

Concept/Applied 107. A five-year-old boy tells you that his kindergarten class has more boys than children.
LO 9   This indicates that he
Page: 449   a. fails to understand the concept of reversibility
Correct = 59%   b. dislikes girls
d   c. cannot yet solve problems involving conservation of number
                    d. cannot handle hierarchical classification problems

Concept/Applied 108. The stage of concrete operations is said to be "concrete" because
LO 9   a. the child attributes human qualities to concrete objects
Page: 449   b. facts are taken to be set in stone, not to be given up easily
Correct = 66%   c. an object must be present for the child to recognize its existence
d   d. children can perform operations only on tangible objects and actual events

Concept/Applied 109. Gerard watched as a researcher placed five toy station wagons and three toy
LO 9   convertibles on a table. The researcher asked him if there were more station wagons
Page: 449   or more cars, and Gerard correctly answered that there were more cars. Gerard's
d   answer indicates that he has mastered
                    a. conservation of number
                    b. object permanence
                    c. preaccommodation
                    d. hierarchical classification problems

Concept/Applied 110. Ten-year-old Sherry watches as you flatten one of two equal-sized balls of clay into
LO 9   a pancake. Sherry says they both still have the same amount of clay, demonstrating
Page: 449   that she understands
Correct = 90%   a. seriation
b   b. conservation
                    c. inductive reasoning
                    d. hierarchical classification

Concept/Applied 111. Eight-year-old Eric watches as you flatten one of two equal-sized balls of clay into a
LO 9   pancake. Eric says they both still have the same amount of clay. When he is asked
Page: 449   how he knows that the ball and the pancake have the same amount of clay, he points
b   out that the pancake could once again be rolled up into a ball demonstrating that he
                    a. is now in the preoperational stage
                    b. understands the concept of reversibility
                    c. is unable to decenter
                    d. is no longer egocentric

Factual   112. During elementary school, children gradually acquire the ability to take the
LO 9   perspective of others. In other words, they
Page: 449   a. develop the ability to classify objects
Correct = 98%   b. come to appreciate the logic of relations
d   c. become less imitative
                    d. become less egocentric

Factual   113. According to Piaget, during the formal operational period of cognitive development,
LO 9   children begin to
Page: 450   a. acquire the concept of conservation
Correct = 64%   b. understand the nature of hierarchical classification
d   c. think primarily in terms of concrete objects or situations
                    d. think in terms of abstract principles and hypothetical possibilities

Concept/Applied LO 9 Page: 450 Correct = 66% **a**	114.	John approaches problems systematically, considering various solutions and the consequences of each before he decides on the implementation of any one solution. John is probably at which level of cognitive development? a. formal operations b. concrete operations c. preoperations d. postoperations
Concept/Applied LO 9 Page: 450 **a**	115.	Byron is planning to ask his parents if he can borrow their car on Friday night. He is thinking about all the possible reasons they might bring up for not letting him use the car, and thinking of a logical reply to each of these possible objections. Based on Piaget's model of cognitive development, Byron's thought processes illustrate a. the use of formal operational thought b. the use of concrete operational thought c. egocentric reasoning d. postconventional reasoning
Factual LO 9 Page: 451 Correct = 70% **b**	116.	One of the criticisms of Piaget's theory of cognitive development is that a. Piaget may have overestimated the cognitive skills of infants and preschool children b. Piaget may have underestimated the influence of cultural factors on cognitive development c. the theory focuses too much on individual differences in development d. evidence for the theory is based on cross-sectional research
Question Type LO 10 Page: 452 **d**	117.	With respect to cognitive abilities, nativists a. strive to understand the adaptive significant of abilities that appear to be prewired b. suggest that infants attend more to novel events because these events require more time for perceptual processing c. assert that abilities which are prewired will be less prone to habituation or dishabituation d. attempt to find out which abilities are prewired, without making any assumptions about why these abilities might be innate
Question Type LO 10 Page: 452 **c**	118.	With respect to cognitive abilities, evolutionary theorists a. suggest that infants attend more to novel events because these events require more time for perceptual processing b. assert that abilities which are prewired will be less prone to habituation or dishabituation c. strive to understand the adaptive significant of abilities that appear to be prewired d. attempt to find out which abilities are prewired, without making any assumptions about why these abilities might be innate
Question Type LO 10 Page: 453 **a**	119.	Maresalysis is 6 years old and she is given a glass that contains some green Kool-Aid. She is surprised when she drinks some and finds it tastes like raspberries. If you ask her what someone else would guess the Kool-Aid would take like, before they have a chance to taste it, Maresalysis will most likely say: "They will guess that it will taste like a. green, lime Kool-Aid b. red, lime Kool-Aid c. green, raspberry Kool-Aid d. red, raspberry Kool-Aid

Factual LO 11 Page: 454 Correct = 43% **a**	120.	Which is the earliest age at which human beings have shown evidence of long-term memory? a. three months b. six months c. nine months d. one year
Factual LO 11 Page: 454 Correct = 56% **c**	121.	Research in the information-processing perspective suggests that children's memory ability improves throughout childhood because children a. pass from the sensorimotor stage to the formal operational stage b. reduce their use of defense mechanisms c. increasingly use deliberate strategies to enhance memory performance d. take more time and expend more effort processing information
Factual LO 11 Page: 454 Correct = 34% **c**	122.	Typically, _____ does not emerge as a memory strategy until a child is at least 11 years old. a. rehearsal b. organization c. elaboration d. repression
Concept/Applied LO 11 Page: 454 **c**	123.	Stacy is 8 years old, and her brother Tyler is 12 years old. If both children are asked to remember a group of seven items, you might expect that a. both children will use rehearsal to aid in remembering the items b. Tyler will rely on rehearsal, while Stacy will use organization to remember the items c. Stacy will rely on rehearsal, while Tyler will use elaboration to remember the items d. both children will use organization to remember the items
Factual LO 12 Page: 454 Correct = 46% **a**	124.	Lawrence Kohlberg believed that moral development is determined by a. cognitive development b. physical development c. emotional development d. social development
Factual LO 12 Page: 454 Correct = 95% **b**	125.	Which of the following is not one of Kohlberg's stages of moral development? a. conventional thought b. midconventional thought c. postconventional thought d. preconventional thought
Concept/Applied LO 12 Page: 454 Correct = 94% **b**	126.	At the preconventional level, the child decides if things are good or bad (moral) on the basis of whether they a. are against the law b. bring punishment or reward c. are in accord with social rules d. fit the child's own sense of "rightness"
Concept/Applied LO 12 Page: 454 **c**	127.	In the 1960s, even though all her friends tried recreational drugs, Maggie refused to experiment with drugs because she was afraid she would get caught and end up in jail. Maggie's reasons for not experimenting with drugs reflect a. conventional moral reasoning b. postconventional moral reasoning c. preconventional moral reasoning d. authoritarian moral reasoning

Concept/Applied LO 12 Page: 454 Correct = 72% **b**	128.	Conventional thinking in moral development bases morality (right or wrong) on a. the risk of punishment b. society's laws c. personal principles d. the potential rewards
Concept/Applied LO 12 Page: 454 **b**	129.	In the 1960s, even though most his friends tried recreational drugs, Sebastian refused to experiment with drugs. He did not think the drugs were likely to be harmful, but using the drugs was illegal and he believes each person has a moral obligation to obey society's rules. Sebastian's reasons for not experimenting with drugs reflect a. preconventional moral reasoning b. conventional moral reasoning c. postconventional moral reasoning d. social moral reasoning
Concept/Applied LO 12 Page: 454 Correct = 46% **b**	130.	If you join your friends in a protest against nuclear power primarily because you want their approval rather than because of any strong conviction you have about nuclear power, you would be said to be at which of the following levels of moral development? a. unconventional b. conventional c. preconventional d. postconventional
Factual LO 12 Page: 455 Correct = 74% **a**	131.	Personal guiding principles take precedence over laws in deciding right or wrong behavior in the _____ stage of moral reasoning. a. postconventional b. preconventional c. conventional d. relativistic
Concept/Applied LO 12 Page: 455 Correct = 81% **a**	132.	Suggesting that a poor man who stole food to feed his family was right, because human life takes precedence over rules, is an example of a. postconventional moral reasoning b. preconventional moral reasoning c. concrete operational thought d. conventional moral reasoning
Concept/Applied LO 12 Page: 455 **a**	133.	The person who objects to war on the basis of higher moral principles and a personal code of ethics would be said to be at which of the following levels of moral development? a. postconventional b. preconventional c. conventional d. unconventional
Concept/Applied LO 12 Page: 455 **a**	134.	Dr. Wilmark prescribes "medical marijuana" for her chemotherapy patients, even though it is in violation of federal law. She believes it is morally wrong to cause unnecessary human suffering and, if necessary, she is willing to serve time in jail rather than watch others suffer needlessly. Dr. Wilmark's reasons for her actions reflect a. postconventional moral reasoning b. conventional moral reasoning c. preconventional moral reasoning d. authoritarian moral reasoning

Factual LO 12 Page: 455 Correct = 41% **a**	135.	Research into Kohlberg's theory of moral development has suggested all of the following <u>except</u> a. most adults reason at stage 6. b. most people show several levels of moral reasoning at one time. c. there are sizable cultural disparities in progression through the stages. d. children generally do progress through the stages in the order he outlined.
Factual LO 13 Page: 456 Correct = 58% **c**	136.	Adolescence, as we know it in the United States today, a. has always existed in the same form throughout our history b. is highly similar to adolescence in all other cultures c. is a byproduct of the modern trend toward increasingly lengthy education and prolonged economic dependence d. does not last as long as it did at the turn of the century
Concept/Applied LO 13 Page: 456 Correct = 53% **b**	137.	Adolescence can be conceptualized as the time period during which individuals are "adults" in terms of their _____ development, but <u>not</u> in terms of their _____ development. a. physical; cognitive b. physical; emotional c. cognitive; emotional d. emotional; cognitive
Factual LO 13 Page: 456 Correct = 89% **b**	138.	Physical features <u>not</u> directly associated with reproduction that are associated with one's gender are referred to as a. primary sexual characteristics b. secondary sexual characteristics c. tertiary sexual characteristics d. nonsexual characteristics
Factual LO 13 Page: 457 Correct = 90% **b**	139.	Females developing wider hips and males developing facial hair are examples of a. primary sexual characteristics b. secondary sexual characteristics c. tertiary sexual characteristics d. peripheral sexual characteristics
Factual LO 13 Page: 457 Correct = 91% **b**	140.	The onset of puberty a. begins approximately two years earlier on the average in boys than in girls b. begins approximately two years earlier on the average in girls than in boys c. begins approximately four years earlier on the average in girls than in boys d. is about the same time for boys and girls
Factual LO 13 Page: 457 Correct = 77% **d**	141.	Which of the following has <u>not</u> decreased over generations? a. age at puberty for boys b. age at puberty for girls c. the age at which the growth spurt begins d. the rate at which the growth spurt proceeds
Factual LO 13 Page: 458 **c**	142.	Evolutionary theories, such as the one proposed by Belsky, suggest that stress in early family relations may a. decelerate sexual maturation, leading to a relatively late onset of puberty b. decelerate sexual maturation, leading to a relatively late onset of menopause c. accelerate sexual maturation, leading to a relatively early onset of puberty d. accelerate sexual maturation, leading to a relatively early onset of menopause

Critical Thinking LO 13 Page: 458 **b**	143.	Tia is 14 years old and has not yet reached puberty. Based on the information in the Featured Study on evolution and the timing of sexual maturation, you might expect to find that a. Tia's father has been relatively uninvolved in her upbringing b. Tia has a warm, loving relationship with her father c. there is a high degree of conflict between Tia's parents d. Tia's parents tend to be harsh disciplinarians
Factual LO 13 Page: 459 Correct = 71% **d**	144.	In both males and females early maturation is associated with a. deterioration of peer relations b. greater risk for eating disorders c. higher levels of moral reasoning d. less self control and emotional stability
Critical Thinking LO 13 Page: 459 **a**	145.	Michael and his twin sister Doreen turned 12 a few months ago. Both Michael and Doreen have begun to go through the early signs of puberty. In this case, it is <u>most</u> likely that, a. compared to Doreen, Michael is at greater risk for using drugs or alcohol because he is maturing early b. compared to Michael, Doreen is at greater risk for using drugs or alcohol because she is maturing early c. both Michael and Doreen are at greater risk for using drugs or alcohol because they are both maturing early d. compared to Doreen, Michael is at lower risk for using drugs or alcohol because he is maturing early
Factual LO 14 Page: 460 Correct = 74% **b**	146.	The ratio of attempted suicides to completed suicides tends to be highest in which of the following age groups? a. preteens b. teenagers c. those at midlife d. the aged
Critical Thinking LO 14 Page: 460 **c**	147.	Relative to older age groups, adolescents a. complete suicide more often b. complete suicide just as often c. attempt suicide more often d. attempt suicide less often
Factual LO 14 Page: 460 **d**	148.	Recent evidence that has investigated the stress and turmoil sometimes associated with adolescence suggests that a. stress and turmoil during adolescence is a universal phenomenon b. very few adolescents actually experience any stress or turmoil c. adolescence is more stressful for those raised in traditional, preindustrial cultures d. storm and stress is more likely during adolescence than at other ages
Concept/Applied LO 15 Page: 461 Correct = 59% **a**	149.	Identity foreclosure suggests that the person is committed to goals he or she a. simply took over from others b. arrived at independently c. believes are apt to last only a short time d. arrived at after a long period of decision making

Concept/Applied 150. Both of Karlee's parents are teachers, and two of her uncles are teachers. For as long
LO 15   as she can remember, she has wanted to be a school teacher, just like these role
Page: 461   models. According to James Marcia, Karlee would be considered to be in a state of
c
   a. identity diffusion
   b. moratorium
   c. foreclosure
   d. identity postponement

Factual   151. James Marcia termed individuals who were delaying commitment and actively
LO 15   exploring alternative ideologies as being in a state of
Page: 461
Correct = 60%
d
   a. identity postponement
   b. identity diffusion
   c. foreclosure
   d. moratorium

Concept/Applied 152. Leanna is 19 years old, but when people ask her what she wants to do when she
LO 15   finishes school she tells them she hasn't really given it much thought. She is
Page: 461   convinced there is lots of time before she even needs to begin thinking about her
a   various career options. According to James Marcia, Leanna would be considered to
                      be in a state of
   a. identity diffusion
   b. moratorium
   c. foreclosure
   d. identity postponement

Concept/Applied 153. Fifteen-year-old Marta has had a relatively smooth adolescent period and, at the
LO 15   urging of her parents, has already decided on a college and a career. If Marta is
Page: 461   simply playing a passive role in relationship to her parents, she may well be in
Correct = 33%
b
   a. a moratorium phase
   b. a foreclosure phase
   c. an identity-diffusion phase
   d. an identity-achievement phase

Concept/Applied 154. Edwin has just started his third year in University and he is still exploring the options
LO 15   for his major. He has taken a number of courses with the intention of obtaining a law
Page: 461   degree, but last semester he also discovered he was very interested in geology. He
d   feels it is important to reach a final decision before the end of the semester, and he
                      has started investigating both career options in great detail. According to James
                      Marcia, Edwin would be considered to be in a state of
   a. identity diffusion
   b. foreclosure
   c. identity postponement
   d. moratorium

Concept/Applied 155. Brock was not sure what he wanted to do while he was in college so he talked to the
LO 15   career counselors last year. His profile showed a strong interest in both medicine and
Page: 461   animals, so he got a part-time job at the local humane society. He also checked the
c   requirements for veterinary school, and he has now completed six of the courses
                      required for the veterinary program. He is convinced that this is the ideal career for
                      him. According to James Marcia, Brock would be considered to be in a state of
   a. identity diffusion
   b. foreclosure
   c. identity achievement
   d. moratorium

Factual LO 15 Page: 461 Correct = 74% **d**	156.	The adolescent who has arrived at a sense of self and direction after consideration of alternative possibilities is at the phase called a. identity diffusion b. foreclosure c. moratorium d. identity achievement
Factual LO 16 Page: 462 Correct = 77% **a**	157.	Which of the following refers to a person's notion of what he or she should have accomplished by certain points in life? a. social clock b. biological clock c. developmental norm d. age stereotype
Factual LO 16 Page: 463 Correct = 53% **d**	158.	Which of the following statements regarding personality changes in adulthood is most accurate? a. Personality stability depends on one's sex and socioeconomic status. b. The overall personality undergoes systematic changes throughout adulthood. c. Personality remains extremely stable after adolescence. d. The adult personality is characterized by both stability and change.
Factual LO 16 Page: 463 Correct = 79% **d**	159.	Midlife crises a. are very common among men, but not women b. are very common among women, but not men c. are nearly universal for both sexes d. occur in only a small minority of subjects
Factual LO 17 Page: 463 Correct = 93% **b**	160.	In early adulthood, the psychosocial crisis centers on establishing close, personal relationships with others. This is the stage of a. generativity versus self-absorption b. intimacy versus isolation c. identity versus confusion d. integrity versus despair
Concept/Applied LO 17 Page: 463 **b**	161.	Jocelyn is 25 years old and she feels very insecure about some of the personal and career choices she has made so far. Consequently, at this point in her life she is unwilling to form a serious, committed relationship with another person. Based on Erikson's theory, Jocelyn may a. become self-indulgent and self-absorbed b. develop a sense of isolation c. experience feelings of despair and bitterness d. develop feelings of inferiority and doubt
Factual LO 17 Page: 463 Correct = 83% **d**	162.	Finding and making commitments to society and future generations mark Erikson's stage of a. integrity versus despair b. identity versus role confusion c. intimacy versus isolation d. generativity versus self-absorption
Concept/Applied LO 17 Page: 463 **d**	163.	Sergio just turned 53, and he feels as though he is not making any real contributions through the career he has chosen. As he sits at his desk each day he fails to find meaning in his life, and feels as though he has no purpose or direction. Based on Erikson's theory, Sergio a. is displaying signs of isolation b. is experiencing feelings of despair and bitterness c. is showing evidence of inferiority and doubt d. is becoming self-indulgent and self-absorbed

Concept/Applied 164. Looking back on her long life, Hilda feels good about herself and her
LO 17   accomplishments and swears that she would do it again the same way if given the
Page: 463   opportunity. According to Erikson's theory, Hilda is at the stage of
Correct = 84%   a. identity versus role confusion
b   b. integrity versus despair
    c. intimacy versus isolation
    d. initiative versus guilt

Concept/Applied 165. Lily is 85 years old and she has recently begun writing her life story. As she thinks
LO 17   back over all that she has done she comes to the conclusion that her life has had no
Page: 463   real meaning or purpose. Based on Erikson's theory, Lily may
b   a. develop a sense of isolation
    b. experience feelings of despair and bitterness
    c. become self-indulgent and self-absorbed
    d. develop feelings of inferiority and doubt

Factual 166. Which of the following is not a current trend regarding marriage?
LO 18   a. an increase in the average age at first marriage
Page: 464   b. an increase in the percentage of couples who voluntarily remain childless
Correct = 79%   c. an increase in the number of single adults
d   d. a decrease in the percentage of couples who cohabit prior to marriage

Factual 167. One recent trend in marriage in this country is
LO 18   a. for marriage to occur at younger ages
Page: 464   b. for most first marriages to occur in the "teen" years
Correct = 90%   c. to increasingly postpone marriage into the late 20s or beyond
c   d. to remain single throughout life

Concept/Applied 168. Mr. and Mrs. McKavick have 3 school-age children. Their next-door neighbors, Mr.
LO 18   and Mrs. Clancy have 3 grandchildren who are about the same age as the
Page: 465   McKavick's children. At the present time, based on research into marital satisfaction
d   across the family life cycle, it is most likely that
    a. the McKavicks are experiencing higher levels of marital satisfaction than the
       Clancys are
    b. both couples are experiencing high levels of satisfaction in their respective
       marriages
    c. both couples are experiencing low levels of satisfaction in their respective
       marriages
    d. the Clancys are experiencing higher levels of marital satisfaction than the
       McKavicks are

Factual 169. Parents overwhelmingly rate _____ as the most difficult stage of child rearing.
LO 18   a. infancy
Page: 465   b. early childhood
Correct = 88%   c. middle childhood
d   d. adolescence

Concept/Applied 170. Walter and Camille have been an "empty nest" couple since their youngest son left
LO 18   for college last year. Now that they are alone, it is likely that Walter and Camille will
Page: 466   find
c   a. their marital satisfaction will drop considerably
    b. the transition to being a "childless" couple will be stressful and depressing
    c. their marital satisfaction will start to increase
    d. they spend less time together than they did when the children were home

HUMAN DEVELOPMENT ACROSS THE LIFE SPAN

Factual LO 18 Page: 466 Correct = 84% a	171.	Today, most couples in the empty nest stage of the family life cycle a. experience an increase in marital satisfaction b. experience post-parental depression c. drift apart and develop separate interests outside the home d. are eager to start a new family and look forward to parenting
Concept/Applied LO 19 Page: 466 Correct = 66% d	172.	Simon, a college senior, has had a few interviews for jobs in engineering. He's pretty sure that's the career field he'll stick with, though he's trying to stay open-minded about other possibilities. Simon is in Super's a. growth stage of vocational development b. maintenance stage of vocational development c. establishment stage of vocational development d. exploration stage of vocational development
Concept/Applied LO 19 Page: 466 a	173.	Juliette is in her last semester at college, and she started working as an intern for an accounting firm last Monday. She is hoping that working as an intern will give her a chance to decide if she really wants to be an accountant for the rest of her life. Based on Super's theory of vocational development, Juliette would be in a. the exploration stage b. the establishment stage c. the growth stage d. the commitment stage
Factual LO 19 Page: 466 Correct = 39% b	174.	In Super's establishment stage of vocational development a. opportunities for occupational mobility have decreased b. the worker may benefit from the guidance of a mentor c. the future worker experiences physical and mental growth, becoming "established" as a future candidate for employment d. the young worker finishes schooling and secures the first job
Concept/Applied LO 19 Page: 466 d	175.	Floyd has worked for seven different advertising agencies in the past 10 years; each time he has moved on to a better job. He now has a high-level of self-confidence and feels he has the managerial skills to open his own agency. Based on Super's theory of vocational development, Floyd would be in a. the exploration stage b. the growth stage c. the commitment stage d. the establishment stage
Factual LO 19 Page: 466 Correct = 62% a	176.	During the maintenance stage of vocational development, one is most likely to a. shift energy and attention from work to family b. experience a midlife crisis c. change careers d. begin to prepare for retirement
Concept/Applied LO 19 Page: 466 b	177.	Gwen has been working as an emergency medical technician for the past 20 years. Lately she has become less concerned with taking classes that will enable her to move up within her field; she is more interested in spending time doing things with her family. Based on Super's theory of vocational development, Gwen would be in a. the commitment stage b. the maintenance stage c. the decline stage d. the mentoring stage

Concept/Applied 178. Richard recently announced that he will be retiring from his teaching position at the
LO 19   end of the year. He is looking forward to his retirement and the chance to travel,
Page: 466   however he is also concerned about whether he will be able to financially support
a   himself without the steady income from his job. Based on Super's theory of
                       vocational development, Richard would be in
                       a. the decline stage
                       b. the maintenance stage
                       c. the accommodation stage
                       d. the postconventional stage

Factual   179. Which is the correct sequencing of Super's stages of vocational development?
LO 19   a. growth, exploration, establishment, maintenance, decline
Page: 466   b. exploration, growth, establishment, maintenance, decline
Correct = 51%   c. exploration, establishment, growth, maintenance, decline
a   d. establishment, exploration, maintenance, growth, decline

Factual   180. Comparison of men and women in their work and career development has found all
LO 19   of the following except
Page: 467   a. career development is more predictable for women than for men
a   b. women experience more career interruptions than do men
                       c. women are less apt to have a mentor than are men
                       d. women show a less clear pattern of development than do men

Factual   181. Dementia occurs in about _____ of people over age 65.
LO 20   a. 60%
Page: 467   b. 45%
Correct = 51%   c. 30%
d   d. 15%

Factual   182. Which of the following statements is false?
LO 20   a. The rate of neuronal loss during adulthood varies in different parts of the brain.
Page: 467   b. It is difficult to measure the rate of the rate of neuronal loss during adulthood.
Correct = 50%   c. Dementia is a normal part of the aging process.
c   d. Neuronal loss in adulthood does not appear to contribute to any of the age-
                          related dementias.

Concept/Applied 183. Marilyn is 65 years old and recently she has begun to notice that her vision has
LO 20   changed significantly. She has most likely noticed that she has become
Page: 472   a. more far-sighted and less able to use monocular depth cues effectively
d   b. more near-sighted and less able to adapt to low illumination
                       c. more near-sighted and less able to use monocular depth cues effectively
                       d. more far-sighted and less able to adapt to low illumination

Factual   184. Which of the following statements is true?
LO 20   a. Menopause for most women typically occurs around age 40.
Page: 472   b. Middle-aged males experience hormonal changes that are equivalent to the
Correct = 63%   female menopause.
d   c. Menopause is almost universally accompanied by severe emotional strain.
                       d. Women's reactions to menopause depend on their expectations.

Concept/Applied 185. Carol is now 50, and she has experienced menopause. This means that
LO 20   a. she will continue to ovulate, but her menstrual cycle will stop
Page: 472   b. she will no longer ovulate, but her menstrual cycle will continue
c   c. she will no longer ovulate, and her menstrual cycle will stop
                       d. her menstrual cycle will continue, but the eggs that are produced will no longer
                          be viable

Concept/Applied LO 21 Page: 472 **a**	186.	Bernard is now 80 years old. When he was 20 years old he took part in a detailed study that assessed various aspects of his intellectual functioning. If Bernard were to complete the same tests today, he would most likely discover that a. his fluid intelligence has declined over time, but his crystallized intelligence has remained stable b. both his fluid and crystallized intelligence have declined over time c. his crystallized intelligence has declined over time, but his fluid intelligence has remained stable d. his fluid intelligence has remained stable over time, and his crystallized intelligence has increased
Factual LO 21 Page: 472 **b**	187.	Recent research on memory in older adults shows a. substantial decreases in memory for conversations and past activities b. age-related declines in the capacity of working memory c. better performance on laboratory tasks than on "real-world" tasks d. insignificant age-related changes in the raw speed of mental processing
Factual LO 21 Page: 473 Correct = 62% **d**	188.	Which of the following is <u>most</u> likely to decline in the later years? a. intellectual accomplishment b. memory c. problem-solving ability d. speed in processing information
Critical Thinking LO 22 Page: 473 Correct = 44% **b**	189.	Differing views on the course and nature of changes in personality across the lifespan illustrates which of the following unifying themes from your text? a. Psychology evolves in a sociohistorical context. b. Psychology is theoretically diverse. c. Heredity and environment jointly influence behavior. d. Our behavior is shaped by our cultural heritage.
Concept/Applied LO 22 Page: 474 Correct = 68% **b**	190.	Investigations of complex, real-world issues, such as the effects of day care and television violence, illustrate which of the textbook's unifying themes? a. Our experience of the world is highly subjective. b. Psychology evolves in a sociohistorical context. c. Our behavior is shaped by our cultural heritage. d. Psychology is theoretically diverse.
Critical Thinking LO 22 Page: 474 Correct = 63% **c**	191.	Gender differences in behavior appear to be influenced by observational learning, operant conditioning, socialization in schools, and role models in the media, among other things. These findings illustrate which of your text's unifying themes? a. Psychology evolves in a sociohistorical context. b. Psychology is theoretically diverse. c. Behavior is determined by multiple causes. d. Our experience of the world is highly subjective.
Factual LO 22 Page: 474 Correct = 62% **c**	192.	The fact that a child's temperament elicits different reactions from each parent, depending on the parents' personalities and expectations, illustrates which of your text's organizing themes? a. the evolution of psychology in a sociohistorical context b. multiple causes of behavior c. interaction of heredity and environment d. cultural diversity

Factual LO 23 Page: 475 **c**	193.	One's sex is _____ determined; one's gender is _____ determined. a. culturally; biologically b. culturally; culturally c. biologically; culturally d. biologically; biologically
Factual LO 23 Page: 475 Correct = 83% **b**	194.	On the average, females perform better than males on tests of a. short-term memory b. verbal skills c. visual-spatial ability d. mathematical ability
Concept/Applied LO 23 Page: 475 **c**	195.	The local school board in Middletown has decided to introduce standardized assessment tests for all students in the sixth grade. The test has separate sections for Math and English. Based on the research into gender differences in cognitive abilities, you should expect that a. the male students will score higher than the female students on both sections of the assessment test b. the female students will score higher than the male students on both sections of the assessment test c. the female students will score higher than the male students on the English section of the assessment test d. the female students will score higher than the male students on the Math section of the assessment test
Factual LO 23 Page: 476 Correct = 89% **a**	196.	Which of the following statements has been supported by research? a. Females are more susceptible to persuasion than males. b. Females are more irrational than males. c. Females are more emotional than males. d. Females are more assertive than males.
Critical Thinking LO 23 Page: 476 **d**	197.	Imagine you have to make a persuasive speech for one of your classes. The teacher will be basing part of your grade on how much the other members of the class are influenced by the views you present in your speech. Based on research into gender differences in personality and social behavior, under these circumstances you would probably prefer a. to have more males than females in your class b. to have an equal number of males and females in the class c. to present the speech using a question-and-answer format d. to have more females than males in your class
Factual LO 23 Page: 476 Correct = 70% **a**	198.	Starting in the grade-school years, females show a slight advantage over males in _____ skills, while males show a slight advantage over females in _____ skills. a. verbal; visual-spatial b. mathematical; verbal c. visual-spatial; mathematical d. mathematical; visual-spatial
Factual LO 23 Page: 476 Correct = 69% **d**	199.	When psychologists say that "males and females differ on Trait X," they mean that a. all males differ from all females on Trait X b. most males differ from most females on Trait X c. a few males differ from a few females on Trait X d. the average male differs from the average female on Trait X

| Concept/Applied
LO 23
Page: 476
b | 200. | The local school board in Middletown recently asked that the Differential Aptitude Test (DAT) be administered to all fifth grade students. They are particularly interested in the scores from the spatial relations and abstract reasoning sections. Based on the research into gender differences in cognitive abilities, you should expect that
a. the male students will score higher than the female students on both these two sections of the test
b. the male students will score higher than the female students on the spatial relations section of the test
c. the female students will score higher than the male students on both these two sections of the test
d. the female students will score higher than the male students on the spatial relations section of the test |
|---|---|---|
| Factual
LO 23
Page: 476
Correct = 67%
a | 201. | The major qualification of the research findings on gender differences is that
a. the data are indicative of group differences and tell us little about individuals
b. the findings are based on only a few studies and are therefore not very representative of the population
c. most of the research has been conducted on white middle-class children
d. there is wide variation from study to study in how the variables have been operationalized |
| Factual
LO 24
Page: 476
Correct = 19%
c | 202. | The better documented gender differences in cognitive abilities, aggression, and sexual behavior appear to be
a. dependent on culture
b. decreasing as more women enter the work force
c. pancultural
d. increasing as more women enter the work force |
| Concept/Applied
LO 24
Page: 477
a | 203. | Imagine Baby S received both an X and a Y chromosome at the time of conception. Near the 7th or 8th week of the pregnancy, Baby S will
a. begin to secrete testosterone, and develop a male reproductive system
b. begin to secrete estrogen, and develop a male reproductive system
c. begin to secrete estrogen, and develop a female reproductive system
d. not secrete any hormones, and will develop a female reproductive system |
| Concept/Applied
LO 24
Page: 477
a | 204. | Imagine Baby P received two X chromosomes at the time of conception. Near the 7th or 8th week of the pregnancy, Baby P will
a. not secrete any hormones, and will develop a female reproductive system
b. begin to secrete testosterone, and develop a male reproductive system
c. begin to secrete estrogen, and develop a male reproductive system
d. begin to secrete estrogen, and develop a female reproductive system |
| Factual
LO 24
Page: 477
b | 205. | Which of the following is not one of the potential concerns regarding the evidence suggesting that prenatal hormones contribute to the shaping of gender differences?
a. Most endocrine disorders have multiple effects.
b. The conclusions are based on large samples from a variety of cultures, making it difficult to draw general conclusions.
c. It is risky to draw causal inferences on the basis of correlational data.
d. The evidence is more voluminous, and the findings are much stronger for females than for males. |

Factual LO 25 Page: 478 Correct = 80% c	206.	_____ is the acquisition of the norms and behaviors expected of people in a particular society. a. Accommodation b. Operant conditioning c. Socialization d. Observational learning
Concept/Applied LO 25 Page: 478 Correct = 84% c	207.	Gender roles tend to be a. based on biological capabilities b. a natural outgrowth of biological gender differences c. based on society's prescriptions of what is proper for each sex d. biology first and social prescription second
Factual LO 25 Page: 478 Correct = 64% d	208.	Which of the following is <u>not</u> one of the key processes that researchers believe to be involved in gender-role socialization? a. observational learning b. self-socialization c. operant conditioning d. classical conditioning
Concept/Applied LO 25 Page: 478 Correct = 97% c	209.	Yesterday little Louis saw his brother climb a tree. Today Louis tried it and fell to the ground, hurting himself. But his mother nevertheless praised him for being a brave boy. Which of the following influences on gender-role socialization are at work here? a. self-socialization and punishment b. self-socialization and extinction c. observational learning and reinforcement d. operant conditioning and classical conditioning
Factual LO 25 Page: 478 Correct = 54% c	210.	According to cognitive theories of gender-role development, self-socialization includes a. being reinforced for gender-appropriate behaviors b. valuing characteristics associated with the opposite gender c. learning to classify oneself as male or female d. responding to praise from parents, teachers and peers
Factual LO 25 Page: 479 Correct = 54% c	211.	Which of the following statements is <u>true</u>? a. Grade school teachers tend to scold girls more often than boys. b. Girls typically receive more pressure to behave in gender-appropriate ways than boys do. c. On TV, physical attractiveness is more important for women than for men. d. Parents' attitudes have very little influence on the gender roles acquired by their children.
Factual LO 25 Page: 479 d	212.	Which of the following is the safest statement to make regarding the origin of gender differences? a. Hormonal differences between the sexes account for the largest proportion of the variation. b. The fact that males tend to exhibit more cerebral specialization than females explains the bulk of the differences. c. The reinforcement children receive for displaying gender-appropriate behavior determines the differences. d. As with anything, the explanation of gender differences is complex and must take into account both biological and environmental factors.

Concept/Applied LO 26 Page: 481 **b**	213.	You and a friend are discussing the importance of fathers in children's overall development. Your friend states that, "If we fail to promote increased involvement of fathers in the parenting process, then we must accept the inevitable breakdown of other social values." This statement is an example of the reasoning fallacy known as a. circular-logic b. a false-dichotomy c. a weak-analogy d. alternative-explanations
Critical Thinking LO 26 Page: 481 **c**	214.	Which of the following critical thinking skills would be least important in evaluating the argument that "Fathers are essential to normal development"? a. understanding the limits of correlational evidence b. recognizing conclusions that are based on common reasoning fallacies c. recognizing how emotions can manipulated through conditioning d. searching for alternative explanations
Integrative Correct = 78% **a**	215.	Trust and optimism are to Erikson's trust versus mistrust stage as _____ is to Piaget's sensorimotor period. a. object permanence b. logical reasoning c. conservation d. separation anxiety
Integrative Correct = 49% **c**	216.	A nine-year-old child would be likely to be in the _____ stage of development according to Piaget and the _____ stage of moral reasoning according to Kohlberg. a. preoperational; preconventional b. concrete operations; preconventional c. concrete operations; conventional d. sensorimotor; postconventional
Integrative Correct = 71% **c**	217.	In relation to age, which of the following does not belong with the others? a. separation anxiety b. babbling c. postconventional moral reasoning d. gradual mastery of object permanence
Integrative Correct = 44% **d**	218.	In relation to age, which of the following does not belong with the others? a. centration b. egocentrism c. telegraphic speech d. development of secondary sex characteristics
Integrative Correct = 65% **a**	219.	In relation to age, which of the following does not belong with the others? a. concrete operations b. generativity versus self-absorption c. midlife transition d. decreased speed in cognitive processes
Integrative Correct = 41% **b**	220.	In relation to age, which of the following does not belong with the others? a. development of secondary sex characteristics b. autonomy versus shame c. formal operations d. postconventional moral reasoning

Study Guide LO 1 Page: 433 **b**	221.	In which prenatal stage do <u>most</u> major birth defects probably have their origins? a. germinal stage b. embryonic stage c. fetal stage d. seminal stage
Study Guide LO 4 Page: 440 **d**	222.	What is the major conclusion from Thomas and Chess's longitudinal study of temperament? a. Children's temperaments tend to go through predictable stages. b. The temperament of the child is not a good predictor of the temperament of the adult. c. Opposites attract. d. Children's temperaments tend to be consistent over the years.
Study Guide LO 7 Page: 445 **c**	223.	According to Belsky's evolutionary viewpoint, the current harshness of an environment affect parent-child attachment, which in turn affects the offspring's later a. accommodation and assimilation b. adaptation to traumatic events c. reproductive strategy d. decision to give birth
Study Guide LO 9 Page: 448 **b**	224.	A child in the early sensorimotor period is shown a ball, which she watches intensely. The ball is then hidden under a pillow. What will the child do? a. ask, "Where is the pillow?" b. stare at the pillow but not pick it up c. move the pillow and pick up the ball d. ignore the pillow, as if the ball didn't exist
Study Guide LO 9 Page: 449 **c**	225.	During which stage in Piaget's system is the child able to understand conservation but unable to handle hierarchical classification? a. sensorimotor b. preoperational c. concrete operations d. formal operations
Study Guide LO 10 Page: 451 **d**	226.	Some research has found that very young children (e.g., 5 months old) appear to be aware of the addition or subtraction of objects from behind a screen. The technique used in these studies was a. sensory preconditioning b. self-socialization c. classical conditioning d. habituation-dishabituation
Study Guide LO 10 Page: 452 **a**	227.	A child is shown a candy box. When asked what he thinks is in it, he says, "Candy." He is then shown that the candy box in fact contains crayons. He is then asked what he thinks another child will say when confronted with the same closed box. He says that he thinks the next child will say, "Crayons." What would be the best guess about the age of the child? a. 3 years b. 5 years c. 6 years d. 7 years

Study Guide
LO 12
Page: 454
d

228. Who developed a stage theory of moral development?
    a. Piaget
    b. Kohlberg
    c. Gould
    d. Bowlby

Study Guide
LO 18
Page: 465
b

229. Which of the following factors tends to be accompanied by a drop in ratings of marital satisfaction?
    a. childlessness during early married life
    b. the birth of the first child
    c. the first child's departure for college
    d. when the last child leaves home

Study Guide
LO 24
Page: 477
a

230. Females exposed to high levels of androgen during prenatal development tend to show
    a. more male-typical behavior than other females
    b. more stereotypic female behavior than other females
    c. less cerebral specialization than other females
    d. a larger corpus collosum than other females

Online Quiz
LO 1
Page: 432
c

231. The _____ stage of prenatal development refers to the first two weeks after conception.
    a. zygote
    b. fetal
    c. germinal
    d. blastula

Online Quiz
LO 3
Page: 437
d

232. Physical growth during infancy tends to be
    a. slow and steady
    b. slow and episodic
    c. rapid and steady
    d. rapid and episodic

Online Quiz
LO 5
Page: 443
d

233. Securely attached children also tend to show all of the following except
    a. more persistence
    b. greater curiosity
    c. greater leadership
    d. less obedience

Online Quiz
LO 6
Page: 444
b

234. Avoidant attachments seem to be _____ common in German infants, and _____ common in Japanese infants, than in American infants.
    a. more; more
    b. more; less
    c. less; more
    d. less; less

Online Quiz
LO 8
Page: 446
c

235. According to Erikson's theory of development, a sense of _____ develops in an infant whose basic biological and emotional needs are adequately met.
    a. warmth
    b. certainty
    c. trust
    d. support

Online Quiz
LO 11
Page: 454
a

236. Typically, the first memory strategy to emerge in young children is
a. rehearsal
b. organization
c. elaboration
d. repression

Online Quiz
LO 12
Page: 454
d

237. If Lawrence Kohlberg were to present you with a moral dilemma, in which of the following would he be most interested?
a. your judgment of right and wrong in this situation
b. what you would do in this situation
c. whether your intended behavior in this situation is consistent with your moral judgment about it
d. your reasons for whatever moral judgment you had about the situation

Online Quiz
LO 13
Page: 456
b

238. Your son has developed facial hair and now needs to shave; he also has developed much wider shoulders. These changes reflect the emergence of
a. primary sexual characteristics
b. secondary sexual characteristics
c. tertiary sexual characteristics
d. peripheral sexual characteristics

Online Quiz
LO 15
Page: 460
a

239. In Erikson's theory, the psychosocial crisis during adolescence is
a. identity versus confusion
b. generativity versus self-absorption
c. industry versus inferiority
d. intimacy versus isolation

Online Quiz
LO 18
Page: 465
b

240. Studies that have measured spouses' overall satisfaction at different stages of the family life cycle have found
a. that marital satisfaction is much higher at the beginning of the cycle than during the middle or end
b. that marital satisfaction tends to be lowest at the middle of the cycle
c. that marital satisfaction tends to be lowest at the end of the cycle
d. that marital satisfaction tends to be lowest at the start of the cycle

ESSAY QUESTIONS

1. Beginning in the late 1970s the concept of <u>bonding</u> became very popular among many psychology and medical professionals, as well as among laypeople. The basic idea was that close physical contact between infant and parents in the hours immediately following birth is necessary for the child's optimal future development. Later research almost completely nullified this conclusion. Why do you think the concept of bonding was so quickly and widely accepted? Hint: One of your text's unifying themes is that psychology evolves in a sociohistorical context. How did the "spirit of the times" in our culture contribute to the "bonding boom"?

   There are various possibilities for approaching this question. One possibility to be elaborated on is the following: Most people in our culture value certain personal characteristics (e.g., autonomy, moral maturity) and therefore try to train their children to develop them. Feelings have been growing during the past few decades that these highly valued qualities are becoming rarer in our society. We are also an impatient culture; we want quick results and we don't want to work very hard to achieve them. We're always on the lookout for quick solutions to problems. The notion that the decline in valued personal characteristics may be due to something as simple as inadequate parent-newborn contact is thus very attractive. It appeared that bonding might be an easy answer to engendering those desired characteristics in our children and combating threatening social problems.

2. Research on adolescence indicates that for girls early maturation is particularly difficult, while for boys late maturation is especially hard. How would you explain this gender difference? Consider how your text's unifying theme that psychology evolves in a sociohistorical context might help to explain it.

   Answers to this question should center on the fact that these differences arise from society's beliefs and expectations about what behaviors are appropriate for males and females. Here's one course an answer to this question could take:

   Boys are socialized toward achievement in the world of action. Physically mature boys appear to be more competent achievers, better able to meet society's expectations for males. Late-maturing boys may appear inept in this regard, and this is threatening to their self-esteem.

   Girls, on the other hand, have traditionally been socialized to become wives and mothers – roles that are closely tied to their biological and sexual characteristics. In short, the traditional role of the female has been to be the source and preserver of the family. Marital and family relationships are therefore threatened by a woman's sexual involvement outside the bounds of marriage. The early-maturing girl, because she arouses sexual feelings in other males and because of her own developing sexual desires, is thus seen as a threat. She is viewed with suspicion and made to feel ashamed of her developing sexuality.

3. The experience of midlife crisis has been likened by some to the adolescent search for identity. In what ways are these two developmental phenomena similar? How are they different?

   Both adolescents and midlife adults are sometimes obsessed with the question, "Who am I?" For adolescents the question arises mainly because they are on the brink of adulthood, when they will be expected to make highly consequential choices based on their understanding of who they are. In addition, the emerging cognitive capacities of adolescence make them both aware of these circumstances and capable of exploring alternative identities.

   Midlife adults are motivated to ask "Who am I?" upon realizing that they are approximately halfway through life's journey and, in most cases, they have not achieved all that they had hoped to by this point in life. Time is seen to be running out. The resultant anxiety provokes some to rethink and reevaluate earlier choices (e.g., occupation, marriage partner) that were predicated on conclusions about one's identity. The feeling may be either "I am not who I thought I was. Who am I?" or "I am no longer who I once was. Who am I?"

4. Research indicates that there are genuine (although often small) gender differences in verbal ability, mathematical ability, spatial ability, aggression, nonverbal communication, and influenceability. There is also some evidence that biological differences between the sexes in hormone levels and brain organization contribute to some or all of these behavioral differences. Adopt a functionalist/evolutionary perspective, and discuss why these biological differences and their consequent behavioral differences might exist.

   Possibilities: Aggressiveness and spatial ability might have served the male in his role as provider, especially as hunter, while the female bore and reared the young. Communicative abilities (verbal ability and nonverbal communication) could conceivably have been useful to females in their roles as preservers of family and other important relationships. In reproductive terms, women are of greater value than men. It may have been adaptive, then, for women to be more influenceable, making it easier to keep them in compliance with group rules and norms designed to guard them from danger. Mathematical ability is a tough one, though creative students will be able to come up with something.

5. According to Carol Gilligan (1982), Kohlberg's theory describes moral development from the "justice perspective," which tends to predominate in males, but neglects to consider the "care perspective," which tends to predominate in females. From the justice perspective, moral decisions are based on considerations of fairness and equal treatment for all. From the care perspective, moral decisions are based on considerations of meeting individuals' personal needs and preserving relationships. Do research findings on gender differences support Gilligan's views?

   Good answers would explore possibilities for how the established behavioral differences between the genders discussed in the Application might lead males to considerations of justice and fairness and females to considerations of individual need and preservation of relationships. A well-rounded answer would also consider how differential socialization practices could contribute to the gender differences that Gilligan posits.

This page intentionally left blank.

Chapter Twelve
Personality: Theory, Research, and Assessment

LEARNING OBJECTIVES

1. Define the construct of personality in terms of consistency and distinctiveness.
2. Explain what is meant by a personality trait and describe the five-factor model of personality.
3. List and describe the three components into which Freud divided the personality and indicate how these are distributed across three levels of awareness.
4. Explain the preeminence of sexual and aggressive conflicts in Freud's theory and describe the operation of defense mechanisms.
5. Outline Freud's psychosexual stages of development and their theorized relations to adult personality.
6. Summarize the revisions of Freud's theory proposed by Jung and Adler.
7. Summarize the strengths and weaknesses of the psychodynamic approach to personality.
8. Discuss how Skinner's principles of operant conditioning can be applied to the structure and development of personality.
9. Describe Bandura's social learning theory and compare it to Skinner's viewpoint.
10. Identify Mischel's major contribution to personality theory and indicate why his ideas have generated so much controversy.
11. Summarize the strengths and weaknesses of the behavioral approach to personality.
12. Explain how humanism was a reaction against both the behavioral and psychodynamic approaches and discuss the assumptions of the humanistic view.
13. Identify the single structural construct in Rogers' person-centered theory and summarize his view of personality development.
14. Explain Maslow's hierarchy of needs and summarize his findings on the characteristics of self-actualizing people.
15. Summarize the strengths and weaknesses of the humanistic approach to personality.
16. Describe Eysenck's theory of personality.
17. Summarize behavioral genetics research on personality and its conclusions.
18. Outline Buss' explanation for why the Big Five traits are important
19. Summarize the strengths and weaknesses of the biological approach to personality.
20. Discuss the meaning of sensation seeking and identify the characteristics of high-sensation seekers.
21. Explain what is meant by self-monitoring and discuss the effects of self-monitoring on interpersonal relationships.
22. Summarize research on the cross-cultural validity of the five-factor model and cultural variations in conceptions of self.
23. Explain how the chapter highlighted three of the text's unifying themes.
24. Outline the four principal uses of personality tests.
25. Describe the MMPI, 16PF, and NEO Personality Inventory and summarize the strengths and weaknesses of self-report inventories.
26. Describe the projective hypothesis and summarize the strengths and weaknesses of projective tests.
27. Discuss how hindsight bias affects everyday analyses of personality, as well as some theoretical analyses of personality.

MULTIPLE-CHOICE QUESTIONS

Factual
LO 1
Page: 486
Correct = 55%
a

1. The two major aspects of people that are studied by personality theorists are
   a. consistency and distinctiveness
   b. situational shifts and interpersonal similarities
   c. commonalties and individual differences
   d. constancy and change

Concept/Applied
LO 1
Page: 486
Correct = 94%
a

2. Joan is an unfailingly polite person who always considers the feelings of others. This tendency to act in a similar manner across situations is indicative of which of the following qualities of personality?
   a. consistency
   b. distinctiveness
   c. reflexivity
   d. social desirability

Concept/Applied
LO 1
Page: 486
Correct = 77%
d

3. In an emergency, we would all react differently from one another because we all have different personalities and experiences. This quality of personality is called
   a. consistency
   b. differentiation
   c. constancy
   d. distinctiveness

Factual
LO 2
Page: 486
d

4. A durable disposition to behave in a particular way in a variety of situations is called
   a. an archetype
   b. an attribution
   c. a reaction formation
   d. a personality trait

Factual
LO 2
Page: 486
Correct = 78%
b

5. _____ is a statistical procedure used by researchers to identify closely related clusters of variables.
   a. Chi-square
   b. Factor analysis
   c. Deviation analysis
   d. Analysis of variance

Factual
LO 2
Page: 486
c

6. Raymond Cattell used factor analysis to reduce a huge list of personality traits compiled by Gordon Allport to _____ basic dimensions of personality.
   a. 5
   b. 10
   c. 16
   d. 27

Factual
LO 2
Page: 486
c

7. Which of the following is <u>not</u> one of the "big five" personality traits?
   a. neuroticism
   b. extraversion
   c. locus of control
   d. openness to experience

Concept/Applied
LO 2
Page: 486
b

8. People who score high in _____ are characterized as outgoing, sociable, upbeat, friendly, and assertive.
   a. neuroticism
   b. extraversion
   c. conscientiousness
   d. openness to experience

370   CHAPTER TWELVE

Concept/Applied LO 2 Page: 487 **a**	9.	People who score high in _____ tend to be anxious, hostile, self-conscious, insecure, and vulnerable. a. neuroticism b. extraversion c. conscientiousness d. openness to experience
Concept/Applied LO 2 Page: 487 **d**	10.	People who score high in _____ tend to be sympathetic, trusting, cooperative, and modest. a. neuroticism b. extraversion c. conscientiousness d. agreeableness
Concept/Applied LO 2 Page: 487 **d**	11.	People who score low in _____ tend to be suspicious, antagonistic, and aggressive. a. neuroticism b. extraversion c. conscientiousness d. agreeableness
Concept/Applied LO 2 Page: 487 **c**	12.	People who score high in _____ tend to be diligent, disciplined, well-organized, and punctual. a. neuroticism b. extraversion c. conscientiousness d. agreeableness
Critical Thinking LO 2 Page: 487 **c**	13.	Which of the following traits is <u>most</u> likely to be associated with high levels of productivity in a job setting? a. neuroticism b. extraversion c. conscientiousness d. agreeableness
Concept/Applied LO 2 Page: 487 **a**	14.	Marcos is very quiet and avoids large groups. Some people consider him unfriendly, and he seldom takes a stand or acts assertively. Based on the five-factor model of personality, Macros would probably score a. low in extraversion b. low in agreeableness c. high in neuroticism d. low in openness
Concept/Applied LO 2 Page: 487 **b**	15.	Janelle is suspicious and uncooperative. Her friends think she is a boastful person who is seldom sympathetic. Based on the five-factor model of personality, Janelle would probably score a. low in openness b. low in agreeableness c. high in neuroticism d. low in extraversion
Concept/Applied LO 2 Page: 487 **c**	16.	Julio is extremely dependable and productive, and his friends think he is great at organizing events. Based on the five-factor model of personality, Julio would probably score a. high in agreeableness b. low in neuroticism c. high in conscientiousness d. high in openness

Critical Thinking LO 2 Page: 487 **b**	17.	Which of the following is <u>not</u> a criticism of the five-factor model of personality? a. It provides no insight into the causes or development of personality. b. It overemphasizes the role of unconscious motivation in personality. c. It is limited by the number of specific traits that are measured in the first place. d. More than five traits are necessary to account for the variation seen in human personality.
Factual LO 3 Page: 488 Correct = 72% **b**	18.	The variety of modern psychodynamic theories of personality all derive from the work of which of the following individuals? a. Albert Bandura b. Sigmund Freud c. Karen Horney d. Wilhelm Wundt
Factual LO 3 Page: 488 **a**	19.	Sigmund Freud received his academic training in which of the following fields? a. medicine b. zoology c. psychology d. philosophy
Factual LO 3 Page: 488 Correct = 94% **c**	20.	Sigmund Freud's method for treating disorders is called a. systematic desensitization b. client-centered therapy c. psychoanalysis d. primal-scream therapy
Concept/Applied LO 3 Page: 488 Correct = 72% **a**	21.	Psychoanalytic theory stresses all of the following except a. conscious thought patterns b. childhood experiences c. internal conflicts d. handling of sexual impulses
Concept/Applied LO 3 Page: 488 **d**	22.	Id is to pleasure principle as a. superego is to desire b. superego is to repetition principle c. ego is to executive principle d. ego is to reality principle
Factual LO 3 Page: 488 **c**	23.	According to Freud, the aspect of personality that is totally unconscious is the a. superego b. ego c. id d. ego ideal
Concept/Applied LO 3 Page: 488 Correct = 57% **a**	24.	According to Freud, the _____ is "like a man on horseback who has to hold in check the superior strength of the horse." a. ego b. id c. superego d. alter ego
Concept/Applied LO 3 Page: 488 Correct = 60% **a**	25.	The portion of the personality that mediates between instinctual demands and the world of reality is the a. ego b. superego c. id d. ego ideal

Concept/Applied LO 3 Page: 488 Correct = 78% **b**	26.	Finding ways to meet instinctual needs and still take into account the conditions of the external, social world defines the _____, the basic operating theme of the _____. a. reality principle; id b. reality principle; ego c. pleasure principle; id d. pleasure principle; ego
Concept/Applied LO 3 Page: 488 **b**	27.	Sarah is torn between the need to study for an exam and her desire to go out with her friends. She decides that she will go out later only if she completes her studying. This realistic decision reflects the functioning of Sarah's a. id b. ego c. superego d. unconscious
Concept/Applied LO 3 Page: 488 **d**	28.	Which of the following is <u>not</u> characteristic of primary-process thinking? a. illogical b. primitive c. irrational d. reality oriented
Concept/Applied LO 3 Page: 488 Correct = 61% **d**	29.	Primary process thinking is associated with the _____ and secondary process thinking is associated with the _____. a. ego; superego b. superego; id c. ego; id d. id; ego
Concept/Applied LO 3 Page: 488 **b**	30.	Cari often has temper tantrums and pouts when she can't have her own way. She often behaves impulsively and becomes extremely impatient if she can't have the things that she wants immediately. According to Freud's view of the personality, Cari's personality appears to be dominated by a. her ego b. her id c. reaction formation d. her superego
Concept/Applied LO 3 Page: 488 **a**	31.	Michael is an executive for a major corporation. He constantly needs to find ways to meet the corporation's goals and objectives while taking into consideration factors such as laws and financial resources. In making these decisions, Michael is acting most like the portion of the personality that Freud referred to as a. the ego b. the superego c. the id d. the preconscious
Critical Thinking LO 3 Page: 489 **b**	32.	Sigmund Freud would have been <u>least</u> likely to make which of the following statements? a. Most behavior is rooted in the unconscious. b. Most of our behavior is rationally directed. c. A great deal of our behavior and thoughts are symbolic of hidden motives. d. Behavior is usually an outcome of an interaction among several components of personality.

Factual LO 3 Page: 489 **d**	33.	The superego is Freud's term for a. the biological impulses b. the mediating agent between "inside" and "outside" c. the defensive aspect of personality makeup d. the moral component of personality
Concept/Applied LO 3 Page: 489 Correct = 74% **a**	34.	Howard sets extremely high standards for both himself and others. He tends to be rigid and inflexible and rarely allows himself to enjoy life. Freud would probably conclude that Howard is dominated by a. his superego b. his id c. his ego d. penis envy
Concept/Applied LO 3 Page: 489 **b**	35.	Which of the following is not characteristic of secondary-process thinking? a. rational b. primitive c. realistic d. oriented toward problem solving
Concept/Applied LO 3 Page: 489 **d**	36.	Janine has extremely strong moral standards. However, whenever she fails to live up to the high standards she sets for herself, she becomes overwhelmed by feelings of guilt. Freud would most likely suggest that Janine's personality is dominated by a. her id b. her ego c. feelings of incongruence d. her superego
Factual LO 3 Page: 489 Correct = 98% **d**	37.	According to Freud, the unconscious can reveal itself through a. dreams b. slips of the tongue c. psychoanalysis d. all of the above
Factual LO 3 Page: 489 **d**	38.	Which of the following is not one of the levels of awareness proposed by Freud? a. conscious b. unconscious c. preconscious d. collective unconscious
Concept/Applied LO 3 Page: 490 **b**	39.	According to Freud's theory, repressed sexual desires are most likely to be found in which level of awareness? a. conscious b. unconscious c. preconscious d. collective unconscious
Factual LO 4 Page: 490 Correct = 77% **a**	40.	A key concept in Freudian theory is a. conflict b. self-actualization c. reinforcement d. personal growth
Concept/Applied LO 4 Page: 491 **a**	41.	Freud ascribed great importance to sexual and aggressive impulses, mainly because a. they tend to be routinely frustrated b. they are essential to the survival of the species c. they dominate our dreams d. they tend to be reinforced by others

Factual LO 4 Page: 491 **b**	42.	According to Freud, conflicts centering on which of the following impulses are especially likely to have far-reaching consequences? a. greed b. aggression c. affiliation d. achievement
Concept/Applied LO 4 Page: 491 Correct = 66% **b**	43.	The impulses that should give rise to the greatest conflicts, according to Freud, are those that are a. biologically the strongest b. most tabooed and regulated by the society c. most basic to survival as a species d. most common in people
Concept/Applied LO 4 Page: 491 Correct = 86% **a**	44.	The impending possibility of a forbidden impulse getting out of control and being expressed in behavior would be most apt to produce _____ in the person. a. anxiety b. impulse gratification c. secondary gain d. depression
Factual LO 4 Page: 491 **a**	45.	Defense mechanisms combat feelings of anxiety and guilt a. through self-deception b. through rational problem solving c. by enhancing self-insight d. by making unconscious urges conscious
Factual LO 4 Page: 491 Correct = 80% **d**	46.	Giving self-justifying plausible excuses that hide the real reasons for our behavior defines the defense mechanism known as a. regression b. reaction formation c. projection d. rationalization
Concept/Applied LO 4 Page: 491 Correct = 77% **a**	47.	Having performed poorly on an exam, Barbara attempts to protect her feelings of self-worth by telling herself that it does not matter because the course really is not that important to her. Barbara is probably a. rationalizing b. displacing c. fantasizing d. using identification
Concept/Applied LO 4 Page: 491 Correct = 79% **d**	48.	The process of pushing distressing thoughts into the unconscious and keeping them there is known as a. neurogenic amnesia b. suppression c. avoidance d. repression
Factual LO 4 Page: 492 Correct = 79% **c**	49.	Attributing one's own thoughts or motives to others defines a. reaction formation b. rationalization c. projection d. regression

Concept/Applied LO 4 Page: 492 **b**	50.	Hal is fearful of men who are friendly toward him, convinced that they are all homosexuals attempting to seduce him. Should it be the case that Hal is himself a latent homosexual fearful of admitting this even to himself, we might conclude that he is using the defense mechanisms of repression and a. reaction formation b. projection c. displacement d. regression
Concept/Applied LO 4 Page: 492 Correct = 62% **c**	51.	A man who has numerous reasons to hate his mother instead lavishes her with unrealistic amounts of attention and love. He is probably exhibiting the defense mechanism of a. regression b. identification c. reaction formation d. displacement
Concept/Applied LO 4 Page: 492 Correct = 68% **a**	52.	Whenever Wanda is denied anything by her husband, she pouts and gives him the silent treatment. This immature way of dealing with reality can be referred to as a. regression b. reaction formation c. displacement d. projection
Concept/Applied LO 4 Page: 492 Correct = 60% **b**	53.	Having a rather poor sense of self worth, Bruce attempts to make himself feel important by driving a European sports car, belonging to an exclusive tennis club, and eating at the best restaurants. Bruce may be using the defense mechanism of a. rationalization b. identification c. projection d. displacement
Concept/Applied LO 4 Page: 492 **a**	54.	John worries about his tendency toward abusing animals, so he joins the Association for the Prevention of Cruelty to Animals. John's behavior can be viewed as an example of a. reaction formation b. projection c. regression d. rationalization
Concept/Applied LO 4 Page: 492 Correct = 27% **d**	55.	Someone with latent homosexual urges strongly and loudly condemns gays. This person may well be using the defense mechanism of a. repression b. projection c. rationalization d. reaction formation
Factual LO 4 Page: 492 Correct = 78% **d**	56.	The defense mechanism of bolstering one's self esteem by forming an imaginary or real alliance with some person or group is referred to as a. compensation b. displacement c. regression d. identification

Factual LO 4 Page: 492 Correct = 83% c	57.	As an adult, going back to an earlier way of gratifying needs defines a. repression b. fixation c. regression d. reaction formation
Concept/Applied LO 4 Page: 492 a	58.	Candice has just joined a sorority as a means of bolstering her self-esteem. Her behavior reflects the use of _____ as a defense mechanism. a. identification b. immersion c. regression d. projection
Concept/Applied LO 4 Page: 492 c	59.	Scott has just been reprimanded by his supervisor. Later on, Scott begins to "stomp around" and throws a tantrum in front of his co-workers. Scott's behavior exemplifies which of the following? a. a fixation b. projection c. regression d. rationalization
Factual LO 4 Page: 493 b	60.	_____ consists of feelings of fear, discomfort, and aversion that some people experience in interacting with gay individuals. a. Gay-bashing b. Homophobia c. Homosexuality d. Homogeneity
Critical Thinking LO 4 Page: 493 b	61.	Which of the following conclusions is most consistent with the results of the Featured Study on homophobia and homosexual arousal? a. Homophobic men showed less physiological arousal to depictions of heterosexual activity. b. Homophobic men were aroused by a depiction of male homosexual activity and nonhomophobic men were not. c. Most of the homophobic men verbally acknowledged their physiological arousal to depictions of homosexual activity. d. Men who rated themselves as nonhomophobic showed high physiological arousal to depictions of male homosexual activity.
Conceptual LO 5 Page: 494 b	62.	Freud used the term "sexual" in his psychosexual stages of development to mean a. genital sexual impulses b. any pleasure-giving urge c. general sexual feelings d. none of these things
Concept/Applied LO 5 Page: 494 b	63.	Freud believed that basic personality structure is developed by approximately _____ years of age. a. three b. five c. ten d. twenty
Factual LO 5 Page: 494 c	64.	Freud's stages of development are associated with a. changes in levels of cognitive sophistication b. psychosocial crises c. the focus of erotic energy d. changes in moral reasoning

Factual
LO 5
Page: 494
Correct = 90%
a

65. Failure to resolve conflict at a particular stage of psychosexual development may lead to failure to move forward psychologically, a phenomenon that Freud called
a. fixation
b. displacement
c. reciprocal determinism
d. compensation

Factual
LO 5
Page: 494
c

66. According to Freud, a person may become fixated at a particular psychosexual stage because of
a. permissiveness on the part of the person's parents
b. a genetic predisposition for fixation
c. either excessive gratification or excessive frustration of needs
d. abnormalities in brain chemistry that develop prenatally

Factual
LO 5
Page: 494
Correct = 78%
c

67. The order of the stages in psychosexual development is
a. anal, oral, phallic, genital, latency
b. oral, anal, latency, phallic, genital
c. oral, anal, phallic, latency, genital
d. anal, oral, genital, latency, phallic

Concept/Applied
LO 5
Page: 495
Correct = 93%
b

68. A Freudian might explain a compulsive smoker's behavior as being the result of fixation at the
a. anal stage
b. oral stage
c. latency stage
d. genital stage

Factual
LO 5
Page: 495
a

69. According to Freud, the crucial event during the anal stage of psychosexual development is
a. toilet training
b. the emergence of the superego
c. resolution of the Oedipal complex
d. having to keep one's room clean and neat

Factual
LO 5
Page: 495
c

70. The Oedipal complex, of such great importance in Freud's thinking, occurs during the _____ stage of psychosexual development.
a. oral
b. anal
c. phallic
d. latency

Factual
LO 5
Page: 495
Correct = 60%
d

71. During the latency stage, children
a. attempt to cope with the desires they have for their same-sex parent
b. begin to focus their sexual energy on their opposite-sex peers
c. turn their biological urges loose
d. begin to expand their social contacts beyond the immediate family

Factual
LO 5
Page: 495
b

72. The stage of psychosexual development that runs from approximately ages three to six is
a. latency
b. phallic
c. genital
d. oral

Factual LO 5 Page: 495 Correct = 65% b	73.	The Freudian period that begins with puberty is the a. anal stage b. genital stage c. phallic stage d. latency stage
Factual LO 5 Page: 495 Correct = 90% c	74.	The idea that a male child desires his mother and fears his father illustrates the a. genital complex b. latency complex c. Oedipal complex d. Electra complex
Factual LO 5 Page: 495 Correct = 92% c	75.	A girl fearing her mother and desiring her father is associated with the a. Meiner's complex b. anal complex c. Oedipal complex d. genital complex
Factual LO 5 Page: 495 Correct = 66% d	76.	Identification of oneself with the proper gender, male or female, would occur during the _____ stage. a. anal b. genital c. oral d. phallic
Factual LO 6 Page: 496 b	77.	Both Carl Jung and Alfred Adler were especially critical of Freud's emphasis on a. the influence of childhood experiences b. sexuality c. the unconscious d. defense mechanisms
Factual LO 6 Page: 496 c	78.	To differentiate his approach from Freud's psychoanalytic theory, Carl Jung used the name a. individual psychology b. depth psychology c. analytical psychology d. existential psychology
Factual LO 6 Page: 496 Correct = 71% b	79.	The theorist who advanced the concept that the unconscious has two layers, the personal unconscious and the collective unconscious, was a. Sigmund Freud b. Carl Jung c. Alfred Adler d. Erik Erikson
Critical Thinking LO 6 Page: 496 b	80.	Freud's concept of the unconscious is most like Jung's a. preconscious b. personal unconscious c. collective unconscious d. archetypes
Factual LO 6 Page: 496 Correct = 51% d	81.	What is the name Carl Jung used to identify the level of the unconscious that stores latent memory traces inherited from our ancestral past? a. personal unconscious b. preconscious c. primeval unconscious d. collective unconscious

Factual LO 6 Page: 496 Correct = 87% **a**	82.	In Jung's theory, emotionally charged images and thought forms that have universal meaning are called a. archetypes b. prototypes c. mandalas d. central memories
Concept/Applied LO 6 Page: 496 **d**	83.	Carl Jung's concept of the collective unconscious includes a. the presence of archetypes b. similarities in the form of myths and dreams throughout the world c. possible biologically based human thought forms d. all of these things
Factual LO 6 Page: 496 **b**	84.	Which of the following individuals was the first to describe the introverted and extraverted personality types? a. Sigmund Freud b. Carl Jung c. Carl Rogers d. Abraham Maslow
Concept/Applied LO 6 Page: 496 **a**	85.	Roberto tends to focus on people and things around him and is outgoing, talkative, and friendly. Jung would refer to Roberto as an a. extravert b. animus-type personality c. external locus of control individual d. iconoclast
Concept/Applied LO 6 Page: 496 Correct = 90% **d**	86.	A person who is occupied with his own thoughts and feelings, aloof, and contemplative exemplifies what Jung described as the _____ type. a. introspective b. extraverted c. reflective d. introverted
Concept/Applied LO 6 Page: 496 **d**	87.	When anthropologists compare ancient artifacts from South America, Europe, and Australia they often find similarities among the images that are depicted. Based on Jung's analytical psychology, some of these apparent similarities may stem from a. the preconscious b. reciprocal determinism c. manifest consciousness d. the collective unconscious
Concept/Applied LO 6 Page: 497 **c**	88.	The central aspect of Adler's theory of personality is that people a. must resolve conflicts between the needs of society and the needs of the self b. have a dynamic interplay between the structures of their mental life that must be maintained in a state of balance and harmony c. strive to adapt and master life's challenges d. have a drive to resolve the discrepancy between their real selves and their ideal selves
Critical Thinking LO 6 Page: 497 Correct = 76% **c**	89.	Adler is to individual psychology as Jung is to a. depth psychology b. existential psychology c. analytical psychology d. Gestalt psychology

Concept/Applied LO 6 Page: 497 Correct = 85% **a**	90.	The sickly child who goes on to become a forceful, physically active adult is engaging in what Adler called a. compensation b. displacement c. fixation d. regression
Factual LO 6 Page: 497 Correct = 87% **b**	91.	According to Alfred Adler, overcompensation may be found in those who a. have a superiority complex b. have an inferiority complex c. are fixated at one of the psychosexual stages d. have not been successful in the use of defense mechanisms
Factual LO 6 Page: 497 **a**	92.	Having exaggerated feeling of weakness and inadequacy is referred to as a. an inferiority complex b. an incongruent personality c. a dysfunctional self-concept d. an Oedipal complex
Factual LO 6 Page: 498 **a**	93.	Which of the following psychodynamic theorists emphasized the social context of personality development? a. Alfred Adler b. Sigmund Freud c. Carl Rogers d. Abraham Maslow
Concept/Applied LO 6 Page: 498 **a**	94.	Natalie is eight years old. Her parents have always spoiled her and given her anything that she has asked for. Based on Adler's theory of individual psychology, this parental pampering may cause Natalie a. to develop exaggerated feelings of weakness and inadequacy b. to develop a weak superego c. to be dominated by her superego as an adult d. to develop feelings of competence and self-sufficiency
Concept/Applied LO 6 Page: 498 Correct = 71% **a**	95.	Research on the influence of birth order on personality can be traced to which of the following theorists? a. Alfred Adler b. Sigmund Freud c. Carl Jung d. John Watson
Critical Thinking LO 7 Page: 498 Correct = 68% **c**	96.	Which of the following is not one of the assumptions of the psychodynamic theories of personality that has obtained considerable acceptance? a. Unconscious forces can influence behavior. b. Early childhood experiences can influence adult personality. c. Sexual and aggressive impulses are the driving force of behavior. d. Internal conflict can play a key role in generating psychological distress.
Factual LO 7 Page: 498 **d**	97.	The psychodynamic theories of personality have been criticized for which of the following? a. sexism b. lack of testability c. inadequate supportive evidence d. all of these reasons

Critical Thinking LO 7 Page: 498 **d**	98.	Which of the following is <u>not</u> a common criticism of psychodynamic theories of personality? a. lack of testability b. sex bias against women c. inadequate supportive evidence d. over-emphasis on the importance of early childhood experiences
Factual LO 8 Page: 499 Correct = 96% **b**	99.	The theoretical orientation that argues that psychology should study only observable behavior is a. rational-emotive b. behaviorism c. humanism d. invasive
Factual LO 8 Page: 499 **a**	100.	Research in the behavioral tradition has focused largely on which of the following? a. learning b. personality c. social behavior d. sensation and perception
Concept/Applied LO 8 Page: 499 **c**	101.	In explaining an individual's aggressiveness, Skinner would look for a. feelings of repressed hostility b. an inadequate sense of self-worth c. early learning experiences and reinforcement history d. instinctual explanations
Factual LO 8 Page: 499 **c**	102.	Which of the following learning theorists proposed the most mechanical view of learning in the sense that little attention is paid to conscious thought in the learning process? a. Albert Bandura b. Walter Mischel c. B. F. Skinner d. Julian Rotter
Critical Thinking LO 8 Page: 499 **c**	103.	Which of the following terms is <u>least</u> closely associated with Skinner's view of personality? a. determinism b. reinforcement c. unconscious motivation d. response tendencies
Concept/Applied LO 8 Page: 500 **b**	104.	Which of the following definitions of "personality" best reflects the views of B. F. Skinner? a. stable behavioral traits that evolve as a function of natural selection b. a collection of response tendencies that are tied to various stimulus situations c. consistent patterns of behavior that occur as a result of unconscious impulses d. innate behavioral tendencies that reflect a unique pattern of genetic predispositions
Factual LO 9 Page: 501 Correct = 62% **a**	105.	The term that Albert Bandura uses to refer to the assumption that internal mental events, external environmental events, and overt behavior all influence each other is a. reciprocal determinism b. mutual dependency c. psychic determinism d. reciprocal relativism

Concept/Applied LO 9 Page: 501 Correct = 86% c	106.	Albert Bandura's concept of reciprocal determinism is best summarized as a. "The environment continually shapes us." b. "Humans continually shape the environment." c. "Environments shape humans and humans shape environments." d. "Each person's world is his or her own."
Concept/Applied LO 9 Page: 501 d	107.	Bandura believes that personality is formed through a. conditioning b. reinforcement c. modeling d. all of these processes
Critical Thinking LO 9 Page: 501 Correct = 41% c	108.	Social learning theory differs from Skinner's approach in giving more weight to a. secondary reinforcers b. respondent conditioning c. cognitive processes d. genetic factors
Concept/Applied LO 9 Page: 501 c	109.	In explaining a person's aggressiveness, a social learning theorist would favor which of the following explanations? a. an inferiority complex b. unconscious forces c. observational learning d. unresolved conflicts
Concept/Applied LO 9 Page: 501 Correct = 77% a	110.	The occurrence of so-called copycat crimes where someone hijacks an airliner after seeing a movie about a hijacking provides anecdotal evidence for which of the following theories? a. Bandura's social learning theory b. Skinner's operant conditioning theory c. Freud's psychoanalytic theory d. Adler's individual psychology
Concept/Applied LO 9 Page: 501 c	111.	A social learning theorist would most likely explain the behavior of a spoiled brat in terms of which of the following? a. personality defects of the child b. unresolved conflicts between the child and the parents c. learning through observation and reinforcement d. a genetic predisposition resulting in a high need for attention
Concept/Applied LO 9 Page: 501 a	112.	According to Albert Bandura's theory of behavior, response tendencies are primarily the product of a. imitation b. punishment c. reinforcement d. unconscious motivation
Factual LO 9 Page: 501 d	113.	Social learning theory has demonstrated that we are most likely to imitate the behavior of a. those whom we like or respect b. those whom we perceive as being similar to ourselves c. those whom we consider to be attractive or powerful d. any of these people

Factual LO 9 Page: 502 Correct = 74% **a**	114.	The belief that one has the ability to perform behaviors that should lead to expected outcomes is referred to as a. self-efficacy b. self-monitoring c. self-control d. self-justification
Factual LO 9 Page: 502 Correct = 89% **d**	115.	Research findings indicate that feelings of greater self-efficacy are associated with which of the following? a. greater success in giving up smoking b. higher levels of academic performance c. enhanced performance in athletic competition d. all of these things
Critical Thinking LO 9 Page: 502 **d**	116.	Which of the following parental behaviors is <u>not</u> likely to foster self-efficacy in children? a. early independence training b. warm support c. providing a stimulating environment d. punitive disciplinary techniques
Factual LO 10 Page: 502 **c**	117.	In explaining behavior, social learning theorist Walter Mischel is <u>most</u> interested in the influence of a. personality traits b. unconscious forces c. the situation d. instincts
Concept/Applied LO 10 Page: 502 Correct = 44% **d**	118.	One of the major points Mischel makes about personality is that a. people behave more consistently across situations than we have thought b. many personal traits are genetically determined c. the idea of traits is fundamental to understanding personality d. people are much less consistent across situations than most theorists have assumed
Concept/Applied LO 10 Page: 502 **b**	119.	Wanda is very quiet around people in authority, but she can be loud and boisterous among her peers. Which of the following theorists would explain the difference in Wanda's behavior in terms of situational factors? a. Carl Rogers b. Walter Mischel c. Alfred Adler d. Sigmund Freud
Factual LO 10 Page: 502 Correct = 93% **a**	120.	The fact that we tend to behave differently in different situations has led Walter Mischel to contend that behavior tends to be a. situationally specific b. situationally consistent c. reliable d. situationally similar
Critical Thinking LO 11 Page: 503 Correct = 60% **c**	121.	Which of the following is <u>not</u> a criticism of the behavioral approach to personality? a. overdependence on animal research b. neglect of biological factors c. use of extensive empirical research d. providing a fragmented view of personality

Critical Thinking LO 11 Page: 503 **a**	122.	Which of the following approaches to personality is most likely to be characterized by the lack of unifying structural concepts that tie all the pieces together? a. behavioral approach b. cognitive approach c. humanistic approach d. psychoanalytic approach
Factual LO 12 Page: 503 **b**	123.	<u>Both</u> the psychoanalytic and behavioral theories of behavior have been criticized for which of the following? a. the belief that behavior is dominated by primitive, animalistic drives b. the failure to recognize the unique qualities of human behavior c. preoccupation with animal research d. fragmented view of personality
Factual LO 12 Page: 503 Correct = 85% **d**	124.	The approach that stresses the individual's freedom, uniqueness, and growth potential is a. social learning theory b. Gestalt theory c. behaviorism d. humanism
Concept/Applied LO 12 Page: 503 Correct = 90% **d**	125.	The <u>most</u> optimistic view of human nature is found in the a. psychoanalytic approach b. behavioral approach c. cognitive approach d. humanistic approach
Factual LO 12 Page: 504 **c**	126.	The term used to refer to an appreciation of an individual's personal, subjective experiences as a way to understand behavior is a. epistemology b. philosophy c. phenomenology d. self-efficacy
Critical Thinking LO 12 Page: 504 **b**	127.	Which of the following statements is <u>least</u> likely to be made by a humanist? a. People are rational. b. People are dominated by unconscious conflicts. c. People can rise above their animal heritage. d. People are unique.
Factual LO 13 Page: 504 **b**	128.	Carl Rogers' view of personality structure centers on a single construct, and that is a. ego b. the self-concept c. the environment d. personality traits
Factual LO 13 Page: 504 Correct = 70% **a**	129.	According to Carl Rogers, if your self-concept is reasonably accurate, it is said to be a. congruent with reality b. self-actualized c. extraverted d. valid
Factual LO 13 Page: 504 Correct = 89% **a**	130.	The collection of beliefs about one's own nature, unique qualities, and typical behavior is referred to as one's _____, according to Rogers. a. self-concept b. phenomenology c. state of incongruence d. level of self-actualization

Factual
LO 13
Page: 504
c

131. According to Rogers, for a child to develop a healthy personality the parents must
a. avoid the use of punishment
b. address the child's ego needs
c. exhibit unconditional love toward the child
d. create an atmosphere of intellectual stimulation

Factual
LO 13
Page: 505
c

132. According to Carl Rogers, troublesome anxiety is caused by
a. unresolved sexual conflicts
b. unconditional love
c. threats to our self-concept
d. the use of defense mechanisms

Factual
LO 13
Page: 505
d

133. According to Carl Rogers, people with highly _____ self-concepts are especially likely to be plagued by recurrent anxiety.
a. objective
b. subjective
c. congruent
d. incongruent

Factual
LO 14
Page: 505
d

134. The correct order of the needs in Maslow's hierarchy, from most basic to highest level, is
a. esteem, physiological, aesthetic, safety, love, cognitive, self-actualization
b. physiological, cognitive, love, safety, aesthetic, esteem, self-actualization
c. safety, physiological, esteem, aesthetic, love, self-actualization
d. physiological, safety, love, esteem, cognitive, aesthetic, self-actualization

Factual
LO 14
Page: 505
a

135. In Maslow's hierarchy of needs, the _____ needs are considered to be the most basic needs and the first priority.
a. physiological
b. safety and security
c. aesthetic and cognitive
d. self-actualization

Concept/Applied
LO 14
Page: 506
b

136. Your needs to live in a crime-free neighborhood, save money, buy insurance, and have a stable job are examples of which of the following kinds of needs?
a. physiological
b. safety and security
c. love and belongingness
d. esteem

Concept/Applied
LO 14
Page: 506
b

137. Imagine a neighborhood in which a hurricane has caused extensive flooding. Many of the residents have had their homes damaged or destroyed. At the time, however, the material loss is unimportant as the residents think only of escaping the flood. Maslow would say this is because the residents' _____ needs are threatened.
a. physiological
b. safety and security
c. esteem
d. self-actualization

Concept/Applied
LO 14
Page: 506
b

138. Your needs for social status and for respect and recognition from others reflect the _____ needs in Maslow's hierarchy.
a. cognitive
b. esteem
c. aesthetic
d. love and belongingness

Concept/Applied LO 14 Page: 506 **c**	139.	Your needs to learn all you can about philosophy, and understand the inner workings of our political system are examples of _____ needs. a. aesthetic b. esteem c. cognitive d. self-actualization
Concept/Applied LO 14 Page: 506 **c**	140.	What need was Abraham Maslow expressing when he said that "what a man can be, he must be"? a. the need for superiority b. the need for unconditional love c. the need to self-actualize d. the need to achieve
Factual LO 14 Page: 506 **c**	141.	Abraham Maslow called the need to fulfill one's potential the need for a. affiliation b. achievement c. self-actualization d. power
Factual LO 14 Page: 507 Correct = 81% **d**	142.	Which of the following is <u>not</u> a characteristic of a self-actualizing person? a. being realistic b. being open and spontaneous c. enjoying peak experiences d. having a strong need to affiliate with many people
Factual LO 14 Page: 507 **c**	143.	Awed by the grandeur of nature, the hiker experienced a profound emotional high. Maslow called such experiences a. ecstatic experiences b. sublimation c. peak experiences d. archetypal experiences
Concept/Applied LO 14 Page: 507 **d**	144.	According to Maslow's theory, the self-actualizing person would be <u>least</u> likely to a. have a limited number of strong friendships b. be spontaneous and neutral in exchanges c. have somewhat mystical experiences d. be uncomfortable when alone or detached
Critical Thinking LO 15 Page: 507 **d**	145.	Which of the following is <u>not</u> one of the major contributions associated with the humanistic theory of personality? a. the importance of a person's subjective views b. focusing attention on what constitutes a healthy personality c. making the self-concept an important construct in psychology d. acknowledging the role that internal conflict plays in generating psychological distress
Critical Thinking LO 15 Page: 507 **b**	146.	Which of the following is one of the major criticisms of the humanistic approach to personality? a. It is too deterministic. b. It is too optimistic about human nature. c. It presents a fragmented view of personality. d. It de-emphasizes the subjective nature of self-concept.

Critical Thinking 147. Which of the following criticisms can be leveled against both the psychoanalytic
LO 15 approach and the humanistic approach to personality?
Page: 507
a
a. poor testability
b. too deterministic
c. overemphasis on the influence of early childhood experiences
d. provide a fragmented view of personality

Concept/Applied 148. Being sociable, assertive, active, and lively is associated with the higher-order trait
LO 16 of _____ according to Eysenck.
Page: 507
Correct = 94%
a
a. extraversion
b. self-monitoring
c. locus of control
d. intraception

Factual 149. According to Han Eysenck, which of the following is not considered a higher-order
LO 16 trait?
Page: 507
d
a. neuroticism
b. extraversion
c. psychoticism
d. agreeableness

Factual 150. According to Han Eysenck, _____ involves being anxious, tense, moody, and low
LO 16 in self-esteem.
Page: 507
a
a. neuroticism
b. psychoticism
c. extraversion
d. introversion

Factual 151. According to Han Eysenck, _____ involves being egocentric, impulsive, cold, and
LO 16 antisocial.
Page: 507
b
a. neuroticism
b. psychoticism
c. extraversion
d. introversion

Factual 152. Which of the following personality theorists contends that personality is determined
LO 16 to a large extent by a person's genes?
Page: 507
Correct = 69%
a
a. Han Eysenck
b. B. F. Skinner
c. Abraham Maslow
d. Sigmund Freud

Factual 153. According to Han Eysenck, people who condition easily are likely to become
LO 16
Page: 508
d
a. neurotic
b. psychotic
c. extraverted
d. introverted

Factual 154. The findings from twin studies indicate that identical twins are much more similar
LO 17 than fraternal twins on which of the following?
Page: 509
d
a. neuroticism
b. extraversion
c. conscientiousness
d. all of the Big Five personality traits

Factual LO 17 Page: 512 **b**	155.	Research on genes and personality indicates that the heritability estimates for personality traits are approximately _____ percent. a. 25 b. 50 c. 75 d. 95
Factual LO 17 Page: 512 **c**	156.	Findings from behavioral genetics research indicate that a. situational factors contributed most to similarities b. family factors contributed most to similarities c. genetic factors contributed most to similarities d. all three components contributed about equally
Factual LO 17 Page: 512 **a**	157.	Research on the heritability of personality shows that _____ appears to have a surprisingly small impact on personality. a. shared family environment b. heredity c. unique experiences d. unconscious motivation
Factual LO 17 Page: 512 **b**	158.	Which of the following techniques is <u>most</u> likely to be used to identify links between specific genes and specific traits? a. twin studies b. genetic mapping c. magnetic resonance imaging d. PET scans
Factual LO 17 Page: 512 **c**	159.	A number of studies have found a link between a gene for a particular type of dopamine receptor and which of the following traits? a. neuroticism b. extraversion c. novelty seeking d. conscientiousness
Factual LO 17 Page: 512 **d**	160.	Which of the following involves being impulsive, exploratory, excitable, and extravagant? a. neuroticism b. extraversion c. agreeableness d. novelty seeking
Factual LO 18 Page: 513 Correct = 28% **b**	161.	Which of the following theorists is <u>most</u> closely associated with the evolutionary approach to personality? a. Albert Bandura b. David Buss c. Abraham Maslow d. Robert Plomin
Critical Thinking LO 18 Page: 513 Correct = 75% **b**	162.	Which of the following statements is <u>most</u> likely to be problematic for theorists who support the evolutionary approach to personality? a. Personality has a biological basis. b. There are a variety of individual differences in personality. c. Various personality traits may contribute to reproductive fitness in humans. d. Natural selection has favored certain traits over the course of human history.

Concept/Applied LO 18 Page: 513 **b**	163.	According to the evolutionary approach to personality, humans have evolved special sensitivity to variations in the ability to bond with others, which is closely associated with which of the following Big Five personality traits? a. neuroticism b. extraversion c. agreeableness d. conscientiousness
Concept/Applied LO 18 Page: 513 **c**	164.	According to the evolutionary approach to personality, humans have evolved special sensitivity to variations in the ability to cooperate and collaborate with others, which is closely associated with which of the following Big Five personality traits? a. neuroticism b. extraversion c. agreeableness d. conscientiousness
Concept/Applied LO 18 Page: 513 **d**	165.	According to the evolutionary approach to personality, humans have evolved special sensitivity to variations in the tendency to be reliable and ethical, which is closely associated with which of the following Big Five personality traits? a. neuroticism b. extraversion c. agreeableness d. conscientiousness
Concept/Applied LO 18 Page: 513 **d**	166.	According to the evolutionary approach to personality, humans have evolved special sensitivity to variations in the capacity to be an innovative problem solver, which is closely associated with which of the following Big Five personality traits? a. neuroticism b. extraversion c. conscientiousness d. openness to experience
Concept/Applied LO 19 Page: 513 **a**	167.	Which of the following is true? a. Efforts to divide behavior into genetic and environmental components are ultimately artificial. b. The evidence suggests that genetic factors do not influence personality. c. The evidence suggests that environmental factors do not influence personality. d. It is only a matter of time before the complicated intertwining of nature and nurture will be understood.
Critical Thinking LO 19 Page: 513 **b**	168.	Which of the following is <u>not</u> one of the main weaknesses in biological approaches to personality? a. conceptual problems with heritability estimates b. an overly optimistic view of human nature c. the difficulty of separating the effects of nature and nurture d. the lack of a comprehensive theory
Factual LO 19 Page: 513 **a**	169.	In comparison to Eysenck's theory of personality, evolutionary theory a. is more limited in scope b. has greater empirical support c. is more popular among behaviorists d. is less applicable to behavior across cultures

Factual   170.   The generalized preference for high or low levels of sensory stimulation is referred
LO 20   to as
Page: 514   a. self-monitoring
b   b. sensation seeking
                         c. locus of control
                         d. level of intraception

Factual   171.   Which of the following researchers is credited for first describing the notion of
LO 20   sensation seeking?
Page: 514   a. Han Eysenck
d   b. Carl Rogers
                         c. Sigmund Freud
                         d. Marvin Zuckerman

Concept/Applied 172.   Jack is an adventuresome fellow who feels most alive when he is putting his life at
LO 20   risk. Marvin Zuckerman would say that Jack is high in
Page: 514   a. self-actualization
c   b. impulse behavior
                         c. sensation seeking
                         d. self-monitoring

Critical Thinking 173.   <u>All but</u> which of the following are characteristic of high sensation seekers?
LO 20   a. uninhibited
Page: 514   b. adventuresome
c   c. low tolerance for stress
                         d. low tolerance for routine and repetition

Critical Thinking 174.   High sensation seeking is <u>least</u> likely to be associated with which of the following
LO 20   behaviors?
Page: 514   a. gambling
b   b. sexual abstinence
                         c. recreational drug use
                         d. criminal behavior

Factual   175.   Which of the following researchers is recognized for his research on self-
LO 21   monitoring?
Page: 514   a. Han Eysenck
b   b. Mark Snyder
                         c. Sigmund Freud
                         d. Marvin Zuckerman

Factual   176.   The degree to which people attend to and try to control the impression they make on
LO 21   others defines the concept of
Page: 514   a. self-consciousness
Correct = 59%   b. extraversion
d   c. self-determination
                         d. self-monitoring

Concept/Applied 177.   For which of the following is the world essentially a stage on which one must act?
LO 21   a. the sensation seeker
Page: 515   b. the person with an internal locus of control
c   c. the person high in self-monitoring
                         d. the self-actualizing person

Concept/Applied LO 21 Page: 515 **b**	178.	The greatest inconsistency between who a person is and the impression he or she creates is likely to be found in a a. sensation seeker b. high self-monitor c. self-actualizer d. person with a realistic self-concept
Concept/Applied LO 21 Page: 515 **b**	179.	Which of the following individuals is <u>most</u> likely to be good at spotting deceptive impression management in other people? a. the sensation seeker b. the high self-monitor c. the low self-monitor d. the self-actualized person
Concept/Applied LO 21 Page: 515 **d**	180.	Gina is good at presenting herself to a group of persons, is able to detect if someone is trying to manipulate her, and has a difficult time making a genuine emotional commitment. Gina is <u>most</u> likely to be classified as a. an introvert b. an extravert c. high in introspection d. a high self-monitor
Concept/Applied LO 21 Page: 515 **b**	181.	Dalton always does well during interviews. He is able to gauge how people react to him, and he can adjust the way he presents himself. As a result of this skill, he invariably makes a good impression on the interviewer. It appears that Dalton a. is low in self-monitoring b. is high in self-monitoring c. has low self-efficacy d. is low in self-enhancement
Concept/Applied LO 21 Page: 515 **a**	182.	Who would you predict would date more, have sex with more partners, and change relationships more? a. the high self-monitor b. the low self-monitor c. the low sensation-seeker d. the introvert
Concept/Applied LO 21 Page: 515 Correct = 35% **a**	183.	Rather than having a few "best friends," Peter tends to select companions based on the event he plans to attend or the activity in which he plans to engage. Peter sounds as if he is a. high in self-monitoring b. someone with an external locus of control c. a sensation seeker d. an extravert
Factual LO 22 Page: 516 Correct = 50% **d**	184.	Research findings indicate that, in general, _____ is fairly consistent across cultures. a. self-monitoring b. locus of control c. conceptions of the self d. the trait structure of personality
Critical Thinking LO 22 Page: 516 **d**	185.	American parents are <u>least</u> likely to teach their children to a. be self-reliant b. feel good about themselves c. view themselves as special individuals d. be modest about their personal accomplishments

Critical Thinking 186. Parents in Asian cultures are most likely to teach their children to
LO 22
Page: 517
b
a. be self-reliant
b. rely on family and friends
c. feel good about themselves
d. view themselves as special individuals

Factual 187. Research suggests that Asian children tend to define themselves in terms of
LO 22
Page: 517
a
a. the groups they belong to
b. their personal accomplishments
c. the accomplishments of their parents
d. their relationships with their teachers

Critical Thinking 188. Which of the following traits is most likely to differ across cultures?
LO 22
Page: 517
c
a. sensation seeking
b. self-monitoring
c. self-enhancement
d. neuroticism

Concept/Applied 189. The fact that there are literally dozens of insightful theories of personality illustrates which of the following unifying themes of your textbook?
LO 23
Page: 517
b
a. Psychology is empirical.
b. Psychology is theoretically diverse.
c. Psychology evolves in a sociohistorical context.
d. Our behavior is shaped by our cultural heritage.

Factual 190. Which of the following demonstrates that psychology has an impact on modern culture?
LO 23
Page: 518
Correct = 88%
d
a. the influence of social learning theory on issues of media violence and aggressive behavior
b. the application of Freud, Adler, and Skinner's ideas to rearing and teaching children
c. the use of Maslow's hierarchy of needs model in the motivation of employees
d. all of these demonstrate psychology's impact on modern culture

Concept/Applied 191. Sigmund Freud's theory of personality was influenced to a degree by his reaction to the hostilities of World War I, a fact that illustrates which of the following unifying themes of your textbook?
LO 23
Page: 518
c
a. Psychology is empirical.
b. Psychology is theoretically diverse.
c. Psychology evolves in a sociohistorical context.
d. Psychology is the study of subjective experience.

Factual 192. The most controversial use of personality assessment is in which of the following areas?
LO 24
Page: 519
a
a. personnel selection
b. clinical diagnosis
c. vocational counseling
d. personal counseling

Factual 193. Which of the following is not one of the main uses of personality scales?
LO 24
Page: 519
c
a. personnel selection
b. clinical diagnosis
c. college admissions
d. psychological research

Concept/Applied 194. You have just taken a test that involved answering pages of questions about your
LO 25   characteristic behavior. You probably responded to a(n)
Page: 519   a. projective test
Correct = 91%   b. intelligence test
c   c. self-report personality inventory
                 d. achievement test

Factual   195. If you needed a personality inventory capable of measuring a person's degree of
LO 25   psychopathology, you would probably use
Page: 519   a. Cattell's 16 Personality Factor Questionnaire
Correct = 59%   b. the Edwards Personal Preference Schedule
c   c. the Minnesota Multiphasic Personality Inventory
                   d. factor analysis

Concept/Applied 196. A friend tells you that he recently responded to a personality inventory with about
LO 25   550 items that indicated that his level of depression was above normal. He probably
Page: 519   took
Correct = 77%   a. the Minnesota Multiphasic Personality Inventory
a   b. Cattell's 16 Personality Factor Questionnaire
                      c. the Edwards Personal Preference Schedule
                      d. the Power Motivation Scale

Concept/Applied 197. A person who is suspicious, aloof, guarded, worrisome, and overly sensitive is likely
LO 25   to score high on which of the following clinical scales of the Minnesota Multiphasic
Page: 519   Personality Inventory (MMPI)?
b   a. hysteria
                      b. paranoia
                      c. depression
                      d. social introversion

Concept/Applied 198. A person who is moody, shy, pessimistic, and distressed is likely to score high on
LO 25   which of the following clinical scales of the Minnesota Multiphasic Personality
Page: 520   Inventory (MMPI)?
c   a. hysteria
                      b. paranoia
                      c. depression
                      d. social introversion

Concept/Applied 199. A person who is social, outgoing, impulsive, overly energetic, and in some cases
LO 25   amoral is likely to score high on which of the following clinical scales of the
Page: 520   Minnesota Multiphasic Personality Inventory (MMPI)?
c   a. hysteria
                      b. paranoia
                      c. hypomania
                      d. social introversion

Concept/Applied 200. A person who is shy, withdrawn, reserved, submissive, tense, and inflexible is likely
LO 25   to score high on which of the following clinical scales of the Minnesota Multiphasic
Page: 520   Personality Inventory (MMPI)?
d   a. hysteria
                      b. paranoia
                      c. depression
                      d. social introversion

Factual LO 25 Page: 520 Correct = 88% c	201.	In order to identify clusters of closely related personality traits and the factors underlying them, Raymond Cattell used a. a factorial anova b. the analysis of variance c. factor analysis d. the normal distribution
Factual LO 25 Page: 520 Correct = 76% b	202.	The personality inventory developed by Raymond Cattell that describes an individual in terms of a limited number of personality source traits is the a. Thematic Apperception Test b. 16 Personality Factor Questionnaire c. Minnesota Multiphasic Personality Inventory d. California Psychological Inventory
Factual LO 25 Page: 520 a	203.	Which of the following personality tests was designed to measure the "Big Five" traits? a. NEO b. TAT c. MMPI d. 16PF
Factual LO 25 Page: 521 Correct = 78% a	204.	One of the problems with self-report personality inventories is that respondents may answer questions in ways that make them look good. This tendency is called a a. social desirability bias b. response set c. perceptual set d. self-serving bias
Factual LO 26 Page: 521 Correct = 70% b	205.	A personality measure that asks you to respond freely to an ambiguous stimulus such as a picture or an inkblot is called a a. self-report personality inventory b. projective test c. behavior rating d. deceptive test
Factual LO 26 Page: 521 Correct = 67% c	206.	The Thematic Apperception Test is composed of a. inkblots b. forced-choice items c. ambiguous pictures d. true-false items
Critical Thinking LO 26 Page: 521 c	207.	Which of the following does not belong with the others? a. the Minnesota Multiphasic Personality Inventory b. Cattell's 16 Personality Factor Questionnaire c. the Thematic Apperception Test d. the Edwards Personal Preference Schedule
Factual LO 26 Page: 521 Correct = 85% d	208.	Projective tests such as the Rorschach Inkblot Test are designed to assess a. your mental abilities b. your behavior patterns c. the way others perceive you d. your characteristic concerns, conflicts, and desires
Critical Thinking LO 26 Page: 521 d	209.	Which of the following does not belong with the other three? a. Rorschach test b. Thematic Apperception Test c. Draw-A-Person Test d. Minnesota Multiphasic Personality Test

Concept/Applied LO 26 Page: 521 **a**	210.	The Rorschach Ink Blot Test presents the person with several rather ambiguously shaped blots of ink. The main assumption behind the test is that a. the person's characteristic needs will structure what he or she sees in the blots b. recent experiences of the person determines what is seen in the blots c. what the person sees in the blots is determined by the physical features of the blots d. "normal" individuals should report the same responses to the blots
Factual LO 26 Page: 522 **b**	211.	Which of the following is considered a major strength of projective tests? a. the degree of standardization in administration and scoring b. the difficulty in engaging in deliberate deception c. the substantial evidence for their validity d. the consistency of the scores provided
Factual LO 26 Page: 523 **c**	212.	Which of the following is one of the main criticisms of projective tests? a. Their accuracy depends on the order in which the stimuli are presented. b. They are deceptive attempts to get at the unconscious. c. There is inadequate evidence for the reliability of projective measures. d. More effort is needed to respond to them than in the case of self-report inventories.
Factual LO 27 Page: 524 **c**	213.	The tendency to mold our interpretation of the past to fit how events actually turned out is called a. projection b. reaction formation c. the hindsight bias d. self-enhancement
Factual LO 27 Page: 524 **a**	214.	The hindsight bias is also known as the _____ effect. a. "I knew it all along" b. "No pain, no gain" c. "Opposites attract" d. "Everyone else is crazy"
Critical Thinking LO 27 Page: 525 **c**	215.	Which of the following statements regarding hindsight bias is <u>not</u> accurate? a. The hindsight bias occurs in many different settings. b. Hindsight bias appears to be pervasive in everyday analyses of personality. c. Hindsight bias is generally restricted to thinking about issues related to personality. d. The notion of hindsight bias has been raised in criticisms of psychoanalytic theory.
Integrative **d**	216.	Sex and aggression are to Sigmund Freud's theory of personality as the tendency for personal growth is to _____ theory. a. Carl Jung's b. B. F. Skinner's c. Han Eysenck's d. Abraham Maslow's
Integrative **c**	217.	The hierarchy of traits is to Maslow's theory of personality as _____ is/are to Freud's theory. a. the self-concept b. the id, ego, and superego c. the inferiority complex d. reward and punishment

Integrative **a**	218.	Unconscious fixations and unresolved conflicts are to Sigmund Freud's theory of personality as _____ is/are to B. F. Skinner's theory. a. faulty learning b. genetic vulnerability c. incongruence between self and actual experience d. innate chemical imbalances in the brain
Integrative **b**	219.	Which of the following theories of personality was developed from laboratory experiments, primarily with animals? a. Sigmund Freud's theory of psychoanalysis b. B. F. Skinner's behavioral view c. Carl Rogers' humanistic view d. Han Eysenck's biological theory
Integrative **d**	220.	Which of the following theories of personality was developed from data collected from family, twin, and adoption studies? a. Sigmund Freud's theory of psychoanalysis b. B. F. Skinner's behavioral view c. Carl Rogers' humanistic view d. Han Eysenck's biological theory
Study Guide LO 4 Page: 492 **d**	221.	Someone attributes his thoughts or feelings to someone else. For example, although he chronically interrupts people, he things that other people interrupt him. What Freudian defense mechanism is illustrated? a. rationalization b. reaction formation c. regression d. projection
Study Guide LO 4 Page: 492 **b**	222.	Although Osmo at an unconscious level has great hatred for Cosmo, he believes that he likes Cosmo and, to the outside world, gives all the appearance of liking him. Which defense mechanism is Osmo using? a. regression b. reaction formation c. projection d. rationalization
Study Guide LO 6 Page: 496 **d**	223.	Which of the following concepts did Carl Jung develop? a. id b. ego c. inferiority complex d. introversion-extraversion
Study Guide LO 9 Page: 501 **c**	224.	Much of the behavior that we call personality results from reinforcement and observational learning, according to a. Jung b. Skinner c. Bandura d. Adler
Study Guide LO 10 Page: 502 **b**	225.	According to Mischel, what is the major factor that predicts human behavior? a. childhood experience b. specifics of the situation c. extraversion and introversion d. central and peripheral traits

Study Guide
LO 12
Page: 503
d

226. Which of the following tends to emphasize freedom and personal growth in its view of human behavior?
    a. the psychoanalytic approach
    b. the biological approach
    c. the behavioral approach
    d. the humanistic approach

Study Guide
LO 13
Page: 504
b

227. According to Rogers, what causes incongruence?
    a. an inherited sense of irony
    b. conditional acceptance or affection
    c. unconditional acceptance or affection
    d. unconditioned stimuli

Study Guide
LO 14
Page: 506
c

228. Herb had the desire and potential to be a violinist but became, instead, a trader in hog futures. He decided never to touch the violin again. What is wrong with Herb, according to Maslow?
    a. He suffers from incongruence.
    b. He suffers from castration anxiety.
    c. He has not achieved self-actualization.
    d. He has an inferiority complex.

Study Guide
LO 18
Page: 513
d

229. Which of the following views personality in terms of the adaptive significance of the Big Five traits?
    a. Abraham Maslow
    b. William James
    c. the behavioral approach
    d. the evolutionary approach

Study Guide
LO 27
Page: 524
a

230. Your friend spends money like water. When you learn that he is from a poverty-stricken background, you attribute his spending patterns to his earlier deprivation. According to the critical thinking analysis, you are likely to do this because of
    a. the hindsight bias
    b. a self-serving attribution
    c. the consistency and distinctiveness of personality
    d. circular reasoning

Online Quiz
LO 2
Page: 486
b

231. When we say that Gordon is quiet and unassuming, we are describing his
    a. unconscious motives
    b. personality traits
    c. philosophy of life
    d. perception of himself

Online Quiz
LO 3
Page: 488
b

232. According to the psychoanalytic view, many important life choices and decisions are based on
    a. rationality and logic
    b. unconscious urges and mechanisms
    c. weighing pros and cons of one's actions before behaving
    d. the distinction between the real self and the ideal self

Online Quiz
LO 6
Page: 496
b

233. According to Jung, one's personal unconscious contains
    a. archetypes
    b. repressed or forgotten information
    c. ancestral memories
    d. none of these things

Online Quiz LO 11 Page: 503 **a**	234.	Which of the following approaches to personality is <u>most</u> firmly rooted in empirical research? a. behavioral approach b. psychoanalytic approach c. humanistic approach d. cognitive approach
Online Quiz LO 13 Page: 504 **d**	235.	The personality theory of Carl Rogers is known as a. the Gestalt approach b. social comparison theory c. rational-emotive theory d. person-centered theory
Online Quiz LO 16 Page: 508 Correct = 78% **a**	236.	According to Han Eysenck, personality is largely a. inherited b. a function of unconscious forces c. shaped by sexual conflicts d. determined by external forces
Online Quiz LO 20 Page: 514 **b**	237.	A desire to engage in activities that involve physical risk and a willingness to volunteer for unusual activities are associated with someone who is high in a. self-monitoring b. sensation seeking c. locus of control d. introspection
Online Quiz LO 22 Page: 516 **c**	238.	Early investigations of the connection between culture and personality were largely guided by which of the following theories? a. Adler's individual psychology b. Bandura's social learning theory c. Freud's psychoanalytic theory d. Skinner's operant conditioning theory
Online Quiz LO 25 Page: 522 **c**	239.	A systematic tendency to respond to questions on a personality inventory in a way that is unrelated to the content of the questions is called a a. perceptual set b. social desirability bias c. response set d. mental set
Online Quiz LO 26 Page: 522 Correct = 55% **c**	240.	The idea that a person's unconscious needs will determine how he or she perceives relatively unstructured stimuli is the basis for a. personality trait tests b. the MMPI c. the TAT d. personal trait checklist

ESSAY QUESTIONS

1. How do you think an operant theorist like Skinner would explain defense mechanisms? Give several examples.

   Answers should demonstrate students' understanding both of several defense mechanisms and of the principles of operant conditioning. In general, an operant theorist would probably explain defense mechanisms as behaviors that one has learned to engage in when confronted by anxiety-arousing stimuli because those behaviors have led to anxiety reduction. This is an example of negative reinforcement. Defense mechanisms might also be explained as examples of escape or avoidance behaviors.

2. Psychodynamic theories have been criticized for their lack of empirical evidence and poor testability. Are there some of Freud's, Jung's, and Adler's ideas that would be easier to test than others? How might you go about designing research studies to test some of these ideas?

   Answers should reveal students' understanding of various research approaches as well as several psychodynamic concepts or hypotheses. Answers should suggest plausible ways to test these concepts or hypotheses. Some starting points might include:

   Using the interview or projective measures, you might be able to test Freud's hypothesis that sexual and aggressive drives are more often frustrated than other basic, biological drives. The same means could be used to probe for the operation of defense mechanisms.

   Modern longitudinal research techniques combined with sophisticated behavioral coding might yield evidence relevant to Freud's and Adler's assertions about childhood experiences molding adult personality.

   Jung's basic approach to testing his hypothesis about the existence of a collective unconscious could be improved on. The presence of archetypes in the unconscious of the individual could be probed using projective techniques. If commonalties across individuals were found, then modern anthropological and archaeological techniques could be used to search for corresponding symbols in other cultures and time periods.

   The concepts of introvert and extravert have been fairly easy to test using psychological tests.

3. On first learning about the different theoretical perspectives on personality, many people like the views of the humanistic theorists best. Why do you think this is? Are these reasons sound, scientific criteria for evaluating a theoretical perspective on personality?

   Reasons for people preferring humanistic views will vary, though a common reason will probably be the humanistic emphasis on free will and choice. More important than the reasons students give for people's preferring humanistic notions are their views on the soundness of these reasons as scientific criteria for evaluating theories. Since the scientific approach places a premium on objectivity, one's merely "liking" the idea of free choice, for instance, should be recognized as an inadequate evaluative criterion. In a good answer, the student will separate preferences from sound, scientific criteria, and recognize that an evaluative argument should be based on the latter.

4. Modern personality research tends to focus on specific traits. Psychologists have moved away from attempting to develop "grand theories" of personality such as those of the psychodynamic and humanistic theorists. Why do you think this has occurred? Do you think the trend toward "minitheories" that focus on specific personality traits is the best way to advance our understanding of personality?

   A good approach to answering this question would be to point to the lack of empirical evidence that's available to support the grand theories of the psychodynamic and humanistic theorists. On the other hand, theories about specific traits have been easier to test.

An insightful response to this question might be one that acknowledges the advances that the minitheories have accomplished – at least some fairly reliable understanding of some of the "pieces" of personality. But a fuller understanding of personality requires that these pieces be arranged in such away that the completed puzzle of personality results. And this might be best accomplished under the direction of an overall blueprint, i.e., a grand theory. So there would seem to be some need for these larger theories as well.

5. Discuss ways in which each of the major perspectives on personality has influenced some aspect of everyday life in modern society.

Answers should demonstrate sound understanding of the broad principles underlying each theoretical approach, and hypotheses about how these principles have influenced everyday life should be well reasoned. Some possibilities include:

Psychodynamic: A tremendous number of notions that comprise "common knowledge" in our society derive from this perspective, especially Freud's work. These include the beliefs that childhood experiences influence later personality and psychological health, that dreams are meaningful, and that the contents of the unconscious can influence behavior.

Behavioral: Behavior-modification techniques are widely used to change habits in oneself and others. Our criminal justice system seems to be based on a belief in the effectiveness of punishment in controlling behavior. Advertising counts on the effectiveness of modeling to help sell products.

Humanistic: The notion of the self is prominent in our society. Most people agree that high levels of self-esteem are important, especially in children, and people sometimes go to great lengths to engender high self-esteem in themselves and others. We greatly value the notion of free choice. Self-actualization is a highly regarded and much sought-after achievement.

Biological: The idea that personality traits are strongly influenced by heredity has become more popular, especially in the wake of the twin research reported in the chapter. It has become more acceptable to hold this intuitively appealing view.

This page intentionally left blank.

Chapter Thirteen
Stress, Coping, and Health

LEARNING OBJECTIVES

1. Discuss the impact of minor stressors.
2. Describe the nature of our appraisals of stress.
3. Describe frustration as a form of stress.
4. Identify the three basic types of conflict and discuss which types are most troublesome.
5. Summarize evidence on life change and pressure as a form of stress.
6. Identify some common emotional responses to stress and discuss the effects of emotional arousal.
7. Describe the fight-or-flight response and the three stages of the general adaptation syndrome.
8. Discuss the two major pathways along which the brain sends signals to the endocrine system in response to stress.
9. Describe and evaluate aggression and self-indulgence as behavioral responses to stress.
10. Discuss the adaptive value of defensive coping and positive illusions.
11. Discuss the effects of stress on task performance and the burnout syndrome.
12. Discuss posttraumatic stress disorder and other psychological problems and disorders that may result from stress.
13. Describe the Type A behavior pattern and summarize the evidence linking it to coronary heart disease.
14. Describe evidence linking emotional reactions and depression to heart disease.
15. Discuss the evidence linking stress to immunosuppression and a variety of physical illnesses.
16. Describe the Featured Study on stress and the common cold.
17. Discuss how social support moderates the impact of stress.
18. Discuss how personality and physiological factors are related to stress tolerance.
19. Discuss the negative impact of smoking, poor nutrition, and lack of exercise on physical health.
20. Discuss the relationship between behavioral factors and AIDS.
21. Explain how health-impairing lifestyles develop.
22. Describe some barriers to effective-patient-provider communication and ways to overcome these problems.
23. Discuss individual differences in the willingness to seek medical treatment.
24. Discuss the extent to which people tend to adhere to medical advice.
25. Explain how this chapter highlighted two of the text's unifying themes.
26. Summarize Albert Ellis' ideas about controlling one's emotions.
27. Discuss the adaptive value of humor and releasing pent-up emotions.
28. Discuss the adaptive value of relaxation and exercise.
29. Describe some important considerations in evaluating health statistics and making health decisions.

MULTIPLE-CHOICE QUESTIONS

Factual
LO 1
Page: 529
Correct = 68%
b

1. _____ refers to the idea that physical illness is caused by a complex interaction of biological, psychobiological, and sociocultural factors.
   a. Disease/medical model
   b. Biopsychosocial model
   c. Psychosociological model
   d. Cognitive model

Factual
LO 1
Page: 530
Correct = 66%
d

2. Your text defined stress as
   a. any unpleasant event
   b. the responses we make to unpleasant events
   c. illness-inducing behavior
   d. circumstances that are perceived as threatening

Factual
LO 1
Page: 531
Correct = 80%
c

3. What does the research have to say about the general effect of everyday problems and the minor nuisances of life?
   a. Minor stresses produce minor effects.
   b. Minor stresses have negative effects only when coupled with major stresses.
   c. Minor stresses may have significant harmful effects on both physical and mental health.
   d. Minor stresses often have significant harmful effects on mental health, but don't affect physical health.

Factual
LO 1
Page: 531
Correct = 73%
a

4. Minor stresses may be more strongly related to mental health than major stressful events largely because
   a. of the cumulative nature of stress
   b. minor stresses lead to more intense physiological arousal than major stresses
   c. we are much more intimately involved with minor stresses
   d. we feel more out of control with minor stresses than we do with major stresses

Concept/Applied
LO 1
Page: 531
a

5. Mason is already late for an important appointment when he realizes he is almost out of gas. He stops to fill up and the clerk has trouble getting approval on his credit card. When he finally pulls out of the service station, the traffic is crawling because of an accident. Inconveniences of this type
   a. can often have a significant effect on physical and mental health
   b. are such routine hassles that they are not perceived as stressful
   c. usually create avoidance-avoidance conflicts
   d. are only stressful to individuals with a Type A personality

Factual
LO 2
Page: 531
Correct = 91%
d

6. When we say that stress "lies in the mind of the beholder" we mean that
   a. our appraisals of stressful events are basically objective
   b. the autonomic nervous system triggers a fight-or-flight response, which then sends messages of stress to the brain
   c. strong-minded persons are better able to handle stressful events than weak-minded persons
   d. our appraisals of stressful events are highly subjective

Concept/Applied
LO 2
Page: 531
d

7. Most of Conrad's friends consider him to be highly neurotic. It is likely that, compared to his friends, Conrad is
   a. less likely to perceive events as stressful
   b. more likely to "choke" under pressure
   c. less likely to use defensive coping strategies
   d. more likely to perceive events as stressful

Factual LO 3 Page: 531 Correct = 88% **a**	8.	Frustration refers to a. being blocked in the pursuit of a desired goal b. the most frequent emotional response to aggression c. being caught between two incompatible motives d. being expected to live up to high standards of performance
Concept/Applied LO 3 Page: 531 Correct = 91% **d**	9.	Virginia has wanted to be a physician for as long as she can remember, but she has been unable to gain entry to medical school. Virginia is probably experiencing a. burnout b. learned helplessness c. regression d. frustration
Concept/Applied LO 3 Page: 531 **c**	10.	Tatiana just finished entering her 10-page term paper into one of the computers in the University's computer lab. She clicks the "Save" command, and the computer unexpectedly locks up. When she reboots the computer she discovers that all but the first two pages of her term paper have been lost. At this point in time Tatiana is <u>most</u> likely experiencing a. pressure b. conflict c. frustration d. burnout
Concept/Applied LO 3 Page: 531 **d**	11.	Steve was excited when he finally landed the lead role in one of the community theater productions. He has been rehearsing his part for the past two months but, on the day that the play is scheduled to open, Steve awakes with a bad case of laryngitis and he is unable to perform in the play. At this point Steve is <u>most</u> likely experiencing a. pressure b. conflict c. burnout d. frustration
Concept/Applied LO 3 Page: 531 **a**	12.	The Sidewinders football team had been down by 36 points at half-time, but they had made a big comeback in the second half. With less than 30 seconds remaining on the clock they had narrowed the other team's lead to a single-point. All their kicker needed to do was kick a field goal, and they would win the game by 2 points. Unfortunately, the kicker missed the kick, and they lost the game. As he watched the kick go wide, the Sidewinders' coach <u>most</u> likely experienced a sense of a. frustration b. pressure c. conflict d. burnout
Concept/Applied LO 3 Page: 531 Correct = 97% **c**	13.	Which of the following does <u>not</u> qualify as a frustrating event? a. being stuck in traffic b. getting a "B" on an exam when you wanted an "A" c. finishing a term paper hours before you expected to finish it d. finding that your car has not yet been repaired even though you left it hours ago
Critical Thinking LO 3 Page: 531 Correct = 73% **b**	14.	The person who is <u>most</u> likely to experience frustration is one who a. can predict the outcome of an event b. is a perfectionist c. sets goals that are too low d. must decide between two equally attractive alternatives

Concept/Applied LO 3 Page: 531 **b**	15.	Miranda started a small craft business in her home three years ago. Last year she finally moved her business into a small store along her town's main street. Last Saturday, most of her store's stock was destroyed as firefighters fought a fire that had started in the vacant office next to her store. As Miranda walks through her ruined store, she is <u>most</u> likely to experience a sense of a. burnout b. frustration c. pressure d. conflict
Factual LO 4 Page: 532 **c**	16.	In general, the <u>least</u> stressful conflict is the a. avoidance-avoidance conflict b. approach-avoidance conflict c. approach-approach conflict d. double approach-avoidance conflict
Concept/Applied LO 4 Page: 532 Correct = 98% **b**	17.	Two blockbuster movies are opening on the same weekend, and Andrea is having trouble deciding which movie to see first. Andrea is experiencing a. a risk-aversion conflict b. an approach-approach conflict c. an avoidance-avoidance conflict d. an avoidance-approach conflict
Concept/Applied LO 4 Page: 532 **d**	18.	Geena has made it to the final round in a game show. She must now choose between accepting the cash that she has earned to date, or risking the cash on the chance to win a new car. As Geena tries to decide between the two available alternatives, she is facing a. an approach-avoidance conflict b. an avoidance-avoidance conflict c. a frustration-pressure conflict d. an approach-approach conflict
Concept/Applied LO 4 Page: 532 **a**	19.	When you find yourself "caught between a rock and a hard place" you are experiencing a. an avoidance-avoidance conflict b. an approach-avoidance conflict c. an approach-approach conflict d. a double approach-avoidance conflict
Concept/Applied LO 4 Page: 532 Correct = 98% **d**	20.	Your gruesome, beastly jailer walks in and offers you the choice of being whipped or clubbed as your form of punishment for the day. Assuming that neither alternative appeals to you, we could assume that you would experience a. an approach-avoidance conflict b. an approach-approach conflict c. a thrill at being given a choice d. an avoidance-avoidance conflict
Concept/Applied LO 4 Page: 532 Correct = 85% **d**	21.	If you cannot decide whether to submit to back surgery, which you dread, to alleviate your back pain or to continue to live with the pain, which you sometimes find unbearable, you are caught in a. an approach-avoidance conflict b. an approach-approach conflict c. a double approach-avoidance conflict d. an avoidance-avoidance conflict

Concept/Applied LO 4 Page: 532 b	22.	Scott is taking a course in American History and his professor has given all the students in the class a choice between completing an in-class final exam that will count for 60% of their final grade, or writing a 25-page term paper that will count for 60% of their final grade. As Scott considers which of these two options he will choose, he is facing a. a frustration-pressure conflict b. an avoidance-avoidance conflict c. an approach-approach conflict d. an approach-avoidance conflict
Concept/Applied LO 4 Page: 532 c	23.	Melissa has an old car that is desperately in need of expensive repairs. She is trying to decide whether she should spend the $1500 she has in her savings account to repair her old clunker, or whether she should use her savings to buy the used car that her neighbor has for sale. As Melissa considers which of these two options she will select, she is facing a. an approach-approach conflict b. an approach-avoidance conflict c. an avoidance-avoidance conflict d. a frustration-pressure conflict
Concept/Applied LO 4 Page: 532 b	24.	Leonard has a job with a small company where he gets along well with everyone and he has 15 years of seniority. Recently a competitor called to offer him a job that would pay more money, but where he would be starting over, with no seniority. As Leonard tries to decide whether to accept the new job because it offers more money, or turn the job offer down because it would mean giving up his seniority, he is facing a. an approach-approach conflict b. an approach-avoidance conflict c. an avoidance-avoidance conflict d. a frustration-pressure conflict
Concept/Applied LO 4 Page: 532 b	25.	Megan is looking at the ballot form for a city-wide referendum and trying to decide whether or not to support the proposed change. If the referendum passes there will be better services available for all the city residents, but it will also mean that residents will pay increased property taxes. As Megan tries to decide whether to support the proposed referendum, she is facing a. an approach-approach conflict b. an approach-avoidance conflict c. an avoidance-avoidance conflict d. a frustration-pressure conflict
Concept/Applied LO 4 Page: 532 Correct = 96% c	26.	A person who loves to eat but at the same time fears becoming overweight is most likely experiencing a. an approach-approach conflict b. an avoidance-avoidance conflict c. an approach-avoidance conflict d. the fight-or-flight response
Factual LO 4 Page: 532 Correct = 26% b	27.	The most likely initial consequence of an approach-avoidance conflict is a. approach b. vacillation c. avoidance d. withdrawal

Concept/Applied LO 4 Page: 532 **a**	28.	Behavioral vacillation would be <u>most</u> apt to go with which type of conflict? a. approach-avoidance b. approach-approach c. avoidance-avoidance d. frustration
Factual LO 5 Page: 533 Correct = 68% **c**	29.	Holmes and Rahe reasoned that major sources of stress for people come from a. failures b. life events involving loss c. changes in one's life that require readjustment d. only those life changes the person sees as negative
Concept/Applied LO 5 Page: 533 **d**	30.	Dr. Gouin believes that getting a promotion at work or getting married is just as stressful as losing a job or getting a divorce. Dr. Gouin's beliefs are <u>most</u> like those of a. Scheier and Carver b. Miller and DiMatteo c. Friedman and Rosenman d. Holmes and Rahe
Factual LO 5 Page: 533 Correct = 83% **a**	31.	The Social Readjustment Rating Scale was designed specifically to measure a. change b. conflict c. control d. aggression
Critical Thinking LO 5 Page: 533 **c**	32.	Rosemary recently married her high school sweetheart, and they moved into a wonderful new condominium. A week after the move Rosemary was offered a job that she had been hoping she would get. At this point in time, Rosemary can't imagine being any happier. According to Holmes and Rahe, Rosemary is likely to be experiencing a. little or no stress b. an approach-approach conflict c. a high level of stress d. overcompensation
Factual LO 5 Page: 534 Correct = 39% **a**	33.	Current research on change and stress suggests that a. change is not inherently or inevitably stressful b. both positive and negative changes are equally stressful c. too much change of whatever sort automatically makes one more vulnerable to physical and psychological problems d. keeping change to a minimum is an effective way to avoid the harmful effects of stress
Factual LO 5 Page: 534 Correct = 53% **b**	34.	People with higher scores on the Social Readjustment Rating Scale have been found to a. react more negatively to stressful events b. be more vulnerable to physical illness and psychological problems c. have a more external locus of control d. cope more effectively with stress
Factual LO 5 Page: 534 Correct = 47% **b**	35.	The major criticism of the Social Readjustment Rating Scale is that a. it is based on a biased sample b. it does not measure change exclusively c. it contains positive events as well as negative ones d. it focuses exclusively on frustrating events

Factual LO 5 Page: 534 Correct = 97% **d**	36.	Demands or expectations to behave in a certain way define the notion of a. stress b. conflict c. frustration d. pressure
Factual LO 5 Page: 534 **c**	37.	In Weiten's studies, _____ turned out to be more strongly related to measures of mental health than scores on the Social Readjustment Rating Scale were. a. frustration b. conflict c. pressure d. change
Concept/Applied LO 5 Page: 534 **d**	38.	The Flashback football team had been down by 35 points at half-time, but they had made a big comeback in the second half. With less than 15 seconds remaining on the clock they made a touchdown that narrowed the other team's lead to a single point. Their quarterback has decided to try for a two-point conversion in an attempt to win the game by a single point in the dying seconds. As the team lines up for the final play of the game, both the quarterback and the intended receiver are likely to be experiencing a. frustration b. conflict c. burnout d. pressure
Concept/Applied LO 5 Page: 534 **a**	39.	Winona has a 10-page term paper due first thing in the morning, and she still has over half the paper left to write. At the same time her boyfriend is insisting that she come to the concert that evening where he will be performing his first violin solo. She knows that she needs to work on the paper, but she also knows her boyfriend will be disappointed if she doesn't attend the concert. Winona is most likely feeling a. pressure b. frustration c. vacillation d. burnout
Concept/Applied LO 6 Page: 536 **b**	40.	What appears to mediate between a potentially stressful event and the emotional, physiological, and behavioral response to that event? a. the magnitude of the event b. the appraisal of the event c. the frequency of occurrence of the event d. the number of other people who are present
Concept/Applied LO 6 Page: 536 Correct = 41% **a**	41.	Emotions resulting from stressful situations a. vary a great deal but are generally unpleasant b. can be positive or negative but are usually strong c. are pretty standard in form across people d. seem to have no pattern at all
Factual LO 6 Page: 536 Correct = 84% **b**	42.	Stressful events are <u>most</u> likely to lead to a. annoyance, anger, and rage b. apprehension, fear, and anxiety c. dejection, sadness, and grief d. guilt, envy, and disgust

Concept/Applied LO 6 Page: 536 Correct = 52% c	43.	The optimal level of arousal for task performance a. is about the same from one task to another b. increases as the tasks become more complex c. decreases as the tasks become more complex d. relates more to personal makeup than to the task
Concept/Applied LO 6 Page: 536 a	44.	Leigh works as a tax accountant and has to complete complex worksheets for each of her clients. Adriana works in a factory where she performs a fairly simple visual inspection of the finished product. Assuming both Leigh and Adriana experienced a high level of arousal after hearing some distressing news, you should expect that a. Leigh's performance will be impaired more than Adriana's performance b. Adriana's performance will be impaired more than Leigh's performance c. both Leigh and Adriana will show significant impairment in the performance of their respective jobs d. neither Leigh nor Adriana will show any impairment in the performance of their respective jobs
Factual LO 7 Page: 537 Correct = 94% c	45.	The physiological reaction to threat in which the autonomic nervous system mobilizes the organism for action is called a. catharsis b. primary appraisal c. the fight-or-flight response d. resistance
Factual LO 7 Page: 537 Correct = 63% b	46.	Cannon's fight-or-flight reaction is mediated by the a. skeletal nervous system b. sympathetic nervous system c. parasympathetic nervous system d. peripheral nervous system
Factual LO 7 Page: 537 Correct = 98% a	47.	The _____ controls the fight-or-flight response as a physiological reaction to a threat. a. autonomic nervous system b. pyramidal system c. central nervous system d. thalamus
Factual LO 7 Page: 537 Correct = 38% b	48.	The name Hans Selye gave to the body's response to stress is a. the fight-or-flight response b. the general adaptation syndrome c. catharsis d. defensive coping
Factual LO 7 Page: 537 Correct = 42% a	49.	Selye believed that the body's reactions to stressful situations a. are nonspecific – that is, the same to different stressors b. vary as a function of the individual c. are specific to the type of stressor involved d. cannot be generalized across individuals
Factual LO 7 Page: 537 Correct = 42% d	50.	The correct order for the three stages of Selye's general adaptation syndrome is a. primary, secondary, tertiary b. recognition, reaction, evaluation c. alarm, adaptation, recovery d. alarm, resistance, exhaustion

Concept/Applied LO 7 Page: 537 Correct = 85% **b**	51.	You have just come face-to-face with a bear on your walk through the woods. Your body automatically mobilizes itself for action in the _____ stage of the general adaptation syndrome. a. resistance b. alarm c. exhaustion d. coping
Concept/Applied LO 7 Page: 537 **d**	52.	Dustin was driving his car on an icy road when the back end started to skid out of control. His car crossed the center line, and he could see the headlights of rapidly approaching, oncoming traffic. His entire body became energized. His heart rate and respiration increased and he began to perspire profusely. According to Selye's general adaptation syndrome, Dustin was experiencing a. a resistance reaction b. physiological exhaustion c. autonomic rebound d. an alarm reaction
Concept/Applied LO 7 Page: 538 **d**	53.	Clarice was in a meeting with several other employees when her boss started to criticize a proposal Clarice had put together for the marketing department. As he started into his critique, Clarice's heart rate and respiration increased, and she could feel her face and hands become flushed and red. According to Selye's general adaptation syndrome, Clarice was experiencing a. a resistance reaction b. physiological exhaustion c. autonomic rebound d. an alarm reaction
Factual LO 7 Page: 538 Correct = 55% **c**	54.	According to Hans Selye's general adaptation syndrome, the stage in which the body appears to be functioning efficiently, although in actuality arousal may continue to be higher than normal, is called a. alarm b. exhaustion c. resistance d. maintenance
Concept/Applied LO 7 Page: 538 Correct = 64% **a**	55.	The stage of Selye's general adaptation syndrome one enters after the body's unsuccessful first attempt at dealing with the stressor is the a. resistance stage b. alarm stage c. third stage d. sympathetic stage
Concept/Applied LO 7 Page: 538 **a**	56.	Tiana was walking down the street late one evening when a stranger suddenly stepped out of the shadows. Her initial reaction was one of total panic, but then she began to think of all her options. Although her heart was still pounding, she quickly crossed to the other side of the street, and began walking in the opposite direction. According to Selye's general adaptation syndrome, Tiana was probably experiencing a. a resistance reaction b. an alarm reaction c. physiological exhaustion d. autonomic rebound

Concept/Applied LO 7 Page: 538 **b**	57.	Travis was piloting a small private jet. He was making his final approach through heavy fog, and when he finally broke through the fog cover at 150 feet he realized that the runway was 20 yards to his left. For an instant he experienced a sensation of total panic, but he quickly took action. With his heart still pounding he gave the plane full throttle in an attempt to clear the rapidly approaching trees. According to Selye's general adaptation syndrome, as Travis took action he was experiencing a. physiological exhaustion b. a resistance reaction c. an alarm reaction d. autonomic rebound
Factual LO 7 Page: 538 Correct = 81% **d**	58.	The final stage of Hans Selye's general adaptation syndrome during which the organism's resources for fighting stress may be depleted is called a. alarm b. fatigue c. resistance d. exhaustion
Concept/Applied LO 7 Page: 538 **c**	59.	Bryce is an army field surgeon who has been operating on wounded soldiers for the past 24 hours, without a break. It seems as if he will never be able to deal with all the wounded soldiers that are already at the field hospital, and more wounded are arriving every hour. Meanwhile, the sound of heavy artillery is getting closer all the time. At this point, Bryce feels completely worn out. His overall energy reserves are totally depleted, and his body just wants to give up. According to Selye's general adaptation syndrome, Bryce is probably experiencing a. a resistance reaction b. an alarm reaction c. physiological exhaustion d. autonomic rebound
Concept/Applied LO 7 Page: 538 **c**	60.	Brooke had been battling the rising flood waters around her home for more than 72 hours. It seemed that no matter how many sandbags she stacked, it wasn't enough. At this point she just feels that there is nothing else that she can do. Her overall energy reserves are totally depleted, and her body just wants to give up. According to Selye's general adaptation syndrome, Brooke is probably experiencing a. a resistance reaction b. an alarm reaction c. physiological exhaustion d. autonomic rebound
Factual LO 8 Page: 538 **a**	61.	The hormones secreted into the bloodstream during times of stress are a. catecholamines and corticosteroids b. endorphins and serotonin c. catecholamines and endorphins d. endorphins and corticosteroids
Factual LO 8 Page: 538 Correct = 52% **c**	62.	Stress effects appear to be moderated by the _____ activating the _____. a. thalamus; pituitary gland b. pituitary gland; hypothalamus c. hypothalamus; sympathetic nervous system d. cerebellum; autonomic nervous system

Factual LO 8 Page: 538 Correct = 46% **b**	63.	In a stress reaction the pituitary gland releases the hormone ACTH, which stimulates a. the gonads b. the adrenal cortex c. the hypothalamus d. the medulla
Concept/Applied LO 8 Page: 538 **d**	64.	Dionne is trapped in an elevator that is stuck between the third and fourth floors of an office building. As maintenance workers try to restart the elevator it suddenly drops ten feet before becoming stuck once more. As the elevator drops Dionne's sympathetic nervous system is activated. This nervous system activation will cause a. the adrenal cortex to begin to release large amounts of catecholamines b. the adrenal medulla to begin to release corticosteroids c. her amygdala to slow the release of acetylcholine d. the adrenal medulla to begin to release large amounts of catecholamines
Concept/Applied LO 8 Page: 538 **a**	65.	Ivan's car began to slip sideways on the rain-slick road. As his car spun out of control, and into the path of oncoming traffic, his pituitary gland began to secrete adrenocorticotropic hormone (ACTH). This would have stimulated the adrenal glands and caused a. the adrenal cortex to begin to release corticosteroids b. the adrenal medulla to begin to release corticosteroids c. the adrenal cortex to begin to release catecholamines d. his amygdala to slow the release of acetylcholine
Factual LO 8 Page: 538 **d**	66.	Which of the following is <u>not</u> a consequence associated with the release of catecholamines in the body? a. heart rate increases b. visual sensitivity increases c. oxygen consumption increases d. digestive processes speed up
Factual LO 8 Page: 538 Correct = 80% **a**	67.	When the adrenal medulla is stimulated a. large amounts of catecholamines are released into the bloodstream b. the hormone ACTH is secreted c. corticosteroids are absorbed by the adrenal glands d. the parasympathetic nervous system is activated
Factual LO 8 Page: 538 **c**	68.	The two major pathways via which the brain may signal the endocrine system are through the a. parasympathetic and sympathetic systems b. circulatory and muscular systems c. pituitary gland and the autonomic nervous system d. autonomic and skeletal nervous systems
Factual LO 9 Page: 538 Correct = 98% **c**	69.	Active efforts to master, reduce, or tolerate the demands created by stress are called a. aggressing b. resisting c. coping d. defending
Factual LO 9 Page: 538 Correct = 68% **c**	70.	Your author takes the position that coping behavior to stress a. is always adaptive b. is always maladaptive c. may be adaptive or maladaptive d. is not "coping" unless it is adaptive

Factual LO 9 Page: 538 Correct = 71% **b**	71.	According to the original frustration-aggression hypothesis put forth by Dollard and his colleagues a. frustration is always a consequence of aggression b. aggression is always caused by frustration c. frustration causes males to be more aggressive than females d. frustration is only a factor in aggressive behavior for non-human species
Factual LO 9 Page: 539 Correct = 63% **a**	72.	The idea that emotional tension can be released through behavior and that this response may be adaptive is known as a. catharsis b. displacement c. an unconditioned response d. the safety-valve effect
Concept/Applied LO 9 Page: 539 Correct = 80% **b**	73.	A police officer gives you a speeding ticket and you take out your frustration and anger on your roommate. This diversion of anger to a substitute target is known as a. catharsis b. displacement c. reaction formation d. overcompensation
Concept/Applied LO 9 Page: 539 **b**	74.	Juli's father borrowed her car to run some errands. When he returned the car the tail light was broken. Juli was angry, but she didn't say anything to her father. Later, when her son dropped cookie crumbs on the floor, Juli yelled at him and sent him to his room with no supper. Juli's behavior toward her son illustrates the concept of a. overcompensation b. displacement c. self-indulgence d. undoing
Concept/Applied LO 9 Page: 539 **d**	75.	Garret is frustrated and angry when his request for a pay raise is turned down. After work Garret goes to his gym and hits the punching bag for 10 minutes. Garret finds that he feels less tense and wound up after his workout. This change in Garret's mood is consistent with the concept of: a. overcompensation b. undoing c. denial d. catharsis
Concept/Applied LO 9 Page: 540 Correct = 71% **b**	76.	When final exam time rolls around, Murray finds himself eating all the time. This reaction to stress can be referred to as a. an eating disorder b. excessive consummatory behavior c. learned helplessness d. constructive coping
Concept/Applied LO 9 Page: 540 **a**	77.	Francis finished writing her Economics final and was convinced that she had failed the exam and would have to repeat the course. She was so stressed out by the thought of taking the course a second time that she drank eight glasses of wine when she got home. Based on this information, it appears that one method that Francis uses to cope with stress is a. self-indulgence b. overcompensation c. learned helplessness d. undoing

Factual LO 9 Page: 540 **d**	78.	Research conducted by Kimberly Young suggests that internet addiction a. is an extremely rare syndrome that is difficult to study empirically b. is mostly limited to shy males with high I.Q. levels c. is decreasing among older adolescents but increasing among young adults d. may be an attempt to escape real-world problems
Factual LO 10 Page: 540 Correct = 94% **d**	79.	Unconscious reactions for dealing with unpleasant emotions such as anxiety or guilt are referred to as a. constructive coping b. rationalizations c. neurosis d. defense mechanisms
Factual LO 10 Page: 541 Correct = 54% **b**	80.	Defense mechanisms are both conscious and unconscious attempts to a. work through problems b. deceive oneself c. enhance self-insight d. constructively cope with stress
Factual LO 10 Page: 541 Correct = 100% **a**	81.	The defense mechanism of protecting oneself from unpleasant reality by refusing to perceive or face it is a. denial of reality b. undercompensation c. overcompensation d. undoing
Concept/Applied LO 10 Page: 541 **b**	82.	There is one week left in the semester and Andre has put off working on his five term papers until the very last minute. Although it has always taken him three to four days to write a single term paper, Andre is convinced that he can write all five papers in the week that remains. In this instance, Andre may be dealing with stress-induced anxiety using a. overcompensation b. denial of reality c. intellectualization d. self-indulgence
Factual LO 10 Page: 541 Correct = 89% **c**	83.	Rick imagines he is secretly admired by women who all wish he would seduce them. Rick, who is socially inept, is using the defense mechanism of a. denial of reality b. intellectualization c. fantasy d. substitution
Concept/Applied LO 10 Page: 541 **c**	84.	Barbara is majoring in English literature, and she has applied for over 100 scholarships during the last year. However, she hasn't received any of the scholarships because her grades are quite low. When she received the latest letter notifying her that a scholarship had gone to someone else, she imagined how humiliated the committee members would be if she were to get one of her short stories published. In this instance, Barbara appears to be dealing with the stress-induced anxiety of being turned down for another scholarship through a. overcompensation b. intellectualization c. the use of fantasy d. displacement

Concept/Applied
LO 10
Page: 541
b

85. Pete is the lead prosecution attorney in a murder case. So far the case has not been going well for him, and the defense attorneys have presented effective rebuttals for most of the points he has raised. The judge adjourned the case for the weekend, and Pete will have to present his closing arguments first thing Monday morning. While he is trying to write his closing statement he daydreams about a surprise eyewitness to the crime suddenly stepping forward and clinching the case for him. In this example, Pete is <u>most</u> likely experiencing
    a. conflict, and he is using overcompensation to deal with the anxiety the conflict has generated
    b. frustration, and he is using fantasy to deal with the anxiety the frustration has generated
    c. conflict, and he is using undoing to deal with the anxiety the conflict has generated
    d. frustration, and he is using intellectualization to deal with the anxiety the frustration has generated

Critical Thinking
LO 10
Page: 541
c

86. In which of the following cases might the use of a defense mechanism be adaptive?
    a. blaming your coworker for mistakes you have made to save your job
    b. justifying cheating on your taxes by pointing out how little the wealthy pay in taxes
    c. jogging five miles a day as a way to release work-related frustrations
    d. refusing to admit flaws in your character, to maintain your self-esteem

Concept/Applied
LO 10
Page: 542
Correct = 59%
c

87. Constructive coping includes all of the following except
    a. confronting a problem directly
    b. inhibiting emotional reactions to stress
    c. reliance on the use of defense mechanisms
    d. making reasonably realistic appraisals of your coping resources

Factual
LO 11
Page: 543
Correct = 81%
a

88. According to Baumeister, the pressure to perform can elevate self-consciousness, which then disrupts our attention by
    a. diverting attention from the demands of the task
    b. causing us to perform too automatically
    c. creating an approach-avoidance conflict
    d. activating our autonomic nervous system

Factual
LO 11
Page: 543
Correct = 82%
c

89. Baumeister and Steinhilber found evidence that, in the final, decisive game of a series in a professional sport such as baseball
    a. the home team has a definite advantage
    b. neither the home team nor the visiting team has an advantage
    c. the home team is under greater pressure than the visiting team, and its performance may decline
    d. the visiting team is under greater pressure than the home team, and its performance may decline

Concept/Applied
LO 11
Page: 543
a

90. Harry is an excellent basketball player who seldom misses a shot during practice. After yesterday's practice Harry's coach told him that some scouts from a big college would be at today's practice. Based on the research by Baumeister, it is likely that this increase in pressure will make Harry
    a. more self-conscious and will interfere with his performance
    b. less self-conscious and will interfere with his performance
    c. more self-conscious, causing him to play even better
    d. less self-conscious, causing him to play even better

Concept/Applied LO 11 Page: 543 Correct = 81% **b**	91.	Natalia is competing in the deciding game of the State basketball finals. According to the research by Baumeister and Steinhilber, Natalia is much more likely to choke a. if the final game is being held in a different city with none of the usual local fans present b. if the final game is being held in her home town in front of local fans c. if the final game is being televised to a large audience d. if the coach changed the usual starting line just before the game began
Concept/Applied LO 11 Page: 543 **d**	92.	Lindsay is acting in her first amateur theater production. She has been practicing, and she has her lines down perfectly, but she is concerned that she will "freeze up" in front of a real audience. According to the research by Baumeister and Steinhilber, Lindsay is more likely to choke on opening night if a. the audience is filled with people whom Lindsay has never met b. the director recommended a small change the night before the play opened c. the opening performance is being videotaped for a cable television network d. there are lots of Lindsay's friends and members of her family in the audience
Factual LO 11 Page: 544 Correct = 95% **b**	93.	The most accurate statement about burnout is that a. it is typically the precursor to full-blow post-traumatic stress syndrome b. it is most apt to result from long-term or chronic stress c. it results mainly from a few highly traumatic events d. it usually develops in individuals with untreated post-traumatic stress disorder
Concept/Applied LO 11 Page: 544 **c**	94.	Kelsey works as an emergency dispatcher. She thought the job would be exciting, but it has turned out to be more stressful than exciting. She works long hours, and seldom receives any recognition. The only time people seem to notice what she does is when the emergency units are slow in responding. She has become disillusioned with her job, and she often calls in sick. In this case, it is quite likely that Kelsey is experiencing a. posttraumatic stress disorder b. general adaptation syndrome c. burnout d. amotivational syndrome
Concept/Applied LO 11 Page: 544 **b**	95.	Wayne was a highly motivated teacher, who really tried to make a difference in the lives of his students. However, the constant budget cutbacks and the long hours that he puts in have taken their toll. He has become disillusioned with teaching, and he often calls in sick. In this case, it is quite likely that Wayne is experiencing a. amotivational syndrome b. burnout c. posttraumatic stress disorder d. general adaptation syndrome
Factual LO 12 Page: 544 Correct = 96% **d**	96.	Disturbed behavior that occurs after a major stressful event is referred to as a. burnout b. a psychosomatic condition c. hypochondriasis d. posttraumatic stress disorder
Factual LO 12 Page: 544 Correct = 79% **c**	97.	Posttraumatic stress disorder involves a. physical, mental and emotional exhaustion attributable to long-term involvement in emotionally demanding situations b. reactions such as sleeplessness or nightmares immediately following a major stressful event c. disturbed behavior that emerges after a major stressful event is over d. the emergence of schizophrenic symptoms in individuals exposed to chronic stress

Critical Thinking LO 12 Page: 544 **d**	98.	Just over a year ago Charlotte went through a very stressful event. Now she has started having difficulty sleeping and she is startled by any small noise or disturbance. Charlotte is most likely to be diagnosed as having posttraumatic stress disorder (PTSD) if the event that triggered her symptoms was a. the birth of her daughter b. an increase in the number of hours of overtime she was required to work c. driving home during a bad snow storm d. being rescued after a tornado destroyed the office where she worked and killed one of her coworkers
Concept/Applied LO 12 Page: 544 **b**	99.	Four years have passed since the death of Bill's eldest son, and still Bill experiences bouts of depression and anxiety when he thinks about the tragic accident that led to his son's death. This lingering depression and anxiety is characteristic of a. burnout b. posttraumatic stress disorder c. Type A behavior d. amotivational syndrome
Factual LO 12 Page: 545 **b**	100.	Research into posttraumatic stress disorder (PTSD) indicates that _____ of people have suffered from PTSD at some point in their lives. a. less than 1% b. approximately 8% c. nearly 20% d. over 50%
Factual LO 12 Page: 545 **c**	101.	In people who experience posttraumatic stress disorder (PTSD), _____ of the cases are long lasting. a. less than 1% b. approximately 25% c. nearly 60% d. over 80%
Concept/Applied LO 12 Page: 545 **a**	102.	Makayla was trapped in the rubble of her house following an earthquake. Ira was the rescue worker who pulled Makayla from the wreckage. Based on the research conducted by Ursano, you would predict that a. both Makayla and Ira are at risk for developing posttraumatic stress disorder (PTSD), because PTSD can develop in rescue workers or survivors b. only Makayla is at risk for developing posttraumatic stress disorder (PTSD), because the disorder is extremely rare in rescue workers c. neither Makayla nor Ira are at risk for developing posttraumatic stress disorder (PTSD), because the disorder is rare following natural disasters d. only Ira is at risk for developing posttraumatic stress disorder (PTSD), because the disorder is more common in rescue workers than in survivors
Factual LO 13 Page: 546 **c**	103.	Psychosomatic illness refers to a. the unconscious faking of physical illness b. the conscious faking of physical illness c. genuine physical illness caused at least partly by psychological factors d. the misinterpretation of minor changes in physiological functioning as symptoms of serious illness
Factual LO 13 Page: 546 Correct = 69% **b**	104.	Physical ailments without a corresponding organic basis that are caused in part by psychological factors are referred to as a. neurotic conditions b. psychosomatic disorders c. hypochondriacal conditions d. anxiety disorders

Factual LO 13 Page: 546 Correct = 84% **b**	105.	Which of the following is <u>not</u> potentially a psychosomatic disease? a. hypertension b. appendicitis c. migraine headaches d. ulcers
Concept/Applied LO 12 Page: 546 **a**	106.	Lola saw her family doctor last week because she had experienced a number of asthma attacks in the preceding month. Her family doctor told Lola that her asthma was a psychosomatic disease. Lola's doctor was telling her that a. her asthma has an organic basis, but that it was caused in part by psychological factors b. the attacks she was having were entirely self-induced c. the problem was all in her head and she will need to see a psychologist, rather than a doctor, to receive effective treatment d. her asthma will disappear if she is able to reduce her level of stress
Factual LO 13 Page: 546 Correct = 79% **a**	107.	The principle cause of coronary heart disease is a. atherosclerosis b. Alzheimer's disease c. diabetes d. burnout
Factual LO 13 Page: 547 Correct = 80% **d**	108.	A person who is hard-driving, ambitious, competitive, and at risk for having a heart attack is said to have _____ personality. a. a Type B b. an internal c. an external d. a Type A
Factual LO 13 Page: 547 Correct = 92% **c**	109.	Which of the following is <u>not</u> characteristic of Type A individuals? a. They are competitive. b. They feel there's never enough time to get everything done. c. They are easygoing and sociable. d. They are strongly achievement-motivated.
Concept/Applied LO 13 Page: 547 Correct = 74% **d**	110.	Jim always comes to the office early, argues his position aggressively during meetings, and frequently feels frustrated when things don't go his way. Jim's behavior is typical of a person with a a. death wish b. Type II self-punishment pattern c. Type B personality d. Type A personality
Concept/Applied LO 13 Page: 547 **c**	111.	Kyle is extremely ambitious. He has been in his current job for 12 months, and he has told everyone that if he doesn't get a promotion at his next evaluation he will move on. He is always in a hurry, and impatient with coworkers who don't have their work done on time. He spends long hours at work, coming in early and staying late. Kyle would <u>most</u> likely be described as having a. a Type B personality b. antisocial personality disorder c. a Type A personality d. dependent personality disorder

Concept/Applied LO 13 Page: 547 c	112.	Mickey is an impatient, highly competitive individual who is easily provoked into angry confrontations. He is suspicious and distrusting of most of the people he works with. Friedman and Rosenman would probably suggest that Mickey's personality puts him at an increased risk for a. ulcers and stomach disorders b. asthma and other respiratory ailments c. high blood pressure and coronary heart disease d. a number of different types of cancer
Concept/Applied LO 13 Page: 547 Correct = 85% a	113.	Christine is relatively relaxed, patient, easygoing, and amicable. Christine would be classified as having a(n) a. Type B personality b. internal locus of control c. external locus of control d. Type A personality
Concept/Applied LO 13 Page: 547 d	114.	Emily is an excellent student. She puts in long hours on her school work, and often gets the top mark in the class. However, she is always relaxed and seems fairly easy going. She does her school work as it is assigned, and doesn't put herself under pressure by leaving things to the last minute. She is also always willing to take the time to patiently explain difficult material to other students in her classes. Emily would <u>most</u> likely be described as having a. a Type A personality b. prosocial personality disorder c. dependent personality disorder d. a Type B personality
Factual LO 13 Page: 547 d	115.	Which of the following is the <u>most</u> accurate conclusion one can draw about Type A behavior and the risk of coronary heart disease? a. The Type A person is six times more likely to suffer from coronary heart disease than the Type B person. b. As it turns out, there is actually very little connection between stress and coronary heart disease. c. The Type A person is more resistant to coronary heart disease than the Type B person. d. The relationship between the two seems more modest than originally thought, with Type A behavior increasing coronary risk only for some.
Factual LO 13 Page: 548 Correct = 34% c	116.	Which of the following is <u>not</u> one of the explanations that has been suggested to explain the link between Type A behavior and coronary risk? a. Type A individuals exhibit greater physiological reactivity. b. Type A individuals tend to have less social support. c. Type A individuals tend to use defensive coping strategies. d. Type A individuals tend to exhibit unhealthy lifestyles.
Factual LO 14 Page: 548 a	117.	Laboratory experiments with cardiology patients have shown that brief period of mental stress a. can trigger acute symptoms of heart disease, such as myocardial ischemia b. have little, or no, impact on overall cardiac function c. can intensify chromic symptoms of heart disease, such as arteriosclerosis d. can trigger emotional responses such as depression and feelings of despair
Factual LO 14 Page: 548 c	118.	Recent research evidence from studies which have investigated the link between depression and heart disease suggests that a. the stress of living with heart disease may cause the onset of depression b. depression and heart disease are not correlated with each other c. the emotional dysfunction of depression may cause heart disease d. depression and heart disease are both caused by the negative effects of smoking

Concept/Applied LO 14 Page: 548 **b**	119.	Rory experienced a massive heart attack, after which he enrolled in a stress management training course. Based on the research reported by Blumental, once Rory has completed the course, he should find that his likelihood of a. developing a depressive disorder will be reduced b. having a second heart attack will be reduced c. having a second heart attack will actually increase d. developing a depressive disorder will actually increase
Factual LO 15 Page: 549 Correct = 92% **a**	120.	Stress and health research suggests that a. stress may relate to the incidence of physical illness in general b. stress effects influence only specific illnesses c. stress relates to physical illness only in predisposed individuals d. stress is very specific in its effects on health
Factual LO 15 Page: 549 **b**	121.	The body's defensive reaction to invasion by bacteria, viral agents, and other foreign substances is referred to as the a. general adaptation syndrome b. immune response c. disease coping response d. body's stress reaction
Factual LO 15 Page: 549 **c**	122.	Studies of the immune system in humans have found that stress a. can lead to increased levels of immune activity b. has very little effect on immune activity c. can lead to decreased levels of immune activity d. can lead to the destruction of lymphocytes
Factual LO 15 Page: 549 Correct = 51% **d**	123.	Studies of the immune system in animals have found that stressors such as crowding a. can lead to increased levels of immune system activity b. can activate the release of aggressive pheromones c. can increase levels of harmful blood lymphocytes d. can reduce various aspects of lymphocyte reactivity
Concept/Applied LO 15 Page: 550 **a**	124.	A number of students often develop colds and other minor illnesses during final exam week. Based on the research into the physical responses to stress, this may happen because the stress of final exams a. raises the level of lymphocytes in the students' blood b. lowers the level of cortisol in the students' blood c. raises the level of cholesterol in the students' blood d. lowers the level of lymphocytes in the students' blood
Critical Thinking LO 15 Page: 550 **b**	125.	Daniel goes to his doctor for a blood test. Two weeks later he returns for a follow-up blood test, and the doctor notes that Daniel's lymphocyte count has increased since his earlier visit. Based on the research into the physical responses to stress, you might conclude that Daniel a. is more likely to develop a physical illness within the next two weeks b. is experiencing more stress at the time of the second blood test c. is experiencing less stress at the time of the second blood test d. has a phobic reaction to medical testing, causing him to experience severe stress
Concept/Applied LO 16 Page: 550 Correct = 67% **b**	126.	In the Featured Study on stress and the common cold, results revealed that stress had a. a dramatic effect on the development of colds b. a moderate effect on the development of colds c. no effect on the development of colds d. more of an effect on women developing colds than on men

Factual LO 16 Page: 550 **a**	127.	The Featured Study by Cohen and his colleagues showed that a. psychological stress can increase people's susceptibility to infectious disease b. when all possible confounding variables are controlled for, there is no longer any association between stress and vulnerability to infection c. the stress-illness association found in other studies is probably the result of an increased frequency of health-impairing habits in stressed subjects d. psychological stress only increases susceptibility to infectious disease in people with Type A personalities
Concept/Applied LO 16 Page: 550 Correct = 91% **c**	128.	The Featured Study by Cohen and his colleagues showed that high-stress subjects had a higher incidence of colds than low-stress subjects. This finding indicates that illness and levels of stress are a. uncorrelated b. negatively correlated c. positively correlated d. multifactorial variables
Factual LO 16 Page: 550 Correct = 95% **d**	129.	In the Featured Study on stress and the common cold, Cohen and his colleagues found that, in the subsample of subjects without an infectious roommate a. there was no difference in the incidence of colds between high-stress and low-stress subjects b. low-stress subjects were more likely to develop colds than high-stress subjects c. the colds developed by low-stress subjects were more severe than the colds in high-stress subjects d. high-stress subjects were more likely to develop colds than low-stress subjects
Factual LO 16 Page: 551 **b**	130.	One of the things that made the Featured Study by Cohen and his colleagues outstanding was a. the use of four separate control groups within the main part of the study b. the enormous effort that the researchers went through to control for possible confounding variables c. the fact that the subjects were followed for two years to determine the long-term impact of their exposure to the stressor d. the fact that only 10% of the subjects developed colds after exposure to a respiratory virus
Factual LO 17 Page: 552 Correct = 93% **b**	131.	Having someone to rely on, provide you with emotional support, and help you preserve your health constitutes a. therapy b. social support c. optimism d. locus of control
Factual LO 17 Page: 552 **a**	132.	Which of the following statements regarding the connection between social support and wellness is true? a. Social support can serve as a buffer in times of high stress. b. Social support typically has negative effects in the absence of stress. c. Social support is only a buffer for people with stress-related illnesses. d. Social support provides more benefits for the elderly.
Concept/Applied LO 18 Page: 552 **a**	133.	Lu Ann exhibits effective problem-focused coping and seeks the help of others when necessary. Her behavior is consistent with someone who is a(n) a. optimist b. Type B personality c. Type A personality d. pessimist

Factual LO 18 Page: 553 **c**	134.	One personality characteristic correlated with good physical health is a. agreeableness b. openness c. conscientiousness d. extraversion
Critical Thinking LO 18 Page: 553 Correct = 77% **b**	135.	Which of the persons described is, on the average, least likely to become ill? a. a person with a Type A personality b. a person with an optimistic personality trait c. a person with high autonomic reactivity d. unknown, as research bearing on relative illness rates is not available
Concept/Applied LO 18 Page: 553 Correct = 67% **c**	136.	The physiological factor hypothesized to mediate one's response to stress is a. neurotransmitter nonuniformity b. hormonal imbalance c. autonomic reactivity d. diet
Factual LO 18 Page: 553 **d**	137.	Individual differences in cardiovascular reactivity a. typically do not emerge until adulthood b. are acquired through classical conditioning c. have not been linked to the occurrence of stress-related illnesses d. probably contribute to susceptibility to heart disease
Factual LO 19 Page: 554 Correct = 99% **a**	138.	Which of the following has been shown to increase the risk of such chronic diseases as lung cancer, emphysema, and stroke? a. smoking b. poor nutrition c. lack of exercise d. obesity
Factual LO 19 Page: 554 **b**	139.	Long-term success rates for those who quit smoking are about _____ percent. a. 15 b. 25 c. 50 d. 75
Factual LO 19 Page: 555 **c**	140.	Research suggests that vulnerability to cardiovascular diseases may be influenced by diet. In particular, low-fiber diets may increase the likelihood of _____, and low consumption of fruit and vegetables may be associated with vulnerability to _____. a. stroke; coronary disease b. peptic ulcers; stroke c. coronary disease; stroke d. coronary disease; peptic ulcers
Concept/Applied LO 19 Page: 555 **c**	141.	Belinda loves to eat cheese omelets or quiche, and she often eats rich, buttery desserts. When she consumes these high-fat, high-cholesterol foods, Belinda is increasing her risk for a. high blood pressure and strokes b. emphysema and other respiratory diseases c. heart disease and some forms of cancer d. gallstones and peptic ulcers

Factual LO 19 Page: 555 Correct = 87% **a**	142.	Alice maintains a diet high in serum cholesterol, eating an abundance of eggs, cheese, butter, and shellfish. Alice may well be increasing her risk of a. heart disease b. emphysema c. arthritis d. hypertension
Factual LO 19 Page: 555 Correct = 99% **d**	143.	Which of the following is <u>not</u> among the advantages of regular exercise? a. reduced cancer risk b. enhanced cardiovascular fitness c. lowered physiological reactivity to stress d. reduced risk of HIV infection
Concept/Applied LO 19 Page: 555 Correct = 48% **b**	144.	Which one of the following is <u>not</u> an effect associated with recreational drug use? a. increased risk for cardiovascular disease b. increased risk for sexual impotence c. increased gastrointestinal problems d. increased risk for neurological disorders
Concept/Applied LO 20 Page: 556 Correct = 95% **b**	145.	Contracting the AIDS virus involves exchange of infected body fluids. Which of the following has <u>not</u> been suggested as a means for reducing such risk? a. use of condoms b. anal intercourse c. reducing the number of partners d. abstinence
Factual LO 20 Page: 556 **d**	146.	In heterosexual relationships a. neither partner is at risk for being infected by the AIDS virus b. the AIDS virus will only be transmitted if one of the partners shows telltale signs of HIV infection c. female-to-male transmission of the AIDS virus is most prevalent d. male-to-female transmission of the AIDS virus is most prevalent
Factual LO 20 Page: 556 **c**	147.	Which of the following statements is <u>true</u>? a. Due to recent efforts to educate the public, misconceptions about AIDS have all but disappeared. b. Many people naively underestimate the risk of contracting the HIV virus through casual contact with infected individuals. c. Many highly sexually active heterosexuals underestimate their risk for HIV infection. d. Taking high doses of immunosuppressants can successfully treat HIV infections and prevent full-blown AIDS from developing.
Concept/Applied LO 21 Page: 557 Correct = 67% **a**	148.	Sonja used to work out five days a week when she was in her late teens. In her twenties she worked out three days a week. Now she is in her forties and she only seems to work out when she has the time. Sonja's pattern of behavior illustrates the idea that a. many health-impairing habits creep up on us b. many health-impairing habits involve activities that are quite pleasant at the time c. the risks associated with health-impairing habits tend to lie in the distant future d. people often underestimate the risks associated with their own health-impairing behaviors

Concept/Applied 149. Sylvester used to keep track of his calorie consumption and fat grams on a daily
LO 21   basis when he was in his early twenties. When he was in his thirties he still counted
Page: 557   calories during the week, but he tended to pay less attention to what he ate on
a   weekends. Now that he is in his forties, Sylvester no longer keeps track of the
                     number of calories or fat grams in the foods that he eats. Sylvester's pattern of
                     behavior illustrates
                     a. the way in which many health-impairing habits creep up on people
                     b. the fact that the risks associated with health-impairing behaviors tend to lie in
                        the distant future
                     c. the fact that the risks associated with health-impairing behaviors are often
                        overstated in the media
                     d. that men are more likely than women to develop health-impairing habits

Concept/Applied 150. Martin knows that excessive exposure to the sun can increase a person's risk of skin
LO 21   cancer and cataracts. However, he can't resist getting out and enjoying a sunny day,
Page: 557   and putting on sun block seems to him to be a major inconvenience. Martin's current
Correct = 65%   pattern of behavior illustrates the idea that
b   a. many health-impairing habits creep up on us
                     b. the risks associated with health-impairing habits tend to lie in the distant future
                     c. people tend to rationalize high-risk behaviors by pointing out healthy habits that
                        offset their unhealthy habits
                     d. people often overestimate the risks associated with their own health-impairing
                        behaviors

Concept/Applied 151. Luigi knows that the surgeon general has determined that smoking increases the risk
LO 21   of various types of cancers, however he is sure he won't develop cancer. Luigi's
Page: 557   pattern of behavior illustrates the idea that
c   a. many health-impairing habits creep up on us
                     b. people tend to rationalize high-risk behaviors by pointing out healthy habits that
                        offset their unhealthy habits
                     c. people often underestimate the risks associated with their own health-impairing
                        behaviors
                     d. people believe the risks associated with health-impairing habits are overstated
                        by media sources

Concept/Applied 152. Beryl has dated ten different men in the past two years, and with each of them she
LO 21   often had unprotected sex. Even though she has read numerous articles about the
Page: 557   dangers of unprotected sexual intercourse, Beryl is not concerned because she has
a   convinced herself that she won't contract the AIDS virus. Beryl's behavior
                     illustrates the idea that
                     a. many people underestimate the risks associated with their own health-impairing
                        behaviors
                     b. many people compensate for health-impairing behaviors by engaging in
                        offsetting low-risk behaviors
                     c. the risks associated with many health-impairing behaviors tend to be overstated
                        by the media
                     d. women are more likely than men to engage in health-impairing habits

Factual   153. One of the largest problems associated with illness confronted by the medical
LO 22   profession is the
Page: 558   a. delay in receiving treatment by persons who need it
Correct = 76%   b. increase in the use of homeopathic intervention
a   c. lack of adequate training in areas of specialties
                     d. overuse of emergency room facilities by persons who do not need it

Factual LO 22 Page: 558 Correct = 97% **a**	154.	People who are _____ tend to report more symptoms of illness. a. high in anxiety b. high in self-esteem c. relatively inattentive to bodily sensations d. high in hardiness
Critical Thinking LO 22 Page: 558 Correct = 92% **c**	155.	Steve has a headache and some muscle stiffness, but he shrugs these symptoms off as a minor inconvenience; Micah has a headache and some muscle stiffness and is so concerned he rushes himself to the urgent care center of the local medical center. If both these individuals had their anxiety and self-esteem levels assessed it is likely that, compared to Micah, Steve would score a. higher in anxiety and self-esteem b. lower in anxiety and self-esteem c. lower in anxiety and higher in self-esteem d. higher in anxiety and lower in self-esteem
Factual LO 23 Page: 558 **d**	156.	Which of the following is <u>least</u> likely to be a barrier to effective provider-patient communication? a. the health care provider's use of technical terminology b. patient evasiveness about real health concerns c. time constraints on the length of the provider-patient interaction d. consulting a health care provider who is not the same-sex as the patient
Factual LO 24 Page: 558 Correct = 73% **b**	157.	Noncompliance with medical advice occurs approximately a. 5 to 10 percent of the time b. 30 to 60 percent of the time c. 75 percent of the time d. 80 to 90 percent of the time
Factual LO 24 Page: 558 Correct = 61% **d**	158.	Which of the following is <u>not</u> typically a reason for noncompliance with medical advice? a. having a negative attitude for physicians b. failing to understand advice or instructions c. the degree of difficulty associated with following advice or instructions d. the cost of the medical treatment program
Factual LO 24 Page: 558 **c**	159.	In which of the following situations are people <u>most</u> likely to follow the instructions they receive from health care professionals? a. when the instructions are complex and include technical medical terms b. when they do not fully understand the instructions but still feel the need to do something c. when they like, respect and understand the health care professional d. when the medication or treatment program is expensive
Concept/Applied LO 25 Page: 559 Correct = 91% **d**	160.	The fact that stress lies in the eye of the beholder illustrates the theme of a. multifactorial causation b. empiricism c. psychology in a sociohistorical context d. the subjectivity of experience
Concept/Applied LO 25 Page: 559 Correct = 93% **a**	161.	The number of variables that are involved in the experience of stress illustrates the theme of a. multifactorial causation b. empiricism c. psychology in a sociohistorical context d. the subjectivity of experience

Concept/Applied LO 25 Page: 559 Correct = 89% **b**	162.	Mary and John are teaming up to make an important sales presentation to 15 executives from a Fortune 500 company. Mary finds the challenge exhilarating, but John is a nervous wreck over the presentation. Their differing reactions illustrate which of your text's unifying themes? a. Psychology is empirical. b. Our experience of the world is highly subjective. c. Psychology is theoretically diverse. d. Behavior is determined by multiple causes.
Concept/Applied LO 25 Page: 559 Correct = 69% **c**	163.	Your text emphasizes that one's physical health and illness is influenced by a complex array of psychological, biological, and social factors. This reality illustrates which of your text's unifying themes? a. Psychology is theoretically diverse. b. Psychology evolves in a sociohistorical context. c. Behavior is determined by multiple causes. d. Our experience of the world is highly subjective.
Concept/Applied LO 26 Page: 560 Correct = 54% **a**	164.	Which of the following strategies for dealing with stress is positively correlated with self-esteem and negatively correlated with anxiety? a. active coping b. turning to religion c. mental disengagement d. venting of emotions
Factual LO 26 Page: 561 Correct = 53% **c**	165.	The therapeutic technique that focuses on altering a client's patterns of irrational thinking to reduce maladaptive emotions and behavior is a. self-monitoring therapy b. constructive coping therapy c. rational-emotive therapy d. behavioral therapy
Concept/Applied LO 26 Page: 561 Correct = 74% **b**	166.	When you tell yourself that you will never be happy again now that your significant other has ended the relationship, you are engaging in what Albert Ellis calls a. catharsis b. catastrophic thinking c. calamitous thinking d. primary appraisal
Factual LO 26 Page: 561 **c**	167.	Catastrophic thinking is characterized as involving a. personality disordered type of thinking b. thinking associated with neuroticism c. exaggeration of the magnitude of one's problems d. focusing on major stressors and ignoring the impact of minor frustrations
Concept/Applied LO 26 Page: 561 **c**	168.	Valerie is doing homework for her statistics class. When she checks the answer she has just calculated for the problem she has been working on, she finds it is incorrect. She is frustrated, and tells her roommate: "I don't know why I'm even trying, I'll never catch on in this course. I should just give up now." According to Albert Ellis, Valerie's statements reflect a. defensive coping b. mental disengagement c. catastrophic thinking d. reality-based coping

Factual LO 26 Page: 561 d	169.	According to Albert Ellis, the key to making realistic appraisals of stress is to a. ignore your feelings b. focus on what you should be doing c. avoid examining your self-talk too closely d. dispute irrational assumptions
Factual LO 27 Page: 562 Correct = 80% c	170.	Finding humor in a stressful situation a. is a counterproductive way of reducing stress b. ignores the reality of the situation and makes it difficult to combat stress c. can help to reduce stress by discharging pent-up emotions d. is an irrational reaction to a serious situation that requires a rational response
Factual LO 27 Page: 562 Correct = 82% b	171.	Humor a. is an example of counterproductive coping b. can relieve stress in normal people c. is used as a defense mechanism by neurotics when dealing with stress d. typically follows catastrophic thinking
Concept/Applied LO 27 Page: 562 a	172.	Sherman's house was almost completely destroyed by fire last week. As he walked through the charred remains with the insurance adjuster, Sherman joked and said: "It's too bad that the only thing that wasn't destroyed is that ugly painting that my brother-in-law gave me for my birthday." In this stressful situation, Sherman's joking attitude a. can help to redefine the situation in a less threatening way b. is an example of overcompensation and intellectualization c. is a counterproductive way of dealing with stress d. will likely cause him to experience stress-rebound in the future
Factual LO 27 Page: 562 Correct = 63% a	173.	Psychological inhibition of anger and other emotions has been linked to a. an increase in health problems b. successful coping with stress-related events c. Type A personalities d. hardy personalities
Factual LO 27 Page: 562 Correct = 95% d	174.	James Pennebaker and his colleagues have shown that a. talking or writing about traumatic events increases overall stress levels b. talking about stress events has beneficial effects, but writing about them has no impact c. psychological inhibition can be an effective coping strategy for most people d. talking or writing about traumatic events can have beneficial effects
Factual LO 27 Page: 562 b	175.	Research suggests that efforts to actively suppress emotions result in _____ automatic arousal and _____ immune function. a. decreased; increased b. increased; decreased c. increased; increased d. decreased; decreased
Factual LO 28 Page: 562 Correct = 84% d	176.	Herbert Benson has demonstrated that if you settle yourself comfortably in a distraction-free environment, focus your attention on a constant stimulus, and adopt a passive attitude, you may well experience what he called a. a hypnotic trance b. an altered state of consciousness c. psychological disinhibition d. the relaxation response

Factual LO 28 Page: 562 Correct = 81% **a**	177.	Herbert Benson devised a simple procedure, called the relaxation response, that can have beneficial health effects. To experience the full benefits, the procedure should be practiced a. on a daily basis b. whenever a person has to deal with a major stressor c. for a minimum of 50 minutes a day, three days per week d. only when traditional medical treatments produce no improvement
Factual LO 28 Page: 562 Correct = 76% **b**	178.	All of the following were cited in the textbook as factors which promote relaxation except for a. developing a passive attitude b. drinking a small amount of alcohol c. being in a comfortable position d. focusing on a constant stimulus
Factual LO 28 Page: 563 **c**	179.	Which of the following is the <u>best</u> piece of advice regarding exercise and its ability to reduce your vulnerability to stress? a. Select a strenuous activity that will stretch you to the limit of your ability. b. Become competitive in a team sport. c. Gradually increase your participation in an enjoyable activity. d. Play to win in competitive activities.
Critical Thinking LO 29 Page: 564 **d**	180.	Imagine that a researcher publishes the results from a study, and the results indicate that there is a statistically significant association between sleep deprivation and coronary disease. This result would mean that a. sleep deprivation causes coronary disease b. coronary disease causes sleep deprivation c. the effect of sleep deprivation on coronary disease is larger than the effect of any other factor d. the findings are not likely to be due to chance fluctuations
Critical Thinking LO 29 Page: 564 **a**	181.	In one study of sodium intake and cardiovascular disease, which used a sample of over 14,000 participants, the researchers found a statistically significant association between high sodium intake and the prevalence of hypertension among normal-weight subjects. The prevalence of hypertension in the group with the lowest sodium intake was 19.1%; the prevalence of hypertension in the group with the highest sodium intake was 21.8%. This data suggests that a. even though the finding was statistically significant, it may not have much practical importance b. the finding has both practical and statistical significance, and should be reviewed in more detail c. the finding has neither practical nor statistical significance, and should be ignored d. one of the main causes of hypertension is a high intake of sodium
Factual LO 29 Page: 564 **d**	182.	Your text outlines a number of ways in which people can think more systematically about health decisions. Which of the following is <u>not</u> one of the suggestions outlined in your text? a. Look for conflicting information. b. Assess the tradeoffs between potential risks and benefits. c. Consider the pros and cons of each alternative. d. Delay making a final decision until you have the opportunity to consult with professionals in the field.

Critical Thinking
LO 29
Page: 564
a

183. A friend shows you an article in the newspaper which indicates a researcher found the prevalence of a specific health disorder increased by 70% in individuals who consumed calcium-enhanced milk products. After reading this article, your friend has decided to stop purchasing any products that are calcium-enhanced. Based on the information provided in the critical thinking application at the end of the chapter, you should tell your friend that
   a. the reported percentage increase may not be important if the overall base rate of the health disorder is quite low
   b. the reported percentage increase may not be important if the overall base rate of the health disorder is quite high
   c. the reported percentage increase probably excludes a number of factors, and the risk may actually be greater than 70%
   d. it is only necessary to cut out milk products, but there is no need to cut out other products which might also contain calcium

Integrative
Correct = 82%
c

184. Janet's husband is dying of cancer, but Janet refuses to acknowledge this obvious reality. Janet is coping with _____ by engaging in _____.
   a. pressure; overcompensation
   b. pressure; denial
   c. frustration; denial
   d. frustration; fantasy

Integrative
Correct = 76%
b

185. Jim is on the brink of flunking out of school. Instead of increasing his studying, he spends his time daydreaming about how he'll win the state lottery so he won't need a degree. Jim is experiencing _____ and is engaging in _____.
   a. conflict; denial
   b. frustration; fantasy
   c. conflict; overcompensation
   d. frustration; acting out

Study Guide
LO 2
Page: 531
d

186. Which of the following statements is incorrect?
   a. stress is a subjective experience
   b. the effects of stress are cumulative
   c. minor hassles may prove more stressful than major ones
   d. one should seek to avoid all stress

Study Guide
LO 4
Page: 532
d

187. You've been invited to dinner at a nice restaurant on the final night of a TV mini-series you've been watching and thus find yourself confronted with
   a. pressure
   b. frustration
   c. an approach-avoidance conflict
   d. an approach-approach conflict

Study Guide
LO 5
Page: 534
a

188. The week of final exams subjects most students to what kind of stress?
   a. pressure
   b. change
   c. frustration
   d. conflict

Study Guide
LO 6
Page: 536
c

189. According to optimal-arousal theories, which of the following situations would be least affected by a high optimal-arousal level?
   a. taking a psychology exam
   b. typing a term paper
   c. buttoning a shirt
   d. learning to drive a car

Study Guide LO 8 Page: 538 a	190.	Which of the following organs is involved in both of the body's two major stress pathways? a. the adrenal gland b. the sympathetic nervous system c. the pituitary gland d. the pineal gland
Study Guide LO 9 Page: 538 b	191.	Aggression is frequently triggered by a. helplessness b. frustration c. loneliness d. change
Study Guide LO 12 Page: 545 a	192.	Rape and seeing someone die are two of the principal causes of a. post-traumatic stress disorder b. burnout c. learned helplessness d. coronary heart disorder
Study Guide LO 13 Page: 546 a	193.	Smoking is to lung cancer as Type A behavior is to a. coronary disease b. AIDS c. defensive coping d. mental disorders
Study Guide LO 15 Page: 549 b	194.	One of the key links between stress and physical illness may be that the body's response to stress a. increases the optimal-arousal level b. suppresses the immune system c. decreases the optimal-arousal level d. suppresses the adrenal gland
Study Guide LO 26 Page: 561 c	195.	A major idea behind Rational-Emotive Therapy is that stress is caused by a. conflict b. frustration c. catastrophic thinking d. pressure
Online Quiz LO 3 Page: 531 b	196.	Being prevented from reaching a goal will cause most individuals to experience a. conflict b. frustration c. pressure d. vacillation
Online Quiz LO 4 Page: 532 a	197.	The pursuit of a goal that has both attractive and unattractive features defines a. an approach-avoidance conflict b. a double-blind conflict c. an approach-approach conflict d. an avoidance-avoidance conflict
Online Quiz LO 5 Page: 534 b	198.	The text defines _____ as expectations and demands that one behave in a certain way. a. stress b. pressure c. conflict d. frustration

Online Quiz LO 6 Page: 536 **d**	199.	As a task becomes more complex, the optimal level of arousal to perform the task best a. increases b. stays the same c. first decreases and then increases d. decreases
Online Quiz LO 8 Page: 538 **b**	200.	The hypothalamus communicates with the endocrine system by way of the a. sebaceous gland b. pituitary gland c. thyroid gland d. pancreas
Online Quiz LO 10 Page: 541 **d**	201.	Which of the following is least accurate in regard to defense mechanisms? a. They are aimed at protecting one from unwelcomed emotions. b. They use self-deception. c. They are normal in that everyone uses them. d. They invariably reduce coping effectiveness.
Online Quiz LO 13 Page: 547 **b**	202.	The component of Type A personality associated with coronary heart disease appears to be a. indecisiveness b. cynical hostility c. time urgency d. ambitiousness
Online Quiz LO 18 Page: 553 **b**	203.	Having a general feeling that "things" will be okay and problems will eventually work out is known as a. internal control b. optimism c. learned helplessness d. hardiness
Online Quiz LO 19 Page: 555 **c**	204.	Which of the following health-impairing habits can, under certain circumstances, kill you directly and immediately? a. poor eating habits b. smoking c. taking drugs d. lack of exercise
Online Quiz LO 26 Page: 561 **b**	205.	Unrealistically pessimistic appraisals of stress that exaggerate the magnitude of one's problems are referred to as a. neuroticism b. catastrophic thinking c. personality dysfunction d. irrational perception

ESSAY QUESTIONS

1. Why do you think posttraumatic stress disorder is more prevalent in women than in men? Is it due to different learning histories, or are the sexes genetically different in the ability to deal with stressors?

   Better answers might be ones in which students refer to material from the Application on gender differences in Chapter 11, and especially the material on gender-role socialization. They might also acknowledge some differences in other types of experiences that males and females face in our society. For instance, is it more dangerous for women to move about in public than it is for men?

2. Many people believe that suicide represents the ultimate failure to cope with life's stresses. Others feel that suicide is, itself, a coping response. What do you think? Is one type of stress more likely to lead to suicide than others?

   Students should refer to the Application on coping with stress and attempt to establish whether suicide fits the bill as an example of constructive coping. To most, the answer will be "obviously not." So the best answers will be those that go further in a creative and insightful way to explore possible arguments for suicide as a coping response, and/or those that thoughtfully explore the notion that suicide is the ultimate failure to cope. Answers should demonstrate understanding of the four types of stress, and provide well-reasoned arguments for one or more types being more likely (or not) to lead to suicide.

3. Describe several recent occasions when you've experienced stress. For each case identify the type(s) of stress you experienced and whatever emotional, physiological, and/or behavioral responses to stress you made.

   Students should accurately classify their examples according to the major types (frustration, conflict, change, and pressure). In better answers, students will recognize that some of their examples contain elements of more than one type.

   Regarding responses to their examples of stress, patterns of responses described should be somewhat different for each example, and each response pattern should include elements from each of the response domains (emotional, physiological, and behavioral).

4. Do you have any favorite or habitual techniques for coping with stress? Explain how your techniques are examples of the categories of coping from this chapter's Application (reappraisal, humor, emotional release, relaxation, lessening physiological vulnerability). Do you use any methods that don't seem to fit into any of these categories?

   Ideally students will provide an example from each, or several, of the coping categories, and their descriptions will reflect accurate understanding of the categories. Some examples should be identified as containing elements of more than one category. For example, a student might describe talking with a friend as a way of coping with stress. This method could be seen as a vehicle for emotional release, and it could also lead to reappraisal. Quite likely the mechanism of humor enters into this technique as well.

   In order to come up with a technique that doesn't fit any of the categories, a student will probably need to be quite creative. Often when students claim that a particular technique doesn't fit into one of the categories, it will be because they don't thoroughly understand the categories.

This page intentionally left blank.

Chapter Fourteen
Psychological Disorders

LEARNING OBJECTIVES

1. Describe and evaluate the medical model of abnormal behavior.
2. Explain the most commonly used criteria of abnormality.
3. List three stereotypes of people with psychological disorders.
4. Summarize the Featured Study on the admission of pseudopatients to mental hospitals.
5. List the five diagnostic axes of DSM-IV.
6. Discuss estimates of the prevalence of psychological disorders.
7. List four types of anxiety disorders and describe the symptoms associated with each.
8. Discuss the contribution of biological, cognitive, and personality factors, conditioning, and stress to the etiology of anxiety disorders.
9. Compare and contrast the three somatoform disorders and discuss their etiology.
10. Describe three dissociative disorders and discuss their etiology.
11. Describe the two major mood disorders.
12. Explain how genetic and neurochemical factors may be related to the development of mood disorders.
13. Explain how cognitive factors, interpersonal factors, and stress may be related to the development of mood disorders.
14. Describe the general characteristics (symptoms) of schizophrenia.
15. Describe two classification systems for schizophrenic subtypes, and discuss the course of schizophrenia.
16. Explain how genetic vulnerability, neurochemical factors, and structural abnormalities in the brain may contribute to the etiology of schizophrenia.
17. Summarize evidence on how neurodevelopmental processes, family dynamics and stress may be related to the development of schizophrenia.
18. Discuss the nature of personality disorders and describe the three broad clusters of such disorders.
19. Describe the antisocial personality disorder and discuss its etiology.
20. Explain the legal concept of insanity and discuss the grounds for involuntary commitment.
21. Discuss the evidence on three issues related to culture and pathology.
22. Explain how this chapter highlighted four of the text's organizing themes.
23. Describe the symptoms and medical complications of anorexia nervosa and bulimia nervosa.
24. Explain how genetic factors, personality, and culture may contribute to eating disorders.
25. Explain how family dynamics and disturbed thinking may contribute to eating disorders.
26. Discuss how mental heuristics can distort estimates of cumulative and conjunctive probabilities.

MULTIPLE-CHOICE QUESTIONS

Factual
LO 1
Page: 570
Correct = 47%
c

1. According to the medical model
   a. all mental illnesses are caused by biological factors
   b. all mental illnesses can be treated using drugs
   c. abnormal behavior can be thought of as a disease
   d. all physical illnesses have a psychological component

Factual
LO 1
Page: 570
c

2. Which of the following statements is true?
   a. Once insanity was recognized as an illness, inhumane treatment of the insane was eliminated.
   b. Scientists now know the cause of every mental illness, and the appropriate treatment.
   c. With the rise of the medical model came gradual progress toward more humane care and scientific investigation of mental disorders.
   d. All mental illnesses can be treated successfully using drug therapy.

Concept/Applied
LO 1
Page: 570
Correct = 68%
c

3. The terms "mental illness" and "psychopathology" are most closely associated with which model of abnormal behavior?
   a. the learning model
   b. the humanistic model
   c. the medical model
   d. the psychodynamic model

Factual
LO 1
Page: 570
b

4. The concept that abnormal behavior is the result of a disease goes with the
   a. humanistic model
   b. medical model
   c. behavioral model
   d. psychological model

Critical Thinking
LO 1
Page: 570
a

5. Dr. Cummings believes that psychological disorders can be diagnosed, treated, and possibly cured, just like physical illnesses. Dr. Cummings' views reflect the point of view suggested by
   a. the medical model of abnormal behavior
   b. the behavioral model of abnormal behavior
   c. the deviance model of abnormal behavior
   d. the psychodynamic model of abnormal behavior

Factual
LO 1
Page: 570
Correct = 71%
d

6. A major criticism of the medical model by Thomas Szasz is that
   a. no evidence exists to support the efficiency of the medical model's treatment approaches
   b. the model is not well understood by its practitioners
   c. uniformity of behavior patterns cannot be established from the medical model viewpoint
   d. most abnormal behavior reflects a moral judgment about what is socially acceptable or unacceptable behavior

Critical Thinking
LO 1
Page: 570
d

7. Diagnosis is to etiology as
   a. where is to when
   b. when is to where
   c. why is to what
   d. what is to why

Factual LO 1 Page: 570 Correct = 71% **a**	8.	The apparent causation and developmental history of an illness is referred to as its a. etiology b. epidemiology c. diagnosis d. prognosis
Factual LO 1 Page: 570 Correct = 65% **b**	9.	Etiology refers to the a. projected course of a condition b. apparent cause of a condition c. study of mental illness d. collection of a group of symptoms
Concept/Applied LO 1 Page: 570 **c**	10.	Dr. Underhill is reviewing the records from a patient who has just been referred for treatment. He is carefully considering the symptoms that have been documented, and is attempting to identify the type of psychological disorder the individual is most likely to have. Dr. Underhill is currently focusing on a. etiology b. prognosis c. diagnosis d. histology
Factual LO 1 Page: 570 Correct = 74% **a**	11.	A prognosis a. is a forecast about the probable course of an illness b. involves distinguishing one illness from another c. refers to the apparent causation and developmental history of an illness d. is a plan for treating an illness
Factual LO 1 Page: 570 **d**	12.	Which of the following terms refers to the future course of a condition or illness? a. etiological forecast b. foreclosure c. diagnosis d. prognosis
Concept/Applied LO 1 Page: 570 **c**	13.	Dr. Wedge is asking her newest client questions about his life history. She is particularly interested in any recent stressful events that the client may have experienced. Dr. Wedge is currently a. developing a prognosis for her client b. trying to determine an appropriate diagnosis c. trying to understand the etiology of her client's current illness d. engaged in naturalistic observation
Concept/Applied LO 1 Page: 570 **b**	14.	Mario has just entered treatment for a major depressive episode and he is told that most patients respond to treatment within a month and many never experience a second depressive episode. This information represents a. an etiology b. a prognosis c. a diagnosis d. a histology
Critical Thinking LO 1 Page: 570 Correct = 81% **b**	15.	Diagnosis is to prognosis as a. why is to what b. what is to outcome c. outcome is to etiology d. ontogeny is to phylogeny

Critical Thinking LO 1 Page: 570 **a**	16.	Prognosis is to etiology as a. outcome is to why b. why is to outcome c. what is to why d. why is to what
Factual LO 2 Page: 570 Correct = 79% **a**	17.	Behavior that does not coincide with cultural norms may be considered to be a. deviant b. maladaptive c. personally distressing d. insane
Concept/Applied LO 2 Page: 571 **d**	18.	Wendy works at Opydyne Corporation. At the last business executive meeting she showed up in pajamas and slippers. When her coworkers commented on the inappropriateness of her outfit, Wendy did not seem the least bit disturbed or embarrassed by their comments. In this example, Wendy's style of dressing would <u>most</u> likely be considered a. maladaptive b. personally distressing c. delusional d. culturally deviant
Concept/Applied LO 2 Page: 571 **a**	19.	Hamilton has embezzled over 3 million dollars from the bank where he is employed as an executive loan officer. He feels no remorse for his actions, and he is looking forward to an early retirement in some South American country with no extradition agreement. In this example, Hamilton's embezzling would <u>most</u> likely be considered a. culturally deviant b. maladaptive c. personally distressing d. legal insanity
Factual LO 2 Page: 571 **b**	20.	Behavior that interferes with an individual's social or occupational functioning may be considered to be a. deviant b. maladaptive c. personally distressing d. insane
Concept/Applied LO 2 Page: 571 **b**	21.	Enright is not a very conscientious individual. He often sleeps late in the morning, and on mornings when he oversleeps, he usually just skips work. He has been fired from four jobs in the past year, but he is not concerned because he feels that there are lots of other jobs available. In this example, Enright's lack of dedication to his various jobs would <u>most</u> likely be considered a. personally distressing b. maladaptive c. culturally deviant d. legal incompetency
Concept/Applied LO 2 Page: 571 **c**	22.	Summer has anorexia nervosa and is slowly starving herself to death. However, when friends or family tell her to seek professional help, she tells them that she feels fine. She can't understand why people won't just leave her alone. In this example, Summer's eating disorder would <u>most</u> likely be considered a. personally distressing b. culturally deviant c. maladaptive d. delusional

Factual LO 2 Page: 571 Correct = 60% **c**	23.	Behavior that causes anxiety or concern for the affected individual may be considered to be a. deviant b. maladaptive c. personally distressing d. insane
Concept/Applied LO 2 Page: 571 **d**	24.	Corrina constantly experiences feelings of dread and despair. Lately, she finds that she is thinking more and more about committing suicide so she can end her feelings of desperation and hopelessness. In this example, Corrina's feelings of dread and despair would <u>most</u> likely be considered a. culturally deviant b. signs of incompetency c. delusions d. personally distressing
Concept/Applied LO 2 Page: 571 **a**	25.	Treit's best friend was seriously injured in a car accident last month. Since that time Treit has been attending all his classes, but he feels like he is unable to pay attention because he is constantly thinking about his friend. Treit finds he can't seem to think about anything else, and he is frequently overwhelmed by feelings of helplessness. In this example, Treit's feelings would <u>most</u> likely be considered a. personally distressing b. culturally deviant c. maladaptive d. compulsive
Concept/Applied LO 2 Page: 571 Correct = 59% **d**	26.	Roger enjoys gambling so much that he does it every day, totally neglecting his family and job. Roger's behavior satisfies which criterion of abnormality <u>most</u> clearly? a. personal distress b. deviance c. persistence d. maladaptive behavior
Factual LO 2 Page: 571 **a**	27.	In an effort to make the criteria of mental illness less value-laden, evolutionary psychologists have proposed that mental disorders ought to be viewed as a. harmful evolutionary dysfunctions b. diseases that can be treated and possibly cured c. the manifestation of unconscious instincts and drives d. culturally maladaptive behaviors learned through social interactions
Factual LO 2 Page: 571 **b**	28.	According to the evolutionary view of mental disorders, a dysfunction occurs when a. an individual's behavior meets at least three of the diagnostic criteria outlined in the DSM-IV b. an evolved psychological mechanism does not perform its naturally selected function adequately or effectively c. a behavior is universally recognized as violating cultural or statistical norms d. the same disorder is evident in at least three generations of the same family
Factual LO 2 Page: 571 **c**	29.	The evolutionary view of mental disorders argues that objective criteria would a. increase the impact of cultural factors in the diagnosis of mental disorders b. result in fewer errors in the diagnosis of major psychological disorders c. protect against arbitrary labeling of socially disvalued conditions as disorders d. remove personality disorders from the DSM-IV categorization system

Factual LO 3 Page: 573 Correct = 93% **b**	30.	Which of the following is <u>not</u> a common stereotype about psychological disorders? a. Psychological disorders are incurable. b. Psychological disorders are a function of biophysiological factors. c. People with psychological disorders are violent and dangerous. d. People with psychological disorders are very different from normal people.
Factual LO 3 Page: 573 **c**	31.	Many people believe that the mentally ill are violence-prone. This is because a. they have personally been the victims of such violence b. there actually is a strong association between mental illness and violent tendencies c. the incidents of violence involving the mentally ill receive a great deal of media attention d. violence is much more common among mental patients than among the general population
Concept/Applied LO 3 Page: 573 **b**	32.	Rosa is the personnel director at Acme Enterprises. If she finds that an individual who has applied for employment has ever been treated for a psychological disorder, she doesn't consider that person for a job. She is concerned that the person will have another breakdown under the stressful conditions that exist at Acme Enterprises. It seems that Rosa holds the largely inaccurate stereotype that a. people with psychological disorders are often dangerous b. all psychological disorders are incurable c. people with psychological disorders behave in bizarre ways d. psychological disorders are often overdiagnosed
Concept/Applied LO 3 Page: 573 **d**	33.	When Erskine found out that his daughter's fifth grade teacher had once been treated for a psychological disorder, he insisted that his daughter be transferred to a different classroom. He was concerned for her safety, and the safety of her classmates, and tried to have the individual barred from teaching in the public school system. Erskine's actions suggest that Erskine holds the largely inaccurate stereotype that a. psychological disorders are incurable b. people with psychological disorders behave in bizarre ways c. psychological disorders often go unrecognized d. people with psychological disorders are often dangerous
Concept/Applied LO 3 Page: 573 **c**	34.	Joanna was somewhat surprised when her study partner postponed a study session because he had an appointment with his psychotherapist. When she was talking to a friend about the postponed study session she commented: "I have been working on projects with this student for several months now, and he has never shown any signs of having a psychological disorder." Joanna's comment suggests that she holds the largely inaccurate stereotype that a. psychological disorders are incurable b. people with psychological disorders are often dangerous c. people with psychological disorders behave in bizarre ways d. the mental health system has a powerful bias toward seeing pathology in everyone
Factual LO 4 Page: 574 **c**	35.	The Featured Study by Rosenhan (1973) showed that a. most mental patients are extensively observed before an initial diagnosis is made b. mental hospital staff often spend a great deal of time interacting with patients c. our mental health system is biased toward seeing mental illness in all potential patients d. it is extremely difficult to successfully fake the symptoms of serious mental illness

Factual LO 4 Page: 574 **b**	36.	One of the findings in the Featured Study by Rosenhan (1973) was that a. patients in psychiatric facilities tend to be overmedicated b. the hospital staff spent a minimal amount of time interacting with patients c. people with genuine mental illnesses act in a deviant manner most of the time d. it is extremely difficult to successfully fake the symptoms of serious mental illness
Concept/Applied LO 4 Page: 574 Correct = 88% **a**	37.	In the Featured Study on "pseudopatients," Rosenhan concluded that a. once one has been diagnosed as abnormal, subsequent behavior gets interpreted in a manner consistent with the diagnosis b. the validity of diagnostic categories in DSM-III-R is very suspect in distinguishing between normal and abnormal persons c. distinguishing between schizophrenic subtypes is almost impossible d. that most behavior patterns are basically the same in people being diagnosed as abnormal
Concept/Applied LO 5 Page: 575 Correct = 09% **d**	38.	The current classification system for psychological disorders (DSM-IV) a. contains fewer disorders than previous systems, making it easier to use b. has been shown to be extremely unreliable c. avoids giving people potentially stigmatizing diagnostic labels d. recognizes the importance of information other than a traditional diagnostic label
Factual LO 5 Page: 575 Correct = 40% **a**	39.	Disorders of mood would be found on a. Axis I of the DSM-IV b. Axis III of the DSM-IV c. Axis IV of the DSM-IV d. Axis X of the DSM-IV
Factual LO 5 Page: 575 **d**	40.	Personality and developmental disorders are found on a. Axis I of the DSM-IV b. Axis V of the DSM-IV c. Axis X of the DSM-IV d. Axis II of the DSM-IV
Concept/Applied LO 5 Page: 575 **c**	41.	Lydia has gone in for a psychiatric assessment. She tells the clinician that lately she has been feeling completely hopeless and dejected, and she no longer enjoys doing any of the things she used to look forward to. The clinician would use a. both Axis IV and Axis V of the DSM-IV to record these symptoms b. Axis III of the DSM-IV to record these symptoms c. either Axis I or Axis II of the DSM-IV to record these symptoms d. Axis X of the DSM-IV to record these symptoms
Concept/Applied LO 5 Page: 575 **d**	42.	Colton has gone in for a psychiatric assessment. He tells the clinician that he is extremely sensitive to humiliation and as a result he has become very socially withdrawn. Colton can't remember feeling confident, even as a child. In this example, the clinician would use a. both Axis IV and Axis V of the DSM-IV to record these symptoms b. Axis III of the DSM-IV to record these symptoms c. Axis X of the DSM-IV to record these symptoms d. either Axis I or Axis II of the DSM-IV to record these symptoms

Concept/Applied LO 5 Page: 575 **d**	43.	Jefferson has gone in for a psychiatric assessment. He tells the clinician that he has been feeling detached from his surroundings since he started taking medication to control his high blood pressure. The clinician would use a. either Axis I or Axis II of the DSM-IV to record this medical information b. both Axis IV and Axis V of the DSM-IV to record this medical information c. Axis X of the DSM-IV to record this medical information d. Axis III of the DSM-IV to record this medical information
Concept/Applied LO 5 Page: 575 **a**	44.	Blair has gone in for a psychiatric assessment. She tells the clinician that she has been feeling extremely depressed for the last month. Blair also tells the clinician that, just before her symptoms began, her husband moved out and she lost her job. The clinician would use a. Axis IV of the DSM-IV to record these environmental factors b. both Axis III and Axis V of the DSM-IV to record these environmental factors c. either Axis I or Axis II of the DSM-IV to record these environmental factors d. Axis X of the DSM-IV to record these environmental factors
Concept/Applied LO 5 Page: 575 **b**	45.	Wesley has gone in for a psychiatric assessment. He tells the clinician that he has been feeling apprehensive and edgy for the last month, but so far his anxiety hasn't seemed to have had a major impact on either his job or his home life. The clinician should use a. both Axis III and Axis IV of the DSM-IV to record Wesley's current level of global functioning b. Axis V of the DSM-IV to record Wesley's current level of global functioning c. either Axis I or Axis II of the DSM-IV to record Wesley's current level of global functioning d. not bother recording Wesley's current level of functioning because Wesley's symptoms do not meet the criteria for abnormality
Factual LO 5 Page: 575 **c**	46.	A code of 90 on Axis V of DSM-IV (global assessment of functioning) is associated with a. behavior considerably influenced by delusions or hallucinations b. serious symptoms or impairment c. absent or minimal symptoms d. persistent danger of severely hurting self or others
Factual LO 5 Page: 575 Correct = 70% **c**	47.	DSM-IV uses five "axes" to describe a person's problem. The actual diagnosis of a disorder is made on a. Axis I only b. Axis II only c. Axis I and II d. Axis V
Factual LO 6 Page: 576 Correct = 76% **a**	48.	Epidemiology is the study of a. the distribution of mental or physical disorders in a population b. treatments for psychological disorders c. sudden "epidemics" involving specific mental or physical disorders d. how cultural values affect judgments of abnormality
Factual LO 6 Page: 576 Correct = 88% **c**	49.	Epidemiological studies of psychological disorders suggest that a. nearly everyone who needs treatment for psychological disorders receives it b. epidemics involving psychological disorders are common c. psychological disorders are more common than many people realize d. there has been a significant decrease in prevalence rates of mental illness in the United States in recent years

Factual LO 6 Page: 576 **b**	50.	The study of the incidence and distribution of mental or physical disorders within a population defines the discipline known as a. etiology b. epidemiology c. psychobiology d. demography
Factual LO 6 Page: 576 Correct = 69% **a**	51.	In regard to psychological disorders, prevalence refers to a. the percentage of a population that exhibits a disorder during a specified time period b. the absolute number of people who are experiencing any psychological disorder at a given point in time c. the reliability of the diagnosis of psychological disorders d. the percentage of a population that has ever been <u>treated</u> for a psychological disorder
Concept/Applied LO 6 Page: 576 **c**	52.	Using the DSM-IV listings and lifetime prevalence, it is estimated that about _____ of the population may experience a psychological disorder. a. 10% b. 25% c. 33% d. 50%
Factual LO 7 Page: 577 Correct = 74% **d**	53.	The disorder that is characterized by worry and fear, muscle tension, trembling, faintness, and difficulty in concentrating is known as a a. conversion disorder b. paranoid disorder c. dissociative disorder d. generalized anxiety disorder
Factual LO 7 Page: 577 Correct = 50% **c**	54.	A generalized anxiety disorder may be associated with all the following physical symptoms <u>except</u> a. dizziness b. diarrhea c. delusions d. trembling
Factual LO 7 Page: 577 **a**	55.	Free-floating anxiety is <u>most</u> characteristic of a. generalized anxiety disorder b. panic disorder c. phobic disorder d. obsessive-compulsive disorder
Concept/Applied LO 7 Page: 577 Correct = 88% **a**	56.	The cartoon character Charlie Brown, with his extreme dread, pessimism, worrying, and brooding, could be diagnosed as having a. a generalized anxiety disorder b. a phobic disorder c. obsessive-compulsive disorder d. panic disorder
Concept/Applied LO 7 Page: 577 Correct = 83% **c**	57.	Jim came home from the office trembling, experiencing shortness of breath, irritable, unable to concentrate, and worrying about whether his business would still be open next week despite the fact that his business was evidencing its highest profit ever. Jim's condition would <u>most</u> likely be diagnosed as a. major depression b. a phobic disorder c. generalized anxiety disorder d. a minor psychotic break

Concept/Applied LO 7 Page: 577 **a**	58.	Stuart feels like he has been worrying constantly for the past 4 months. He is worried about making his car payments, losing his job, and how his children are doing in school. He has also started to experience dizziness and occasional heart palpitations. In this case, Stuart's symptoms are <u>most</u> consistent with a. generalized anxiety disorder b. panic disorder c. obsessive-compulsive disorder d. hypochondriasis
Concept/Applied LO 7 Page: 577 Correct = 100% **b**	59.	Charlie cannot tolerate heights. When walking up several flights of stairs, he breaks out in a cold sweat, shakes, and believes he is going to fall and seriously injure himself. Consequently, Charlie avoids any type of height at all costs. Charlie's condition would be diagnosed as a a. dissociative disorder b. phobic disorder c. somatoform disorder d. conversion disorder
Concept/Applied LO 7 Page: 577 Correct = 74% **b**	60.	The major difference between a phobic disorder and a generalized anxiety disorder is that a. the phobic disorder is more severe and more difficult to treat b. anxiety is specific to one object or situation in a phobic disorder, but is "free floating" in a generalized anxiety disorder c. the generalized anxiety disorder occurs primarily in men and the phobic disorder occurs primarily in women d. only the generalized anxiety disorder depends on past conditioning
Concept/Applied LO 7 Page: 577 **d**	61.	Ann is so terrified of fire that she cannot light a match or even enjoy dinner by candlelight. Ann is <u>most</u> likely suffering from a. generalized anxiety disorder b. panic disorder c. obsessive-compulsive disorder d. phobic disorder
Concept/Applied LO 7 Page: 577 **b**	62.	Elise is so terrified of enclosed places that she had to quit her new job because her office had no windows. She knows that her fear is irrational, but she can't seem to control her anxiety. In this case, Elise's symptoms are <u>most</u> consistent with a. generalized anxiety disorder b. a phobic disorder c. obsessive-compulsive disorder d. a conversion disorder
Factual LO 7 Page: 578 Correct = 87% **d**	63.	The condition characterized by recurrent, intense, and sudden onset of anxiety is a. a histrionic reaction b. obsessive-compulsive disorder c. a neurotic split d. panic disorder
Concept/Applied LO 7 Page: 578 **c**	64.	Damian has brief attacks of overwhelming anxiety in which his heart pounds and he can't control his breathing. He never knows when the next attack is going to occur. In this case, Damian's symptoms are <u>most</u> consistent with a. generalized anxiety disorder b. a conversion disorder c. panic disorder d. schizophrenia

Concept/Applied LO 7 Page: 578 Correct = 69% **c**	65.	Doris feels terrified every time she leaves her house, and avoids doing so whenever possible. Doris is <u>most</u> likely suffering from a. generalized anxiety disorder b. claustrophobia c. agoraphobia d. obsessive-compulsive disorder
Factual LO 7 Page: 578 Correct = 81% **b**	66.	Agoraphobia is a fear of a. heights b. going out to public places c. closed spaces d. fluffy sweaters
Factual LO 7 Page: 578 **b**	67.	An unwanted thought that repeatedly intrudes upon an individual's consciousness is called a. a delusion b. an obsession c. a compulsion d. a hallucination
Concept/Applied LO 7 Page: 579 **a**	68.	Jack thinks constantly about dirt and germs. He washes his hands hundreds of times a day. Jack is <u>most</u> likely suffering from a. obsessive-compulsive disorder b. hypochondriasis c. phobic disorder d. somatization disorder
Concept/Applied LO 7 Page: 579 **a**	69.	Selena constantly thinks about climbing up the stairs to the roof of her building and jumping into the street below. Selena's uncontrollable thoughts could be considered as an example of a. an obsession b. a compulsion c. a hallucination d. a delusion
Concept/Applied LO 7 Page: 579 Correct = 50% **a**	70.	A person who checks his alarm clock 20 times before going to sleep is being a. compulsive b. obsessive c. phobic d. amnesiac
Concept/Applied LO 7 Page: 579 **d**	71.	Grayson seems to be preoccupied with the possibility that he might miss an important message from someone in his family. He checks for new messages on his answering machine every 15 minutes. Grayson's constant checking for messages could be considered an example of a. an obsession b. a hallucination c. a delusion d. a compulsion
Concept/Applied LO 7 Page: 579 **d**	72.	Kate constantly thinks about jumping in front of an oncoming car when she is walking. The only way she seems to be able to stop these self-destructive thoughts is to say Mother Goose nursery rhymes over and over to herself. In this case, Kate's symptoms are <u>most</u> consistent with a. generalized anxiety disorder b. panic disorder c. bipolar disorder d. obsessive-compulsive disorder

Factual LO 7 Page: 579 Correct = 44% **b**	73.	People who suffer from an obsessive-compulsive disorder usually a. find their thoughts and acts reassuring, as they lead to reduction in anxiety b. feel they have lost control of their thoughts or actions c. are treatable with a form of aversive conditioning d. are institutionalized, as they cannot function in society in an appropriate manner
Factual LO 8 Page: 579 Correct = 65% **a**	74.	A concordance rate indicates a. the percentage of twin pairs or other pairs of relatives who exhibit the same disorder b. agreement rates between physicians in diagnosing psychological disorders c. the degree to which psychological factors affect physical health d. the degree to which biological factors affect psychological adjustment
Factual LO 8 Page: 580 **b**	75.	Altering neurotransmitter activity at _____ synapses can reduce excessive anxiety. a. dopamine b. GABA c. acetylcholine d. endorphin
Concept/Applied LO 8 Page: 580 **b**	76.	Ali has a psychological disorder, and her doctor has prescribed a drug that affects the levels of GABA in her nervous system. Based on this information, it is most likely that Ali is being treated for a. a schizophrenic disorder b. an anxiety disorder c. a dissociative disorder d. a somatoform disorder
Factual LO 8 Page: 580 **c**	77.	Abnormalities in neural circuits that use _____ have recently been implicated in panic and obsessive-compulsive disorders. a. dopamine b. acetylcholine c. serotonin d. endorphin
Concept/Applied LO 8 Page: 580 Correct = 49% **d**	78.	Anique is being treated for a psychological disorder. As part of her treatment program she is taking medication that alters the activity of GABA synapses. It is likely that Anique has a. a somatoform disorder b. a schizophrenic disorder c. a personality disorder d. an anxiety disorder
Factual LO 8 Page: 580 Correct = 79% **a**	79.	According to Mowrer, phobic responses are acquired through _____ conditioning and maintained through _____ conditioning. a. classical; operant b. classical; classical c. operant; classical d. operant; operant
Factual LO 8 Page: 580 Correct = 68% **a**	80.	Preparedness is a term coined by Seligman that refers to a. a biological predisposition to be easily conditioned to fear certain things b. the physical state or condition associated with a panic attack c. psychological processes that accompany obsessive-compulsive behavior patterns d. a particular type of learning situation in which negatively reinforced behaviors reduce the level of one's generalized anxiety disorder

Concept/Applied 81. According to Seligman's concept of "preparedness," which of the following stimuli
LO 8   should one develop a phobia toward most easily?
Page: 580   a. chairs
c   b. monkeys
                  c. heights
                  d. certain numbers

Factual   82. The concept that people are biologically set to acquire some fears more easily than
LO 8   others is the concept of
Page: 580   a. genetic drift
c   b. constitutional susceptibility
                  c. preparedness
                  d. temperamental predisposition

Concept/Applied 83. Conditioning theories of anxiety disorders are being revised to include more
LO 8   emphasis on
Page: 580   a. constitutional factors
d   b. genetic factors
                  c. neurotransmitter factors
                  d. cognitive factors

Concept/Applied 84. Quninton's father had an irrational fear of railroad crossings and would sometimes
LO 8   spend hours planning family trips so that all railroad crossings were avoided. If
Page: 580   Quinton also develops a fear of railroad crossings, the process that would best
c   explain the acquisition of his phobia would be
                  a. classical conditioning
                  b. operant conditioning
                  c. observational learning
                  d. reciprocal stress

Factual   85. Which of the following personality traits appears to be related to the likelihood of
LO 8   developing anxiety disorders?
Page: 581   a. neuroticism
Correct = 78%   b. extraversion
a   c. agreeableness
                  d. conscientiousness

Concept/Applied 86. Yesenia has an anxiety disorder. Based on research that has investigated the
LO 8   correlations between psychological disorders and personality traits, it is likely that
Page: 581   Yesenia will score
c   a. low in openness
                  b. low in extroversion
                  c. high in neuroticism
                  d. high in agreeableness

Factual   87. A physical ailment that results from psychological factors without any
LO 9   accompanying physical basis is referred to as
Page: 582   a. a somatoform disorder
a   b. a psychosomatic illness
                  c. an anxiety disorder
                  d. malingering

| Concept/Applied
LO 9
Page: 582
d | 88. | Griffin didn't have time to study for his philosophy midterm so he called the professor and claimed he had strep throat, even though he was not really ill. He was hoping that the professor would allow him to write the midterm one day later. In this case, Griffin's "faked" illness could be considered
a. a psychosomatic illness
b. conversion disorder
c. panic disorder
d. malingering |

| Factual
LO 9
Page: 582
Correct = 40%
a | 89. | Which of the following is not an example of a somatoform disorder?
a. neuroticism
b. somatization disorder
c. conversion disorder
d. hypochondriasis |

| Concept/Applied
LO 9
Page: 582
Correct = 52%
b | 90. | The major difference between a somatization disorder and a conversion disorder is that
a. a somatization disorder involves intentional faking of physical illness, while conversion symptoms are unconsciously created
b. somatization disorders involve a wide variety of organs and symptoms; conversion disorders involve loss of function in a single organ system
c. a somatization disorder involves apparent physical illness, and conversion disorder involves genuine physical illness
d. somatization disorders occur only in adults, while conversion disorders occur only in children |

| Concept/Applied
LO 9
Page: 582
a | 91. | Lillian sees her doctor nearly every week, and each time she has something different that is bothering her. Two weeks ago she had back pains, last week she had shortness of breath, and this week she has abdominal cramps. If Lillian has a psychological disorder, rather than an actual physical disorder, her symptoms are most consistent with
a. somatization disorder
b. hypochondriasis
c. conversion disorder
d. obsessive-compulsive disorder |

| Factual
LO 9
Page: 582
Correct = 79%
a | 92. | When one experiences a loss of use of some part of the body with no accompanying organic problems, the diagnosis is a
a. conversion disorder
b. hypochondriasis
c. somatization disorder
d. panic attack |

| Concept/Applied
LO 9
Page: 582
b | 93. | Three months ago Sheldon's 7-year-old daughter was killed when a car swerved out of control and hit her as she waited to cross the street. As the police told Sheldon about the accident he felt everything start to go black, and then he found he couldn't see at all. Since then he has been to a number of specialists, but none of the specialists can find anything wrong with his visual system. Sheldon's pupils respond normally to light, and there is activity in the visual cortex when images are presented. Still, Sheldon claims that he cannot see anything. In this case, Sheldon's symptoms are most consistent with
a. somatization disorder
b. conversion disorder
c. hypochondriasis
d. dissociative identity disorder |

Concept/Applied LO 9 Page: 582 Correct = 69% **c**	94.	Jim is unable to move his left arm despite the fact there is nothing physically wrong with him. Jim will <u>most</u> likely be diagnosed as having a. hypochondriasis b. somatization disorder c. conversion disorder d. a parasomnia
Factual LO 9 Page: 583 Correct = 83% **d**	95.	Hypochondriasis involves a. the deliberate faking of physical illness b. apparent physical illness caused by psychological factors c. genuine physical illness caused in part by psychological factors d. a tendency to misinterpret minor bodily changes as being indicative of serious illness
Concept/Applied LO 9 Page: 583 Correct = 75% **c**	96.	Karen believes she has a rare tropical disease. Her physicians can find no evidence of the disease, yet Karen continues to insist she has it. Karen's condition is best classified as a. a psychotic episode b. a somatoform disorder c. a hypochondriasis d. a psychosomatic conversion reaction
Concept/Applied LO 9 Page: 583 **b**	97.	Jack always complains of being sick. He is convinced he is dying. His physicians have all told him that there is nothing wrong with him and he should live well into his 80s. Jack does not believe the physicians and continues to search for a doctor who will confirm that he is sick. Jack's behavior is <u>most</u> consistent with the symptoms of a. an anxiety disorder b. a somatoform disorder c. a dissociative disorder d. a schizophrenic disorder
Concept/Applied LO 9 Page: 583 **d**	98.	Sophie takes over 40 different vitamins and herbal remedies each day to keep herself in top physical health. Recently she had some severe dizziness, but her family doctor assured her that it was just a minor ear infection that would clear up in a few days. Sophie is concerned because she is sure the ear infection is the sign of something much more serious, such as a brain tumor, and she has made appointments with three different specialists to have more testing done. In this case, Sophie's symptoms are <u>most</u> consistent with a. somatization disorder b. conversion disorder c. panic disorder d. hypochondriasis
Factual LO 9 Page: 584 Correct = 77% **a**	99.	Which of the following personality traits appears to be related to the likelihood of developing a somatoform disorder? a. neuroticism b. extraversion c. agreeableness d. conscientiousness
Concept/Applied LO 10 Page: 584 Correct = 80% **c**	100.	Frank witnessed a horrible car accident but cannot remember anything about it. Frank appears to have a. psychosis-induced repression b. dissociative fugue c. dissociative amnesia d. conversion disorder

Concept/Applied LO 10 Page: 584 **b**	101.	Chantel's four children were killed in an automobile accident which Chantel survived. When police question her about the events surrounding the accident, Chantel is unable to remember anything. She remembers getting into her car to drive her children to school, and she remembers her trip by ambulance to the local hospital, but everything in between is a complete "blank." In this case, Chantel's symptoms are most consistent with a. dissociative fugue b. dissociative amnesia c. panic disorder d. generalized anxiety disorder
Concept/Applied LO 10 Page: 584 **a**	102.	Simon recently walked into a hospital emergency room in Florida. He had no identification, and although he didn't appear to be hurt in anyway, he had no idea who he was or where he lived. A check of missing person reports showed that Simon had walked away from his home in Brooklyn ten days earlier. In this case, Simon's symptoms are most consistent with a. dissociative fugue b. dissociative amnesia c. panic disorder d. generalized anxiety disorder
Concept/Applied LO 10 Page: 585 **b**	103.	Alexia started a new job on Monday morning. For the first three days she showed up in bright colors and was outgoing and extroverted. However, on Thursday she showed up in a dark suit and appeared shy and introverted. She insisted that her name was Clara, and she couldn't understand why her coworkers kept calling her Alexia. In this example, Alexia is showing symptoms that are consistent with: a. bipolar disorder b. dissociation identity disorder c. disorganized schizophrenia d. antisocial personality disorder
Factual LO 10 Page: 585 **c**	104.	Psychogenic amnesia and fugue most likely result from a. a neurotransmitter imbalance b. a neurotic personality c. extreme stress d. unconscious recollections of childhood trauma
Factual LO 11 Page: 586 **d**	105.	Emotional disturbances that affect one's physical, perceptual, social, and thought processes are referred to as a. somatoform disorders b. dissociative disorders c. anxiety disorders d. mood disorders
Factual LO 11 Page: 586 Correct = 58% **b**	106.	Depression is an example of a _____ mood disorder. a. bipolar b. unipolar c. cyclical d. dissociative
Factual LO 11 Page: 586 Correct = 88% **a**	107.	Which of the following symptoms is not associated with a depressive disorder? a. impulsive behavior b. altered appetite c. insomnia d. feelings of worthlessness

Concept/Applied 108. Carrie has been sad a lot lately. She is down on herself, evidences very little appetite,
LO 11   can't sleep, and doesn't want to be around her friends or family. Carrie's condition is
Page: 587   most likely
Correct = 95%   a. schizophrenia
d   b. dissociative identity disorder
                 c. hypochondriasis
                 d. a depressive disorder

Concept/Applied 109. Janae is an 18-year-old college freshman. She has missed almost all her classes for
LO 11   the past month, and she spends most of her time in her bedroom. Frequently, she is
Page: 587   still not dressed when her parents come home from work, and she often hasn't eaten
b   anything all day. She thinks her whole life is a failure, and she blames herself for
               being a social misfit whom everyone hates. Janae's symptoms are most consistent
               with those seen in
                 a. antisocial personality disorder
                 b. major depression
                 c. generalized anxiety disorder
                 d. hypochondriasis

Concept/Applied 110. For the past month Lawrence seems to have lost interest in most of his normal
LO 11   activities. He feels irritable and he has had difficulty sleeping. He also finds that he
Page: 587   has difficulty making decisions. Lawrence's symptoms are most consistent with
b   those seen in
                 a. bipolar disorder
                 b. depressive disorder
                 c. generalized anxiety disorder
                 d. disorganized schizophrenia

Concept/Applied 111. Art always seems to be grumpy and irritable. He has a poor self-image and is usually
LO 11   socially withdrawn. Although he never feels totally dejected and out of control, he
Page: 587   feels that life is not very exciting or enjoyable. Art's symptoms are most consistent
a   with those seen in
                 a. dysthymic disorder
                 b. cyclothymic disorder
                 c. antisocial personality disorder
                 d. generalized anxiety disorder

Factual   112. The median duration of depressive episodes is
LO 11   a. 7 to 14 days
Page: 587   b. 4 to 6 weeks
d   c. 1 year
                 d. 5 months

Factual   113. For individuals who suffer from depression, the median number of depressive
LO 11   episodes they will experience over the course of their lifetime is
Page: 587   a. 1 episode
c   b. 10 episodes
                 c. 4 episodes
                 d. 25 episodes

Concept/Applied 114. Victor has been diagnosed with a depressive disorder. He has already experience two
LO 11   episodes of major depression. If Victor's depressive disorder follows the median
Page: 587   pattern, he should expect to experience
a   a. up to 2 more episodes, because 4 episodes is the median
                 b. up to 8 more episodes, because 10 episodes is the median
                 c. no more episodes, because 2 episodes is the median
                 d. periods of mania in between any subsequent depressive episodes

Factual LO 11 Page: 588 Correct = 90% **c**	115.	Individuals who alternate between periods of depression and periods of being manic are diagnosed as having a a. multiple personality disorder b. conversion disorder c. bipolar disorder d. dissociative disorders
Factual LO 11 Page: 588 Correct = 48% **d**	116.	Which of the following symptoms is <u>not</u> associated with someone who has a bipolar disorder? a. sexually reckless behavior b. inflated self-esteem c. decreased need for sleep d. hallucinations
Concept/Applied LO 11 Page: 588 **c**	117.	Tina has been extremely hyperactive for the past week, and she has been getting by with only 3 hours of sleep each night. Her thoughts seem to be racing out of control and she is convinced that the novel she started last week will become a best seller and win a Pulitzer Prize, even though she has never had any of her writing published in the past. Tina's symptoms suggest that she is currently experiencing a. dysthymic disorder b. generalized anxiety disorder c. a manic episode d. dissociative fugue
Concept/Applied LO 11 Page: 588 **d**	118.	After several weeks of feeling gloomy and being socially withdrawn, Marco has suddenly become extremely sociable and talkative. He doesn't seem to need any sleep, and he becomes irritated when his friends tell him to slow down. Marco's behavior is consistent with a. obsessive-compulsive disorder b. schizophrenia c. histrionic personality disorder d. bipolar disorder
Concept/Applied LO 11 Page: 588 **a**	119.	Carina is 50 years old, and she never seems to be on an even keel. Some days she is excited and happy, other days she is sad and withdrawn. Her symptoms seem fairly mild, but she has had mood swings of this type since she was in her early 20s. Carina's symptoms are <u>most</u> consistent with those seen in a. cyclothymic disorder b. dysthymic disorder c. undifferentiated schizophrenia d. dissociative identity disorder
Concept/Applied LO 11 Page: 588 Correct = 53% **a**	120.	Dysthymic disorder is to _____ as cyclothymic disorder is to _____. a. depressive disorder; bipolar disorder b. bipolar disorder; unipolar mood disorder c. manic-depressive disorder; depressive disorder d. bipolar disorder; depressive disorder
Concept/Applied LO 11 Page: 588 **c**	121.	Charlotte is in a heightened emotional state and hasn't been sleeping much lately. Additionally, she is making plans to solve the world's hunger problem while simultaneously composing music (even though she's never had musical training). Charlotte would <u>most</u> likely be diagnosed as having a. antisocial personality disorder b. dissociative identity disorder c. bipolar disorder d. seasonal affective disorder

Factual LO 11 Page: 588 Correct = 54% **a**	122.	Bipolar disorders occur in _____ of the population. a. a little over 1% b. nearly 33% c. approximately 7% d. around 15%
Concept/Applied LO 11 Page: 588 Correct = 74% **c**	123.	Carol finds she is no longer interested in things she used to do, is sad most of the time, and thinks she is a terrible person. Additionally, she has recently lost a lot of weight and doesn't sleep very much. Carol's behavior would be diagnosed as a. an anxiety disorder b. a dissociative disorder c. a mood disorder d. a personality disorder
Factual LO 12 Page: 588 Correct = 38% **d**	124.	Studies that have evaluated concordance rates for various mood disorders have found a. only unipolar disorder has a genetic component b. the influence of genetic factors appears to be slightly stronger for unipolar disorders than for bipolar disorders c. the influence of genetic factors is the same for both bipolar disorders and unipolar disorders d. the influence of genetic factors appears to be slightly stronger for bipolar disorders than for unipolar disorders
Factual LO 12 Page: 588 **a**	125.	Recent studies suggest that genetic vulnerability a. may play a larger role in women's depression than in men's b. may play a larger role in men's depression than in women's c. plays an equal role in both men's and women's depression d. does not play a role in either women's or men's depression
Critical Thinking LO 12 Page: 589 **a**	126.	Sarah is a 23-year-old woman whose sister has recently been diagnosed with a depressive disorder. Jacob is a 25-year-old man whose brother has recently been diagnosed with a depressive disorder. Based on studies which have investigated genetic vulnerability, you should predict that a. Sarah is at a higher risk than Jacob for developing a depressive disorder b. Jacob is at a higher risk than Sarah for developing a depressive disorder c. both Sarah and Jacob are equally likely to develop a depressive disorder d. neither Sarah nor Jacob is likely to develop a depressive disorder
Factual LO 12 Page: 589 **b**	127.	Which of the following neurotransmitters has been implicated in mood disorders? a. GABA b. serotonin c. dopamine d. endorphins
Concept/Applied LO 12 Page: 589 **d**	128.	Jose has a psychological disorder, and his doctor has prescribed a drug that affects both the levels of norepinephrine and serotonin in Jose's nervous system. Based on this information, it is most likely that Jose is being treated for a. an anxiety disorder b. a schizophrenic disorder c. a somatoform disorder d. depression

Factual
LO 13
Page: 589
d

129. In his investigations of the cognitive factors that might contribute to depression, Seligman found that people with a pessimistic explanatory style are especially vulnerable to depression. These individuals tend to attribute their setbacks to _____, and draw _____ conclusions about their personal inadequacies.
   a. situational factors; narrow, specific
   b. personal flaws; narrow, specific
   c. situational factors; global, far-reaching
   d. personal flaws; global, far-reaching

Critical Thinking
LO 13
Page: 589
a

130. Darla was fired from her most recent job. Based on Seligman's investigations into the cognitive factors that might contribute to depression, Darla will be most prone to depression if she attributes her firing to
   a. her lack of ability to do her job successfully
   b. the bad mood that her boss was in on the day she was fired
   c. a general downturn in the economy which resulted in massive layoffs
   d. her coworker who started a number of false rumors about Darla

Factual
LO 13
Page: 589
Correct = 76%
c

131. Which of the following statements is false?
   a. Correlations have been found between poor social skills and depression.
   b. Depressed people tend to be evaluated negatively by others.
   c. There is no relationship between depression and environmental stress.
   d. Depressed people gravitate towards people who reinforce their negative views of themselves.

Factual
LO 13
Page: 590
b

132. According to Susan Nolen-Hoeksema, excessive _____ tends to prolong and intensify depressive episodes.
   a. norepinephrine
   b. rumination
   c. stress
   d. anxiety

Factual
LO 13
Page: 590
d

133. Lauren Alloy and her colleagues investigated the link between negative thinking and vulnerability to depression. Their study involved a group of first-year college students who had no prior history of depression. Over a 2.5 year period, they found that _____ of those students with a negative cognitive style developed a major depressive disorder, compared to _____ of those students who did not have a negative cognitive style.
   a. 98%; 16%
   b. 12%; 33%
   c. 23%; 12%
   d. 17%; 1%

Factual
LO 13
Page: 590
a

134. Lauren Alloy and her colleagues investigated the link between negative thinking and vulnerability to depression. Their study involved a group of first-year college students who had no prior history of depression. Over a 2.5 year period, they found that _____ of those students with a negative cognitive style experienced minor depressive episodes, compared to _____ of those students who did not have a negative cognitive style.
   a. 39%; 6%
   b. 12%; 2%
   c. 8%; 42%
   d. 98%; 18%

Concept/Applied LO 13 Page: 591 **a**	135.	The evidence available today suggests a. a moderately strong link between stress and the onset of mood disorders b. a very weak link between stress and the onset of mood disorders c. no link between stress and the onset of mood disorders d. an inverse link between stress and the onset of mood disorders
Critical Thinking LO 14 Page: 592 Correct = 76% **d**	136.	The basic problem in the mood disorders is disturbed _____; the basic problem in the schizophrenic disorders is disturbed _____. a. thought; emotion b. perception; thought c. thought; perception d. emotion; thought
Concept/Applied LO 14 Page: 592 **d**	137.	Schizophrenia is characterized by a. emotional disturbances and high levels of anxiety b. the presence of two or more distinct personalities c. loss of memory or personal identity d. a fragmentation of thought processes
Factual LO 14 Page: 592 Correct = 85% **b**	138.	A person who maintains bizarre, false beliefs that have no basis in reality is said to have a. hallucinations b. delusions c. obsessions d. illusions
Concept/Applied LO 14 Page: 592 Correct = 93% **c**	139.	Johnny believes he is the president of the United States. Johnny's belief is referred to as a. a hallucination b. a compulsion c. a delusion d. an obsession
Factual LO 14 Page: 592 Correct = 90% **a**	140.	A delusion is a. a false belief that is maintained even though it is not supported by reality b. the consequence of loosening of associations c. a perceptual experience without a sensation d. the major symptom associated with dissociative disorders
Concept/Applied LO 14 Page: 592 **c**	141.	Cooper is an auto mechanic at a local garage. However, he is convinced that his phone line is tapped and all the rooms in his house have listening devices planted, so that enemy agents can learn all his secret conversations. He never takes the same route to work two days in a row, to prevent the enemy agents from following him and learning where he works. In this case, it appears that Cooper is experiencing a. hallucinations b. obsessions c. delusions of persecution d. loosening of associations
Concept/Applied LO 14 Page: 592 **a**	142.	Ivy excitedly tells you that she has been invited to sing at the coronation of the new King of Cyprus. You find this difficult to believe considering Ivy sings terribly, and Cyprus has an elected government, not a monarchy. Ivy's statements are clearly out of touch with reality. It appears that Ivy is experiencing a. delusions of grandeur b. hallucinations c. compulsions d. loosening of associations

Factual LO 14 Page: 593 Correct = 86% **a**	143.	A person who perceives stimuli that aren't there is said to have a. hallucinations b. delusions c. obsessions d. illusions
Concept/Applied LO 14 Page: 593 Correct = 61% **a**	144.	Kevin hears voices singing even though none are present. Kevin suffers from a. hallucinations b. delusions c. obsessions d. loosening of associations
Concept/Applied LO 14 Page: 593 **d**	145.	Norton hears disembodied voices all the time that give him strange commands. Yesterday he finished building a concrete landing pad in his backyard for a UFO. The voices have told him that the spacecraft will land over the weekend and take him to a more advanced civilization 27 light years from earth. In this case, the voices that Norton hears are a. delusions b. obsessions c. compulsions d. hallucinations
Concept/Applied LO 14 Page: 593 **b**	146.	Abby was watching a documentary on some of the horrors of the Viet Nam War. Even when she saw soldiers being blown up after stepping on land mines, she showed no emotional reaction or response. In this case, Abby is displaying symptoms of a. catatonic stupor b. blunted or flat affect c. antisocial personality disorder d. conversion disorder
Factual LO 15 Page: 593 Correct = 79% **d**	147.	The subtype of schizophrenia marked by delusions of persecution and grandeur is a. hebephrenic b. disorganized c. catatonic d. paranoid
Concept/Applied LO 15 Page: 593 **a**	148.	Tony believes that he is Thomas Edison, and he is convinced that his neighbors are spies who are trying to steal his inventions. He believes the neighbors break into his house and search for plans for new inventions when he is not home. Tony's symptoms are most consistent with those seen in a. paranoid schizophrenia b. undifferentiated schizophrenia c. catatonic schizophrenia d. disorganized schizophrenia
Concept/Applied LO 15 Page: 593 Correct = 90% **b**	149.	Jill will sit in one position for long periods of time, evidencing muscular rigidity. Jill is exhibiting symptoms of a. paranoid schizophrenia b. catatonic schizophrenia c. disorganized schizophrenia d. undifferentiated schizophrenia

Concept/Applied LO 15 Page: 593 Correct = 54% **b**	150.	Roy alternates between periods in which he remains motionless and seems oblivious to his environment, and periods of hyperactivity and frenzied excitement. Roy would <u>most</u> likely be diagnosed as having a. paranoid schizophrenia b. catatonic schizophrenia c. disorganized schizophrenia d. undifferentiated schizophrenia
Concept/Applied LO 15 Page: 593 **d**	151.	Hope often sits for hours in extremely rigid positions; during these times she seems to lose contact with the external world and does not respond to people who try to speak to her. At other times she becomes extremely hyperactive and rambles on incoherently. Hope's symptoms are <u>most</u> consistent with those seen in a. paranoid schizophrenia b. undifferentiated schizophrenia c. disorganized schizophrenia d. catatonic schizophrenia
Concept/Applied LO 15 Page: 593 Correct = 55% **c**	152.	Harold sits all day alone on a park bench, babbling incoherently and giggling to himself. Harold would <u>most</u> likely be diagnosed as having a. paranoid schizophrenia b. catatonic schizophrenia c. disorganized schizophrenia d. undifferentiated schizophrenia
Concept/Applied LO 15 Page: 593 **c**	153.	Tyberius wears a hat 24 hours a day and becomes extremely agitated if anyone tries to remove it. He is convinced that small robots made of Lego blocks nibbled his ears off while he was sleeping, and if he removes his hat his brains will leak out through the holes in the sides of his head. Tyberius' delusion is the type of delusion typically seen in a. catatonic schizophrenia b. paranoid schizophrenia c. disorganized schizophrenia d. undifferentiated schizophrenia
Factual LO 15 Page: 593 Correct = 67% **d**	154.	Which of the following is <u>not</u> a type of schizophrenia according to DSM-IV? a. paranoid b. undifferentiated c. disorganized d. frenetic
Factual LO 15 Page: 594 Correct = 70% **a**	155.	People who are clearly schizophrenic but who cannot be placed into any of the three main categories for schizophrenic disorders are said to have a. undifferentiated schizophrenia b. borderline schizophrenia c. disorganized schizophrenia d. schizophrenia in remission
Factual LO 15 Page: 594 Correct = 44% **a**	156.	Negative symptoms in schizophrenia include a. behavioral deficits such as flattened emotion, apathy, and poverty of speech b. behavioral excesses such as hallucinations, delusions, and bizarre behavior c. antisocial behaviors such as violence and rage reactions d. dissociative behaviors and the emergence of multiple personalities

Factual LO 15 Page: 594 Correct = 61% **b**	157.	Positive symptoms in schizophrenia include a. behavioral deficits such as flattened emotion, apathy, and poverty of speech b. behavioral excesses such as hallucinations, delusions, and bizarre behavior c. compliant behavior such as medication monitoring d. dissociative behaviors and the emergence of multiple personalities
Concept/Applied LO 15 Page: 594 **b**	158.	Individuals with schizophrenic disorders tend to show a greater responsiveness to treatment when a. positive and negative symptoms are both evident at the same time b. the predominant symptoms include behavioral excesses or peculiarities c. positive and negative symptoms alternate throughout the schizophrenic episodes d. the predominant symptoms include behavioral deficits
Factual LO 15 Page: 594 **d**	159.	Nancy Andreasen has proposed a classification scheme for schizophrenia which divides schizophrenic disorders into two categories, based on the predominance of negative versus positive symptoms. Results from research studies which have investigated this method of classification suggest that most patients a. exhibit mainly positive symptoms b. alternate between positive and negative symptoms c. exhibit mainly negative symptoms d. exhibit both types of symptoms
Concept/Applied LO 16 Page: 595 Correct = 82% **c**	160.	Which of the following statements is <u>true</u>? a. Concordance rates for schizophrenia are near 100 percent for identical twins. b. Schizophrenia is caused by a single recessive gene that must be contributed by both parents. c. Some people inherit a polygenetically transmitted vulnerability to schizophrenia. d. Concordance rates for schizophrenia are the same for fraternal twins and identical twins.
Critical Thinking LO 16 Page: 595 **b**	161.	Enos and Amir are both currently 30 years old. Enos' biological mother has schizophrenia, but neither of his adoptive parents have the disorder. In contrast, neither of Amir's biological parents have schizophrenia, however his adoptive mother has schizophrenia. Based on research that has investigated the role of genetic vulnerability in schizophrenic disorders, you should predict that a. Enos is unlikely to develop schizophrenia, but Amir has an increased risk of developing schizophrenia b. Amir is unlikely to develop schizophrenia, but Enos has an increased risk of developing schizophrenia c. Enos and Amir are both at high risk for developing schizophrenia d. neither Enos nor Amir is likely to develop schizophrenia
Factual LO 16 Page: 596 **b**	162.	At this time the major neurotransmitter that has been related to schizophrenia is a. norepinephrine b. dopamine c. GABA d. serotonin
Concept/Applied LO 16 Page: 596 **a**	163.	Mayra has a psychological disorder, and her doctor has prescribed a drug that affects the levels of dopamine in her nervous system. Based on this information, it is <u>most</u> likely that Mayra is being treated for a. a schizophrenic disorder b. an anxiety disorder c. a dissociative disorder d. a somatoform disorder

Concept/Applied LO 16 Page: 596 Correct = 83% **a**	164.	The finding that many schizophrenics have difficulty in focusing their attention implies that schizophrenia may be caused by a. neurological defects b. exposure to deviant communication patterns c. a specific recessive gene d. traumatic childhood experiences
Factual LO 16 Page: 596 **c**	165.	Research with CT scans and MRI scans suggests that there is an association between chronic schizophrenic disturbance and a. shrunken brain ventricles b. atrophied cells in the corpus callosum c. enlarged brain ventricles d. enlarged temporal lobes
Concept/Applied LO 16 Page: 596 **c**	166.	Renata recently had a magnetic resonance imaging (MRI) scan done. The results showed that her brain has enlarged ventricles and a thalamus that is smaller than normal. If Renata has a psychological disorder, the results of her MRI scan would suggest that the disorder is most likely a. obsessive-compulsive disorder b. bipolar disorder c. schizophrenia d. dissociative identity disorder
Factual LO 16 Page: 596 Correct = 75% **d**	167.	Researchers have found that in schizophrenic patients, as compared to normal control subjects, the thalamus is: a. larger, and shows more metabolic activity b. smaller, but shows more metabolic activity c. larger, but shows less metabolic activity d. smaller, and shows less metabolic activity
Factual LO 17 Page: 596 **b**	168.	The neurodevelopmental hypothesis of schizophrenia suggests that schizophrenia may be caused, in part, by a. low levels of expressed in emotion in the family of the schizophrenic patient b. disruptions in the normal maturational process of the brain before or at birth c. genetic factors that interact with environmental stressors during infancy d. abnormal levels of dopamine and serotonin in the cerebral cortex
Factual LO 17 Page: 597 **a**	169.	Several research studies have found an elevated incidence of schizophrenia among individuals whose mothers a. were exposed to influenza during the second trimester of their pregnancy b. were exposed to high levels of stress during the second trimester of their pregnancy c. drank heavily during the second trimester of their pregnancy d. took narcotic drugs during the second trimester of their pregnancy
Factual LO 17 Page: 597 **b**	170.	Some research studies have found that, compared to control subjects, schizophrenic patients are a. less likely to have a history of obstetrical complications b. more likely to have a history of obstetrical complications c. more likely to have experienced impoverished living conditions during infancy d. more likely to have developed influenza while they were in preschool
Factual LO 17 Page: 597 Correct = 40% **c**	171.	The prognosis is poorer for schizophrenics who return to families characterized by a. low expressed emotion b. low communication deviance c. high expressed emotion d. high interpersonal support

Concept/Applied LO 17 Page: 597 **d**	172.	Jazmine has just returned home after receiving treatment for schizophrenia. The clinician who is supervising her case is aware that Jazmine's family is high in expressed emotion. Under these conditions, Jazmine a. has a low risk of relapse b. is likely to develop symptoms of bipolar disorder c. will need little or no medication because she will have high levels of social support d. has a high risk of relapse
Concept/Applied LO 17 Page: 598 **d**	173.	Mohammed was recently treated for a mood disorder. The clinician who is supervising his case is aware that Mohammed's family is high in expressed emotion. Under these conditions, Mohammed a. has a low risk of relapse b. is likely to develop positive symptoms of schizophrenia c. is at a high risk for developing a personality disorder d. has a high risk of relapse
Concept/Applied LO 17 Page: 598 Correct = 47% **c**	174.	The "vulnerability" model of schizophrenia suggests that schizophrenia occurs because of a. psychological weakness or vulnerability b. inherent physical weakness of the brain to deal with stress c. predisposing factors that interact with stressful life events d. a genetic-based deficiency of certain neurotransmitters
Concept/Applied LO 18 Page: 598 Correct = 31% **a**	175.	Personality disorders are characterized by a. extreme, inflexible personality traits b. hallucinations and delusions c. an inability to function outside of a hospital setting d. extremely inconsistent behavior across a variety of situations
Concept/Applied LO 18 Page: 598 **d**	176.	Lukas does not trust anyone. He is convinced that no one around him is truthful, and everything they say to him is a lie. He is extremely suspicious of other people's motives, and he often flies into a jealous rage when his wife speaks to other men. If Lukas has a personality disorder, his symptoms are most consistent with those associated with disorders in a. the anxious/fearful cluster b. the dramatic/impulsive cluster c. the neurotic/dissociative cluster d. the odd/eccentric cluster
Concept/Applied LO 18 Page: 598 **a**	177.	Killian lets her husband keep all the financial records for the family, and she expects him to make all the decisions that affect the family. She refuses to make any decisions on her own, and if anything unexpected occurs she calls her husband at work to ask for his advice. If Killian has a personality disorder, her symptoms are most consistent with those associated with disorders in a. the anxious/fearful cluster b. the odd/eccentric cluster c. the dramatic/impulsive cluster d. the neurotic/dissociative cluster
Concept/Applied LO 18 Page: 598 **a**	178.	Erick is impulsive and unpredictable. His moods seem to be constantly changing and all his interpersonal relationships seem to be very unstable. If Erick has a personality disorder, his symptoms are most consistent with those associated with disorders in a. the dramatic/impulsive cluster b. the odd/eccentric cluster c. the anxious/fearful cluster d. the neurotic/dissociative cluster

Factual LO 18 Page: 599 Correct = 69% **b**	179.	What do the avoidant, dependent, and obsessive-compulsive personality disorders have in common? a. mistrustfulness and the inability to connect emotionally with others b. maladaptive efforts to control anxiety and fear c. highly impulsive behavior d. a flair for overdramatizing events
Concept/Applied LO 18 Page: 599 Correct = 65% **c**	180.	A person who withdraws socially because of an intense fear of rejection would most likely be diagnosed as _____ personality, while a person who withdraws socially due to a lack of interest in interpersonal intimacy would most likely be diagnosed as _____ personality. a. a schizoid; a paranoid b. a dependent; a schizotypal c. an avoidant; a schizoid d. an avoidant; a paranoid
Concept/Applied LO 18 Page: 599 **b**	181.	Sophia has always been preoccupied with schedules, lists, and trivial details. She plans everything down to the last detail, and becomes very upset if things don't work out the way she has planned. Last week Sophia went in for a psychological assessment, and based on that assessment, she was told that she may have a personality disorder. Based on her behavior, it is most likely that Sophia has a. schizotypal personality disorder b. obsessive-compulsive personality disorder c. borderline personality disorder d. histrionic personality disorder
Concept/Applied LO 18 Page: 599 **c**	182.	Adam always expects special treatment, and he seems to be preoccupied with his own success. His interpersonal relationships are generally superficial because he seems to lack the ability to understand how others feel. Last week Adam went in for a psychological assessment, and based on that assessment, he was told that he may have a personality disorder. Based on his behavior, it is most likely that Adam has a. schizotypal personality disorder b. obsessive-compulsive personality disorder c. narcissistic personality disorder d. avoidant personality disorder
Factual LO 18 Page: 599 **d**	183.	What do the histrionic, narcissistic, borderline, and antisocial personality disorders have in common? a. mistrustfulness and the inability to connect emotionally with others b. maladaptive efforts to control anxiety and fear c. high levels of communication deviance d. highly impulsive behavior and a flair for overdramatizing events
Concept/Applied LO 18 Page: 599 Correct = 35% **b**	184.	Ellen is self-centered, immature, and excitable. She craves attention, especially from men, with whom she is flirtatious and seductive. Ellen would most likely be diagnosed as having a. avoidant personality disorder b. histrionic personality disorder c. schizoid personality disorder d. dependent personality disorder

Factual LO 18 Page: 599 **c**	185.	The dimensional approach to describing personality disorders a. has been incorporated into DSM-IV b. assumes that people can reliably be placed into nonoverlapping diagnostic categories c. assumes that personality disorders involve maladaptive variants of normal personality traits d. provides a much more complete description of the dynamics of personality disorders
Concept/Applied LO 19 Page: 602 Correct = 48% **b**	186.	Which of the following is not a common characteristic of the antisocial personality? a. manipulative behavior b. excessive guilt c. social charm d. aggressiveness
Factual LO 19 Page: 602 Correct = 81% **c**	187.	A person who does not conform to the accepted norms of morality and behavior and is impulsive, callous, and manipulative is referred to as having a. borderline personality disorder b. paranoid personality disorder c. antisocial personality disorder d. histrionic personality disorder
Concept/Applied LO 19 Page: 602 **d**	188.	Ruth was convicted of five separate counts of fraud. She had used her charm to persuade elderly pensioners to sign their life savings over to her. She confessed to the crimes, but she showed no remorse for her actions. She even bragged at the trial that she would do it all again when she had the chance. In this case, Ruth's behavior is consistent with that seen in a. narcissistic personality disorder b. bipolar disorder c. avoidant personality disorder d. antisocial personality disorder
Concept/Applied LO 19 Page: 602 **a**	189.	In the past 9 months Andrew has been fired by three different employers. He was unreliable and often missed work, and each employer finally let him go when they found he had been stealing money and materials. Andrew feels no remorse over his actions, but he has managed to convince each of his former employers that he is sorry for his actions, and none of the employers plan to press any charges. In this case, Andrew's behavior is consistent with that seen in a. antisocial personality disorder b. bipolar disorder c. dissociative identity disorder d. avoidant personality disorder
Concept/Applied LO 19 Page: 602 Correct = 64% **a**	190.	Which of the following statements is true? a. Although they may be superficially charming, antisocial personalities rarely experience genuine affection for anyone. b. Antisocial personalities are, by definition, violent criminals. c. Antisocial personalities act as they do out of terror of punishment or humiliation. d. Antisocial personalities tend to have an excessively high tolerance for frustration.

Factual LO 19 Page: 602 Correct = 90% a	191.	Investigation into the causes of antisocial behavior has been hampered by the fact that a. there is little available data on the backgrounds of antisocial personalities because they so rarely seek voluntary treatment for the disorder b. most antisocial personalities are in prison and so are unavailable as research subjects c. our courts of law rarely refer antisocial personalities for psychotherapy d. antisocial personality disorder is extremely rare
Factual LO 20 Page: 603 Correct = 88% c	192.	Insanity is a legal status indicating that a. a defendant is unable to understand the nature and purpose of legal proceedings b. an individual is dangerous to themselves or to others c. a person cannot be held responsible for his or her actions because of mental illness d. a person has a chronic mental illness that is not responsive to treatment
Concept/Applied LO 20 Page: 603 b	193.	Jeffrey Dahmer was judged to be legally sane, even though he admitted to butchering, cannibalizing, and then having sex with the dead bodies of over a dozen young men. The judgment of legal sanity meant that a. his actions failed to meet the criteria of cultural deviance b. he was able to appreciate the fact his actions were legally or morally wrong at the time of the crime c. he had recovered from his psychological disorder by the time the trial took place d. his actions failed to meet the criteria of personal distress
Factual LO 20 Page: 604 Correct = 71% c	194.	All of the following people might be subject to involuntary commitment <u>except</u> a. John, who is suicidal b. Samantha, who has threatened her neighbors with a gun c. Ruth, who embezzled $1,000,000 from the bank where she works d. Steve, who is severely disoriented and in need of treatment
Concept/Applied LO 20 Page: 604 b	195.	Valerie has attempted suicide on four separate occasions in the past month. Her family is concerned and they have approached a judge asking for legal intervention to protect Valerie from hurting herself. In this case, it is likely that the judge will a. declare Valerie legally insane and sentence her to time in a psychiatric facility b. order that Valerie be involuntarily committed to a psychiatric facility c. find Valerie is not competent, and postpone the civil hearing until she recovers d. refuse to intervene because Valerie does not pose a risk to others
Concept/Applied LO 21 Page: 604 b	196.	The pancultural view of psychological disorders suggests that a. Western diagnostic concepts have limited validity or utility in other cultural contexts b. basic standards of normality and abnormality are universal across cultures c. culture-bound disorders demonstrate the subjectivity of psychological diagnosis d. there are no universal standards of normality and abnormality
Critical Thinking LO 21 Page: 604 a	197.	Anorexia nervosa is an eating disorder than seems to occur only in Western cultures. The discovery of culture-bound disorders, such as anorexia nervosa, lends support to a. the relativistic view of psychological disorders b. the pancultural view of psychological disorders c. the stress-vulnerability model of psychological disorders d. the idiosyncratic view of psychological disorders

Critical Thinking LO 21 Page: 604 **d**	198.	The prevalence estimates of both schizophrenia and bipolar disorders are roughly comparable across diverse cultures. This finding lends support to a. the relativistic view of psychological disorders b. the stress-vulnerability model of psychological disorders c. the idiosyncratic view of psychological disorders d. the pancultural view of psychological disorders
Factual LO 21 Page: 605 Correct = 68% **d**	199.	Which of the following disorders is seen <u>only</u> in affluent Western cultures? a. schizophrenia b. depression c. bipolar illness d. anorexia nervosa
Critical Thinking LO 21 Page: 605 **a**	200.	The key symptoms of depression in Western cultures are often cognitive symptoms, such as guilt and self-blame. The key symptoms of depression in non-Western cultures are often somatic symptoms, such as headaches and fatigue. The fact that the same disorder can manifest itself in different ways in Western and non-Western cultures lends support to the a. relativistic view of psychological disorders b. pancultural view of psychological disorders c. stress-vulnerability model of psychological disorders d. idiosyncratic view of psychological disorders
Concept/Applied LO 21 Page: 605 Correct = 74% **c**	201.	Which of the following is <u>not</u> an example of a culture-bound disorder? a. koro b. anorexia nervosa c. bipolar disorder d. windingo
Factual LO 21 Page: 605 Correct = 52% **b**	202.	Of the major disorders, symptom patterns are probably <u>most</u> culturally variable for a. schizophrenia b. depression c. bipolar illness d. dissociative disorders
Concept/Applied LO 22 Page: 606 Correct = 87% **d**	203.	According to the stress-vulnerability models for mood disorders and schizophrenic disorders a. vulnerability to these disorders is determined by the environment alone b. vulnerability to these disorders is determined by heredity alone c. traumatic stress is the major cause of these disorders d. these disorders emerge when high biological vulnerability combines with high stress
Critical Thinking LO 22 Page: 606 Correct = 85% **c**	204.	The development of schizophrenia involves a complex interplay among a variety of psychological, biological, and social factors. This illustrates which of your text's unifying themes? a. Our experience of the world is highly subjective. b. Psychology evolves in a sociohistorical context. c. Behavior is determined by multiple causes. d. Psychology is theoretically diverse.
Concept/Applied LO 22 Page: 606 **d**	205.	The stress-vulnerability models that have been developed for mood disorders and schizophrenic disorders illustrate which of your text's unifying themes? a. Our experience of the world is highly subjective. b. Our behavior is shaped by our cultural heritage. c. Psychology is empirical. d. Heredity and environment jointly influence behavior.

Concept/Applied LO 23 Page: 607 **a**	206.	Claire has been diagnosed with anorexia nervosa. Based on the physical symptoms listed in your text, you should expect that Claire will show evidence of a. amenorrhea and low blood pressure b. dental problems and cardiac arrhythmias c. cardiac arrhythmias and elevated blood pressure d. metabolic disturbances and dental problems
Concept/Applied LO 23 Page: 607 **b**	207.	Fiona has been diagnosed with bulimia nervosa. Based on the physical symptoms listed in your text, you should expect that Fiona will show evidence of a. amenorrhea and low blood pressure b. dental problems and cardiac arrhythmias c. cardiac arrhythmias and osteoporosis d. dental problems and elevated blood pressure
Factual LO 23 Page: 607 **c**	208.	Of the following, which is the most accurate statement regarding eating disorders? a. Bulimia nervosa is a more life-threatening condition than anorexia nervosa. b. Both bulimia nervosa and anorexia nervosa lead to death in 2-10% of patients. c. Anorexia nervosa is a more life-threatening condition than bulimia nervosa. d. While bulimia nervosa and anorexia nervosa are both serious conditions, neither is a life-threatening condition.
Concept/Applied LO 23 Page: 608 **d**	209.	Scarlett has anorexia nervosa and Bridget has bulimia nervosa. Based on the research into these two disorders, you should predict that a. Scarlett will be more likely to recognize that her eating behavior is pathological b. both individuals are likely to deny that their eating behavior as pathological c. both individuals will recognize their eating behavior is pathological, but neither will be willing to seek treatment d. Bridget will be more likely to recognize that her eating behavior is pathological
Factual LO 24 Page: 608 **a**	210.	Of the individuals who develop either anorexia nervosa or bulimia nervosa, approximately _____ are females. a. 90-95% b. 70-75% c. 50-55% d. 20-25%
Factual LO 24 Page: 608 **b**	211.	Studies of young women suggest that about _____ develop anorexia nervosa and about _____ develop bulimia nervosa. a. 10%; 20% b. 1 to 1.5%; 2 to 3% c. 2 to 3%; 1 to 1.5% d. 20%; 5%
Factual LO 24 Page: 608 **c**	212.	When individuals enter treatment programs for eating disorders, about _____ experience a full recovery, while about _____ show little or no improvement. a. 20-25%; 40-50% b. 10-15%; 75-80% c. 40-50%; 20-25% d. 75-80%; 10-15%
Concept/Applied LO 25 Page: 609 **d**	213.	Melissa has been diagnosed with anorexia nervosa. If Melissa were to complete a personality assessment, it is likely that her personality profile would list her as a. impulsive, overly sensitive, and low in self-esteem b. rigid, low in self-esteem, and introverted c. impulsive, extroverted, and obsessive d. obsessive, rigid, and emotionally restrained

Concept/Applied LO 25 Page: 609 **a**	214.	Jacqueline has been diagnosed with bulimia nervosa. If Jacqueline were to complete a personality assessment, it is likely that her personality profile would list her as a. impulsive, overly sensitive, and low in self-esteem b. obsessive, rigid, and emotionally restrained c. rigid, low in self-esteem, and introverted d. impulsive, extroverted, and obsessive
Factual LO 25 Page: 609 **b**	215.	Which of the following is <u>not</u> one of the factors that has been linked to the development of anorexia nervosa or bulimia nervosa in young women? a. Mothers who model unhealthy dieting behaviors for their daughters. b. Parents who are negligent or uninvolved in their children's lives. c. The presence of rigid, all-or-none thinking and maladaptive beliefs. d. A genetic vulnerability to eating disorders.
Critical Thinking LO 28 Page: 610 **d**	216.	Stanley was surprised to hear that Jennifer had been treated by a psychiatrist ten years ago. When he first met Jennifer she seemed to be calm and rational, and she certainly didn't look "psychotic." If you were to ask Stanley to estimate the overall prevalence of psychological disorders, you should predict that a. the representativeness heuristic would cause him to overestimate the overall prevalence rate b. the conjunction fallacy would cause him to overestimate the overall prevalence rate c. the availability heuristic would cause him to underestimate the overall prevalence rate d. the representativeness heuristic would cause him to underestimate the overall prevalence rate
Critical Thinking LO 28 Page: 610 **a**	217.	In determining the probabilities associated with comorbidity (the coexistence of two or more psychological disorders), epidemiologists would need to work with a. conjunctive probabilities b. cumulative probabilities c. point prevalence rates d. disjunctive probabilities
Critical Thinking LO 28 Page: 611 **c**	218.	Often, cases of dissociative identity disorder (multiple personality disorder) receive wide press coverage, leading people to believe this disorder is a relatively common psychological problem when, in fact, it is quite rare. People's estimates of the prevalence of dissociative identity disorder may be influenced to a large extent by a. the representativeness heuristic b. the conjunction fallacy c. the availability heuristic d. the hindsight bias
Integrative Correct = 59% **c**	219.	A phobic disorder is to anxiety disorders as a _____ disorder is to somatoform disorders. a. depressive b. multiple-personality c. conversion d. panic
Integrative **b**	220.	The likelihood a person would be declared legally incompetent would be highest for a. a generalized anxiety disorder b. a schizophrenic disorder c. a substance-abuse disorder d. an antisocial personality disorder

Study Guide LO 1 Page: 570 **b**	221.	Which of the following concepts or people asserts that abnormal behavior is best thought of as an illness? a. the behavioral model b. the medical model c. Thomas Szasz d. Arthur Staats
Study Guide LO 4 Page: 573 **a**	222.	In Rosenhan's study involving admission of pseudopatients to psychiatric facilities, most of the "patients" were a. diagnosed as seriously disturbed b. diagnosed as suffering from a mild neurosis c. dismissed within two days d. misdiagnosed by the ward attendants but correctly diagnosed by the professional staff
Study Guide LO 7 Page: 578 **d**	223.	An individual gets sudden, paralyzing attacks of anxiety and fears going out in public away from her house. Which anxiety disorder does this describe? a. generalized anxiety disorder b. phobic disorder c. obsessive-compulsive disorder d. agoraphobia
Study Guide LO 8 Page: 580 **a**	224.	Human beings may have evolved to be more easily conditioned to fear some stimuli than others. This is Seligman's notion of a. preparedness b. anxiety differentiation c. somatization d. learned helplessness
Study Guide LO 9 Page: 582 **b**	225.	Paralysis or loss of feeling that does not match underlying anatomical organization is a symptom of a. somatization disorder b. conversion disorder c. hypochondriasis d. malingering
Study Guide LO 12 Page: 588 **d**	226.	The concordance rate for mood disorders has been found to be about 67% among identical twins and 17% among fraternal twins. Thee data suggest that the mood disorders a. are caused primarily by stress b. have an onset at an early age c. are due primarily to family environment d. are caused in part by genetic factors
Study Guide LO 15 Page: 593 **a**	227.	The disorder marked by striking motor disturbances ranging from rigidity to random motor activity and incoherence is termed a. catatonic schizophrenia b. multiple personality c. dissociative disorder d. paranoid schizophrenia
Study Guide LO 20 Page: 603 **a**	228.	A court declares that because of a mental illness, an individual is not responsible for his criminal actions. The individual is a. insane b. psychopathic c. psychotic d. schizophrenic

Study Guide LO 21 Page: 605 **c**	229.	Which of the following are disorders that occur cross-culturally? a. generalized anxiety disorder and panic disorder b. hypochondriasis and somatization disorder c. schizophrenia and bipolar mood disorder d. bulimia and anorexia nervosa
Study Guide LO 24 Page: 608 **d**	230.	A disorder that was extremely rare prior to the last half of the 20th century is a. manic-depressive disorder b. schizophrenia c. obsessive-compulsive disorder d. anorexia nervosa
Online Quiz LO 1 Page: 570 **a**	231.	Prior to the 18th century, people who exhibited abnormal behavior were thought to be _____ and were treated through _____. a. possessed by evil spirits; exorcism b. mentally ill; exorcism c. mentally ill; verbal psychotherapy d. possessed by evil spirits; drug therapy
Online Quiz LO 5 Page: 575 **b**	232.	The DSM classification system is said to be "multiaxial." This means that the system a. permits multiple diagnoses of a single individual b. asks for judgments about individuals on numerous separate dimensions c. allows many different potential methods of diagnosing people d. is characterized by poor reliability
Online Quiz LO 6 Page: 576 **d**	233.	The most common psychological disorders in the United States are a. schizophrenic disorders b. personality disorders c. mood disorders d. anxiety disorders
Online Quiz LO 7 Page: 579 **c**	234.	Dave washes his hands at least 50 times per day, even though his hands are rarely dirty. Dave's behavior is an example of a. an obsession b. a phobia c. a compulsion d. a delusion
Online Quiz LO 9 Page: 582 **b**	235.	Somatoform disorders involve a. the deliberate faking of physical illness b. apparent physical illness caused by psychological factors c. genuine physical illness caused in part by psychological factors d. psychological disorders that respond to medical intervention
Online Quiz LO 10 Page: 585 **b**	236.	Most authentic cases of multiple-personality disorder have in common a background of a. extremely overprotective parents b. a traumatic childhood characterized by physical, emotional, or sexual abuse c. extremely distorted communication patterns in the family d. having been reinforced for "crazy" behavior
Online Quiz LO 11 Page: 588 **b**	237.	Inflated self-esteem, distractibility, heightened emotionality, and grandiose planning are all symptoms associated with a. fugue states b. bipolar disorders c. dissociative disorders d. obsessive-compulsive disorders

Online Quiz LO 15 Page: 594 **b**	238.	A two-category scheme for classification of schizophrenia has been suggested as an alternative to the older four categories. These two categories are based on a. presence or absence of delusions b. predominance of positive or negative symptoms c. early or late age of onset d. slow or fast developing symptoms
Online Quiz LO 18 Page: 598 **d**	239.	The class of disorders marked by extreme and inflexible characteristics that cause subjective distress or impaired social and occupational functioning are referred to as a. mood disorders b. affective disorders c. conduct disorders d. personality disorders
Online Quiz LO 21 Page: 605 **b**	240.	Which of the following statements is <u>false</u>? a. Prevalence estimates for schizophrenia and bipolar disorder appear to be roughly comparable across diverse cultures. b. Prevalence estimates for most diagnostic categories appear to be quite similar across cultures. c. Disorders that have a strong biological component tend to exhibit greater cross-cultural similarity in prevalence. d. Environmental factors at work in specific cultures probably foster some disorders more readily that others.

ESSAY QUESTIONS

1. It has been said that not all deviant behavior is maladaptive, but all maladaptive behavior is deviant. Discuss this idea, based on what you've learned about the definition and criteria of abnormal behavior.

    Good answers should reflect an understanding of the various ways of defining and characterizing abnormal behavior. A deviant behavior is one that deviates from the norm and is considered inappropriate in one's society. Most students can come up with several examples of such deviant behavior that may, nevertheless, be adaptive in certain circumstances. Such deviant behavior is not maladaptive. On the other hand, behavior is maladaptive when it interferes with one's functioning in one or more of the various arenas of life (social, occupational, etc.). Most societies have evolved in such a way that these kinds of behaviors are both uncommon and considered inappropriate, thus deviant. There may be exceptions here, too, however.

2. There appear to be some similarities between posttraumatic stress disorder (Chapter 13) and the dissociative disorders in that most cases of each type of disorder are thought to result from extreme stress. How would you justify creating separate classifications for these disorders?

    Students should demonstrate an understanding of the characteristics of each type of disorder, and should focus on the differences between them that justify classifying them separately. Stress plays a role in the etiology of both, but reactions to the stress experienced are quite different for the two types of disorder. Characteristic of posttraumatic stress disorder is the inability to get the traumatic experience out of mind and other evidences of being "overinvolved" with the stressful situation. Symptoms may persist for quite some time.

    In cases of dissociative disorders, rather than being overinvolved with the stressful situation, patients use various means to escape involvement and its attendant anxieties and conflicts. These means involve somehow altering consciousness in order to blot out the stressful experience. Often dissociative disorders begin and end suddenly. These cases are often traced to traumatic events in childhood, though the disorder may not appear until adulthood.

3. Freud believed that most, if not all, psychological disorders are mainly the result of anxiety. However, Freudian explanations of the anxiety disorders receive much less attention today than they once did. From what you've learned of Freudian theory, how would a Freudian explanation of the etiology of the anxiety disorders differ from the types of explanations presented in your text?

    Freud would say that the anxiety disorders result from internal events and drives and motivations that the patient is not conscious of. We normally feel anxiety when we are threatened, but in the case of anxiety disorders, anxiety is experienced even when we're not aware of any dangerous threat. Often there's just the feeling of danger or a threat being present. Everyone uses defense mechanisms to alleviate feelings of anxiety, but in clinical cases, these mechanisms are not effective enough to provide relief. Anxiety that's severe enough to be considered abnormal may be caused by unacceptable impulses that are on the verge of breaking into consciousness, threatened disapproval, withdrawal of love, and fear of abandonment. These are examples of events that might be threatening to a small child and which might be thrust into the unconscious, only to emerge later in the form of the symptoms of an anxiety disorder.

    Getting more specific, a phobic object or situation would symbolically stand for something that the patient is frightened of, either consciously or unconsciously. Obsessions and compulsions function by directing attention away from fearful, unconscious thoughts.

4. According to the DSM-IV, individuals should not be diagnosed as having a personality disorder before they're 18 years old because personality is not well established before then. From what you know about personality development (Chapters 11 and 12), can you support this position? You may wish to answer from the particular viewpoint of one of the personality theorists covered in your text (e.g., Erikson, Mischel, Maslow, or others).

Answers should reveal an understanding of the category of personality disorders as well as something about personality development. A couple of examples of outlines for answers follow:

In personality disorders the individual shows extreme, inflexible personality traits that cause subjective distress or impaired social and occupational functioning. It's reasonable to think that these extreme traits develop in basically the same way that more normal personality traits develop. According to Erikson, certain crises arise at predictable life stages within a society, and individuals are faced with the challenge of dealing satisfactorily with them if their personality and emotional status are to be healthy. Less than optimal coping with the challenges of a particular life crisis might lead to a personality disorder. Most of the personality disorders seem to involve traits that Erikson believes are influenced by social experiences during the years before the age of eighteen. So he might agree that we're unlikely to see personality disorders before that age.

The social learning theorists would point to observational learning as the prime mechanism by which maladaptive personality traits might develop. From material in the text, we're given no clear indication that Bandura believed that personality development occurred mainly in childhood, although his best-known research has been with children. Like others in the larger learning-theory camp, social learning theorists believe that learning continues to occur throughout life. So there's no principled reason why they'd restrict the emergence of extreme personality traits to any particular life stage.

5. Some of the most prominent modern theories of the mood disorders focus primarily on cognitive factors. You learned in Chapter 10 that some theorists believe the experience of emotion is heavily influenced by cognitive factors. In what ways do some of these cognitive theories of emotion agree with theories about cognitive factors in the etiology of the mood disorders?

Essentially, cognitive theories of the mood disorders say that depression, in particular, results from a particular kind of thinking, especially a negative attributional style. Schachter's two-factor theory of emotion states that we experience particular emotions through interpreting physiological arousal in accordance with the current environment. If situational cues appear to be in accord with an explanation of negative events that places the blame on the individual, then one may experience unpleasant emotions and depression may result. If this pattern of interpreting physiological arousal hardens into one's habitual attributional style, then clinical depression may result.

This page intentionally left blank.

Chapter Fifteen
Psychotherapy

LEARNING OBJECTIVES

1. Identify the three major categories of therapy and discuss how various demographic variables relate to the likelihood of treatment.
2. Describe the various types of mental health professionals involved in the provision of therapy.
3. Explain the logic of psychoanalysis and describe the techniques by which analysts probe the unconscious.
4. Discuss resistance and transference in psychoanalysis.
5. Identify the elements of therapeutic climate and discuss therapeutic process in Rogers' client-centered therapy.
6. Discuss the logic, goals, and techniques of cognitive therapy.
7. Describe how group therapy is generally conducted and identify some advantages of this approach.
8. Discuss Eysenck's critique of insight therapy and more recent evidence on the efficacy of insight therapies.
9. Summarize the general principles underlying behavioral approaches to therapy.
10. Describe the goals and procedures of systematic desensitization and aversion therapy.
11. Describe the goals and techniques of social skills training and biofeedback.
12. Discuss evidence on the effectiveness of behavior therapies.
13. Describe the principal categories of drugs used in the treatment of psychological disorders.
14. Discuss evidence on the effects and problems of drug treatments for psychological disorders.
15. Describe ECT and discuss its therapeutic effects and its risks.
16. Summarize the concerns that have been expressed about the impact of managed care on the treatment of psychological disorders.
17. Discuss the pros and cons of empirically validated treatments.
18. Discuss the merits of blending or combining different approaches to therapy.
19. Discuss the barriers that lead to underutilization of mental health services by ethnic minorities and possible solutions to the problem.
20. Explain why people grew disenchanted with mental hospitals and describe the community mental health movement.
21. Describe the deinstitutionalization trend and evaluate its effects.
22. Explain how this chapter highlighted two of the text's unifying themes.
23. Discuss when and where to seek therapy, and the potential importance of a therapist's sex, professional background, and cost.
24. Discuss the importance of a therapist's theoretical approach.
25. Summarize what one should look for in a prospective therapist and what one should expect out of therapy.
26. Explain how placebo effects and regression toward the mean can complicate the evaluation of therapy.

MULTIPLE-CHOICE QUESTIONS

Factual
LO 1
Page: 616
Correct = 74%
a

1. Which of the following statements is <u>true</u>?
   a. The first systematic psychotherapy procedure was Freud's psychoanalysis.
   b. Since Freud's time, all forms of treatment for psychological disorders have involved verbal interaction.
   c. All psychotherapies employ essentially the same method of treatment.
   d. Insight therapy is the most effective method for treating psychological disorders.

Factual
LO 1
Page: 616
Correct = 57%
a

2. A psychotherapist who participates in complex verbal interactions with clients in order to enhance clients' understanding of themselves and their problems would be classified as a(n) _____ therapist.
   a. insight
   b. behavior
   c. biomedical
   d. aversive

Concept/Applied
LO 1
Page: 616
a

3. Vicki is seeing a therapist in an attempt to work through the troubles in her relationship with her father. During her meetings with her therapist, the two of them often engage in lengthy verbal interactions, and her therapist tries to help Vicki work through a variety of potential solutions for the problems she is facing. In this case, her therapist's approach to treatment would <u>most</u> likely be classified as
   a. insight therapy
   b. behavior therapy
   c. biomedical therapy
   d. homeopathic therapy

Concept/Applied
LO 1
Page: 616
d

4. Claude has been seeing a therapist in an attempt to finally stop smoking. The therapist has described a number of techniques that they might try to eliminate Claude's behavior of smoking. In this case, his therapist's approach to treatment would <u>most</u> likely be classified as
   a. insight therapy
   b. biomedical therapy
   c. homeopathic therapy
   d. behavior therapy

Factual
LO 1
Page: 616
Correct = 97%
b

5. Which of the following is <u>not</u> one of the main categories of treatment?
   a. insight therapies
   b. revelation therapies
   c. behavior therapies
   d. biomedical therapies

Concept/Applied
LO 1
Page: 616
c

6. Leslie has been feeling depressed for a number of weeks. She thinks she may need to see a therapist to help her overcome her depression, but she doesn't want to see anyone who is going to dwell on her childhood and try to work through any problems she experienced years ago. She wants to see someone who will focus on her current symptoms. In this example, it appears that Leslie is looking for a therapist whose approach to treatment would be classified as
   a. insight therapy
   b. non-invasive therapy
   c. biomedical therapy
   d. hypnotherapy

Factual LO 1 Page: 616 Correct = 89% **d**	7.	The two most common problems among those who seek psychotherapy are a. marital conflicts and a sense of emptiness b. loneliness and boredom c. low self-esteem and irrational thinking d. anxiety and depression
Factual LO 1 Page: 617 **c**	8.	Which of the following statements is <u>true</u>? a. Men are more likely than women to enter therapy. b. People from the lower socioeconomic classes are more likely to enter therapy than those from the upper classes. c. Many people who need therapy don't receive it. d. Only people who have an identifiable mental disorder are eligible for therapy.
Factual LO 2 Page: 618 Correct = 47% **a**	9.	Which of the following academic degrees is <u>not</u> associated with being a psychologist? a. M.D. b. Ph.D. c. Psy.D. d. Ed.D.
Concept/Applied LO 2 Page: 618 Correct = 84% **b**	10.	Which of the following psychologists is <u>most</u> likely to deal with the most severe mental health problems? a. counseling psychologist b. clinical psychologist c. school psychologist d. research psychologist
Factual LO 2 Page: 618 Correct = 97% **b**	11.	The theoretical difference between a clinical psychologist and a counseling psychologist is that a. the clinical psychologist has a doctorate; the counseling psychologist has a master's degree b. the clinical psychologist specializes in the treatment of mental disorders; the counseling psychologist specializes in the treatment of everyday adjustment problems c. only the clinical psychologist can prescribe drugs d. clinical psychologists are trained to provide behavior therapy; counseling psychologists are trained to provide insight therapy
Factual LO 2 Page: 618 Correct = 74% **c**	12.	Psychiatrists a. have essentially the same education as clinical psychologists b. are less likely to use psychoanalytic methods than psychologists c. are physicians who specialize in the treatment of mental disorders d. focus exclusively on biomedical therapies in treating psychological disorders
Concept/Applied LO 2 Page: 618 **c**	13.	Clive is a clinical psychologist and his sister Grace is a psychiatrist. The main difference between these two professionals would be the fact that Clive would a. typically deal with patients who have more severe problems than the patients Grace usually sees b. normally treat young children while Grace would treat more adults c. have a degree in psychology while Stephanie would have a medical degree d. take a psychoanalytic approach in treating patients while Grace would take a behavioral approach

Concept/Applied LO 2 Page: 618 Correct = 76% **d**	14.	Which of the following disorders would be <u>least</u> apt to be treated by psychiatrists? a. schizophrenia b. mood disorder c. anxiety disorder d. marital problems
Concept/Applied LO 2 Page: 618 **b**	15.	Gilbert just graduated from medical school and has entered a four-year residency at a local hospital. He plans to specialize in the treatment of mental disorders. Gilbert would <u>most</u> likely be classified as a. a psychiatric nurse b. a psychiatrist c. a clinical psychologist d. a counseling psychologist
Factual LO 2 Page: 618 **d**	16.	Today psychoanalysis is <u>most</u> likely to be practiced by a. clinical psychologists b. counseling psychologists c. social workers d. psychiatrists
Concept/Applied LO 2 Page: 618 **d**	17.	Berle has her master's degree and she provides counseling and support to patients who have recently received treatment at a mental health facility. Berle would <u>most</u> likely describe herself as a. a psychiatric nurse b. a counseling psychologist c. a psychiatrist d. a clinical social worker
Concept/Applied LO 3 Page: 619 **d**	18.	The idea that interactions designed to help a client develop self-knowledge and thus progress to healthy changes in personality and behavior is the basis for a. psychopharmacological therapy b. emotive therapy c. behavioral therapy d. insight therapy
Concept/Applied LO 3 Page: 619 Correct = 85% **b**	19.	What do psychoanalytic, client-centered, and cognitive therapies have in common? a. They all deal with psychotic problems. b. They all stress insight into the self. c. They all require an M.D. degree to practice. d. They all use drugs as part of the treatment.
Concept/Applied LO 3 Page: 619 Correct = 78% **a**	20.	In treating an abnormal behavior, the main concern of a <u>psychoanalyst</u> would be to discover the a. childhood unconscious conflict that led to the behavior b. environmental conditions that are maintaining the behavior at its current frequency c. ways in which the behavior keeps the client from becoming self-actualized d. inappropriate thought patterns that underlie the behavior
Critical Thinking LO 3 Page: 619 **a**	21.	Dr. Stroetz believes that most psychological disorders can be successfully treated by bringing unconscious conflicts and defenses into conscious awareness. Knowing this, you might expect that Dr. Stroetz's bookshelves contain a large number of books written by a. Sigmund Freud b. Hans Eysenck c. Carl Rogers d. Joseph Wolpe

Critical Thinking LO 3 Page: 619 **b**	22.	You make an appointment to see a therapist and as you are waiting, you notice that a large number of the books on the therapist's shelves deal with the work of Sigmund Freud. You might expect that this therapist will a. use counterconditioning to reverse maladaptive behaviors b. emphasize the need to bring unconscious conflicts and defenses into conscious awareness c. provide a supportive emotional environment while allowing you to determine the pace and direction of your therapy d. help you recognize and change negative thoughts and maladaptive beliefs
Factual LO 3 Page: 619 Correct = 78% **b**	23.	According to Freud, neurosis usually results from unconscious conflicts over a. power and aggression b. sex and aggression c. sex and achievement d. power and achievement
Concept/Applied LO 3 Page: 620 **c**	24.	Mario recently started seeing a therapist. At the start of each session Mario lies down and starts talking about anything that comes to mind. He often rambles, and he sometimes thinks that the things he describes seem trivial or silly, but his therapist encourages him to say whatever comes into his mind. This therapeutic technique is common among therapists who use a. a client-centered approach in therapy b. a cognitive approach in therapy c. a psychoanalytic approach in therapy d. a holistic approach to therapy
Concept/Applied LO 3 Page: 620 **d**	25.	Miriam has been in psychotherapy for five years. At the start of each session she describes any dreams that she has had since her last session. Her therapist analyzes the symbolism in these dreams, and helps Miriam understand the unconscious conflicts that underlie the dreams. In this case, Miriam is most likely seeing a therapist who is trained in a. the client-centered approach b. rational-emotive therapy c. biofeedback therapy d. psychoanalysis
Factual LO 3 Page: 620 Correct = 82% **d**	26.	All of the following are Freudian techniques to bring unconscious material to consciousness except a. free association b. analysis of transference c. dream analysis d. directed confrontation
Concept/Applied LO 3 Page: 620 **a**	27.	Free association and dream analysis were held to be major methods to discover the makeup of a. the unconscious b. the conscious c. irrational thoughts d. maladaptive behaviors
Factual LO 3 Page: 620 Correct = 91% **c**	28.	In free association a. clients relate the events of their dreams as they remember them b. clients are restricted to talking about their sexual conflicts only c. clients spontaneously express their thoughts and feelings exactly as they occur d. therapists openly express their interpretations of clients' thoughts and feelings

Factual LO 3 Page: 620 **b**	29.	Which of the following would Freud consider to be the most direct means of access to the unconscious mind? a. transference b. the content of dreams c. the client's feelings toward the therapist d. the client's attempts to hinder the progress of therapy
Factual LO 3 Page: 620 Correct = 31% **c**	30.	According to Freud, the events in dreams a. have no connection to the client's real life and thus are irrelevant in therapy b. are symbolic representations of recent events in the client's life c. need to be analyzed by the therapist and interpreted for the client d. are logical interpretations of random neural activation
Concept/Applied LO 3 Page: 620 **a**	31.	Michelle has been having a recurring dream for the past four months, and during a session with her psychotherapist the therapist proposed one possible explanation that might give meaning to the images in Michelle's dream. In providing an explanation for the meaning of the dream, the therapist is engaged in a. interpretation b. transference c. clarification d. free association
Factual LO 4 Page: 621 **c**	32.	Resistance a. consists primarily of conscious efforts to hinder the progress of therapy b. refers to the client's reaction to sexual advances from the therapist c. involves largely unconscious defensive maneuvers intended to hinder the progress of therapy d. refers to the subtle, primarily unconscious ways in which young children rebel against their parents' demands
Concept/Applied LO 4 Page: 621 **c**	33.	A client in psychoanalysis has been arriving late for sessions, acting hostile to the analyst, and making up dreams. This is <u>most</u> likely a. transference b. frustration c. resistance d. projection
Concept/Applied LO 4 Page: 621 **b**	34.	Jimmy has been in psychotherapy for several months, but during the last few sessions he has been distracted and inattentive. When his therapist asks him to describe any dreams he has had recently, Jimmy insists that he doesn't remember any of his dreams. According to Freud, Jimmy's behavior may be a sign of a. defensive neurosis b. resistance c. transference d. insight
Factual LO 4 Page: 621 Correct = 90% **b**	35.	Transference a. occurs when the client makes conscious attempts to hinder the progress of therapy b. refers to the client's redirection toward the therapist of unconscious emotional reactions originally felt toward others c. involves transferring memories of past traumatic experiences to current dreams d. occurs when the therapist treats the client as though the client was an important authority figure

Concept/Applied LO 4 Page: 621 c	36.	Transference in psychoanalytic therapy may reveal itself when the patient a. transfers from one stage of analysis to another b. changes the way the patient feels about people close to the patient c. responds to the therapist as though he or she were the patient's parent d. shifts social roles during the course of therapy
Concept/Applied LO 4 Page: 621 b	37.	After several months of psychoanalysis, Andy begins to feel intensely angry at his therapist, although the therapist has been consistently warm and supportive. Andy's feelings are probably a. due to a misinterpretation of the therapist's behavior b. a result of transference c. a sign of an impending psychosis d. a result of sudden insight about some childhood experience
Concept/Applied LO 4 Page: 621 Correct = 98% a	38.	Treating the therapist as though he were a very important person from one's past, such as a parent, defines a. transference b. resistance c. frustration d. reaction formation
Concept/Applied LO 4 Page: 621 a	39.	Tasha has been in psychotherapy for just over a year. Lately she has started to express a strong sexual desire for her therapist. Unconsciously she is acting toward him the way she wishes she could act toward her own husband. According to Freud, Tasha's behavior may be a sign of a. transference b. resistance c. free association d. defensive neurosis
Concept/Applied LO 4 Page: 621 d	40.	George has been in psychotherapy for several months. When he first started therapy George had a very positive relationship with his therapist. However, over the past two weeks he has shown increasing hostility and he often yells and becomes threatening when his therapist offers her interpretations of the things that George says during therapy. According to Freud, George's behavior may be a. evidence that his psychological problems are worsening b. a sign of repressed free association c. evidence of defensive neurosis d. a sign of transference
Concept/Applied LO 4 Page: 621 Correct = 79% d	41.	The psychoanalytic therapist deals with transference by a. modeling new behavior for the client b. moving to a new topic for discussion c. ignoring it and recentering on the real problem d. allowing the patient to work through the feelings associated with transference
Concept/Applied LO 5 Page: 621 Correct = 88% a	42.	Rogers named his technique "client-centered therapy" to emphasize his belief that a. clients should play a major role in determining the pace and direction of their therapy b. clients should always be the center of attention c. therapists should always share all of their thoughts, feelings, and experiences with clients d. the client is in a position of natural status and authority over the therapist

Factual LO 5 Page: 621 c	43.	Carl Rogers' client-centered therapy grew from the _____ tradition. a. psychoanalytic b. behaviorist c. humanistic d. cognitive
Factual LO 5 Page: 621 Correct = 93% b	44.	The therapeutic technique that focuses on providing a supportive emotional climate for clients, who in turn play a major role in determining the pace and direction of therapy, is referred to as a. rational-emotive therapy b. client-centered therapy c. psychoanalytic therapy d. Gestalt therapy
Concept/Applied LO 5 Page: 622 Correct = 71% c	45.	According to Rogers, personal distress occurs when a. unconscious conflicts threaten to rise to the surface of conscious awareness b. a person engages in negative thinking c. there is incongruence between a person's self-concept and reality d. a person is lacking in self-control
Concept/Applied LO 5 Page: 622 a	46.	An important goal of client-centered therapy is to a. help clients realize they don't have to worry constantly about approval from others b. help clients achieve a greater understanding of how long-repressed childhood conflicts can affect their adult behavior c. change the ways clients think d. modify clients' maladaptive behavior patterns
Concept/Applied LO 5 Page: 622 b	47.	Dr. Benz always tries to be honest with her clients, and she never becomes defensive, even if the clients ridicule her feedback or her methods of therapy. According to Carl Rogers, Dr. Benz is displaying the quality of a. empathy in dealing with her clients b. genuineness in dealing with her clients c. unconditional positive regard in dealing with her clients d. validity in dealing with her clients
Concept/Applied LO 5 Page: 622 c	48.	Charlene is talking with her father, and she confesses that she lied about where she had been on the weekend. Her father tells Charlene that he loves her, but that he doesn't approve of her lying. According to Carl Rogers, Charlene's father is displaying the quality of a. empathy b. validity c. unconditional positive regard d. selective abstraction
Concept/Applied LO 5 Page: 622 b	49.	Which of the following statements best represents the approach of a <u>client-centered</u> therapist in treating a chronically anxious client? a. "Let's look for ways in which you might actually be benefiting from your anxiety." b. "So, you feel that your world is a very scary place to be." c. "Let's see if we can identify the irrational beliefs that are producing your anxiety." d. "Do you feel that your mother adequately met your need for emotional support when you were a child?"

Concept/Applied LO 5 Page: 622 Correct = 62% c	50.	Client: "I've had a bad week. I'm really down." Therapist: "You've had some unpleasant experiences lately and are feeling quite depressed as a result." The therapist's statement in this interaction is intended to communicate _____ to the client. a. genuineness b. unconditional positive regard c. empathy d. disapproval
Concept/Applied LO 5 Page: 622 d	51.	Lange tells his therapist: "My whole world is a mess and nobody cares for me or is concerned about what happens to me." Lange's therapist knows that he has many friends who are concerned about him, but she tells him: "I understand why you might feel that way right now, and it must be difficult for you to deal with your feelings of abandonment." In this interaction, Lange's therapist is displaying the quality that Carl Rogers termed a. unconditional positive regard b. genuineness c. clarification d. empathy
Concept/Applied LO 5 Page: 622 c	52.	The characteristics of client-centered therapy that are necessary to encourage client growth include all but which of the following? a. empathy b. genuineness c. directedness d. unconditional positive regard
Concept/Applied LO 5 Page: 622 d	53.	Dr. Nenning is a psychotherapist who is extremely supportive of all his clients. He encourages his clients to talk about their concerns, and he often acts as a sounding board, restating and clarifying the themes that come to the surface as his clients speak freely about their concerns and problems. Dr. Nenning appears to be a. a therapist who uses a modern psychodynamic approach b. a therapist who uses Beck's cognitive approach to therapy c. a therapist who uses existential therapy methods d. a client-centered therapist
Factual LO 5 Page: 623 Correct = 76% a	54.	In client-centered therapy the therapist's key task is a. clarification b. interpretation c. behavior modification d. cognitive evaluation
Concept/Applied LO 6 Page: 623 a	55.	Cognitive therapy emphasizes a. recognizing and changing negative thought patterns b. reliving of traumatic childhood experiences c. increasing the client's self-awareness and self-acceptance d. modifying maladaptive behaviors
Critical Thinking LO 6 Page: 623 a	56.	Dr. Guralski believes that most psychological disorders are a result of negative thoughts and maladaptive beliefs. Knowing this, you might expect that Dr. Guralski's bookshelves contain a large number of books written by a. Aaron Beck b. Sigmund Freud c. Hans Eysenck d. Carl Rogers

Factual
LO 6
Page: 623
c

57. Cognitive therapy originally developed as a treatment approach to
    a. marital problems
    b. anxiety problems
    c. depression
    d. schizophrenia

Critical Thinking
LO 6
Page: 623
b

58. You make an appointment to see a therapist and, as you are waiting, you notice that a large number of the books on the therapist's shelves deal with the work of Aaron Beck. You might expect that this therapist will
    a. emphasize the need to bring unconscious conflicts and defenses into conscious awareness
    b. help you recognize and change negative thoughts and maladaptive beliefs
    c. provide a supportive emotional environment while allowing you to determine the pace and direction of your therapy
    d. use counterconditioning to reverse maladaptive behaviors

Factual
LO 6
Page: 623
Correct = 97%
c

59. According to Beck, which types of thought processes tend to produce depression?
    a. blaming setbacks on circumstantial factors
    b. focusing selectively on positive experiences
    c. drawing negative conclusions about one's personal worth based on insignificant events
    d. failing to accept responsibility for one's own actions

Concept/Applied
LO 6
Page: 623
Correct = 64%
c

60. Which of the following statements best represents the approach of a cognitive therapist in treating a chronically anxious client?
    a. "So, you feel that your world is a very scary place to be."
    b. "Let's look for ways in which you might actually be benefiting from your anxiety."
    c. "Let's see if we can identify the irrational thoughts that are producing your anxiety."
    d. "Do you feel that your mother adequately met your need for emotional support when you were a child?"

Concept/Applied
LO 6
Page: 624
d

61. Dr. Varsho is a psychotherapist who often argues openly with her clients. She is very assertive, and tries to persuade her clients to alter their patterns of thinking. Dr. Varsho is
    a. using a client-centered approach to therapy
    b. probably not very successful as a therapist
    c. using a modern psychodynamic approach to therapy
    d. a therapist who uses Beck's cognitive approach

Factual
LO 6
Page: 624
b

62. Cognitive therapy borrows many techniques from _____ therapy.
    a. group
    b. behavior
    c. client-centered
    d. psychodynamic

Concept/Applied
LO 6
Page: 624
d

63. Bryson was surprised by his first psychotherapy session. When the session was over the therapist gave Bryson a homework assignment. She asked Bryson to record any thoughts that came to his mind when he experienced a setback at home or in his job. In this case, it appears that Bryson is seeing a therapist who uses
    a. client-centered therapy
    b. a psychoanalytic approach to therapy
    c. social skills training
    d. Beck's cognitive therapy

Factual LO 7 Page: 625 Correct = 92% **d**	64.	Which of the following statements about group therapy is <u>false</u>? a. Therapy groups typically consist of 4 to 15 participants. b. The therapist may share his or her personal experiences and feelings with the group. c. Group participants essentially function as therapists for each other. d. Group therapy is typically more expensive than individual therapy.
Factual LO 7 Page: 625 **b**	65.	Which of the following is <u>not</u> among the advantages of group therapy? a. Participants often come to realize that their misery is not unique. b. It produces a significantly higher recovery rate than individual therapy. c. It provides an opportunity for participants to work on social skills in a safe environment. d. Certain kinds of problems are especially well-suited to group treatment.
Concept/Applied LO 7 Page: 625 Correct = 93% **a**	66.	The <u>most</u> important aspect of group therapy is that group members a. provide acceptance and emotional support b. challenge one another's false belief structures c. increase conformity and compliance d. reduce both transference and resistance
Factual LO 8 Page: 625 **c**	67.	The recovery from a disorder without formal treatment is referred to as a. a placebo effect b. reified recovery c. spontaneous remission d. countertransference
Factual LO 8 Page: 625 Correct = 69% **a**	68.	With regard to psychological disorders, spontaneous remission refers to a a. recovery from a disorder that occurs without formal treatment b. recovery from a disorder that occurs as a result of formal treatment c. sudden recurrence of a disorder in a client who had apparently been cured d. failure to recover despite extensive treatment
Concept/Applied LO 8 Page: 625 **a**	69.	Carolyn worked for the same company for twelve years. Six months ago the company closed down. Carolyn had been feeling extremely depressed over the loss of her job, and she had considered seeing a therapist for help with her depression. However, for the past week she has been feeling much better, and has decided that she doesn't need professional treatment after all. In this case, Carolyn appears to have experienced a. spontaneous remission b. personal insight c. the placebo effect d. transference
Factual LO 8 Page: 625 **c**	70.	Hans Eysenck is famous for studying the outcome of insight therapies. Which of the following was <u>not</u> one of his findings? a. Neurotics who were treated showed about a two-thirds recovery rate. b. Untreated neurotics showed about a two-thirds recovery rate. c. Neurotics in therapy showed a significantly higher recovery rate than untreated neurotics. d. Treatment seemed to produce little difference over nontreatment in recovery of neurotics.

Concept/Applied LO 8 Page: 626 Correct = 84% **b**	71.	Clients' subjective ratings of changes in their feelings, measures of clients' behavioral change, and therapists' subjective ratings of change in clients' adaptive functioning could all be used as measures of a. therapists' professional competence b. the effectiveness of therapy c. placebo effects d. personality differences among clients
Factual LO 9 Page: 626 Correct = 79% **a**	72.	Behavior therapy is derived from a. research by B. F. Skinner, Hans Eysenck, and Joseph Wolpe b. cognitive research c. psychodynamic research d. Gestalt psychology
Concept/Applied LO 9 Page: 626 **c**	73.	According to behavior therapists, pathological behaviors a. are signs of an underlying emotional or cognitive problem b. should be viewed as the expression of an unconscious sexual or aggressive conflict c. can be modified directly, through the application of established principles of conditioning d. are the product of irrational thinking
Concept/Applied LO 9 Page: 626 **b**	74.	A <u>behavior</u> therapist's major concern in treating an abnormal behavior would be to discover a. the childhood unconscious conflict that led to the behavior b. how situational factors are evoking the troublesome behavior c. the ways in which the behavior keeps the client from becoming self-actualized d. the inappropriate thought patterns that underlie the behavior
Critical Thinking LO 9 Page: 626 **a**	75.	Behavior therapy requires that a. the client's vague complaints be translated into concrete behavioral goals b. the client develop insight into his or her irrational thought processes c. the client passively accept suggestions for change d. the client's concrete complaints be translated into abstract constructs
Critical Thinking LO 9 Page: 626 **b**	76.	Dr. Stroetz believes that most psychological disorders can be successfully treated if clients' vague complaints are translated into concrete behavioral goals. Knowing this, you might expect that Dr. Stroetz's bookshelves contain a large number of books written by a. Carl Rogers and Abraham Maslow b. B. F. Skinner and Joseph Wolpe c. Sigmund Freud and Carl Jung d. Aaron Beck and Albert Ellis
Critical Thinking LO 9 Page: 627 **c**	77.	You make an appointment to see a therapist and, as you are waiting, you notice that a large number of the books on the therapist's shelves deal with the work of Joseph Wolpe. You might expect that this therapist will a. emphasize the need to bring unconscious conflicts and defenses into conscious awareness b. provide a supportive emotional environment while allowing you to determine the pace and direction of your therapy c. use counterconditioning to reduce anxiety responses d. help you recognize and change negative thoughts and maladaptive beliefs

Factual LO 10 Page: 627 Correct = 46% **d**	78.	Joseph Wolpe launched behavior therapy in 1958 with his description of a. aversion therapy b. social skills training c. the token economy d. systematic desensitization
Concept/Applied LO 10 Page: 627 Correct = 45% **b**	79.	Systematic desensitization is a technique based on a. instrumental conditioning b. classical conditioning c. operant conditioning d. aversive conditioning
Concept/Applied LO 10 Page: 627 Correct = 53% **a**	80.	The basic learning principle used in Wolpe's systematic desensitization is a. counterconditioning b. negative reinforcement c. positive reinforcement d. operant conditioning
Concept/Applied LO 10 Page: 627 **c**	81.	Viewing a phobia for snakes in classical conditioning terms, the snake is a(n) _____ and the fear is a(n) _____. a. unconditioned stimulus; conditioned response b. unconditioned stimulus; unconditioned response c. conditioned stimulus; conditioned response d. conditioned stimulus; unconditioned response
Concept/Applied LO 10 Page: 627 **c**	82.	When Brett was only six years old, his older sister hid in his closet, then unexpectedly jumped out and scared him when he came into his dark bedroom. As an adult, Brett is still terrified of the dark. Based on principles of classical conditioning, Brett's current fear of the dark is a. an unconditioned response b. a result of observational learning c. a conditioned response d. a result of counterconditioning
Concept/Applied LO 10 Page: 627 **b**	83.	When Yayoi was only six years old, her older brother hid in her closet, then unexpectedly jumped out and grabbed her when she came into her dark bedroom. This terrified Yayoi, and even though she is now 25, she is still frightened in dark places. Based on principles of classical conditioning, being grabbed unexpectedly by her bother a. acted as a conditioned stimulus b. acted as an unconditioned stimulus c. produced transference d. resulted in counterconditioning
Concept/Applied LO 10 Page: 627 **d**	84.	When Cary was eight years old she was startled and began to cry when a car backfired just as she was walking under a ladder. As an adult, Cary is still terrified of ladders. Based on principles of classical conditioning, the sound of the car backfiring a. acted as a conditioned stimulus b. produced transference c. resulted in counterconditioning d. acted as an unconditioned stimulus

Concept/Applied LO 10 Page: 627 **d**	85.	When Donovan was four years old he was startled and began to cry when a car backfired just as he was walking past a fire hydrant. As an adult, Donovan is still fearful of fire hydrants and avoids walking near them. Based on principles of classical conditioning, Donovan's current fear of fire hydrants is a. an unconditioned response b. a result of observational learning c. a conditioned response d. a result of counterconditioning
Concept/Applied LO 10 Page: 627 Correct = 72% **a**	86.	In systematic desensitization, a new _____ response is substituted for the old _____ response. a. relaxation; fear b. undesirable; desirable c. unpleasant; pleasant d. conditioned; unconditioned
Concept/Applied LO 10 Page: 627 Correct = 91% **a**	87.	The use of the anxiety hierarchy in systematic desensitization allows for the a. gradual approach to the feared object b. direct confrontation with the feared object c. use of real objects instead of imagination d. transfer of treatment to real-life situations
Factual LO 10 Page: 627 Correct = 69% **b**	88.	The idea that you can't be profoundly relaxed and fearful at the same time is basic to a. behavior modification b. systematic desensitization c. successive goal approximations d. psychodynamic activation
Concept/Applied LO 10 Page: 628 Correct = 58% **c**	89.	The "behavior" that is incompatible with anxiety, and that systematic desensitization tries to recondition to phobic cues is a. an imagined fear b. an imagined pleasant experience c. deep muscle relaxation d. vigorous exercise
Concept/Applied LO 10 Page: 628 **b**	90.	Beth is so terrified of snakes that even walking on sidewalks covered with earthworms after a rain storm makes her feel anxious. Her behavioral therapist has been helping Beth overcome her fear by having her work through an anxiety hierarchy while she maintains a state of deep relaxation. In this case, her therapist is using a. hypnotherapy to help Beth overcome her fear of snakes b. systematic desensitization to help Beth overcome her fear of snakes c. aversion therapy to help Beth overcome her fear of snakes d. biofeedback to help Beth overcome her fear of snakes
Concept/Applied LO 10 Page: 628 **d**	91.	Aversion therapy is designed to remove unwanted a. negative associations using classical conditioning techniques b. pleasant associations using observational learning techniques c. negative associations using operant learning techniques d. pleasant associations using classical conditioning techniques
Concept/Applied LO 10 Page: 628 **b**	92.	A therapist cures a man of his sexual attraction to children by pairing pictures of children with painful electric shocks. The procedure being used here is a. systematic desensitization b. aversion therapy c. extinction d. social skills training

Concept/Applied
LO 10
Page: 628
Correct = 73%
a

93. George is a child molester. In therapy, George is shown pictures of children, and every time he begins to evidence physiological arousal he is shocked. George is undergoing
    a. aversion therapy
    b. systematic desensitization
    c. biofeedback therapy
    d. rational-emotive therapy

Concept/Applied
LO 10
Page: 628
Correct = 76%
b

94. Giving an alcoholic an emetic drug so that each time she takes a drink she becomes nauseous and ill is a form of
    a. systematic desensitization
    b. aversive conditioning
    c. behavioral redirection
    d. negative reinforcement therapy

Concept/Applied
LO 10
Page: 628
c

95. Bryant loves rich deserts, but he knows that eating high-fat, calorie-laden deserts is bad for his heart. However, he was unable to control his desire for these tasty treats until he read an article in a magazine. The article suggested that every time a person looked at a tempting, but forbidden food, he or she should form a mental image of something disgusting. Bryant has been doing this for the past month and he finds deserts no longer have pleasant associations for him. In this case, Bryant used
    a. systematic desensitization to overcome his desire for rich deserts
    b. observational learning to overcome his desire for rich deserts
    c. aversion therapy to overcome his desire for rich deserts
    d. negative reinforcement to overcome his desire for rich deserts

Concept/Applied
LO 10
Page: 628
b

96. Heather is a smoker who is unable to quit, even though she knows that smoking is ruining her health. Finally, she decides to enter therapy in an attempt to control her desire for cigarettes. In this case, the best behavioral therapy technique to use in helping Heather eliminate her smoking habit would be
    a. negative reinforcement
    b. aversion therapy
    c. systematic desensitization
    d. social skills training

Factual
LO 11
Page: 629
Correct = 46%
b

97. Which of the following is <u>not</u> a component of social skills training?
    a. modeling
    b. aversive stimuli
    c. behavioral rehearsal
    d. shaping

Factual
LO 11
Page: 629
Correct = 82%
b

98. A critical component associated with social skills training is
    a. transference
    b. behavioral rehearsal
    c. biofeedback
    d. classical conditioning

Factual
LO 11
Page: 629
Correct = 42%
d

99. Modeling, behavioral rehearsal, and shaping are the major tools of
    a. insight-rehearsal training
    b. rational-emotive therapy
    c. cognitive restructuring
    d. social skills training

Concept/Applied LO 11 Page: 629 **a**	100.	Earl is an extremely aggressive child who often hits other children when he can't get his own way. Earl is now seeing a behavioral therapist who has discussed appropriate ways of interacting with peers, and shown Earl several videotapes of children resolving conflicts in non-aggressive ways. Earl has also engaged in "role play" during which the therapist has provided corrective feedback and positive reinforcement. In this case, the therapist is using a. social skills training to develop Earl's ability to interact with his peers b. biofeedback to develop Earl's ability to interact with his peers c. aversion therapy to develop Earl's ability to interact with his peers d. systematic desensitization to develop Earl's ability to interact with his peers
Factual LO 11 Page: 629 Correct = 87% **a**	101.	Biofeedback is a. a technique in which information about a bodily function is monitored and fed back to a person b. based on the assumption that people have no voluntary control over any of their physiological processes c. a treatment method developed by Joseph Wolpe d. a behavioral technique that combines classical conditioning and observational learning
Factual LO 11 Page: 629 **d**	102.	An electromyograph measures a. brain-wave patterns b. heart rate c. electrical conductivity of the skin d. muscle tension
Concept/Applied LO 11 Page: 629 Correct = 63% **a**	103.	Georgina is attempting to control her anxiety by altering a tone from a device monitoring her physiological arousal. Georgina is <u>most</u> likely undergoing a. biofeedback therapy b. counterconditioning c. systematic desensitization d. aversion therapy
Concept/Applied LO 11 Page: 629 **b**	104.	Holly finds her job to be extremely stressful, and she often develops tension headaches by the end of the day. Her behavioral therapist has been trying to help Holly control the anxiety she feels when problems arise at work. During her therapy sessions Holly is connected to an electromyograph (EMG). When Holly is deeply relaxed, the tone from the EMG recorder decreases in volume. In this case, her therapist is using a. aversion therapy to help Holly control her level of anxiety b. biofeedback to help Holly control her level of anxiety c. systematic desensitization to help Holly control her level of anxiety d. observational learning to help Holly control her level of anxiety
Critical Thinking LO 11 Page: 629 **c**	105.	Jari works as a hostage negotiator for the local police force. The extreme tension and stress associated with his job often cause Jari to experience migraine headaches. The medication that Jari has been taking is not able to control his headaches, so his family doctor has suggested that Jari try behavioral therapy. In this case, the best behavioral therapy technique to use in helping to eliminate Jari's migraine headaches is likely to be a. aversion therapy b. systematic desensitization c. biofeedback d. negative reinforcement

Critical Thinking LO 11 Page: 629 Correct = 36% **d**	106.	Biofeedback would be <u>least</u> successful in the treatment of a. migraine headaches b. high blood pressure c. anxiety d. bipolar disorder
Factual LO 12 Page: 630 Correct = 43% **a**	107.	In direct comparisons of the effectiveness of behavior therapy and insight therapy a. the differences are usually small, but tend to favor behavior therapy b. the differences are usually small, but tend to favor insight therapy c. behavior therapy tends to be significantly more effective d. insight therapy tends to be significantly more effective
Factual LO 12 Page: 630 **c**	108.	Behavior therapies appear to be particularly effective in the treatment of a. major depression b. antisocial personality disorder c. phobias d. multiple-personality disorders
Factual LO 12 Page: 630 Correct = 64% **b**	109.	Which of the following statements is <u>true</u>? a. Behavior therapists have historically placed little emphasis on measuring therapeutic outcomes. b. Behavior therapies can make important contributions in treating obsessive-compulsive disorder, schizophrenia, eating disorders, and hyperactivity. c. Insight therapists generally can measure progress more precisely than behavior therapists because of the nature of their therapeutic goals. d. The evidence for the effectiveness of insight therapy is stronger than the evidence for the effectiveness of behavior therapy.
Factual LO 13 Page: 630 Correct = 98% **c**	110.	Psychopharmacotherapy involves the treatment of mental disorders with a. electroconvulsive shock b. insight therapy c. medication d. surgery
Factual LO 13 Page: 631 Correct = 78% **b**	111.	Valium is a. an antidepressant drug b. an antianxiety drug c. an antipsychotic drug d. an MAO inhibitor
Factual LO 13 Page: 631 **b**	112.	The two major antianxiety drugs or tranquilizers are a. Thorazine and Haldol b. Valium and Xanax c. Elavil and Nardil d. Prozac and Zoloft
Concept/Applied LO 13 Page: 631 **b**	113.	Frank has just been to a therapist who prescribed an antianxiety medication. Frank should expect to experience some relief from his symptoms of anxiety a. within 24 hours of taking the drug for the first time b. almost immediately after taking the drug for the first time c. only after 1-2 weeks of taking the prescribed amount of the drug d. only after 6-8 weeks of taking the prescribed amount of the drug

Factual LO 13 Page: 631 Correct = 73% **a**	114.	The most commonly cited side effect associated with antianxiety drugs is a. drowsiness b. tachycardia c. blurred vision d. insomnia
Concept/Applied LO 13 Page: 631 **a**	115.	Mary has a psychological disorder, and her doctor has prescribed a drug from the benzodiazepine family to reduce the severity of Mary's symptoms. In this case, Mary's therapist is most likely treating her for a. an anxiety disorder b. depression c. schizophrenia d. bipolar disorder
Concept/Applied LO 13 Page: 631 **c**	116.	Brian has been feeling anxious and tense as his final exams approach. He schedules an appointment with his doctor to find out if there is something he can take to help him feel more relaxed and less anxious. If Brian's doctor prescribes a medication for the symptoms that Brian is experiencing, it would most likely be a. Thorazine b. Nardil c. Xanax d. Prozac
Factual LO 13 Page: 631 **b**	117.	Thorazine is classed as a. an antianxiety drug b. an antipsychotic drug c. an antidepressant drug d. a mood-altering drug
Factual LO 13 Page: 631 **a**	118.	Antipsychotic drugs a. gradually reduce psychotic symptoms such as hallucinations and delusions b. are effective in about 95 percent of psychotic patients c. tend to produce an immediate, but short-lasting, effect d. are often prescribed even for individuals who have no clinical psychotic disorder
Factual LO 13 Page: 631 Correct = 66% **d**	119.	About _____ of psychotic patients respond favorably to traditional antipsychotic medication. a. 10-15% b. 1-3% c. 40-50% d. 70-90%
Concept/Applied LO 13 Page: 631 **a**	120.	Cyndi has just been to a therapist who prescribed an antipsychotic medication. Cyndi should expect to experience a noticeable reduction in her symptoms of schizophrenia a. only after 1-2 weeks of taking the prescribed amount of the drug b. within 2-3 hours of taking the drug for the first time c. within 24 hours of taking the drug for the first time d. only after 6-8 weeks of taking the prescribed amount of the drug
Concept/Applied LO 13 Page: 631 **d**	121.	Gil has a psychological disorder, and his doctor has prescribed an antipsychotic drug to reduce the severity of Gil's symptoms. In this case, Gil's therapist is most likely treating him for a. panic disorder b. mild depression c. generalized anxiety disorder d. schizophrenia

Concept/Applied LO 13 Page: 631 **c**	122.	Eartha has been experiencing mental confusion, hallucinations, and delusions. Her parents schedule an appointment with a therapist to find out if there is something she can take to reduce her symptoms. In this case, the doctor will <u>most</u> likely prescribe a. Xanax b. Nardil c. Thorazine d. Prozac
Concept/Applied LO 13 Page: 631 **b**	123.	Jennifer's doctor has recently prescribed a drug that alters the activity in dopamine synapses. Her doctor is <u>most</u> likely treating Jennifer for symptoms of a. depression b. schizophrenia c. bipolar disorder d. an anxiety disorder
Concept/Applied LO 13 Page: 632 **d**	124.	Colton has been taking a drug to control a psychological disorder. Some of the side effects that he has been experiencing include drowsiness, constipation, and tardive dyskinesia. In this case, Colton is <u>most</u> likely being treated for a. depression b. bipolar disorder c. an anxiety disorder d. schizophrenia
Concept/Applied LO 13 Page: 632 Correct = 72% **b**	125.	Nelson, a schizophrenic patient, has just begun taking antipsychotic medication. He took his first dose about 12 hours ago, but so far his family sees no change in his condition. What advice should they be given? a. If he doesn't show improvement in another 12 hours, a different kind of medication should be tried. b. Patients usually don't begin responding to antipsychotic drugs for at least a couple of days. c. He may have been misdiagnosed as schizophrenic. d. Early changes due to antipsychotic medication are usually not apparent to nonprofessionals, who are unfamiliar with the signs of improvement.
Factual LO 13 Page: 632 **c**	126.	Antipsychotic drugs typically do all but which of the following? a. reduce hyperactivity b. reduce delusions c. increase mental confusion d. decrease activity at dopamine synapses
Factual LO 13 Page: 632 **a**	127.	Tardive dyskinesia a. is a neurological disorder marked by involuntary writhing and tic-like movements b. is a serious side effect of long-term use of antidepressant drugs c. can be cured with the same medication used to treat Parkinson's disease d. can emerge after long-term use of lithium
Factual LO 13 Page: 632 Correct = 81% **b**	128.	The side effect associated with taking traditional antipsychotic drugs, that is characterized by chronic tremors and involuntary spastic movements, is a. infindibular recidivism b. tardive dyskinesia c. tachycardia palpitations d. MAO inhibition

Factual
LO 13
Page: 632
c
	129.	In comparison to traditional antipsychotic drugs, atypical antipsychotic drugs
		  a. yield higher relapse rates while patients are taking the medication, but have much lower relapse rates once patients discontinue their drug regimen
		  b. yield lower relapse rates for patients following a drug regimen and for patients who have discontinued their drug regimen
		  c. yield lower relapse rates while patients maintain their drug regimen, but have much higher relapse rates if patients discontinue their drug regimen
		  d. yield higher relapse rates for patients following a drug regimen and for patients who have discontinued their drug regimen

Factual
LO 13
Page: 632
d
	130.	Compared to traditional antipsychotic drugs, the newer atypical antipsychotic drugs
		  a. seem to produce more severe side effects, but they work much more quickly
		  b. are more effective in treating the negative symptoms of schizophrenia
		  c. can be used to treat depression and anxiety, in addition to schizophrenia
		  d. seem to produce fewer side effects

Factual
LO 13
Page: 632
b
	131.	The tricyclics and the MAO inhibitors
		  a. are both classified as antipsychotic drugs
		  b. are the two principal classes of antidepressants
		  c. have an immediate mood-elevating effect
		  d. are the two main classes of antianxiety drugs

Factual
LO 13
Page: 632
a
	132.	Which of the following drugs is <u>not</u> an antidepressant?
		  a. Valium
		  b. Elavil
		  c. Nardil
		  d. Prozac

Concept/Applied
LO 13
Page: 632
b
	133.	William has just been to a therapist who prescribed an antidepressant medication. William should expect to experience a noticeable reduction in his symptoms of depression
		  a. within 24 hours of taking the drug for the first time
		  b. only after 1-2 weeks of taking the prescribed amount of the drug
		  c. within 2-3 hours of taking the drug for the first time
		  d. only after 6-8 weeks of taking the prescribed amount of the drug

Concept/Applied
LO 13
Page: 632
a
	134.	Kayla has a psychological disorder, and her doctor has prescribed an MAO inhibitor to reduce the severity of Kayla's symptoms. In this case, Kayla's therapist is <u>most</u> likely treating her for
		  a. depression
		  b. an anxiety disorder
		  c. schizophrenia
		  d. bipolar disorder

Concept/Applied
LO 13
Page: 632
c
	135.	Lancaster has been feeling worthless and unmotivated since he lost his job six months ago. He schedules an appointment with his doctor to find out if there is some physical problem that is causing his symptoms. His doctor tells Lancaster that he has a psychological disorder that should respond well to medication. The doctor will <u>most</u> likely treat Lancaster's symptoms by prescribing
		  a. Xanax
		  b. Thorazine
		  c. Zoloft
		  d. Valium

Factual LO 13 Page: 632 Correct = 33% **c**	136.	The newest antidepressant drugs, such as Prozac a. increase levels of dopamine in the brain b. act as MAO inhibitors c. slow the reuptake process at serotonin synapses d. also reduce the manic symptoms associated with bipolar disorder
Concept/Applied LO 13 Page: 632 **d**	137.	Ariana's doctor has recently prescribed a drug that slows the reuptake process at serotonin synapses. Her doctor is <u>most</u> likely treating Ariana for symptoms of a. schizophrenia b. bipolar disorder c. an anxiety disorder d. depression
Factual LO 13 Page: 632 **b**	138.	Which of the following statements is <u>most</u> accurate concerning the antidepressant drugs known as selective serotonin reuptake inhibitors (SSRIs)? a. There are few, if any, negative side effects, and patients can safely terminate their use of the drug at any time without experiencing withdrawal symptoms. b. The drugs have negative effects on sexual functioning, and patients experience withdrawal symptoms if treatment is terminated abruptly. c. The drugs reduce the symptoms of depression, but they often increase levels of anxiety and which can lead to aggressive or suicidal behavior. d. They are broad-spectrum drugs than can successfully treat depression, bipolar disorder and schizophrenia.
Factual LO 13 Page: 633 **d**	139.	Lithium is a chemical used to treat a. major depression b. schizophrenia c. multiple-personality disorders d. bipolar mood disorders
Factual LO 13 Page: 633 Correct = 51% **a**	140.	A major drug that has been used to control mood swings in bipolar mood disorders is a. lithium b. Thorazine c. Prozac d. Xanax
Concept/Applied LO 13 Page: 633 Correct = 35% **c**	141.	Charlie alternates between periods of elation and depression. Which of the following medications is he <u>most</u> likely to receive to control his condition? a. Thorazine b. Prozac c. lithium d. Xanax
Concept/Applied LO 13 Page: 633 **c**	142.	Price has had several episodes of severe depression, but for the past week he has been euphoric and hyperactive, and he hasn't slept for the past four nights. His family is concerned, and they have brought him to a mental health clinic for treatment. If the doctor who sees him prescribes medication to reduce Price's current symptoms, the medication that will <u>most</u> likely be prescribed is a. a selective serotonin reuptake inhibitor b. a tricyclic drug c. lithium d. a drug from the benzodiazepine family

Concept/Applied LO 14 Page: 633 Correct = 52% **b**	143.	Which of the following is <u>not</u> a criticism of drug therapy? a. The side effects may be worse than the illnesses they are supposed to cure. b. The therapy is typically expensive. c. They temporarily relieve symptoms without addressing the real problem. d. Many drugs are overprescribed and many patients are overmedicated.
Factual LO 15 Page: 634 **a**	144.	Electroconvulsive shock therapy (ECT) a. involves the use of electric shock to produce a cortical seizure and convulsions b. is used primarily for the treatment of schizophrenia c. has been used increasingly often since the 1940s d. is one of the key components in aversion therapy
Critical Thinking LO 15 Page: 634 Correct = 61% **d**	145.	The <u>most</u> accurate statement about why ECT works to the degree that it does is that a. it acts as a form of aversion therapy b. it alters neural circuits in the brain c. it alters neurotransmitter activity in the brain d. no one is really certain why it works
Critical Thinking LO 15 Page: 634 **d**	146.	You are watching a television documentary that shows a patient who is undergoing electroconvulsive therapy (ECT). If this documentary is depicting psychotherapy in the late 1930s or early 1940s, you should conclude that a. the patient is being treated for severe depression that has not responded to medication b. the patient is being treated for epilepsy c. the doctor is using a form of aversion therapy to reduce compulsive behaviors in a patient with obsessive-compulsive disorder (OCD) d. the patient is being treated for schizophrenia
Critical Thinking LO 15 Page: 634 **a**	147.	You are watching a television documentary that shows a patient who is undergoing electroconvulsive therapy (ECT). If this documentary is depicting psychotherapy in the 1990s, you should conclude that a. the patient is being treated for severe depression that has not responded to medication b. the patient is being treated for severe schizophrenia that has not responded to medication c. the documentary is inaccurate because electroconvulsive shock therapy hasn't been used since the 1970s d. the documentary is an "undercover expose," and the doctor administrating the treatment is in violation of current ethical guidelines
Factual LO 15 Page: 635 Correct = 70% **b**	148.	The risks of ECT a. have been completely eliminated by modern improvements in the procedure b. may include both short- and long-term intellectual impairment c. are so severe that the use of ECT has been banned by law d. are negligible, as long as appropriate precautions are taken
Factual LO 16 Page: 638 **a**	149.	Which of the following is <u>not</u> one of the criticisms that has been raised concerning the impact of managed care on mental health care? a. Delays in providing service result in spontaneous remission of psychological disorders in nearly 25% of cases. b. Mental health care has seen severe service cuts because the question of what is medically necessary can be subjective. c. Patients who are denied psychotherapy services are relatively unlikely to complain. d. Cost containment may cause physicians to prescribe older, less-expensive drugs which are less effective.

Factual LO 16 Page: 638 **b**	150.	Health maintenance organizations (HMOs) can hold down costs by restricting mental health services. According to critics, these restrictions may include <u>all but</u> which of the following? a. underdiagnosing mental health conditions b. requiring re-certification of the service providers within the HMO c. railing to make needed referrals to mental health specialists d. arbitrarily limiting the length of treatment
Factual LO 16 Page: 638 **c**	151.	Many managed care systems hold down casts by erecting barrier to access. These barriers may include <u>all but</u> which of the following? a. requiring referrals from primary care physicians b. authorizing only a few sessions of therapy c. requiring service providers to be re-certified every six months d. re-routing patients from highly trained providers to less well-trained providers
Factual LO 16 Page: 638 **d**	152.	In one national survey _____ of the psychologists indicated that managed care had negatively affected the quality of their treatment efforts and _____ reported that some of their clients had experienced adverse consequences due to treatment delays or denials. a. all; half b. half; all c. 57%; 81% d. 72%; 49%
Factual LO 17 Page: 639 **c**	153.	Which of the following is <u>not</u> one of the qualifications for an empirically validated treatment? a. The treatment must have been found to be superior to a placebo or no treatment. b. The treatment must have been tested for a specific type of problem or disorder. c. Carefully controlled experiments must have been conducted by at least two independent research teams. d. The treatment program must include new drug therapies, such as SSRIs or atypical antipsychotics.
Concept/Applied LO 17 Page: 639 **a**	154.	Psychologists have worked toward identifying empirically validated treatments. In undertaking this research there is a general tendency to <u>exclude</u> a. behavioral approaches to therapy b. psychodynamic approaches to therapy c. client-centered approaches to therapy d. eclectic approaches to therapy
Factual LO 17 Page: 639 **d**	155.	The movement toward empirically validated treatments has raised some concerns. Critics have raised all of the following objections <u>except</u> a. manualized application of pure treatments do not reflect the fact that most patients come with unique mixtures of multiple problems b. identifying a limited number of validated therapies will give HMO managers even more control over how therapy is conducted c. the movement toward empirically validated treatments runs counter to the eclectic blending of therapeutic approaches d. very few empirically validated treatments exist and, as a result, many patients are being denied access to necessary therapy
Critical Thinking LO 17 Page: 639 **b**	156.	Cleon is part of the experimental group in a study that is attempting to empirically validate one psychological treatment program. Under these circumstances, the therapist who is treating Cleon is <u>least</u> likely to utilize a. a behavioral approach to therapy b. a client-centered approach to therapy c. an eclectic approach to therapy d. a psychodynamic approach to therapy

Factual LO 18 Page: 639 **c**	157.	Which of the following statements is <u>false</u>? a. An individual client may be treated with several different kinds of therapy. b. A combination of therapeutic approaches is often more effective than a single approach. c. Therapy is generally more effective if a single approach is used consistently throughout the treatment of an individual client. d. Generally speaking, the majority of clinical psychologists use an eclectic approach to therapy.
Factual LO 18 Page: 640 Correct = 72% **a**	158.	Which of the following is <u>not</u> among recent trends in the field of psychotherapy? a. a decrease in eclecticism b. an increased emphasis on public education about mental disorders c. deinstitutionalization d. an increased number of crisis intervention services and facilities
Factual LO 18 Page: 640 **a**	159.	In the Featured Study which investigated the impact of combining insight therapy and medication, the researchers found that the relapse rate for participants who received the combination of interpersonal therapy and medication was a. lower than that for either medication alone or interpersonal therapy alone b. higher than that for either medication alone or interpersonal therapy alone c. lower than that for medication alone but higher than that for interpersonal therapy alone d. higher than that for medication alone but lower than that interpersonal therapy alone
Factual LO 18 Page: 640 **b**	160.	In the Featured Study which investigated the impact of combining insight therapy and medication, the researchers found that the combination of interpersonal therapy and medication was a. most valuable to patients over 70 years of age b. least valuable to patients over 70 years of age c. most valuable to patients under 40 years of age d. least valuable to patients under 40 years of age
Factual LO 18 Page: 640 **a**	161.	In the Featured Study which investigated the impact of combining insight therapy and medication, the researchers speculate that the combined treatment they tested may be best-suited for dealing with a. both the biological and psychosocial substrates of old-age depression b. the biological substrate, but not the psychosocial substrate of old-age depression c. the psychosocial substrate, but not the biological substrate of old-age depression d. the genetic substrate, but not the biological substrate of old-age depression
Concept/Applied LO 18 Page: 640 **d**	162.	Ethel is 75 years old, and for the past six months she has been coping with major depression. Based on the results reported in the Featured Study which investigated the impact of combining insight therapy and medication, you should predict that Ethel will show the best response to treatment if her therapist combines a. a tricyclic antidepressant with electroconvulsive shock therapy b. interpersonal psychotherapy with electroconvulsive shock therapy c. group therapy with antipsychotic medication d. interpersonal psychotherapy with a tricyclic antidepressant
Concept/Applied LO 18 Page: 640 Correct = 40% **b**	163.	Generally speaking, the majority of clinical psychologists describe themselves as using _____ approach to therapy. a. a psychoanalytic b. an eclectic c. a Gestalt d. a behavioral

Concept/Applied LO 18 Page: 640 **d**	164.	Dr. Brannigen often treats individuals who have symptoms of major depression. During the initial treatment Dr. Brannigen often prescribes antidepressants, but during the course of therapy he also encourages patients to recognize and change negative thoughts and maladaptive beliefs. He believes that drug treatment can be effective in reducing the symptoms of depression, but only by understanding the causes of their depression will individuals be able to prevent relapses. Dr. Brannigen's approach to therapy could best be described as a. a humanistic approach b. a behavioral approach c. a deinstitutional approach d. an eclectic approach
Critical Thinking LO 18 Page: 640 **c**	165.	Imagine that during 1997 the American Psychological Association (APA) sent a survey to all the clinical and counseling psychologists who were on their mailing list. When the results were compiled, the APA most likely found that the greatest proportion of the individuals who were surveyed identified themselves as having a. a psychodynamic approach to therapy b. a biomedical approach to therapy c. an eclectic approach to therapy d. a humanistic approach to therapy
Factual LO 19 Page: 641 **b**	166.	Which of the following is not among the reasons that American minority groups typically underutilize therapeutic services? a. a reluctance to turn to formal, professional sources of assistance b. the complete unavailability of therapeutic services to those who have no health insurance c. language and communication barriers d. the inability of many therapists to provide culturally responsive forms of treatment
Factual LO 19 Page: 642 Correct = 36% **c**	167.	Suggestions for improving mental health services for American minority groups have included all of the following except a. recruitment and training of more ethnic minority therapists b. pretherapy education programs for minority clients to familiarize them with the process of therapy c. the provision of free therapeutic services for all ethnic clients d. giving therapists special training in cultural sensitivity
Factual LO 20 Page: 642 Correct = 89% **b**	168.	Which of the following was not a problem with state mental hospitals in the United States during the 1950s and 1960s? a. The hospitals were underfunded. b. The hospitals were overstaffed. c. The hospital staff was undertrained. d. The hospitals were overcrowded.
Factual LO 21 Page: 643 Correct = 88% **b**	169.	Deinstitutionalization means that a. hospitalization for mental illness has become a thing of the past b. whenever possible, the mentally ill should be treated at community-based facilities that emphasize outpatient care c. the environment inside mental hospitals is designed to be less structured and rigid d. mental hospitals should take increased responsibility for the treatment of all clients, even those who are not seriously ill

Factual LO 21 Page: 643 Correct = 94% **d**	170.	The transferring of treatment of mental illness from inpatient institutions to community-based facilities is referred to as a. mainstreaming b. exit-transfer therapy c. decentralization d. deinstitutionalization
Concept/Applied LO 21 Page: 644 **d**	171.	Dinah has just been released from the hospital after being treated for schizophrenia. Based on what is known about the effectiveness of current treatments and the impact of deinstitutionalization, you should predict that a. there is a 50% chance that Dinah will be readmitted to the hospital for further treatment within one month of her release b. there is an 80% chance that Dinah will never need to be readmitted to the hospital for further treatment c. there is a 50% chance that Dinah will develop symptoms of another psychological disorder, such as bipolar disorder, following her release d. there is a 50% chance that Dinah will be readmitted to the hospital for further treatment within one year of her release
Factual LO 21 Page: 644 **b**	172.	Which of the following has not been an outcome of deinstitutionalization? a. a decrease in the average inpatient population in state and county mental hospitals b. an increase in the average length of stay in state and county mental hospitals c. an increase in the number of mentally ill patients in local general hospitals d. more outpatient care of psychological disorders
Factual LO 21 Page: 644 Correct = 69% **a**	173.	Which of the following is not true of trends in mental hospitals in this country? a. The length of stay has increased since the 1950s. b. They serve mainly the chronically ill patient. c. More patients are now placed in local facilities instead of the mental hospital. d. The number of patients in mental hospitals has declined since the 1950s.
Concept/Applied LO 21 Page: 644 Correct = 85% **a**	174.	Which of the following statements is most accurate? a. Although many people have benefited from deinstitutionalization by avoiding unnecessary hospital stays, there have been some unanticipated problems. b. Deinstitutionalization has been an outstanding success, resulting in better care for all clients. c. Deinstitutionalization has been a failure, resulting in poorer treatment for both inpatients and outpatients. d. Deinstitutionalization hasn't had much of an impact on mental health care at all.
Factual LO 21 Page: 644 **c**	175.	What percentage of psychiatric inpatient admissions are readmission of former patients? a. approximately 1% b. approximately 15% c. approximately 65% d. approximately 95%
Factual LO 21 Page: 644 **a**	176.	Taken as a whole, the evidence suggests that roughly _____ of the homeless suffer from severe mental illness (schizophrenic and mood disorders), and that another _____ or more are struggling with alcohol and drug problems. a. one-third; one-third b. one-half; one-third c. one-third; one-quarter d. one-quarter; one-third

Factual LO 21 Page: 644 **b**	177.	Taken as a whole, the results from studies investigating mental illness among the homeless suggest that a. the homeless population is made up primarily of elderly male alcoholics b. many of the homeless suffer from some form of psychological disorder c. most of the homeless have family or friends they could go to, if they chose d. deinstitutionalization has been largely successful in getting mental patients off the streets
Factual LO 21 Page: 644 **c**	178.	Taken as a whole, the results from studies investigating mental illness among the homeless indicate that, compared to the non-homeless, homeless persons are a. less likely to suffer from mental health problems or substance abuse problems b. equally likely to suffer from mental health problems c. more likely to suffer from mental health problems d. less likely to suffer from mental health problems, but more likely to exhibit substance abuse problems
Concept/Applied LO 21 Page: 645 Correct = 94% **c**	179.	To deal with the problems deinstitutionalization has created, most experts advocate a. returning to the era of mental hospitals as custodial warehouses b. eliminating shelters for the homeless in urban areas c. increasing the quality and availability of intermediate care facilities d. increasing the number of traditional mental hospitals
Factual LO 22 Page: 645 Correct = 57% **b**	180.	The different approaches to psychotherapy a. overlap so much that there is little basis for differentiating one from another b. have developed due to tension between competing theories c. are all equally appropriate for all kinds of psychological problems d. can be used interchangeably for the majority of psychological disorders
Concept/Applied LO 22 Page: 645 **b**	181.	Many specific therapies have turned out to be irrelevant or counterproductive when used with different cultural groups. This finding illustrates that a. psychology is theoretically diverse. b. our behavior is shaped by our cultural heritage. c. psychology evolves in a sociohistorical context. d. our experience of the world is highly subjective.
Concept/Applied LO 22 Page: 645 **c**	182.	Today there are many alternative approaches to treatment, including client-centered therapy, cognitive therapy, behavior therapy, and biomedical therapies. This wide range of alternatives illustrates that a. behavior is determined by multiple causes. b. psychology evolves in a sociohistorical context. c. psychology is theoretically diverse. d. heredity and environment jointly influence behavior.
Factual LO 23 Page: 646 Correct = 82% **a**	183.	In looking for therapeutic services, keep in mind that a. community mental health centers and human service agencies are good sources of information b. most therapists are in private practice c. the therapeutic services available are essentially the same in most American communities d. the therapist's professional background should be your number one concern
Factual LO 23 Page: 646 **c**	184.	Which of the following is <u>not</u> a primary source of therapeutic services? a. community mental health centers b. private practitioners c. employers d. human service agencies

Concept/Applied LO 24 Page: 647 **b**	185.	In a review of the overall effectiveness of psychotherapy, Smith and Glass (1977) found that a. eclectic therapy had better outcomes than all other types of therapy b. based on estimates of overall effectiveness, most approaches to therapy are similar in their effectiveness c. systematic desensitization is the least effective approach to therapy d. rational-emotive therapy has a poor overall success rate
Factual LO 25 Page: 648 **a**	186.	What should you look for in a prospective therapist? a. personal warmth, empathy, and self-confidence b. low fees and accessible office hours c. a Ph.D. or M.D. degree and a private practice d. a therapist who works in an established clinic or hospital
Factual LO 25 Page: 649 **c**	187.	If you feel that your therapy isn't progressing, you should a. get a new therapist immediately b. assume you are not a good candidate for therapy, and drop the idea c. first consider the possibility of your own resistance to therapy d. first question your therapist's competence
Concept/Applied LO 25 Page: 649 Correct = 96% **b**	188.	Hiding information or things from your therapist can be evidence for a. displacement b. resistance to therapy c. transference d. counterconditioning
Factual LO 25 Page: 649 Correct = 97% **b**	189.	Which of the following statements is <u>true</u>? a. The therapists' role is to run their clients' lives for them. b. Therapists are only facilitators, not producers, of change. c. Therapy typically produces immediate, major improvements in clients' psychological functioning. d. The best outcomes in therapy are seen when the therapist and the client are the same sex and are similar in age.
Factual LO 26 Page: 650 **a**	190.	Placebo effects occur when a. people's expectations lead them to experience some change, even though they receive a fake or ineffective treatment b. people recover from a mental or physical illness without any form of intervention c. people who originally score extremely high or low on some trait are measured a second time, and their new score falls closer to the average d. people who originally score near the average on some trait are measured a second time, and their new score falls at the extreme high or low end of the scale
Factual LO 26 Page: 650 **b**	191.	Regression toward the mean occurs when a. people's expectations lead them to experience some change, even though they receive a fake or ineffective treatment b. people who originally score extremely high or low on some trait are measured a second time, and their new score falls closer to the average c. people recover from a mental or physical illness without any form of intervention d. people who originally score near the average on some trait are measured a second time, and their new score falls at the extreme high or low end of the scale

Concept/Applied LO 26 Page: 651 c	192.	Felicity scored 98% on her first statistics exam, while Baxter scored only 35%. Felicity studied really hard in an attempt to score 100% on the next exam. Baxter decided he wasn't going to be successful in the course, so he didn't study at all. On the second exam Felicity scored 89%, while Baxter scored 42%. One explanation for this might be a. both Felicity and Baxter experienced a placebo effect b. Felicity is experiencing a "sophomore slump," while Baxter is experiencing a "junior jump" c. both Felicity's and Baxter's scores reflect regression toward the mean d. both Felicity's and Baxter's scores reflect the impact of a self-fulfilling prophecy
Concept/Applied LO 26 Page: 651 d	193.	Professor Newton gave a midterm exam where the scores ranged from 28% to 89%; the average score for the exam was 69%. Based on the phenomenon known as regression toward the mean, you should expect that a. almost all students will score lower on the final than they did on the midterm b. almost all students will score higher on the final than they did on the midterm c. the students who scored near the average on the midterm will score lower on the final d. the students who earned the highest scores on the midterm will not do as well on the final
Factual LO 26 Page: 651 b	194.	Researchers can try to control for regression toward the mean and placebo effects through the use of a. double-blind testing, correlational research, and random sampling b. control groups, random assignment, and statistical adjustment c. cross-sectional studies, statistical adjustment, and case-study research d. longitudinal testing, random assignment, and naturalistic observation
Integrative Correct = 35% c	195.	Freud is to unconscious conflicts as Rogers is to a. catharsis b. maladaptive habits c. incongruence d. clarification
Integrative d	196.	Cognitive therapy is to negative thinking as drug therapy is to a. ECT b. incongruence c. maladaptive learning d. abnormal neurotransmitter activity
Integrative Correct = 72% d	197.	Of the following, which is not a closely related pair of terms? a. psychoanalysis and free association b. client-centered therapy and clarification c. behavior therapy and systematic desensitization d. biomedical therapy and aversion therapy
Integrative a	198.	Which of the following therapies are mainly intended to eliminate symptoms rather than alter personality? a. behavior and drug therapies b. psychoanalysis and client-centered therapy c. client-centered therapies and behavior therapies d. psychoanalysis and drug therapies

Integrative **b**	199.	Which of the following shows the <u>most</u> appropriate matching of therapy to psychological problem? a. lithium treatment for phobic disorder b. cognitive therapy for panic disorder c. Xanax for depression d. systematic desensitization for bipolar mood disorder
Integrative Correct = 69% **a**	200.	Which of the following is <u>not</u> a closely related set of concepts? a. aversion therapy, ECT, tardive dyskinesia b. free association, dream analysis, transference c. genuineness, empathy, unconditional positive regard d. antipsychotic, antianxiety, antidepressant
Study Guide LO 1 Page: 617 **b**	201.	Which of the following is <u>not</u> a true statement? a. Women seek psychotherapy more than men. b. The two most common problems that lead to psychotherapy are sexual problems and depression. c. Persons seeking psychotherapy don't always have identifiable problems. d. Many people feel that seeking psychotherapy is an admission of personal weakness.
Study Guide LO 4 Page: 621 **a**	202.	When a client begins relating to his psychoanalyst as though she were his mother, we have an example of a. transference b. free association c. catharsis d. restructuring
Study Guide LO 5 Page: 622 **c**	203.	The major emphasis in client-centered therapy is to provide the client with a. interpretation of unconscious thinking b. cognitive restructuring c. feedback and clarification d. good advice
Study Guide LO 6 Page: 623 **a**	204.	Which of the following is likely to be found in cognitive therapy? a. a search for automatic negative thoughts b. dream interpretation c. free association d. an emphasis on childhood conflicts
Study Guide LO 7 Page: 625 **c**	205.	Which kind of therapists are likely to play the <u>least</u> active (most subtle) role in conducting therapy? a. behavior therapists b. cognitive therapists c. group therapists d. pychoanalytic therapists
Study Guide LO 9 Page: 626 **c**	206.	Which of the following therapies is <u>most</u> likely to see the symptom as the problem? a. psychoanalysis b. client-centered therapy c. behavior therapy d. cognitive therapy

Study Guide LO 10 Page: 627 **b**	207.	Which of the following behavior therapy techniques would <u>most</u> likely be used to treat a fear of flying? a. systematic desensitization b. aversive conditioning c. modeling d. biofeedback
Study Guide LO 10 Page: 628 **b**	208.	Which of the following therapies would be <u>most</u> likely to employ aversive conditioning? a. psychoanalysis b. behavior therapy c. biomedical therapies d. client-centered therapy
Study Guide LO 15 Page: 634 **c**	209.	Electroconvulsive therapy (ECT) is now primarily used to treat patients suffering from a. anxiety b. phobias c. severe mood disorders d. psychosis
Study Guide LO 20 Page: 643 **b**	210.	The trend toward deinstitutionalization mainly came about because large mental institutions a. were becoming too expensive b. were actually worsening the condition of many patients c. were overstaffed d. were becoming too political
Online Quiz LO 1 Page: 616 **b**	211.	Drug therapy is classified as _____ therapy; electroconvulsive shock therapy is classified as _____ therapy. a. an aversion; a biomedical b. a biomedical; a biomedical c. a biomedical; a behavior d. a behavior; an insight
Online Quiz LO 2 Page: 618 **a**	212.	Compared to psychologists, in their provision of therapy psychiatrists tend to a. emphasize biomedical treatments more b. use group therapies more often c. use behavior therapies more often d. spend less time working with severely disturbed patients
Online Quiz LO 3 Page: 620 **a**	213.	A therapist's attempt to explain the significance of a client's thoughts, feelings, and behaviors is referred to as a. interpretation b. debriefing c. confrontation d. clarification
Online Quiz LO 5 Page: 622 **d**	214.	Rogers believed that client-centered therapists must provide unconditional positive regard for their clients. In other words, they must a. provide warmth and caring only when clients' behavior is appropriate b. communicate with clients in an honest and spontaneous manner c. understand the client's world from the client's point of view, and be able to communicate this d. show complete, nonjudgmental acceptance of the client as a person

Online Quiz LO 6 Page: 623 **a**	215.	Uncovering the patterns of thinking and assumptions behind maladaptive behavior and then assessing their validity is at the core of a. cognitive therapy b. reality therapy c. behavioral therapy d. client-centered therapy
Online Quiz LO 9 Page: 626 **b**	216.	Therapists who tend to see symptoms as the problem rather than as signs of more internal, underlying problems are a. cognitive therapists b. behavior therapists c. psychodynamic therapists d. humanists
Online Quiz LO 10 Page: 628 **d**	217.	Therapy that involves pairing a stimulus that leads to an undesirable behavior with an unconditioned stimulus that is unpleasant is a. biofeedback training b. systematic desensitization c. reverse countertransference d. aversion therapy
Online Quiz LO 13 Page: 631 **c**	218.	A major drug used to reduce the symptoms of schizophrenia is a. Valium b. Elavil c. Thorazine d. lithium
Online Quiz LO 18 Page: 640 **c**	219.	Eclectic therapists a. commit themselves to just one theoretical approach b. utilize only the insight approaches to therapy c. use ideas and techniques from a variety of therapeutic approaches d. refuse to adjust their techniques to the unique needs of each client
Online Quiz LO 23 Page: 646 **c**	220.	With regard to a therapist's sex a. it is generally better to choose a therapist the same sex as yourself b. it is generally better to choose a therapist the opposite sex as yourself c. you should feel free to look for a therapist of one sex or the other if it is personally important to you d. both men and women report better outcomes when seeing female therapists

ESSAY QUESTIONS

1. Compare and contrast the psychoanalytic and humanistic brands of insight therapy.

    The main similarity is that both seek to enlighten the individual about internal structures and mechanisms that may be contributing to one's distress.

    Differences center on assumptions about the causes of that distress. Psychoanalysis focuses on uncovering unconscious conflicts, motives, and defenses that are not merely adaptive, but which cause distress or dysfunction. Client-centered therapy, a representative humanistic therapy, centers on the notion that distress results from incongruence between one's self-concept and reality, which causes one to behave in maladaptive ways. The aim is for the individual to "get in touch" with one's own individual nature and to value it appropriately.

    Another difference is in techniques. Psychoanalysis employs free association, dream analysis, and other techniques aimed at allowing and encouraging the emergence of material from the unconscious, which is then interpreted by the analyst. The general approach in client-centered therapy is for the therapist to establish a climate that feels safe enough so that the client is free to examine his or her true nature without feeling it necessary to employ defensive maneuvers.

2. In light of the differences between the various psychological disorders and their hypothesized etiologies, it would seem that for each disorder, a particular type of therapy might work best. Discuss this notion, and give examples using specific disorders and specific approaches to therapy to support your arguments.

    This proposition makes sense, and there is some evidence to support it. A related point is that the particular symptoms of particular disorders probably mean particular therapies are better suited to treat them. Here are some points that might be included in good answers

    To the extent that biological factors have been shown to be involved in the etiology of a disorder, it would seem that biomedical treatments ought to be most effective. And, in fact, biomedical treatments have been more effective than insight and behavior therapies in treating especially the more severe disorders, such as schizophrenia, and some mood disorders, for which there is significant evidence for biological causes.

    Insight therapies work best for clients who are highly motivated and who have positive attitudes about therapy. This would seem to eliminate depressed individuals as good candidates for insight therapies. Sufferers from the anxiety disorders seem to best fit the description of ideal candidates for insight therapy.

    Behavior therapies have been successful with a wide variety of disorders. This is probably because most disorders manifest in maladaptive behaviors, and if these behaviors can be targeted specifically enough to design a behavior modification program, then the prognosis may be good. Behavior therapy would likely be least successful when the undesirable behavior is pervasive, vague, and hard to pinpoint. This may be the case with some of the anxiety disorders and some of the mood disorders.

3. It is believed by some that all psychological disorders can be traced to some sort of biological malfunction, especially malfunctions in the nervous system. In other words, in a perfectly formed and perfectly functioning biological organism, there could be no psychological disorder. If this were true, then the "ultimate cure" for any psychological disorder would be a biomedical cure. Explain why this position does or does not make sense to you.

   If your set of philosophical assumptions includes the belief that all psychological phenomena are products of biological activity, then this position will make sense to you. It says, in essence, that the nervous system is the "organ" of thought, emotion, and personality. So disturbances in these domains should be traceable to malfunctions in the nervous system. Psychological disorders may follow from biological problems that are inborn, or environmental events may lead to biological damage, which then leads to psychological disorder. Most modern psychologists are in this camp. This explains, at least in part, why the search for biomedical (especially drug) cures is progressing at a rapid pace and, apparently, quite successfully.

   Other psychologists, and students, aren't comfortable with this position. One argument is that psychological disorders may indeed be caused by biological malfunction but, just as environmental events or subjects' behaviors may lead to biological damage, in some cases environmental events or behavior changes (including changes in cognitive patterns) may actually lead to repairs of the biological malfunction.

   Those who don't agree that the mind is a dependent product of the body may believe that some psychological disorders can exist in a perfectly healthy (biological) organism. In these cases, therapies that focus on changing behavior or thought may be considered the most appropriate.

4. Persons suffering from different psychological disorders differ from each other in the extent to which they admit they need help and the extent to which they are resistant to therapy. For which disorders are patients most likely and least likely to cooperate with therapeutic interventions?

   Answers should reveal and elaborate upon an understanding of characteristics of the various types of disorders that would influence compliance. For example, patients having disorders in which subjective distress is the main problem should be least resistant, since their pain will motivate them to seek relief. Anxiety disorders are good examples. Patients with problematic thinking processes might be resistant, depending on the nature of their thought patterns. So certain psychotic delusions would lead to resistance, and a depressed patient whose negative attributional style was well entrenched might be resistant. Certain personality disordered individuals would certainly be resistant.

5. A major difference between insight therapies and behavior therapies is in their position about whether it's necessary or useful to seek out the origin of psychological difficulties. A compromise position might be that this kind of information is important for patients with some disorders, but not for patients with other disorders. Explain why this kind of information might be more helpful for some kinds of patients than for others.

   Answers to this question also should reveal students' understanding of the characteristics of the various types of disorders. Insight therapists have argued that if symptoms are removed, as through behavior modification, but underlying causes are not treated, then the disorder is likely to manifest again in the same or a different guise. Behavior therapists have argued that there are no "underlying" causes, but that maladaptive behavior has simply been learned and ought to be unlearned.

   For some patients, it's difficult to pinpoint a particular behavior that needs to be unlearned or modified because the maladaptive pattern has become so pervasive. This may be true in some cases of anxiety, mood, and personality disorders. For these patients, it may be more beneficial to seek out the "roots" of the pervasive maladaptive style and, perhaps, to destroy the many offshoots stemming from these roots. When particularly troublesome behaviors can be identified, however, and when those behaviors are such that a behavior modification program can be designed, then this may be the best approach. If successful in changing the problem behavior, the patient and therapist might then want to remain on the lookout for future signs that an underlying problem is manifesting via new symptoms. If so, then insight therapy may be called for.

Chapter Sixteen
Social Behavior

LEARNING OBJECTIVES

1. Describe how various aspects of physical appearance may influence our impressions of others.
2. Explain how schemas, stereotypes, and other factors contribute to subjectivity in person perception.
3. Explain the evolutionary perspective on bias in person perception.
4. Explain what attributions are and why we make them.
5. Describe the distinction between internal and external attributions.
6. Summarize Kelley's and Weiner's theories of attribution.
7. Describe several types of attributional bias and cultural variations in attributional tendencies.
8. Summarize evidence on the role of physical attractiveness in attraction.
9. Summarize evidence on the role of similarity and reciprocity in attraction.
10. Describe various distinctions regarding love described by Berscheid and Hatfield, Sternberg.
11. Summarize the evidence on love as a form of attachment.
12. Discuss cross-cultural research on romantic relationships and evolutionary analyses of mating patterns.
13. Describe the components and dimensions of attitudes and the correlates of attitude strength.
14. Discuss the relations between attitudes and behavior.
15. Summarize evidence on source factors, message factors, and receiver factors that influence the process of persuasion.
16. Discuss how learning processes can contribute to attitudes.
17. Explain how cognitive dissonance can account for the effects of counterattitudinal behavior and effort justification.
18. Relate self-perception theory and the elaboration likelihood model to attitude change.
19. Summarize research on the determinants of conformity.
20. Describe the Featured Study on obedience to authority and the ensuing controversy generated by Milgram's research.
21. Discuss cultural variations in conformity and obedience.
22. Discuss the nature of groups and the bystander effect.
23. Summarize evidence on group productivity, including social loafing.
24. Describe group polarization and groupthink.
25. Explain how the chapter highlighted three of the text's unifying themes.
26. Relate person perception processes and attributional bias to prejudice.
27. Relate principles of attitude formation and group processes to prejudice.
28. Discuss some useful criteria for evaluating credibility and some standard social influence strategies.

MULTIPLE-CHOICE QUESTIONS

Factual
LO 1
Page: 656
c

1. The topics of aggression, altruism, conformity, and attitudes are most likely to be studied by a _____ psychologist.
   a. structural
   b. attributional
   c. social
   d. clinical

Concept/Applied
LO 1
Page: 656
b

2. Which of the following research questions is most likely to be studied by a social psychologist?
   a. How is reinforcement related to the speed with which one acquires a new behavior?
   b. What are the factors that make people likely to conform to the behavior of others?
   c. What is the relationship between heredity and intelligence?
   d. What role does stress play in the onset of psychological disorders?

Factual
LO 1
Page: 656
Correct = 85%
a

3. Person perception refers to the process of
   a. forming impressions of others
   b. developing an implicit personality theory
   c. predicting the behavior of others
   d. monitoring the impressions you make on other people

Factual
LO 1
Page: 657
d

4. People with baby-faced features (e.g., large eyes, smooth skin) tend to be viewed as
   a. competent
   b. dominant
   c. intelligent
   d. honest

Factual
LO 1
Page: 657
b

5. Which of the following people are most likely to be viewed as honest and trustworthy?
   a. older people
   b. baby-faced people
   c. people who are physically attractive
   d. people who mimic our own mannerisms

Factual
LO 1
Page: 657
b

6. The chameleon effect illustrates which of the following principles?
   a. Children tend to model the behavior of their same-gender parents.
   b. Some aspects of interpersonal behavior can occur with little or no conscious awareness.
   c. Inferences about other people based on their nonverbal behavior tend to be fairly accurate.
   d. Our initial inferences about those who are dissimilar to ourselves tend to be negative.

Concept/Applied
LO 2
Page: 657
Correct = 61%
d

7. Your unique ideas about how a college class should be run, what a typical straight "A" student is like, and how a typical professor will act are all examples of
   a. prejudices
   b. attitudes
   c. attributions
   d. social schemas

Factual LO 2 Page: 657 **d**	8.	Organized clusters of ideas about categories of social events and people are referred to as a. attributions b. illusory correlations c. covariation inferences d. social schemas
Factual LO 2 Page: 657 **b**	9.	Social schemas are best defined as a. patterns of social behavior one is most likely to perform b. organized clusters of ideas about people or social events c. tendencies to view those who are different than us in a negative way d. widely held beliefs that people have certain characteristics because of their membership in a particular group
Factual LO 2 Page: 657 Correct = 94% **c**	10.	Widely held beliefs about groups of people based on their group membership defines a. cognitive structuring b. cultural direction c. stereotypes d. schematizing
Concept/Applied LO 2 Page: 658 Correct = 71% **c**	11.	George believes all white males are snobbish, standoffish, cold, and money hungry. George's belief about white males can be viewed as a. a prototype b. a schema c. a stereotype d. all of these things
Factual LO 2 Page: 658 **c**	12.	Research has revealed that the gender stereotype associated with women is composed of all of the following except for seeing women as a. submissive b. illogical c. asexual d. emotional
Concept/Applied LO 2 Page: 658 **c**	13.	The illusory correlation effect occurs when we a. incorrectly assume that one social trait is the cause of another, simply because we have observed that they are correlated b. are motivated to accurately estimate the frequency with which some pattern of social traits occurs c. see correlations between social traits that really aren't there, because our expectations distort our memories d. fail to see true correlations between social traits, because our expectations distort our memories
Concept/Applied LO 2 Page: 658 Correct = 94% **a**	14.	John observed Gracie, an executive for a large accounting firm, behave in an aggressive and pushy manner with her subordinates. John now believes that most women executives are basically aggressive and pushy with their subordinates. John's overestimation of the relationship between women executives and the social traits of "pushy" and "aggressive" is referred to as a(n) a. illusory correlation b. contravened stereotype c. heuristic overbias d. self-serving attribution

Concept/Applied LO 2 Page: 658 **a**	15.	You believe that short men have a tendency to be insecure. The concept of illusory correlation implies that you will a. overestimate the frequency of insecure short men b. underestimate the frequency of insecure short men c. accurately estimate the frequency of insecure short men d. falsely assume that tall men are naturally secure
Factual LO 3 Page: 659 **a**	16.	Evolutionary psychologists argue that many of the biases seen in social perception a. were adaptive in humans' ancestral environment b. can be attributed mainly to illusory correlations c. are a function of our tendency to be egocentric d. are counterproductive in the natural selection of social behavior
Critical Thinking LO 3 Page: 659 Correct = 71% **d**	17.	Which of the following statements best reflects an evolutionary explanation of why we tend to be influenced by physical attractiveness in our perception of others? a. We have a tendency to identify with those we perceive as attractive. b. Physical attractive individuals are also likely to be intelligent and hard-working. c. Being around attractive people tends to make us view ourselves more favorably. d. At one time in our history, physical attractiveness was associated with reproductive potential.
Factual LO 3 Page: 659 Correct = 87% **d**	18.	A group that one belongs to and identifies with is known as a(n) a. stereotype b. social schema c. outgroup d. ingroup
Factual LO 3 Page: 659 Correct = 93% **d**	19.	According to evolutionary psychologists, we tend to view members of outgroups a. as role models b. as superior to us c. as potential mates d. in terms of various negative stereotypes
Factual LO 3 Page: 659 Correct = 57% **b**	20.	Evolutionary psychologists ascribe much of the bias in person perception to cognitive mechanisms that have been shaped by a. parental attitudes b. natural selection c. childhood experiences d. relationships with others
Factual LO 4 Page: 659 **c**	21.	The inferences that people draw about the causes of events, others' behavior, and their own behavior are called a. prejudices b. attitudes c. attributions d. social schemas
Factual LO 4 Page: 659 **a**	22.	What is the main reason we tend to make attributions about the causes of events, others' behavior, and our own behavior? a. We have a strong need to understand our experiences. b. Attribution-making was selected for at some point in our ancestral past. c. We have an unconscious urge to psychoanalyze the behavior of others. d. Having access to information about others tends to fulfill our need for power.

Factual LO 5 Page: 660 c	23.	Which of the following individuals was the first to describe how people make attributions? a. Albert Bandura b. Sigmund Freud c. Fritz Heider d. Harold Kelley
Concept/Applied LO 5 Page: 660 Correct = 37% c	24.	A father suggests that his son's low marks in school are due to the child's laziness. The father has made _____ attribution. a. an external b. a distinctive c. an internal d. a situational
Concept/Applied LO 5 Page: 660 a	25.	Celine just heard that her neighbor, Rodney, was involved in an automobile accident. If Celine concludes that Rodney's children distracted him for a few seconds, and that was the reason for the accident, she has a. made an external attribution b. made an internal attribution c. made the fundamental attribution error d. been influenced by an illusory correlation
Concept/Applied LO 5 Page: 660 c	26.	Blaming your friend's auto accident on the weather conditions is an example of a. a self-serving attribution b. a defensive attribution c. an external attribution d. a dispositional attribution
Factual LO 6 Page: 660 Correct = 41% a	27.	An actor's behavior being the same over time and across situations defines the covariation information referred to as a. consistency b. convergence c. consensus d. criterial
Factual LO 6 Page: 660 Correct = 33% b	28.	People responding similarly as an actor did to the same situation defines the item of covariation information referred to as a. distinctiveness b. consensus c. divergence d. convergence
Factual LO 6 Page: 660 a	29.	A person responding uniquely to someone or something defines the item of covariation information referred to as a. distinctiveness b. divergence c. disjunctiveness d. criterial
Factual LO 6 Page: 660 b	30.	Which of the following individuals proposed the covariation model of attribution? a. Fritz Heider b. Harold Kelley c. Albert Bandura d. Sigmund Freud

Factual LO 6 Page: 660 **b**	31.	According to Kelley's theory of attribution, the dimension of consistency refers to whether a. the cause of a behavior is internal or external b. an actor's behavior in a situation is the same over time c. a person's behavior is unique to the specific entity that is the target of the person's actions d. other people in the same situation tend to respond similarly to each other
Factual LO 6 Page: 660 Correct = 57% **d**	32.	In Kelley's attributional model, the dimension of consensus refers to whether a. the cause of a behavior is internal or external b. an actor's behavior in a situation is the same over time c. a person's behavior is unique to the specific entity that is the target of the person's actions d. other people in the same situation tend to respond like the actor
Concept/Applied LO 6 Page: 660 **b**	33.	Laura is afraid of bees. In fact, Laura is afraid of all insects. Laura's fear of bees is a case where there is a. high distinctiveness b. low distinctiveness c. high consensus d. low consensus
Concept/Applied LO 6 Page: 660 Correct = 86% **c**	34.	Martin just adores the newest album by the Space Invaders. So do all his friends. Martin's adoration of the new album is a case where there is a. high distinctiveness b. low distinctiveness c. high consensus d. low consensus
Concept/Applied LO 6 Page: 660 **a**	35.	You pass one of your classmates, Manny, in the hall. Although you greet Manny with a friendly "Hi," he ignores you. On thinking about Manny's failure to respond, you realize he always ignores you. According to Kelley's theory of attribution, Manny's behavior would be characterized as being _____ in _____. a. high; consistency b. low; consistency c. high; distinctiveness d. low; distinctiveness
Concept/Applied LO 6 Page: 660 **c**	36.	Like everyone else in her botany class, Rosa is anxious just before the weekly quizzes. Based on Kelley's covariation model, in this example there is a. low distinctiveness b. low consistency c. high consensus d. high consistency
Concept/Applied LO 6 Page: 660 Correct = 22% **b**	37.	Janet went out of her way this morning to give you a ride to school. To evaluate the consistency of Janet's behavior, you need to think about her past helpfulness toward _____; to evaluate the distinctiveness of Janet's behavior, you need to think about her past helpfulness toward _____. a. a specific other person; you b. you; others in general c. a specific other person; others in general d. others in general; you

Concept/Applied LO 6 Page: 660 **c**	38.	Mark tells you he dislikes his economics professor. If you know that Mark has disliked the professor since the beginning of the semester, that the other students generally like the professor, and that Mark dislikes all of his professors, you will probably make a(n) _____ attribution about Mark's behavior. a. positive b. objective c. internal d. external
Factual LO 6 Page: 660 Correct = 50% **a**	39.	According to Kelley, a behavior is most likely to be attributed to situational factors under conditions of a. high consistency, high distinctiveness, and high consensus b. high consistency, low distinctiveness, and low consensus c. low consistency, low distinctiveness, and low consensus d. low consistency, low distinctiveness, and high consensus
Concept/Applied LO 6 Page: 661 **a**	40.	If a behavior shows high consistency, but distinctiveness and consensus are both low, then an observer is very apt to make _____ attribution. a. an internal b. an external c. a situational d. all are equally likely
Concept/Applied LO 6 Page: 661 **b**	41.	If a behavior shows high consistency and distinctiveness, and consensus is also high, an observer is apt to make _____ attribution. a. an internal b. an external c. a personal d. a trait
Concept/Applied LO 6 Page: 661 Correct = 75% **a**	42.	You've just been awarded a full scholarship for next year, which you perceive as confirmation of your superior intellectual ability. According to Weiner's model, you are making an _____ attribution about your success. a. internal-stable b. internal-unstable c. external-stable d. external-unstable
Concept/Applied LO 6 Page: 661 **d**	43.	Martha wins three games of backgammon in a row, even though she has never played before. If Martha assumes she has "beginner's luck," she is making an _____ attribution about her success; if she decides backgammon is an easy game, she is making an _____ attribution about her success. a. internal-stable; internal-unstable b. internal-unstable; external-unstable c. external-unstable; internal-stable d. external-unstable; external-stable
Concept/Applied LO 6 Page: 661 Correct = 79% **c**	44.	An unstable internal cause for an event would be a. one's intelligence b. one's ability c. one's mood d. any of these things
Factual LO 7 Page: 662 **b**	45.	The fundamental attribution error refers to the tendency of a. observers to favor external attributions in explaining the behavior of others b. observers to favor internal attributions in explaining the behavior of others c. actors to favor external attributions in explaining the behavior of others d. actors to favor internal attributions in explaining the behavior of others

Factual LO 7 Page: 662 **c**	46.	According to the fundamental attribution error, actors tend to attribute their own behavior to _____ factors, and observers tend to attribute the behavior of others to _____ factors. a. personal; personal b. personal; situational c. situational; personal d. situational; situational
Concept/Applied LO 7 Page: 662 Correct = 49% **d**	47.	If you tend to overemphasize internal characteristics in explaining the behavior of others, you are evidencing the a. false consensus effect b. situational attributional tendency c. self-serving bias d. fundamental attribution error
Factual LO 7 Page: 662 **d**	48.	Actors and observers tend to give different explanations for the same instance of behavior because a. only actors themselves can accurately explain their own behavior b. only outside observers can accurately explain actors' behavior c. observers tend to possess more knowledge than the actors d. situational pressures may not be readily apparent to an observer
Factual LO 7 Page: 662 Correct = 51% **a**	49.	According to the notion of defensive attribution, we tend to explain the setbacks that befall other people in terms of _____ causes. a. internal b. external c. stable d. defensive
Factual LO 7 Page: 663 Correct = 62% **b**	50.	Attributing one's successes to dispositional factors and one's failures to situational factors is referred to as a. the fundamental attribution error b. a self-serving bias c. the actor-observer bias d. a self-enhancing strategy
Concept/Applied LO 7 Page: 663 Correct = 82% **b**	51.	A self-serving bias is a tendency to attribute our positive outcomes to _____ and negative outcomes to _____. a. situational causes; dispositional causes b. dispositional causes; situational causes c. consensus; uniqueness d. ego strength; ego weakness
Concept/Applied LO 7 Page: 663 Correct = 92% **a**	52.	You are likely to attribute your own failing grade on a test to _____; your roommate is more likely to attribute your failing grade to _____. a. an unfair test; your poor study habits b. your poor study habits; an unfair test c. a poor teacher; an unfair test d. your own stupidity; a poor teacher
Concept/Applied LO 7 Page: 663 **c**	53.	Attributing one's success on an exam to one's intelligence and one's failure to the unfairness of the test is an example of a. a defensive attribution b. an actor-observer bias c. a self-serving bias d. the fundamental attributional error

Factual
LO 7
Page: 664
a

54. Which of the following individuals suggested that cultural differences in individualism and collectivism tend to influence attributional tendencies?
    a. Harry Triandis
    b. Harold Kelley
    c. Albert Bandura
    d. Sigmund Freud

Concept/Applied
LO 7
Page: 664
d

55. Carisa was born and raised in Peru; Olga was born and raised in the Netherlands. Based on evidence from cross-cultural studies comparing individualistic and collectivist cultures, Carisa is likely to be
    a. more prone to the fundamental attribution error
    b. less likely to experience cognitive dissonance
    c. more likely to experience cognitive dissonance
    d. less prone to the fundamental attribution error

Factual
LO 7
Page: 664
a

56. Putting group goals ahead of personal goals and defining one's identity in terms of the groups one belongs to is called
    a. collectivism
    b. functionalism
    c. individualism
    d. attributionism

Factual
LO 7
Page: 664
Correct = 54%
d

57. Putting personal goals ahead of group goals and defining one's identity in terms of personal attributes is referred to as
    a. hedonism
    b. dispositional attributional bias
    c. egocentrism
    d. individualism

Critical Thinking
LO 7
Page: 664
Correct = 88%
b

58. Individualism is to collectivism as _____ is to _____.
    a. external; internal
    b. personal; group
    c. communism; capitalism
    d. All of these complete the analogy correctly.

Concept/Applied
LO 7
Page: 664
Correct = 79%
a

59. Individuals from Western societies are more likely to evidence a(n) _____ in their causal attributions relative to individuals from non-Western societies.
    a. self-serving bias
    b. self-effacing bias
    c. actor-observer bias
    d. fundamental attribution error

Factual
LO 7
Page: 664
Correct = 70%
c

60. Which of the following are Japanese subjects more likely to engage in than American subjects?
    a. individualism
    b. self-serving bias
    c. self-effacing bias
    d. fundamental attribution error

Factual
LO 8
Page: 665
c

61. Which of the following factors is *not* one that influences a person's initial attraction to someone else?
    a. similarity
    b. reciprocity
    c. attributional style
    d. physical attractiveness

Factual LO 8 Page: 665 Correct = 96% **b**	62.	Research has shown that initial attraction a. to someone is minimally influenced by that person's physical attractiveness b. is greatly influenced by that person's physical attractiveness c. is more influenced by personality similarity than by physical attractiveness d. is greatly influenced by perceived intellectual similarity
Factual LO 8 Page: 665 Correct = 77% **a**	63.	The idea that males and females of approximately equal physical attractiveness are likely to select each other as partners refers to the a. matching hypothesis b. propinquity hypothesis c. attitude-behavior consistency principle d. attributional outcome principle
Factual LO 8 Page: 665 **d**	64.	The matching hypothesis proposes that males and females of approximately equal _____ are likely to select each other as partners. a. intelligence b. income c. personality d. physical attractiveness
Concept/Applied LO 9 Page: 665 Correct = 77% **b**	65.	Which of the following statements is true concerning attitudes? a. People are more likely to be attracted to someone with dissimilar attitudes: "Opposites attract." b. People are more likely to be attracted to someone with similar attitudes: "Birds of a feather flock together." c. People are equally likely to be attracted to people with similar and dissimilar attitudes. d. People are not attracted to others based on their attitudes because attitudes and attraction are independent.
Concept/Applied LO 9 Page: 666 Correct = 83% **b**	66.	Research on factors contributing to building relationships seems to support the adage a. "similarity breeds contempt" b. "similarity breeds liking" c. "similarity builds uncertainty" d. "similarity builds discrimination"
Concept/Applied LO 9 Page: 666 **d**	67.	The fact that we tend to like people who like us illustrates which of the following principles involved in interpersonal attraction? a. equity b. reification c. dyadic interaction d. reciprocity
Concept/Applied LO 9 Page: 666 **a**	68.	Which of the following statements best reflects the principle of reciprocity? a. We tend to like others who seem to like us. b. We tend to be attracted to people who seem to dislike us initially. c. We tend to be attracted to people who are generous to others. d. We are attracted to people whose attitudes seem to be similar to our own.
Critical Thinking LO 9 Page: 666 **b**	69.	Which of the following statements regarding the reciprocity effect in romantic relationships is <u>not</u> accurate? a. Relationships are more likely to persist when partners idealize each other. b. An accurate view of one's partner is the best foundation for a satisfying relationship. c. Most people view their partners more favorably than the partners view themselves. d. Individuals' perceptions of their romantic partners seem to reflect their ideals for a partner more than reality.

Factual LO 10 Page: 666 **a**	70.	A complete absorption in another that includes tender sexual feelings and the agony and ecstasy of intense emotion is called _____ love. a. passionate b. sexual c. platonic d. lustful
Concept/Applied LO 10 Page: 666 Correct = 52% **d**	71.	Joe has been calling Jill each evening and talking with her everyday at lunch, but now he is deeply despondent because she is out of town. Joe is in the throws of a. companionate love b. sexual infatuation c. communal love d. passionate love
Concept/Applied LO 10 Page: 666 **a**	72.	Whenever Scott sees Diana he can feel his heart start to pound with excitement. Even though Scott and Diana have only dated a few times, Scott often becomes jealous when Diana talks to other men. He also finds he can't get her out of his mind when they are apart. According to Hatfield and Berscheid, Scott is experiencing _____ love. a. passionate b. companionate c. consummate d. reciprocal
Factual LO 10 Page: 666 Correct = 54% **c**	73.	According to Sternberg (1988), companionate love can be subdivided into a. friendship and sexuality b. sexuality and commitment c. commitment and intimacy d. intimacy and friendship
Factual LO 10 Page: 666 **a**	74.	The element of intimacy in Sternberg's triangular view of love is defined by a. feelings of closeness and warmth in a relationship b. sexual feelings for the other person c. feelings of infatuation for the other person d. all of these things
Concept/Applied LO 10 Page: 666 Correct = 67% **c**	75.	According to Sternberg, long-term, older relationships are dominated by a. passion and romantic love b. commitment and passion c. commitment and intimacy d. fatuous and companionate love
Factual LO 10 Page: 666 Correct = 98% **a**	76.	In Sternberg's triangular theory of love, _____ refers to an intention to maintain a relationship in spite of the difficulties and costs that may arise. a. commitment b. passion c. consummation d. secureness
Factual LO 11 Page: 667 **a**	77.	According to Hazan and Shaver, romantic love is an attachment process, and people's intimate relationships in adulthood follow the same form as their attachments a. in infancy b. to their preschool playmates c. to their adolescent peers d. to their same-gender parent

Concept/Applied
LO 11
Page: 668
a

78. According to Hazan and Shaver's model of infant attachment and romantic love, adults with which of the following attachment styles are most likely to have satisfying, interdependent, and long-lasting relationships?
   a. secure
   b. insecure
   c. avoidant
   d. anxious-ambivalent

Concept/Applied
LO 11
Page: 668
d

79. According to Hazan and Shaver's model of infant attachment and romantic love, adults with which of the following attachment styles are most likely to report more intense emotional highs and lows in their romantic relationships?
   a. secure
   b. insecure
   c. avoidant
   d. anxious-ambivalent

Concept/Applied
LO 11
Page: 668
d

80. According to Hazan and Shaver's model of infant attachment and romantic love, adults with which of the following attachment styles are most likely to feel negative about their relationships after dealing with conflict?
   a. secure
   b. insecure
   c. avoidant
   d. anxious-ambivalent

Concept/Applied
LO 11
Page: 668
c

81. According to Hazan and Shaver's model of infant attachment and romantic love, adults with which of the following attachment styles are most likely to engage in casual sex?
   a. secure
   b. insecure
   c. avoidant
   d. anxious-ambivalent

Concept/Applied
LO 11
Page: 668
Correct = 45%
b

82. According to Hazan and Shaver, an adult who reports that his or her love relations are volatile, jealous, and full of expected rejection was probably a(n) _____ child.
   a. avoidant attachment
   b. anxious-ambivalent attachment
   c. secure attachment
   d. tentatively attached

Concept/Applied
LO 11
Page: 668
Correct = 96%
d

83. Natasha has always felt at ease confiding in other people, and she and Boris have described their relationship as one based on trust. Hazan and Shaver (1987) would hypothesize that when Natasha was a baby, her relationship with her parents would have been described by Ainsworth as
   a. nonattachment
   b. anxious-ambivalent attachment
   c. avoidant attachment
   d. secure attachment

Concept/Applied
LO 11
Page: 668
c

84. Milton has always been "in love with the idea of being in love," yet his romances have been threatened by his feelings of jealousy. His current girlfriend, Emilia, often assures him that she'll love him forever, but he's not so sure about that. Hazan and Shaver (1987) would say that Milton is
   a. perfectly normal
   b. avoidant
   c. anxious-ambivalent
   d. secure

Factual LO 12 Page: 668 **a**	85.	Which of the following factors is likely to be the most important for a female seeking a prospective mate? a. social status b. youthfulness c. physical strength d. physical attractiveness

Factual LO 12 Page: 668 **d**	86.	Which of the following factors is likely to be the most important for a male seeking a prospective mate? a. ambition b. social status c. financial resources d. physical attractiveness

Factual LO 12 Page: 668 **d**	87.	Love as the basis for marriage is a. unique to the United States b. a product of Asian collectivism c. virtually universal across all cultures d. an 18th-century invention of Western culture

Factual LO 12 Page: 668 **b**	88.	Marriages arranged by families and other go-betweens remain common in cultures high in a. individualism b. collectivism c. self-perception d. self-monitoring

Concept/Applied LO 12 Page: 669 Correct = 31% **d**	89.	According to evolutionary psychologists, which of the following characteristics in a prospective mate would be the least important consideration for a woman seeking a mate? a. ambition b. social status c. financial potential d. physical attractiveness

Concept/Applied LO 12 Page: 670 **c**	90.	A psychologist with which of the following orientations is most likely to analyze romantic relationships in terms of the adaptive problems they have presented over the course of human history? a. behavioral b. humanistic c. evolutionary d. psychodynamic

Factual LO 13 Page: 671 **c**	91.	Which of the following is <u>not</u> one of the major components of an attitude? a. beliefs that one holds about the object of an attitude b. emotional feelings stimulated by an object of thought c. genetic tendencies toward specific biases d. predispositions to act in certain ways

Concept/Applied LO 13 Page: 671 **d**	92.	Virginia has a favorable attitude toward aerobics and working out. Just the thought of her daily workout is enough to make Virginia feel good, and she finds that when she is at the gym she feels much more relaxed and much less stressed. These emotional responses form part of the _____ component of Virginia's attitude toward working out. a. cognitive b. behavioral c. physiological d. affective

Concept/Applied LO 13 Page: 671 **b**	93.	Eric has a favorable attitude toward the "Twisted Lizards" rock band. He buys every CD they release, as soon as it is available. He also has both of the band's music videos, and he has been to six of the band's live concerts. These actions form part of the _____ component of Eric's attitude toward the "Twisted Lizards." a. affective b. behavioral c. cognitive d. physiological
Factual LO 13 Page: 671 **d**	94.	Which of the following is <u>not</u> one of the crucial dimensions of attitudes? a. strength b. ambivalence c. accessibility d. distinctiveness
Factual LO 13 Page: 671 **c**	95.	How often one thinks about an attitude and how quickly it comes to mind refer to the _____ of an attitude. a. strength b. ambivalence c. accessibility d. distinctiveness
Factual LO 13 Page: 671 **d**	96.	Attitudes that are _____ are quickly and readily available. a. strong b. ambivalent c. distinctive d. highly accessible
Factual LO 13 Page: 671 **b**	97.	Which of the following dimensions of attitudes are most likely to be correlated? a. strength and ambivalence b. accessibility and strength c. accessibility and ambivalence d. distinctiveness and ambivalence
Factual LO 13 Page: 671 **d**	98.	Which of the following dimensions of an attitude refers to whether the attitude relates to an issue that can affect an individual's personal outcomes? a. strength b. ambivalence c. accessibility d. vested interest
Factual LO 14 Page: 672 **a**	99.	A number of studies have shown that attitudes are only mediocre predictors of behavior. One explanation for this finding is that a. researchers failed to take variations in attitude strength into account b. researchers failed to operationalize the concept of an atttude c. subjects often intentionally lie about both their attitudes and their behavior d. general beliefs and feelings aren't likely to predict specific behaviors very well
Factual LO 15 Page: 672 **d**	100.	Which of the following is <u>not</u> considered one of the basic elements of the persuasion process? a. source b. receiver c. channel d. intensity

Critical Thinking LO 15 Page: 673 c	101.	Which of the following characteristics is most likely to enhance the credibility of the source of a persuasive message? a. height b. friendliness c. trustworthiness d. physical attractiveness
Factual LO 15 Page: 673 a	102.	Persuasion is most likely to be successful when the source of the persuasive communication a. is perceived as trustworthy b. will personally benefit from changing the receiver's attitudes c. is perceived as highly ingratiating d. is highly dissimilar to the receiver
Concept/Applied LO 15 Page: 673 b	103.	You would be most likely to accept the suggestion that the country needs a reduction in corporate taxes if the suggestion were made by a. the CEO of a major company b. a noted economics professor c. a manufacturer's representative d. a well know television actor
Concept/Applied LO 15 Page: 673 c	104.	Sean Jones is a basketball player who was been hired by a major cereal manufacturer to promote one of their brands of cereal. Last week Sean received national coverage when he was arrested for drunk driving. This week the cereal manufacturer canceled the remainder of his contract. Based on the research into factors which influence persuasion, the contract was most likely canceled because, as a result of his arrest a. Sean's trustworthiness will probably decrease b. people will now perceive Sean as being less of an expert on nutrition c. Sean's likability will probably decrease d. people will now perceive Sean as being less physically attractive
Concept/Applied LO 15 Page: 673 b	105.	You would be most apt to accept the suggestion that the country needs a reduction in corporate taxes if given by a. E15on's CEO b. a noted economics professor c. a manufacturer's representative d. the Republican president
Concept/Applied LO 15 Page: 673 Correct = 90% a	106.	Alan has been known to stretch the truth in the past. Therefore, when he tries to convince you to adopt a particular attitude, you are somewhat resistant. Alan has lost _____ in his ability to persuade you. a. the characteristic of trustworthiness b. the characteristic of group identification c. the characteristic of expertness d. all of these characteristics
Concept/Applied LO 15 Page: 673 Correct = 84% c	107.	Barbara's car has been running poorly lately. Whose advice is Barbara most likely to follow in order to make her car run better? a. her physician b. her uncle c. her mechanic d. her physics instructor

Critical Thinking 108. Which of the following statements regarding the effectiveness of two-sided
LO 15   arguments is accurate?
Page: 673
               a. Presenting a two-sided argument often confuses the receiver and decreases a
c   source's persuasiveness.
               b. Two-sided arguments should be avoided, since the receiver shouldn't be
                   informed that there is an alternative to the source's view.
               c. Overall, two-sided arguments tend to be more effective than one-sided
                   arguments.
               d. Two-sided arguments tend to be effective with women, but not with men.

Critical Thinking 109. Which of the following statements regarding the use of weak arguments in
LO 15   persuasive communication is accurate?
Page: 673
               a. The more arguments one presents, the more effective the message will be,
b   regardless of the strength of the arguments.
               b. Adding weak arguments to a persuasive message will likely do more harm than
                   good to one's case.
               c. The key determinant of the effectiveness of a persuasive message seems to be
                   the ratio of strong arguments to weak arguments.
               d. Weak arguments will enhance the effectiveness of a persuasive communication
                   as long as they are presented clearly.

Factual   110. Simply repeating a message causes it to be perceived as more true. This finding is
LO 15   known as the _____ effect.
Page: 674
               a. validity
a   b. contrast
               c. exposure
               d. reiteration

Concept/Applied 111. If you are trying to persuade others to your point of view on AIDS research, you
LO 15   would be wise to
Page: 674
               a. give only a one-sided, fear-invoking argument
c   b. stress only the personal threat of getting AIDS
               c. give a two-sided argument, arouse fear, and offer a solution
               d. emphasize arguments directed at the opposing view

Factual   112. Fear arousal is likely to be an effective persuasive tactic
LO 15
Page: 674   a. as long as the negative consequences to be avoided are perceived as fairly
                   unlikely
d   b. as long as the receiver thinks the source's advice is reasonable
               c. with people who are familiar with both sides of the issue
               d. if the negative consequences are extremely unpleasant, fairly probable if the
                   receivers don't follow the source's advice, and avoidable if they do

Factual   113. Which of the following factors is (are) associated with one being resistant to a
LO 15   persuasive attempt?
Page: 674
               a. believing in a just world
c   b. high self-monitoring
               c. forewarning
               d. all of these factors

Critical Thinking 114. Arguments that are in conflict with one's prior attitudes are scrutinized longer and
LO 15   subjected to more skeptical analysis than are arguments that are consistent with
Page: 674   one's prior beliefs. This finding is most consistent with which of the following
               concepts?
a
               a. disconfirmation bias
               b. the matching hypothesis
               c. cognitive dissonance
               d. the fundamental attribution error

Factual LO 16 Page: 675 **b**	115.	Classical conditioning could account for the formation of the _____ component of an attitude. a. cognitive b. affective c. behavioral d. perceptual
Concept/Applied LO 16 Page: 675 **d**	116.	A recent anti-smoking campaign on television showed graphic images of the internal effects of smoking. Twelve-year-old Kandice has seen a number of these ads, and they made her feel nauseated. Now she finds that she has developed an unfavorable attitude toward smoking. In this case, Kandice's attitude appears to have developed as a result of a. observational learning b. operant conditioning c. cognitive dissonance d. classical conditioning
Concept/Applied LO 16 Page: 675 Correct = 50% **b**	117.	When advertisers use extremely attractive models to demonstrate their products, they are relying, in part, on the power of _____ to change consumers' attitudes. a. observational learning b. classical conditioning c. reinforcement d. punishment
Concept/Applied LO 16 Page: 675 **c**	118.	If Matthew's mother praises his "good sense" every time he says that money is important, then Matthew's attitude will be strengthened by a. observational learning b. classical conditioning c. reinforcement d. punishment
Concept/Applied LO 16 Page: 675 **c**	119.	Rodney has an unfavorable attitude toward his astronomy professor. In explaining Rodney's attitude, a psychologist who took an operant conditioning perspective would consider a. the astronomy professor's personality and general attitude toward Rodney b. how other students in the class feel about this particular professor c. Rodney's history of reinforcement and punishment in dealing with his astronomy professor d. how Rodney feels about his other professors
Concept/Applied LO 16 Page: 675 **a**	120.	Matthew often hears his parents discussing the importance of making lots of money. Eventually, Matthew himself begins to value a high income. Matthew's attitude about money was acquired through a. observational learning b. classical conditioning c. reinforcement d. punishment
Factual LO 17 Page: 676 **c**	121.	Which of the following individuals is noted for developing the theory of cognitive dissonance? a. Albert Bandura b. Daryl Bem c. Leon Festinger d. Sigmund Freud

Factual LO 17 Page: 676 Correct = 69% **a**	122.	Cognitive dissonance a. is a state of tension produced when related cognitions are inconsistent b. is a feeling of discomfort experienced by receivers of persuasive communications c. is a feeling of guilt produced by engaging in counterattitudinal behavior d. occurs only when cognitions are unrelated to each other
Factual LO 17 Page: 676 Correct = 42% **a**	123.	In the study by Festinger and Carlsmith (1959), subjects who were paid $1 for "lying" exhibited _____ attitude change; subjects who were paid $20 for "lying" exhibited _____ attitude change. a. much; little b. much; much c. little; much d. little; little
Factual LO 17 Page: 676 Correct = 56% **d**	124.	Cognitive dissonance theory accounts for Festinger and Carlsmith's (1959) results by proposing that subjects paid a. $1 to "lie" felt little cognitive dissonance b. $1 to "lie" had sufficient justification for their counterattitudinal behavior c. $20 to "lie" felt high cognitive dissonance d. $20 to "lie" had sufficient justification for their counterattitudinal behavior and experienced little dissonance
Concept/Applied LO 17 Page: 676 Correct = 43% **c**	125.	Minimizing the imbalance of inconsistent attitudes is a technique used to a. resist persuasion b. counteract self-handicapping c. reduce the discomfort associated with cognitive dissonance d. maintain psychological control in situations in which great pressure exists to behave counter-attitudinally
Concept/Applied LO 17 Page: 676 **a**	126.	According to Festinger's cognitive dissonance research, you would predict greatest attitudinal change in a person who is led to lie by a(n) a. simple request to do so b. offer of one dollar to do so c. offer of extra grade points to do so d. offer of $50 to do so
Concept/Applied LO 17 Page: 676 **a**	127.	Scott spent a great deal of time and money on becoming a member of a certain club, yet later discovered that the members of the club were boring. According to dissonance theory, Scott would most likely a. continue to extol the virtues of the club to his friends b. now "bad mouth" the club to his friends c. engage in denial and disengagement as part of his defensive attribution d. try to modify the behavior of the current club members
Factual LO 17 Page: 677 **b**	128.	Elliot Aronson views inconsistency as the key to dissonance, but maintains that it is inconsistency between one's _____ and one's _____ that motivates dissonance. a. emotions; behavior b. self-concept; behavior c. behavior; attributions d. self-concept; unconscious urges

Critical Thinking LO 17 Page: 677 **a**	129.	Which of the following statements regarding the research on dissonance theory is most accurate? a. Research has generally supported dissonance theory. b. Research has generally not supported dissonance theory. c. Research has supported dissonance theory, but only with regard to social behavior. d. Research on dissonance theory has been favorable, but only when the subjects have been young children.
Factual LO 18 Page: 677 **b**	130.	Which of the following individuals is recognized for developing self-perception theory? a. Albert Bandura b. Daryl Bem c. David Buss d. Leon Festinger
Factual LO 18 Page: 677 **d**	131.	Which of the following theories proposes that we often infer our attitudes from observations of our own behavior? a. cognitive dissonance theory b. learning theory c. balance theory d. self-perception theory
Concept/Applied LO 18 Page: 677 Correct = 29% **d**	132.	Self-perception theory suggests that a. one develops attitudes from discerning what others think the attitudes should be b. one's self-concept is tied to the feedback one gets from others c. self-handicapping is a strategy used to deal with the negative outcomes one experiences d. one infers attitudes from observing one's own behavior
Concept/Applied LO 18 Page: 677 Correct = 49% **c**	133.	John notices he's been eating carrots a lot lately. From this John infers that he must like carrots. John's positive attitude toward carrots can be explained by a. attribution theory b. the actor-observer bias c. self-perception theory d. the lens model of attitude-behavior relationships
Concept/Applied LO 18 Page: 677 Correct = 38% **d**	134.	In recent election campaigns, there has been much criticism that campaign ads focus too much on building attractive images for candidates and too little on substantive issues of genuine importance. These two ways of trying to influence voters are dealt with by the approach to persuasion called a. balance theory b. dissonance theory c. self-perception theory d. the elaboration likelihood model
Concept/Applied LO 18 Page: 677 **a**	135.	The makers of the new Adobe automobile are sick and tired of TV commercials that rely on images of sex and life in the fast lane to sell cars. Besides, they believe that if their commercials simply present the true facts about why their car is the best on the market, potential buyers are more likely to develop a long-lasting preference for the Adobe. According to the elaboration likelihood model, this approach exemplifies the _____ route to persuasion. a. central b. peripheral c. autonomic d. somatic

Critical Thinking LO 18 Page: 677 Correct = 47% **b**	136.	If you are attempting to persuade someone to purchase your soft drinks, according to the elaboration likelihood model it would be best to use the a. central route b. peripheral route c. tertiary route d. reified route
Factual LO 18 Page: 678 **c**	137.	According to the elaboration likelihood model, messages that focus on the _____ are more likely to produce lasting attitude change. a. primary path b. parasympathetic route c. central route d. generic path
Factual LO 18 Page: 678 **c**	138.	The elaboration likelihood model of attitude change suggests that a. the peripheral route gives more enduring attitude change b. attitude change from the peripheral route better predicts behavior c. the central route gives more enduring attitude change d. none of these is correct
Concept/Applied LO 18 Page: 678 **b**	139.	Maureen was trying to decide which one of two national brand computers to buy. She was pretty well set on buying the "Brand A" computer when one of her friends mentioned that Kevin Costner did commercials endorsing "Brand B." Maureen decides to buy the "Brand B" computer, based on the assumption that Kevin Costner wouldn't endorse anything that wasn't top quality. In this instance, Maureen has reached her decision using a. a self-serving route to persuasion b. the peripheral route to persuasion c. the cognitive dissonance model of persuasion d. the central route to persuasion
Factual LO 19 Page: 678 **d**	140.	Yielding to real or imagined social pressure defines which of the following terms? a. cognitive dissonance b. obedience c. groupthink d. conformity
Factual LO 19 Page: 678 Correct = 93% **d**	141.	Conformity occurs when people change their behavior a. as a result of positive reinforcement b. as a result of negative reinforcement c. after observing a model being reinforced for a particular response d. in response to real or imagined social pressure
Factual LO 19 Page: 678 **a**	142.	Which of the following psychologists is known for conducting classic research on conformity? a. Solomon Asch b. Daryl Bem c. Leon Festinger d. Stanley Milgram
Factual LO 19 Page: 679 **c**	143.	In Asch's studies of conformity, subjects a. were ordered to deliver painful electric shocks to a stranger b. became the recipients of painful electric shocks delivered by an experimental accomplice c. indicated which of three lines matched a "standard line" in length d. were ordered to give consistently wrong answers to simple questions

Factual LO 19 Page: 679 Correct = 77% **d**	144.	In Asch's studies, _____ were found to be the key determinants of conformity. a. group size and the subjects' intelligence b. the group leader's personality and group unanimity c. task difficulty and group size d. group size and group unanimity
Factual LO 19 Page: 680 **b**	145.	Asch found that group size made little difference if a. the task was easy b. just one accomplice failed to go along with the rest of the group c. the experimenter ridiculed the group's wrong answers d. the task was difficult
Factual LO 19 Page: 680 **d**	146.	In his research on conformity in making perceptual judgments, Asch found that a. conformity did not change much with group size b. group size affected conformity, but unanimity did not c. increasing group size reduced conformity d. both group size and unanimity affected the degree of conformity
Factual LO 19 Page: 680 **a**	147.	In his studies on conformity, Asch found that if a group of persons espouses an opinion contradictory to one's own opinion, one is most likely to a. voice the group's opinion b. echo the opinion of the nearest group member c. voice one's own opinion, even though it's contradictory d. show mild symptoms of learned helplessness
Factual LO 20 Page: 680 **d**	148.	Which of the following psychologists is known for conducting classic research on obedience to authority? a. Solomon Asch b. Daryl Bem c. Leon Festinger d. Stanley Milgram
Factual LO 20 Page: 680 Correct = 85% **a**	149.	Obedience is a form of compliance in which people change their behavior in response to a. direct commands b. implied pressure c. requests from others d. persuasive communications
Factual LO 20 Page: 681 Correct = 77% **a**	150.	In Milgram's (1963) study of obedience, subjects a. were ordered to deliver painful electric shocks to a stranger b. became the recipients of painful electric shocks delivered by an experimental accomplice c. indicated which of three lines matched a "standard line" in length d. were ordered to give consistently wrong answers to simple questions
Factual LO 20 Page: 681 **c**	151.	In Milgram's (1963) study, what percentage of the subjects fully obeyed the experimenter? a. 5 percent b. 35 percent c. 65 percent d. 95 percent
Factual LO 20 Page: 681 **b**	152.	In Milgram's research on obedience, the "teacher" routinely a. resisted the authority figure b. obeyed the authority figure c. resisted the authority figure, but obeyed the confederate d. resisted the authority figure when the learner appeared to be injured

Factual LO 20 Page: 681 **a**	153.	In Milgram's research on obedience, what was the teacher's perception of what would happen when the learner made a mistake? a. The learner would receive a shock. b. The learner would be negatively reinforced. c. The teacher would be asked to change places with the learner. d. The experiment would have to be terminated.
Factual LO 20 Page: 681 **c**	154.	In Milgram's research on obedience, what did the experimenter do to the teacher when the teacher questioned whether the experiment should continue? a. The teacher was verbally abused. b. The teacher was shocked. c. The teacher was given verbal prompts to continue. d. The teacher was requested to change places with the learner.
Factual LO 20 Page: 682 **c**	155.	As Milgram studied factors affecting obedience to the research authority, the only factor which seemed to markedly reduce obedience was a. agreement of other "teachers" with the directions of the researcher b. moving the research away from the university to rundown quarters c. other "teachers" defying the experimenter and supporting subject objections d. no variable was found that greatly reduced obedience
Factual LO 20 Page: 682 **c**	156.	Milgram found that subjects' obedience declined dramatically when a. an innocent stranger was harmed by the subjects' actions b. group size was increased beyond seven members c. another "teacher" defied the experimenter's order d. the study was conducted in a run-down, dilapidated building
Concept/Applied LO 20 Page: 682 **b**	157.	Maria is driving along her normal route to work when a police officer stops her and directs her to take a different route. She is not sure why she has to take the detour, but she does what the police officer tells her to do. The process that best explains Maria's actions in this instance is a. conformity b. obedience c. ingratiation d. reciprocity
Factual LO 20 Page: 682 **d**	158.	Milgram's study was criticized on a. the grounds that the results wouldn't generalize to the real world b. the grounds that subjects were exposed to extensive deception c. the grounds that subjects had to face some disturbing truths about themselves d. all of these grounds
Factual LO 20 Page: 682 **c**	159.	Which of the following is <u>not</u> one of the criticisms directed toward Milgram's research on obedience to authority? a. The findings generalize very poorly to the "real" world. b. Subjects were exposed to extensive deception without prior consent. c. The independent and dependent variables were not clearly defined. d. Subjects were exposed to severe stress that could leave emotional scars.
Factual LO 21 Page: 683 **a**	160.	A recent review of 133 conformity studies drawn from 17 countries found higher levels of conformity in _____ cultures than in _____ cultures. a. collectivistic; individualistic b. individualistic; collectivistic c. Western; non-Western d. Western; Asian

Critical Thinking LO 21 Page: 683 c	161.	Which of the following statements about cross-cultural variations in conformity and obedience is <u>not</u> accurate? a. Results of Milgram's experiment have been fairly consistent across different cultures. b. In some replications of Milgram's study conducted in other cultures, obedience rates of over 80 percent have occurred. c. Replications of the Asch experiment have found higher levels of conformity in individualistic cultures than in collectivistic cultures. d. All of these statements are accurate.
Factual LO 21 Page: 683 c	162.	Which of the following statements regarding the influence of culture on conformity and obedience is accurate? a. Conformity and obedience appear to be unique to American culture. b. Replications of Milgram's study in other countries have generally resulted in low levels of obedience. c. Collectivistic cultures tend to encourage more conformity than individualistic cultures. d. Studies of conformity and obedience have yielded virtually identical results across a variety of cultures.
Factual LO 22 Page: 683 Correct = 73% c	163.	According to social psychologists, a group a. exists whenever two or more people are in spatial proximity to each other b. consists of three or more people who interact on a regular basis c. consists of two or more people who interact and are interdependent d. will not affect the behavior of its members
Critical Thinking LO 22 Page: 684 Correct = 72% b	164.	Which of the following meet(s) the definition of a group? a. all single mothers in the United States b. the members of the Yearbook Club c. people traveling together on a city bus d. all of these could meet the definition
Critical Thinking LO 22 Page: 684 b	165.	Which of the following is <u>not</u> a defining feature of a group? a. It consists of two or more people. b. The members must meet face-to-face. c. Group members must interact with each other. d. The group members are interdependent.
Factual LO 22 Page: 684 c	166.	The "bystander effect" is the finding that a. the probability that a witness to an emergency will help increases as the number of bystanders increases b. a group of witnesses to an emergency will all tend to cooperate to provide help c. the probability that a witness to an emergency will help decreases as the number of bystanders increases d. bystanders' willingness to help depends on the seriousness of the emergency
Factual LO 22 Page: 684 Correct = 79% a	167.	The bystander effect is a. greater the more people there are in the group b. less the more people there are in the group c. unaffected by the size of the group d. greatest when the observer is the only one present
Factual LO 22 Page: 684 a	168.	Evidence from numerous studies of the bystander effect suggests that a. it is a widespread phenomenon b. it is limited to contrived laboratory situations c. it occurs only in urban ghetto areas d. there is much truth to the old saying that "there is safety in numbers"

Concept/Applied LO 22 Page: 685 Correct = 56% **a**	169.	The bystander effect should be strongest in a. a large group when need for help is ambiguous b. a large group when need for help is unambiguous c. a smaller group when need for help is ambiguous d. a smaller group when need for help is unambiguous
Concept/Applied LO 22 Page: 685 Correct = 80% **a**	170.	Diffusion of responsibility refers to the a. tendency of others to assume that someone else will take responsibility in a crisis b. basis for performing prosocial behavior c. halo effect in aggression d. loss of identity one experiences in mob violence/aggression
Concept/Applied LO 22 Page: 685 **d**	171.	Jeff, Greg, Dan, and Ray all watched as the building across the street burned to the ground. They kept waiting for the fire trucks to show up, even though none of them had called 911. In this case, the fact that none of the four friends phoned to report the fire illustrates the phenomenon known as a. social loafing b. a self-fulfilling prophecy c. group polarization d. the bystander effect
Concept/Applied LO 22 Page: 685 **d**	172.	Phoebe saw the passenger in the seat across the aisle suddenly slump forward in her seat. While the other passengers looked around for a flight attendant, Phoebe immediately started to administer CPR. In this case, Phoebe's actions are the opposite of what would be expected based on a. the actor-observer effect b. social loafing c. group polarization d. the bystander effect
Factual LO 23 Page: 685 **a**	173.	Individuals' productivity typically _____ in larger groups, partly due to _____. a. declines; reduced efficiency due to the loss of coordination among group members' efforts b. declines; positive reinforcement from other group members for reduced productivity c. increases; concern about being observed and evaluated by other group members d. increases; commitment to the group's goals
Factual LO 23 Page: 685 **c**	174.	Which of the following is generally <u>not</u> considered a factor in explaining why individuals' performance in groups declines? a. loss of coordination between members b. social loafing c. unequal numbers of male and female members d. duplication of effort by group members
Factual LO 23 Page: 685 **d**	175.	The reduction in effort by individuals when they work in groups is referred to as a. bystander apathy b. diffusion of responsibility c. extroverted effort d. social loafing

Factual LO 23 Page: 685 Correct = 83% **b**	176.	Social loafing refers to a. increases in socializing among members of larger groups b. the reduction of effort by individuals when they work in groups c. the loss of coordination among group members' efforts d. a tendency to blame others for the group's poor performance
Critical Thinking LO 23 Page: 686 **a**	177.	Which of the following statements regarding social loafing is <u>not</u> accurate? a. Social loafing is an inevitable outcome of group projects. b. As group size increases, social loafing becomes more likely. c. Recent evidence indicates that fatigue tends to increase social loafing. d. The social-loafing effect has been replicated in a number of studies using a variety of tasks.
Concept/Applied LO 23 Page: 686 **b**	178.	When Jerry thought he was the only person who was assigned the job of contacting alumni for a 15-year reunion, he spent several hours on the phone each evening trying to reach members of his graduating class. When he learned that eight other people were also working on contacting the alumni he spent only 30 minutes each night making phone calls. The process that would best explain the decrease in Jerry's effort when he learned that he was working as part of a larger group, is a. social interference b. social loafing c. the bystander effect d. social dissonance
Factual LO 24 Page: 686 **c**	179.	When Stoner (1961) compared the average decision of a group's members against their group decision generated through group discussion, he found that a. group members ignored the discussion and maintained their original decision b. individuals arrived at riskier decisions than groups c. groups arrived at riskier decisions than individuals d. the longer the discussion continued, the riskier the group's decisions
Factual LO 24 Page: 686 **a**	180.	A shift toward more extreme decisions in a group as a function of discussion is referred to as a. group polarization b. biased decision making c. the bystander effect d. diffusion of responsibility
Critical Thinking LO 24 Page: 686 **a**	181.	The group polarization effect implies that a. when most of the group members initially favor a cautious decision, discussion will cause the group to adopt an even more cautious decision b. the gap between two opposing factions will be narrowed after group discussion c. when most of the group members initially favor a cautious decision, discussion will cause the group to adopt a risky decision d. group decisions will always be better than individual decisions
Factual LO 24 Page: 686 **b**	182.	Group discussion resulting in strengthening a group's dominant view and shifting it to a greater extreme is known as a. groupthink b. polarization c. group diffusion d. reinforcement

Concept/Applied LO 24 Page: 686 **d**	183.	When the jury entered the jury room most of the jurors thought that the defendant in the case was probably innocent, but some weren't certain. After discussing the case for four hours, all twelve jurors are now firmly convinced that the defendant did not commit the crime. The strengthening of the jurors' opinions following group discussion is consistent with which of the following processes? a. group think b. the bystander effect c. reciprocity d. group polarization
Factual LO 24 Page: 687 **d**	184.	Censoring dissent, pressuring to conform, omitting contradictory evidence, and polarizing ingroup and outgroup are basic features of which of the following? a. social loafing b. group polarization c. social diffusion d. groupthink
Factual LO 24 Page: 687 **c**	185.	Which of the following is not characteristic of groupthink? a. dividing the world into the ingroup and the outgroup b. censoring dissent from group members c. gathering all the relevant information before making a decision d. censoring information that contradicts the group's views
Critical Thinking LO 24 Page: 687 **b**	186.	Which of the following statements regarding group decision making is <u>not</u> accurate? a. Groupthink seems to promote incomplete gathering of information. b. Groups tend to focus on information that is unique to the individual members. c. Groups have a tendency to emphasize information that the members already share. d. Sound decision making depends on group members combining their information effectively.
Factual LO 24 Page: 687 **b**	187.	Group cohesiveness refers to the a. degree to which group members agree about an issue b. strength of the liking relationships linking group members to each other and to the group itself c. extent of polarization that occurs after group discussion d. tendency of groups to make more cautious decisions than individuals
Factual LO 24 Page: 688 Correct = 76% **c**	188.	Groupthink is more likely when the group a. does not have a designated leader b. must justify their decision to other groups in the same organization c. is under pressure to make a major decision d. experiences any of these things
Factual LO 25 Page: 688 **a**	189.	Psychology is committed to the reliance on systematic observation through research, to arrive at conclusions. That is, psychology is committed to a. empiricism b. objectivity c. subjectivity d. functionalism
Factual LO 25 Page: 689 **d**	190.	Which of the following behaviors is likely to be variable across cultures? a. attitudes about conformity b. the tendency to obey authority figures c. the role of love in mating relationships d. all of these behaviors

Factual LO 25 Page: 689 **d**	191.	Which of the following are potential sources of subjectivity in our perceptions of ourselves and others? a. the impact of their physical appearance b. our social schemas c. pressure to conform d. all of these factors
Factual LO 26 Page: 690 Correct = 75% **a**	192.	Prejudice a. refers to a negative attitude toward members of a group b. refers to unfair behavior toward the members of a group c. is the same thing as discrimination d. refers to all of these things
Factual LO 26 Page: 690 Correct = 78% **c**	193.	Harboring negative thoughts and feelings about a person simply because of his or her membership in a particular group defines a. discrimination b. social judgment c. prejudice d. chauvinism
Critical Thinking LO 26 Page: 690 Correct = 59% **b**	194.	Prejudice is to discrimination as a. feeling is to thinking b. attitude is to action c. thought is to perception d. behavior is to motive
Concept/Applied LO 26 Page: 690 **a**	195.	Denying a person equal social treatment based on his or her group membership defines a. discrimination b. social scaling c. prejudice d. chauvinism
Concept/Applied LO 26 Page: 690 **a**	196.	Kevin is the human resource manager for a large company. He actually has a favorable attitude toward the handicapped in general. However, he hasn't hired anyone who has a visible disability for any position that has come open in the company because his boss told him not to consider applicants who are handicapped. In this case Kevin a. shows evidence of discrimination, but not prejudice b. shows evidence of prejudice, but not discrimination c. is displaying both prejudice and discrimination d. is showing neither prejudice nor discrimination
Factual LO 26 Page: 690 **d**	197.	Which of the following statements regarding stereotypes is accurate? a. Stereotypes are inevitably negative and unflattering. b. Ethnic and racial groups are the only targets of widespread prejudice. c. We see members of our own ingroup as more alike than the members of outgroups. d. Stereotypes are so pervasive that they are often activated automatically.
Concept/Applied LO 26 Page: 691 **b**	198.	A man who believes that "women just don't make good leaders" may dwell on his female supervisor's mistakes and quickly forget about her achievements. This scenario illustrates which of the following concepts? a. defensive attribution b. the illusory correlation effect c. the fundamental attribution error d. the bystander effect

Factual LO 26 Page: 692 Correct = 67% **a**	199.	Observers tend to favor _____ attributions about the success of males; observers tend to favor _____ attributions about the success of females. a. internal; external b. internal; internal c. external; internal d. external; external
Factual LO 26 Page: 692 **a**	200.	The fundamental attribution error leads observers to attribute the crime and poverty of urban ethnic neighborhoods to the a. personal qualities of the residents b. job discrimination experienced by the residents c. poor police protection in such areas d. crowded living conditions in these neighborhoods
Concept/Applied LO 27 Page: 693 Correct = 72% **a**	201.	After repeatedly hearing her parents say that "all fat people are slobs," Cindy begins to express the same belief. In this case, Cindy's prejudice against fat people was acquired due to a. observational learning b. classical conditioning c. reinforcement d. punishment
Concept/Applied LO 27 Page: 693 **c**	202.	If Cindy's parents heartily agree with her each time she says that "all fat people are slobs," Cindy's prejudice will be strengthened due to a. observational learning b. classical conditioning c. reinforcement d. punishment
Factual LO 27 Page: 693 **b**	203.	Ethnocentrism refers to the tendency to a. focus on one's own needs as opposed to what is best for the group b. evaluate people in one's own group as superior to others c. model the attitudes of members of one's immediate family d. identify with members of a popular outgroup
Critical Thinking LO 27 Page: 693 Correct = 63% **d**	204.	Which of the following is <u>not</u> characteristic of ethnocentric thinking? a. a tendency to evaluate outgroup members less favorably than ingroup members b. a tendency to overestimate the similarity of outgroup members c. a tendency to think simplistically about outgroups d. a tendency to evaluate people in an outgroup from the perspective of a member of that outgroup
Factual LO 28 Page: 694 **a**	205.	In deciding what to believe, we also need to decide whom to believe, a task that requires assessing the _____ of the source of the information. a. credibility b. attractiveness c. collectivism d. cognitive dissonance
Factual LO 28 Page: 694 **a**	206.	The purveyors of miracle tonics and psychic advice tend to rely on which of the following forms of evidence? a. anecdotal evidence b. findings from observational research c. results from laboratory experiments d. findings from surveys and questionnaires

Factual LO 28 Page: 695 **d**	207.	Which of the following social influence techniques involves getting people to agree to a small request to increase the chances that they will agree to a larger request later? a. lowball technique b. highball technique c. reciprocity norm d. foot-in-the-door technique
Concept/Applied LO 28 Page: 695 **c**	208.	Groups seeking donations often ask people to simply sign a petition first. This approach illustrates which of the following social influence techniques? a. lowball technique b. highball technique c. foot-in-the-door technique d. reciprocity norm
Factual LO 28 Page: 695 **b**	209.	The rule that we should pay back in kind what we receive from others is known as the a. display rule b. reciprocity norm c. principle of collectivism d. law of cognitive dissonance
Concept/Applied LO 28 Page: 695 **d**	210.	Groups seeking donations routinely send address labels and other small gifts with their pleas. This approach illustrates which of the following social influence techniques? a. lowball technique b. highball technique c. foot-in-the-door technique d. reciprocity norm
Factual LO 28 Page: 695 **a**	211.	Which of the following social influence techniques involves getting someone to commit to an attractive proposition before its hidden costs are revealed? a. lowball technique b. highball technique c. reciprocity norm d. foot-in-the-door technique
Concept/Applied LO 28 Page: 695 **b**	212.	A car dealer may offer a customer a terrific deal on a car, but once the customer commits to buying the car the dealer reveals that there are some hidden costs. This approach illustrates which of the following social influence techniques? a. feigned scarcity b. lowball technique c. foot-in-the-door technique d. reciprocity norm
Concept/Applied LO 28 Page: 695 **a**	213.	Advertisements that include phrases like "limited supply available" or "for a limited time only" are making use of which of the following social influence techniques? a. feigned scarcity b. lowball technique c. foot-in-the-door technique d. reciprocity norm
Integrative **c**	214.	The studies by Asch and by Milgram indicate that both conformity to group pressure and obedience to commands are reduced by a. group cohesiveness b. group polarization c. the presence of a dissenter d. centralized communication

Integrative **c**	215.	In terms of underlying causes, which of the following share the most kinship? a. group polarization and cognitive dissonance b. discrimination and ingratiation c. the bystander effect and social loafing d. social loafing and the illusory correlation effect
Study Guide LO 1 Page: 657 **b**	216.	Which of the following characteristics do we tend to attribute to physically attractive people? a. coldness b. friendliness c. unpleasantness d. low intelligence
Study Guide LO 7 Page: 661 **d**	217.	Which of the following could be an example of the fundamental attribution error? a. Ralph described himself as a failure. b. Ralph thought that the reason he failed was that he was sick that day. c. Jayne said Ralph failed because the test was unfair. d. Sue explained Ralph's failure in terms of his incompetence and laziness.
Study Guide LO 7 Page: 663 **c**	218.	Bruce performed very well on the examination, which he attributed to native ability and hard work. Which bias does this illustrate? a. the fundamental attribution error b. the actor-observer bias c. the self-serving bias d. illusory correlation
Study Guide LO 12 Page: 669 **a**	219.	According to this viewpoint, men emphasize physical attractiveness in mate selection while women emphasize the ability to acquire resources. Which theory does this describe? a. evolutionary theory b. cognitive dissonance theory c. sexual propensity theory d. attribution theory
Study Guide LO 15 Page: 674 **b**	220.	Which of the following is, in general, likely to reduce the persuasiveness of a message? a. The receiver's viewpoint is already fairly close to that of the message. b. The receiver has been forewarned about the message. c. A two-sided appeal is used. d. The source is physically attractive.
Study Guide LO 17 Page: 676 **b**	221.	Subjects in Group A are paid $1 for engaging in a dull task. Subjects in Group B are paid $20 for the same task. Which theory would predict that Group A subjects would enjoy the task more? a. balance b. cognitive dissonance c. self-perception d. observational learning
Study Guide LO 18 Page: 677 **b**	222.	In making a decision you rely on the opinion of experts and the behavior of your best friends. According to the elaboration likelihood model, which route to persuasion have you used? a. central b. peripheral c. attributional d. 66

Study Guide LO 20 Page: 682 **b**	223.	Which of the following is the best statement of conclusion concerning Milgram's classic study involving the learner, teacher, and ostensible shock? a. Under certain circumstances, people seem to enjoy the opportunity to be cruel to others. b. People have a strong tendency to obey an authority even if their actions may harm others. c. The more people there are who observe someone in need of help, the less likely any one is to help. d. Aggression seems to be a more potent force in human nature than had previously been suspected.
Study Guide LO 22 Page: 683 **c**	224.	Which of the following is most likely to function as a group? a. shoppers at a mall b. the audience in a theater c. the board of trustees of a college d. passengers in an airplane
Study Guide LO 22 Page: 684 **a**	225.	Someone witnesses a car accident. In which of the following cases is that individual most likely to stop and render assistance? a. Only that individual saw the accident. b. That individual and one other individual saw the accident. c. That individual and 18 others saw the accident. d. The other observers are pedestrians.
Online Quiz LO 1 Page: 657 **c**	226.	Research on physical attractiveness has shown that a. most people disregard physical attractiveness when forming first impressions of people b. judgments of women's personalities are affected by their physical attractiveness, but judgments of men's personalities are not c. we tend to ascribe desirable personality characteristics to good-looking people d. men are more likely than women to make biased judgments of others based on physical appearance
Online Quiz LO 2 Page: 658 **d**	227.	Which of the following is <u>not</u> a variable people use to stereotype other people? a. ethnicity b. gender c. occupation d. Any of these variables may be used.
Online Quiz LO 5 Page: 660 **d**	228.	In making a causal attribution, we first tend to decide if an event was due to _____ causes. a. subjective or objective b. usual or unusual c. positive or negative d. internal or external
Online Quiz LO 7 Page: 663 **b**	229.	Making excuses for problems (blaming something else) reflects a a. fundamental attribution error b. self-serving bias c. halo effect d. self-handicapping strategy
Concept/Applied LO 10 Page: 666 **b**	230.	Which of the following types of love relationships is most likely to have a sexual component? a. companionate love b. passionate love c. fatuous love d. attributional love

Online Quiz
LO 12
Page: 670
d

231. Findings from recent studies suggest that people adjust their tactics of attraction as a function of which of the following?
   a. their own physical attractiveness
   b. the number of previous relationships they've had
   c. the quantity of financial resources at their disposal
   d. whether they are pursuing a short-term or long-term relationship

Online Quiz
LO 14
Page: 672
b

232. Research has revealed that attitudes are
   a. very reliable predictors of behavior
   b. mediocre predictors of behavior
   c. very reliable predictors of behavior in men but not women
   d. very reliable predictors of behavior in women but not men

Online Quiz
LO 17
Page: 676
b

233. Cognitive dissonance refers to the state one is in when
   a. beliefs are contrary to one's peer group
   b. cognitions are inconsistent
   c. behaviors are socially undesirable
   d. interpersonal relationships are unbalanced

Online Quiz
LO 19
Page: 679
b

234. In Asch's studies, what was the relationship between group size and conformity?
   a. Conformity did not change with group size.
   b. Conformity increased steadily as group size went from two to four, and then leveled off.
   c. Conformity increased as group size went from two to four, and then decreased.
   d. Conformity increased steadily as group size was increased up to fifteen.

Online Quiz
LO 26
Page: 692
d

235. Unjustly blaming victims of misfortune for their misfortune defines a(n)
   a. ingroup/outgroup effect
   b. stereotypic response
   c. risky shift
   d. defensive attribution

ESSAY QUESTIONS

1. Daryl Bem's self-perception theory suggests that behavior determines attitudes. This counterintuitive notion is reminiscent of the James-Lange theory of emotion. How are the two theories similar yet different from each other?

   Obviously, Bem's theory purports to explain the origins of attitudes, and the James-Lange theory tries to do the same for emotions. Interestingly, though, attitudes are considered to contain an affective component, which suggests a closer tie to James-Lange than might at first be expected. Bem suggests that we observe our behavior in a situation and infer our attitude about the situation, including its affective component, from the observed behavior. Similarly, the James-Lange theory suggests that our behavior in an emotion-arousing situation, especially our autonomic behavior, leads to inferences about the emotion we're experiencing. We could elaborate on the James-Lange view by assuming that as we "choose" an emotion on the basis of autonomic arousal pattern, along with it come certain associated ideas and beliefs (a cognitive component) and certain predispositions to act (a behavioral component). Put them all together and you've got an attitude. So it may not be too great a stretch to suggest that the James-Lange theory is, like Bem's theory, a self-perception theory of attitude formation.

2. It's commonly believed that most political elections are determined by the public's impressions of the candidates rather than the candidates' views on the issues. What are some possible reasons for this irrational voting behavior? If the public were more knowledgeable about factors that affect person perception and attitudes, how might that knowledge influence voting behavior?

   Answers should reflect students' understanding of factors that influence person perception and attitude formation and change. With regard to person perception, students should discuss such things as the effects of physical appearance and the halo effect, stereotypes, and illusory correlation.

   With regard to attitudes, students should discuss source, message, and receiver factors in persuasion, as well as what various theoretical approaches have to say about attitude change.

   Presumably if voters were aware of these ways in which their voting decisions can be influenced, they'd be on guard against undue influences of this type, and would attend more to substantive issues when choosing who to vote for.

3. How could you explain the matching hypothesis in terms of operant conditioning?

   A simple explanation is that if someone pursues a relationship with another who is more attractive than oneself, he or she is more likely to be rebuffed and thereby punished for the attempt. The likelihood of this kind of behavior would then decrease. Presumably we're more likely to approach someone who is relatively more attractive because of the rewards that come with being around attractive people.

   If, however, we pursue a relationship with another whom we and others believe matches our level of attractiveness, we are more likely to be rewarded by the other's encouragement and by the approval of our peers.

4. Evidence suggests that women tend to be more self-disclosing (telling another person private information about oneself) than men. Explain how self-disclosure might help or hinder the development of interpersonal attraction. Which theorist(s) investigating love would be most likely to consider self-disclosure as an important element in love?

Self-disclosure may help by signaling trust. Trust and liking tend to go together, so if someone trusts us, they probably like us and we will probably reciprocate by liking them. Through self-disclosure, persons may learn about ways in which they're similar, and the more similar people feel to each other, the more likely they are to be attracted to each other.

Hatfield and Berscheid would probably see self-disclosure playing more of a role in companionate rather than passionate love.

Sternberg would include self-disclosure as an element in intimacy, and therefore more important in relationships in which intimacy is strong (romantic, liking, companionate).

5. Why do you think so many of the "teachers" in Milgram's "shocking" experiment on obedience administered the highest levels of shock to their "learners"? In answering this question you undoubtedly made some sort of attributions of the teachers' behavior. Analyze the attributions you made in terms of what you've learned about attribution theory from the text.

The task here is to analyze one's own attributions or explanations for the behavior of Milgram's teachers. Answers should reflect an understanding of attribution processes, especially the dimensions of internal versus external, consistency, distinctiveness, consensus, and stability.

Appendix B
Statistical Methods

LEARNING OBJECTIVES

1. Describe several ways to use frequency distributions and graphs to organize numerical data.
2. Describe the measures of central tendency and variability discussed in the text.
3. Describe the normal distribution and its use in psychological testing.
4. Explain how the magnitude and direction of a correlation are reflected in scatter diagrams and how correlation is related to predictive power.
5. Explain how the null hypothesis is used in hypothesis testing and relate it to statistical significance.

MULTIPLE-CHOICE QUESTIONS

Concept/Applied
LO 1
Page: A-7
a

1. A frequency distribution
   a. is a way to present data visually in a table
   b. depicts a correlation between two variables using a histogram
   c. is the same thing as a scattergram
   d. typically lists the frequency of each score on the horizontal axis

Concept/Applied
LO 1
Page: A-7
c

2. Before you construct a histogram you need to
   a. calculate an inferential statistic
   b. calculate a correlation
   c. create a frequency distribution
   d. create a series of percentile ranks

Factual
LO 1
Page: A-7
d

3. A histogram
   a. provides a p value of statistical significance
   b. is necessary before one can calculate a standard deviation
   c. is the same thing as a frequency polygon
   d. is a visual depiction of a frequency distribution

Factual
LO 1
Page: A-7
c

4. A bar graph that presents data from a frequency distribution is called a
   a. scatterplot
   b. histoplot
   c. histogram
   d. frequency polygon

Concept/Applied
LO 1
Page: A-7
b

5. In both bar graphs and frequency polygons, the vertical axis is typically used to indicate
   a. all the possible scores in a data set
   b. the frequency of each score in a data set
   c. the average scores for the entire data set
   d. the strength of the correlation among the scores in a data set

Concept/Applied
LO 1
Page: A-7
a

6. In both bar graphs and frequency polygons, the horizontal axis is typically used to indicate
   a. all the possible scores in a data set
   b. the frequency of each score in a data set
   c. the average scores for the entire data set
   d. the strength of the correlation among the scores in a data set

Factual
LO 2
Page: A-8
a

7. Statistics used to organize and summarize data are
   a. descriptive statistics
   b. inferential statistics
   c. correlational statistics
   d. significant statistics

Factual
LO 2
Page: A-8
c

8. The most frequently occurring score in a group of scores is the
   a. mean
   b. median
   c. mode
   d. harmonic mean

542   APPENDIX B

Factual LO 2 Page: A-8 **b**	9.	The median is a. the most frequently occurring score in a group of scores b. the score that divides a distribution of data in half c. the arithmetic average for a group of scores d. typically greater than the mean
Factual LO 2 Page: A-8 **a**	10.	The mean in a set of scores is a. the arithmetic average for a group of scores b. the most frequently occurring score c. the basis for calculating the range d. the score that divides a distribution of scores in half
Concept/Applied LO 2 Page: A-8 **c**	11.	Which measure of central tendency is obtained by adding all the scores and dividing that total by the number of scores? a. mode b. median c. mean d. range
Concept/Applied LO 2 Page: A-8 **a**	12.	The three measures of central tendency tend to converge in a a. symmetrical distribution b. asymmetrical distribution c. positively skewed distribution d. negatively skewed distribution
Factual LO 2 Page: A-8 **b**	13.	Scores pile up at the low end of the scale in a. a negatively skewed distribution b. a positively skewed distribution c. any skewed distribution d. a normal distribution
Concept/Applied LO 2 Page: A-8 **b**	14.	Professor Latimore gives an exam that turns out to be exceptionally easy and everyone does well, yielding a a. normal distribution b. negatively skewed distribution c. positively skewed distribution d. bimodal distribution
Concept/Applied LO 2 Page: A-8 **d**	15.	The marketing agent for a professional sports franchise conducts a survey asking people how much they support the construction of a new sports stadium. Almost everyone who takes part in the survey indicates they are strongly in favor of a new stadium; there are just a few respondents who think a new stadium would be a bad idea. When the results from the survey are plotted in a histogram the distribution will be a. positively skewed b. symmetrical c. impossible to predict without more information d. negatively skewed
Concept/Applied LO 2 Page: A-8 **a**	16.	Dr. Kleiman gives an exam where most of the students receive failing grades and only a few students receive high scores. When the exam scores are plotted the distribution will be a. positively skewed b. negatively skewed c. symmetrical d. impossible to predict without more information

STATISTICAL METHODS

Factual LO 2 Page: A-8 **b**	17.	In a strongly skewed distribution, the best indicator of central tendency is usually the a. mean b. median c. mode d. standard deviation
Concept/Applied LO 2 Page: A-9 **b**	18.	When scores are "bunched up" in the center of a distribution a. the mean will be relatively low b. the standard deviation will be relatively low c. the correlation coefficient will be a negative number d. the standard deviation will be relatively high
Concept/Applied LO 2 Page: A-9 **c**	19.	Aster knows that the distribution of incomes for university students has a strong positive skew. In this case the best index of central tendency for Aster to use a. would be the median b. would be the mode c. would be the mean d. would be the standard deviation
Factual LO 2 Page: A-9 **a**	20.	The standard deviation a. indicates the average difference between each score in a group and the mean for that group of scores b. reveals the degree of skew for a group of scores c. is sensitive to scores at the extremes of a distribution of scores d. is used to determine whether a data set is positively or negatively skewed
Concept/Applied LO 2 Page: A-9 **a**	21.	Al and Marilyn have the same bowling average, but Al is much more erratic than Marilyn. If we compute the standard deviations for their respective distributions of bowling scores, which of the following will be true? a. Al's standard deviation will be higher than Marilyn's. b. Marilyn's standard deviation will be higher than Al's. c. Both standard deviations will be the same. d. Al's scores will be symmetrical while Marilyn's will be positively skewed.
Concept/Applied LO 2 Page: A-9 **c**	22.	When a frequency polygon has a sharp peak near the center, and very few scores away from the center, you would expect that a. the mode for the data set will be greater than the mean b. the standard deviation for the data set will be high c. the standard deviation for the data set will be low d. the mean for the data set will be less than the median
Factual LO 3 Page: A-9 **b**	23.	In a normal distribution, most scores fall near the _____ of the distribution, and the number of scores gradually _____ as one moves away from the mean. a. low end; increases b. center; declines c. center; increases d. high end; declines
Factual LO 3 Page: A-10 **c**	24.	In a normal distribution, _____ of the scores fall within plus or minus 1 standard deviation of the mean. a. 24 percent b. 50 percent c. 68 percent d. 99 percent

Concept/Applied LO 3 Page: A-10 **d**	25.	When scores from a personality scale designed to measure agreeableness are plotted, the scores follow a normal distribution. This means that a. the scores are evenly distributed across the entire range of possible scores b. people who score high in agreeableness tend to score high in other personality traits c. people who score high in agreeableness tend to score low in other personality traits d. most people score near the middle of the scale and there are fewer people who score extremely high or extremely low in agreeableness
Concept/Applied LO 3 Page: A-10 **b**	26.	Scores on standardized intelligence tests are normally distributed with a mean of 100 and a standard deviation of 15. This means that a. 50% of the population scores between 70 and 100 on standardized intelligence tests b. only 5% of the population scores higher than 130 or lower than 70 on standardized intelligence tests c. only 5% of the population scores higher than 115 or lower than 85 on standardized intelligence tests d. 95% of the population scores between 100 and 130 on standardized intelligence tests
Concept/Applied LO 3 Page: A-10 **b**	27.	Julia has an IQ of 130. If the mean for IQ is 100 with a standard deviation of 15, what percentage of the population has an IQ greater than Julia's (assume a normal distribution)? a. 0 percent b. 2.5 percent c. 32 percent d. 50 percent
Concept/Applied LO 3 Page: A-10 **d**	28.	Frank scored 30 on a test of assertiveness. Assuming that assertiveness is normally distributed with a mean of 20 and a standard deviation of 5, what percentage of people are less assertive than Frank? a. 50 percent b. 68.5 percent c. 95.5 percent d. 97.5 percent
Concept/Applied LO 3 Page: A-10 **d**	29.	If you take a test in which the scores are normally distributed and you score at the 40th percentile, you have scored _____ the mean and _____ the median. a. above; above b. above; below c. below; above d. below; below
Concept/Applied LO 3 Page: A-10 **c**	30.	If you take a test and score at the 70th percentile, you have a. answered 70 percent of the questions correctly b. scored lower than 70 percent of the people taking the test c. scored higher than 70 percent of the people taking the test d. scored higher than 30 percent of the people taking the test
Concept/Applied LO 3 Page: A-10 **d**	31.	On the SAT, the mean is 500 and the standard deviation is 100. If you scored 2 standard deviations above the mean, your score would be a. 300 b. 400 c. 600 d. 700

Factual LO 4 Page: A-11 **a**	32.	An inverse relationship between two variables will yield a a. negative correlation b. positive correlation c. weak correlation d. spurious correlation
Concept/Applied LO 4 Page: A-11 **b**	33.	High scores on variable X are associated with high scores on variable Y and low scores on variable X are associated with low scores on variable Y. Hence, the correlation between variables X and Y will be a. negative b. positive c. zero d. spurious
Concept/Applied LO 4 Page: A-11 **c**	34.	A positive correlation is to a direct relationship as a negative correlation is to a. an ascending relationship b. a descending relationship c. an inverse relationship d. an inferential relationship
Concept/Applied LO 4 Page: A-11 **a**	35.	Which of the following correlation coefficients represents the <u>strongest</u> association between two variables? a. -.88 b. -.42 c. +.30 d. +.65
Concept/Applied LO 4 Page: A-11 **c**	36.	Which of the following correlation coefficients represents the <u>weakest</u> association between two variables? a. +.74 b. -.43 c. +.09 d. -.85
Critical Thinking LO 4 Page: A-11 **c**	37.	Jackie correlates the number of hours spent studying with final grades in a course and finds the correlation is +0.55. When Phil correlates the number of classes missed with final grades in a course, he finds the correlation is -0.75. You should predict that, when the results are plotted using a scatter diagram a. Jackie's data points will cluster more tightly than Phil's data points b. all Phil's data points will fall on a flat horizontal line running from left to right c. Phil's data points will cluster more tightly than Jackie's data points d. all Jackie's data points will fall on a vertical line running from top to bottom
Factual LO 4 Page: A-11 **d**	38.	A graph in which paired X and Y scores for each subject are plotted as single points is called a a. correlational plot b. histogram c. frequency distribution d. scatter diagram
Concept/Applied LO 4 Page: A-11 **b**	39.	When a correlation is perfect, the data points in a scatter diagram a. form a bell-shaped curve b. fall in a straight, line c. scatter in a symmetric oval d. scatter in a perfect circle

Concept/Applied LO 4 Page: A-11 **b**	40.	As the magnitude of a correlation coefficient increases a. the data points in a scatter diagram become more dispersed b. the data points in a scatter diagram become less dispersed c. the correlation coefficient changes from a positive to a negative number d. the correlation coefficient changes from a negative to a positive number
Critical Thinking LO 4 Page: A-12 **b**	41.	Imagine that Jenilee earned the highest score in the entire class on the midterm exam, and the correlation between midterm exam scores and final exam scores is -0.02. If the final exam grades for Jenilee's class are 92, 84, 79, 65, and 54 a. Jenilee most likely earned the score of 54 b. it is impossible to predict Jenilee's final exam score because the correlation coefficient is so small c. Jenilee most likely earned the score of 92 d. Jenilee most likely earned the score of 79
Factual LO 4 Page: A-12 **b**	42.	Multiplying a correlation coefficient by itself will give you the a. standard deviation b. coefficient of determination c. percentile rank d. cross-product of the sum of squares
Concept/Applied LO 4 Page: A-12 **d**	43.	You find a correlation of .44 between a measure of subjects' extraversion and their reports of how many people they have dated in the last two years. This finding means that a. 44 percent of extraverts date a lot b. extraversion accounts for 44 percent of the variation in the amount of subjects' dating c. high extraversion is associated with infrequent dating d. high extraversion is associated with more frequent dating
Critical Thinking LO 4 Page: A-12 **a**	44.	Nelson's company manufactures computer games, and Nelson is interested in the relationship between the price of a game and people's ratings of the game's quality. He surveys 1000 customers, selected at random, and finds the correlation between price and quality is +0.50. Based on this information, Nelson can conclude a. people perceive the quality of a game to be better when the price is high than when the price is low b. increasing the price of a game will increase the perceived quality of the game for approximately 50% of consumers c. people perceive the quality of a game to be better when the price is low than when the price is high d. decreasing the price of a game will increase the perceived quality of the game for approximately 50% of consumers
Concept/Applied LO 4 Page: A-12 **c**	45.	If two variables are correlated, the percentage of variation in one variable that can be predicted from the other variable a. increases for positive correlations and decreases for negative correlations b. increases for negative correlations and decreases for positive correlations c. increases as the magnitude of the correlation coefficient increases d. decreases as the magnitude of the correlation coefficient increases
Concept/Applied LO 4 Page: A-12 **b**	46.	If the correlation between intelligence and college grade point average is .60, then intelligence appears to account for about _____ of the variation in grade point average. a. 40 percent b. 36 percent c. 60 percent d. 90 percent

Concept/Applied LO 4 Page: A-12 **a**	47.	Which of the following correlations will yield the highest coefficient of determination? a. -.70 b. -.40 c. .30 d. .50
Factual LO 5 Page: A-13 **d**	48.	Statistics designed to help one draw conclusions from a set of data are referred to as a. descriptive statistics b. frequency statistics c. nonparametric statistics d. inferential statistics
Concept/Applied LO 5 Page: A-13 **d**	49.	Helen conducted a study in which she measured the response time for males and females to complete a spatial task. She found that the mean response time was 1.48 minutes for males and 1.63 minutes for females. For Helen to be confident that an actual difference exists between males and females in her study she must a. calculate a correlation b. retest the participants in her study c. obtain a larger sample d. calculate an inferential statistic
Factual LO 5 Page: A-13 **b**	50.	In a study, a researcher observes a _____ to draw conclusions about a much larger _____. a. population; sample b. sample; population c. sample; sample d. population; inferential group
Factual LO 5 Page: A-13 **b**	51.	Technically speaking, in hypothesis testing, researchers evaluate the a. plausibility of the sample b. null hypothesis c. representativeness of the results d. acceptability of the descriptive statistics
Factual LO 5 Page: A-13 **b**	52.	In research, the assumption that no relationship exists between two variables is referred to as the a. alternative hypothesis b. null hypothesis c. inferential hypothesis d. research hypothesis
Critical Thinking LO 5 Page: A-13 **a**	53.	Astin believes that people will be more persuaded by an argument if the person presenting the argument is tall, rather than if the presenter is short. Astin wants to test her belief in an experiment. In this instance, Astin should state her null hypothesis as a. a presenter's height will have no impact on persuasion b. a short presenter will be more persuasive than a tall presenter c. a tall presenter will be less persuasive than a short presenter d. a tall presenter will be more persuasive than a short presenter
Factual LO 5 Page: A-14 **d**	54.	Statistically significant results occur when the probability that the observed results are due to chance is a. very high b. moderately high c. moderately low d. very low

Concept/Applied LO 5 Page: A-14 a	55.	Statistically significant results a. usually support the research hypothesis b. typically support the null hypothesis c. indicate the observed findings are due to chance d. indicate that the researcher has not made any errors in the calculations
Factual LO 5 Page: A-14 c	56.	The probability that observed results are due to chance is _____ when the results are statistically significant. a. zero b. unknown c. very low d. very high
Factual LO 5 Page: A-14 b	57.	Generally, the <u>minimum</u> requirement for statistical significance is that there is less than _____ that the observed results are due to chance. a. 1 chance in 1000 b. 5 chances in 100 c. 20 chances in 100 d. 50 chances in 100
Factual LO 5 Page: A-14 d	58.	If there is less than a 1 in 1000 chance that observed findings are attributable to sampling error, the results are a. insignificant b. impossible c. significant at the .01 level d. significant at the .001 level
Factual LO 5 Page: A-14 a	59.	When you reject the null hypothesis a. you have statistically significant results b. you have statistically insignificant results c. you have a 50% chance of making an error d. you also reject the research hypothesis
Concept/Applied LO 5 Page: A-14 a	60.	Having a statistically significant result allows one to infer that a. a real difference exists between groups b. no errors were made in the calculations c. the factors in the study are positively correlated d. the data came from a normal distribution

STATISTICAL METHODS

This page intentionally left blank.

Appendix C
Industrial/Organizational Psychology

LEARNING OBJECTIVES

1. Discuss the settings and content areas of I/O psychology.
2. Discuss how the systems approach relates to the subfields of I/O psychology.
3. Describe how the three subfields of I/O psychology emerged historically.
4. Discuss job analysis and psychological testing in personnel psychology.
5. Summarize I/O psychologists theories of work motivation.
6. Summarize research on job satisfaction.
7. Discuss the concepts of work teams, transformational and charismatic leadership, and organizational culture.
8. Discuss how human engineering can enhance work environments.

MULTIPLE-CHOICE QUESTIONS

Factual
LO 1
Page: A-15
a

1. Which of the following is <u>not</u> one of the primary areas of interest for an industrial/organizational psychologist?
   a. occupational therapy
   b. personnel psychology
   c. organizational psychology
   d. human factors

Factual
LO 1
Page: A-16
b

2. The area of psychology dealing with the assessment of people's knowledge, skills, and abilities in the work environment is
   a. human factors psychology
   b. personnel psychology
   c. social psychology
   d. associated with all of these areas

Factual
LO 1
Page: A-16
d

3. The area of psychology concerned with how people adapt emotionally and socially to the work environment is
   a. personnel psychology
   b. human factors psychology
   c. systems psychology
   d. organizational psychology

Concept/Applied
LO 1
Page: A-16
b

4. Which of the following topics would be of the <u>least</u> concern for an industrial/organizational psychologist?
   a. human motivation
   b. psychotherapy
   c. psychological testing
   d. employment discrimination

Factual
LO 1
Page: A-16
a

5. The area of performance evaluation and job training is associated <u>most</u> closely with
   a. personnel psychology
   b. human factors psychology
   c. psychodiagnostics
   d. NIOSH

Concept/Applied
LO 1
Page: A-16
d

6. Valerie has been working on a program to improve motivation in the employees at her company. Valerie will <u>most</u> likely have had her training in
   a. clinical psychology
   b. counseling psychology
   c. physiological psychology
   d. organizational psychology

Concept/Applied
LO 1
Page: A-16
a

7. Kevin has been working on a test to predict the performance of new employees at the company he works for. Kevin is <u>most</u> likely a
   a. personnel psychologist
   b. counseling psychologist
   c. human factors psychologist
   d. developmental psychologist

Factual
LO 1
Page: A-16
c

8. The area of psychology that focuses on designing machines to match the capabilities or characteristic of humans is
   a. personnel psychology
   b. biopsychology
   c. human factors psychology
   d. tests and measurements

Concept/Applied LO 1 Page: A-16 **d**	9.	Henri has been working on developing a process control panel for his company that takes into account the human visual system's capabilities and limitations. Henri is <u>most</u> likely a. a personnel psychologist b. a developmental psychologist c. an applied clinical psychologist d. a human factors psychologist
Critical Thinking LO 2 Page: A-16 **a**	10.	The fact that the three areas of I/O psychology are not mutually exclusive is <u>most</u> consistent with which of the following approaches to behavior in the workplace? a. systems approach b. behavioral approach c. cognitive approach d. social learning approach
Factual LO 3 Page: A-17 **a**	11.	The first Ph.D. in I/O psychology was granted in 1915 to a. Lilian Gilbreth b. William James c. Hugo Munsterberg d. Frederick Taylor
Factual LO 3 Page: A-17 **c**	12.	Which of the following individuals was instrumental in the development of testing techniques in industry? a. Alfred Binet b. Lilian Gilbreth c. Hugo Munsterberg d. Wilhelm Wundt
Factual LO 3 Page: A-17 **b**	13.	Which of the following was the first I/O subfield to appear? a. occupational therapy b. personnel psychology c. organizational psychology d. human factors
Factual LO 3 Page: A-17 **a**	14.	Which of the following was a major factor in industry's adopting testing as part of personnel work? a. the positive experiences with testing by the military during World War I b. the development of appropriate statistical techniques to evaluate test findings c. the enactment of several federal laws concerning job analysis and testing d. the emerging strength of labor unions in the early part of the 20th century
Factual LO 3 Page: A-18 **d**	15.	Which of the following individuals developed the theory of "scientific management" that was dominant in the early 1900s? a. William James b. Elton Mayo c. Hugo Munsterberg d. Frederick Taylor
Critical Thinking LO 3 Page: A-18 **d**	16.	Which of the following is <u>not</u> one of the main tenets of Taylor's scientific management? a. Identify the most efficient way to complete a task. b. Select a worker capable of performing the required task. c. Pay workers in proportion to the amount produced. d. Reward workers based on loyalty and seniority.

Concept/Applied LO 3 Page: A-18 **a**	17.	The focus of Taylor and similar theorists was on a. applying methods of industrial engineering to the work environment to increase efficiency b. individual differences and how they contribute to the overall production system c. organizational climate, communication, and related factors d. employees' attitudes toward their supervisors and co-workers
Factual LO 3 Page: A-18 **c**	18.	As a result of research conducted by Elton Mayo and his colleagues at a Western Electric facility near Chicago in 1930, the scientific management approach was replaced by a. the "Theory Z" model b. a cognitive dissonance model c. the human relations movement d. the natural selection paradigm
Factual LO 3 Page: A-18 **b**	19.	Research and application of modern human factors psychology began with a. World War I b. World War II c. the Korean War d. the Vietnam War
Concept/Applied LO 3 Page: A-19 **b**	20.	Administering a series of tests that determine the mental and physical ability and emotional stability of candidates for the New York City Police Academy is an application of which of the following subfields of I/O psychology? a. occupational therapy b. personnel psychology c. organizational psychology d. human factors
Factual LO 4 Page: A-19 **c**	21.	Breaking a job into its constituent components is a. a personnel feature analysis b. a systems analysis c. a job analysis d. an exigency analysis
Factual LO 4 Page: A-20 **a**	22.	The most widely used device in personnel selection is a. the interview b. the reference check c. a personality test d. a mental ability test
Factual LO 4 Page: A-20 **c**	23.	For the purpose of personnel selection, structured interviews have been found to be a. reliable, but not valid b. valid, but not reliable c. both valid and reliable d. neither valid nor reliable
Factual LO 4 Page: A-20 **a**	24.	If a test is an accurate predictor of job performance, then it is said to be a. valid b. reliable c. standardized d. correlated

Factual LO 4 Page: A-20 **a**	25.	Which of the following statistical techniques would be used to test the hypothesis that people who score better on a particular test will perform better on the job? a. correlation b. mean squares c. factor analysis d. analysis of variance
Concept/Applied LO 4 Page: A-20 **d**	26.	In order for a test to be considered a valid predictor of job performance, the correlation between scores on the test and measures of performance should be a. near zero b. curvilinear c. strong and negative d. strong and positive
Critical Thinking LO 4 Page: A-20 **d**	27.	In order to determine if a test can accurately predict job performance one could a. correlate IQ with productivity levels b. correlate mechanical aptitude with quality of production c. correlate verbal ability with sales d. do any of these things
Factual LO 4 Page: A-21 **b**	28.	The _____ is responsible for determining if the use of tests in industrial/ organizational situations is fair to all applicants. a. Department of Transportation b. Equal Employment Opportunity Commission c. National Occupational Safety Board d. Better Business Bureau
Concept/Applied LO 4 Page: A-21 **b**	29.	The debate concerning the "adverse impact" of testing in hiring situations tends to focus on the a. reliability of the measurements b. validity of the measurements c. lack of a legitimate criterion for acceptable work behavior d. overwhelming costs associated with the testing programs
Factual LO 4 Page: A-22 **d**	30.	Today, applicants for police work are <u>most</u> likely to be given which of the following tests? a. an intelligence test b. a test of physical abilities c. a test that measures communication skills d. any of these of tests
Concept/Applied LO 5 Page: A-22 **c**	31.	Psychologists who study the social and emotional factors of workers are referred to as a. personnel psychologists b. human factors psychologists c. organizational psychologists d. personality psychologists
Concept/Applied LO 5 Page: A-22 **d**	32.	James is conducting research in the company he works for in order to determine the level of job satisfaction in the work force. James is <u>most</u> likely a. a developmental psychologist b. a human factors researcher c. a clinical psychologist d. an organizational psychologist

Factual LO 5 Page: A-22 **b**	33.	Which of the following individuals is credited with developing job enrichment theory as an explanation for worker motivation? a. Albert Bandura b. Frederick Herzberg c. B. F. Skinner d. Frederick Taylor
Factual LO 5 Page: A-22 **c**	34.	Which of the following individuals is most closely associated with reinforcement theory as an explanation for worker motivation? a. Albert Bandura b. Frederick Herzberg c. B. F. Skinner d. Frederick Taylor
Concept/Applied LO 5 Page: A-22 **d**	35.	The notion that worker motivation depends on whether or not the job is interesting is most consistent with which of the following theories of employee motivation? a. self-efficacy theory b. expectancy theory c. reinforcement theory d. job enrichment theory
Concept/Applied LO 5 Page: A-22 **a**	36.	The notion that work is motivating primarily through its association with external rewards is most consistent with which of the following theories of employee motivation? a. reinforcement theory b. self-efficacy theory c. expectancy theory d. job enrichment theory
Concept/Applied LO 5 Page: A-23 **d**	37.	The idea that individuals choose to work hard (or not work hard) based on a consideration of the reward they will receive and the likelihood of receiving it forms the basis of the _____ theory of worker motivation. a. self-efficacy b. psychodynamic c. job enrichment d. expectancy
Concept/Applied LO 5 Page: A-23 **c**	38.	When employers make sure that workers have a clear understanding that successful performance will be followed by desired rewards, they are applying the principles found in which of the following theories of employee motivation? a. reinforcement theory b. self-efficacy theory c. expectancy theory d. job enrichment theory
Critical Thinking LO 5 Page: A-23 **a**	39.	Which of the following statements is most consistent with goal setting theory of motivation? a. Goals should be general enough to ensure some degree of flexibility. b. Even if you do not reach your goal, you will work harder than if you had not set a goal. c. The most effective goals are ones that are relatively easy to achieve. d. For goals to be effective motivating forces, it's necessary that someone other than yourself set them.

Factual LO 6 Page: A-23 **d**	40.	Which of the following factors is <u>not</u> associated with high job satisfaction? a. having supportive supervisors b. having pleasant co-workers c. having interesting work d. All three of these factors contribute to high job satisfaction.
Critical Thinking LO 6 Page: A-23 **b**	41.	Based on findings from studies of job satisfaction, which of the following statements is <u>most</u> accurate? a. Job satisfaction causes productivity. b. Productivity causes job satisfaction. c. Job satisfaction and productivity are independent. d. Job satisfaction is more important for women than men in the workplace.
Factual LO 6 Page: A-24 **d**	42.	In general, stressful work environments are characterized by _____ levels of uncertainty and conflict, and _____ levels of control. a. low; low; b. high; high c. high; low d. low; high
Factual LO 7 Page: A-24 **a**	43.	Work teams began to be used in North America in the 1980s mainly as a result of which of the following factors? a. the downsizing that took place in many organizations b. research findings demonstrating high satisfaction among members of teams c. an influx of college graduates with experience in collaborative work d. pressure from international companies that had been using work teams for years
Concept/Applied LO 7 Page: A-24 **c**	44.	An organizational leader who has a compelling vision of what he or she wants to accomplish and molds workers' beliefs, values, and needs so that they are consistent with this vision is demonstrating _____ leadership. a. charismatic b. developmental c. transformational d. incentive-based
Concept/Applied LO 7 Page: A-24 **a**	45.	_____ leadership depends mainly on the sheer force of a leader's personality, as opposed to the appeal of the leader's vision. a. Charismatic b. Developmental c. Transformational d. Incentive-based
Concept/Applied LO 7 Page: A-25 **b**	46.	"Time urgency," "zero defects," and "customer-friendly" are all examples of a. issues in human factors b. organizational cultures c. job incentive programs d. effective company mottos
Factual LO 8 Page: A-25 **c**	47.	A psychologist who designs environments and equipment to match the capabilities of humans would <u>most</u> likely be considered _____ psychologist. a. a personnel b. an organizational c. a human factors d. a developmental

Concept/Applied LO 8 Page: A-25 **d**	48.	Cheryl is designing a control panel that she hopes will allow workers to function more efficiently. Cheryl is most likely a. an organizational psychologist b. a developmental psychologist c. a personnel psychologist d. a human factors psychologist
Concept/Applied LO 8 Page: A-25 **b**	49.	The speedometer on a car is an example of which of the following components of the human-machine system? a. control b. display c. interface d. readout
Concept/Applied LO 8 Page: A-25 **a**	50.	Assume that the instrument panel in an airplane were designed in such a way that a dial providing important information was located outside of the pilot's line of vision. This scenario exemplifies which of the following problems? a. faulty display b. faulty control c. faulty interface d. faulty feedback loop
Factual LO 8 Page: A-26 **b**	51.	Response stereotypy refers to the a. same response being repeated over and over b. expectation on people's part for a control to work in a particular fashion c. range of motion that people have for their limbs d. ability of a person to integrate sensory information with motor behavior
Factual LO 8 Page: A-26 **c**	52.	The expectation people have concerning how a control device will work is referred to as a. functional fixedness b. perceptual angst c. response stereotypy d. none of these things
Concept/Applied LO 8 Page: A-27 **c**	53.	The guiding principle in work design is a. Use all sensory systems available to avoid perceptual conflict. b. Always have overlapping or redundant control mechanisms. c. Never design a job that exceeds the resources of the person doing the job. d. All of these are guiding principles.

PART II

Psyk.trek: A Multimedia Introduction to Psychology

Unit 1	History & Methods	561
Unit 2	Biological Bases of Behavior	569
Unit 3	Sensation & Perception	580
Unit 4	Consciousness	592
Unit 5	Learning	599
Unit 6	Memory & Thought	609
Unit 7	Testing & Intelligence	616
Unit 8	Motivation & Emotion	623
Unit 9	Human Development	630
Unit 10	Personality Theory	637
Unit 11	Abnormal Behavior & Therapy	643
Unit 12	Social Psychology	652

Unit 1
History & Methods

Factual
Module 1a
a

1. Psychology was first established as an independent discipline
   a. in 1879 when Wundt established a research laboratory to study conscious experience
   b. in the first century when Greek philosophers first questioned the nature of the human soul
   c. in 1892 when G. Stanley Hall founded the American Psychological Association
   d. in 1956 when Chomsky, Miller, and Simon showed that cognitive processes could be studied using empirical methods

Concept/Applied
Module 1a
b

2. From 1880 through 1890 the study of psychology focused mainly on
   a. understanding the purpose of conscious experience
   b. investigating the basic elements of conscious experience
   c. discovering the nature of stimulus-response associations
   d. discovering how personality was shaped by unconscious thoughts and urges

Concept/Applied
Module 1a
c

3. Dr. Branford believes that to truly understand emotional responses we must understand what purpose emotional responses serve. Dr. Branford's views most closely mirror those of
   a. the structuralists school
   b. the behavioral school
   c. the functionalist school
   d. the humanistic school

Concept/Applied
Module 1a
d

4. The stage was set for the emergence of Concept/Applied psychology
   a. in 1904 when Ivan Pavlov discovered classical conditioning
   b. in 1971 when B. F. Skinner published Beyond Freedom and Dignity
   c. in the 1920s when the Gestalt school of psychology was established
   d. in 1905 when Alfred Binet published the first intelligence test

Factual
Module 1a
b

5. The psychoanalytic view in psychology is most clearly associated with
   a. Carl Rogers
   b. Sigmund Freud
   c. John B. Watson
   d. Max Wertheimer

Factual
Module 1a
a

6. John B. Watson is the individual most closely associated with the psychological view known as
   a. behaviorism
   b. structuralism
   c. Gestalt psychology
   d. cognitive psychology

Factual
Module 1a
d

7. The Gestalt view in psychology is based on the belief that
   a. consciousness must be broken down into its component parts
   b. each person has a unique potential for personal growth
   c. mental processes cannot be objectively observed or measured
   d. the whole is greater than the sum of its parts

Concept/Applied Module 1a c	8.	During the 1940s the most rapid growth in psychology was in the fields of a. cognitive and applied psychology b. cross-cultural and evolutionary psychology c. clinical psychology and psychological disorders d. structuralism and functionalism
Factual Module 1a c	9.	Carl Rogers and Abraham Maslow are most closely associated with a. behavioral psychology b. psychoanalysis c. humanism d. structuralism
Factual Module 1a b	10.	The school of thought which emphasizes the unique qualities of humans and their potential for personal growth is a. psychoanalysis b. humanism c. functionalism d. behaviorism
Factual Module 1a d	11.	At a conference held in 1956 Noam Chomsky, George Miller, and Herbert Simon presented papers on language, memory, and problem-solving. This event sparked a. the behavioral revolution in psychology b. the field of cross-cultural psychology c. the humanist revolution in psychology d. the cognitive revolution in psychology
Factual Module 1a a	12.	Social psychology emerged as a major area of research in the field of psychology in a. 1963 when Stanley Milgram published his work on obedience to authority b. 1971 when B. F. Skinner published *Beyond Freedom and Dignity* c. 1905 when Alfred Binet published the first intelligence test d. 1908 when Margaret Floy Washburn published *The Animal Mind*
Factual Module 1b b	13.	The research method in which an investigator manipulates one variable under carefully controlled conditions and observes whether any changes occur in a second variable as a result is called a. correlational research b. an experiment c. a case study d. naturalistic observation
Factual Module 1b a	14.	The first step in conducting an experimental study is to a. formulate a research hypothesis b. randomly assign subjects to different conditions c. measure the effects of the independent variable d. state what the final outcome of the experiment will be
Concept/Applied Module 1b d	15.	Dr. Holbrook predicts that reducing the level of lighting at a computer station will increase a computer operator's level of productivity. Dr. Holbrook's prediction is an example of a. an operational definition b. a dependent variable c. a random manipulation d. a hypothesis

Critical Thinking Module 1b **c**	16.	Dr. Watson believes people who are under stress will develop more colds than people who are not under stress. When he randomly selects 10 participants and exposes them to high levels of stress, he finds that 9 of the participants develop colds. Based on his results he concludes that stress causes an increase in colds. Dr. Watson's reasoning may be flawed because in his study a. there was no dependent variable in his study b. he didn't formulate a hypothesis before he collected his data c. there was no control group for comparison d. he didn't measure the independent variable when the study ended
Factual Module 1b **a**	17.	The control group in an experiment is the group that a. does not receive any special treatment in regard to the independent variable b. receives some special treatment in regard to the independent variable c. receives the lowest score on the dependent variable d. is not exposed to the dependent variable in the study
Concept/Applied Module 1b **b**	18.	Harry and Samantha both take part in a research study that is investigating the effects of sleep deprivation on reaction time. Harry is kept awake for 24 hours straight while Samantha follows her normal sleep routine. In this study Harry is part of a. the control group b. the experimental group c. the dependent variable group d. the hypothesis group
Factual Module 1b **a**	19.	The independent variable in an experiment is a. the variable that the researcher varies systematically in order to determine its impact on another variable b. the variable that is thought to be affected or changed by the experimental manipulation c. any variable that changes randomly during the course of an experiment d. any variable that is held constant or doesn't change during an experiment
Concept/Applied Module 1b **b**	20.	Peter believes listening to relaxing music will improve memory. He designs a study in which 15 people listen to relaxing music while studying for 30 minutes and 15 people study in a quiet room for 30 minutes. He measures how much they remember from the material they studied. In this example the independent variable is a. the amount that the participants remember from the material they study b. what the participants hear while they study (relaxing music or no music) c. the number of people who take part in the experiment d. the length of time the participants were allowed to study the material
Concept/Applied Module 1b **d**	21.	Researchers studying the effects of alcohol consumption tested the physical coordination skills of 21-year-old men who were first assigned to drink a beverage with either 4, 2, or 0 ounces of alcohol in the laboratory. In this study, the independent variable would be a. the age of the men who took part in the study b. the physical coordination of the participants at the start of the study c. the physical coordination of the participants after drinking the beverage d. the amount of alcohol contained in the beverage
Factual Module 1b **c**	22.	In an experiment the variable that is thought to be affected or changed by the experimental manipulation is called a. the independent variable b. a placebo c. the dependent variable d. a random factor

Concept/Applied 23. Eloise believes people will form better initial impressions of people dressed in
Module 1b   business clothes than of people dressed in casual clothes. She designs a study in
d   which 10 people meet "Angela" when she is wearing a business suit and 10 people
                meet "Angela" when she is wearing jeans and a scruffy t-shirt. She measures the
                impressions people have of "Angela" after talking with her for 5 minutes. In this
                example the dependent variable is
                a. Angela's style of dress (business clothes or casual)
                b. the length of time that the participants meet with Angela
                c. the number of people who take part in the study
                d. the impressions people form of Angela

Concept/Applied 24. To determine whether two variables interact (for example, room temperature and
Module 1b   distracting noise), a researcher should set up an experiment in which
c   a. two different dependent variables are measured in a single study
                b. the same group of individuals are used for both the experimental and the control
                    group
                c. two different independent variables are manipulated in a single study
                d. there are two experimental groups and no control group

Concept/Applied 25. To visually present the number of hours that a group of children spend watching
Module 1c   television, a researcher could
d   a. calculate a mean and standard deviation
                b. create a histogram or calculate a measure of variability
                c. create a frequency polygon or calculate a measure of central tendency
                d. create a histogram or a frequency polygon

Factual   26. In a frequency polygon all the possible scores are listed
Module 1c   a. on the vertical axis
b   b. on the horizontal axis
                c. in a table
                d. in a box set into the graph

Factual   27. The mean for a distribution of scores
Module 1c   a. is the arithmetic average of the scores
a   b. is the score that occurs most frequently
                c. is the score that falls at the center of the distribution
                d. indicates how much variability there is in the data set

Factual   28. The score that occurs most frequently in a data set is called
Module 1c   a. the median
d   b. the mean
                c. the standard deviation
                d. the mode

Critical Thinking 29. Carmen is in a class of 15 students. On the most recent exam, 7 students earned
Module 1c   scores lower than Carmen's score, and 7 student scored higher than Carmen did.
b   Based on this information, you can conclude that Carmen's score is
                a. equal to the mode for her class
                b. the same as the median score for her class
                c. equivalent to the mean for her class
                d. the same as all three measures of central tendency for that particular exam

Factual   30. In a negatively skewed distribution most of the scores
Module 1c   a. pile up at the low end of the distribution
c   b. are less than the mean for the distribution
                c. pile up at the high end of the distribution
                d. pile up above the standard deviation for the distribution

Critical Thinking Module 1c **c**	31.	Dr. Kleiman gives an exam where most of the students receive failing grades and only a few students receive high scores. When the exam scores are plotted the distribution will be a. negatively skewed b. symmetrical c. positively skewed d. impossible to predict without more information
Factual Module 1c **d**	32.	In a highly skewed distribution of scores a. the median may be misleading and the mean often provides the best index of central tendency b. the mode may be misleading and the mean often provides the best index of central tendency c. the median may be misleading and the mode often provides the best index of central tendency d. the mean may be misleading and the median often provides the best index of central tendency
Concept/Applied Module 1c **b**	33.	Sarah knows that the distribution of incomes for university students has a strong positive skew. In this case the best index of central tendency for Sarah to use would be a. the mean b. the median c. the mode d. the standard deviation
Factual Module 1c **a**	34.	The standard deviation is an index of a. the amount of variability in a set of scores b. the amount of skew in a set of scores c. how many scores there are in a data set d. the degree of correlation among scores in two separate data sets
Concept/Applied Module 1c **d**	35.	Dr. Penopolis gives an exam where all the students in the class receive scores between 45 and 55. Dr. Grath gives an exam where the scores for the class range from 20 to 80. In this example a. the standard deviation in Dr. Penopolis' class should be higher than the standard deviation in Dr. Grath's class b. the standard deviation in Dr. Penopolis' class should be the same as the standard deviation in Dr. Grath's class c. the scores in Dr. Penopolis' class will be negatively skewed and the scores in Dr. Grath's class will be positively skewed d. the standard deviation in Dr. Penopolis' class should be lower than the standard deviation in Dr. Grath's class
Concept/Applied Module 1c **c**	36.	When a frequency polygon has a sharp peak near the center, and very few scores away from the center, you would expect that a. the standard deviation for the data set will be high b. the mode for the data set will be greater than the mean c. the standard deviation for the data set will be low d. the mean for the data set will be less than the median
Factual Module 1d **a**	37.	A correlation coefficient is a numerical index of a. the degree of relationship between two variables b. the amount of variability in a data set c. the amount of skew in a data set d. the degree to which one variable will cause a change in an unrelated variable

Factual Module 1d **b**	38.	A positive correlation indicates there is a. an inverse relationship between two variables b. a direct relationship between two variables c. a very strong relationship between two variables d. a causal relationship between two variables
Concept/Applied Module 1d **a**	39.	As the unemployment rate goes down the number of new car sales increase. This indicates that these two variables are a. negatively correlated b. positively correlated c. directly correlated d. only weakly correlated
Factual Module 1d **b**	40.	In a scatter diagram a. the frequency for each score is plotted on the horizontal axis of the graph b. paired X and Y scores for each subject are plotted as single points c. a frequency polygon is used to plot the direction and strength of the relationship d. high scores are plotted on the X axis and low sores are plotted on the Y axis
Concept/Applied Module 1d **c**	41.	Dr. Bolton predicts that if parents are nurturant their children are less likely to act aggressively. In this case Dr. Bolton is suggesting that parental nurturance and a child's level of aggression are a. positively correlated b. uncorrelated c. negatively correlated d. both dependent variables
Factual Module 1d **d**	42.	When a correlation coefficient has a negative sign a. the two factors being measured tend to move in the same direction b. there is no relationship between the two factors being measured c. the factor with the lowest scores is the dependent variable d. the two factors being measured tend to move in opposite directions
Concept/Applied Module 1d **b**	43.	Dr. Marquette has found a correlation of +0.70 between snoring and weight. This indicates that a. overweight individuals tend to snore less than underweight individuals b. overweight individuals tend to snore more than underweight individuals c. there is no relationship between weight and snoring d. individuals who go on a diet will most likely begin to snore
Concept/Applied Module 1d **a**	44.	Of the following, the correlation coefficient that would be associated with the <u>tightest</u> cluster of data points on a scatter diagram would be a. −0.92 b. +0.73 c. 0.00 d. −2.15
Factual Module 1d **a**	45.	The coefficient of determination is a numerical index that indicates a. the percent of variation in one variable that can be predicted based on another variable b. the strength and direction of a relationship between two variables c. the degree of variability within a set of scores d. the amount of skew within a set of scores

Factual Module 1d **d**	46.	As the coefficient of determination increases a. the accuracy of prediction begins to decrease b. the accuracy of prediction does not change c. the likelihood that variable X causes the observed changes in variable Y increases d. the accuracy of prediction also increases
Concept/Applied Module 1d **c**	47.	Dr. Johnson surveys 50 university students to discover the relationship between textbook price and ratings of readability. Dr. Johnson finds that for these two variables the correlation coefficient is +0.70. Based on this information Dr. Johnson could report that a. increasing a textbook's price will produce a decrease in readability ratings b. students will be willing to pay more for a book that is difficult to read c. approximately 50% of the variability in ratings readability can be predicted based on a textbook's price d. 70% of the variability in ratings readability can be predicted based on a textbook's price
Critical Thinking Module 1d **b**	48.	Identifying that a strong correlation exists between two variables allows a researcher a. to determine which of the variables is the independent variable b. to accurately predict the value of one variable from known values of the second variable c. to conclude that a positive, direct relationship exists between the two variables d. to calculate the strength of the cause-and-effect relationship between the two variables
Factual Module 1e **c**	49.	Journals are periodicals that publish a. general research hypotheses and ideas for potential studies b. personal views and opinions in a variety of scientific areas c. technical and scholarly research in a narrowly defined area of study d. nontechnical articles written for the general public
Factual Module 1e **d**	50.	An abstract contained in *Psychological Abstracts* would typically be a. a listing of the article's title and the names and addresses of the main authors for the research study b. an expanded 5000-10000 word interpretation of several different studies in a single area c. an exact reprint of the original research article that was published d. a concise 75-175 word summary of the hypothesis, methods, results, and implications of a research study
Concept/Applied Module 1e **c**	51.	Gaston is looking for a recent journal article that deals with treatment options for dyslexia. Brooke is looking for similar information, but she wants to find a book that deals with treatments for dyslexia. In this situation a. Gaston can check *PsychINFO* but Brooke can't, because *PsychINFO* only indexes journal articles b. Brooke can check *PsychINFO* but Gaston can't, because *PsychINFO* only indexes book chapters c. both students can check *PsychINFO*, because *PsychINFO* indexes both journal articles and book chapters d. neither student is likely to find the information they need in *PsychINFO*, unless they know the author of the article or the book

Concept/Applied Module 1e **b**	52.	Georgelle wants to locate a number of recent articles that relate to a specific area in psychology. The most efficient way for her to conduct her search would be to a. manually search through *Psychological Abstracts* b. use the computer database called *PsychINFO* c. access the *Virtual Psychology* web page d. read several articles in the area she is interested in, and back-trace the references provided by the authors of those articles
Factual Module 1e **a**	53.	The author index for *Psychological Abstracts* a. lists all the work for a variety of authors for a given time period b. highlights different authors each month and lists all the research they have ever completed c. provides the names, institutional addresses, and contact phone numbers for current researchers in the field of psychology d. lists all the authors who have written on a given topic in the past five years
Factual Module 1e **d**	54.	*PsychLIT* is a. a computerized data base containing the results of studies that are currently being reviewed by other researchers b. a condensed version of the studies published in *Psychology Today* c. a journal that contains research articles dealing with the psychology of literary interpretation d. a CD-ROM version of *Psychological Abstracts*

Unit 2
Biological Bases of Behavior

Factual
Module 2a
c
1. The two major divisions of the human nervous system are
   a. the glial and neuronal systems
   b. the autonomic and somatic nervous systems
   c. the central and peripheral nervous systems
   d. the sensory and motor systems

Factual
Module 2a
b
2. The neurons in the autonomic nervous system connect to
   a. the heart and blood vessels
   b. smooth muscles and glands
   c. glial cells and interneurons
   d. skeletal muscles and receptors in the skin

Factual
Module 2a
b
3. The three main types of neurons are
   a. glial cells, interneurons, and neurotransmitters
   b. interneurons, sensory neurons, and motor neurons
   c. sensory neurons, motor neurons, and terminal buttons
   d. sodium neurons, potassium neurons, and chloride neurons

Concept/Applied
Module 2a
a
4. James wrinkled his nose when he caught a whiff of the odor from the pulp mill. The message to wrinkle his nose was carried from his spinal cord to his face along
   a. motor neurons
   b. sensory neurons
   c. inhibitory neurons
   d. glial cells

Concept/Applied
Module 2a
a
5. When an interneuron receives information from another neuron, the first structure(s) to be activated
   a. are the dendrites
   b. is the axon
   c. is the soma
   d. is the myelin sheath

Concept/Applied
Module 2a
d
6. Eleanor has multiple sclerosis. If you could view her nervous system you would find
   a. areas where the dendrites are severely damaged
   b. a lack of neurotransmitters in some neurons
   c. a reduction in the number of chloride ions in her peripheral nervous system
   d. areas where the myelin sheath has degenerated

Concept/Applied
Module 2a
c
7. When a neuron is <u>not</u> transmitting a neural impulse
   a. sodium ions are concentrated inside the neuron and potassium ions are concentrated outside the neuron
   b. sodium ions and potassium ions are both concentrated inside the neuron
   c. sodium ions are concentrated outside the neuron and potassium ions are concentrated inside the neuron
   d. sodium ions and potassium ions are both concentrated outside the neuron

Factual Module 2a **a**	8.	As an action potential travels along the axon a. there is a sequential opening of sodium gates in the axon b. there is a sequential closing of chloride gates in the axon c. the signal becomes weaker as it nears the terminal buttons d. the signal becomes stronger as it nears the terminal buttons
Factual Module 2a **b**	9.	When a neuron is at rest, the inside of the neuron has a slight electrical charge called a resting potential. This electrical charge is a. zero millivolts for all neurons b. approximately -70 millivolts for all neurons c. approximately +70 millivolts for all neurons d. -70 millivolts for sensory neurons and +70 millivolts for motor neurons
Concept/Applied Module 2a **d**	10.	Anastasia is deeply relaxed and her muscles are not moving at all. This suggests that for Anastasia's motor neurons a. potassium ions are concentrated outside the neurons and sodium ions are concentrated inside the neurons b. sodium ions and potassium ions are both concentrated outside the neurons c. sodium ions and potassium ions are both concentrated inside the neurons d. sodium ions are concentrated outside the neurons and potassium ions are concentrated inside the neurons
Concept/Applied Module 2a **a**	11.	The neurons in Jake's arm just sent a neural impulse. It will be 1-2 milliseconds before another neural impulse can be generated. This brief time period when another neural impulse cannot occur is called a. the absolute refractory period b. a resting potential c. the post-synaptic discharge d. the all-or-none period
Concept/Applied Module 2a **b**	12.	Clarice is holding Franklin's hand during a scary movie. Suddenly she squeezes his hand very hard. When she does this the neurons in Franklin's hand will a. send strong signals to the central nervous system b. start to fire at a faster rate c. enter an absolute refractory period d. release more chloride ions
Factual Module 2b **c**	13.	A synapse is a. the structure that pumps ions into and out of the soma b. the part of the neuron that stores the neurotransmitters c. a junction where neural signals are transmitted between cells d. a receptor molecule on a sensory or motor neuron
Factual Module 2b **d**	14.	Neurotransmitters are synthesized in a. the receptor channels of the postsynaptic neuron b. the myelin sheath of the presynaptic neuron c. the dendrites of the central nervous system d. the terminal buttons of the presynaptic neuron
Critical Thinking Module 2b **a**	15.	A good analogy for the way in which a neurotransmitter binds to receptor sites on the postsynaptic neuron is a. a key fitting into the lock on a door b. lowering a drawbridge to permit traffic to cross c. opening or closing a window to regulate air movement d. pulling the trigger on a gun to fire a bullet

Critical Thinking Module 2b **b**	16.	When a neurotransmitter is released, but it does not fit into a suitable receptor channel on the postsynaptic neuron, a. an inhibitory postsynaptic potential will be generated b. the firing potential of the postsynaptic neuron will not be affected c. an excitatory postsynaptic potential will be generated d. the strength of the action potential in the presynaptic neuron will increase
Factual Module 2b **a**	17.	Reuptake occurs when a. unused neurotransmitters are absorbed and recycled by the presynaptic neuron b. excess neurotransmitters are inactivated by enzymes c. neurotransmitters remain in the synaptic cleft and continue to simulate the postsynaptic neuron d. excess neurotransmitters are absorbed by the postsynaptic neuron and stored in the dendrites for future use
Factual Module 2b **d**	18.	Postsynaptic potentials a. follow the all-or-none principle b. always cause the postsynaptic neuron to move toward threshold c. always cause the postsynaptic neuron to increase its electrical charge d. can vary in size
Factual Module 2b **c**	19.	An excitatory postsynaptic potential moves the postsynaptic neuron a. closer to threshold and decreases the likelihood that the neuron will fire b. away from threshold and increases the likelihood that the neuron will fire c. closer to threshold and increases the likelihood that the neuron will fire d. away from threshold and decreases the likelihood that the neuron will fire
Factual Module 2b **c**	20.	When many signals from one neuron pile up at the same receptor site, the signals are combined through the process of a. spatial summation b. synaptic synthesis c. temporal summation d. the all-or-none principle
Concept/Applied Module 2b **d**	21.	Raul is sitting quietly when the muscles in his left leg begin to "twitch." This activation of movement in his voluntary muscles is most likely due to the release of the neurotransmitter a. serotonin b. dopamine c. norepinephrine d. acetylcholine
Concept/Applied Module 2b **a**	22.	Francesca has a sleep disorder, and her waking and sleep cycles are disrupted. In this situation, it is <u>most</u> likely that there is a problem with the neural pathways that release and utilize a. serotonin b. GABA c. norepinephrine d. acetylcholine
Critical Thinking Module 2b **b**	23.	Cocaine is a stimulant drug that acts by blocking the reuptake of dopamine in the nervous system. This means that dopamine stays in the synapse longer and continues to stimulate the postsynaptic neuron. Based on this information you could infer that dopamine affects the postsynaptic neuron by a. producing inhibitory postsynaptic potentials b. producing excitatory postsynaptic potentials c. canceling out excitatory potentials generated by other neurons d. blocking the receptors channels in the postsynaptic neuron

Concept/Applied Module 2b **a**	24.	Fatima is currently in the midst of major depression. It is most likely that she has a. reduced activity at norepinephrine synapses b. excess levels of the neurotransmitter dopamine c. reduced levels of the neurotransmitter GABA d. increased activity at serotonin synapses
Factual Module 2c **d**	25.	An electroencephalogram (EEG) is used to a. destroy specific brain structures to determine the effect on behavior b. produce color coded maps showing areas of high brain activity c. produce high resolution images of specific brain structures d. monitor the electrical activity of the brain over time
Concept/Applied Module 2c **c**	26.	Crystabel is wide awake and studying for an upcoming exam. While she is studying her brain activity is being recorded using an EEG. The EEG recording is most likely to be dominated by a. alpha waves b. theta waves c. beta waves d. delta waves
Concept/Applied Module 2c **d**	27.	Dr. White is monitoring a patient's brain wave activity using an EEG. At the present time, the EEG read-out is dominated by alpha waves. From this information, Dr. White should conclude that the patient is a. alert and actively thinking about events or problems b. sleeping very lightly c. currently dreaming about an exciting event d. deeply relaxed or meditating
Factual Module 2c **a**	28.	The research method in which specific structures in the brain are destroyed or disabled using a mild electrical current is called a. brain lesioning b. electrical stimulation of the brain (ESB) c. positron emission topography (PET scan) d. computerized tomography (CT scan)
Factual Module 2c **b**	29.	Researchers who studied brain function by lesioning areas of the hypothalamus in rats found that when the lateral hypothalamus was inactivated the rats would a. eat more frequently and become obese b. lose interest in food and stop eating c. eat larger portions and become obese d. cross a shock grid to press a lever that stimulated pleasure centers in the brain
Factual Module 2c **a**	30.	Electrical stimulation of the brain (ESB) is used to a. artificially activate specific brain structures b. destroy or inactivate specific areas of the brain c. produce low level brain waves in electroencephalogram (EEG) recordings d. map activity in the brain over time
Factual Module 2c **b**	31.	Computerized tomography (CT) scans are used to a. map patterns of activity in the brain over time b. produce computer enhanced X-ray images of brain structures c. monitor the overall level of activity in the brain d. map the relation between brain activity and observed behavior

Concept/Applied Module 2c **c**	32.	Carlotta is going in for neurological testing. The doctors will using an X-ray machine to create images of horizontal slices through her brain. These X-ray images will be enhanced by a computer to show specific brain structures. This procedure is called a. positron emission topography (a PET scan) b. magnetic resonance imaging (an MRI scan) c. computerized tomography (a CT scan) d. an electroencephalogram (EEG)
Concept/Applied Module 2c **d**	33.	Sterling is going in for neurological testing. He knows that during the test a radioactive isotope will be injected that will allow his doctor to record the metabolic activity in his brain, but he can't remember the name of the test he is having. It appears that Sterling's doctors are planning to use a. computerized tomography (a CT scan) b. magnetic resonance imaging (an MRI scan) c. electrical stimulation of the brain (an ESB scan) d. positron emission topography (a PET scan)
Factual Module 2c **b**	34.	The brain imaging technique that has been used to study neurotransmitter activity and map out dopamine pathways within the brain is a. computerized tomography (a CT scan) b. positron emission topography (a PET scan) c. magnetic resonance imaging (an MRI scan) d. electrical stimulation of the brain (an ESB scan)
Concept/Applied Module 2c **a**	35.	The brain imaging technique that will produce the highest resolution images of actual brain structures is a. magnetic resonance imaging (an MRI scan) b. positron emission topography (a PET scan) c. computerized tomography (a CT scan) d. an electroencephalogram (EEG)
Concept/Applied Module 2c **c**	36.	Psychologists have used MRI scans to compare the brains of schizophrenic and non-schizophrenic patients. These MRI scans have indicated that the patients who show symptoms of schizophrenia are more likely to have a. abnormal activity levels in their dopamine pathways b. excess activity in their frontal and parietal lobes c. enlarged ventricles within their brain d. an excess number of delta waves during sleep
Factual Module 2d **d**	37.	The structures of the hindbrain, midbrain, and forebrain can first be differentiated in a human embryo at a. 11 weeks b. 52 weeks c. the time of birth d. 3 weeks
Factual Module 2d **c**	38.	The hindbrain in the human brain is comprised of a. the pons, the reticular formation, and the thalamus b. the medulla, the substantia nigra, and Broca's area c. the cerebellum, medulla, and pons d. the cerebellum, Wernicke's area, and the corpus callosum

Factual Module 2d **c**	39.	The cerebellum is the hindbrain structure that is most directly involved with a. control of breathing and circulation b. sleep and arousal c. coordination and balance d. the perception of pain
Concept/Applied Module 2d **d**	40.	Jessica damaged her cerebellum when she slipped on some stairs and struck her head. The most likely impact of this injury will be a. disruption of Jessica's sleep and wake cycles b. difficulty in interpreting verbal instructions c. visual and auditory hallucinations d. an impairment in Jessica's fine motor skills
Factual Module 2d **b**	41.	The hindbrain structure that is most directly involved with the control of breathing and circulation is a. the cerebellum b. the medulla c. the thalamus d. the pons
Concept/Applied Module 2d **a**	42.	Clifton has been in a coma since he was in a serious car accident three weeks ago. He is still on medial life support because he is unable to breathe and his heart will not beat without assistance. It is likely that the accident caused damage to Clifton's a. medulla b. cerebellum c. hypothalamus d. midbrain
Factual Module 2d **a**	43.	The pons is a bridge of fibers that helps to regulate a. sleep and arousal b. unconscious reflexes such as breathing c. coordination and balance d. the perception of pain
Factual Module 2d **c**	44.	One function of the midbrain is a. regulation of unconscious reflexes such as breathing, heart beat, and blood pressure b. control of fine motor skills and general coordination c. processing of certain types of sensory information, such as locating where things are in space d. regulation of sleep and wake cycles, and general levels of arousal
Factual Module 2d **d**	45.	Parkinson's disease results from the degeneration of dopamine-releasing neurons located in a. the reticular formation b. the cerebellum c. the left cerebral cortex d. the midbrain
Factual Module 2d **c**	46.	The reticular formation runs through a. the midbrain and the forebrain b. the hindbrain and the forebrain c. the hindbrain and the midbrain d. the corpus callosum

Concept/Applied Module 2d	47.	Dr. Pustanyk has implanted electrodes in the brain of a rabbit. When currents of different frequencies are passed through the electrodes the rabbit will fall into a deep sleep, or suddenly awaken. Based on this information, the electrodes are most likely stimulating the rabbit's

b

    a. medulla
    b. reticular formation
    c. cerebellum
    d. occipital lobe

Concept/Applied Module 2d

a

48. If an individual's reticular formation were damaged, the most likely behavioral effect would be
    a. a disruption of sleep and wake cycles
    b. a loss of fine motor coordination
    c. the inability to accurately locate objects in space
    d. the degeneration of dopamine-releasing neurons

Factual Module 2e

a

49. The main structures of the forebrain are
    a. the thalamus, the hypothalamus, the limbic system, and the cerebrum
    b. the medulla, the pons, and the cerebellum
    c. the tectum, the hippocampus, and the endocrine system
    d. the autonomic and somatic nervous systems

Factual Module 2e

b

50. All sensory information, except for smell, passes through the
    a. hypothalamus
    b. thalamus
    c. ventromedial nucleus
    d. septum

Concept/Applied Module 2e

c

51. Bertha just caught sight of a blue butterfly. The neural impulses from her eye will eventually travel to her occipital lobe, but first they must pass through her
    a. hypothalamus
    b. amygdala
    c. thalamus
    d. hippocampus

Factual Module 2e

c

52. The thalamus is
    a. a passive relay station for sensory inputs
    b. a major link between the brain and the endocrine system
    c. an active processor of sensory information
    d. the center of all complex thought and emotion

Critical Thinking Module 2e

b

53. Imagine that you have stumbled across a secret laboratory where an evil scientist is conducting unauthorized brain research. By altering brain structures he has created superheroes who have specialized powers or abilities. One of these superheroes seldom feels hungry or thirsty, and can go for days without feeling the need to eat or drink. In this case, the brain structure that the scientist most likely altered would be
    a. the hippocampus
    b. the hypothalamus
    c. the reticular formation
    d. the thalamus

Factual Module 2e

d

54. Researchers who studied brain function by lesioning areas of the hypothalamus in rats found that rats will eat more frequently and become obese when
    a. the lateral hypothalamus is destroyed
    b. the amygdala is destroyed
    c. the reticular formation is destroyed
    d. the ventromedial hypothalamus is destroyed

Factual Module 2e	55.	The link between the brain and the endocrine system is provided by the
b		a. thalamus
		b. hypothalamus
		c. limbic system
		d. septum

Concept/Applied Module 2e	56.	Monica is in a state of high arousal. Her heart is beating quickly and she is perspiring. These automatic responses are largely controlled by activity in her
a		a. hypothalamus
		b. temporal lobe
		c. limbic system
		d. hippocampus

Factual Module 2e	57.	The limbic system is a set of loosely defined structures that includes
c		a. the hypothalamus, the thalamus, and the tectum
		b. the brain stem, the pons, and the medulla
		c. the hippocampus, the amygdala, and the septum
		d. the corpus callosum, the pons, and the temporal lobe

Concept/Applied Module 2e	58.	Tyler had severe epilepsy, and surgeons had to remove portions of his hippocampus to control the severity of his seizures. It is quite likely that Tyler will find that the surgery has also affected his ability to
d		a. control his urges to eat and drink
		b. interpret sensory information accurately
		c. experience pleasure
		d. form new memories

Concept/Applied Module 2e	59.	Xavier has learned to fear thunder and lightening storms. When Xavier's fear was first acquired there was probably a significant amount of neural activity in
c		a. his left temporal lobe
		b. Wernicke's area
		c. his amygdala
		d. the midbrain

Factual Module 2e	60.	The pleasure centers located in rat brains, by researchers who used electrical brain stimulation (ESB), are found in the
d		a. midbrain
		b. hindbrain
		c. spinal cord
		d. limbic system

Factual Module 2f	61.	The corpus callosum is
b		a. the major center for speech comprehension, found in the temporal lobe
		b. a thick bundle of fibers that connects the two cerebral hemispheres
		c. the portion of the cortex associated with representational memory
		d. the link between the subcortical brain structures and the cortex

Factual Module 2f	62.	In the cerebral cortex voluntary muscle movements are initiated in the
a		a. frontal lobe
		b. temporal lobe
		c. parietal lobe
		d. occipital lobe

Concept/Applied Module 2f d	63.	If an animal had a very small portion of its primary motor cortex devoted to its toes it is most likely that the animal would a. be able to initiate very intricate and well-controlled movements with its toes b. have a limited sense of touch in its toes c. constantly feel pain in its toes d. not have very fine motor control over its toes
Factual Module 2f c	64.	In humans a large part of the frontal lobe, known as the prefrontal cortex, is associated with a. emotional control b. fine motor coordination c. representational memory d. basic life support functions
Factual Module 2f a	65.	The parietal lobe of the brain is where a. our sense of touch is primarily located b. voluntary muscle movements are initiated c. auditory processing occurs d. visual processing occurs
Factual Module 2f d	66.	The portion of the cerebrum that plays a part in monitoring the body's position in space is a. the temporal lobe b. the midbrain c. the primary motor cortex d. the parietal lobe
Concept/Applied Module 2f b	67.	Maximillian had a stroke and he now finds that he has little feeling in his right hand and arm. It is likely that Maximillian's stroke destroyed some of the neurons in his a. right frontal lobe b. left parietal lobe c. left temporal lobe d. corpus callosum
Factual Module 2f a	68.	In humans, the primary auditory cortex is located in a. the temporal lobes b. the parietal lobes c. the occipital lobes d. the lateral fissure
Concept/Applied Module 2f b	69.	Gillian has been told she has a small tumor in her left hemisphere. The symptom that first concerned her was the fact she constantly heard a buzzing sound in her ears. In this case it is likely that the tumor is located in Gillian's a. occipital lobe b. temporal lobe c. cerebellum d. corpus callosum
Factual Module 2f c	70.	In humans, the occipital lobes contain the a. motor homunculus b. primary somatosensory cortex c. primary visual cortex d. vestibular system

Concept/Applied Module 2f **d**	71.	When Omar slipped on the stairs and hit his head he saw "stars" for several minutes. The "stars" were most likely a result of activity in Omar's a. temporal lobes b. prefrontal cortex c. primary somatosensory cortex d. occipital lobes
Critical Thinking Module 2f **c**	72.	Imagine that you have stumbled across a secret laboratory where an evil scientist is conducting unauthorized brain research. In one of his patients the scientist has artificially shrunk the occipital lobes until they are only one half their normal size. You might expect that this individual will a. have difficulty processing auditory information b. be less responsive to sensations of touch c. have difficulty processing visual information d. sometimes display uncontrollable rages
Factual Module 2g **b**	73.	The area in the left hemisphere, known as Broca's area, is important in a. the comprehension of spoken language b. speech production c. visual-spatial tasks d. perception of melodies
Concept/Applied Module 2g **d**	74.	Dr. Waddell is treating a patient with a closed head injury. This patient seems to understand all the questions that Dr. Waddell is asking, but is having difficulty answering the questions. Prior to the head injury the patient had no trouble speaking. If the head injury caused damage to the patient's cerebral cortex, the area that was most likely damaged would be a. Wernicke's area b. the prefrontal cortex c. the reticular formation d. Broca's area
Concept/Applied Module 2g **a**	75.	Walter is unable to comprehend spoken language, although he has no problems speaking. It appears that Walter may have damage to the area known as a. Wernicke's area b. Broca's area c. the corpus callosum d. Sperry's area
Factual Module 2g **d**	76.	The left hemisphere of the brain primarily controls and communicates with a. the left side of the body in right-handed people and the right side of the body in left-handed people b. the left side of the body c. both sides of the body d. the right side of the body
Factual Module 2g **c**	77.	When images of common household objects are flashed in the visual fields of split-brain patients, these subjects a. can only name objects that appear in the left visual field b. can name objects in either visual field accurately c. can only name objects that appear in the right visual field d. do not see the objects that appear in the right visual field

Concept/Applied Module 2g **c**	78.	Imagine that a picture of a banana was briefly flashed in the left visual field of an individual with a severed corpus callosum. At the same time a picture of a rabbit was briefly flashed in the right visual field. Based on Roger Sperry's work with split brain patients, you could predict that this individual would say a. "I saw a banana." b. "I'm not sure what I saw, it looked like a long-eared banana." c. "I saw a rabbit." d. "I didn't see anything."
Critical Thinking Module 2g **b**	79.	Imagine that a plastic cup is placed in the left hand of an individual with a severed corpus callosum. At the same time a metal spoon is placed in the individual's right hand. Based on Roger Sperry's work with split-brain patents, you could predict that this individual will say that he or she is holding a. a metal cup with a long handle b. a metal spoon c. a plastic cup d. a plastic spoon with no handle
Factual Module 2g **d**	80.	Roger Sperry's work with split brain subjects found that the right hemisphere was superior to the left at a. naming objects that flashed briefly on a screen b. recognizing objects using only touch c. performing mathematical calculations d. puzzle assembly and copying drawings
Factual Module 2g **b**	81.	In most individuals the left hemisphere of the cerebral cortex appears to be superior to the right hemisphere at handling a. musical tasks b. verbal processing c. complex motor coordination d. visual-spatial tasks
Factual Module 2g **a**	82.	Perceptual asymmetries refer to a. imbalances between the cerebral hemispheres in the speed of cognitive processing b. differences in the structural makeup of the two cerebral hemispheres c. gender-based differences in specific cognitive abilities d. the tendency for perception to remain stable as sensory input changes
Factual Module 2g **d**	83.	Doreen Kimura tested the degree to which the hemispheres of normal subjects differed in their ability to handle cognitive tasks. When subjects were required to recognize faces or melodies Kimura found that a. recognition was faster when the information went primarily to the left hemisphere b. recognition was most rapid when the information was directed to both hemispheres simultaneously c. faces were recognized faster by the left hemisphere, but melodies were recognized faster by the right hemisphere d. recognition was faster when the information went primarily to the right hemisphere
Critical Thinking Module 2g **c**	84.	Jasmine is using a single earphone to listen in on a conversation. Based on the work by Doreen Kimura you might suggest that she will recognize the words she hears most quickly if she a. puts the earphone in her left ear b. closes her eyes while she listens to the conversation c. puts the earphone in her right ear d. keeps switching the earphone from ear to ear

Unit 3
Sensation & Perception

Factual Module 3a **a**	1.	The environmental stimulus for vision is a. electromagnetic radiation b. mechanical energy c. chemical energy d. neurochemical energy
Concept/Applied Module 3a **b**	2.	If the human eye was not sensitive to differences in wavelengths of electromagnetic energy, people would not be able to perceive differences in a. saturation b. color c. brightness d. distance
Concept/Applied Module 3a **c**	3.	Sarah is wearing a red shirt and Joan is wearing a blue shirt. In this case, Sarah's shirt is reflecting a. shorter light waves than Joan's shirt b. higher amplitude light waves than Joan's shirt c. longer light waves than Joan's shirt d. lower amplitude light waves than Joan's shirt
Concept/Applied Module 3a **b**	4.	The Cyborgs who on planet Gamma-Delta-II are able to see infrared, in addition to the normal visual spectrum. This means that, compared to humans, the Cyborgs can detect a. light waves that have a higher amplitude b. longer wavelengths of light c. light waves that have a lower amplitude d. shorter wavelengths of light
Factual Module 3a **b**	5.	Our perception of an object's brightness is affected by a. the wavelength of the reflected light waves b. the amplitude of the light waves reflected from the object c. the number of light waves that are mixed together d. the position of the object in our visual field
Factual Module 3a **a**	6.	The mixture or purity of wavelengths in electromagnetic energy influences our perception of an object's a. saturation or richness of color b. brightness c. actual color d. sharpness or focus
Factual Module 3a **d**	7.	The retina is a. the transparent structure that focuses incoming light waves b. the opening that helps regulate the amount of light entering the eye c. the structure in the thalamus that integrates the neural signals from each eye d. the light-sensitive surface at the back of the eye

Factual Module 3a **c**	8.	The lens focuses light on the retina because muscles in the eye a. stretch the lens so it becomes thinner when objects are close b. move the lens closer to the retina when objects are close c. stretch the lens so it becomes thinner when objects are farther away d. move the lens closer to the retina when objects are more distant
Critical Thinking Module 3a **b**	9.	As people age the lens of the eye loses its ability to accommodate and it tends to remain flat instead of becoming fat and round. This suggests that as people age they a. will be more likely to detect differences in brightness and hue b. will lose their ability to focus on objects that are close c. will be less likely to detect differences in light purity d. will lose their ability to focus on objects in the distance
Concept/Applied Module 3a **a**	10.	Lannie wears glasses to correct the near-sightedness in his right eye. If he were not wearing his glasses a. the lens would focus images in front of the retina in his right eye b. the pupil in his right eye would dilate and let in too much light energy c. the lens would focus images behind the retina in his right eye d. the pupil in his right eye would constrict and not let in sufficient light energy
Factual Module 3a **d**	11.	The path of a light wave entering the human eye is through a. the cornea, the lens, then the pupil b. the lens, the pupil, then the cornea c. the pupil, the cornea, then the lens d. the cornea, the pupil, then the lens
Concept/Applied Module 3a **c**	12.	Ursla is having her eyes examined, and the doctor has put drops in her eyes that cause her pupils to dilate. As the drops begin to work Ursla will probably notice that a. her vision becomes clearer with objects appearing more highly focused b. she becomes more sensitive to mid-range wavelengths, such as green and yellow c. her vision becomes blurry with objects appearing less well focused d. she becomes less sensitive to binocular cues for depth
Factual Module 3b **c**	13.	The optic disk is a. a tiny spot in the center of the retina that contains only cones b. another name for the lens c. a hole in the retina where the optic nerve fibers exit the eye d. the neural tissue that lines the back surface of the eye
Factual Module 3b **d**	14.	Rods are the cells in the retina that a. are necessary for color vision b. provide sharp and highly detailed vision c. are found exclusively in the fovea of the eye d. play a key role in peripheral vision
Concept/Applied Module 3b **b**	15.	Imagine that the cones in a human eye ceased to function. If this were to happen a person would have a. poor vision in low illumination b. no color vision c. poor peripheral vision d. more accurate depth perception
Factual Module 3b **a**	16.	The visual receptors that play a key role in daylight vision and color perception are a. cones b. rods c. lateral cells d. antagonistic cells

Critical Thinking Module 3b c	17.	Imagine you were investigating the eye structure in an animal that spent most of its life burrowing through the ground and that seldom ever emerged from its dark underground tunnels. From what is known about the function of the cells in the human eye, you would expect that, compared to humans, this animal would have a higher proportion of a. cones to provide good color vision b. rods to provide better peripheral vision c. rods to provide good vision in low illumination d. cones to facilitate faster dark adaptation
Factual Module 3b d	18.	The tiny spot in the center of the retina that contains only cones is called a. the optic disk b. the blind spot c. the iris d. the fovea
Factual Module 3b a	19.	The eyes become more sensitive to light in low illumination through the process of a. dark adaptation b. light adaptation c. lateral inhibition d. lateral antagonism
Concept/Applied Module 3b c	20.	Helen has just entered a darkened room. After 10 minutes in these low light conditions her vision will a. continue to improve because, even though her rods will have fully adapted, her cones will continue to adapt to the reduced light b. continue to improve because both her rods and cones will continue to adapt for another 10 to 20 minutes c. continue to improve because, even though her cones will have fully adapted, her rods will continue to adapt to the reduced light d. be at its best because both the rods and cones will be fully adapted at this point
Factual Module 3b b	21.	The collection of rod and cone receptors that funnel signals to a particular visual cell in the retina make up that cell's a. neural network b. receptive field c. optic disk d. retinal web
Factual Module 3b b	22.	If a retinal cell has a center-surround receptive field, then that cell's rate of firing will increase the most when a. no light falls in the center of the receptive field but light falls in the surround b. light falls in the center of the receptive field but no light falls in the surround c. equal amounts of light fall in both the center and the surround d. no light falls in either the center or the surround
Factual Module 3b a	23.	Lateral antagonism occurs when a. neural activity in one cell opposes activity in surrounding cells b. dark adaptation in the rods interferes with light adaptation in the cones c. a single cell alternates between sending rapid and slow neural signals to the brain d. the pupil constricts and allows less light to enter the eye

Factual Module 3b **a**	24.	The Hermann grid provides perceptual evidence to support the existence of a. lateral antagonism b. the optic chiasm c. dark adaptation d. the optic disk
Factual Module 3c **c**	25.	The optic chiasm is a. a structure in the main visual pathway through the thalamus b. a structure in the secondary visual pathway through the midbrain c. the point at which the optic nerves from the inside half of each eye cross over and project to the opposite half of the brain d. a hole in the retina where the optic nerve fibers exit the eye
Concept/Applied Module 3c **d**	26.	There was a brief flash of light in Teray's left visual field. This information would have registered on the a. left side of each retina before traveling to the right occipital lobe b. right side of each retina before traveling to the left occipital lobe c. left side of each retina before traveling to both the left and right occipital lobes d. right side of each retina before traveling to the right occipital lobe
Factual Module 3c **b**	27.	Visual signals that project from the optic chiasm to the thalamus and finally synapse in the lateral geniculate nucleus (LGN) are traveling along the a. secondary visual pathway b. main visual pathway c. temporal-parietal visual pathway d. peripheral visual pathway
Concept/Applied Module 3c **a**	28.	Sabine injured her head and there was some damage to portions of her secondary visual pathway. It is most likely that this will affect Sabine's ability to a. localize objects in space b. perceive both form and color c. perceive brightness and contrast d. accurately perceive depth
Factual Module 3c **d**	29.	Before it reaches the occipital lobes, information relating to the perception of form, color, brightness, motion and depth is processed in the a. superior colliculus b. hypothalamus c. hippocampus d. lateral geniculate nucleus
Factual Module 3c **b**	30.	Hubel and Wiesel identified three main types of feature detector cells: a. short, medium, and long cells b. simple, complex, and hypercomplex cells c. color, form, and depth cells d. linear, curvilinear, and angular cells
Factual Module 3c **c**	31.	The complex cells identified by Hubel and Wiesel are cells that respond best to a. bars of a particular orientation in the visual field b. bars of a particular length moving in a particular direction across the visual field c. movement of correctly oriented bars across the visual field d. bars of a specific color located at a specific distance from the eye

| Concept/Applied Module 3c
c | 32. | If a 1-inch line moving from left to right causes a neural cell in the visual cortex to fire, but a 2-inch line moving in the same direction does not cause the cell to fire, you could conclude that the cell in question is
a. a complex cell
b. a simple cell
c. a hypercomplex cell
d. an antagonistic surround cell |

Factual Module 3c
d
33. Feature analysis assumes that form perception involves a progression from
a. forming perceptual hypotheses to the identification of a stimulus
b. identification of a stimulus to detecting specific stimulus elements
c. secondary to tertiary processing of a stimulus input
d. detecting specific elements to the identification of a stimulus

Factual Module 3c
c
34. When your perception of objects progresses from the identification of individual elements to recognition of the whole object, your perception has been guided by
a. top-down processing
b. two-stage processing
c. bottom-up processing
d. parallel processing

Critical Thinking Module 3c
b
35. Dean is a strong believer in UFOs, and the other night he saw three streaks of light flash across the sky in a group. They were actually planes from the local air base, but Dean was convinced he had just seen three spaceships. Dean's perception of the strange lights in the sky illustrates the influence of
a. bilateral inhibition
b. top-down processing
c. bottom-up processing
d. lateral antagonism

Concept/Applied Module 3c
a
36. Individuals sometimes perceive contours or edges that are not really present. This phenomenon is called subjective contours, and it lends support to the idea that perception involves
a. top-down processing
b. two-stage processing
c. bottom-up processing
d. parallel processing

Factual Module 3d
b
37. Perception of hue depends primarily on
a. a complex blend of all three properties of light
b. light wavelength
c. the purity of the light mixture
d. the amplitude of the light waves

Factual Module 3d
d
38. With subtractive color mixing, when all wavelengths are mixed together the result is
a. white
b. gray
c. green
d. black

Concept/Applied Module 3d
c
39. At the rock concert she attended over the weekend Veronica noticed that when the red and green spotlights overlapped they seemed to change to a yellow spotlight. This can be explained using the principles of
a. subtractive color mixing
b. complementary colors
c. additive color mixing
d. hypercomplex feature detection

Factual Module 3d **a**	40.	Human processes of color perception most closely parallel a. additive color mixing b. subtractive color mixing c. multiplicative color mixing d. tertiary color mixing
Factual Module 3d **b**	41.	The theory of color vision that proposes the human eye has three types of receptors with differing sensitivities to different wavelengths of light is a. lateral inhibition theory b. trichromatic theory c. opponent-process theory d. frequency theory
Concept/Applied Module 3d **a**	42.	Television sets are able to recreate the entire visible spectrum by additively mixing three primary colors. This process is similar to the view of human color vision called a. trichromatic theory b. saturation theory c. opponent-process theory d. complementary color theory
Factual Module 3d **b**	43.	Complementary colors are pairs of colors that produce a. white when they are mixed together b. gray tones when they are mixed together c. black when they are mixed together d. one of the three primary colors when they are mixed together
Factual Module 3d **c**	44.	The opponent-process theory of color vision proposes that a. the human eye has three types of receptors with differing sensitivities to different light wavelengths b. the final color that we perceive depends on the specific rods that are activated in the retina c. color perception depends on receptors that make antagonistic responses to three pairs of colors d. human color perception closely parallels principles of subtractive color mixing
Concept/Applied Module 3d **d**	45.	Dexter had his picture taken, and the photographer used a soft blue flash. For sometime afterwards Dexter saw spots in front of his eyes. Based on the opponent-process theory of color vision, it is most likely that the spots that Dexter saw were a. blue b. green c. red d. yellow
Factual Module 3d **b**	46.	Physiological support for trichromatic theory is provided by research which demonstrated that a. ganglion cells in the retina that increase their firing rate in response to red will decrease their firing rate in response to green b. the eye has three types of cones which are each sensitive to different wavelengths of light c. neurons in the optic nerve fire at the same frequency as the incoming light wave d. the periphery of the retina is more sensitive to color than the fovea

Factual Module 3d **a**	47.	The discovery of ganglion cells that increase their rate of firing when stimulated by yellow and decrease their rate of firing when stimulated by blue provides support for a. the opponent-process theory of color vision b. the subtractive-mixing theory of color vision c. the trichromatic theory of color vision d. the feature-detection theory of color vision
Concept/Applied Module 3d **b**	48.	Currently, the best description of the way in which color is encoded in the visual pathways is that color vision begins as a. a bottom-up process and then switches to a top-down process b. an opponent process and then switches to a trichromatic process c. a top-down process and then switches to a bottom-up process d. a trichromatic process and then switches to an opponent process
Concept/Applied Module 3d **c**	49.	The principle of perceptual organization that the Gestalt psychologists named the "phi phenomenon" helps to explain why individuals a. tend to perceive shapes in the simplest way possible b. tend to continue in the direction they were originally led c. may perceive movement when visual stimuli are presented in rapid succession d. sometimes perceive contours or edges that are not really present
Concept/Applied Module 3e **d**	50.	Movies are created by rapidly projecting a series of still pictures onto a screen. This creates the illusion that the people and objects that appear on the screen are actually moving. This illusion illustrates the principle that the Gestalt psychologists called a. figure-ground differentiation b. the principle of good form c. bottom-up processing d. the phi phenomenon
Concept/Applied Module 3e **c**	51.	Carson is looking at a reversible figure which first appears to be a vase and then appears to be two faces. His perception of the figure keeps switching between these two interpretations. This switching perception is caused by the fact that a. the Gestalt principle of simplicity doesn't work for reversible figures b. the Gestalt principles of proximity and closure are both at work in reversible figures c. the figure-ground distinction in reversible figures is often ambiguous d. reversible figures cause people to experience the phi phenomenon
Factual Module 3e **c**	52.	The fact that most people tend to perceive visual elements that are close to each other as being a single group illustrates the Gestalt principle of a. similarity b. continuity c. proximity d. good form
Concept/Applied Module 3e **d**	53.	Ray sat on his porch looking out at his field of corn. The fact that Ray perceived the corn in the field as being grouped into a series of separate rows is consistent with the Gestalt principle of a. closure b. good form c. similarity d. proximity

Factual Module 3e **b**	54.	The Gestalt principle of similarity suggests that visual elements a. that are close to one another will be perceived as being a single group b. that share common features or properties will be perceived as a single group c. that contain gaps will be perceived as complete objects d. will be perceived in the simplest way possible
Concept/Applied Module 3e **a**	55.	Gwen was at a basketball game, and even though people wearing red shirts were spread evenly through the stands, she perceived all the red shirts as a single group of visiting fans. Gwen's perception is most consistent with the Gestalt principle of a. similarity b. closure c. proximity d. good form
Factual Module 3e **c**	56.	The Gestalt principle of good form suggests that people tend to a. close up gaps in incomplete objects b. connect points into straight or gently curving lines c. perceive forms in the simplest way possible. d. pay more attention to dark objects when they appear against light backgrounds
Concept/Applied Module 3e **d**	57.	Zoe was walking through the woods when the path she was on broke into two separate branches. One branch turned off at a 90-degree angle, the second branch appeared to continue in the same general direction she was currently heading. If Zoe takes the second branch her actions would be consistent with the Gestalt principle of a. connectedness b. closure c. proximity d. continuity
Concept/Applied Module 3e **c**	58.	Raylin held a small earthworm in each hand and then held her hands together so that only one end of each of the earthworms could be seen. In this way, she was able to fool her little brother into thinking she had one gigantic earthworm in her hands. Raylin's trick illustrates the Gestalt principle of a. similarity b. proximity c. continuity d. closure
Factual Module 3e **a**	59.	Perceiving figures that contain gaps as complete figures illustrates the Gestalt principle of a. closure b. good form c. proximity d. connectedness
Concept/Applied Module 3e **b**	60.	When Wade looked up at the night sky he perceived the seven stars that made up the Big Dipper as a single complete figure, rather than as individual stars. Wade's perception of the night sky illustrates the Gestalt principle of a. similarity b. closure c. proximity d. figure-ground

Factual Module 3f **a**	61.	One monocular cue for depth is linear perspective. This cue for depth occurs because a. parallel lines appear to converge in the distance b. smaller objects appear to be farther away than larger objects c. closer objects appear coarser than distant objects d. closer objects overlap objects that are more distant
Concept/Applied Module 3f **b**	62.	Wilda was painting a country scene. In her painting the sides of the country road slowly came together. Wilda was trying to create an impression of depth in her painting by using the monocular depth cue of a. convergence b. linear perspective c. motion parallax d. height in plane
Factual Module 3f **c**	63.	The monocular cue to depth perception that is based on the amount of detail a person is able to detect is a. interposition b. motion parallax c. texture gradient d. light and shadow
Concept/Applied Module 3f **b**	64.	Annabel was building a model village on a narrow shelf. She bought 3 inch high houses to put at the front of the shelf and smaller houses to put at the back of the shelf. Annabel was trying to increase the impression of depth in her model village through the use of a. texture gradient b. relative size c. light and shadow d. convergence
Factual Module 3f **d**	65.	Height in plane is a cue for depth because a. closer objects appear to be higher in our field of vision than distant objects b. parallel lines appear to converge in the distance c. closer objects will partly obscure our view of more distant objects d. distant objects appear to be higher in our field of vision than closer objects
Factual Module 3f **b**	66.	As objects we are viewing move closer or farther away, the lens in the eye changes shape, in order to keep the object focused on the retina. This change in the shape of the lens is the monocular cue for depth known as a. motion parallax b. accommodation c. interposition d. convergence
Concept/Applied Module 3f **a**	67.	As Justin drove down the highway the fence posts beside the highway moved past him in a blur but the mountains in the distance didn't appear to move at all. Justin was experiencing a. the monocular cue for depth called motion parallax b. the pictorial cue for depth called texture gradient c. the binocular cue for depth called convergence d. the binocular cue for depth called retinal disparity

| Factual
Module 3f
d | 68. | Binocular depth cues are clues about distance that
a. can be detected in paintings or photographs
b. can be derived from the active use of either eye on its own
c. are based on Gestalt principles of perception
d. are based on the differing views of the two eyes |
|---|---|---|
| Concept/Applied
Module 3f
c | 69. | Simon had an operation on his left eye and had to wear an eye patch for three weeks. While he is wearing the patch Simon will lose his ability to
a. perceive any depth cues
b. perceive colors accurately
c. utilize binocular depth cues
d. perceive motion parallax |
| Concept/Applied
Module 3f
c | 70. | As the large butterfly flew toward Michelle she could tell it was getting closer because she could feel her eyes turning inward toward her nose as she watched it. In this instance Michelle was able to judge how far away the butterfly was based on the depth cue of
a. retinal disparity
b. accommodation
c. convergence
d. relative size |
| Factual
Module 3f
d | 71. | The principal binocular depth, which results from the fact that objects project slightly different images to the left and right retinas, is called
a. convergence
b. accommodation
c. motion parallax
d. retinal disparity |
| Concept/Applied
Module 3f
b | 72. | Fergus and Deidre are watching a great blue heron. Fergus is standing 15 feet from the heron, while Deirdre is standing 5 feet away. From what is known about binocular depth cues you should conclude that, as these two friends watch the heron,
a. Deidre will experience less binocular disparity than Fergus, because she is closer to the heron
b. Fergus will experience less binocular disparity than Deidre, because he is farther from the heron
c. Deidre and Fergus will both experience the same amount of binocular disparity, because they are less than 25 feet from the heron
d. neither Deidre nor Fergus will experience any binocular disparity, because binocular disparity only occurs when objects are more than 25 feet away |
| Factual
Module 3g
a | 73. | In the Müller-Lyer illusion, the vertical line in the figure that has the same characteristics as the outside corner of a building appears to be
a. shorter than the line that looks like an inside corner
b. longer than the line that looks like an inside corner
c. wider than the line that looks like an inside corner
d. narrower than the line that looks like an inside corner |
| Factual
Module 3g
d | 74. | The Ponzo illusion can be attributed to a misperception of depth based on
a. relative height
b. light and shadow
c. binocular disparity
d. linear perspective |

SENSATION & PERCEPTION

Factual Module 3g c	75.	In the Ames room the person who is standing closest to the viewer a. appears to be a midget b. is perceived as constantly changing in size c. appears to be a giant d. appears to be moving rapidly across the visual field
Factual Module 3g d	76.	Impossible figures are a. drawings that are compatible with two different interpretations that shift back and forth b. drawings that make sense when analyzed with top-down processing, but not when analyzed with bottom-up processing c. optical illusions that result from a misinterpretation of binocular cues for the perception of depth d. objects that can be represented in two-dimensional pictures, but which cannot exist in three-dimensional space
Concept/Applied Module 3g a	77.	The initial illusion that impossible figures make sense is most likely a result of a. bottom-up processing b. top-down processing c. Gestalt principles of organization d. a misperception of depth
Factual Module 3g b	78.	The moon illusion, in which the full moon appears much larger when it is on the horizon than when it is directly overhead, is mostly likely caused by a. top-down processing b. a misperception of distance c. a figure-ground mismatch d. the phi phenomenon
Factual Module 3h a	79.	The purity of a sound wave affects our perception of a sound's a. timbre b. pitch c. amplitude d. location
Factual Module 3h d	80.	For the most part, sounds that have a higher frequencies are perceived as a. having a lower pitch b. being louder c. being softer d. having a higher pitch
Concept/Applied Module 3h b	81.	When a trumpet plays a high-C followed by a low-C, these two notes sounds are perceived differently because they differ in a. amplitude b. frequency c. purity d. complexity
Factual Module 3h b	82.	Humans can hear sounds ranging between a. 5 to 5,000 Hz b. 20 to 20,000 Hz c. 20,000 to 50,000 Hz d. 320 to 780 Hz

Factual Module 3h a	83.	The frequencies between 500 and 5000 Hz yield the _____ absolute thresholds, because the human ear is _____ sensitive to sounds in this range. a. lowest; most b. lowest; least c. highest; most d. highest; least
Concept/Applied Module 3h c	84.	If the human ear could not detect differences in the amplitude of sound waves, people would not be able to detect differences in a. the pitch of sounds b. the timbre of sounds c. the loudness of sounds d. the saturation of sounds
Factual Module 3h a	85.	A rough guide for the relationship between the perceived loudness of sound and sound amplitude is that perceived loudness a. doubles for every 10 decibel increase in amplitude b. doubles each time the amplitude is doubled c. increases by one half when the amplitude is doubled d. is unaffected by changes in overall amplitude
Factual Module 3h d	86.	Very loud sounds can jeopardize hearing, and exposure to loud sounds can be perceived as being painful. With respect to hearing, human threshold for pain a. hovers around 120 Hz b. is generally between 500 and 5,000 Hz c. is between 50 to 55 decibels d. hovers around 120 decibels
Factual Module 3h d	87.	As sound waves enter the human ear they travel from a. the eardrum, to the auditory canal and though the middle ear b. the middle ear, to the eardrum and through the auditory canal c. the auditory canal, through the middle ear to the eardrum d. the auditory canal, to the eardrum and through the middle ear
Factual Module 3h c	88.	The three-stage lever system in the inner ear a. transduces sound waves into neural signals b. encodes the purity of the incoming sound wave c. amplifies tiny changes in air pressure d. creates pressure against the eardrum which causes the auditory neurons to fire
Factual Module 3h c	89.	The structure in the ear that contains the auditory receptors is a. the vestibular sacs b. the middle ear c. the cochlea d. the auditory canal
Factual Module 3h d	90.	The basilar membrane is located in the a. pinna and contains the vestibular sacs b. eardrum and contains the auditory nerve c. auditory canal and contains the hammer, anvil, and stirrup d. cochlea and contains the auditory receptors

Unit 4
Consciousness

Factual
Module 4a
a

1. Birds beginning a winter migration and bears going into hibernation show the influence of
   a. yearly cycles in biological rhythms
   b. circadian rhythms in species other than humans
   c. the suprachiasmatic nucleus in adjusting the body's biological clock
   d. seasonal adjustments in circadian rhythms

Factual
Module 4a
d

2. People's biological rhythms include cycles corresponding roughly to periods of
   a. 5 years, 1 year, 28 days, and 24 hours
   b. 48 hours, 24 hours, 12 hours, and 6 hours
   c. 28 days, 7 days, 24 hours, and 1 hour
   d. 1 year, 28 days, 24 hours, and 90 minutes

Factual
Module 4a
c

3. Physiological functions tend to rise and fall according to a 24-hour cycle known as
   a. a biorhythm
   b. a nuclear rhythm
   c. a circadian rhythm
   d. a hyperbolic rhythm

Concept/Applied
Module 4a
b

4. Imagine that you are taking your roommate's temperature every 30 minutes. After staying fairly steady for the past 4 hours her temperature has now started to drop. Based on research studies, it is likely that your roommate
   a. is halfway through the day and won't fall asleep for several more hours
   b. will fall asleep soon
   c. is just about to wake up
   d. is halfway through the night and won't wake up for several more hours

Factual
Module 4a
c

5. Studies of individuals who have been cut off from all external time cues have shown that circadian rhythms
   a. persist, but drift toward a slightly shorter 22-hour cycle
   b. become even stronger and more closely follow a 24-hour cycle
   c. persist, but drift toward a slightly longer 25-hour cycle
   d. break down and sleep-wake patterns become highly irregular

Critical Thinking
Module 4a
a

6. When the first astronauts travel to Mars they will be traveling for long period of time with no external time cues. Based on what research has shown, you should predict that the circadian rhythms for these astronauts would
   a. drift toward a longer 25-hour cycle
   b. drift toward a shorter 23-hour cycle
   c. stay synchronized with a 24-hour cycle
   d. become sporadic and show no definite pattern

Factual
Module 4a
c

7. When people are isolated from all external time cues they tend to
   a. go to sleep and awaken a little earlier each day
   b. go to sleep a little earlier and awaken a little later each day
   c. go to sleep and awaken a little later each day
   d. go to sleep a little later and awaken a little earlier each day

Factual Module 4a **d**	8.	Exposure to light seems to readjust the 24-hour biological clock by acting on a small structure in the a. thalamus called the lateral geniculate nucleus (LGN) b. midbrain called the superior colliculus c. brain stem called the reticular formation d. hypothalamus called the suprachiasmatic nucleus (SCN)
Concept/Applied Module 4a **b**	9.	Based on what is known about circadian rhythms and jet lag, you might expect that a flight attendant would experience the most jet lag on a flight from a. Seattle to Los Angeles (north to south) b. San Francisco to New York (west to east) c. New York to San Francisco (east to west) d. Los Angeles to Seattle (south to north)
Concept/Applied Module 4a **c**	10.	Morley is a news anchor who just flew from San Diego to Paris, crossing 8 time zones. Based on what is know about the time it takes for circadian rhythms to adjust and for psychomotor performance to recover when time zones change in this manner, you should predict that a. it should take less than a week for his psychomotor performance to recover b. it will take about 24 hours (1 circadian rhythm) for his psychomotor performance to recover c. it may take more than two weeks for his psychomotor performance to recover d. no adjustment time will be required because the flight was not a westbound flight
Concept/Applied Module 4a **a**	11.	George is a nurse who is currently on the midnight to 8 a.m. shift; tomorrow he will be shifting to the 8 a.m. to 4 p.m. shift. George's wife Melva is a factory worker who is also currently working on the midnight to 8 a.m. shift; however, tomorrow she will be shifting to the 4 p.m. to midnight shift. You should suspect that: a. George will adjust better to the shift change than Melva b. Melva will adjust better to the shift change than George c. neither worker will adjust to the shift change for at least three weeks d. neither George nor Melva will have any trouble adjusting to the shift change
Concept/Applied Module 4a **d**	12.	The Acme factory rotates their workers' shifts once every three weeks. The Widget factory rotates their workers' shifts every Wednesday. Based on the work by Charles Czeisler, you would predict that a. neither schedule will disrupt the circadian rhythm of the workers if progressively earlier starting times are used in both cases b. the Widget schedule is less disruptive for the workers c. both schedules will be equally disruptive for the workers d. the Acme schedule is less disruptive for the workers
Factual Module 4b **b**	13.	The 8-12 cycle per second brain waves associated with deep relaxation are called a. beta waves b. alpha waves c. theta waves d. delta waves
Concept/Applied Module 4b **a**	14.	Bernard is at a sleep lab and an electroencephalogram (EEG) is recording his brain wave patterns. As the researcher watches, alpha waves begin to appear in the EEG recording. Based on this information the researcher can assume that Bernard is a. deeply relaxed, but has not yet fallen asleep b. currently in light Stage 1 sleep c. currently in the slow wave sleep of Stage 3 or 4 d. dreaming

Factual Module 4b **d**	15.	Theta waves are brain waves with a frequency of a. 13-24 cycles per second which are associated with alert problem solving b. 8-12 cycles per second which are associated with mediation or deep relaxation c. less than 4 cycles per second which occur during deep sleep d. 4-7 cycles per second which are seen during light sleep
Critical Thinking Module 4b **b**	16.	Victoria is listening to a lecture in a hot lecture hall, late on a Friday afternoon. She starts to feel drowsy, and then falls into a light sleep. If her brain wave patterns were being monitored they would show a shift from a. alpha waves to beta waves and finally to delta waves b. beta waves to alpha waves and finally to theta waves c. beta waves to theta waves and finally to alpha waves d. theta waves to beta waves and finally to alpha waves
Factual Module 4b **c**	17.	Sleep spindles are a. high-amplitude low-frequency brain waves that appear during REM sleep b. low-amplitude high-frequency brain waves that appear during deep sleep c. brief bursts of high-frequency brain waves that appear during Stage 2 sleep d. brief bursts of theta waves that sometimes occur during deep concentration
Concept/Applied Module 4b **d**	18.	Winston is hooked up to an electroencephalograph (EEG) in a sleep lab. As the researcher watches the printout from the EEG, delta waves appear. Based on this information, the researcher can conclude that Winston a. has just entered Stage 1 sleep b. is still awake, but is becoming relaxed and drowsy c. is currently experiencing REM sleep d. has just entered Stage 3 sleep
Concept/Applied Module 4b **a**	19.	Rhonda is at a sleep lab and she has been sleeping for just over an hour. The electroencephalogram is now showing high-frequency beta waves and Rhonda's eyes are moving back and forth beneath closed eyelids. The researcher monitoring Rhonda's sleep can conclude that Rhonda a. has just entered REM sleep b. has just entered Stage 3 or Stage 4 sleep c. is experiencing an unusual sleep disturbance and may need medical help d. is just about to wake up
Factual Module 4b **b**	20.	During the course of a night, people usually repeat the sleep cycle a. only once b. about four times c. about ten times d. close to 40 times
Factual Module 4b **a**	21.	During the first cycle of sleep in an evening a. the REM period is relatively short, lasting only a few minutes b. REM sleep lasts about 40-60 minutes c. people typically skip Stage 2 sleep d. people experience their most vivid dreams
Concept/Applied Module 4b **b**	22.	Olivia has trouble staying asleep for more than four hours at a time. Olivia is likely to experience a. less deep sleep than people who sleep for a full 8 hours b. less REM sleep than people who sleep for a full 8 hours c. less REM sleep and less deep sleep than people who sleep for a full 8 hours d. more sleep spindles during Stages 3 and 4 of the sleep cycle

| Factual
Module 4b
c | 23. | When compared to adults, newborn infants
a. spend more total time sleeping, and spend a greater proportion of their sleep time in deep sleep
b. spend less total time sleeping, but spend a greater proportion of their sleep time in REM sleep
c. spend more total time sleeping, and spend a greater proportion of their sleep time in REM sleep
d. spend less total time sleeping, but spend a greater proportion of their sleep time in deep sleep |
|---|---|---|
| Concept/Applied
Module 4b
d | 24. | Roger was twelve when his grandfather came for a visit. The grandfather used the spare bed in Roger's room. Several times during the night the grandfather awoke briefly, and then fell back to sleep. Roger didn't awaken at all during the night. This different in sleep patterns can best be explained by research which shows that during adulthood the proportion of time spent in _____ increases, while the proportion of time spent in _____ decreases.
a. slow-wave sleep; light sleep
b. REM sleep; non-REM sleep
c. non-REM sleep; REM sleep
d. light sleep; slow-wave sleep |
| Concept/Applied
Module 4c
a | 25. | Brenda broke her pelvis and dislocated her shoulder in a car accident. She was in the hospital for several weeks, and during that time she was in a great deal of pain. To help her deal with the pain while her injuries healed, Brenda's doctor most likely prescribed
a. opiate-based drugs (narcotics)
b. barbiturates
c. hallucinogens
d. amphetamines |
| Factual
Module 4c
c | 26. | Over the past several decades the overall use of heroin has
a. decreased considerably
b. increased dramatically
c. remained relatively stable with less than 1% of young adults using the drug
d. remained relatively stable with about 15% of young adults using the drug |
| Factual
Module 4c
d | 27. | In general, heroin has
a. a moderate risk for physical dependence but a low risk for psychological dependence
b. a low risk for physical dependence but a high risk for psychological dependence
c. a low risk for both physical and psychological dependence
d. a high risk for both physical and psychological dependence |
| Factual
Module 4c
b | 28. | The drug that is associated with the greatest increase in the risk for infectious diseases, including AIDS, is
a. cocaine
b. heroin
c. hashish
d. mescaline |
| Factual
Module 4c
a | 29. | Sedative abuse among young adults
a. peaked in the early 1970s
b. peaked in the 1980s
c. is still increasing today
d. has remained stable over the past several decades |

Factual Module 4c **d**	30.	Sedative effects include a. euphoria, pain relief, and enhanced awareness b. elation, excitement, increased energy, and reduced fatigue c. increased sensory awareness, euphoria, and altered perceptions d. euphoria, relaxation, anxiety reduction, and reduced inhibitions
Factual Module 4c **c**	31.	Among young adults, the use of amphetamines and other similar stimulants a. was stable at 10% until 1985, but has increased significantly in recent years b. has increased steadily since the 1950s c. was stable at 10% until 1985, but has dropped in recent years d. has decreased steadily since the 1950s
Concept/Applied Module 4c **b**	32.	Wyatt has been feeling extremely tired for the past six months, even though he is getting lots of sleep. His chronic tiredness has started to affect his job, and his boss has threatened to fire Wyatt if his job performance doesn't improve. Wyatt sees his family doctor and asks if there is something that can be prescribed to help him feel more alert, and to give him more energy. If the doctor prescribes a medication for Wyatt, it is most likely to be a. a narcotic b. an amphetamine c. a hallucinogen d. a sedative
Factual Module 4c **c**	33.	Overall, the highest percentage of drug-related deaths is associated with the use of a. heroin b. alcohol c. cocaine d. sedatives
Concept/Applied Module 4c **d**	34.	Cassandra has just taken a drug that has altered her perceptions and increased her sensory awareness. It is most likely that Cassandra has taken a. morphine or heroin b. barbiturates or Quaaludes c. cocaine or amphetamines d. LSD or mescaline
Factual Module 4c **b**	35.	When an individual takes hallucinogenic drugs there is a. a high risk for dependence but almost no risk of overdose b. little risk for dependence and almost no risk of overdose c. little risk for dependence but a high risk of overdose d. a high risk for dependence and also a high risk of overdose
Factual Module 4c **a**	36.	The drug that is most likely to increase a user's risk for respiratory and pulmonary diseases is a. marijuana b. cocaine c. heroin d. psilocybin
Factual Module 4d **a**	37.	Cocaine exerts its effects at norepinephrine and dopamine synapses where it interferes with a. reuptake, causing more post-synaptic potentials than normal b. neurotransmitter binding, causing more post-synaptic potentials than normal c. reuptake, causing fewer post-synaptic potentials than normal d. neurotransmitter binding, causing fewer post-synaptic potentials than normal

Factual Module 4d **b**	38.	The powerful reinforcing effects of cocaine are thought to stem from a. decreased activation in GABA-releasing neural circuits that originate near the substantia nigra b. increased activation in dopamine-releasing neural circuits that originate near the substantia nigra c. increased activation in benzodiazepine neural circuits in the hippocampus d. decreased activation in THC neural circuits in the cerebellum
Concept/Applied Module 4d **a**	39.	Ivy has taken a drug that has increased the release of dopamine and norepinephrine while at the same time slowing the reuptake of these same neurotransmitters. Ivy has most likely taken some type of a. amphetamine b. narcotic drug c. antianxiety drug d. hallucinogenic drug
Concept/Applied Module 4d **c**	40.	Dr. Ware has developed a new drug that blocks the reuptake of dopamine and norepinephrine within the brain. It is likely that Dr. Ware's new drug will a. act as a sedative and induce sleep b. function as an effective pain killer c. have stimulant effects and produce mild euphoria d. produce hallucinations and distorted perceptions
Factual Module 4d **b**	41.	Users often crash into a depressed state a few hours after taking stimulant drugs. This depression occurs because, over time, stimulants a. increase the overall availability of dopamine and norepinephrine b. lead to a depletion of dopamine and norepinephrine c. inactivate GABA synapses d. inhibit the release of substance P within the central nervous system
Concept/Applied Module 4d **c**	42.	Assume that you want to increase the activity within an individual's GABA system. The type of drug that would have this effect is a. an amphetamine drug b. an opiate drug c. an antianxiety drug d. any drug containing THC, such as marijuana or hashish
Concept/Applied Module 4d **d**	43.	When the activity within the GABA system is increased, an individual will experience a. a reduction in the perception of pain b. hallucinations and sensory alterations c. euphoria and excitement d. a reduction in overall levels of anxiety
Factual Module 4d **b**	44.	Some psychoactive drugs help in the reduction of pain by inhibiting the release of substance P. These drugs a. bind to GABA receptor sites b. bind to opiate receptor sites c. block norepinephrine receptor sites d. block dopamine receptor sites
Factual Module 4d **a**	45.	The euphoric effects of opiate drugs are probably due to the indirect activation of a. the same dopamine circuits that account for the reinforcing effects of cocaine b. GABA receptor sites throughout the peripheral nervous system c. norepinephrine receptor sites in the hippocampus d. substance P receptor channels in the brain

Factual Module 4d **d**	46.	LSD seems to work by a. blocking the reuptake of dopamine b. binding to THC receptors and inactivating them c. blocking GABA receptors d. increasing activity at some serotonin synapses
Critical Thinking Module 4d **d**	47.	Dr. Kruse has developed a new drug that increases the activity in some serotonin synapses. Based on what is known about the neurological impact of various drugs, you might expect that Dr. Kruse's new drug will a. act as an effective sedative and induce sleep b. function as an effective pain killer by blocking the release of substance P c. have stimulant effects and produce mild agitation d. produce hallucinations or distorted perception
Factual Module 4d **c**	48.	Receptors that are activated by THC have been located in a. the hypothalamus and the substantia nigra b. the frontal lobe and the occipital lobe c. the hippocampus and the cerebellum d. the cerebellum and the substantia nigra

Unit 5
Learning

Factual Module 5a c	1.	Classical conditioning is a type of learning in which a. voluntary responses come to be controlled by their consequences b. an organism's responding is influenced by the observation of others c. a neutral stimulus acquires the ability to evoke a response that was originally evoked by another stimulus d. there is a long-lasting decrease in the neural excitability along specific neural pathways
Factual Module 5a d	2.	As Pavlov's research progressed, he noticed that dogs who were accustomed to the procedure would a. start salivating after the meat powder was presented b. stop salivating as soon as the meat powder was presented c. bark if the presentation of the meat powder was delayed d. start salivating before the meat powder was presented
Factual Module 5a b	3.	An unconditioned stimulus a. is an unlearned reaction that occurs without any previous conditioning b. evokes a response without any previous conditioning c. acquires the capacity to evoke a response through conditioning d. is a learned reaction that occurs as a result of previous conditioning
Factual Module 5a a	4.	An unlearned reaction that occurs without any previous conditioning is called a. an unconditioned response b. an unconditioned stimulus c. a conditioned response d. a conditioned stimulus
Factual Module 5a d	5.	In Pavlov's original demonstration, the unconditioned response was a. salivation to the tone b. the meat powder c. the sound of the tone d. salivation to the meat powder
Factual Module 5a a	6.	An conditioned response a. is a learned reaction that occurs as a result of previous conditioning b. is an unlearned reaction that occurs without any previous conditioning c. evokes a response without any previous conditioning d. acquires the capacity to evoke a response through conditioning
Concept/Applied Module 5a c	7.	When Ricardo was small, he was standing under a tree that was struck by lightening. Now every time he walks under trees along the street he feels terrified. In this example the conditioned stimulus is a. the lightening that struck the original tree b. Ricardo's original fear when the lightening struck c. walking under trees d. the fear Ricardo now experiences whenever he walks under trees

Concept/Applied Module 5a	8.	Ann Marie received a small blue package last Christmas that had a beautiful bracelet in it. Now every time Ann Marie sees small blue boxes she feels a little twinge of excitement. In this example the excitement that Ann Marie experiences when she sees small blue boxes now is
a		a. a conditioned response
		b. a conditioned stimulus
		c. an unconditioned response
		d. an unconditioned stimulus

Concept/Applied
Module 5a
b

9. When Lewis was younger he was on a bridge that collapsed. Today he feels very nervous every time he has to drive across bridges. The learning process that could best account for Lewis' fear and anxiety is
   a. operant conditioning
   b. classical conditioning
   c. observational learning
   d. delayed reinforcement

Concept/Applied
Module 5a
a

10. Advertisers often try to take advantage of classical conditioning by presenting their product in association with an attractive person. When they do this, the attractive person is acting as
    a. a conditioned stimulus
    b. an unconditioned stimulus
    c. a role model
    d. a positive reinforcer

Factual
Module 5a
b

11. In immunosuppression studies animals were injected with a drug that caused immunosuppression. At the same time they were given an unusual-tasting liquid to drink. Several days later the animals were again given the unusual-tasting liquid and the researchers found that
    a. the immune response increased when the animals drank the liquid
    b. the immune response decreased when the animals drank the liquid
    c. the immune response did not change because physiological responses are not affected by conditioning techniques
    d. the animals refused to drink the liquid

Concept/Applied
Module 5a
b

12. If you allow a rat to drink a unique tasting liquid, while you simultaneously inject the rat with an immunosuppressing drug, the conditioned response would be
    a. the unique taste of the liquid
    b. immune suppression
    c. the pain associated with the injection
    d. the drug injection

Factual
Module 5b
c

13. During acquisition, the strength of a conditioned response generally
    a. increases slowly for the first few trials, followed by a sudden increase
    b. starts off near its maximum and then slowly decreases over time
    c. increases rapidly and then levels off near its maximum
    d. increases rapidly and then slowly decreases over time

Concept/Applied
Module 5b
c

14. Dr. Dyle has classically conditioned a dog to salivate to a clicking noise. If Dr. Dyle continues to play the clicking noise all by itself, over and over again, the dog will
    a. begin to salivate even more to the clicking sound
    b. develop secondary conditioned responses
    c. respond for a while, and then stop responding
    d. also become operantly conditioned to the clicking noise

Factual Module 5b **d**	15.	The loss of a conditioned response following the repeated presentation of a conditioned stimulus on its own, without the unconditioned stimulus, is called a. discrimination b. generalization c. higher-order conditioning d. extinction
Concept/Applied Module 5b **b**	16.	Bernice classically conditioned her cat to purr whenever the phone rang. One day the phone rang for nearly two hours straight when Bernice wasn't home and the cat's conditioned purring response underwent extinction. Today the response has spontaneously recovered, but if the conditioned purring response were to undergo extinction again Bernice should expect that it will a. take more time to extinguish than it took for the original extinction b. take less time to extinguish than it took for the original extinction c. take the same amount of time to extinguish as it took for the original extinction d. not be possible to extinguish the response now that spontaneous recovery has occurred
Concept/Applied Module 5b **a**	17.	The phenomenon of spontaneous recovery suggests that a. even if a person is able to extinguish a conditioned response, there is a chance that it will reappear later b. once a conditioned response has been extinguished a person will also stop responding to other stimuli that are similar c. when a conditioned response is extinguished, higher-order responses replace the original response d. classical conditioning can only be used to condition biologically meaningful responses
Factual Module 5b **d**	18.	When an organism that has learned a response to one specific stimulus responds in the same way to a new stimulus that is similar, the process at work is a. discrimination b. higher-order conditioning c. spontaneous recovery d. generalization
Concept/Applied Module 5b **c**	19.	When Petra was 4 years old the neighbor's parrot bit Petra's hand quite badly. Today Petra is afraid of almost all birds, including robins and hummingbirds. Petra's fear illustrates the classical conditioning process of a. discrimination b. higher-order conditioning c. generalization d. spontaneous recovery
Factual Module 5b **c**	20.	In classical conditioning, stimulus discrimination occurs when a. an organism that has learned a response to one specific stimulus responds in the same way to a new stimulus that is similar b. a previously extinguished response reappears after a period of nonexposure to the conditioned stimulus c. an organism that has learned a response to one specific stimulus does *not* respond in the same way to a new stimulus that is similar d. a conditioned stimulus functions as if it were an unconditioned stimulus

LEARNING

Concept/Applied Module 5b **d**	21.	Frank fell off his red tricycle last week and he would cry whenever his parents tried to put him back on the tricycle. This week his father painted Frank's tricycle blue, and now Frank doesn't cry when his parents put him on the tricycle. Frank's reaction to the painted tricycle illustrates the classical conditioning process of a. generalization b. higher-order conditioning c. negative reinforcement d. discrimination
Factual Module 5b **b**	22.	The basic law governing discrimination in classical conditioning is: a. the more similar new stimuli are to the original conditioned stimuli, the greater the likelihood of discrimination b. the less similar new stimuli are to the original conditioned stimuli, the greater the likelihood of discrimination c. discrimination can only occur when extinction has already taken place d. once spontaneous recovery has occurred, discrimination cannot take place
Factual Module 5b **a**	23.	A conditioned stimulus can sometimes function as if it were an unconditioned stimulus. When this happens, the process at work is a. higher-order conditioning b. stimulus generalization c. spontaneous recovery d. operant conditioning
Critical Thinking Module 5b **d**	24.	Five-year-old Antonio is afraid of balloons because a balloon once popped in his face while he was holding it. Last week Antonio went to the circus and there was a clown holding a large assortment of helium balloons. Now Antonio is also afraid of clowns, even though none of the balloons that the clown was holding popped. Antonio's fear of clowns illustrates the classical conditioning process known as a. stimulus discrimination b. spontaneous recovery c. negative reinforcement d. higher-order conditioning
Factual Module 5c **d**	25.	The type of learning in which voluntary responses come to be controlled by their consequences: is a. classical conditioning b. observational learning c. dichotic conditioning d. operant conditioning
Factual Module 5c **c**	26.	One of the first people to outline the basic principles of operant conditioning was a. Sigmund Freud b. Ivan Pavlov c. B. F. Skinner d. Albert Bandura
Factual Module 5c **a**	27.	When an event or stimulus that follows a response increases an organism's tendency to perform the response, the event or stimulus is called a. a reinforcer b. a conditioned stimulus c. an unconditioned stimulus d. a discriminative stimulus

Concept/Applied Module 5c **a**	28.	Bernard is attempting to teach his dog to fetch a baseball when it is hit into the outfield. He will be most successful in teaching his dog this behavior if he uses a. operant conditioning b. classical conditioning c. observational learning d. higher-order conditioning
Factual Module 5c **b**	29.	The key dependent variable in most research on operant conditioning is a. the number of reinforcers that the subject receives b. the subjects' response rate over time c. the number of responses that produce no immediate consequences d. the type of stimulus used to signal that a response should be made
Factual Module 5c **a**	30.	On a cumulative recorder a rapid response rate produces a. a steep slope b. a shallow slope c. a flat, horizontal line d. a downward sloping line
Concept/Applied Module 5c **b**	31.	Adrien is watching the cumulative recorder that is connected to a box where a rat is pressing a lever to receive food reinforcement. The slope of the line is becoming flatter and flatter over time. Based on this output, Adrien can conclude that the rat's response rate a. is increasing over time b. is decreasing over time c. will soon show spontaneous recovery d. is caused by inadequate stimulus generalization
Factual Module 5c **c**	32.	In operant conditioning, the process of shaping involves a. demonstrating a desired response and then reinforcing it whenever it occurs b. positively reinforcing correct responses and negatively reinforcing incorrect responses c. delivering reinforcement for closer and closer approximations to the final desired response d. switching to classical conditioning once a behavior is well established
Concept/Applied Module 5c **d**	33.	Elizabeth is a telephone salesperson. When she was first training for her job she was paid for every call she made. Later, she was only paid if a customer requested an information package. Now she is only paid when she actually closes a sale. Elizabeth's telephone sales skills were developed using the process of a. generalization b. discrimination c. higher-order conditioning d. shaping
Factual Module 5c **b**	34.	When the extinction process is begun in operant conditioning there is usually a. a significant drop in the rate of the operant response b. a brief surge in responding, followed by a gradual decline c. a slow decline in the response followed by an rapid upsurge in responding d. no change in the overall response rate
Concept/Applied Module 5c **b**	35.	Louisa has discovered that her classmates don't tease her if she simply ignores them, and doesn't pay attention to their harassment. Louisa's discovery illustrates the concept of a. shaping b. extinction c. acquisition d. stimulus discrimination

Concept/Applied Module 5c a	36.	When resistance to extinction is high it means that a. responding will continue for a long time after reinforcement is discontinued b. responding will taper off quickly when reinforcement is discontinued c. responding will fail to show spontaneous recovery following a period of extinction d. shaping was done incorrectly when the initial response was acquired
Factual Module 5d d	37.	Partial or intermittent reinforcement occurs when a. reinforcers are provided whether or not an appropriate response occurs b. reinforcers are sometimes provided for inappropriate responses c. when classical conditioning and operant conditioning are combined d. a designated response is reinforced only some of the time when it occurs
Factual Module 5d c	38.	Compared to continuous reinforcement schedules, intermittent reinforcement a. makes a response less resistant to extinction b. makes a response more resistant to shaping c. makes a response more resistant to extinction d. makes a response easier to shape
Factual Module 5d c	39.	When a fixed-ratio schedule of reinforcement is in place a response will only be reinforced after a. a varying number of nonreinforced responses have occurred b. a fixed time interval has elapsed since the last reinforced response c. a fixed number of nonreinforced responses have occurred d. an unpredictable period of time has elapsed since the last reinforced response
Concept/Applied Module 5d d	40.	Eve has taken on a home-employment job which involves stuffing envelopes for a mass marketing firm. She receives $1.00 for every 50 envelopes she stuffs. In this example, the mass marketer is utilizing a. a variable-ratio schedule b. a fixed-interval schedule c. a variable-interval schedule d. a fixed-ratio schedule
Factual Module 5d b	41.	When a response is only reinforced after a variable number of nonreinforced responses have occurred, the type of schedule that is in place is a. a variable-interval schedule b. a variable-ratio schedule c. a fixed-ratio schedule d. a fixed-interval schedule
Concept/Applied Module 5d a	42.	Anthony is a free-lance author who submits short news articles to various magazines. He never knows for sure which news stories will be purchased by the magazines, but the more stories he submits the more likely he is to have a story accepted. In this example, Anthony is being reinforced for his writing on a. a variable-ratio schedule b. a fixed-ratio schedule c. a fixed-interval schedule d. a variable-interval schedule
Factual Module 5d a	43.	When a reinforcer is given for the first response after a changing time interval has elapsed, with the interval varying around some predetermined average a. a variable-interval schedule of reinforcement is in place. b. a variable-ratio schedule of reinforcement is in place. c. a fixed-interval schedule of reinforcement is in place. d. a fixed-ratio schedule of reinforcement is in place.

Concept/Applied Module 5d c	44.	Marion's mail arrives at 2:00 p.m. every day. For the past two weeks Marion has been waiting for a $500 rebate check to arrive in the mail. Each day she looks out her window periodically to see if the mail has arrived yet. In this example, Marion's behavior of "watching for the mail" should match the pattern of behavior that emerges on a. fixed-ratio schedules b. variable-ratio schedules c. fixed-interval schedules d. variable-interval schedules
Concept/Applied Module 5d b	45.	Jonilee has been trying to reach her mother for the past 45 minutes, but her mother's phone keeps ringing busy. She redials every few minutes, but she still hasn't been able to get through. In this example, Jonilee's redialing behavior should match the pattern of behavior that emerges on a. fixed-ratio schedules b. variable-interval schedules c. variable-ratio schedules d. fixed-interval schedules
Concept/Applied Module 5d d	46.	Kaylee and Bryce are both enrolled in an Experimental Psychology class. Their task is to train a rat to press a lever, using food pellets as a reinforcer. Kaylee uses a fixed-interval schedule of reinforcement and Bryce uses a variable-ratio schedule of reinforcement. From what is known about the patterns of responding on different types of schedules you should predict that, compared to Kaylee's rat, Bryce's rat will a. show faster responding, because Bryce is using a ratio schedule b. show less stable responding, because Bryce is using a variable schedule c. show less resistance to extinction, because Bryce is using a ratio schedule d. take longer to learn the response, because Bryce is using a variable schedule
Factual Module 5d c	47.	In general the two types of schedules which tend to generate the most stable response rates, and which lead to the greatest resistance to extinction are a. fixed-ratio and fixed-interval b. fixed-ratio and variable-ratio c. variable-ratio and variable-interval d. fixed-interval and variable-interval
Concept/Applied Module 5d d	48.	You are watching a rat pressing a lever for food reinforcement. The rat makes very few lever presses right after the food has been delivered, but gradually increases to a rapid rate of lever pressing just before the next food pellet is delivered. In this example it appears that a a. variable-interval schedule of reinforcement is in place b. fixed-ratio schedule of reinforcement is in place c. variable-ratio schedule of reinforcement is in place d. fixed-interval schedule of reinforcement is in place
Factual Module 5e a	49.	When a response is strengthened because it is followed by the presentation of a rewarding stimulus the process at work is a. positive reinforcement b. classical conditioning c. negative reinforcement d. punishment
Concept/Applied Module 5e b	50.	Every time Jason cried his mother picked him up. Now Jason is a real crybaby. In this case when Jason's mother picked him up she was a. presenting an unconditioned stimulus for crying b. positively reinforcing his crying c. presenting a conditioned stimulus for crying d. negatively reinforcing his crying

Concept/Applied Module 5e c	51.	Vern really enjoys cutting the lawn using the new riding lawn mower, but his dad will only let him cut the lawn if Vern has finished his homework. Consequently Vern rushes home right after school every day and does his homework. In this example a. cutting the lawn acts as a negative reinforcer for finishing homework b. finishing homework acts as a positive reinforcer for cutting the lawn c. cutting the lawn acts as a positive reinforcer for finishing homework d. finishing homework acts as a negative reinforcer for cutting the lawn
Factual Module 5e b	52.	Negative reinforcement occurs when a response is a. weakened because it is followed by the presentation of an aversive stimulus b. strengthened because it is followed by the removal of an aversive stimulus c. strengthened because it is followed by the presentation of a rewarding stimulus d. strengthened because it is followed by the presentation of an aversive stimulus
Concept/Applied Module 5e d	53.	Every time Amanda cried her mother picked her up and the crying would stop. Now Amanda is a real crybaby. In this case when the crying stopped it was a. a positive reinforcer for picking Amanda up b. a conditioned stimulus for picking Amanda up c. a conditioned response to Amanda's crying d. a negative reinforcer for picking Amanda up
Concept/Applied Module 5e a	54.	Hamilton often stays late at the office because he needs the extra money that he gets for working over time. Bethany often stays late at the office because she is hoping that the extra work she gets done will mean she won't lose her job if the company downsizes. In this example, Hamilton's behavior of "staying late" is influenced by _____ and Bethany's behavior of "staying late" is influenced by _____. a. positive reinforcement; negative reinforcement b. negative reinforcement; positive reinforcement c. positive reinforcement; punishment d. negative reinforcement; punishment
Concept/Applied Module 5e a	55.	Cynthia loves to go to the gym for a 30-minute aerobic workout at the end of the day because she finds the exercise helps to eliminate any stress or tension she might be feeling. In this example a. eliminating stress acts as a negative reinforcer for the aerobic workout b. the aerobic workout acts as a negative reinforcer for stress reduction c. eliminating stress acts as a positive reinforcer for the aerobic workout d. the aerobic workout acts as a conditioned response for stress reduction
Factual Module 5e c	56.	If you were explaining the concept of punishment to another student, the most accurate explanation would be that punishment a. increases the probability of an undesirable response b. has the same effects as negative reinforcement c. decreases the probability of a response d. affects the probability of an unconditioned response occurring in the future
Factual Module 5e b	57.	When a behavior is punished, once the behavior has occurred a. an aversive stimulus is removed from the situation b. an aversive stimulus is added to the situation c. a negative reinforcer is added to the situation d. a positive reinforcer is removed from the situation

Critical Thinking
Module 5e
d

58. Typically, most people would
   a. dislike being negatively reinforced or punished
   b. enjoy being negatively reinforced or punished
   c. enjoy being punished and dislike being negatively reinforced
   d. enjoy being negatively reinforced and dislike being punished

Concept/Applied
Module 5e
c

59. Paul has a history of poor driving including speeding and failing to obey traffic signals. At his most recent court appearance the judge suspended Paul's license for six months, hoping that this would help to decrease his poor driving behavior. The judge is basing his actions on the operant conditioning process of
   a. positive reinforcement
   b. negative reinforcement
   c. punishment
   d. higher-order conditioning

Concept/Applied
Module 5e
d

60. Jessica was roller blading last week when she fell and skinned her knees quite badly. When her friends ask her to come roller blading now she is not interested in joining them. Jessica's roller blading behavior has been modified through
   a. positive reinforcement
   b. higher-order conditioning
   c. negative reinforcement
   d. punishment

Factual
Module 5f
b

61. Escape learning is a type of learning in which an animal or a person learns that an operant response will
   a. prevent some aversive stimulation from occurring
   b. decrease or end some aversive stimulation
   c. produce some type of aversive stimulation
   d. have no effect

Concept/Applied
Module 5f
a

62. Marion has a headache and has just taken some pain killers. If the pain killers take away Marion's headache, taking the pain killers would be considered to be
   a. an escape response
   b. an avoidance response
   c. an unconditioned response
   d. positive reinforcement

Factual
Module 5f
d

63. When a person or an animal learns that an operant response will prevent some aversive stimulation from occurring, the process at work is
   a. escape learning
   b. observational learning
   c. non-reinforced learning
   d. avoidance learning

Concept/Applied
Module 5f
c

64. Tyrone's cat, Phoebe, always hides under the couch whenever Tyrone's 3-year-old nephew, Jacob, comes for a visit. On one of Jacob's first visits to his uncle's house, he kept trying to carry Phoebe around by her tail or her ears. Phoebe's current behavior is an example of
   a. a conditioned response
   b. positive reinforcement
   c. an avoidance response
   d. an unconditioned response

Concept/Applied Module 5f **c**	65.	Fabian knows that eating chili tends to give him heartburn so before he digs into his mom's "3-alarm" chili he takes an antacid that prevents heartburn. In this case, when Fabian takes the antacid before he eats the chili he is displaying a. an escape response b. an unconditioned response c. an avoidance response d. non-contingent learning
Factual Module 5f **a**	66.	The paradox that occurs in avoidance learning is that the learning a. is a function of the nonoccurrence of an event b. involves a response that increases, even though it is punished c. involves a response that decreases, even though it is reinforced d. disappears and reappears in a random pattern
Critical Thinking Module 5f **d**	67.	According to the basic principles of operant conditioning theory, avoidance responses should a. become stronger over time because they successfully prevent the occurrence of an unconditioned stimulus b. show spontaneous recovery each time a unconditioned stimulus is presented on its own, without a conditioned stimulus c. slowly extinguish because they are no longer followed by the presentation of an external aversive event d. slowly extinguish because they are no longer followed by removal of an external aversive event
Factual Module 5f **b**	68.	Mowrer's explanation for avoidance learning integrates the processes of a. positive and negative reinforcement b. classical and operant conditioning c. positive reinforcement and punishment d. punishment and negative reinforcement
Factual Module 5f **a**	69.	According to Mowrer's explanation, when a light comes on in a shuttle box to indicate a shock is about to be turned on, the light is functioning as a. a conditioned stimulus b. an unconditioned stimulus c. a negative reinforcer d. a punisher
Factual Module 5f **b**	70.	In Mowrer's two-process theory of avoidance, the avoidance response a. is punished because it increases conditioned fear b. produces negative reinforcement because it reduces conditioned fear c. produces negative reinforcement because it increases an unconditioned response d. produces positive reinforcement because it reduces unconditioned fear
Factual Module 5f **c**	71.	Mowrer's two-process theory of avoidance helps to explain why a. phobias seldom last for more than a few months b. people continue to respond, even when they are being punished c. phobias are so resistant to extinction d. people stop responding, even when they are being reinforced
Factual Module 5f **d**	72.	Phobias are thought to be highly resistant to extinction because a. the avoidance response is punished each time it is made b. the avoidance response is maintained by both positive reinforcement and higher-order conditioning c. the person is continually exposed to the conditioned stimulus, and this prevents extinction from occurring d. the avoidance behavior prevents any opportunity to extinguish the phobic conditioned response

Unit 6
Memory & Thought

Factual
Module 6a
b

1. The key processes involved in memory are
   a. rehearsal, organization, and interference
   b. encoding, storage, and retrieval
   c. listening, learning, and attention
   d. structure, sound and meaning

Concept/Applied
Module 6a
a

2. The memory process that is analogous to the use of a keyboard to enter data into a computer is
   a. encoding
   b. storage
   c. retrieval
   d. linking

Concept/Applied
Module 6a
a

3. Shayla is able to retain the vocabulary she learned in her first-semester Spanish class after the class has ended. The main memory process that accounts for the fact that Shayla can hold information in her memory for extended periods of time is
   a. storage
   b. retrieval
   c. encoding
   d. attention

Factual
Module 6a
d

4. Craik and Lockhart proposed that incoming information would be processed at three different levels. When individuals emphasize the way a words sounds, they are using
   a. structural encoding
   b. semantic encoding
   c. linked encoding
   d. phonemic encoding

Concept/Applied
Module 6a
c

5. Scarlett was trying to remember three words she had heard. Instead of remembering "ship, professor, and infant" she recalled the words as "boat, teacher, and baby." Based on her errors in recall, it appears that Scarlett originally encoded the words using
   a. structural encoding
   b. phonemic encoding
   c. semantic encoding
   d. auditory encoding

Factual
Module 6a
c

6. In an experimental test of the levels of processing theory, researchers found that subjects had the best memory for words when they had been asked if the words
   a. rhymed with other words
   b. were written in capital or lower case letters
   c. would fit into an incomplete sentence
   d. were nouns or verbs

Concept/Applied Module 6a **b**	7.	Two students took a memory test. Twenty nouns were shown sequentially on a television monitor. Ava tried to think of rhymes for each word as it appeared on the monitor. Calvin tried to think of ways each word could be used in a sentence. Based on Craik and Lockhart's levels-of-processing theory, you should predict that a. Ava will have better recall of the words because she used phonemic encoding b. Calvin will have better recall of the words because he used semantic encoding c. both students should have equivalent recall of the words d. Calvin will have poorer recall of the words because he used structural encoding
Factual Module 6a **d**	8.	Researchers have found that individuals have better recall for words when they are able to form images of the words. In general, it is easier to create images for a. abstract concepts b. scientific terms c. foreign terms d. concrete objects
Factual Module 6a **b**	9.	Paivio and his colleagues asked subjects to learn lists of word pairs in which they manipulated whether the words were concrete, high-imagery words or abstract, low-imagery words. They found that a. recall was unaffected by the type of words used in the list b. the best recall was for high-high pairings c. the best recall was for low-low pairings d. the best recall was for mixed high-low or low-high pairings
Factual Module 6a **a**	10.	Many popular mnemonic devices depend on the use of a. visual imagery b. semantic encoding c. abstract encoding d. phonemic encoding
Concept/Applied Module 6a **d**	11.	Stanley forms an image of his dog, wearing a suit, and foaming at the mouth. He is hoping that creating this interactive image will help him remember to pick-up dog food, his dry cleaning, and shaving cream. Stanley's strategy illustrates the use of a. the method of loci b. structural encoding c. passive encoding d. the link method
Concept/Applied Module 6a **c**	12.	Greg is trying to remember his lines in a play. While he is practicing his six lines he stands in a different location in his apartment as he reads each line out loud. Later, when he is on stage, he visualizes himself walking around his apartment and he is able to successfully remember all his lines. Greg's rehearsal strategy is most similar to the mnemonic device known as a. the link method b. semantic encoding c. the method of loci d. abstract encoding
Factual Module 6b **a**	13.	Sensory memory is a. a memory buffer that preserves information in its original form for a brief time b. a limited-capacity store that maintains unrehearsed information for 20-30 seconds c. a store with unlimited capacity that can hold information for long time periods d. a memory store that contains information about actions and skills

Factual Module 6b **b**	14.	George Sperling tested the limits of sensory memory by flashing three rows of letters on a screen and then sounding a tone to signal which row of letters should be reported. In this experiment the independent variable was a. the number of acoustic confusions the participants made b. the length of the delay before the tone was sounded c. the number of letters the participants were able to recall d. the actual sound of the tone (high, medium, or low)
Factual Module 6b **a**	15.	The memory system that is a limited-capacity store capable of maintaining unrehearsed information for approximately 20-30 seconds is a. short-term memory b. long-term memory c. sensory memory d. articulatory memory
Concept/Applied Module 6b **c**	16.	As Mallory was introduced to the ten members of the sorority she hoped to join, she silently repeated all the names to herself several times to help her try to remember them. Mallory was using a. chunking to increase the capacity of her long-term memory b. acoustic encoding to help her process the names semantically c. rehearsal to temporarily store the names in short-term memory d. linking to form a conceptual hierarchy of the names
Concept/Applied Module 6b **b**	17.	When Clara recalled letters from a list after 60 seconds had passed she mistakenly recalled an "E" instead of a "P," and a "C" instead of a "T." Her errors indicate that the letters had been encoded a. semantically b. phonemically c. structurally d. visually
Concept/Applied Module 6b **d**	18.	Bart is listening as his roommate lists 14 things that they need to buy for their apartment, before the end of the week. Based on research into the capacity of short-term memory, if Bart doesn't write the items down as he hears them he is most likely to remember a. the entire list of items b. approximately 10 to 12 items from the list c. less than 5 of the items from the list d. between 5 and 9 items from the list
Factual Module 6b **c**	19.	Rearranging incoming information into meaningful or familiar patterns would be an example of a. rehearsal b. networking c. chunking d. linking
Factual Module 6b **b**	20.	Baddeley developed a model of working memory that consists of three components. The component that corresponds to all of short-term memory in early models of memory is the a. sensory buffer b. articulatory rehearsal loop c. visuospatial sketchpad d. executive control system

Concept/Applied Module 6b **d**	21.	Graham has selected four different universities that he might like to attend, and now he is trying to decide which of the four he should submit applications to. He has all the material spread out in front of him and he is carefully considering all the advantages and disadvantages associated with each campus. According to Baddeley's model of working memory, Graham is utilizing a. the rehearsal loop to repeat only the most important aspects of each campus b. the visuospatial sketchpad to manipulate the pros and cons for each campus c. the method of loci to mentally place the information in the best order d. the executive control system to juggle all the information he needs to consider
Factual Module 6b **a**	22.	A conceptual hierarchy is a. a multilevel classification system based on common properties among items b. a set of nodes that represent concepts, joined together by pathways that link related concepts c. a temporary storage system that allows people to manipulate visual images d. an organized cluster of knowledge about a particular object or event that is abstracted from previous experience
Concept/Applied Module 6b **d**	23.	In a semantic network, concepts that are strongly associated will a. have longer pathways linking them together b. have a greater number of pathways linking them together c. be easier to chunk d. have shorter pathways linking them together
Concept/Applied Module 6b **c**	24.	Alicia was describing the inside of her doctor's office to one of her friends. In her description she mentioned two diplomas that were on the wall, even though this doctor does not have any diplomas hanging on the wall. Alicia's error in recall illustrates a. the role of semantic networks in long-term memory b. the need for conceptual hierarchies in long-term memory c. the role of schemas in long-term memory d. the need for an executive control system in short-term memory
Factual Module 6c **a**	25.	Kandel and his colleagues studied conditioned reflexes in sea slugs and showed that some forms of learning result in a. an increase or decrease in the release of neurotransmitters by presynaptic neurons b. a decrease in the release of neurotransmitters by postsynaptic neurons c. a decrease in the synthesis of acetylcholine d. an increase in the synthesis of specific protein molecules
Factual Module 6c **c**	26.	Research into the biochemistry of memory has found that Alzheimer's disease may be due, in part, to a. overproduction of acetylcholine b. the destruction of dopamine synapses in the substantia nigra c. inadequate synthesis of the neurotransmitter acetylcholine d. structural defects in the hippocampus
Concept/Applied Module 6c **a**	27.	The Pharmex Corporation is currently developing a new drug that increases levels of acetylcholine in the brain. Based on research into the biochemistry of memory, when this new drug is available, people who take it may find that a. they experience impairments in their long-term memory b. their sensory memory improves, but their short-term memory is impaired c. their procedural memory is enhanced, but their declarative memory is impaired d. their long-term memory is enhanced

Factual Module 6c **b**	28.	Researchers who were studying the eyeblink response in rabbits suggested that specific memories may depend on localized neural circuits within the brain. Specifically, they found that when a microscopic spot in the cerebellum was destroyed a. spontaneous recovery of previously extinguished responses occurred b. the conditioned stimulus no longer elicited the eyeblink response c. the unconditioned stimulus no longer elicited the eyeblink response d. the conditioned stimulus began to elicit an unconditioned response
Factual Module 6c **d**	29.	Researchers who studied the anatomy of rat brains after the rats had learned to run a series of mazes found that the rats showed evidence of a. increased axon width in certain neurons b. increased synaptic vesicles in motor neurons that controlled leg muscles c. neural growth within the cerebellum d. new branches in the dendritic trees of certain neurons
Factual Module 6c **b**	30.	Organically-based amnesia that involves memory loss for events that happened prior to the time of the injury is called a. proactive amnesia b. retrograde amnesia c. declarative amnesia d. anterograde amnesia
Concept/Applied Module 6c **b**	31.	Kelly struck her head when she fell down the stairs last week, and since then she has had difficulty remembering things like the names of new people she meets, or where she has parked her car. It appears that Kelly has a. proactive amnesia b. anterograde amnesia c. retrograde amnesia d. Alzheimer's disease
Concept/Applied Module 6c **a**	32.	The profound anterograde amnesia that H. M. experienced after surgery to control his epilepsy suggests that a. the hippocampus plays a key role in the consolidation of long-term memories b. the prefrontal lobes are the storage area for most long-term memories c. the cortex houses exact tape recording of past experiences and events d. long-term memories are processed and stored in the cerebellum
Factual Module 6c **c**	33.	Our memory for factual information, such as names, dates, faces and ideas, is called a. procedural memory b. working memory c. declarative memory d. articulatory memory
Concept/Applied Module 6c **c**	34.	Dr. McGrath is demonstrating a new computer program to his students. As he shows them how to launch the application and create a new file Dr. McGrath is largely relying on his a. declarative memory b. sensory memory c. procedural memory d. articulatory rehearsal loop

Factual Module 6c **d**	35.	Consolidation refers to a hypothetical process that involves a. the creation of a multilevel classification system based on common properties among items b. the formation of a network of interlinked nodes joined by semantic pathways c. using information from previous experiences to create an organized cluster of knowledge about a particular object or event d. the gradual conversion of information into durable memory codes stored in long-term memory
Factual Module 6c **d**	36.	The current thinking regarding memories is that memories are probably stored a. in the hippocampus and cerebellum b. primarily in the temporal lobe of the brain c. in the brain stem, medulla, and other subcortical areas d. in the same cortical areas that were originally involved in processing the sensory input that led to the memories
Factual Module 6d **b**	37.	Problems of inducing structure require people to a. clearly specify all the constraints that are present in the problem situation b. discover relations among numbers, words, symbols, or ideas c. arrange the parts of a problem in a way that satisfies some criterion d. carry out a sequence of transformations in order to reach a specific goal
Concept/Applied Module 6d **a**	38.	On some types of intelligence tests people are asked to solve series completion problems. These types of problems are examples of the type of problem Greeno called a problem of a. inducing structure b. arrangement c. transformation d. constrained information
Concept/Applied Module 6d **c**	39.	Steven is taking an aptitude test in his college career center. A number of the questions ask questions such as: Glove is to hand as sock is to _____. Based on Greeno's classification system, problems such as this would be considered a. problems of arrangement b. problems of transformation c. problems of inducing structure d. problems of constraint
Factual Module 6d **a**	40.	When the parts of a problem can be arranged in many ways, but only one or a few of the potential combinations provides a solution, an individual is working on a. an arrangement problem b. a transformation problem c. a problem of inducing structure d. a non-heuristic problem
Concept/Applied Module 6d **c**	41.	Lila is trying to rearrange the letters DCDIARS into a common English word. This is an example of the type of problem Greeno called a problem of a. transformation b. inducing structure c. arrangement d. constrained information
Factual Module 6d **d**	42.	The type of problem that is most likely to be solved through a planned sequence of steps, rather than through sudden insight, is a. a functional fixedness problem b. an arrangement problem c. a problem of inducing structure d. a transformation problem

Factual Module 6d **b**	43.	When solving problems containing numerical information most people a. start by figuring out which information is relevant to the problem b. assume that all of the information will be needed to solve the problem c. start by trying to figure out how to use the numerical information d. rely on insight to produce the fastest, most accurate solution to the problem
Factual Module 6d **a**	44.	Functional fixedness refers to the tendency to a. perceive an item only in terms of its most common use b. persist in using an inappropriate problem-solving strategy that has been successful in the past c. rely on insight as a basic problem solving strategy d. impose unnecessary constraints on a problem-solving situation
Concept/Applied Module 6d **b**	45.	Theresa spent an uncomfortable night on her first camp-out because she forgot to bring along a pillow. Even though she had a knapsack filled with several shirts, she didn't think to use that as a substitute pillow. Theresa showed evidence of a. introducing unnecessary constraints b. functional fixedness c. mental set d. reverse insight
Concept/Applied Module 6d **c**	46.	Dominique learned how to reformat documents one specific way with his old word processing software. His new software has been rewritten to make it easier to reformat documents, but Dominique continues to use the cumbersome method he learned with his old software package. In this case Dominique is displaying a. functional fixedness b. introducing unnecessary constraints c. mental set d. second-order processing
Concept/Applied Module 6d **d**	47.	Harriet was reading a puzzle magazine. One of the puzzles was a group of nine dots set out in three rows of three dots. To successfully solve the puzzle it was necessary to connect all the dots using only four lines. The lines had to be drawn without lifting the pencil off the paper. Harriet worked on the puzzle for 30 minutes before declaring it unsolvable. In this case it is most likely that Harriet a. was experiencing mental set b. was showing functional fixedness c. was focusing on irrelevant information in her solution of the problem d. imposed unnecessary constraints on the solution for the problem
Factual Module 6d **d**	48.	Of the following, the one would be least likely to be a barrier to efficient problem solving is a. imposing unnecessary constraints b. utilizing a mental set c. focusing on irrelevant information d. overcoming functional fixedness

Unit 7

Testing & Intelligence

Factual
Module 7a
c

1. Tests of mental abilities include
   a. projective tests, creativity tests, and aptitude tests
   b. intelligence tests, personality tests, and projective tests
   c. intelligence tests, aptitude tests, and achievement tests
   d. aptitude tests, achievement tests, and self-report inventories

Factual
Module 7a
d

2. Intelligence tests are designed to measure
   a. previous learning and accumulated knowledge rather than intellectual potential
   b. specific types of mental abilities
   c. various aspects of personality, including interests, values, and attitudes
   d. intellectual potential rather than previous learning or accumulated knowledge

Concept/Applied
Module 7a
a

3. Sarah is taking a psychological test in which she has to select a figure that would be the next logical component in a series of similar figures. This test is most likely designed to measure Sarah's
   a. abstract reasoning skills
   b. perceptual speed and accuracy
   c. mechanical reasoning skills
   d. spatial relation skills

Concept/Applied
Module 7a
b

4. On a psychological test that Bertram completed recently there were a series of questions that asked him to determine how a pattern would look once it was folded into a box. Questions of this type are designed to measure
   a. perceptual speed and accuracy
   b. spatial relations
   c. numerical reasoning
   d. mechanical reasoning

Concept/Applied
Module 7a
d

5. If you wanted to gauge a person's mastery and knowledge in a specific area, such as mathematics, you would need to administer
   a. an aptitude test
   b. the Wechsler Adult Intelligence Scale (WAIS)
   c. a self-report inventory
   d. an achievement test

Concept/Applied
Module 7a
a

6. Madisen has just completed a two-year internship with a law firm. She takes a test that is designed to assess her current knowledge of general legal principles. In this case, the test that Madison takes would most likely be classified as
   a. an achievement test
   b. an aptitude test
   c. an intelligence test
   d. a projective test

Factual
Module 7a
c

7. Self-report inventories and projective tests are used to
   a. assess general intellectual potential
   b. measure potential in one specific area
   c. assess personality
   d. measure previous learning and accumulated knowledge

Concept/Applied Module 7a **b**	8.	David recently completed the 16PF. His results indicated that he was more emotionally stable, controlled, tough-minded, and relaxed than the average person. This type of personality profile is consistent with those found in a. artists b. airline pilots c. writers d. teachers
Concept/Applied Module 7a **a**	9.	Donovan just took a personality test designed to measure his assertiveness. He tells you that his final score on the test was 35. He knows you are taking a psychology class so he asks you what that score means. You should tell Donovan a. that you can't interpret his score without knowing the norms for the test b. 35 is probably a high score since most tests have a maximum score of 40 c. 35 is probably a low score since most tests have an average score of 100 d. he will need to take the test again before his score can be accurately interpreted
Factual Module 7a **b**	10.	The Rorschach test and the Thematic Apperception Test (TAT) are both examples of a. aptitude tests b. projective tests c. self-report inventories d. achievement tests
Concept/Applied Module 7a **b**	11.	Daryl uses a software package on his computer to create a number of abstract images. He finds that each person who looks at the images sees something different in them. If Daryl records the responses that each person provides, he may find that the answers are similar to those that would be obtained using a. the 16 personality factor test (16PF) b. the Rorschach test c. the Thematic Apperception Test (TAT) d. the Differential Aptitude Test (DAT)
Concept/Applied Module 7a **a**	12.	Stella is taking a personality test in which she is shown a series of simple scenes. She is supposed to tell a story about what is happening in each scene and suggest what the characters are feeling. The test that Stella is taking is a. the Thematic Apperception Test (TAT) b. the Rorschach test c. the 16PF test d. the Wechsler Adult Intelligence Scale (WAIS)
Factual Module 7b **c**	13.	When uniform procedures are used in the administration and scoring of a test, the test is a. reliable b. valid c. standardized d. comprehensive
Concept/Applied Module 7b **d**	14.	Arvind and Salah were enrolled in different sections of the same history course. Arvind's class met three days a week and Salah's class met twice a week. Arvind had 50 minutes to write the mid-term exam for the course and Salah was allowed 75 minutes, even though both tests were identical. In this case, the administration of the mid-term exam a. would have poor construct validity b. did not have adequate reliability c. has low content validity d. was not standardized across the course sections

Critical Thinking Module 7b **c**	15.	When Renata took the ACT Assessment this past year she was allowed to use a graphing calculator on the mathematics portion of the exam. Her older sister is surprised because seven years ago, when she took the test, calculators were not allowed for any portion of the exam. This suggests that a. the current form of the ACT Assessment has poor construct validity b. Renate probably earned a higher score on the exam than her sister did c. it may be difficult to meaningfully compare Renate's score with the score her sister obtained on the test d. Renate's score is probably less reliable than her sister's score
Concept/Applied Module 7b **a**	16.	Diantha scored at the 85th percentile on the verbal component of the Scholastic Aptitude Test (SAT). This means that, for the verbal section of the SAT a. she scored higher than 85% of the sample used to establish the test norms b. she answered 85% of the questions correctly on the exam c. she obtained a raw score of 85 correct answers on the exam d. she scored lower than 85% of the sample used to establish the test norms
Concept/Applied Module 7b **b**	17.	In psychological testing the most appropriate synonym for reliability would be a. comprehensiveness b. consistency c. accuracy d. validity
Concept/Applied Module 7b **d**	18.	Manfred recently completed the Musical Aptitude Test (MAT) for the third time in three months. The first time he took the test his score was near the top of the scale. The second time he scored near the bottom of the scale and in the most recent test he scored near the middle of the scale. Manfred's scores for this test indicate that a. the test has not been properly standardized b. the test has poor construct validity c. the test is measuring something other than musical aptitude d. the test has low reliability
Concept/Applied Module 7b **d**	19.	Dr. Tremblay has had 17 students repeat his advanced Calculus class over the past five years. Each time, the student's grade for the second attempt in the course was nearly identical to the grade received on the first attempt. This leads Dr. Tremblay to conclude that his testing procedures a. provide valid measures of student ability b. are well standardized c. successfully measure abstract reasoning skills d. provide reliable measures of student ability
Factual Module 7b **c**	20.	Content validity refers to a. the degree to which scores on the test correlate with scores on an independent criterion b. the extent to which there is evidence that the test measures a particular hypothetical construct c. the degree to which the content of a test is representative of the domain it is supposed to cover d. the degree to which people's scores are relatively consistent across different administrations of the same test
Concept/Applied Module 7b **c**	21.	Instructors who are creating classroom exams should be especially concerned with a. criterion-related validity b. construct validity c. content validity d. test-retest reliability

Factual Module 7b **d**	22.	A test that can be used to accurately estimate future performance in a given area is said to have high a. content-validity b. test-retest reliability c. test norms d. criterion-related validity
Concept/Applied Module 7b **b**	23.	Micah took the Airline Pilot Aptitude Test (APAT) because he wanted to become an airline pilot. Micah earned one of the top scores on the test, however he is a terrible pilot who consistently gets poor on-the-job ratings. This suggests that the APAT a. is a valid test, but lacks reliability b. is not a valid test of occupational aptitude c. is not a reliable test of occupational aptitude d. has been poorly standardized
Concept/Applied Module 7b **a**	24.	If a test designed to measure extraversion correlates negatively with measures of social discomfort, correlates positively with measures of sociability, and has low correlations with measures of intelligence and tolerance, you can conclude that the test has a. high construct validity b. low construct validity c. high test-retest reliability d. low test norms
Factual Module 7c **d**	25.	The first successful intelligence test was developed by a. David Wechsler in the 1950s b. Sigmund Freud in the late 1800s c. Lewis Terman in the early 1900s d. Alfred Binet and Theodore Simon in the early 1900s
Factual Module 7c **c**	26.	In the Binet-Simon scale, a child's mental age referred to a. the child's actual age stated as a deviation score b. the ratio of the child's intellectual ability to his or her actual age c. the child's mental ability relative to other children of various ages d. the ratio of a child's actual age to his or her intellectual ability
Factual Module 7c **b**	27.	In Binet's original scoring system a. children of different ages could only be compared when the child's chronological age exceeded his or her mental age b. comparing children of different ages was awkward c. children of different ages could only be compared when the child's mental age exceeded his or her chronological age d. children could be compared using the concept of deviation IQ scores
Concept/Applied Module 7c **a**	28.	Twelve-year-old Rita received an IQ score of 75 on the original Stanford-Binet intelligence test. Her mental age would be a. 9 b. 16 c. 12 d. impossible to determine without more information
Concept/Applied Module 7c **a**	29.	Bonnie's IQ score was calculated using the formula developed by Lewis Terman, and the result was 92. This indicates that a. Bonnie's chronological age is greater than her mental age b. Bonnie's mental age is greater than her chronological age c. Bonnie's mental age and chronological age are the same d. the IQ score calculation was done incorrectly

Factual Module 7c	30.	The distinction between verbal and nonverbal abilities in intelligence was incorporated into intelligence testing by
b		a. Theodore Simon
		b. David Wechsler
		c. Alfred Binet
		d. Lewis Terman

Concept/Applied Module 7c
b

31. Joel is completing the Wechsler Adult Intelligence Scale, and one section of the test evaluates his arithmetic reasoning skills using story problems. His score on this section of the test will be used in the computation of his score on the
   a. aptitude scale
   b. verbal scale
   c. performance scale
   d. practical scale

Factual Module 7c
d

32. In a normal distribution of test scores
   a. all the scores fall within ±1 standard deviation of the mean
   b. approximately 68% of the scores fall within ±2 standard deviations of the mean
   c. approximately 50% of the scores fall within ±1 standard deviation of the mean
   d. approximately 68% of the scores fall within ±1 standard deviation of the mean

Factual Module 7c
a

33. One of the innovations that David Wechsler introduced to intelligence testing was
   a. the use of deviation IQ scores
   b. the use of repeated testing to increase the criterion-related validity of his test
   c. the use of an intelligence quotient that was the ratio of mental age to chronological age
   d. the use of mental age to compare children to chronological age norms

Concept/Applied Module 7c
c

34. Nan recently completed the Wechsler Adult Intelligence Scale and was told her score was 115. This scores means that
   a. Nan scored below the average for the test
   b. Nan scored higher than 98% of the sample used to establish norms for the test
   c. Nan scored one standard deviation above the mean
   d. the test was scored incorrectly because the highest possible score is 100

Concept/Applied Module 7c
b

35. Willard recently took an intelligence test and was told that he scored at the 50th percentile. This means that
   a. Willard's score falls below the average for the test
   b. Willard's IQ score would be 100
   c. Willard's IQ score would also be 50
   d. Willard answered half the questions on the exam correctly

Factual Module 7c
a

36. One of the criteria that may be used to classify an individual as gifted is
   a. a score higher than 130 on a standardized intelligence test
   b. a score higher than 100 on a standard intelligence test
   c. a score more than 1 standard deviation from the mean on a standardized intelligence test
   d. a mental age that exceeds chronological age by more than 3 years

Factual Module 7d
d

37. In family studies researchers assess hereditary influences by examining
   a. the resemblance of identical and fraternal twins with respect to a specific trait
   b. the resemblance between adopted children and their biological parents
   c. the resemblance between adopted children and their adoptive parents
   d. blood relatives to see how much they resemble one another on a specific trait

Critical Thinking Module 7d **c**	38.	If heredity affects intelligence then researchers should expect to find that a. cousins are more similar in intelligence than siblings b. fraternal twins are more similar in intelligence than identical twins c. siblings are more similar in intelligence than cousins d. adoptive siblings reared in the same home will have similar intelligence scores
Concept/Applied Module 7d **d**	39.	Family studies have found that the average correlation between biological parents and the children they raise is +.42. This indicates that a. the average correlation between family members is somewhat lower than would be expected by chance b. intelligence does not appear to run in families c. biological parents and their children have a genetic overlap of only 42% d. to some degree intelligence does run in families
Concept/Applied Module 7d **c**	40.	Family studies can indicate whether a trait runs in families, however they cannot provide conclusive evidence that the trait is influenced by heredity because a. random assignment is impossible in family studies b. there are no independent variables in family studies c. family members share not only genes but also similar environments d. there are too many dependent variables in family studies
Factual Module 7d **a**	41.	Twin studies of intelligence have found that average correlation reported for identical twins reared together is a. +.86 b. +.68 c. -.68 d. +1.00
Factual Module 7d **b**	42.	The results from studies that have compared correlations in intelligence between identical twins reared apart and fraternal twins reared together support the notion that a. intelligence is entirely determined by environmental factors b. intelligence is inherited to a considerable degree c. heredity does not contribute to similarities in intelligence scores d. shared environment explains most of the similarity in family intelligence scores
Concept/Applied Module 7d **c**	43.	The fact that the correlation in IQ scores between identical twins reared apart is higher than that between fraternal twins reared together suggests that intellectual development is a. influenced more by environmental factors than by genetics b. affected equally by genetics and environmental factors c. influenced more by genetics than by environmental factors d. not affected by either genetics or environmental factors
Factual Module 7d **d**	44.	Adoption studies indicate that a. siblings reared apart are more similar in intelligence than siblings reared together b. siblings reared together have the same correlation in intelligence scores as those seen in siblings reared apart c. biological siblings reared together are more similar in intelligence than children and their biological parents d. siblings reared together are more similar in intelligence than siblings reared apart

TESTING & INTELLIGENCE

Factual Module 7d **c**	45.	Most experts suggest that the heritability ratio for intelligence is a. approximately 75% b. less than 50% c. approximately 60% d. more than 90%
Factual Module 7d **b**	46.	The concept of a reaction range suggests that a. the environment sets upper and lower limits on intelligence, while genetic factors determine where a person will fall within that range b. heredity sets upper and lower limits on intelligence, while environment factors determine where a person will fall within that range c. intelligence is almost completely determined by environmental influences d. intelligence is almost completely determined by genetic factors
Concept/Applied Module 7d **c**	47.	According to the reaction range model a. children with average IQ scores will not have very wide reaction ranges b. children with average IQ scores are being raised in average-quality environments c. children raised in high-quality environments should score near the top of their reaction range d. children raised in high-quality environments will have higher IQ scores than children raised in poor-quality environments
Concept/Applied Module 7d **d**	48.	Kai has been raised in an intellectually-impoverished environment, with no access to books and very few age-appropriate toys. The reaction range model suggests that Kai will a. show a steady decrease in IQ score during early childhood and adolescence b. perform worse than the majority of his peers on standardized tests of intelligence c. have a narrower intellectual reaction range than children raised in more stimulating environments d. score near the bottom of his potential IQ range

Unit 8
Motivation & Emotion

Factual
Module 8a
b

1. In rats, electrical stimulation of the lateral hypothalamus generally leads to
   a. undereating and a significant weight loss
   b. overeating and a significant weight gain
   c. overeating, but a continual loss of weight
   d. undereating, but a significant increase in weight

Factual
Module 8a
a

2. Laboratory rats tend to eat more and balloon to several times their normal weight following lesioning of the
   a. ventromedial hypothalamus
   b. lateral hypothalamus
   c. pancreas
   d. vagus nerve

Concept/Applied
Module 8a
b

3. Dr. McCardle has implanted an electrode in the hypothalamus of a rat. When the rat's brain is electrically stimulated the rat stops eating. The electrode is most likely activating the
   a. magnocellular hypothalamus
   b. ventromedial hypothalamus
   c. lateral hypothalamus
   d. parvocellular hypothalamus

Factual
Module 8a
c

4. Closer examination of rats with lesions to the ventromedial hypothalamus revealed that they
   a. would eat any available food, including foods they had previously avoided
   b. showed a distinct preference for high-calorie foods
   c. became picky and would reject food that didn't taste good
   d. developed a binge-and-purge style of eating

Factual
Module 8a
d

5. The current view of the role of the hypothalamus in the regulation of hunger is
   a. the lateral hypothalamus starts the experience of hunger and the ventromedial stops the experience of hunger
   b. the ventromedial hypothalamus starts the experience of hunger and the lateral stops the experience of hunger
   c. the paraventricular nucleus is the key to understanding the role of ventromedial and lateral hypothalamus
   d. the notion that the lateral and ventromedial hypothalamus are on-off centers for hunger is too simplistic

Concept/Applied
Module 8a
a

6. When blood glucose levels start to fall, people are most likely to
   a. feel hungry
   b. lose interest in food
   c. become sexually aroused
   d. become agitated

Concept/Applied
Module 8a
b

7. Secretion of insulin by the pancreas is associated with
   a. increased blood flow to the lateral hypothalamus
   b. increased hunger
   c. decreased hunger
   d. decreased blood flow to the ventromedial hypothalamus

Concept/Applied Module 8a **d**	8.	For most individuals, insulin levels are higher at midday than late in the evening. This would help to explain why most people are a. thirstier in the late evening than in the middle of the day b. more active in the middle of the day than late in the evening c. sleepier in the late evening than in the middle of the day d. hungrier in the middle of the day than in the late evening
Concept/Applied Module 8a **b**	9.	Mr. Knez is trying to get his 7-year-old daughter to eat some vegetable-fried rice for the first time. Mr. Knez should be most successful in getting his daughter to sample the new dish if he a. tells his daughter she won't get any desert until she tries some of the fried rice b. eats some of the fried rice first, and shows a favorable reaction while he eats it c. carefully describes all the ingredients that are in the fried rice d. mixes it in with some other food that she enjoys eating
Factual Module 8a **c**	10.	Stanley Schachter conducted a study to determine whether hunger could be influenced by environmental cues. He manipulated the apparent time by altering a clock so that it ran fast. He found that when the subjects erroneously thought it was late in the afternoon a. both obese and nonobese subjects ate less than people who had not been mislead about the time b. both obese and nonobese subjects ate more than people who had not been mislead about the time c. obese subjects ate more than nonobese subjects d. nonobese subjects ate more than obese subjects
Factual Module 8a **c**	11.	Judith Rodin demonstrated that external cues, such as the sight, smell, or sound of a grilling steak can a. cause the glucostats to send signals to the hypothalamus b. reduce activity in the lateral hypothalamus c. elicit insulin secretions which lead to increased hunger d. directly activate the ventromedial hypothalamus
Factual Module 8a **d**	12.	Studies that investigated the link between stress and eating have found that a. stress leads to decreased eating in a substantial portion of people b. there is no link between stress and eating for most people c. there is only a link between stress and eating in overweight individuals d. stress leads to increased eating in a substantial portion of people
Concept/Applied Module 8b **a**	13.	Allison has the need to master difficult challenges, to outperform others, and to meet high standards of excellence. According to researchers such as McClelland and Atkinson, Allison most likely a. is high in achievement motivation b. is low in achievement motivation c. has a high fear of failure d. has high affiliation needs
Factual Module 8b **b**	14.	In Maslow's hierarchy of needs, achievement is found at a. the fifth level, among the cognitive needs b. the fourth level, among the esteem needs c. the third level, among the belongingness needs d. the seventh level, along with the need for self-actualization

Factual Module 8b **d**	15.	The need for achievement is usually measured with a. the Rorschach test b. the MMPI c. the 16 Personality Factor Assessment (16PF) d. the Thematic Apperception Test (TAT)
Concept/Applied Module 8b **c**	16.	Beecher is telling a story about a character on a TAT card. In this story Beecher focuses on the individual's desire to win, and how unhappy the person will be if she does not succeed in reaching her goal. Beecher's answer suggests that he most likely has a. a low need for achievement b. a high need for affiliation c. a high need for achievement d. a low need for affiliation
Factual Module 8b **b**	17.	David McClelland and his colleagues found that estimates of the need for achievement in the United States a. was lowest during the 1890s when inventive activity was at its peak b. peaked during the 1890s when inventive activity also peaked c. peaked during the 1820s when inventive activity was at its lowest d. shows no reliable correlation with the U. S. patent index
Concept/Applied Module 8b **a**	18.	Imagine that a sociologist had been tracking the patent index in a developing country for the past 30 years. Over that time the number of patents applied for has been steadily increasing. Based on David McClelland's work, it is likely that this country's need for achievement a. will also have steadily increased over the past 30 years b. will have shown a steady decline over the past 30 years c. will not have changed over the past 30 years d. will have fluctuated randomly over the past 30 years
Factual Module 8b **a**	19.	Research has shown that people who score high in the need for achievement a. are more likely to delay gratification in order to pursue long-term goals b. prefer non-competitive occupations c. show less persistence on difficult tasks d. are more likely to select tasks that have a high probability of success
Concept/Applied Module 8b **b**	20.	David is an individual who has a high need for achievement. If he were asked to play a ring-toss game you would expect that David would a. stand as close to the target peg as possible, to maximize his chance for success b. stand at an intermediate distance from the target peg c. stand as far from the target peg as possible, to maximize the task difficulty d. refuse to take part in such an easy task
Concept/Applied Module 8b **b**	21.	Cynthia is an individual who has a high need for achievement. She is trying to decide which one of four possible courses she should take as her final elective course for her degree. One of the courses is supposed to be an easy course with an "A" practically guaranteed for very little effort; one course is supposed to be moderately difficult, but with effort an "A" is possible; one course is supposed to be a "killer" course with little chance of earning a grade higher than a "B"; the fourth course is a seminar-style course with no grades assigned. You should expect that Cynthia will choose a. the course that has no assigned grades b. the moderately difficult course that requires effort for a high grade c. the easy course which practically guarantees a high grade d. the "killer" course to maximize her level of task difficulty

Factual Module 8b **a**	22.	The determinant of achievement that does not vary from situation to situation is a. the individual's motivation to achieve success b. the probability of success for the task c. the incentive value of success d. the negative value placed on failure
Concept/Applied Module 8b **c**	23.	The determinant of achievement that increases when a student is enrolled in a university course that is required for graduation is a. the probability of success b. the need for achievement c. the incentive value of success d. the need to avoid failure
Factual Module 8b **d**	24.	As tasks become easier, the probability of success a. decreases, and the incentive value for the task decreases b. increases, and the incentive value for the task increases c. decreases, and the incentive value for the task increases d. increases, and the incentive value for the task decreases
Factual Module 8c **a**	25.	The component of emotion that involves the conscious experience of intense feelings that can be difficult to control is the a. cognitive component b. physiological component c. behavioral component d. innate component
Concept/Applied Module 8c **b**	26.	Nadine has been waiting for her car to be serviced for over two hours and the mechanic has just told her that it will be at least another hour before the car is ready. Nadine feels furious when the mechanic tells her this. Nadine's reaction is part of a. the subcortical component of her emotional experience b. the cognitive component in her emotional experience c. the behavioral component in her emotional experience d. the physiological component in her emotional experience
Factual Module 8c **d**	27.	Activation of the sympathetic nervous system in the experience of emotions would be part of the a. cognitive component b. behavioral component c. adaptive component d. physiological component
Factual Module 8c **c**	28.	The autonomic responses that accompany emotion appear to be controlled by a. the frontal lobe in the cerebral cortex b. the brain stem and the reticular formation c. the hypothalamus, amygdala, and adjacent structures in the limbic system d. the cerebellum and the spinal cord
Concept/Applied Module 8c **c**	29.	Daniel decides to try sky diving. As he steps out of the airplane door for the first time his blood pressure rises rapidly and he can feel his heart start to pound. These reactions are part of a. the behavioral component in Daniel's emotional experience b. the cognitive component in Daniel's emotional experience c. the physiological component in Daniel's emotional experience d. the overt expression of Daniel's emotional experience

Factual Module 8c **b**	30.	One problem that has been identified with the use of polygraph tests is that the test a. is not accurate in detecting changes in blood pressure or respiration rate b. can sometimes produce false positives, indicating truthful people are lying c. often fails to use adequate control questions d. is only accurate if the individual being tested is highly aroused
Concept/Applied Module 8c **b**	31.	Victoria is extremely upset because she has been falsely accused of stealing money from her employer. Her lawyer has suggested that Victoria take a polygraph test to prove her innocence. She asks you whether she should agree to the test. Based on the research into the accuracy of polygraphs, you should tell Victoria that polygraphs a. are extremely accurate, and if Victoria is truly innocent she will pass with no problem b. can wrongly indicate that innocent people are guilty, or that guilty people are innocent c. sometimes wrongly indicate that innocent people are guilty, but are 100% accurate in detecting guilt d. sometimes wrongly indicate that guilty people are innocent, but are 100% accurate in detecting innocence
Factual Module 8c **d**	32.	The behavioral component of an emotional experience could include a. activation of the parasympathetic nervous system b. a subjective experience that is evaluative c. an increase in blood pressure and heart rate d. a smile or a frown
Concept/Applied Module 8c **a**	33.	Melissa is watching a slapstick comedy, and she can't stop herself from laughing and holding her sides while she watches the action. Melissa's reactions are part of a. the behavioral component in her emotional experience b. the physiological component in her emotional experience c. the cognitive component in her emotional experience d. the subcortical component of her emotional experience
Factual Module 8c **d**	34.	The facial feedback hypothesis suggests that a. the subjective experience of emotions creates the facial expression associated with that emotion b. the facial expression of others can affect our subjective emotional responses c. people innately mimic facial expressions that they see in photographs d. facial expressions help create the subjective experience of various emotions
Concept/Applied Module 8c **c**	35.	Eugene was posing for his girlfriend while she painted a picture for her art class. She had asked him to hold his mouth in a frown because she was trying to depict someone who was sad and dejected. Now that he has finished posing, Eugene finds that he is feeling somewhat unhappy, but he is not really sure why. This type of reaction is consistent with a. the two-factor theory of emotion b. the James-Lange theory of emotion c. the facial feedback hypothesis d. the common-sense view of emotion
Concept/Applied Module 8c **c**	36.	One piece of evidence that suggests the expression of some emotions may be innate is the finding that a. the same types of experience make people feel angry, regardless of their cultural background b. the same types of experience make people feel happy, regardless of their cultural background c. there is universal recognition of some emotional expressions d. people produce facial expressions that are not seen in nonhuman primates

Factual Module 8d **a**	37.	The theory of emotion which suggests that the conscious experience of an emotion results from an individual's perception of autonomic arousal is a. the James-Lange theory b. the Cannon-Bard theory c. Schachter's two-factor theory d. Plutchik's evolutionary theory
Factual Module 8d **b**	38.	The common sense view of emotions, based on everyday logic suggests that a. our cognitive interpretation of events determines our emotional response b. the conscious experience of an emotion leads to physiological arousal c. physiological arousal produces the conscious experience of an emotion d. both physiological arousal and the conscious experience of an emotion happen simultaneously
Concept/Applied Module 8d **b**	39.	As Vivian is walking down the street she hears a loud crash behind her. Based on the James-Lange theory of emotion, Vivian should report a. "My pulse is racing so I must be scared." b. "I feel scared because my pulse is racing." c. "That noise caused my pulse race and made me feel scared." d. "My racing pulse means I am scared because I interpret this as a dangerous situation."
Critical Thinking Module 8d **d**	40.	Imagine that an individual has taken medication that has lowered his or her overall level of autonomic arousal. If this person reports less intense emotional experiences it would provide some support for a. the Cannon-Bard theory of emotion b. the common-sense view of emotion c. the facial feedback hypothesis d. the James-Lange theory of emotion
Factual Module 8d **a**	41.	The Cannon-Bard theory of emotion suggests that a. emotions occur when the thalamus sends signals simultaneously to the cortex and the autonomic nervous system b. the conscious experience of an emotion results from an individual's perception of autonomic arousal c. the experience of emotion depends on autonomic arousal and a cognitive interpretation of that arousal d. humans are equipped with a small number of innate emotions with proven adaptive value
Factual Module 8d **c**	42.	According to the Cannon-Bard theory of emotion a. different patterns of autonomic activation lead to the experience of different emotions b. emotions are innate reactions that originate in subcortical brain structures c. people experiencing very different emotions exhibit almost identical patterns of autonomic arousal d. both arousal and a cognitive interpretation must be present before an emotion will be labeled
Concept/Applied Module 8d **d**	43.	Recent studies that have detected some subtle differences in the patterns of autonomic arousal that accompany basic emotions such as happiness, anger and fear lend some support to a. the Cannon-Bard theory of emotion b. Schachter's two-factor theory of emotion c. Izard's evolutionary theory of emotion d. the James-Lange theory of emotion

Factual Module 8d **a**	44.	The view of emotion which suggests we may attach different labels to physiological arousal on the basis of our cognitive interpretation of environmental cues, is a. Schachter's two-factor theory of emotion b. the James-Lange theory of emotion c. the Cannon-Bard theory of emotion d. Izard's evolutionary theory of emotion
Concept/Applied Module 8d **a**	45.	Barry takes an antihistamine, but he doesn't realize that the medication will also increase his overall level of autonomic arousal. Thirty minutes after he has taken the medication he is introduced to Danielle. If Barry incorrectly attributes his increased arousal as attraction for Danielle it would lend support to a. Schachter's two-factor theory of emotion b. the James-Lange theory of emotion c. the Cannon-Bard theory of emotion d. Izard's evolutionary theory of emotion
Factual Module 8d **b**	46.	Evolutionary theories assume that a. the conscious experience of an emotion results from the labeling of discrete physiological states of arousal b. emotions should be immediately recognizable under most conditions without much thought c. the conscious experience of an emotion depends on the cognitive interpretation we place on the situation d. emotions are learned responses that develop from environmental interactions
Factual Module 8d **d**	47.	Tomkins, Izard and Plutchik have all identified eight to ten primary emotions. Three of the emotions that appear on all their lists are a. joy, contempt, and guilt b. shame, distress, and sadness c. surprise, fear, and sadness d. fear, anger, and surprise
Concept/Applied Module 8d **c**	48.	When the strikers learned that their union's latest offer had been turned down by management, Roger was annoyed, Sylvester was angry, and Clyde was enraged. Robert Plutnik would suggest that these three men were a. experiencing different unique secondary emotions b. experiencing different unique primary emotions c. experiencing different intensities of the same primary emotion d. each labeling their emotions differently due to differences in experience

Unit 9
Human Development

Factual Module 9a c	1.	The first two weeks of the prenatal period are called a. the fetal stage b. the embryonic stage c. the germinal stage d. the placental stage
Concept/Applied Module 9a d	2.	Melissa conceived a baby three days ago, and does not yet know she is pregnant. Her pregnancy is currently at the a. embryonic stage b. fetal stage c. placental stage d. germinal stage
Factual Module 9a a	3.	The embryonic stage of prenatal development occurs during a. weeks 3 through 8 of the pregnancy b. the first two weeks of the pregnancy c. the last seventh months of the pregnancy d. the second trimester of the pregnancy
Factual Module 9a b	4.	The final stage of prenatal development is the a. stage of the zygote b. fetal stage c. embryonic stage d. germinal stage
Factual Module 9a c	5.	The period of greatest vulnerability during the prenatal period, and the time when most miscarriages occur is a. the germinal stage b. the fetal stage c. the embryonic stage d. once the fetus has reached the age of viability
Factual Module 9a d	6.	Most major structural birth defects are due to problems that occur a. during the germinal stage of prenatal development b. during the fetal stage of prenatal development c. once the fetus has reached the age of viability d. during the embryonic stage of prenatal development
Concept/Applied Module 9a b	7.	Sally is currently pregnant and she is concerned about taking some over-the-counter medication for a cold she has. She should be most concerned if her pregnancy is currently at the a. placental stage b. embryonic stage c. germinal stage d. fetal stage

| Factual
Module 9a
a | 8. | Brain cells develop most rapidly
a. during the fetal stage of prenatal development
b. during the embryonic stage of prenatal development
c. during the germinal stage of prenatal development
d. before the zygote is formed |

| Concept/Applied
Module 9a
a | 9. | Jennifer is pregnant, and when her husband Michael comes home form work she tells him that she felt the baby kick for the first time. Based on this information you could conclude that Jennifer's pregnancy is currently in the
a. fetal stage
b. embryonic stage
c. germinal stage
d. sensorimotor stage |

| Factual
Module 9a
b | 10. | The fetus typically reaches the age of viability sometime between
a. the 14th and the 18th week of the pregnancy
b. the 22nd and the 26th week of the pregnancy
c. the 8th and the 12th week of the pregnancy
d. the 34th and the 38th week of the pregnancy |

| Critical Thinking
Module 9a
b | 11. | The 24th week of pregnancy is often set as the legal upper limit for medical abortions. At this point in time, the milestone reached by the developing fetus is
a. the heart and circulatory systems begin to function
b. the age of viability has been reached
c. spontaneous movement is apparent for the first time
d. the fetus begins to show periods of sleep and wakefulness |

| Factual
Module 9a
a | 12. | Cross-cultural comparisons of infant mortality rates have shown that the United States
a. ranks 21st in the prevention of infant mortality
b. ranks 1st in the prevention of infant mortality
c. ranks 98th, and has the highest overall infant mortality rates
d. ranks 4th in the prevention of infant mortality |

| Concept/Applied
Module 9b
c | 13. | Juanita is 3 months old and her parents take care of her basic needs poorly. Sometimes they are very attentive, but often they are less attentive, and she can cry for some time before they take care of her. Based on Erikson's theory, it is likely that Juanita will develop
a. a sense of inadequacy and inferiority
b. role confusion
c. a mistrusting, pessimistic personality
d. feelings of guilt |

| Factual
Module 9b
c | 14. | According to Erikson, during the first year of life young infants must resolve the psychosocial crisis of
a. initiative versus guilt
b. accommodation versus assimilation
c. trust versus mistrust
d. generativity versus stagnation |

| Factual
Module 9b
d | 15. | According to Erikson, the key question, "Can I do things myself or must I always rely on others?" emerges during the stage of
a. identity versus role confusion
b. industry versus inferiority
c. generativity versus self-absorption
d. autonomy versus shame and doubt |

Factual Module 9b **d**	16.	According to Erickson, the psychosocial crisis of autonomy versus shame and doubt occurs a. during the first year of life b. between the ages of 6 and 12 c. during the middle adult years d. between the ages of 1 and 3
Factual Module 9b **a**	17.	According to Erikson, the stage during which parents need to support their children's emerging independence while maintaining appropriate controls is the stage of a. initiative versus guilt b. industry versus inferiority c. trust versus mistrust d. intimacy versus isolation
Concept/Applied Module 9b **b**	18.	Dimitri is 8 years old and is learning to function effectively in school. He receives good grades and generally feels that he can be successful at tasks he attempts. According to Erikson, Dimitri is likely in the process of developing a sense of a. autonomy b. industry c. integrity d. trust
Factual Module 9b **d**	19.	The rapid physical changes that occur during adolescence, along with changes in cognitive processes that promote personal introspection may trigger the psychosocial crisis that Erikson referred to as a. intimacy versus isolation b. integrity versus despair c. trust versus mistrust d. identity versus role confusion
Factual Module 9b **c**	20.	James Marcia suggested that people who simply refuse to confront the challenge of charting a life course and committing to an ideology are in a state of a. identity achievement b. moratorium c. identity diffusion d. foreclosure
Concept/Applied Module 9b **c**	21.	Dinah is near the end of her second year in University and she is still exploring the options for her major. She is starting to think seriously about pursuing an engineering degree, but she is also interested in medicine. She feels it is important for her to reach a final decision before the end of the school year, and she is investigating both career options in great detail. According to James Marcia, Dinah would considered to be in a state of a. foreclosure b. identity diffusion c. moratorium d. identity postponement
Factual Module 9b **d**	22.	According to Erikson, the key question that emerges during early adulthood is a. "Have I lived a full life or have I failed?" b. "Will I produce something of real value?" c. "Am I successful or am I worthless?" d. "Shall I share my life with others or should I live alone?"

Factual Module 9b **a**	23.	According to Erikson, the psychosocial stage of development associated with middle adulthood is the stage of a. generativity versus self-absorption b. identity versus role confusion c. initiative versus guilt d. integrity versus despair
Concept/Applied Module 9b **b**	24.	Conrad is 73 years old. Lately he has been dwelling on mistakes he made in the past and also on his imminent death. According to Erikson, Conrad is likely experiencing a sense of a. self-absorption b. despair c. integrity d. isolation
Factual Module 9c **a**	25.	According to Piaget, the process of interpreting new experiences in terms of existing mental structures without changing them is called a. assimilation b. accommodation c. centration d. conservation
Concept/Applied Module 9c **b**	26.	Often new environments and experiences have characteristics in common with experiences people have encountered in the past. In these types of situations people can often respond appropriately by applying the process Piaget referred to as a. object permanence b. assimilation c. accommodation d. centration
Concept/Applied Module 9c **c**	27.	Five-year-old Brittany thought that her friend's new pet was a kitty until she realized it hopped and it didn't purr. The change in Brittany's understanding of her friend's new pet illustrates the process that Piaget referred to as a. assimilation b. centration c. accommodation d. object permanence
Factual Module 9c **a**	28.	According to Piaget, the sensorimotor period of development lasts from a. birth through the age of 2 b. the age of 11 through adulthood c. the age of 2 through the age of 7 d. the start of the fetal stage through to the time of birth
Factual Module 9c **d**	29.	According Piaget, from the age of 7 through to age 11 a child is in the a. preoperational period of cognitive development b. assimilation versus accommodation period of cognitive development c. formal operational period of cognitive development d. concrete operational period of cognitive development
Factual Module 9c **d**	30.	According to Piaget, object permanence develops when a child recognizes that a. physical quantities remain constant in spite of changes in appearance or shape b. it is sometimes necessary to focus on more than one aspect of a problem c. assimilation is typically more useful that accommodation d. objects continue to exist, even when they are no longer visible

Concept/Applied Module 9c **b**	31.	Franklin's mother hides his teddy bear under a pillow. Franklin acts as though the teddy bear no longer exists, and he makes no attempt to search for it. Based on this information, Franklin should be in a. the formal operational period of cognitive development b. the sensorimotor period of cognitive development c. the concrete operational period of cognitive development d. the preoperational period of cognitive development
Factual Module 9c **a**	32.	Egocentrism in thinking is characterized by a. a limited ability to share another person's point of view b. the tendency to focus on just one feature of a problem c. the inability to envision reversing an action d. changing existing mental structures to explain new experiences
Concept/Applied Module 9c **d**	33.	Allen watches as a researcher pours water from a short, fat beaker into a tall, skinny beaker. He confidently announces that the tall, skinny beaker now has more water because the water is higher in that beaker. Allen's response illustrates the concept that Piaget referred to as a. object permanence b. hierarchical classification c. egocentrism d. centration
Factual Module 9c **c**	34.	The typical order that children master various aspects of conservation is a. number, then area, and finally mass b. mass, then area, and finally number c. number, then mass, and finally area d. area, then number, and finally mass
Concept/Applied Module 9c **c**	35.	Amanda watched as a researcher placed four apples and two oranges on the table. The researcher asked her if there were more apples or more pieces of fruit, and Amanda correctly answered that there were more pieces of fruit. Amanda's answer indicates that she has mastered a. conservation of number b. object permanence c. hierarchical classification problems d. preaccommodation
Factual Module 9c **d**	36.	During the formal operational period a. object permanence emerges b. the principle of conservation is finally mastered c. children can successfully use centration to solve problems d. abstract reasoning skills emerge
Factual Module 9d **a**	37.	In general, preconventional moral reasoning a. declines continually as children mature b. emerges at about age 10 and increases steadily after that c. remains constant from age 7 through age 16 d. increases to a peak at age 13 and then begins to decline
Factual Module 9d **b**	38.	At the preconventional level of moral reasoning, children a. generally don't comply with rules b. comply with rules to avoid punishment or to obtain rewards c. begin to draw distinctions between what is legal and what is moral d. comply with rules to promote harmony or social order

Concept/Applied Module 9d **a**	39.	If an individual at the preconventional level or moral reasoning had to choose between stealing and letting a loved one die, that person might a. refuse to steal because getting caught would mean they would go to jail b. steal because friends would think they were a coward if they didn't try to save the loved one c. steal because you have a duty to save people who you love and care for d. steal because something that is legally wrong can still be the morally correct thing to do
Concept/Applied Module 9d **d**	40.	During the Viet Nam War Percy volunteered for the Marines. He wanted to go to war because he thought he might become a hero and win a medal. Percy's reasons for going to war reflect a. an authority orientation in moral reasoning b. a social contract orientation in moral reasoning c. an individual principles orientation in moral reasoning d. a naive reward orientation in moral reasoning
Factual Module 9d **d**	41.	In general, conventional moral reasoning a. declines continually as children mature b. emerges at about age 10 and increases steadily after that c. remains constant from age 7 through age 16 d. increases to a peak at age 13 and then begins to decline
Factual Module 9d **c**	42.	Children comply with rules to promote harmony and social order at the a. preconventional level of moral reasoning b. postconventional level of moral reasoning c. conventional level of moral reasoning d. concrete level of moral reasoning
Concept/Applied Module 9d **a**	43.	If an individual at the conventional level or moral reasoning had to choose between stealing and letting a loved one die, that person might a. refuse to steal because society's rules and laws should always be obeyed b. refuse to steal because getting caught would mean they would go to jail c. steal because something that is legally wrong can still be the morally correct thing to do d. steal because human life is more important than social laws
Concept/Applied Module 9d **b**	44.	During the Viet Nam War Mark was in the Air Force. He was scared to go to war, but he believed that a person has an obligation to follow society's rules and laws. Mark's reasons for going to war reflect a. an individual principles orientation in moral reasoning b. an authority orientation in moral reasoning c. a naive reward orientation in moral reasoning d. a good boy/good girl orientation in moral reasoning
Factual Module 9d **b**	45.	In general, postconventional moral reasoning a. declines continually as children mature b. emerges at about age 10 and increases steadily after that c. remains constant from age 7 through age 16 d. increases to a peak at age 13 and then begins to decline
Factual Module 9d **a**	46.	At the postconventional level of moral reasoning, people a. begin to draw distinctions between what is legal and what is moral b. comply with rules to avoid punishment or to obtain rewards c. comply with rules to promote harmony or social order d. generally don't comply with rules

Concept/Applied 47. If an individual at the postconventional level or moral reasoning had to choose
Module 9d   between stealing and letting a loved one die, that person might
b
    a. steal because friends would think they were a coward if they didn't try to save the loved one
    b. steal because something that is legally wrong can still be the morally correct thing to do
    c. steal because you have a duty to save people who you love and care for
    d. refuse to steal because getting caught would mean they would go to jail

Concept/Applied 48. Wilfred registered as a conscientious objector during the Viet Nam War. He
Module 9d   believed that it was wrong to take the life of another person, and if it was necessary
c   he was willing to go to jail, rather than take part in an armed conflict. Wilfred's
                    reasons for not going to war reflect
    a. an authority orientation in moral reasoning
    b. a good boy/good girl orientation in moral reasoning
    c. an individual principles orientation in moral reasoning
    d. a punishment orientation in moral reasoning

Unit 10
Personality Theory

Concept/Applied
Module 10a
a

1. Annie is currently thinking about all the things she has to do before she goes to her first class. She is mentally making lists of all these things so she will remember to do them on her way to school. According to Freud, these thoughts are contained in
   a. Annie's conscious mind
   b. Annie's preconscious mind
   c. Annie's unconscious mind
   d. Annie's superego

Factual
Module 10a
a

2. According to Freud, the preconscious contains
   a. material which is not in current awareness, but which can easily be retrieved
   b. thoughts and memories that are well inaccessible to conscious awareness
   c. thoughts that occupy the focus of current attention
   d. the decision-making component of our personality

Concept/Applied
Module 10a
b

3. When Jacob was five he was burned quite badly while he was playing in the kitchen. Jacob is now 30 years old, and he has no memory of the accident or the hospital stay. When his parents talk to him about it he is convinced they are confused and that the accident must have happened to one of his brothers. According to Freud, the memory of the accident is in Jacob's
   a. preconscious
   b. unconscious
   c. conscious
   d. subconscious

Factual
Module 10a
c

4. According to Freud, the id is the portion of our personality that
   a. operates according to the reality principle and makes decisions
   b. incorporates social standards of right and wrong
   c. houses raw biological urges and operates according to the pleasure principle
   d. houses material which is not in current awareness, but which can be easily retrieved

Factual
Module 10a
d

5. According to Freud, the portion of our personality which seeks to delay gratification until appropriate outlets and situations can be found is the
   a. the preconscious
   b. the id
   c. the superego
   d. the ego

Concept/Applied
Module 10a
b

6. Roland has extremely strong moral standards. However, whenever he fails to live up to the high standards he sets for himself, Roland becomes overwhelmed by feelings of guilt and anxiety. Freud would most likely suggest that Roland's personality is dominated by
   a. feelings of incongruence
   b. his superego
   c. his id
   d. his ego

Concept/Applied Module 10a **b**	7.	Donavon hates his boss. To deal with the anxiety of working for someone he dislikes intensely Donavon has convinced himself that his boss can't stand him, and that his boss purposely gives Donavon all the bad assignments in the company. According to Freud, Donavon may be unconsciously dealing with the anxiety caused by his feelings toward his boss by using the defense mechanism of a. reaction formation b. projection c. displacement d. denial
Factual Module 10a **a**	8.	Rationalization is a defense mechanism in which a. false but plausible excuses are created to justify unacceptable behavior b. distressing thoughts and feelings are buried in the unconscious c. an individual reverts to immature pattern of behavior d. a person refuses to face up to unpleasant realities
Factual Module 10a **d**	9.	The defense mechanism that is at work when a person diverts emotional feelings (such as anger) from their original source to a substitute target is a. projection b. denial c. reaction formation d. displacement
Factual Module 10a **c**	10.	According to Freud, the handling of a child's feeding experiences is crucial to subsequent development during the a. anal stage b. phallic stage c. oral stage d. latency stage
Concept/Applied Module 10a **c**	11.	Garth has just turned four, and he has starting acting with hostility toward his father. At the same time, he wants his mother's undivided attention all the time. According to Freud, Garth would currently be in the a. genital stage of personality development b. latency stage of personality development c. phallic stage of personality development d. anal stage of personality development
Factual Module 10a **d**	12.	According to Freud, the latency period a. emerges when the child enters puberty b. emerges around age 4 and lasts until about age 6 c. unfolds during the second year of life d. lasts from age six through puberty
Factual Module 10b **a**	13.	In terms of personality development, Skinner a. made no provision for internal personality structures that couldn't be observed b. argued that private, unobservable cognitive processes were the basis for all observable behavior c. believed that unconscious motivation was shaped by reinforcers and punishers d. suggested that to understand an individual's personality you had to look at the person's role models
Factual Module 10b **b**	14.	In Skinner's view, personality is a. a product of unconscious motivation and conflict b. a collection of response tendencies that are tied to various stimulus situations c. the result of observational learning and role models d. a function of internal biological processes

Concept/Applied Module 10b **c**	15.	Dr. Que believes that early childhood experiences have no more influence on personality than later experiences have, and she thinks that our personality is simply a collection of response tendencies that are emitted in different situations. Dr. Que's views most closely mirror those of a. Sigmund Freud b. Carl Rogers c. B. F. Skinner d. Sidney Sheldon
Concept/Applied Module 10b **c**	16.	Alex is a shy person who seldom socializes with other people. He has found that if he keeps to himself he seldom feels anxious or worried about what other people might be thinking. Based on principles of operant conditioning, Alex's shyness is most likely a result of a. positive reinforcement b. punishment c. negative reinforcement d. extinction
Concept/Applied Module 10b **d**	17.	Sara is a dishonest individual who has a tendency to lie. She has found that when she lies she is usually able to get what she wants from other people. Based on principles of operant conditioning, the dishonest aspect of Sara's personality is most likely a result of a. negative reinforcement b. punishment c. extinction d. positive reinforcement
Concept/Applied Module 10b **b**	18.	Deirdre used to monopolize meetings and constantly interrupt other people when they were talking. In her new job the people who she works with simply ignore her when she interrupts during meetings, and carry on as if she hadn't spoken. Consequently, Deirdre has become less assertive and outspoken. Based on principles of operant conditioning, Deirdre's new non-assertive characteristics are most likely a result of a. positive reinforcement b. extinction c. negative reinforcement d. punishment
Concept/Applied Module 10b **a**	19.	Kermit used to be a fairly generous individual, but it seemed that whenever he would loan money to one of his friends he was never repaid. Consequently, Kermit is no longer a generous individual. Based on principles of operant conditioning, Kermit's lack of generosity is most likely a result of a. punishment b. positive reinforcement c. negative reinforcement d. extinction
Factual Module 10b **a**	20.	Skinner's theory of personality views personality development as a. a continuous, lifelong journey b. a series of discrete stages that unfold from birth through old age c. a series of stages that unfold in the first few years of life d. a biological process that is largely unaffected by environment or culture

Factual Module 10b **c**	21.	The main difference between Bandura's social learning theory of personality development and Skinner's view of personality development is that Bandura a. does not believe that personality is shaped through learning b. focused on unconscious determinants of external behavior c. suggests that much of what people learn is acquired through observational learning d. believed that personality continued to develop during adolescence and adulthood
Concept/Applied Module 10b **b**	22.	Roberta is an impulsive child who seldom waits for her turn when playing with other children. Roberta's mother is also an impulsive individual often seems to act before she thinks. The theorist who would most likely suggest that Roberta has learned to be impulsive from watching her mother is a. B. F. Skinner b. Albert Bandura c. Sigmund Freud d. Carl Rogers
Concept/Applied Module 10b **d**	23.	Mr. Valento is a very patient individual who always has time for any questions his children might ask. If Mr. Valento's children grow up to be patient individuals, the development of this personality trait would be best explained using the concept of a. positive reinforcement b. extinction c. rationalization d. observational learning
Concept/Applied Module 10b **d**	24.	In explaining why Robert is cheerful, conscientious, and willing to share, a psychologist who took an observational learning perspective toward personality development would consider Robert's a. previous learning experiences and his history of reinforcement b. unconsciously repressed feelings of anxiety c. self concept and his interactions with others d. role models
Factual Module 10c **d**	25.	The theoretical orientation to personality that emphasizes humans' unique potential for personal growth is a. the psychodynamic approach b. the behavioral approach c. the biological approach d. the humanistic approach
Factual Module 10c **b**	26.	According to Carl Rogers, two processes that tend to add stability to personality are a. denial and resistance to discordant information b. self-fulfilling prophecies and resistance to discordant information c. self-fulfilling prophecies and rationalization d. incongruence and self-actualization
Factual Module 10c **a**	27.	If your self-concept is reasonably accurate, it is said to be a. congruent with reality b. incongruent with reality c. conditional on acceptance d. unconditional on acceptance

Factual Module 10c **a**	28.	Carl Rogers was concerned with a. the way in which childhood experiences promoted congruence or incongruence b. the way in which the individual learns to balance the demands of the id, the ego and the superego c. how adult role models shape personality characteristics in children d. the way environmental contingencies influence personality development
Factual Module 10c **c**	29.	According to Carl Rogers, incongruence will develop when a. parental love is unconditional b. basic physiological needs cannot be adequately met c. parental love seems conditional d. the personality destabilizes during adolescence
Concept/Applied Module 10c **b**	30.	Fourteen-year-old Elsie knows that she has made some bad choices at times, and these choices have gotten her into serious trouble on a number of occasions. However, she is confident that her parents love her, in spite of her mistakes. Based on the theory developed by Carl Rogers, Elsie perceives her parents' affection as _____ and she is likely to develop _____ in her self-concept. a. conditional; incongruence b. unconditional; congruence c. unconditional; incongruence d. conditional; congruence
Concept/Applied Module 10c **b**	31.	According to Carl Rogers, when parents make their affection unconditional and show affection to their children, they are promoting a. observational learning and identification b. congruence between their children's self concept and their actual experiences c. incongruence between their children's self concept and their actual experiences d. the resolution of the Oedipal conflict
Factual Module 10c **d**	32.	According to Maslow, human needs can be represented a. using an interlinked chain b. using a circle c. in the form of a closed feedback loop d. in the form of a pyramid
Concept/Applied Module 10c **a**	33.	As we move up in Maslow's needs hierarchy, the needs that emerge become a. more social and less biological b. more congruent and less incongruent c. more biological and less social d. more incongruent and less congruent
Concept/Applied Module 10c **c**	34.	Ramon is homeless and he is never certain from one day to the next whether or not he will have enough to eat or find a warm place to sleep. According to Maslow, Ramon is most likely a. functioning at the top tier of the needs hierarchy b. experiencing incongruence in his self-concept c. functioning at the bottom tier of the needs hierarchy d. acting in a way that promotes a self-fulfilling prophecy
Factual Module 10c **a**	35.	According to Maslow, growth needs such as the need for knowledge, understanding, and aesthetic beauty will not become activated until a. the need for love and belongingness, and esteem needs have been met b. a person's need for self-actualization has been activated c. a person develops a congruent self-concept d. other people begin to provide unconditional love and acceptance

Factual Module 10c **c**	36.	Maslow suggested that the characteristics of self-actualizing individuals include a. total congruence and a strong superego b. extroversion, openness, and agreeableness c. spontaneity and a balance between polarities in personality d. dependence on others and a need to belong
Concept/Applied Module 10d **c**	37.	Drew Carrey has a soft, round body. Based on Sidney Sheldon's theory of personality, you would expect that Drew would be a. energetic, competitive, and aggressive b. apprehensive, self-conscious, and introverted c. sociable, relaxed, and even-tempered d. egocentric, impulsive, and moody
Concept/Applied Module 10d **d**	38.	Jose is energetic, competitive and aggressive. Based on Sheldon's theory of personality, Jose is most likely to have a. an endomorphic physique b. an ectomorphic physique c. a transmorphic physique d. a mesomorphic physique
Concept/Applied Module 10d **b**	39.	According to Sheldon's theory of personality, a person who has a thin, frail body type would most likely display personality characteristics such as a. apprehension, affection, and competitiveness b. inhibition, apprehension, and self-consciousness c. sociability, even-temperedness, and affection d. aggression, boldness, and competitiveness
Factual Module 10d **a**	40.	According to Eysenck, people who condition easily are more likely to develop the personality trait of a. introversion b. extroversion c. mesomorphism d. altruism
Concept/Applied Module 10d **b**	41.	The strongest evidence that would support the theory that personality has a genetic basis would be the finding that personality traits correlated more highly among a. identical twins reared together than among fraternal twins reared together b. identical twins reared apart than among fraternal twins reared together c. fraternal twins reared apart than among identical twins reared together d. fraternal twins reared together than among fraternal twins reared apart
Factual Module 10d **c**	42.	A landmark study conducted at the University of Minnesota assessed the correlations in personality traits between pairs of identical and fraternal twins. Some of the twins were reared together and some were reared apart. This study found the strongest heritability for the personality trait of a. positive emotionality b. extroversion c. constraint d. aggressiveness

Unit 11
Abnormal Behavior & Therapy

Factual
Module 11a
d

1. Anxiety disorders are
   a. fairly common, occurring in over 50% of the population
   b. relatively rare, occurring in approximately 7% of the population
   c. relative rare, occurring in less than 2% of the population
   d. fairly common, occurring in approximately 17% of the population

Factual
Module 11a
a

2. Which of the following is not an example of an anxiety disorder?
   a. bipolar disorder
   b. panic disorder
   c. obsessive-compulsive disorder
   d. phobic disorder

Concept/Applied
Module 11a
c

3. For the past year Melvin has been worrying constantly about minor things. He has a chronic, high level of anxiety and has been experiencing dizziness, sweating, and heart palpitations. Melvin's symptoms are consistent with those seen in
   a. phobic disorder
   b. panic disorder
   c. generalized anxiety disorder
   d. obsessive-compulsive disorder

Factual
Module 11a
b

4. A phobic disorder is marked by
   a. persistent, uncontrollable thoughts and the urge to engage in senseless rituals
   b. a persistent and irrational fear of objects or situations that present no real danger
   c. chronic, high anxiety levels that are not tied to any specific threats
   d. recurrent attacks of overwhelming anxiety that occur suddenly and unexpectedly

Concept/Applied
Module 11a
a

5. Kass has experienced several recurrent attacks of overwhelming anxiety that occurred suddenly and unexpectedly. She is now concerned about being in public because she is never sure when or where she will be overcome by anxiety. In this case Kass is displaying symptoms consistent with
   a. agoraphobia
   b. claustrophobia
   c. bipolar disorder
   d. obsessive-compulsive disorder

Concept/Applied
Module 11a
c

6. Elbert finds that he can't stop thinking about all the germs that could contaminate him when he touches something. No matter where he is, or what he is doing, he finds he can't stop thinking about possible contamination. Elbert's uncontrollable and unwanted thoughts illustrate the concept of
   a. a compulsion
   b. a delusion
   c. an obsession
   d. brontophobia

Concept/Applied Module 11a a	7.	Ginny has been diagnosed with an anxiety disorder, and she is being treated with a drug that blocks the reuptake of serotonin. It is most likely that Ginny is being treated for a. obsessive-compulsive disorder b. generalized anxiety disorder c. a specific phobic disorder d. a schizophrenic disorder
Factual Module 11a d	8.	Therapeutic drugs that reduce excessive anxiety appear to a. decrease activity at GABA receptor sites b. increase activity at norepinephrine receptor sites c. decrease activity at norepinephrine receptor sites d. increase activity at GABA receptor sites
Factual Module 11a b	9.	Many phobias appear to be acquired through a. observational learning and maintained through classical conditioning b. classical conditioning and maintained through operant conditioning c. operant conditioning and maintained through classical conditioning d. classical conditioning and maintained through observational learning
Factual Module 11a b	10.	According to cognitive theories, some people are more likely to suffer from problems with anxiety because they tend to a. misinterpret threatening situations as harmless b. selectively recall information that seems threatening c. focus insufficient attention on perceived threats d. show signs of communication deviance
Factual Module 11a b	11.	In one research study anxious and nonanxious subjects read sentences that could be interpreted in either a threatening or a nonthreatening way. The researchers found a. both groups were equally likely to interpret the sentences in a threatening way b. that the anxious subjects were more likely to interpret the sentences in a threatening way c. that the anxious subjects were less likely to interpret the sentences in a threatening way d. neither group tended to interpret the sentences in a threatening way
Concept/Applied Module 11a a	12.	Hugo was recently diagnosed with panic disorder. In taking Hugo's case history at the time the diagnosis was made, his therapist most likely found a. a dramatic increase in Hugo's stress levels in the previous month b. chronic high stress that had been present for several years c. unresolved unconscious conflicts stemming from Hugo's early childhood d. high self-esteem and a tendency toward extroversion
Factual Module 11b c	13.	Mood disorders tend to be a. chronic, with few periods when the individual is unaffected b. escalating, with each successive episode having more severe symptoms than the previous episode c. episodic, interspersed among periods of normality d. diminishing, with each successive episode having less severe symptoms than the previous episode
Factual Module 11b c	14.	An individual who shows disordered mood shifts in two directions is likely to be classified as having a. schizophrenia b. obsessive-compulsive disorder c. bipolar disorder d. hyperdelusional disorder

Factual Module 11b **d**	15.	Age-related trends in the onset of mood disorders indicate that a. the onset of depression is age-related but the onset of bipolar disorder is not strongly related to age b. the onset of both bipolar disorder and depression are strongly related to age c. neither bipolar disorder nor depression have an onset strongly related to age d. the onset of bipolar disorder is age-related but the onset of depression is not strongly related to age
Factual Module 11b **d**	16.	Which of the following statements is <u>not</u> accurate in relation to depressive disorders? a. They are quite common and affect approximately 7% of the population. b. Individuals with depressive disorders often show insomnia and loss of appetite. c. Individuals with depressive disorders often show slowed thinking and speech. d. They are age related, with onset typically occurring during adolescence.
Concept/Applied Module 11b **a**	17.	For the past month Akiem seems to have lost interest in most of his normal activities. He feels constantly gloomy and unable to make decisions. He has had difficulty sleeping and he is constantly fatigued. Akiem's symptoms are most consistent with those seen in a. depressive disorder b. bipolar disorder c. generalized anxiety disorder d. a schizophrenic disorder
Concept/Applied Module 11b **c**	18.	Evelyn has been extremely hyperactive for the past three days, and she has been getting by with only 3 hours sleep each night. Her thoughts seem to be going off in all directions, and she is convinced that she can pilot a hot-air balloon non-stop around the world, even though she has never actually been in a hot-air balloon before. Evelyn's symptoms suggest that she is currently experiencing a. a schizophrenic episode b. generalized anxiety disorder c. a manic episode d. a psychotic depression
Factual Module 11b **d**	19.	Studies that have investigated genetic links in mood disorders have found that a. fraternal twins have a concordance rate of 67%, compared to a concordance rate of 15% for identical twins b. both identical twins and fraternal twins have a concordance rate of 67% c. both identical twins and fraternal twins have a concordance rate of 15% d. identical twins have a concordance rate of 67%, compared to a concordance rate of 15% for fraternal twins
Factual Module 11b **b**	20.	The two neurotransmitters that have been most closely linked to the onset of depressive disorders are a. GABA and dopamine b. norepinephrine and serotonin c. norepinephrine and GABA d. serotonin and GABA
Concept/Applied Module 11b **c**	21.	Based on Seligman's learned helplessness model of depression, an individual would be <u>least</u> vulnerable to depression if he or she tended to make a. internal, stable, global attributions b. external, stable, global attributions c. external, unstable, specific attributions d. internal, stable, specific attributions

Concept/Applied Module 11b d	22.	Everett has just taken the SAT test and he did very poorly on the English portion of the test. If Everett has a helpless attributional style he would be most likely to make the following type of attribution for his poor performance a. "The English sections on standardized tests just aren't realistic." b. "I lost my concentration during the English portion of the test." c. "The heat in the room distracted me during that portion of the test." d. "I'm stupid and I'll never make it in college."
Factual Module 11b b	23.	According to behavioral approached to understanding depression, depression-prone people experience a. an excess of negative reinforcers which leads to negative emotions and depression b. a scarcity of reinforcers which leads to negative emotions and depression c. a scarcity of conditioned stimuli which leads to negative emotions and depression d. an excess of unconditioned stimuli which leads to negative emotions and depression
Factual Module 11b a	24.	Recent studies into the link between stress and mood disorders suggest that a. stress can cause sleep loss which leads to neurochemical changes that can induce mood disorders b. sleep loss can cause neurochemical changes which lead to the stress that induces mood disorders c. sleep loss can cause stress which induces mood disorders that produce neurochemical changes d. neurochemical changes can cause sleep loss which leads to stress that can induce mood disorders
Factual Module 11c b	25.	In comparing different types of psychological disorders, schizophrenia occurs a. less frequently than anxiety disorders, but more frequently than mood disorders b. less frequently than either anxiety or mood disorders c. more frequently than either anxiety or mood disorders d. more frequently than anxiety disorders, but less frequently than mood disorders
Factual Module 11c c	26.	Delusions involve a. perceptual distortions such as hearing nonexistent voices b. jumbled, vague, fragmented speech patterns c. false beliefs that are maintained even though they are out of touch with reality d. a deterioration in routine functioning and personal care
Concept/Applied Module 11c d	27.	Charlotte believes that she is a member of the Russian royal family, and that her neighbors are American agents who want to destroy her. Charlotte's symptoms are most consistent with those seen in a. catatonic schizophrenia b. disorganized schizophrenia c. undifferentiated schizophrenia d. paranoid schizophrenia
Concept/Applied Module 11c a	28.	Chester sometimes sits for hours in extremely rigid positions. At other times he displayed frenzied motor activity. Chester's symptoms are most consistent with those seen in a. catatonic schizophrenia b. paranoid schizophrenia c. undifferentiated schizophrenia d. disorganized schizophrenia

Concept/Applied Module 11c **a**	29.	Jana has almost completely withdrawn from all social interactions. When she talks she is incoherent, and she no longer attends to her own personal care. Jana's symptoms are most consistent with those seen in a. disorganized schizophrenia b. catatonic schizophrenia c. undifferentiated schizophrenia d. paranoid schizophrenia
Concept/Applied Module 11c **c**	30.	Jerome's doctors have decided that Jerome has schizophrenia. But he shows delusions, social withdrawal, and frenzied motor activity, so they can't decide which category of schizophrenia should be used to describe his symptoms. In this case Jerome will most likely be diagnosed with a. manic schizophrenia b. bipolar schizophrenia c. undifferentiated schizophrenia d. disorganized schizophrenia
Factual Module 11c **b**	31.	One of the potential neurochemical factors that has been implicated as a possible cause of schizophrenia is a. reduced dopamine activity in the brain b. excess dopamine activity in the brain c. excess serotonin levels in the brain d. reduced norepinephrine levels in the brain
Factual Module 11c **d**	32.	MRI scans of schizophrenic and nonschizophrenic individuals have shown that schizophrenic patients may have a. shrunken brain ventricles b. an enlarged hypothalamus c. reduced activity across the corpus callosum d. enlarged brain ventricles
Factual Module 11c **c**	33.	Communication deviance refers to a. highly critical attitudes toward schizophrenic patients b. emotional overinvolvement with schizophrenic patients c. vague, muddled, fragmented communication within a family group d. auditory hallucinations that emerge in nonschizophrenic patients
Factual Module 11c **b**	34.	Exposure to deviant communication patterns during childhood a. decreases an individual's vulnerability to schizophrenia b. increases an individual's vulnerability to schizophrenia c. increases an individual's vulnerability to bipolar disorder d. has no effect on an individual's risk for developing a psychological disorder
Factual Module 11c **d**	35.	The rates of schizophrenic relapse are three times higher in schizophrenic patients who return to families a. low in expressed emotion b. low in communication deviance c. high in social interaction d. high in expressed emotion
Factual Module 11c **a**	36.	Which of the following would not be a potential reason for someone developing symptoms of schizophrenia? a. experiencing traumatic life events in early childhood that interrupted the stages of psychosexual development b. inheriting a genetic predisposition for the disorder c. an interaction occurring between predisposing factors and stressful life events d. being exposed to deviant communication patterns within the family

Factual Module 11d **a**	37.	Psychoanalysis is based on the assumption psychological problems are caused by a. unconscious conflicts left over from early childhood b. incongruence between a person's self-concept and reality c. environmental conditions that support maladaptive behaviors d. imbalances among key neurotransmitters in the brain
Factual Module 11d **b**	38.	During free association, clients are encouraged to a. remember and describe the content of any dreams they have recently had b. spontaneously express their thoughts and feelings with as little censorship as possible c. relate to their therapist in ways that mimic critical relationships in their lives d. actively confront irrational beliefs and negative thoughts
Concept/Applied Module 11d **c**	39.	Clifford has been in psychoanalysis for several months but lately he has been late for most of his appointments, and in some cases has simply not shown up for appointments. Clifford's behavior is hindering the progress of his therapy. According to Freud, Clifford's behavior may be evidence of a. insight b. incongruence c. resistance d. transference
Factual Module 11d **b**	40.	Transference refers to a. unconscious attempts to subvert or hinder the therapeutic process b. relating to the therapist in ways that mimic critical relationships in the client's life c. conscious attempts to extend therapy once insight has been achieved d. active confrontation of irrational beliefs and negative thoughts
Concept/Applied Module 11d **b**	41.	Alexis has been in psychoanalysis for just over a year. Up until this point she and her therapist have had a very positive relationship. However in today's session she began to act in a domineering, aggressive manner, similar to the way she treats her husband and her children. According to Freud, this change in Alexis' behavior may be a sign of a. incongruence b. transference c. resistance d. insight
Factual Module 11d **a**	42.	Psychoanalysis is a. a slow, painful process of self-examination requiring 3 to 5 years of hard work b. a non-directive form of therapy that keeps interpretation and advice to a minimum c. the only effective way to deal with most psychological disorders d. used less frequently than client-centered therapy
Factual Module 11d **d**	43.	Modern therapies based on Freud's principles of psychoanalysis are known collectively as a. client-centered approaches to therapy b. behavioral approaches to therapy c. free-ranging approaches to therapy d. psychodynamic approaches to therapy

Factual Module 11d **b**	44.	The person who developed the humanistic approach to therapy, known as client-centered therapy, was a. Alfred Adler b. Carl Rogers c. Sigmund Freud d. B. F. Skinner
Factual Module 11d **a**	45.	Carl Rogers maintained that most personal distress is due to a. incongruence between a person's self-concept and reality b. unconscious conflicts left over from early childhood c. environmental conditions that support maladaptive behaviors d. imbalances among key neurotransmitters in the brain
Factual Module 11d **c**	46.	According to Rogers, the emotional climate in which therapy takes place a. is not as important as the therapeutic process which is used b. has little impact on the success of therapy, as long as transference is resisted c. is more important than the therapeutic process which is used d. should be challenging, confrontational, and threatening
Factual Module 11d **c**	47.	According to Carl Rogers, the three critical components in therapy are a. incongruence, transference, and resistance b. free association, empathy, and directive feedback c. genuineness, unconditional positive regard, and empathy d. clarification, unconditional positive regard, and social reinforcement
Concept/Applied Module 11d **d**	48.	Dr. Quimby is a psychotherapist who is nonjudgmental and who communicates honestly and spontaneously with her clients. She encourages them to talk openly about their concerns but she keeps her interpretation and advice to a minimum. She feels her job is to provide feedback that helps her clients sort out their own feelings. Dr. Quimby is most likely a. a psychodynamic therapist b. a behavioral therapist c. an unsuccessful psychotherapist d. a client-centered therapist
Critical Thinking Module 11e **a**	49.	The basic idea behind various forms of behavior therapy is that problem behaviors a. have been learned, and can therefore be "unlearned" b. result from unresolved unconscious conflicts c. can be traced to problems in the individual's self-concept d. stem from a lack of personal responsibility
Factual Module 11e **d**	50.	The goal of systematic desensitization is to a. weaken the association between the conditioned stimulus and the unconditioned stimulus b. strengthen the association between the unconditioned stimulus and the unconditioned response c. strengthen the association between the conditioned response and the unconditioned response d. weaken the association between the conditioned stimulus and the conditioned response
Factual Module 11e **a**	51.	The behavioral therapy which attempts to replace learned anxiety with learned relaxation is a. systematic desensitization b. aversion therapy c. insight therapy d. operant conditioning

Concept/Applied Module 11e **b**	52.	When Karina was seven years old, her older brother was hiding under some stairs and he grabbed her ankle unexpectedly as she started to walk up the stairs. As an adult Karina is still terrified of stairs. Based on principles of classical conditioning, Karina's current fear of stairs is a. an unconditioned response b. a conditioned response c. a conditioned stimulus d. an unconditioned stimulus
Concept/Applied Module 11e **c**	53.	Maurice is so terrified of heights that he recently turned down a job promotion that would require him to work on the second floor of his office building. In this case, the most effective technique to help Maurice overcome his phobia is likely to be a. the use of antipsychotic mediation b. psychoanalysis c. systematic desensitization d. aversion therapy
Factual Module 11e **b**	54.	The second step in systematic desensitization involves a. helping the client to deal with transference and resistance b. training the client in deep muscle relaxation c. helping the client to build an anxiety hierarchy d. working through an anxiety hierarchy
Factual Module 11e **c**	55.	Aversion therapy is a behavioral therapy in which a. an aversive stimulus is paired with a stimulus that elicits an desirable response b. a pleasant stimulus is paired with a stimulus that elicits an undesirable response c. an aversive stimulus is paired with a stimulus that elicits an undesirable response d. a pleasant stimulus is paired with a stimulus that elicits an undesirable response
Concept/Applied Module 11e **a**	56.	Ivala is a smoker who has been unable to quit, even though she knows that smoking is ruining her health. The behavioral therapy technique that would be most useful in helping Ivala to stop smoking would be a. aversion therapy b. the use of antianxiety medication c. systematic desensitization d. client-centered therapy
Factual Module 11e **d**	57.	Antianxiety drugs a. can permanently cure anxiety disorders b. can produce symptoms such as tardive dyskensia c. reduce mental confusion and delusions d. can temporarily alleviate feelings of anxiety
Concept/Applied Module 11e **d**	58.	Trent has a psychological disorder, and his doctor has prescribed a drug that will bind to Trent's benzodiazepine receptor sites. In this case, Trent most likely has a. a depressive disorder b. a schizophrenic disorder c. bipolar disorder d. an anxiety disorder
Factual Module 11e **a**	59.	One serious side effect of the drug Thorazine is tardive dyskinesia, which produces a. involuntary writhing and tic-like movements b. hallucinations and delusions c. confusion and severe loss of memory d. depression and extreme nausea

Factual
Module 11e
b

60. Two antidepressant drugs that work primarily by increasing norepinephrine levels in the brain are
    a. Thorazine and Nardil
    b. Elavil and Nardil
    c. Xanax and Prozac
    d. Prozac and Valium

Unit 12
Social Psychology

Concept/Applied
Module 12a
d

1. Belle watches Jose slip on the stairs of their apartment building. If Belle decides that Jose is an uncoordinated "klutz" who wasn't paying attention to what he was doing, she has made
   a. an external attribution
   b. a self-serving attribution
   c. an attributional error
   d. an internal attribution

Factual
Module 12a
c

2. An external attribution occurs when individuals attribute the cause of another person's behavior to
   a. personal dispositions, traits, abilities, and feelings
   b. factors that the individual has no control over
   c. situational demands or environmental factors
   d. factors that the individual is able to control

Concept/Applied
Module 12a
d

3. Tina recently lost over half the money she had put away for her retirement. If Webster concludes that Tina lost the money because the stock market took a significant downturn, he has
   a. made an internal attribution
   b. made the fundamental attribution error
   c. been influenced by an illusory correlation
   d. made an external attribution

Factual
Module 12a
d

4. One type of information that individuals weigh when attempting to infer the causes of a person's behavior is consistency. This means that individuals attempt to determine whether
   a. the person's behavior is unique to one specific entity
   b. other people in the same situation tend to respond in the same way
   c. other people react in different ways when the situation changes
   d. the person's behavior in a given situation is the same over time

Concept/Applied
Module 12a
b

5. Francesca tends to daydream in her Chemistry class. Her professor asks some of the other professors about Francesca and it turns out that she also daydreams in her Psychology class, her English class and her Sociology class. In this example, Francesca's behavior shows
   a. high consensus
   b. low distinctiveness
   c. low consistency
   d. high distinctiveness

Concept/Applied
Module 12a
a

6. Like everyone else in his neighborhood, Alistair is terrified of his next-door neighbor's pit bull. In this example there is
   a. high consensus
   b. low distinctiveness
   c. high consistency
   d. low consistency

Concept/Applied Module 12a	7.	Parker is sometimes extremely well prepared for discussion classes, but other times he skims the assigned material in the first few minutes of the class and doesn't make any meaningful contributions to the ongoing discussions. Based on Kelley's covariation model, Parker's behavior has
c		a. low distinctiveness
		b. high consensus
		c. low consistency
		d. low consensus

Concept/Applied Module 12a
c

7. Parker is sometimes extremely well prepared for discussion classes, but other times he skims the assigned material in the first few minutes of the class and doesn't make any meaningful contributions to the ongoing discussions. Based on Kelley's covariation model, Parker's behavior has
   a. low distinctiveness
   b. high consensus
   c. low consistency
   d. low consensus

Factual Module 12a
c

8. People tend to make internal attributions for a behavior when that behavior is
   a. high in consistency, distinctiveness and consensus
   b. low in consistency, but high in distinctiveness and consensus
   c. high in consistency but low in distinctiveness and consensus
   d. high in consensus, but low in distinctiveness and consistency

Concept/Applied Module 12a
c

9. Imagine that you recently applied for a job, but the job went to someone else. According to Weiner's attributional model, if you state: "It was bad luck that the boss had a neighbor who applied the same day that I did," you have made
   a. an internal-unstable attribution
   b. an external-stable attribution
   c. an external-unstable attribution
   d. an internal-stable attribution

Concept/Applied Module 12a
b

10. Rendel heard that Lydia was involved in a minor car accident. Rendel decides that Lydia must be a terrible driver, even though he knows that the roads were slick with rain on the day of the accident. In this case Rendel's attribution for the cause of the accident is consistent with
    a. discrepancy bias
    b. the fundamental attribution error
    c. a self-serving bias
    d. a self-fulfilling prophecy

Factual Module 12a
d

11. In general, actors are more likely than observers to attribute the cause of their behavior to
    a. personal traits, abilities or dispositions
    b. unstable, global factors
    c. stable, specific factors
    d. situational demands and environmental factors

Concept/Applied Module 12a
a

12. Winifred earns an "A" on the first psychology exam, and proudly tells her parents how good she is in psychology. However, on the second exam she only earns a "C," and she explains to her parents that she didn't study as much for that test because she had to work overtime at her job. Winifred's attributions for her grades in psychology are consistent with
    a. a self-serving bias
    b. the fundamental attribution error
    c. a self-fulfilling prophecy
    d. a high level of cognitive dissonance

Factual Module 12b
b

13. According to Berscheid and Hatfield, passionate love involves
    a. an intent to maintain a relationship in spite of difficulties that may arise
    b. a complete absorption in another that includes the agony and ecstasy of intense emotion
    c. a warm, trusting, tolerant affection for another whose life is deeply intertwined with one's own
    d. warmth, closeness and sharing in a relationship

Concept/Applied Module 12b a	14.	Whenever Trent sees Diana he can feel his heart start to pound with excitement. Even though Trent and Diana have only dated a few times, Trent often becomes jealous when Diana talks to other men. He also finds he can't get her out of his mind when they are apart. According to Hatfield and Berscheid, Trent is experiencing a. passionate love b. companionate love c. consummate love d. reciprocal love
Concept/Applied Module 12b b	15.	Greer and Neil have been married for 15 years. They have an extremely warm and trusting relationship and, even though Neil frequently travels on business, Greer never worries about him seeing other women. According to Hatfield and Berscheid, Greer and Neil share a. reciprocal love b. companionate love c. passionate love d. consummate love
Factual Module 12b d	16.	According to Sternberg, the emotional component of a relationship that involves warmth, closeness, and sharing is a. commitment b. passion c. companionship d. intimacy
Concept/Applied Module 12b a	17.	Phyllis and Chester feel a strong physical passion for each other, and they freely confide in each other and share their feelings. However, they have not yet made a long-lasting commitment to continuing their relationship. According to Sternberg, Phyllis and Chester share a. romantic love b. fatuous love c. empty love d. infatuation
Concept/Applied Module 12b c	18.	Long-term marriages in which there is still a strong sense of intimacy and commitment, but in which the passion has faded, involve the type of love that Sternberg described as a. consummate love b. empty love c. companionate love d. fatuous love
Factual Module 12b a	19.	Sternberg suggested that a. passion reaches its zenith in the early phases of love and then erodes b. intimacy peaks early in a relationship and then begins to decline c. commitment reaches a peak late in a relationship and then declines over time d. intimacy and passion typically both peak at the same time in a relationship
Factual Module 12b d	20.	According to John Alan Lee, ludus involves a. slow-burning love in which the person prefers stable, calm relationships b. altruistic love in which the person is very giving in intimate relationships c. possessive love in which the person is prone to jealousy d. game-playing love in which the person seldom develops long-term involvements

Concept/Applied Module 12b **c**	21.	Melva is always looking for areas of compatibility and shared interests and values when she is developing a relationship with someone. According to John Alan Lee, Melva's style of loving is a. eros b. agape c. pragma d. storge
Concept/Applied Module 12b **b**	22.	A person who selects potential companions on the basis of their looks, rather than their personality or their intelligence is demonstrating the style of loving that John Alan Lee referred to as a. ludus b. eros c. storge d. mania
Concept/Applied Module 12b **a**	23.	Anastasia always seems to become involved in volatile love relationships. She constantly expects to be rejected and she is extremely jealous in her relationships. Hazan and Shaver would suggest that Anastasia most likely a. developed an anxious-ambivalent attachment with her parents during infancy b. developed an avoidant attachment with her parents during infancy c. developed a secure attachment with her parents during infancy d. failed to develop any type of attachment relationship
Concept/Applied Module 12b **b**	24.	Esa is uncomfortable being close to others. He finds it difficult to trust them and he does not feel that he has ever experienced any real intimacy in his relationships. According to Hazan and Shaver, this type pattern is evident in a. less than 10% of adult love relationships b. approximately 24% of adult love relationships c. approximately 40% of adult love relationships d. approximately 56% of adult love relationships
Concept/Applied Module 12c **c**	25.	Merlyn saw a television advertisement in which a new long distance carrier showed a vignette of pleasant family scenes while some relaxing music played in the background. Later, when Merlyn is asked about this particular long distance carrier he has a positive attitude toward their service, even though he actually uses a different carrier. Merlyn's attitude appears to have developed through the process of a. operant conditioning b. observational learning c. classical conditioning d. cognitive dissonance
Critical Thinking Module 12c **c**	26.	Foster has an unfavorable attitude toward his astronomy professor. In explaining Foster's attitude, a psychologist who took an operant conditioning perspective would consider a. the astronomy professor's personality and general attitude toward Foster b. how other students in the class feel about this particular professor c. Foster's history of reinforcement and punishment in dealing with his astronomy professor d. how Foster feels about his other professors
Concept/Applied Module 12c **d**	27.	Carmella has a negative attitude toward most lawyers because she has often heard her parents speak poorly of lawyers in general. Carmella's attitude appears to have developed through the process of a. classical conditioning b. operant conditioning c. cognitive dissonance d. observational learning

Application Module 12c **d**	28.	Jonna really likes Rusty. Rusty really likes horseback riding, but Jonna can't stand horseback riding. Based on Heider's balance theory, in this situation Jonna will a. be unmotivated to change her attitudes because the attitude triangle is balanced b. experience a high degree of cognitive dissonance c. be most successful in changing Rusty's attitude if she uses classical conditioning d. be motivated to change her attitude toward either Rusty or horseback riding
Factual Module 12c **b**	29.	One of the problems with Heider's balance theory is that it a. focuses only on peripheral elements in attitude change b. doesn't allow for efforts to change the attitude of the other person in the relationship c. overemphasizes differences in degrees of liking d. incorporates too many different elements
Factual Module 12c **c**	30.	According to Festinger, when related cognitions are inconsistent with each other, individuals will experience a. imbalance b. low self-perception c. cognitive dissonance d. negative reinforcement
Factual Module 12c **a**	31.	Festinger and Carlsmith paid subjects either $1 or $20 to lie and say that a boring task was fun. Later they found a. subjects who were paid $1 rated the task as being more enjoyable than subjects who were paid $20 b. subjects who were paid $1 rated the task as being less enjoyable than subjects who were paid $20 c. both groups changed their attitude and later rated the task as being enjoyable d. subject paid $1 had less enduring attitudes toward the task than subjects who were paid $20
Factual Module 12c **c**	32.	The theory which suggests we infer our attitudes from an observation of our own behavior is a. cognitive dissonance theory b. balance theory c. self-perception theory d. elaboration-likelihood theory
Application Module 12c **a**	33.	Bernie notices that whenever he is riding in his car alone he always tunes the radio to a soft rock station. Consequently, Bernie concludes he must like soft rock music. Bernie's attitude in this example can be best explained using a. self-perception theory b. cognitive dissonance theory c. balance theory d. principles of operant conditioning
Factual Module 12c **b**	34.	When people focus on nonmessage factors, such as attractiveness or credibility of a speaker, the message is being processed using a. balanced processing b. the peripheral route to persuasion c. the central route to persuasion d. cognitive distortions

Concept/Applied Module 12c **a**	35.	Julio had planned to buy a national brand computer when one of his friends suggested that he look into the computers available through a local "no-name" outlet store. Julio carefully reviewed the relevant reports about the various computer components as well as the statistics on service reliability, and decided his friend was correct. Julio bought his computer from the local "no-name" outlet store. In this case, Julio reached his decision using a. the central route to persuasion b. the peripheral route to persuasion c. the cognitive dissonance model of persuasion d. a self-serving route to persuasion
Application Module 12c **d**	36.	Sylvester listens carefully to the content of an infomercial for a new product, Ryan focuses on the fact that the product has three different celebrity endorsers who are really excited about the product. After the infomercial has ended, both Sylvester and Ryan think the product is worth purchasing. According to the elaboration likelihood model a. Ryan will have a more enduring attitude toward the product than Sylvester b. Sylvester will experience more cognitive dissonance than Ryan c. Ryan will have less balance in his attitudes than Sylvester d. Sylvester will have a more enduring attitude toward the product than Ryan
Factual Module 12d **b**	37.	Prejudice involves a. behaving negatively toward members of a group b. holding a negative attitude toward members of a group c. experiencing cognitive dissonance in interactions with someone from an outgroup d. central processing of information about outgroup members
Factual Module 12d **d**	38.	When we behave differently toward someone, just because he or she is a member of a particular group, we are displaying a. prejudice b. stereotypic behavior c. the fundamental attribution error d. discrimination
Concept/Applied Module 12d **c**	39.	Mort actually has a favorable attitude toward women in general, but he doesn't hire any women because his boss has told him not to consider women for any open positions in the company. In this case Mort is showing a. prejudice, but not discrimination b. both prejudice and discrimination c. discrimination, but not prejudice d. neither prejudice nor discrimination
Concept/Applied Module 12d **c**	40.	Marsha believes that all news reporters are cynical, doubting individuals who would sell their souls for an exclusive story. In this case, Marsha's beliefs about the traits and behaviors of news reporters are one example of a. the fundamental attribution error b. a confirmation bias c. stereotypes d. the matching hypothesis

SOCIAL PSYCHOLOGY

Factual Module 12d **a**	41.	In one study, designed to determine if stereotypes would affect perceptions, researchers had subjects watch and evaluate interactions on a TV monitor. In the videotaped presentation two people began arguing and one person gave the other a slight shove. The shove was coded as "violent behavior" by a. 73% of the subjects when the person who gave the shove was black b. 13% of the subjects when the person who gave the shove was black c. 73% of the subjects when the person who gave the shove was white d. 50% of the subjects, no matter who gave the shove
Concept/Applied Module 12d **d**	42.	When a member of an ethnic minority is successful, people are least likely to attribute that success to a. sheer effort b. luck or opportunity c. ease of the task d. ability or intelligence
Concept/Applied Module 12d **a**	43.	In trying to understand why some ethnic neighborhoods are dominated by poverty, people often infer that the residents are lazy and unmotivated. This type of inference illustrates a. the fundamental attribution error b. a stable global attribution c. inverse discrimination d. a stable external attribution
Factual Module 12d **b**	44.	When people claim that homosexuals have brought the AIDS crisis on themselves, and they deserve the consequences for their deviant behavior, a. self-perceptions have been inactivated b. defensive attributions are being made c. cognitive dissonance is at work d. offensive attributions are being made
Concept/Applied Module 12d **c**	45.	Although Jasmine has never actually met anybody who is Irish, she is convinced that all Irish individuals are lazy drunks who can't hold a job. She has heard her father make these types of statements for as long as she can remember. In this case, Jasmine's prejudice appears to have formed through the process of a. classical conditioning b. operant conditioning c. observational learning d. cognitive dissonance
Concept/Applied Module 12d **d**	46.	Eric has joined a new fraternity. Based on the research conducted by Krebs and Denton, if the other fraternity members now consider Eric as part of their ingroup they are more likely to a. view him in somewhat negative terms b. pay less attention to his actions and ideas c. remember things that he does with greater accuracy d. view him in a generally positive light
Concept/Applied Module 12d **c**	47.	Leonard is a basketball fan and he loves to attend all the home games for the local team. When he is at the game, Leonard's outgroup would most likely consist of a. fans for the home team b. the referee and game officials c. fans for the visiting team d. the sports announcer and the news crew

Factual
Module 12d
a

48. In general, people tend to
    a. see diversity among the members of their ingroup, but overestimate the homogeneity of the outgroup
    b. see diversity among the members of the outgroup, but overestimate the homogeneity of their ingroup
    c. make the fundamental attribution error when explaining ingroup behavior, but not outgroup behavior
    d. make defensive attributions for ingroup behavior, but not for outgroup behavior